THE HAMLYN WORLD ENCYCLOPEDIA OF FOOTBALL

HAMLYN
London · New York · Sydney · Toronto

ENDPAPERS: ***A sensible Swiss engine driver parked his locomotive alongside the Basel ground for much of the 1979 European Cup Winners Cup final. He chose well, for the game was one of the better European finals of the past decade, Barcelona eventually defeating Fortuna Dusseldorf 4-3.***
PREVIOUS PAGES: ***Ajax of Amsterdam, three times winners of the European Cup, Flamengo of Rio de Janeiro, World Club Champions of 1981, and Cruzeiro of Belo Horizonte, Libertadores Cup winners in 1976, three of the greatest club sides in the world.***
RIGHT: ***Marinho of Fluminense is tackled by Rondineli of Flamengo during a Flu-Fla derby in the world's largest stadium, the Maracana in Rio. The competition between these two clubs is among the most intense in the world and both have been Brazilian champions since the national championship was first instituted in 1967. Flamengo have won the crown three times since 1980 alone. In the first 78 years since the separate Rio League was founded in 1906, Fluminense have won it 23 times and Flamengo 22. Flamengo, leading the tournament mid-way through 1984, were poised to equal their rivals' record by year-end.***
OVERLEAF: ***Ricky Villa in his much-publicised Tottenham days. When he was signed from Racing Club of Buenos Aires on 7 July 1978 by Keith Burkinshaw he was, at £400,000, the most expensive player ever sold by a South American club. Since then Diego Maradona's transfer from Argentinos Juniors to Barcelona for $7,700,000 has dwarfed all other fees in football history.***

Written, compiled and edited by
Phil Soar, Martin Tyler and Richard Widdows
Designed by Phil Bush and Gordon Robertson
Artwork and Diagrams by Paul Buckle
Editorial and production assistance by Robert Pryce and Dennis Hovell

Published by
The Hamlyn Publishing Group Limited
London New York Sydney Toronto
Astronaut House, Feltham, Middlesex, England

Produced by
Marshall Cavendish Books Limited
58 Old Compton Street
London W1V 5PA

First published 1980
Completely revised and updated edition published in 1984

ISBN 0 600 34730 3

Printed and bound in Milan, Italy by New Interlitho, SpA.

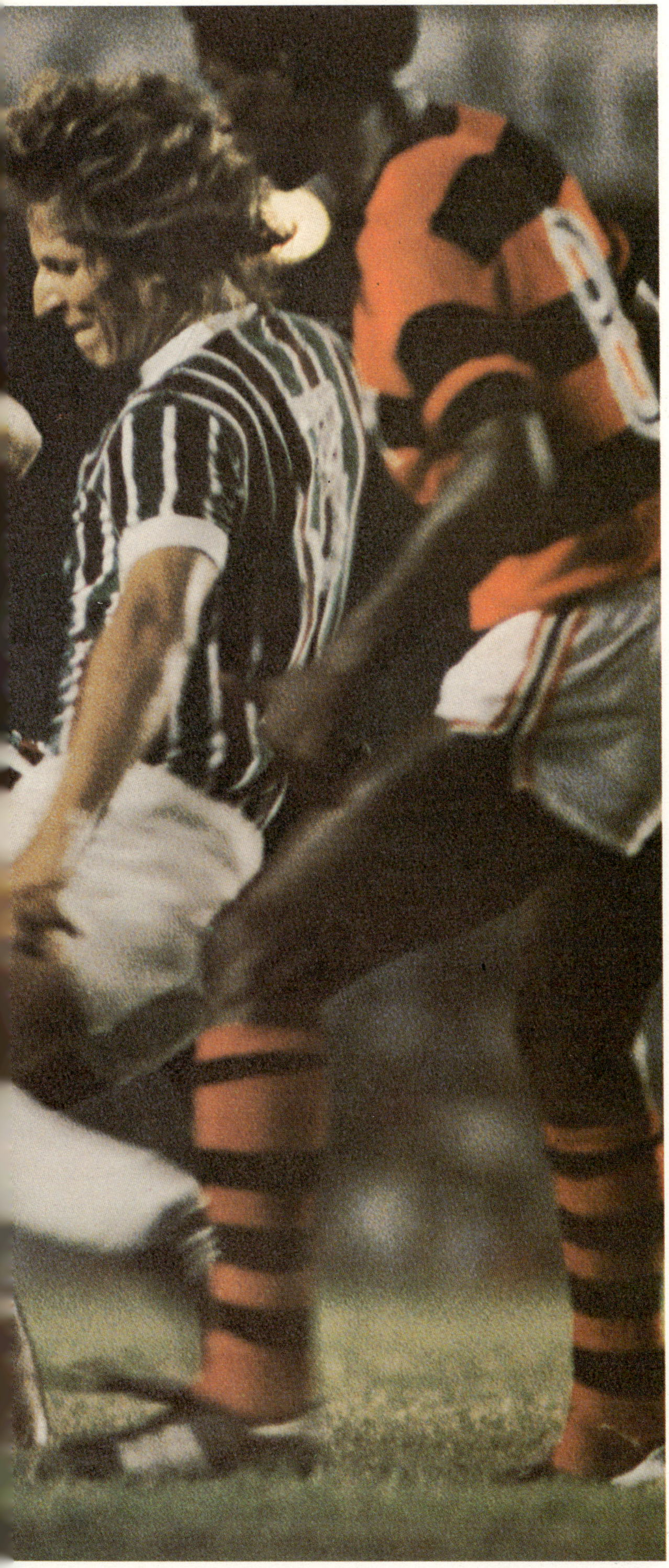

INTRODUCTION

The 1982 World Cup final in Madrid was watched by a television audience of over one thousand million people. Not only was this the greatest audience for any single event in the history of mankind, it was also an event that generated more column inches, more emotion, more excitement, more commitment, and more widespread interest than any other sporting event ever. Such is the role of football in the world today.

From its clumsy origins in the public (meaning private) schools of Great Britain in the nineteenth century, soccer became codified as association football and then, from the start of the twentieth century onwards, spread throughout the world. And there were very few parts of the world which did not take it to their hearts. Only North America held out, but in the last decade even that bastion has shown signs of falling with the stars of Europe and South America travelling to New York, Florida and Chicago to compete during the summer season in the world's richest country.

It is a game which can unite nations, a common currency from Chile to Finland, from China to Tahiti. All over the world men and women know the names of Pele, Cruyff, Maradona and Zico. Football is a universal language; it is a game for today, it is a game that the whole world can play. Beyond all doubt, it is *the* world game.

CONTENTS

THE BIRTH OF FOOTBALL

Like so many inventions in the nineteenth century, football as we know it today first saw light of day in Britain. But, although it was on the playing fields of England's public (meaning very private) schools that the game was first codified, it had been played all over the world for as long as man could remember.

If Britain manufactured association football, it was a product for which the raw materials could have been drawn from all over the world. From the time when the invention of the wheel made man aware of the properties of a curved surface, every land has had its pastime in which some type of ball played a part. Britain's virtue lay only in formalising some of these earlier games into organised sport, and, having fashioned the article, in ultimately exporting it around the globe.

Exactly where the first ball was kicked is buried deep in history, and no single individual or society can be said to have 'invented' football. But it is certain that, in both the ancient cultures of Greece and Rome, organised games formed part of sporting spectacles, though the Athenian League remained a concept for English amateur football in the twentieth century and the contest performed between rival Roman legions probably had more in common with contemporary rugby league or American football than the game we now refer to as soccer.

In civilisations as distant as China and ancient Mexico, records point to competitions of high skill and technique which would be beyond many a professional footballer of later years. The Far East has always been the traditional home of the juggler and the early version of football in those lands encouraged such virtues; points were not scored via the traditional medium of 'goals' but were awarded when the performers directed the ball through holes in curtains, or, as in Mexico, through rings set up high in a wall. Heading and kicking were both permitted methods of propulsion. In the light of such a heritage the suppleness and the co-ordination shown by the North Koreans in the 1966 World Cup finals should have come as no surprise, and, indeed, in Japan a game is still played which rewards participants who can juggle and manipulate

Street football was for centuries little more than a disorganised brawl or formless contest between local villages. They began as long ago as pre-Norman times.

with their feet, heads, thighs and shoulders a ball made out of wickerwork.

Such dexterity held little place in the English ball games of the early Christian era. You risked your life if you took part in the violent skirmishes, often between neighbouring communities, which characterised the prototype sports of that time. Every Shrove Tuesday in Ashbourne, Derbyshire, remembrance is still paid to this type of sport with a contest between the two halves of the town; the goals are the gates of Ashbourne Hall and the parish church. Records suggest that the first of these trials of strength took place around AD 217, and they also refer to similar mass contests across open countryside in Cornwall, Cumberland and Brittany.

As the game in all its forms was later to do, these early versions of football provided a means for release of tension; a public brawl in the middle ages could end in death for any person blamed for the incident, so there was a healthy interest in playing a game in which even severe violence passed unpunished. And while football flourished, there was also a considerable increase in the numbers who suffered often permanent injury during this sprawling, brawling pastime which spread itself across the countryside like a hunt in full cry.

Inevitably its anti-social aspects attracted criticism. Both Scottish and English monarchs—among them Edward III, Richard II and Henry IV—became anxious about the large number of supposedly fit young men who became unfit for army training as a result of damage sustained while playing football rather than at valuable pursuits such as archery. The game was banned by royal decree. Later the Puritans, alarmed that the participants in this rough sport might actually be enjoying themselves, spoke out against it. The game was banned by ecclesiastical decree.

ABOVE: ***A later artist's impression of a street match (more like a street brawl) in London probably around the fourteenth century, a period when the game was regularly banned.***
TOP RIGHT: ***A soldiers' friendly from a print dated in 1827.***
RIGHT CENTRE: ***The oldest regularly contested football match in the country is thought to be that played on Shrove Tuesday in Ashbourne, Derbyshire. The game reputedly originated with roman soldiers in AD 217.***
FAR RIGHT: ***A letter which appeared in*** THE TIMES ***on 5 October 1863 pleading for a single set of rules and outlining the problem.***

Both types of order were sensibly ignored by the masses. And eventually royalty and academics realised the virtues of the game. By the turn of the seventeenth century the students of Cambridge University were allowed to broaden their bodies as well as their minds by playing football. Certain thinkers of the day found that the rough and tumble of this often thirty-a-side sport lacked sophistication and hived off their interest into an Italian hybrid game called *calcio*. History recalls *calcio* as a game which needed speed and balance as well as physical resolution but it does not record whether its Italian ancestors played with the defensive attitudes of their twentieth century descendants; it seems unlikely.

And so football prospered—but in a whole variety of forms and with such inconsistency of rules (when there were any at all) that competition, except between local opponents, was impossible. Kicking the ball was always allowed, so was handling in varying styles; goals came in different sizes, and shapes; the playing area had diverse definitions; and above all no one could exactly agree what atrocities one player could commit on another. But whatever form prevailed in a locality it now engendered sufficient thrilling activity that not only was there no shortage of participants but those too old, too scared, or of the wrong sex to take part would attend as spectators.

But the game still had one more damp fuse to survive before it exploded into immense and eventually world-wide popularity. The advent of the Industrial Revolution disrupted the social climate, particularly the pattern of working that had allowed rural villagers the time to play. As Britain urbanised, farm labourers became factory

workers—exploited labour forces who toiled long hours in oppressive conditions; on the few public holidays, those who had indulged in sporting activities rarely has the energy or inclination to organise or participate. As a game of the common people, football was in decline.

This trend was redressed by the more educated classes. The game of the public became the sport of the public (meaning private) schools. Increasingly the purpose of these establishments was to breed a succession of generations of responsible young gentlemen, and the headmasters of all

The public schools seek a common set of rules

believed in the dictum of a healthy body breeding a healthy mind; football in some form or another was always on the curriculum. As a game it was expedient, too, because facilities were much cheaper than the traditional pastimes of the young aristocrat—hunting, shooting and fishing.

But there still remained little uniformity. At Charterhouse, for example, the rules did not permit handling, the players all being skilled dribblers on the stony surface of the cloisters (where the game was played), and teams consisted of twenty players per side.

FOOTBALL.

TO THE EDITOR OF THE TIMES.

Sir,—A letter having lately appeared in the columns of one of your contemporaries on the subject of football, and the inconvenience consequent upon there being no general and universally acknowledged rules of this game, I seize this opportunity of making a few remarks on a subject so fraught with interest for public schools. I am myself an Etonian, and the game of football as played by us differs essentially in most respects from that played at Westminster, Rugby, Harrow, and most of the London clubs. Now, this difference prevents matches being made or played between either school or club; and, furthermore, prevents a player from gaining the credit of playing well anywhere but among his own associates. For instance, an Etonian who attempts to play at the Rugby game finds himself quite unable to touch the ball at all, and so *vice versâ*. The Etonians have now for two years played against the Westminsters in Vincent-square; the game is a kind of compromise between the two, more closely resembling the Westminster game than ours; the display is therefore below mediocrity—neither of the sides can practice any of their favourite "dodges" without infringing the rules of the other, and an advantage gained by one side is not lawful by the rules of the opposite party. The results of the two matches have been that in 1861, at the eleventh hour, we fluked a goal, and in 1862, at the eleventh hour, also, one of our best players was knocked over, and broke his arm in the fall; and, while I am on this subject, I think it but just to do what I am afraid has not been done before—viz., acknowledge on behalf of my school the great kindness and consideration, as well as courtesy, on the part of the Westminsters on this occasion, for which they were, I dare say, thanked individually, though not collectively.

Now, Sir, all these annoyances might be prevented by the framing of set rules for the game of football to be played everywhere. Say, let the captains of the football elevens at Eton, Westminster, and Rugby, and the presidents of one or two London clubs meet, with members of either University, and frame rules for one universal game.

The public schools would no doubt be very unwilling to give up their old game, and so they might very well keep it up among themselves, while the new rules might be observed at any match between schools or clubs, and, the advantages being thus equalized, football might then stand a chance of occupying, among other games, the rank which so healthy and manly a sport deserves to hold, while all the inconvenience consequent upon playing a game with no fixed rules would be avoided.

I would suggest, in conclusion, that the new rules should be framed before the match between Eton and Westminster, as, with the present state of things, to whichever side victory may incline, it brings with it no glory, but a great deal of dissatisfaction.

With apologies for thus trespassing on your valuable space, I am, Sir, yours obediently,

Oct. 3. ETONENSIS.

At Harrow football was an eleven-a-side game on muddy terrain at the bottom of the school's hill. At Rugby, where radical change was imminent, boys could handle the ball but could not run with it in their hands. Meanwhile Eton fashioned a totally unique experience, the famed Wall Game with goals (one a small door, the other a tree) at either end of a wall which was 120 yards long; scrimmages were long and fierce and goals were very scarce, the pitch being only six yards wide. The goalscoring rate in all games at Eton this century has been approximately one every two years, not exactly the kind of attack-minded displays likely to threaten the spectator appeal of soccer. Westminster based its game of football on a similar pattern to that of Charterhouse, while the Winchester version of football existed without any goals at all, points being awarded when the ball was kicked over the goal-line.

It was hardly a situation conducive to competition between the schools. Each generation of schoolboys handed down the codes of practice at their particular establishment (largely determined by the physical layout of the games area) and even

ABOVE: ***Some of the many faces of football—rugby union, gaelic football and the North American variety, on this occasion Canadian rather than American. South Wales, where the left hand picture was taken, is perhaps the only part of Britain where youngsters still prefer to play rugby.***

within the major schools formal rule-books were rare. When one participant improvised in any way condemnation was hard to substantiate. So it was at Rugby School in 1823. There, on the wide reaches of The Close, William Webb Ellis made the transition from anonymous schoolboy to immortal. Ignoring the custom of his school, he picked up the ball, clasped it in both hands and ran with it towards the opposing goal-line. Just how his fellows reacted to such behaviour is a matter of conjecture, but he had broken only convention, not a set of written rules; his rather obvious action constituted not a foul but a matter for debate. And within twenty years Webb Ellis's interpretation had become an accepted feature of the game of football played at Rugby.

But still there could be no inter-school matches, nor indeed could those who had left school participate in organised football. And it was the need of the latter group which finally stimulated the first serious attempts to create set of unified regulations. In 1848 fourteen students at Cambridge University met for this purpose, among them a former pupil of Rugby School who had played his football in the post-Webb Ellis vein. The areas for argument were vast and the meeting stretched on and on, but in the final outcome the delegate from Rugby

William Webb Ellis makes a name for himself and Rugby

could not have received much support. The use of the hands was only permitted in arresting the flight of the ball and the rules outlawed the practice of running with it.

The first mould of what was to become association football had been cast. A goal could be scored by kicking the ball between two posts and under a piece of string which joined them; tripping, kicking or grabbing an opponent was to be penalised; the ball

Rules had not found universal acceptance. Within a few years of the founding of the first Sheffield teams, the area could boast as many as fifteen football clubs. Both players and onlookers were becoming aware of the extra thrills that competition stimulated; but though Sheffield had its code of laws, there was still a faltering step or two to be taken even before any small consensus could be achieved.

Not many miles south of Sheffield, Uppingham School in Rutland performed their variation on this theme. The Headmaster, Edward Thring, and his younger brother J C Thring, formalised their game in a set of rules entitled *The Simplest Game*; for the boys of their school there was no physical violence, no kicking of the ball when it was off the ground, no attacker allowed in front of the ball. If the regulations sounded a little unattractive there was surely no shortage of goals, for the Thrings decreed that the goal should stretch across the width of the pitch, defined by two sticks joined by a long piece of tape.

But all the minor variations and interpretations of football boiled down to one major division of opinion—should players be permitted to propel or carry the ball with their hands. If you had chosen to watch a contest in 1860 it might have fallen into one of two kinds of spectacle. Either foot or hand would dominate. In the former, you would witness a game of dribbling, in which there would be a succession of individual

By 1860 the choice had come down to two— the dribbling game or the handling game

could be passed forwards as long as the receiver had three opponents between him and the goal. Some common basis for competition had been laid down.

As football at Oxford and Cambridge blossomed under the new regulations, the game had re-emerged outside the playing fields of the academic institutions. The spread of industry had not simply perpetuated the polarisation of classes of feudal times; it had created a new breed, a middle-class of professional men who had the luxury of leisure time. Men such as these turned to football as a newly respectable outlet.

The industrial atmosphere of Sheffied gave birth to the first football club of modern definition, and in the mid-1850s matches were allowed to take place on the ground of the Sheffield Cricket Club at Bramall Lane, a site which, over a hundred years later, was to reverse the process and become solely devoted to the use of Sheffield United FC to the exclusion of Yorkshire cricket. The Sheffield club was almost certainly in existence in some form as early as 1854, but its first rulebook was not produced until 1857. The original players

ABOVE: ***Rugby League at Wembley; this is the only other professional version of football that is regularly played in the British Isles and it was the payment of players which caused the game's break from rugby union at the turn of the century. Nonetheless, soccer has no real competitor outside the USA and New Zealand.***

were from the Old Collegiate School in Sheffield, with a probable sprinkling of Old Etonians. Sheffield are the oldest club still in existence, having preceded the first of the London clubs (Hampstead Heathens and Forest, later Wanderers, were both probably formed in 1858) and their proud history contains one major honour—the Amateur Cup of 1904. At first they played to the basis of the Cambridge Rules, but the protagonists were allowed to hit the ball forwards with their hands; the practice of pushing away an opponent with the hands was also allowed. And there was no denying the spectator appeal; when Sheffield met their local rivals Hallam in 1861, 600 followers attended.

The experience of Sheffield typified the upsurge of interest in the game—and the still differing versions that were being played up and down a land in which the Cambridge

forays into the opposing territory, and when possession had been lost an opponent would set up his sole counter-attack. Passing was an art as yet unborn, and the swift runner who could manipulate the ball with his feet was the coveted player. In the latter instance the spectator would see a match of scrimmaging, of long punts from one end of the field to the other, of players running with the ball under their arms while opponents could push them off balance. Many local versions were really a combination of both handling and kicking though, interestingly, never heading. It must be stressed that there was no soccer or rugby at this stage—merely 'football', though, for the game as played at Rugby School, this was already a misnomer.

If, as history turned the corner into the 1860s, the situation seemed rife for a split between the two methods of propulsion, there was little indication as to which emphasis of play had more adherents. The social environment, rather than individuals, had created two prototypes of a product for which there was a great demand. But late in 1863 a selection was to be made, and the process of sophisticating the product was to begin.

THE FIRST ORGANISATIONS

The Football Association's foundation was essentially a local meeting of public schoolboys living in London. If they had any national ambitions at the time, they remained well hidden. Their aim appears to have been simply to agree on a single set of basic rules so that they did not have to waste time at the start of games between the old boys of different schools. They did not invite any representatives from Sheffield or Nottingham, the major provincial centres, nor anyone from Cambridge University. Despite all this, within 20 years it was to become the organisation which completely dominated football and which, within 50 years, spread the code throughout the world.

ABOVE: ***The 15-man Uppingham School team poses in front of one of its idiosyncratic pitch-wide goals at the Rutland school in the 1860s. The 'Simplest Game' had been codified there by J. C. Thring in 1862 but spread no further.***

Football changed from a game to a sport on 26 October 1863. Representatives of eleven clubs in the London area gathered that day at the Freemasons' Tavern in Holborn with the explicit intentions of founding an association. Their reasons were essentially mundane. They were not seeking to spread their old school games to the far corners of the earth, nor to take the first step in a movement that was to develop into the world's premier sport. Rather they were simply trying to establish a uniform set of rules and so avoid the long debates which always preceded any game between teams which operated under different codes.

Most of the clubs involved had been founded by old boys from public schools—as a result they all played to the rules operating at their old schools, and this explains the continuing lack of uniformity among codes. Almost as significant, in a sense, as those who did attend were those who did not. Notable absentees were any representatives from Cambridge University (where one of several revisions of the 1848 rules had just been drawn up), the major public schools (as distinct from their old boys), and anyone from the two major provincial centres of the game, Sheffield and Nottingham.

It was essentially a local meeting of ex-public schoolboys living in London. At the time there were no national ambitions—or, if there were, they remained unadmitted. Most of the clubs involved subscribed more or less to variations of the Harrow School and Cambridge Rules, several of the more prominent sides, such as Forest (nothing to do with Nottingham Forest) and Kilburn No Names, being comprised of Old Harrovians. There was also a sprinkling of Old Rugbeians, led by the Blackheath club, who were to disagree with the Harrow party almost at once. One A Pember of Kilburn No Names was elected the first chairman, F M Campbell of Blackheath briefly became treasurer and E C Morley, of Barnes, secretary.

Some of the other clubs represented were: Crystal Palace, a short lived side (named after the Great Exhibition Hall of 1851 which had been moved to South London in 1854) having nothing to do with the present League team and playing in blue and white with blue serge knickerbockers; two Blackheath schools which were closely associated with the Old Rugbeian Blackheath Club; Kensington Grammar

School, represented by their captain William Macintosh, which had not so much an undistinguished career as no career at all in the years to come; Morley and the club's secretary P D Gregory represented Barnes, who played 'in a field belonging to J Johnstone Esq near the White Hart'; the War Office, represented by E Wawn, and a selection of representatives of various other sides including Forest, the Crusaders, an observer from Charterhouse, several other observers from undisclosed clubs and, even at this stage, at least one member of the press. Few of these clubs have survived in any shape or form; only Blackheath still exist at any remotely senior level—and then playing rugby union!

Blackheath's Campbell and Barnes' Morley clashed almost immediately in the subsequent series of meetings arranged to draw up the all-important formal rules, and

Only Blackheath survive from foundation —playing rugby!

the two were to remain the figureheads of the soccer versus rugby clash. Draft rules nine and ten were the stumbling blocks. The former allowed a player to run with the ball '. . . if he makes a fair catch', a basic ingredient of the Rugby game since William Webb Ellis's day. Draft rule ten, however, was far more contentious. It would allow players to 'charge, hold, trip or hack (an opponent) . . .' but generously allowed that '. . . no player shall be held and hacked at the same time.'

In the end the issue was black and white. Blackheath and the Rugbeians insisted on the inclusion of these rules, the rest on their exclusion. At a decisive meeting on 1 December 1863, Morley insisted that if hacking were allowed '. . . men of business would be unwilling to play football.' Campbell retorted that: 'Hacking is the true foot-

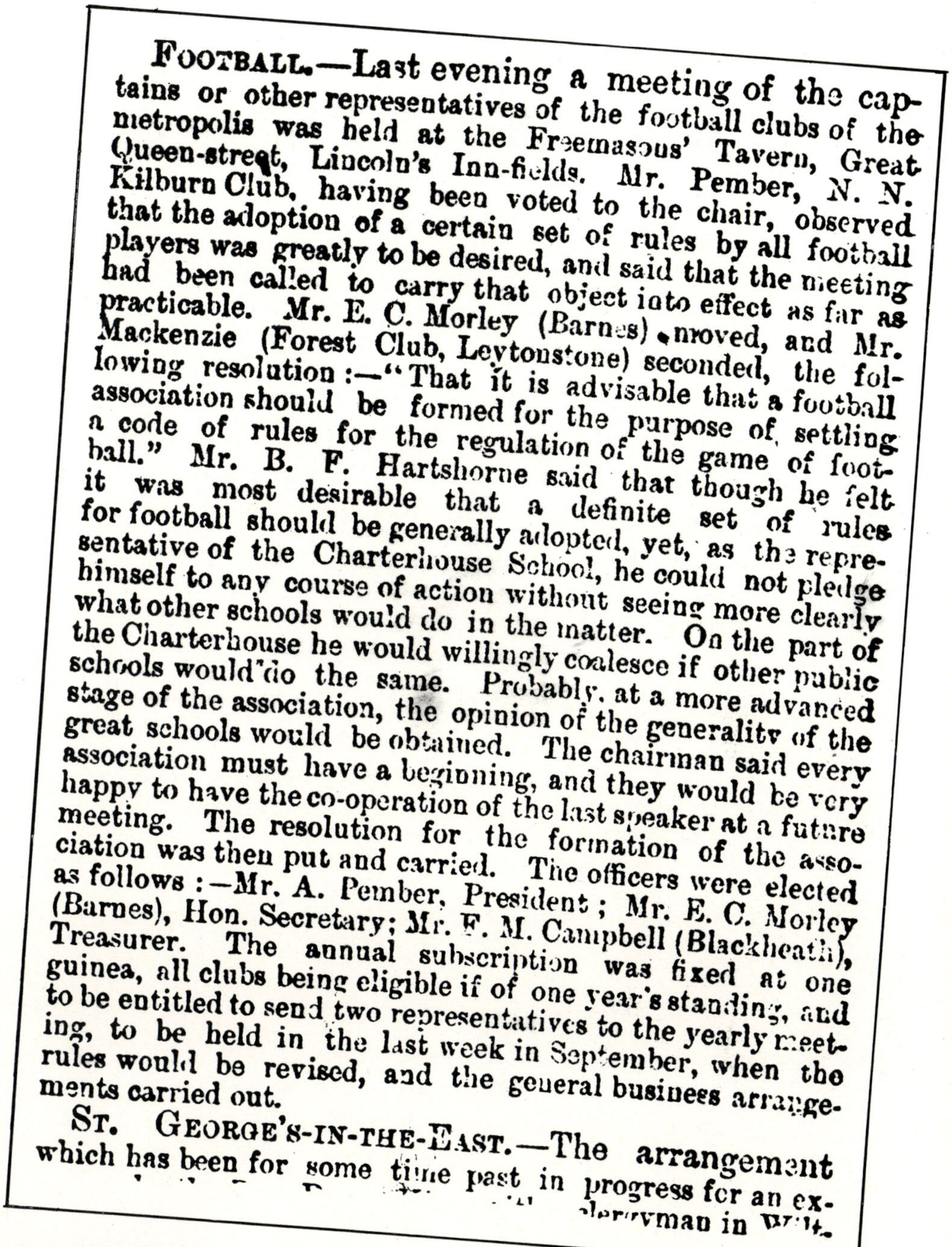

FOOTBALL.—Last evening a meeting of the captains or other representatives of the football clubs of the metropolis was held at the Freemasons' Tavern, Great Queen-street, Lincoln's Inn-fields. Mr. Pember, N. N. Kilburn Club, having been voted to the chair, observed that the adoption of a certain set of rules by all football players was greatly to be desired, and said that the meeting had been called to carry that object into effect as far as practicable. Mr. E. C. Morley (Barnes) moved, and Mr. Mackenzie (Forest Club, Leytonstone) seconded, the following resolution :—"That it is advisable that a football association should be formed for the purpose of settling a code of rules for the regulation of the game of football." Mr. B. F. Hartshorne said that though he felt it was most desirable that a definite set of rules for football should be generally adopted, yet, as the representative of the Charterhouse School, he could not pledge himself to any course of action without seeing more clearly what other schools would do in the matter. On the part of the Charterhouse he would willingly coalesce if other public schools would do the same. Probably, at a more advanced stage of the association, the opinion of the generality of the great schools would be obtained. The chairman said every association must have a beginning, and they would be very happy to have the co-operation of the last speaker at a future meeting. The resolution for the formation of the association was then put and carried. The officers were elected as follows :—Mr. A. Pember, President; Mr. E. C. Morley (Barnes), Hon. Secretary; Mr. F. M. Campbell (Blackheath), Treasurer. The annual subscription was fixed at one guinea, all clubs being eligible if of one year's standing, and to be entitled to send two representatives to the yearly meeting, to be held in the last week in September, when the rules would be revised, and the general business arrangements carried out.

ST. GEORGE'S-IN-THE-EAST.—The arrangement which has been for some time past in progress for an ex- ...

WORLD CLUB CHAMPIONSHIP

1960	Real Madrid *(Spain)* beat *Penarol *(Uruguay)* 0-0, 5-1
1961	Penarol *(Uruguay)* beat *Benfica *(Portugal)* 0-1, 5-0, †2-1
1962	*Santos *(Brazil)* beat Benfica *(Portugal)* 3-2, 5-2
1963	Santos *(Brazil)* beat *AC Milan *(Italy)* 2-4, 4-2, ‡1-0
1964	Inter-Milan *(Italy)* beat *Independiente *(Argentina)* 0-1, 2-0, §1-0
1965	*Inter Milan *(Italy)* beat Independiente *(Argentina)* 3-0, 0-0
1966	*Penarol *(Uruguay)* beat Real Madrid *(Spain)* 2-0, 2-0
1967	Racing Club *(Argentina)* beat *Celtic *(Scotland)* 0-1, 2-1, †1-0
1968	*Estudiantes *(Argentina)* beat Manchester United *(England)* 1-0, 1-1
1969	*AC Milan *(Italy)* beat Estudiantes *(Argentina)* 2-2, 1-0
1970	Feyenoord *(Holland)* beat *Independiente *(Argentina)* 2-2, 1-0
1971	Nacional *(Uruguay)* beat *Panathinaikos *(Greece)* 1-1, 2-1
1972	Ajax *(Holland)* beat *Independiente *(Argentina)* 1-1, 3-0
1973	Independiente *(Argentina)* beat Juventus *(Italy)* 1-0 [in Rome]
1974	Atletico Madrid *(Spain)* beat *Independiente *(Argentina)* 0-1, 2-0
1975	*Independiente and Bayern Munich could not agree dates*
1976	*Bayern Munich *(W. Germany)* beat Cruzeiro *(Brazil)* 2-0, 0-0
1977	*Boca Juniors *(Argentina)* beat B'sia M'gladbach *(W. Germany)* 2-2, 3-0
1978	*Not played*
1979	Olimpia Asuncion *(Paraguay)* beat *Malmo FF *(Sweden)* 1-0, 2-1
1980	Nacional *(Uruguay)* beat Nottingham Forest *(England)* 1-0 [in Tokyo]
1981	Flamengo *(Brazil)* beat Liverpool *(England)* 3-0 (in Tokyo]
1982	Penarol *(Uruguay)* beat Aston Villa *(England)* 2-0 [in Tokyo]
1983	Gremio *(Brazil)* beat Hamburg *(W. Germany)* 2-1 [in Tokyo]

*home team in first leg †decider in Montevideo ‡decider in Rio de Janeiro §decider in Madrid (aet)
Note: Panathinaikos (1971) & Juventus (1973), as beaten European Cup finalists, took place of Ajax; Atletico Madrid (1974) took place of Bayern Munich; Moenchengladbach (1977) took place of Liverpool; Malmo (1979) took place of Nottingham Forest

ABOVE: ***Organised football arrives; the foundation of the FA warranted just three column inches in*** *THE TIMES* ***of 27 October 1863 and was ignored elsewhere.*** *LEFT:* ***A century later the game had spread so far and wide that the ultimate club competition was introduced—the World Club Championship between the champions of Europe and South America. In spirit and sportsmanship it also proved a century apart.***

ball game and if it is done away with all the pluck and courage of the game will be at an end.' Campbell did not help his cause with tactless remarks directed, among other things, at Morley's lack of a public school education, thus implying that he was scared of the rough and tumble of the games as played at these institutions as well as suggesting some sort of social inferiority.

It is unlikely that Campbell would have won the argument anyway, and the vote went so firmly against the Rugbeians that they immediately left the Association. The rival Rugby Union, in keeping with its history of loose and informal organisation, was not actually formed until 1871. It immediately outlawed hacking.

The major public schools themselves (from where, it was assumed, the majority of future players would come) had already been asked their opinions on a uniform code of rules. Harrow replied: 'We cling to our present rules and should be sorry to alter

EUROPEAN FOOTBALLER OF THE YEAR

Year	Winner	Runner-up	Third
1956	Stanley Matthews *(Blackpool & England)*	Alfredo di Stefano *(Real Madrid* & Spain)*	Raymond Kopa *(Stade de Reims & France)*
1957	Alfredo di Stefano *(Real Madrid* & Spain)*	Billy Wright *(Wolverhampton W. & England)*	Raymond Kopa *(Real Madrid* & France)*
1958	Raymond Kopa *(Real Madrid* & France)*	Helmut Rahn *(Rot-Weiss Essen & West Germany)*	Just Fontaine *(Stade de Reims & France)*
1959	Alfredo di Stefano *(Real Madrid* & Spain)*	Raymond Kopa *(Real Madrid* & France)*	John Charles *(Juventus & Wales)*
1960	Luis Suarez *(Barcelona‡ & Spain)*	Ferenc Puskas *(Real Madrid,* Hungary & Spain)*	Uwe Seeler *(SV Hamburg & W. Germany)*
1961	Omar Sivori *(Juventus & Italy)*	Luis Suarez *(Inter-Milan & Spain)*	Johnny Haynes *(Fulham & England)*
1962	Josef Masopust *(Dukla Prague & C'slovakia)*	Eusebio *(Benfica* & Portugal)*	Karl-Heinz Schnellinger *(Cologne & W. Germany)*
1963	Lev Yashin *(Dynamo Moscow & USSR)*	Gianni Rivera *(AC Milan* & Italy)*	Jimmy Greaves *(Tottenham Hotspur† & England)*
1964	Denis Law *(Manchester U. & Scotland)*	Luis Suarez *(Inter-Milan* & Spain§)*	Amancio *(Real Madrid & Spain§)*
1965	Eusebio *(Benfica & Portugal)*	Giacinto Facchetti *(Inter-Milan* & Italy)*	Luis Suarez *(Inter-Milan* & Spain)*
1966	Bobby Charlton *(Manchester U. & England**)*	Eusebio *(Benfica & Portugal)*	Franz Beckenbauer *(Bayern & W. Germany)*
1967	Florian Albert *(Ferencvaros & Hungary)*	Bobby Charlton *(Manchester United & England)*	Jimmy Johnstone *(Celtic* & Scotland)*
1968	George Best *(Manchester United* & N. Ireland)*	Bobby Charlton *(Manchester United* & England)*	Dragan Dzajic *(Partizan Belgrade & Yugoslavia)*
1969	Gianni Rivera *(AC Milan* & Italy)*	Gigi Riva *(Cagliari & Italy)*	Gerd Muller *(Bayern Munich & W. Germany)*
1970	Gerd Muller *(Bayern Munich & W. Germany)*	Bobby Moore *(West Ham United & England)*	Gigi Riva *(Cagliari & Italy)*
1971	Johan Cruyff *(Ajax* & Holland)*	Sandro Mazzola *(Inter-Milan & Italy)*	George Best *(Manchester United & N. Ireland)*
1972	Franz Beckenbauer *(Bayern & W. Germany)*	Gerd Muller *(Bayern Munich & W. Germany§)*	Gunter Netzer *(Bor. M'gladbach & W. Germany§)*
1973	Johan Cruyff *(Ajax*/Barcelona & Holland)*	Dino Zoff *(Juventus & Italy)*	Gerd Muller *(Bayern Munich & W. Germany)*
1974	Johan Cruyff *(Barcelona & Holland)*	Franz Beckenbauer *(Bayern* & W. Germany**)*	Kazimierz Deyna *(Legia Warsaw & Poland)*
1975	Oleg Blokhin *(Dynamo Kiev† & USSR)*	Franz Beckenbauer *(Bayern* & W. Germany)*	Johan Cruyff *(Barcelona & Holland)*
1976	Franz Beckenbauer *(Bayern* & W. Germany)*	Rob Rensenbrink *(Anderlecht & Holland)*	Ivo Viktor *(Dukla Prague & Czechoslovakia§)*
1977	Allan Simonsen *(Bor. M'gladbach & Denmark)*	Kevin Keegan *(Liverpool*/Hamburg & England)*	Michel Platini *(Nantes & France)*
1978	Kevin Keegan *(SV Hamburg & England)*	Hans Krankl *(Rapid Vienna/Barcelona & Austria)*	Rob Rensenbrink *(Anderlecht† & Holland)*
1979	Kevin Keegan *(SV Hamburg & England)*	Karl-Heinz Rummenigge *(Bayern & W. Germany)*	Ruud Krol *(Ajax & Holland)*
1980	Karl-Heinz Rummenigge *(Bayern & W. Germany)*	Bernd Schuster *(Barcelona & W. Germany)*	Michel Platini *(St Etienne & France)*
1981	Karl-Heinz Rummenigge *(Bayern & W. Germany)*	Paul Breitner *(Bayern Munich & W. Germany)*	Bernd Schuster *(Barcelona & W. Germany)*
1982	Paulo Rossi *(Juventus & Italy)*	Alain Giresse *(Bordeaux & France)*	Zbignew Boniek *(Juventus & Poland)*
1983	Michel Platini *(Juventus & France)*	Kenny Dalglish†† *(Liverpool & Scotland)*	Allan Simonsen†† *(Vejle & Denmark)*

*European Cup winners †European Cup Winners Cup winners ‡European Fairs Cup winners §European Champions **World Cup winners ††joint second

ABOVE: ***The European Footballer of the Year is elected by a panel of journalists in December, not at the end of each season.***

them in any respect.' Charterhouse's observer at the original meeting had replied similarly. The rest were non-commital.

By 8 December 1863 general agreement had been reached among the clubs and the new Association's first laws clearly followed those of Cambridge which 'embraced the true principles of the game' and had, in turn, derived much from Harrow. There were still some local variations but it probably seemed that all would soon be standardised. In fact it was to be nearly twenty years before the whole country was playing to an accepted set of rules—and even as late as the 1884 Cup final there were bitter disputes over basic interpretations.

The rules as finally agreed were:

1 The maximum length of the ground shall be 200 yds; the maximum breadth shall be 100 yds; the length and breadth shall be marked off with flags; and the goals shall be defined by two upright posts, 8 yds apart, without any tape or bar across them.

2 The winners of the toss shall have the choice of goals. The game shall be commenced by a place-kick from the centre of the ground by the side losing the toss. The other side shall not approach within 10 yds of the ball until it is kicked off.

3 After a goal is won, the losing side shall kick off, and goals shall be changed.

4 A goal shall be won when the ball passes between the posts of over the space bet-

Offside if you were in front of the ball!

ween the posts (at whatever height), not being thrown, knocked on, or carried.

5 When the ball is in touch, the first player who touches it shall throw it from the point on the boundary-line where it left the ground in a direcion at right angles with the boundary-line, and it shall not be in play until it has touched the ground.

6 When a player has kicked the ball, any one of the same side who is nearer the opponents' goal-line is out of play, and may not touch the ball himself nor in any way whatever prevent any other player from doing so until the ball has been played; but no player is out of play when the ball is kicked from behind the goal-line.

7 In case the ball goes behind the goal-line, if a player on the same side to whom the goal belongs first touches the ball, one of his side shall be entitled to a free-kick

The rules allowed throwing and catching the ball!

from the goal-line at the point opposite the place where the ball shall be touched. If a player of the opposite side first touches the ball, one of his side shall be entitled to a free-kick (but at the goal only) from a point 15 yds from the goal-line opposite the place where the ball is touched; the opposing side shall stand behind the goal-line until he has had his kick.

8 If a player makes a fair catch, he shall be entitled to a free-kick, provided he claims it by making a mark with his heel at once; and in order to take such a kick he may go as far back as he pleases, and no player on the opposite side shall advance beyond his mark until he has kicked.

9 No player shall carry the ball.

10 Neither tripping nor hacking shall be allowed, and no player shall use his hands to hold or push an adversary.

11 A player shall not throw the ball or pass it to another.

12 No player shall take the ball from the ground with his hands while it is in play under any pretence whatever.

13 A player shall be allowed to throw the ball or pass it to another if he made a fair catch or catches the ball on the first bounce.

14 No player shall be allowed to wear projecting nails, iron plates or gutta percha on the soles or heels of his boots.

Laws one to eight remain the basis of rugby union to the present day. As they imply, much was left unregulated and it is immediately noticeable that there is no reference to the size and shape of the ball, referees, goalkeepers, free-kicks for infringements, penalties or even the number of players! The laws were meant to lay down *basics* which were common to all mat-

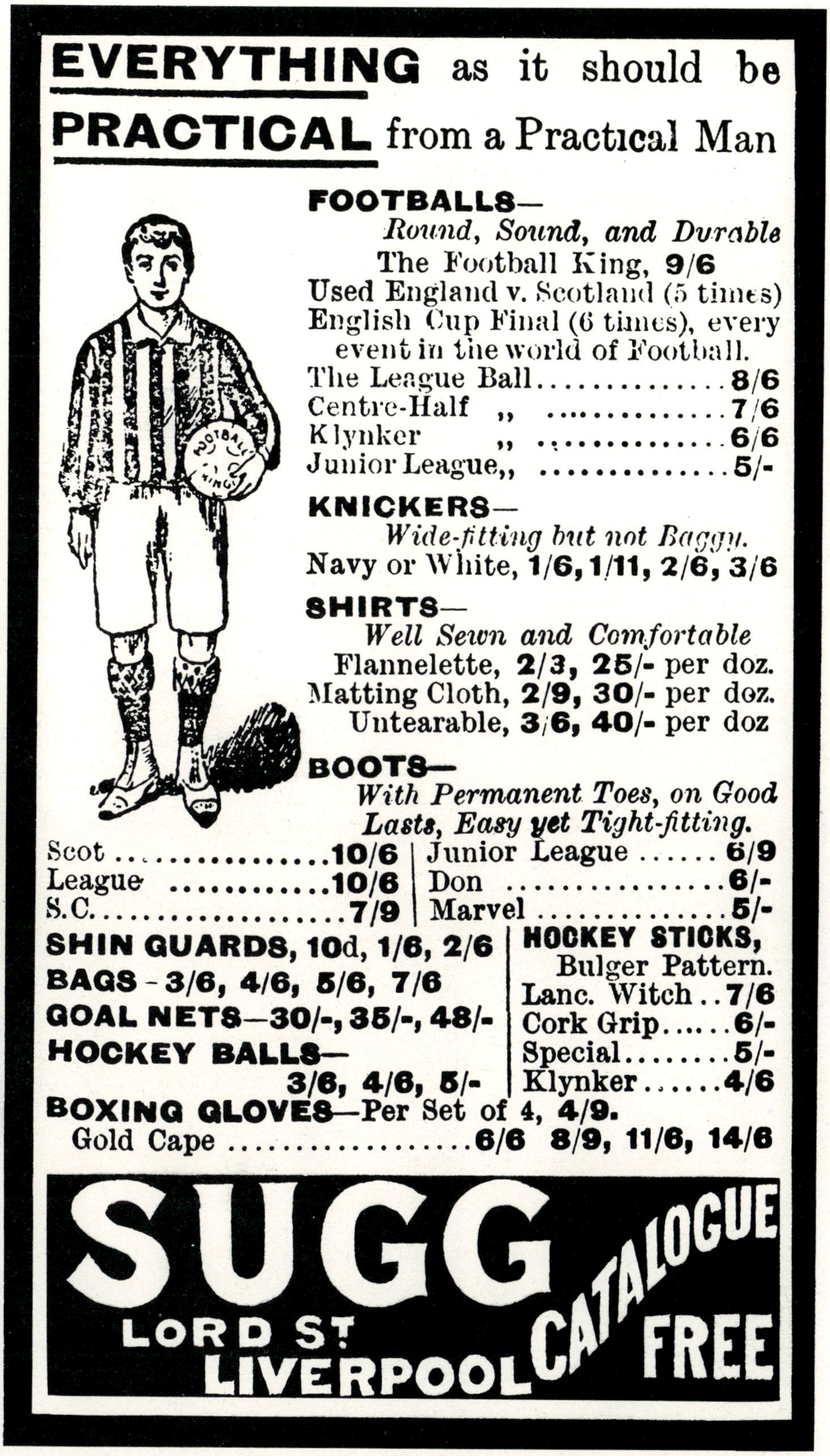

LEFT: Perhaps the most idiosyncratic of all the individual school games was that played (and still played) at Eton. The famous Wall Game has a pitch six yards wide, a tree and a door as goals and scores are recorded approximately once every two years. The individual public schools were almost uniformly reluctant to give up their own codes.

ABOVE: Sugg and Company were one of the leading manufacturers of the 1890s, from which decade this advertisement comes. Their major claim to fame had been the kitting out of the Blackburn Rovers side of the 1880s, the team that won 5 FA Cup finals in 8 seasons and one of only two to have won three consecutive FA Cups.

ches—'additional' restrictions could still be agreed by captains before games began. Even today certain variations are still allowed—there is no directive on the precise size of the pitch or shape of goalposts for instance. The original offside law (number 6) is particularly interesting—it was thirty years before anyone noticed that 'kicking' does not include heading and changed the law to 'played' rather than 'kicked'.

The twenty-year lag before these laws became universally accepted was due largely to the lethargy of the new Association. It was not until 1866 that a truly representative game was arranged and, up to that time, the strong provincial groupings were effectively ignored. Sheffield had approached the newly founded Association as early as 1863 in an attempt to formalise a single code, but received absolutely no encouragment and barely even a formal reply. It is vital to remember that, at this time, the Football Association controlled only the handful of clubs in membership. Most provincial clubs bore no more allegiance to it than the Rugby League does to the Rugby Union today.

But on 31 March 1866 London (in reality the Football Association) did finally take on Sheffield at Battersea Park, winning easily by 2 goals and 4 touch-downs to nil (see law 7). During the match one Charles W Alcock had the distinction of being the first man ruled offside in an official Football Association fixture. The same year Alcock joined the FA Committee and things began to move ahead again.

Born in Sunderland but educated at Harrow, Alcock seems to have had a much wider, national, vision than his contemporaries. He may have been aware that the Association was already being overtaken in the provinces and was instrumental in bringing the first Yorkshire representative on to the FA Committee in 1868. Sheffield

The first ever picture of a Cup final team was taken of the Royal Engineers before the 1872 final, which they lost 1-0. Their captain, Major Francis Marindin, who played in two finals and refereed eight, is standing in the centre.

already had a thriving group of clubs and was about to establish its own association. If Alcock had hoped to forestall this rival he failed, which was probably for the good, as the local associations which were to come into being during the next decade had a vital administrative role to play and in no way ever threatened the ultimate control of the original body in London.

There was already an annual representative game between Sheffield and Nottingham, the other major centre, which had first been played on 2 January 1865 and won by the eighteen-man Sheffield side. The number of players, incidentally, was one of the biggest bones of contention between rival codes in the early years and obviously related to the size of the playing area. Notts County (often known as plain Nottingham before 1880) had been founded in 1862 and are the oldest of the surviving senior clubs. Second in genealogy, and founded in 1865, come rivals Nottingham Forest. The Nottingham clubs sprang from the County Cricket club—then the strongest in England—and some 'shinney' (a form of hockey) players. Both used Trent Bridge as a venue for major matches until the end of the century and thus retained their original links with the Cricket Club. The suffix Forest came from a clearing to the north of Nottingham, once part of renowned Sherwood Forest, where some games were also played.

That was the venue of the Nottingham clubs' first clash (also the first between any two Football League clubs though in 1865 Sheffield had played County) in 1866 which ended in a 1-0 win for Nottingham Forest when, according to a guide of 1871, '. . . there was a sort of steeple chase across the goal-line and over the grandstand railings where W H Revis touched down. The place-kick, 15 yards at right-angles from the goal-line, was taken by the same player.' As can be deduced, the Nottingham game was a hybrid, relying on a mixture of Sheffield, Rugby and London rules with a few Nottingham perversions probably thrown in. Most codes required a try and goal (as in rugby union today) for a proper score until the end of the 1860s.

Elsewhere Chesterfield, midway between Sheffield and Nottingham, was founded in 1866. Stoke have long claimed to have been founded in 1863, but there is no satisfactory evidence of their existence before 1867 and they come next in the ranks of current League clubs (City was added in 1925). Other than Sheffield, the major local associations—such as the Scottish, Lancashire and Birmingham—were not founded until the 1870s and individual provincial clubs tended to vary their rules according to their opponents.

The contact between the FA and Sheffield

Goal-kicks in 1869, Corner kicks in 1872, Umpires in 1874

in 1866 inevitably provoked further efforts to standardise laws throughout the country. The fair catch (and thus handling) was abolished and a tape was soon stretched between the posts (thus returning to the Cambridge Rules) after a goal had been scored at Reigate '. . . from a balloon kick which had passed quite 90 feet in the air between the posts' according to the FA Chairman. Sheffied wanted a bar, but this was not made obligatory until 1882. Free-kicks for infringements had been incorporated in the laws by the 1873-74 season; before this date the game had apparently functioned on the presumption that gentlemen did not commit fouls.

Other law changes gradually followed, although Sheffield continued to play to their own rules when at home until April 1877. Goal-kicks were introduced in 1869, corner-kicks in 1872, umpires in 1874. It was not until 1870 that all clubs accepted eleven-a-side as the norm and, in the same year, came what has been described as the law-makers' master stroke, the innovation of a goalkeeper who was governed by a largely different set of laws from other players. Before this date, whichever player was closest to the goal took the responsibility and, as penalty-kicks were still two decades away, tended to handle regularly.

Strangely, the change of law that was to affect the game most significantly in the next dozen years was not regarded as being

GOLDEN BOOT AWARD (Europe's leading league scorer)

Season	Winner	Gls	Second	Gls	Third	Gls
1967-68	Eusebio *(Benfica)*	43	Antal Dunai *(Ujpest Dozsa)*	36	Bobby Lennox *(Celtic)*	32
1968-69	Petar Jekov *(CSKA Sofia)*	36	George Sideris *(Olympiakos Piraeus)*	35	Antal Dunai *(Ujpest Dozsa)*	32
					Helmut Kogelberger *(FK Austria)*	31
1969-70	Gerd Muller *(Bayern Munich)*	38	*Jan Devillet *(Spora Luxembourg)*	(22)31	Petar Jekov *(CSKA Sofia)*	(30)31
1970-71	Josip Skoblar *(Olympique Marseille)*	44	Salif Keita *(St Etienne)*	42	Georges Dedes *(Panionios, Athens)*	28
1971-72	Gerd Muller *(Bayern Munich)*	40	Antonis Antoniadis *(Panathinaikos)*	39	Joe Harper *(Aberdeen)*	33
					Francis Lee *(Manchester City)*	33
					Slobodan Santrac *(OFK Belgrade)*	33
1972-73	Eusebio *(Benfica)*	40	Gerd Muller *(Bayern Munich)*	36	Petar Jekov *(CSKA Sofia)*	29
1973-74	Hector Yazalde *(Sporting Lisbon)*	46	Hans Krankl *(Rapid Vienna)*	36	Carlos Bianchi *(Stade de Reims)*	30
					Jupp Heynckes *(Borussia M'gladbach)*	30
					Gerd Muller *(Bayern Munich)*	30
1974-75	Dudu Georgescu *(Dynamo Bucharest)*	33	Ruud Geels *(Ajax)*	30	Willy van der Kuylen *(PSV Eindhoven)*	28
			Delio Onnis *(AS Monaco)*	30		
			Hector Yazalde *(Sporting Lisbon)*	30		
1975-76	Sotiris Kaiafas *(Omonia Nicosia)*	39	Carlos Bianchi *(Stade de Reims)*	34	Peter Risi *(FC Zurich)*	33
1976-77	Dudu Georgescu *(Dynamo Bucharest)*	47	Bela Varadi *(Vasas Budapest)*	36	Ruud Geels *(Ajax)*	34
					Dieter Muller *(1FC Cologne)*	34
1977-78	Hans Krankl *(Rapid Vienna)*	41	Carlos Bianchi *(Paris St Germain)*	37	Ruud Geels *(Ajax)*	34
1978-79	Kees Kist *(AZ 67 Alkmaar)*	34	Laszo Fekete *(Ujpest Dozsa)*	31	Hans Krankl *(Barcelona)*	29
			Thomas Mavros *(AEK Athens)*	31		
1979-80	Erwin Vandenbergh *(Lierse)*	39	Laszlo Fazekas *(Ujpest Dozsa)*	36	Walter Schachner *(FK Austria)*	34
1980-81	Georgi Slavkov *(Trakia Plovdiv)*	31	Tibor Nyilasi *(Ferencvaros)*	30	Karl-Heinz Rummenigge *(Bayern Munich)*	29
1981-82	Wim Kieft *(Ajax)*	32	Kees Kist *(AZ 67 Alkmaar)*	29	Allan Hansen *(Odense)*	28
			Delio Onnis *(Tours)*	29		
1982-83	Fernando Gomes *(Porto)*	36	Peter Houtman *(Feyenoord)*	30	Nikos Anastopoulos *(Olympiakos Piraeus)*	29

*took second place on less matches played

of any great importance when it was approved in 1867 and, indeed, it did not affect football materially for several years. This was the alteration of the offside law from the old Harrow (and current rugby) rule that, basically, a player was offside unless he was behind the ball. It was changed to the more relaxed Charterhouse, Westminster and Cambridge version under which an attacker was onside unless there were fewer than three defenders between himself and the goal.

For nearly a century the early English footballers have been criticised for their slavish devotion to the 'dribbling' game. This has often been seen as an ill-considered manifestation of the public school ethic of self-reliance—quite unfairly if viewed alongside the rules adhered to by most schools and the FA before 1866. Under this code a player really had few alternatives. He could either pass back or dribble forwards, and this very simple fact explains the existence of the dribbling game. Its persistence is probably attributable to the conservatism of the sport, in that English teams had developed tactics suited to the old offside law and prized good dribblers above all others. The best of them all, and the first 'Prince of Dribblers', was the Reverend Vidal, who played for Wanderers in the first FA Cup final and who once scored three goals without an opponent touching the ball. This was in a game where the local code had the side which scored kicking off and Vidal simply dribbled straight from the off three times running.

It was not until the English came into contact with Scotland's Queen's Park in 1872 that they began to question their outdated methods. Queen's Park, in determining their own laws, had never been influenced by a repressive history and, from the beginning, had played the more complex 'combination' short passing game. Queen's Park also suffered far less from the competition and influence of the Rugby game. That school was, after all, a long way from Glasgow although the relative success of soccer over its competitors in Scotland is more often put down to the fact that it can be played on literally any surface and, with a little imagination, on any shaped area. Rugby generally requires a soft landing and the Scottish central lowlands had precious few open grassy areas within its towns.

OPPOSITE: ***The oldest programme of which a copy is known to exist today. It was for a friendly between Wanderers and Queen's Park in Glasgow. Queen's Park were still undefeated at the time, 8 years after their foundation, and it was not until the return of this match, played in London in February 1876, that they were first to meet defeat at the feet of the Wanderers.***

The game had had as distinguished a history in Scotland as in England (Sir Walter Scott was a particularly notable fan, writing in 1815: 'Then strip lands, and to it, though sharp be the weather, And if, by mischance you should happen to fall, There are worse things in life than a tumble on heather, And life is itself but a game of football!') but there had been no formal codification. The centres of population were in the central lowlands, and in Glasgow the keenest players eventually gravitated to one of the three public parks—Queen's Park.

On 9 July 1867, together with some local YMCA members and, according to legend, caber-tossing Highlanders who also used the park, the Queen's Park Football Club was founded at number 3 Eglinton Terrace. To begin with, their interests did not extend outide their own domain, matches being arranged between their own members and recorded as 'North of the Clyde' versus 'South of the Clyde' and such like. But gradually outside opposition was discovered and games organised—the first on 1 August 1868 against Thistle (nothing to do with Partick Thistle). Later Queen's Park were to have an influence all pervading north of the border and quite important south of it, but, for the time being, it suffices to say that their interpretation of the rules automatically became the Scottish interpretation.

Back in England, the contacts with Sheffield had awakened the proselytizing spirit in the Football Association and, for the first time, serious efforts were made to recruit new members. The Sheffield club joined in 1867, with teams from as far afield as Hull, Lincolnshire and South Wales. In 1870 Charles Alcock became secretary (at the age of twenty-eight) and the next ten years were to become the most significant in the history of the game, just as Alcock is arguably the most important figure in that history.

Alcock was soon to turn his attention to formally competitive events rather than informally arranged friendlies—and his immediate interest was attracted by the reputation of mighty Queen's Park, who had still not had a goal scored against them! They actually remained unbeaten until February 1876 when Wanderers (the club of which Alcock was secretary and with which he won a Cup winner's medal) finally despatched them in a friendly. However, back in 1870 they were attracting all Scotland's best players but had little contact with England

The Inter-American Cup is an occasional extra fixture between the winners of the Libertadores Cup and its CONCACAF equivalent. That the South Americans do not take it too seriously can be seen from the results.

INTER-AMERICAN CUP

1968† Estudiantes *(Argentina)* beat Toluca *(Mexico)* 1-2, 2-1, 3-0
1971† Nacional *(Uruguay)* beat Cruz Azul *(Mexico)* 2-1, 1-1
1972† Independiente *(Argentina)* beat Olimpia *(Honduras)* 2-0, 2-1
1974 Independiente* *(Argentina)* beat Dep. Municipal *(Guatemala)* 1-0, 0-1
1975† Independiente* *(Argentina)* beat Atletico Espanol *(Mexico)* 2-2, 0-0
1977† America *(Mexico)* beat Boca Juniors *(Argentina)* 0-3, 1-0, 2-1
1979 Olimpia Asuncion *(Paraguay)* beat America *(Mexico)* 0-0, 1-0
1981 Universidad Autonoma *(Mexico)* beat Nacional *(Uruguay)* 3-1, 1-3, 2-1‡
1983 America *(Mexico)* beat Internacional Porto Alegre *(Brazil)* 5-2

*won on penalties †played the following year ‡play off in Los Angeles

FOOTBALL MATCH,

WANDERERS, London, v. QUEEN'S PARK,

Played on Hampden Park, Mount Florida, Glasgow, on Saturday, 9th October, 1875

H. W. CHAMBERS,
*
Goal Keeper

A. H. STRATFORD,
X
Back.

A. F. KINNAIRD,
Right X *Half-back*
Blue and white cap

W. S. RAWSON
Left X *Half-back*
Blue cap

J. TURNER,
Left X *Wing.*

W. D. GREIG,
Right X *Wing*
Blue stockings

R. L. GEAVES,
X
Centre
Red and white cap

C. W. ALCOCK,
Captain X *and Centre.*
Cap—blue and white chequers.

H. S. OTTER,
X
Centre
Pink cap

HUBERT HERON,
Left X *Wing*
Grey stockings and orange, violet, and black cap

J. KENRICK,
Right X *Wing*
Cerise and French grey cap

UMPIRE—ROBERT GARDINER, CLYDESDALE CLUB.
REFEREE—THOMAS HASWELL, 3RD L.R.V. CLUB
UMPIRE—W. C. MITCHELL, QUEEN'S PARK CLUB

HENRY M'NEILL,
Left X *Front*
Orange and black stockings.

W. MACKINNON,
Centre X *Front*
Red stockings.

JAMES B. WEIR,
Right X *Front.*
Red and white stockings.

M. M'NEIL,
Left X *Back-up*
Blue and white stockings.

C. HERRIOT,
Centre X *Back-up*
Black and white cap—no stocking.

THOMAS LAWRIE,
Right X *Back-up.*
White stockings.

JAS. PHILIPS
Left X *Half-back*
Red and black stockings.

CHAS. CAMPBELL,
Right X *Half-back*
Red, white, and black stockings.

R. W. NEIL,
Left X *Back*
Heather mixture stockings

JOSEPH TAYLOR,
Captain and X *Right Back*
Black and white stockings.

JOHN DICKSON,
*
Goal Keeper.

Colours: Wanderers, White Jersey — Queen's Park, Black and White Stripe.

Play will begin at 3.30 p.m, and end at 5 p.m.

PLEASE DO NOT STRAIN THE ROPES.

or the Football Association.

On 3 November that year, Alcock wrote to the *Glasgow Herald* announcing that the FA intended to select teams of English and Scottish players to compete against one another at Kennington Oval on 19 November. He invited nominations, stating: 'In Scotland, once essentially the land of football, there should still be a spark left of the old fire and I confidently appeal to Scotsmen. . . .' Alcock did not expect this challenge to be ignored, nor was it. Queen's Park nominated Robert Smith, one of three brothers who were founder members of Queen's Park and who now lived in London, and he effectively represented Scotland in the capital over the next two years.

The team that eventually lost 1-0 at the Oval was hardly representative of Scotland. W H Gladstone, son of the Prime Minister, was a Member of Parliament himself, Quintin Hogg was father and grandfather of Lord Chancellors of the same name, Lord Kinnaird was later High Commissioner for the Church of Scotland. The whole team was comprised of Scots living in England, and in some cases with only very tenuous links with Scotland at all. Nonetheless, unofficial and unrepresentative though the game was, it was counted a success and three more followed. England won two, the other being drawn 1-1.

In the meantime, at Raeburn Place in Edinburgh, there had been an 'official' international football match—but at rugby, the defecting code. Provoked by this, Alcock and Kinnaird sought to arrange an official soccer equivalent. Wanderers teammates, they had already forged links with Queen's Park during the first FA Cup semi-final early in 1872, and the Glaswegians therefore organised everything from the Scottish side of the border. Their whole team was comprised of Queen's Park or ex-Queen's Park (two of the brothers Smith) men, adequately reflecting their standing in the game at the time.

The momentous event was arranged for 30 November 1872 at the West of Scotland Cricket Club in Partick, and the English went north intending to give the Scots an object lesson in the game. Nothing could have been further from reality. The Scots obviously had an understanding the English could not match, but neither side could score and the game ended in the last goalless draw in a peacetime match for ninety-eight years. Four thousand people turned up to watch, at one shilling a time, and Queen's Park immediately started to look for a larger ground.

Glasgow Corporation agreed to lend them Hampden Park, Mount Florida, which, although the exact location has moved twice, has remained the home of Queen's Park and, by and large, the Scots international team ever since.

As was briefly mentioned, the men of Queen's Park were not unfamiliar to many of the England side. Earlier in the year, they had travelled to London for a game which was (probably correctly) described as: 'the most remarkable event in modern football'. This was that first semi-final of the first ever Football Association Challenge Cup.

The Cup was another of Alcock's innovations and was unashamedly based on a similar competition between the school houses at Harrow (where Alcock has been a pupil between 1855 and 1859). There, the winners of a knock-out competition became 'Cock House'. He put a resolution that such a competition be established on 20 July 1871. It was enthusiastically agreed; the committee were nearly all ex-public school men and shared similar memories from their own schools—although their counterparts at the Rugby Union refused to institute such an idea for another century.

A Cup was purchased for £20 and entries were invited. There were only fifteen, of which two, Maidenhead and Marlow, have entered every year since. Most were home county clubs, but Donington School came from Lincolnshire (though they scratched, never entered again, and thus established the shortest Cup history on record) and the ubiquitous Queen's Park not only entered but also sent a guinea (reputedly one-sixth of their income that year) towards the cost of the trophy.

Queen's Park remained a more or less enthusiastic member of the Football Association for over a decade and the founding of the Scottish FA, the Scottish Cup, and the formal codification of the laws are all very closely linked to their regular contact with the Association in London.

The FA Cup was an imitation of Harrow's house cup

For the first few years all semi-finals and finals had to be played in London, and Queen's Park therefore travelled to Surrey County Cricket Club's ground at Kennington Oval for their game against the Wanderers, the renamed Forest of 1863. Their opponents had also arrived by a less than strenuous route. In the first round opponents Harrow Chequers (an old boys club) had scratched, in the second they defeated Clapham Rovers 3-1, in the third they drew with Crystal Palace but both teams went through to provide four semi-finalists.

Thus, on 4 March 1872, Charles Alcock's Wanderers faced Queen's Park in the first ever semi-final—between them having won only one game to get there!

The match was something of an anti-climax—the dribbling Wanderers and the short passing Scotsmen effectively neutralising each other for a 0-0 draw. Queen's Park had to go home before the decider, could not afford to travel the 400 miles again, and Wanderers went through to the final. They had gone through four rounds by winning only one game, but history only remembers the victors and they won the one that mattered on 16 March 1872.

Their opponents in that first Cup final, of any competition, anywhere, were Royal Engineers, 7-4 favourites and probably the best team of their time. Engineers were unlucky in that Lieutenant Cresswell broke his collar bone in the first ten minutes and, though he played on, they could not equal Wanderers' one goal scored by M P Betts. Betts, for many years subsequently a member of the FA Committee, was down on the team sheet as A H Chequer, meaning that he had played for the same Harrow Chequers that had scratched to Wanderers in the first round.

Why Betts played under this pseudonym has never been established—but he has found a place in history under both names. The long-term significance of the Cup was not what it initially seemed; what it did do was to force the provincial clubs to play to FA rules. It was the most prized trophy, so if a club from Nottingham or Scotland wished to contest it, they had to play to FA rules. It did not matter what they did normally; in a Cup match the rules were uniform. The benefits of such an arrangement were soon clear to everyone, but without the Cup who knows how long it would have been before the whole country, and later the world, recognised the fact and played a single game.

ABOVE: The first clear picture taken of an FA Cup final in progress at Crystal Palace. The game had moved there in 1895 and this picture was taken in 1897 during the famous final between Aston Villa and Everton on 10 April 1897. Villa had already secured the League Championship, eventually winning it by a then record 11-point margin from Sheffield United. In the Cup final, which Villa needed for the Double of course, all the goals were scored in the 25 minutes before half-time. Campbell, Devey and Crabtree scored for Villa, Bell and Hartley for Everton and Villa thus became only the second Double winners.
RIGHT: The Home International Championship (renamed the British Championship in the 1980s) finally staggered to an end after exactly 100 years in 1984 when both England and Scotland declared that they could no longer spare the dates for games against Wales and Northern Ireland.

UEFA YOUTH TOURNAMENT FINALS

Year	Venue	Winners		Runners-up	
1948	London	England	3	Holland	2
1949	Rotterdam	France	4	Holland	1
1950	Vienna	Austria	3	France	2
1951	Cannes	Yugoslavia	3	Austria	2
1952	Barcelona	*Spain	0	Belgium	0
1953	Brussels	Hungary	2	Yugoslavia	0
1954	Cologne	*Spain	2	West Germany	2
1955	Italy†				
1956	Hungary‡				
1957	Madrid	Austria	3	Spain	2
1958	Luxembourg	Italy	1	England	0
1959	Sofia	Bulgaria	1	Italy	0
1960	Vienna	Hungary	2	Rumania	1
1961	Lisbon	Portugal	4	Poland	0
1962	Bucharest	Rumania	4	Yugoslavia	1
1963	London	England	4	Northern Ireland	0
1964	Amsterdam	England	4	Spain	0
1965	Essen	East Germany	3	England	2
1966	Belgrade	§Italy	0	§USSR	0
1967	Istanbul	USSR	1	England	0
1968	Cannes	Czechoslovakia	2	France	1
1969	Leipzig	*Bulgaria	1	East Germany	1
1970	Glasgow	*East Germany	1	Holland	1
1971	Prague	England	3	Portugal	0
1972	Barcelona	England	2	West Germany	0
1973	Florence	England	3	East Germany	2
1974	Malmo	Bulgaria	1	Yugoslavia	0
1975	Berne	England	1	Finland	0
1976	Budapest	USSR	1	Hungary	0
1977	Brussels	Belgium	2	Bulgaria	1
1978	Krakow	USSR	3	Yugoslavia	0
1979	Vienna	Yugoslavia	1	Bulgaria	0
1980	Leipzig	England	2	Poland	1
1981	Dusseldorf	West Germany	1	Poland	0
1982	Helsinki	Scotland	3	Czechoslovakia	1
1983	London	France	1	Czechoslovakia	0

*won on toss of a coin †played in groups only (group winners: Bulgaria, Czechoslovakia, Hungary, Italy and Rumania) ‡played in groups only (group winners: Czechoslovakia, Hungary, Rumania and Italy) §joint holders

EUROPEAN UNDER-23/UNDER-21 CHAMPIONSHIP

1970-72†	Czechoslovakia v USSR* (2-2, 3-1)	5-3
1972-74†	Hungary v East Germany* (2-3, 4-0)	6-3
1974-76†	USSR v Hungary* (1-1, 2-1)	3-2
1976-78‡	Yugoslavia* v East Germany (1-0, 4-4)	5-4
1978-80	East Germany* v USSR (0-0, 1-0)	1-0
1980-82	England* v West Germany (3-1, 2-3)	5-4

*home team in first leg †Under-23 ‡Under-21 from 1976 onwards

HOME INTERNATIONAL CHAMPIONSHIP

Season	Winners	Pts
1883-84	Scotland	6
1884-85	Scotland	5
1885-86	England/Scotland	5
1886-87	Scotland	6
1887-88	England	6
1888-89	Scotland	5
1889-90	England/Scotland	5
1890-91	England	6
1891-92	England	6
1892-93	England	6
1893-94	Scotland	5
1894-95	England	5
1895-96	Scotland	5
1896-97	Scotland	5
1897-98	England	6
1898-99	England	6
1899-1900	Scotland	6
1900-01	England	5
1901-02	Scotland	5
1902-03	England/Scotland Ireland	4
1903-04	England	5
1904-05	England	5
1905-06	England/Scotland	4
1906-07	Wales	5
1907-08	England/Scotland	5
1908-09	England	6
1909-10	Scotland	4
1910-11	England	5
1911-12	England/Scotland	5
1912-13	England	4
1913-14	Ireland	5
1915-18	*No competition*	

Season	Winners	Pts
1919-20	Wales	4
1920-21	Scotland	6
1921-22	Scotland	4
1922-23	Scotland	5
1923-24	Wales	6
1924-25	Scotland	6
1925-26	Scotland	6
1926-27	England/Scotland	4
1927-28	Wales	5
1928-29	Scotland	6
1929-30	England	6
1930-31	England/Scotland	4
1931-32	England	6
1932-33	Wales	5
1933-34	Wales	5
1934-35	England/Scotland	4
1935-36	Scotland	4
1936-37	Wales	6
1937-38	England	4
1938-39	England/Scotland/ Wales	4
1940-45	*No competition*	
1946-47	England	5
1947-48	England	5
1948-49	Scotland	6
1949-50	England	6
1950-51	Scotland	6
1951-52	England/Wales	5
1952-53	England/Scotland	4
1953-54	England	6
1954-55	England	6
1955-56	England/Scotland/ Wales/N. Ireland	3

Season	Winners	Pts
1956-57	England	5
1957-58	England/N. Ireland	4
1958-59	England/N. Ireland	4
1959-60	England/Scotland/ Wales	4
1960-61	England	6
1961-62	Scotland	6
1962-63	Scotland	6
1963-64	England/Scotland/ N. Ireland	4
1964-65	England	5
1965-66	England	5
1966-67	Scotland	5
1967-68	England	5
1968-69	England	6
1969-70	England/Scotland/ Wales	4
1970-71	England	5
1971-72	England/Scotland	4
1972-73	England	6
1973-74	England/Scotland	4
1974-75	England	4
1975-76	Scotland	6
1976-77	Scotland	5
1977-78	England	6
1978-79	England	5
1979-80	N. Ireland	5
1980-81	*Not completed*	
1981-82	England	6
1982-83	England	5
1983-84		

Competition not contested after 1984

Tango
5

WORLD CUP

With the Olympics struggling to preserve their very being, the FIFA World Cup could now claim to be the world's most important sporting competition. It is, after all, the major event of man's most popular recreation: millions of people watch thousands of players from over 140 countries take more than two years to complete it . . .

For all its present status and popularity, the World Cup had a laboured beginning. At the first meeting of FIFA in Paris in 1904 the seven member countries—Switzerland, Belgium, Denmark, France, the Netherlands, Spain, and Sweden—did include a provision in the constitution stating that only FIFA had the right to organize such a tournament. Yet it was not until 1920, at the Antwerp Congress, that the principle of the cup was agreed.

At the 1926 Congress, the secretary of the French Federation, Henri Delaunay, maintained that the Olympic Games no longer represented the best (the professionals) from many nations. And two years later, at the FIFA meeting during the Amsterdam Olympics, it was decided to hold a world championship every fourth year. The following year, at Barcelona, Uruguay won approval to stage the initial tournament in 1930.

The Uruguayans had several claims to be the hosts: they had won the Olympic gold medals of 1924 and 1928, they celebrated their centenary in 1930, and they promised to pay every team's full expenses and install a crash programme to build a new 100,000-capacity stadium.

As the new competition approached, however, European enthusiasm evaporated, and with only eight weeks to go no country had entered. The prominent soccer powers—Austria, Czechoslovakia, Germany, Hungary, Italy, Spain, and Switzerland—all declined, and the British contingent were ineligible, having withdrawn from FIFA in 1928 over the question of broken-time payments. Europe was represented by four nations, though none could be rated as a major force in continental football.

The South Americans, on the other hand, provided seven entries, with Argentina, Bolivia, Brazil, Chile, Peru, and Paraguay joining the hosts. The United States, who were to do surprisingly well, and Mexico made up the motley 13.

Luque, skipper Passarella, Ardiles and Larrosa with the FIFA World Cup after Argentina's 3-1 extra-time win over Holland in the 11th final.
OPPOSITE: An aggressive Joe Jordan during Scotland's 3-2 victory over Holland in 1978.

Uruguay, 1930

Because the tournament lacked the number of sides necessary for the planned knock-out system, the organizers seeded the teams and grouped them in four sections, with four in one and three in each of the others.

The competition proved an exercise for the South Americans, Uruguay and Argentina repeating their 1928 Olympic final, though Yugoslavia and the United States were the losing semi-finalists. The Americans were the surprise of the series. Nicknamed 'the shot-putters' by the French because of their bulky build, the side included six British ex-professionals.

The first ever World Cup match saw France beat Mexico 4-1 in a Group 1 fixture on the 13 July 1930. The French triumphed despite losing goalkeeper Thépot, but they failed to keep up that standard, and subsequently lost to South American champions Argentina and Chile. The seeded Argentinians, with Guillermo Stabile scoring five times, comfortably removed Mexico and Chile to lead the group.

In Group 2 Yugoslavia surprised Brazil, the seeds, by 2-1, and then qualified for the last four by beating Bolivia 4-0. Uruguay scraped home 1-0 against Peru and then beat Rumania 4-0 to head Group 3. Meanwhile, the United States lived up to their unexpected seed rating with 3-0 wins over both Belgium and Paraguay.

The semi-finals proved illuminating. An experienced Argentina exposed the brave but limited qualities of the Americans and won 6-1, though five of their goals came in the second half. Uruguay dealt with Yugoslavia by the same score, Cea getting three goals.

Thus the final, played in front of 90,000 people on 30 July, involved traditional and bitter rivals. Uruguay had beaten Argentina 2-1 in the replayed Olympic final of 1928.

It was expected to be a tough, explosive game, with temperament a key factor. Boatloads of Argentinians crossed the River Plate and were searched for arms. The rivalry of the two sides was such that, after an argument, the two halves of the match were played with different balls—one manufactured in each country.

Uruguay, who started without their star young centre-forward Pelegrin Anselmo, won 4-2. Outside-right Pablo Dorado put them ahead in the 12th minute, but the Argentinians equalized through Carlos Peucelle and then took the lead with a disputed goal by Stabile, his eighth of the series.

In the second half, however, Uruguay began to capitalize on their technical superiority, especially at half-back. Cea made it 2-2 after a fine dribble. Iriarte gave them a lead with a fine opportunist goal, and then Castro, deputizing for Anselmo, put the issue virtually beyond doubt with a long-range drive.

Montevideo went wild, and the following day was declared a national holiday. The Argentinians demonstrated in the streets of Buenos Aires, slated Uruguay in their press, and finally broke off relations with the Football Association in Montevideo.

With its limited European entry, violent play, and indifferent refereeing, the initial competition for the Jules Rimet Trophy was hardly an unqualified success. It had, nevertheless, made the long-awaited break into intercontinental national competition, and adequately laid the basis for the contests of the future.

Different balls for the two halves of the final

TOP: ***Jules Rimet, president of the French Football Federation, was elected president of FIFA in 1920 and held that position until 1954. Nobody did more to gain support for the idea of a world championship, and it was fitting that the first trophy was named after him.***
ABOVE: ***Guillermo Stabile gives Argentina a 2-1 lead in the 1930 final, but hosts Uruguay went on to win 4-2.***

1st WORLD CUP, URUGUAY, 1930

POOL 1

France 4 Mexico 1
Argentina 1 France 0
Chile 3 Mexico 0
Chile 1 France 0
Argentina 6 Mexico 3
Argentina 3 Chile 1

	P	W	D	L	F	A	P
Argentina	3	3	0	0	10	4	6
Chile	3	2	0	1	5	3	4
France	3	1	0	2	4	3	2
Mexico	3	0	0	3	4	13	0

POOL 2

Yugoslavia 2 Brazil 1
Yugoslavia 4 Bolivia 0
Brazil 4 Bolivia 0

	P	W	D	L	F	A	P
Yugoslavia	2	2	0	0	6	1	4
Brazil	2	1	0	1	5	2	2
Bolivia	2	0	0	2	0	8	0

POOL 3

Rumania 3 Peru 1
Uruguay 1 Peru 0
Uruguay 4 Rumania 0

	P	W	D	L	F	A	P
Uruguay	2	2	0	0	5	0	4
Rumania	2	1	0	1	3	5	2
Peru	2	0	0	2	1	4	0

POOL 4

United States 3 Belgium 0
United States 3 Paraguay 0
Paraguay 1 Belgium 0

	P	W	D	L	F	A	P
United States	2	2	0	0	6	0	4
Paraguay	2	1	0	1	1	3	2
Belgium	2	0	0	2	0	4	0

SEMI-FINALS

Uruguay 6 Yugoslavia 1
Argentina 6 United States 1

FINAL

Uruguay 4 Argentina 2
(Montevideo, 30.7.30, 90,000)

Uruguay: Ballesteros, Nasazzi, Mascheroni, Andrade, Fernandez, Gestido, Dorado, Scarone, Castro, Cea, Iriarte

Argentina: Botasso, Della Torre, Paternoster, J. Evaristo, Monti, Suarez, Peucelle, Varallo, Stabile, Ferreira, M. Evaristo

Scorers: Dorado, Cea, Iriarte, Castro; Peucelle, Stabile

Italy, 1934

Impressed by the first series, but more enticed by the decision to hold the tournament in their continent, the European nations responded well in 1934. The entry list rose to 34, grouped in 10 sections to produce 16 finalists.

The composition of the final series was very different from that of 1930. Of the teams of the initial tournament only Argentina, Brazil, Belgium, France, and the United States were present, and the Argentinians, frightened of losing more players to Italian clubs, did not compete at full strength. The most notable absentee was Uruguay, no doubt annoyed by the European reaction of four years earlier but also troubled by domestic matters.

The Italians had the most improved side in Europe. Team manager Vittorio Pozzo had brought in three Argentinians of Italian extraction Guaita, Orsi, and Luisito Monti, who played in the 1930 final.

A simple knock-out system was employed, with half the 16 sides seeded. Italy started proceedings on 27 May by beating the United States—who had

An early end to the South American challenge in Europe

only three of their 1930 team left—7-1 in Rome, one of eight venues used for the series. At Florence the Germans, thorough as ever in preparation but somewhat uninspired, took Belgium 5-2, with a hat-trick from Cönen, after being 1-2 down at halftime. Austria made heavy weather of beating France at Turin.

A workmanlike Swedish team overcame Argentina (with none of the 1930 final side present) by the same margin at Bologna, and with Brazil missing a penalty in their 3-1 defeat by Spain in Genoa, the South American challenge came to an early end.

On the whole the first round had been free from incident, but the quarter-finals were a different story. The worst, perhaps, was at Florence, where a splendid display by Zamora enabled Spain to hold Italy to a 1-1 draw. For the replay the following day seven Spaniards, including the roughly handled Zamora, and four Italians were non-starters because of injury. The hosts got through with a Meazza goal in a game even more badly refereed than the first—so much so that the Swiss official, M. Mercet, was suspended by his national federation.

Fancied Austria bow out in the Milan mud

At Bologna, what promised to be a classic duel between neighbours Austria and Hungary degenerated into an ill-tempered scramble. Hungary's outside-right Markos was sent off after a fight, and Austria held on to win 2-1.

Germany beat a Swedish side reduced for much of the game at Milan to 10 men. By far the best match of the round was in Turin, where Czechoslovakia played Switzerland. The Swiss swarmed all over their opponents but the Czechs, with Planicka again superb in goal, kept their head and won 3-2 with a Nejedly goal seven minutes from time.

One semi-final saw the favourites clash. The Italians had Schiavio and Ferrari back after the debacle against Spain, but Austria lacked Horwath, who had come into the side against Hungary and scored in the opening minutes. The traditional game of the Austrians was, however, lost in a sea of mud at Milan, and Italy, showing considerable staying power only two days after their replay with Spain, won with a first-half goal from Guaita.

In Rome, the improving Czechs were too clever for the Germans, and won with two goals from Nejedly and one from Kreil. In the third place match at Naples a dejected Austria lost 3-2 to Germany.

Three days later, in a final remarkable for its two great goalkeeper-captains, Czechoslovakia surprised Italy with the standard of their neat, short-passing game. With Antonin Puc causing havoc on the left, and Planicka supreme in goal, they had slightly the better of a goalless first half. The 55,000 spectators saw Puc score from a corner 20 minutes from time, and the Czechs should then have clinched it, Sobotka missing a good chance and Svoboda hitting a post. But with Schiavio and Guaita changing positions the Italians came more into the game, and Orsi equalized eight minutes from time with a goal that was either genius or fluke, his swerving shot curling over the hands of a groping Planicka (in practice the next day he could not repeat it). After seven minutes of extra time the ball went from the injured Meazza, on the wing, to Guaita and on to Schiavio, who scored the winner. The hosts had again secured the Jules Rimet Trophy.

2nd WORLD CUP, ITALY, 1934

FIRST ROUND

Italy 7 United States 1
Spain 3 Brazil 1
Hungary 4 Egypt 2
Austria *3 France 2
Germany 5 Belgium 2
Sweden 3 Argentina 2
Switzerland 3 Holland 2
Czechoslovakia 2 Rumania 1

SECOND ROUND

Italy 1:1 Spain 1:0
Austria 2 Hungary 1
Germany 2 Sweden 1
Czechoslovakia 3 Switzerland 2

SEMI-FINALS

Italy 1 Austria 0
Czechoslovakia 3 Germany 1

THIRD PLACE MATCH

Germany 3 Austria 2†

FINAL

Italy 2 Czechoslovakia 1 [aet]
(Rome, 10.6.34, 55,000)

Italy: Combi, Monzeglio, Allemandi, Ferraris, Monti, Bertolini, Guaita, Meazza, Schiavio, Ferrari, Orsi

Czechoslovakia: Planicka, Zenisek, Ctyroky, Kostalek, Cambal, Krcil, Junek, Svoboda, Sobotka, Nejedly, Puc

Scorers: Orsi, Schiavio; Puc

*after extra time †in Naples

ABOVE RIGHT: ***The Italian side that beat Czechoslovakia 3-1 at Rome in the 1934 final.*** *Back:* ***Pozzo (coach), Combi, Monzeglio, Allemandi, Ferraris, Monti;*** *Front:* ***Bertolini, Guaita, Meazza, Schiavio, Ferrari, Orsi. Luisito Monti had played in the 1930 final for Argentina.***

RIGHT: ***Inter's star Giuseppe Meazza, one of only two players to gain winner's medals with Italy in 1934 and 1938. The other was Giovanni Ferrari.***

France, 1938

Argentina wish to stage the 1938 World Cup, but in spite of the mounting political tension in Europe, France was chosen—and Argentina would have to wait 40 years for their turn to come. The competition attracted 36 entries, with 16 qualifying for the finals. Uruguay, still worried by the crisis of professionalism, again refused to participate, as did a peeved Argentina. Spain was in the throes of civil war, and Austria, having qualified, were forcibly withdrawn when she was swallowed up by an increasingly belligerent Germany. No less than 11 of the countries who competed four years earlier were present, and the newcomers were Poland, Norway, Cuba, and the Dutch East Indies.

Champions Italy were thought by manager Pozzo to have a stronger side than in 1934. Only Meazza and Ferrari survived from that team, and between them Schiavio had been replaced by the powerful Silvio Piola.

A much-changed Hungary, conquerors of Czechoslovakia by 8-3 the previous September, had an in-form Sarosi getting good support from the young inside-left Szengeller. Planicka, Kostalek, Nejedly, and Puc survived from the Czech side of 1934, and they were well fancied, but Germany, now under Sepp Herberger, were smarting from the 6-3 defeat by England in Berlin only a few weeks before—their first loss in 15 matches.

Leonidas stars for Brazil in a 6-5 special

The straight elimination system was again employed, but after England had refused a generous offer to take Austria's place, Sweden won a bye through to the quarter-finals. The first round was close fought, with two matches requiring replays and three being decided in extra time.

Three fancied countries were extended to extra time by less endowed sides. At Le Havre, Czechoslovakia were perhaps lucky that the Dutch lacked their leading scorer Bakhuijs; Italy were almost upset by gallant Norway at Marseille; and Poland really surprised Brazil, South America's sole representatives, in a remarkable game at Strasbourg. Brazil, with six players winning their first cap, took a 3-1 half-time lead, but at the end of 90 minutes Poland had pulled back to 4-4. In extra time both Leonidas and Ernest Willimowski took their personal tallies to four goals each, but another by Romeu proved decisive: 6-5.

Two matches went to a replay. Germany, now fielding four Austrians, were held 1-1 by the Swiss, and in the replay Switzerland came back from 2-0 down to win 4-2 against a side with six new players.

The greatest surprise of the round was Cuba's elimination of Rumania in Toulouse, 2-1 after a 3-3 draw.

3rd WORLD CUP, FRANCE, 1938

FIRST ROUND

Italy *2 Norway 1
France 3 Belgium 1
Czechoslovakia *3 Holland 0
Brazil 6 Poland 5
Cuba *3:2 Rumania 3:1
Switzerland *1:4 Germany 1:2
Hungary 6 Dutch East Indies 0
[Sweden received bye]

SECOND ROUND

Italy 3 France 1
Brazil *1:2 Czechoslovakia 1:1
Sweden 8 Cuba 0
Hungary 2 Switzerland 0

SEMI-FINALS

Italy 2 Brazil 1
Hungary 5 Sweden 1

THIRD PLACE MATCH

Brazil 4 Sweden 2†

FINAL

Italy 4 Hungary 2
(Paris, 19.6.38, 65,000)

Italy: Olivieri, Foni, Rava, Serantoni, Andreolo, Locatelli, Biavati, Meazza, Piola, Ferrari, Colaussi

Hungary: Szabo, Polger, Biro, Szalay, Szucs, Lazar, Sas, Vincze, Sarosi, Szengeller, Titkos

Scorers: Colaussi 2, Piola 2; Titkos, Sarosi

*after extra time †at Bordeaux

TOP: Italy coach Vittorio Pozzo holds the Jules Rimet Trophy aloft after his side had retained the world championship by beating Hungary 4-2 at Paris in 1938.
ABOVE: Titkos equalizes for Hungary in the final. Italy scored twice more before half-time, however, and went on to become the first country to win the trophy outside their own borders.

In the quarter-finals, Italy, with three changes, looked more like champions in beating France 3-1 in front of 58,000 at the Stade Colombes. Delfour and Mattler were playing in their third World Cup for France but it was Piola, with two goals, who stole the limelight. Sweden aligned freshness with experience to end the Cuban dream 8-0 at Antibes, with Gustav Wetterstroem accounting for half the score.

At the new municipal stadium in Bordeaux, Czechoslovakia took on Brazil in what proved to be the one large blot on the 1938 copybook. Two Brazilians and a Czech were sent off by referee von Hertzka, while Planicka (broken arm) and Nejedly (broken leg) ended in hospital—the latter after he had equalized Leonidas' goal from a penalty. The match finished at 1-1 after extra time. The replay, under M. Capdeville of France, was remarkably well tempered, with only seven players remaining from the first encounter. Leonidas, one of the two surviving Brazilians, and Roberto erased Kopecky's half-time lead.

For the semi-final against Italy at Marseille two days later, Brazil unaccountably omitted Leonidas and Tim, and paid the price. In the other game, Hungary exposed Sweden 5-1 at Stade Colombes.

The final, watched by 65,000 at Stade Colombes on 19 June, was a good one, the Italians playing with speed and energy, the Hungarians with grace and precision. Colaussi, for the third successive match, put Italy ahead, but a tremendous cheer went up when Titkos equalized less than a minute later. Meazza, given too much space, then made two goals—one for Piola and a second for Colaussi—and the holders went in 3-1 up at half-time. Sarosi scrambled one in after the break to raise hopes of a revival, but Piola restored the two-goal difference and Italy had retained the trophy.

Brazil, 1950

The 1950 series in Brazil, the first for 12 years, was in many ways an inconsistent one: on the one hand it had only 31 entries, a number of withdrawals, and an illogical organization; on the other it produced some fine football and some eye-catching shocks.

Only four of the nations who were present in 1938 attended, and that group (Brazil, Italy, Sweden, and Switzerland) included the hosts and the holders. Several of the notable absentees—Hungary, Czechoslovakia, Austria, and West Germany (who were not yet in FIFA and had not played a full international)—were in turmoil.

England entered for the first time. Britain had rejoined FIFA in 1946, and the 1949-50 Home International Championship was generously designed as a qualifying group, with two teams going through. Scotland, with inexplicable narrow-mindedness, stated they would go to Brazil only as champions, so after England beat them 1-0 at Hampden Park they stayed at home.

The groups were left as one of four, two of three, and one of two sides. Uruguay and Bolivia (France having withdrawn). The cup was to be decided on a league basis, and won by the country finishing top of a final

First-timers England are seeded—and then humiliated

pool. Four sides—Brazil, England, Italy, and Uruguay—were seeded.

In the giant shell of the still uncompleted Maracana Stadium, Brazil kicked off against Mexico on 24 June preceded by a 21-gun salute, firecrackers, balloons, and pigeons. Mexico's keeper Carbajal, playing in what proved to be the first of five consecutive World Cups, let in four goals, including two from Ademir, and Brazil had an easy passage. It was a different story, however, when the Brazilians travelled to São Paulo to play Switzerland. Costa included several local players to please the crowd, but Switzerland proved no easy opponents and Brazil were booed off after the Swiss had squared the match at 2-2 a few minutes before time.

With an in-form Yugoslavia having produced two convincing wins over Switzerland and Mexico, Brazil had to win in Rio to qualify. Zizinho played his first match and scored the second in the 2-0 win.

The sensations were reserved for Group 2. In their opening game at Maracana, England had a laboured win over a Chile side that included George Robledo, the Newcastle United star, at centre-forward; Mortensen and Mannion got the goals. At Curitiba the Americans aroused memories of 1930 by taking the lead against Spain and holding it until 10 minutes from time before going down to goals from Basora (2) and Zarra. The same players then scored one each against Chile in Rio to give Spain maximum points from two games.

Meanwhile, up at Belo Horizonte, there occurred one of the biggest upsets in the history of international football: England were beaten 1-0 by the United States—and despite all the excuses beaten fair and square.

Thus England had to beat Spain handsomely in Rio to keep in the hunt, and they made wholesale changes: Milburn took over from Bentley at centre-forward, Matthews came in on the right-wing with Finney moving over to dislodge Mullen on the left. Two new caps, left-back Roy Eckersley and inside-left Eddie Baily, displaced Aston and Mannion. But it was all to no avail: Milburn's 14th-minute goal was disallowed for offside, and Spain won with a header from Zarra in the second half. Chile beat the Americans 5-2 in Recife to emphasize England's plight.

Giant-killers emerged from Group 3 in the shape of Sweden. English coach George Raynor had rebuilt the 1948 Olympic winners with players such as Hasse Jeppson and Nacka Skoglund. Italy, with managerial and selection rows and still suffering from the Torino club's air crash of 1949, were unsettled, but managed to take the lead

4th WORLD CUP, BRAZIL, 1950

POOL 1

Brazil 4 Mexico 0
Yugoslavia 3 Switzerland 0
Yugoslavia 4 Mexico 1
Brazil 2 Switzerland 2
Brazil 2 Yugoslavia 0
Switzerland 2 Mexico 0

	P	W	D	L	F	A	P
Brazil	3	2	1	0	8	2	5
Yugoslavia	3	2	0	1	7	3	4
Switzerland	3	1	1	1	4	6	3
Mexico	3	0	0	3	2	10	0

POOL 2

Spain 3 United States 1
England 2 Chile 0
United States 1 England 0
Spain 2 Chile 0
Spain 1 England 0
Chile 5 United States 2

	P	W	D	L	F	A	P
Spain	3	3	0	0	6	1	6
England	3	1	0	2	2	2	2
Chile	3	1	0	2	5	6	2
United States	3	1	0	2	4	8	2

POOL 3

Sweden 3 Italy 2
Sweden 2 Paraguay 2
Italy 2 Paraguay 0

	P	W	D	L	F	A	P
Sweden	2	1	1	0	5	4	3
Italy	2	1	0	1	4	3	2
Paraguay	2	0	1	1	2	4	1

POOL 4

Uruguay 8 Bolivia 0

FINAL POOL

Uruguay 2 Spain 2
Brazil 7 Sweden 1
Uruguay 3 Sweden 2
Brazil 6 Spain 1
Sweden 3 Spain 1
Uruguay 2 Brazil 1*

	P	W	D	L	F	A	P
Uruguay	3	2	1	0	7	5	5
Brazil	3	2	0	1	14	4	4
Sweden	3	1	0	2	6	11	2
Spain	3	0	1	2	4	11	1

*last game in pool became unofficial final, with Brazil needing only to draw to win the series; (Rio de Janeiro, 16.7.50, 199,854):

Uruguay: Maspoli, Gonzales, Tejera, Gambetta, Varela, Andrade, Ghiggia, Perez, Miguez, Schiaffino, Moran

Brazil: Barbosa, Augusto, Juvenal, Bauer, Danilo, Bigode, Friaca, Zizinho, Ademir, Jair, Chico

Scorers: Schiaffino, Ghiggia; Friaca

The appeals of Uruguay's right-half Schubert Gambetta were irrelevant as Ademir's shot in the 1950 'final' went wide. Brazil only had to draw in Rio to win the cup—but lost 2-1.

through their captain, Carapallese, in front of a Sao Paulo crowd full of Italo-Brazilians. The Swedes retaliated with three goals, two of them by Jeppson, and though Muccinelli pulled one back Italy had lost. Sweden could only draw 2-2 with Paraguay at Curitiba, but Italy's 2-0 win over the South Americans at São Paulo three days later put Sweden through.

The odds-on favourites fall to their old bogey team

In the fourth group, if that was what it was, Uruguay humbled Bolivia 8-0 at Belo Horizonte, with four coming from Juan Schiaffino. The final pool thus comprised two seeds, Brazil and Uruguay, with Sweden and Spain.

Brazil opened at Rio by swamping Sweden 7-1, and received a bonus the same day when Uruguay, their obvious rivals, were held to a 2-2 draw by Spain at Sao Paulo.

Spain travelled up to Rio to face Brazil, and were beaten 6-1. At Sao Paulo Uruguay came from behind twice to beat Sweden, but having won through with goals from Ghiggia and Miguez (2), they had to beat Brazil to win the World Cup.

For the 'final' on 16 July, nearly 200,000 squeezed into the unfinished Maracana Stadium, despite only 150,000 tickets being sold. Brazil were 1-10 favourites, and were on £10,000 a man even if they drew, which would give them the trophy. But they knew as well as anyone that Uruguay were their 'bogey' team. And so it proved. Yet early on it was all Brazil, who for 45 minutes pounded an iron Uruguayan defence superbly controlled by Varela and with Maspoli in remarkable form in goal. Two minutes after half-time it cracked. Friaça scored, and the passionate home fans waited for the deluge. It did not come. Uruguay, with Varela moving up, came more into the play. After 65 minutes he sent Ghiggia down the right, and the tiny winger crossed to an unmarked Schiaffino, who beat Barbosa with his shot. With 11 minutes to go Ghiggia took a return pass from Perez and ran on to score the winner.

The Uruguayans obviously knew Brazil. They absorbed the pressure, stayed cool, and when the moment arrived took the initiative with clinical precision. Brazil had been robbed, but legally. They had to wait eight years for compensation, and 20 years for revenge, when they won the semi-final in Mexico.

The United States centre-forward Larry Gaetjens is chaired off the pitch at Belo Horizonte after his goal had beaten England in what was then—and possibly still is—the biggest upset in World Cup history.

Switzerland, 1954

If Brazil had been favourites in 1950, Hungary were virtual certainties in 1954. They were unbeaten in four years, during which they had played the cream of Europe, scoring 104 goals against 25 in 25 matches. They had thrashed England 6-3 at Wembley in November 1953 and 7-1 in Budapest the following May—three weeks before the World Cup.

The Home International Championship was again employed as a qualifying group, and this time Scotland, who again came second to England, condescended to enter. They were, however, without any players from Rangers, who considered a club tour more important.

The Latin American representation dwindled from six to three—Brazil, Uruguay, and Mexico—with Uruguay, twice winners and yet to lose a match, at last entering a European World Cup.

In Group 2, which was to provide both finalists, Hungary started by swallowing Korea 9-0 at Zurich, and West Germany beat Turkey 4-1 in Berne. Then came the match which, in its subtle way, was to decide the series: Germany against Hungary at Basle.

Hungary, apart from Toth for Budai at outside-right, were at full strength, but Sepp Herberger fielded a side that included at least six reserves. His reasoning seems to have been that Germany would easily dispose of Turkey in the play-off, and then, if the Hungarians met his side again in the final, they would know little of them. As it was, it worked, but he had an unexpected piece of fortune. Puskas, after a clash with Werner Liebrich, had to go off with an injury that was to keep him out until the final. Hungary won the initial encounter 8-3 (four from Kocsis, whose heading was superb).

Germany throw a game—in order to win the final

Turkey, as expected, beat South Korea (7-0), and West Germany, as planned, beat Turkey in the play-off, by 7-2.

ABOVE: ***Brazil's Julinho comes up against Yugoslavia's Horvat in the group 1 game at Lausanne.***
ABOVE RIGHT: ***Zoltan Czibor put Hungary 2-0 up after only eight minutes in the final.***
RIGHT: ***Less than a minute later Morlock replied for the Germans and put them on the road to a remarkable win, a goal in each half from Helmut Rahn snatching victory from the favourites.***

Austria and Uruguay were the seeds in Group 3. Uruguay found Czechoslovakia difficult to master in the Berne mud, and were seen through only by two late goals, while at Zurich Austria were a little fortunate to beat Scotland 1-0. Team manager Andy Beattie then resigned following criticism, and the Scots were in no mental state to face classy Uruguay at Basle. An unchanged side crashed 7-0, giving away five in the second-half.

In Group 4, seeded England drew a fluctuating game with Belgium at Basle despite being 3-1 up with only a quarter of an hour left.

At the same time, Italy were being upset 2-1 by Switzerland at Lausanne.

For England's game with Switzerland at Berne three days later, new men Jimmy Mullen and Denis Wilshaw of Wolves both scored in a dull encounter to enable England to qualify. At

Lugano, Italy beat Belgium 4-1 to secure a play-off with Switzerland in Basle, but lost the chance to reassert themselves when they went down 4-1.

The first two quarter-finals, Uruguay v England at Basle and Austria against Switzerland at Lausanne, produced no less than 18 goals. England, with Matthews and Lofthouse back,

Two penalties and three players sent off in the 'Battle of Berne'

lost 4-2 after a well-fought game.

At the same time Austria and Switzerland were involved in a record 12-goal classic at Lausanne. The Swiss took a 3-0 lead, but Austria, prompted by Ocwirk and using the speed of the Koerners down the wings, produced some magnificent football to win 7-5 despite a missed penalty. The next day, a full-strength West Germany beat Yugoslavia 2-0 at Geneva.

In the meantime the fourth quarter-final provided the most violent World Cup scenes since the Brazil-Czechoslovakia affair of 1938. Brazil were again involved, this time against Hungary, in what became known as the 'Battle of Berne'—a match with two Penalties and three sendings-off. After Hungary's 4-2 win the battle was continued in the dressing-rooms.

For Hungary's semi-final against Uruguay, steel-helmeted police ringed the Lausanne pitch. The game, however, proved not a brawl but a delight, rich in the skills of football, and all in pouring rain. Hungary won the game with two headers from Kocsis, who took his tally to 11.

In the other semi-final, at Basle, the Austrian defence collapsed against a West German attack superbly generalled by Fritz Walter, and lost 6-1.

The final, played at Berne on 14 July, again in rain, proved a dramatic match. Puskas insisted on playing (against medical orders), and Hungary opened in traditional style, Puskas following up to score from Kocsis' blocked shot in the sixth minute, and Czibor adding a second two minutes later. But the Germans replied first through Morlock, within a minute, and then through Rahn, after 18 minutes, and the game was wide open. In the second-half Hungary put the pressure on: Hidegkuti hit the bar, Kocsis the post, and Turek made some tremendous saves.

With five minutes to go, Boszik untypically mispassed: Schaefer found Walter, his cross was cleared, but Rahn cracked the ball home. A revived Puskas put the ball in the next, and it looked like extra-time, but linesman Mervyn Griffiths had his flag up for offside—and Hungary had lost. West Germany, unseeded, had beaten Hungary, undefeated. in four years and clear favourites.

5th WORLD CUP, SWITZERLAND, 1954

GROUP 1

Yugoslavia 1 France 0
Brazil 5 Mexico 0
France 3 Mexico 2
Brazil *1 Yugoslavia 1

	P	W	D	L	F	A	P
Brazil	2	1	1	0	6	1	3
Yugoslavia	2	1	1	0	2	1	3
France	2	1	0	1	3	3	2
Mexico	2	0	0	2	2	8	0

GROUP 2

Hungary 9 South Korea 0
West Germany 4 Turkey 1
Hungary 8 West Germany 3
Turkey 7 South Korea 0

	P	W	D	L	F	A	P
Hungary	2	2	0	0	17	3	4
Turkey	2	1	0	1	8	4	2
West Germany	2	1	0	1	7	9	2
South Korea	2	0	0	2	0	16	0

Play-off: West Germany 7 Turkey 2

GROUP 3

Austria 1 Scotland 0
Uruguay 2 Czechoslovakia 0
Austria 5 Czechoslovakia 0
Uruguay 7 Scotland 0

	P	W	D	L	F	A	P
Uruguay	2	2	0	0	9	0	4
Austria	2	2	0	0	6	0	4
Czechoslovakia	2	0	0	2	0	7	0
Scotland	2	0	0	2	0	8	0

GROUP 4

England *4 Belgium 4
England 2 Switzerland 0
Switzerland 2 Italy 1
Italy 4 Belgium 1

	P	W	D	L	F	A	P
England	2	1	1	0	6	4	3
Italy	2	1	0	1	5	3	2
Switzerland	2	1	0	1	2	3	2
Belgium	2	0	1	1	5	8	1

Play-off: Switzerland 4 Italy 1

QUARTER-FINALS

West Germany 2 Yugoslavia 0
Austria 7 Switzerland 5
Uruguay 4 England 2
Hungary 4 Brazil 2

SEMI-FINALS

West Germany 6 Austria 1
Hungary 4 Uruguay 2

THIRD PLACE MATCH

Austria 3 Uruguay 1†

FINAL

West Germany 3 Hungary 2
(Berne, 4.7.54, 55,000)

West Germany: Turek, Posipal, Kohlmeyer, Eckel, Liebrich, Mai, Rahn, Morlock, O. Walter, F. Walter, Schaefer

Hungary: Grosics, Buzansky, Lantos, Bozsik, Lorant, Zakarias, Czibor, Kocsis, Hidegkuti, Puskas, Toth

Scorers: Morlock, Rahn 2; Puskas, Czibor

*after extra time †in Zurich

Sweden, 1958

In their sixth consecutive series, and after the anti-climax of 1950, Brazil at last won the cup, and in a style that secured them a place at the peak of world football history.

Though there was no seeding, the 16 finalists (whittled down from an original 53) fell into an arrangement of one team from Britain, one from Western Europe, one from Eastern Europe and one from Latin America in each group.

All teams played each other, with those level on points playing off.

After the opening ceremony in Stockholm, Sweden beat Mexico 3-0 in Group 3. At Sandviken, John Charles equalized for Wales after Boszik had given the lead to Hungary, but then they could only draw with Mexico at Stockholm.

The following day, on the same ground, goals from Hamrin took an unimpressive Sweden past Hungary 2-1, but against Mexico at Sandviken the Hungarians came to life. Lajos Tichy, who had played well and scored against Sweden, started a 4-0 drubbing with two good goals. Meanwhile, in the capital, Sweden fielded five reserves against Wales, and were quite content with a goalless draw—one that gave Dave Bowen's Welshmen a play-off with Hungary.

Play-offs for second place also resulted in Groups 1 and 4. In the former, Northern Ireland started in spirited style by beating Czechoslovakia at Halmstad with a goal from Wilbur Cush. The Germans also kicked off well, beating Argentina 3-1 at Malmö. Rahn, star of the 1954 final, scored two of the goals, and he was again on song with another to secure a draw for West Germany against Czechoslovakia at Hälsingborg. The Irish, meantime, had the wind taken out of their sails at Halmstad with a defeat by Argentina.

Wales and Northern Ireland enjoy their finest hour

That glory was short-lived. At Hälsingborg Argentina crashed 6-1 to Czechoslovakia, and had Germany then beaten Ireland at Malmö, the Czechs would have been safe. But Peter McParland twice put the Irish ahead, twice the Germans equalized, through Rahn and Uwe Seeler, and Czechoslovakia, despite a much better goal average, had to play-off with Ireland.

The strongest section, Group 4, saw Brazil, without Pelé (injured) or Garrincha, beat Austria 3-0 at Boras, and England and Russia, who had drawn 1-1 in Moscow three weeks before, draw 2-2 at Gothenburg. The Russians took a 2-0 lead, but then Derek Kevan and Tom Finney, from a penalty, beat Lev Yashin to square it.

On the same pitch England then produced a fine defensive display against Brazil, who had Vavà back, but in place of Dida. Colin McDonald was cool in goal, while Bill Slater virtually erased Didì from the game. Meanwhile, at Boras, Russia had a comfortable 2-0 win over a dull Austria.

Assuming Brazil beat Russia at Gothenburg, England had to beat Austria at Boras to be sure of qualifying, but weak in front of goal, an unchanged side stumbled to a 2-2 draw. Brazil, with Zito, Garrincha, and Pelé replacing Dino, Joel and Altafini, duly beat Russia with two goals from Vavà to give England a play-off.

It was left to Group 2 to come up with two clear qualifiers, and it was apparent from the first match, when France beat Paraguay 7-3 at Norrköping, who would be one. Just Fontaine, whose 13 goals (many stemming from his fine understanding with Kopa) were to be a record, started with three. At Västeras, Scotland pulled their game with Yugoslavia out of the fire to draw 1-1, but in their next game at Norrköping they went down 3-2 to Paraguay.

Yugoslavia, remaining at Västeras, beat France 3-2 against the run of play, with Fontaine scoring both French goals. Scotland brought in new cap Bill Brown in goal and had Dave Mackay at left-half for the game with France at Örebro, but first-half goals by Kopa and Fontaine put them out of the competition.

The three play-offs, held on 17 June, all involved British teams. At Malmö in Group 1, Northern Ireland repeated their earlier win over Czechoslovakia with two McParland goals, the second coming in extra time, while in Group 3 at Stockholm, Wales also beat a team superior on goal average, Hungary, with goals from Ivor Allchurch and Terry Medwin.

The Group 4 play-off saw England and Russia meet for the third time within a month. Brabrook hit the post twice and had a goal disallowed, but when Ilyin hit the post the ball went in—and England were out.

In the quarter-finals, Northern Ireland, with Harry Gregg not really fit, were beaten 4-0 at Norrköping by France, with the unstoppable Fontaine adding two more to his total. Wales, too, went out, but not before giving Brazil (without Vavà) a real defensive fight at Gothenburg, despite the absence of John Charles. The only goal came in the second half from Pelé. At Malmö, West Germany repeated their 1954 quarter-final win over Yugoslavia, and again it was Rahn who scored the all-important goal. Sweden beat Russia 2-0 in Stockholm.

At Stockholm in the semi-final, Fontaine became the first player to score against Brazil when, after a superb move with Kopa, he equalized Vavà's first-minute goal. But after France lost centre-half Robert Jonquet in the 37th minute Didi got number two, and Pelé scored a hat-trick in the second-half. In Gothenburg, Sweden upset West Germany 3-1.

On the same ground four days later France beat West Germany 6-3 for third place. The inevitable Rahn scored again but it was the four from Fontaine (taking him past Kocsis' World Cup finals record) that formed the star turn.

In the final the following day in the Rasunda Stadium, Sweden, seeking revenge for the 7-1 defeat in 1950, seemed to have a great start, with rain affecting the pitch and Liedholm picking his way through to score after five minutes. The Brazilians, to the surprise of many, remained unflustered, and Garrincha, after a lovely dribble, made the equalizer for Vavá. With their full-backs (Djalma Santos replacing De Sordi for his first match of the series) bottling up Hamrin and Skoglund, and Zagalo dropping back to assist Zito and Didì in midfield, Brazil got on top. In the 32nd minute Garrincha repeated his act and Vavà once again beat Svensson. In the second-half Pelé coolly scored, and Zagalo added a fourth before Simonsson reminded the crowd of Sweden's attack. Pelé made it five right on time with a brilliant header to crown a devastating display.

Vavà and Pelé turn on the skill for Brazil

Brazil's winning side in 1958. *Back: Feola (coach), Djalma Santos, Zito, Bellini, Nilton Santos, Orlando, Gilmar; Front: Garrincha, Didi, Pelé, Vavà, Zagalo. Eight of this team—Bellini, Orlando and Pelé were the exceptions—retained the trophy in 1962.*

Didi and Gilmar console the 17-year-old Pelé, overcome with emotion after the final—in which he scored two coolly-taken goals.

6th WORLD CUP, SWEDEN, 1958

GROUP 1

West Germany 3 Argentina 1
N. Ireland 1 Czechoslovakia 0
West Germany 2 Czechoslovakia 2
Argentina 3 Ireland 1
West Germany 2 N. Ireland 2
Czechoslovakia 6 Argentina 1

	P	W	D	L	F	A	P
West Germany	3	1	2	0	7	5	4
Czechoslovakia	3	1	1	1	8	4	3
N. Ireland	3	1	1	1	4	5	3
Argentina	3	1	0	2	5	10	2

Play-off: N. Ireland *2 Czech'vakia 1

GROUP 2

France 7 Paraguay 3
Yugoslavia 1 Scotland 1
Yugoslavia 3 France 2
Paraguay 3 Scotland 2
France 2 Scotland 1
Yugoslavia 3 Paraguay 3

	P	W	D	L	F	A	P
France	3	2	0	1	11	7	4
Yugoslavia	3	1	2	0	7	6	4
Paraguay	3	1	1	1	9	12	3
Scotland	3	0	1	2	4	6	1

GROUP 3

Sweden 3 Mexico 0
Hungary 1 Wales 1
Wales 1 Mexico 1
Sweden 2 Hungary 1
Hungary 4 Mexico 0
Sweden 0 Wales 0

	P	W	D	L	F	A	P
Sweden	3	2	1	0	5	1	5
Hungary	3	1	1	1	6	3	3
Wales	3	0	3	0	2	2	3
Mexico	3	0	1	2	1	8	1

Play-off: Wales 2 Hungary 1

GROUP 4

England 2 USSR 2
Brazil 3, Austria 0
Brazil 0 England 0
USSR 2 Austria 0
Brazil 2 USSR 0
England 2 Austria 2

	P	W	D	L	F	A	P
Brazil	3	2	1	0	5	0	5
England	3	0	3	0	4	4	3
USSR	3	1	1	1	4	4	3
Austria	3	0	1	2	2	7	1

Play-off: USSR 1 England 0

QUARTER-FINALS

Brazil 1 Wales 0
France 4 Northern Ireland 0
West Germany 1 Yugoslavia 0
Sweden 2 USSR 0

SEMI-FINALS

Brazil 5 France 2
Sweden 3 West Germany 1

THIRD PLACE MATCH

France 6 West Germany 3†

FINAL

Brazil 5 Sweden 2
(Stockholm, 29.6.58, 49,737)

Brazil: Gilmar, D. Santos, N. Santos, Zito, Bellini, Orlando, Garrincha, Didi, Vava, Pele, Zagalo

Sweden: Svensson, Bergmark, Axbom, Boerjesson, Gustavsson, Parling, Hamrin, Gren, Simonsson, Liedholm, Skoglund

Scorers: Vava 2, Pele 2, Zagalo; Liedholm, Simonsson

*after extra time †in Gothenburg

Chile, 1962

The 1962 competition, in Chile, is remembered as the one everyone wants to forget. Poor standards, defensive football and vicious tackling made it the most disappointing of all the modern World Cups.

The selection of Chile, hardly a major footballing nation, was in itself surprising, particularly as the country was just recovering from a disastrous earthquake. Nevertheless, Chile organized the series well, having constructed several new stadiums.

England were the only British representatives, Scotland having been eliminated by Czechoslovakia, Wales by Spain, and Northern Ireland by West Germany. But England, without a settled centre-forward, looked apprehensive.

Chile started well enough in Group 2 by beating Switzerland 3-1 in the new stadium at Santiago. The next match on the ground, between West Germany and Italy, produced an early example of the typical 1962 match: a defensive, goalless draw.

Group 2 was then host to the most violent game in the series, between Chile and Italy, where two Italians were sent off and some of the acting was worthy of a bad western. Chile won 2-0 against nine men and qualified with West Germany, who beat Switzerland and the hosts.

In Group 1, at waterless Arica in the far north, the European sides emerged unbeaten against Uruguay and Colombia, Russia winning the decider against Yugoslavia. This group, too, was plagued by violence on the field.

At Viña del Mar, in Group 3, Brazil opened (as they had in 1950 and 1954) by beating Mexico, this time by 2-0. But they were not in form, and Pelé, making the first and scoring the second, was the only spark. The next day Czechoslovakia had a good win over a 'Spanish' side that included Santamaria and

Pelé out—but another prodigy takes his place

Puskas but missed an injured Di Stefano. The Czechs, with goalkeeper Schroiff and Popluhar outstanding, then held Brazil to a goalless draw, but in the 25th minute the champions lost Pelé for the rest of the game—and the tournament—with a severely pulled muscle.

Spain, despite their talented line-up, only squeezed through against Mexico with a last-minute goal by Peiro. Then Brazil and Spain drew the largest crowd of the group (18,715), and Amarildo, Pelé's teenage deputy, score twice in the last 10 minutes to wipe out Spain's early lead.

Group 4, at Rancagua, started with Argentina scoring the only goal of a mundane encounter with Bulgaria. The following day Hungary beat a pedestrian England side 2-1. The best crowd of the group—but still under 10,000—turned up to see an improved England beat Argentina 3-1. The Hungarians then

Armfield, Springett and Wilson see Albert's shot squeeze home to give Hungary a 2-1 victory over England at Viña del Mar in 1962.

trounced Bulgaria 6-1, Albert scoring a brilliant hat-trick and Tichy two, but the last two games were both goalless.

Of the quarter-finals the highest scoring was at Vinã del Mar, where England met a Brazil side playing 'at home'. Garrincha, springing to life after a quiet time in the qualifiers, headed a 31st minute lead. Hitchens, replacing the injured Peacock, equalized after Greaves hit the bar, but Garrincha won the game in the second-half: first Springett failed to hold his shot and Vavà followed up to score, and then he scored the third with a long, swerving shot.

At Arica, Chile caught Yashin on a bad day and he should have

The Czechs hand the holders the title on a plate

saved both goals, from Sanchez and Rojas. Hungary had Czechoslovakia pinned down at Rancagua, but the Czechs held on tenaciously to Scherer's 13th minute goal to go through. In Santiago, Yugoslavia at last beat Germany in a quarter-final, Radakovic scoring from Galic's pass with only four minutes left.

Garrincha again inspired Brazil in the semi-final against Chile, played in front of 76,594 (the biggest crowd of the series) at Santiago. He scored from 20 yards after nine minutes, and then headed another from a corner. Brazil ran out 4-2 winners, but the match was spoilt when Landa and Garrincha were sent off.

The cat-and-mouse tactics of the Czechs came off again against Yugoslavia at Vinã del Mar, and they won 3-1 against the general run of play.

In the final, Czechoslovakia took on Brazil for the second time in the competition. With Kvasnak dictating a steady pace in midfield, the Czechs took a lead when Josef Masopust (later voted European Footballer of the Year) scored after Scherer had made the opening. They then broke down in the position they least expected—goalkeeper. Amarildo equalized with an amazing shot from on the byline; Zito headed in Amarildo's cross from close-in 13 minutes from time; and Schroiff dropped Djalma Santos' high cross into the sun to present Vavà with number three.

TOP: Garrincha rounds England's Ray Wilson in the quarter-final. at Vinã del Mar. After a quiet time in the qualifiers, he virtually won the game on his own, scoring twice and setting up a third.
ABOVE: Amarildo (left) proved an admirable deputy after Brazil lost Pelé with a pulled muscle against the Czechs. His two goals in the last 10 minutes beat Spain, and it was his remarkable goal that equalized Masopust's shock lead in the final—against Czechoslovakia.

7th WORLD CUP, CHILE, 1962

GROUP 1

Uruguay 2 Colombia 1
USSR 2 Yugoslavia 0
Yugoslavia 3 Uruguay 1
USSR 4 Colombia 4
USSR 2 Uruguay 1
Yugoslavia 5 Columbia 0

	P	W	D	L	F	A	P
USSR	3	2	1	0	8	5	5
Yugoslavia	3	2	0	1	8	3	4
Uruguay	3	1	0	2	4	6	2
Colombia	3	0	1	2	5	11	1

GROUP 2

Chile 3 Switzerland 1
West Germany 0 Italy 0
Chile 2 Italy 0
West Germany 2 Switzerland 1
West Germany 2 Chile 0
Italy 3 Switzerland 0

	P	W	D	L	F	A	P
West Germany	3	2	1	0	4	1	5
Chile	3	2	0	1	5	3	4
Italy	3	1	1	1	3	2	3
Switzerland	3	0	0	3	2	8	0

GROUP 3

Brazil 2 Mexico 1
Czechoslovakia 1 Spain 0
Brazil 0 Czechoslovakia 0
Spain 1 Mexico 0
Brazil 2 Spain 1
Mexico 3 Czechoslovakia 1

	P	W	D	L	F	A	P
Brazil	3	2	1	0	4	1	5
Czechoslovakia	3	1	1	1	2	3	3
Mexico	3	1	0	2	3	4	2
Spain	3	1	0	2	2	3	2

GROUP 4

Argentina 1 Bulgaria 0
Hungary 2 England 1
England 3 Argentina 1
Hungary 6 Bulgaria 1
Hungary 0 Argentina 0
England 0 Bulgaria 0

	P	W	D	L	F	A	P
Hungary	3	2	1	0	8	2	5
England*	3	1	1	1	4	3	3
Argentina	3	1	1	1	2	3	3
Bulgaria	3	0	1	2	1	7	1

QUARTER-FINALS

Brazil 3 England 1
Chile 2 USSR 1
Yugoslavia 1 West Germany 0
Czechoslovakia 1 Hungary 0

SEMI-FINALS

Brazil 4 Chile 2
Czechoslovakia 3 Yugoslavia 1

THIRD PLACE MATCH

Chile 1 Yugoslavia 0†

FINAL

Brazil 3 Czechoslovakia 1
(Santiago, 17.6.62, 69,068)

Brazil: Gilmar, D. Santos, N. Santos, Zito, Mauro, Zozimo, Garrincha, Didi, Vava, Amarildo, Zagalo

Czechoslovakia: Schroiff, Tichy, Novak, Pluskal, Popluhar, Masopust, Pospichal, Scherer, Kvasnak, Kadraba, Jelinek

Scorers: Amarildo, Zito, Vava; Masopust

*qualified on goal difference †in Santiago

England, 1966

England staged the 1966 World Cup, and became the first hosts to win it since Italy in 1934. They did so by team spirit on and off the field, by faith in themselves and their manager, and by calculated, bland, hard-working, stereotyped football.

The tournament left mixed feelings. On the credit side there were the record figures for gates and receipts, the success of, and support for, the little North Koreans, the prowess of Eusebio and a nail-biting final. But as an overall spectacle it was poor. As in 1962, 89 goals were scored in 32 matches, but football had become even more negative and defensive, with most teams employing a sweeper behind the defence. Five players were sent off, four of them against West Germany.

Group 1 of the finals was scheduled to be played in London, with England playing all three games at Wembley. After Queen Elizabeth had opened the tournament, it started on 11 July with an archetypal match—a goalless draw between England and an uninspired Uruguay.

Mexico, somewhat surprisingly, then took a point off a disappointing France. Two days later, in the only game played at London's White City Stadium, Uruguay beat France 2-1.

The following day, England, with Paine and Peters coming in for Ball and Connelly, beat Mexico 2-0. The defensive Mexicans held out until the 37th minute, when Bobby Charlton ended the stalemate with a magnificent individual goal. In the second

Brazil lose their first game in the finals since 1954

half Hunt put in Greaves' blocked shot to score another. Uruguay then played for a draw against Mexico and secured it. France, however, had to attack England (who had Callaghan in for Paine) and it suited Ramsey's tactics well. Herbin, already bandaged about the leg, fell awkwardly and was a passenger from an early stage. A Greaves goal was disallowed for offside, and just before the interval Hunt put England ahead after Jack Charlton had headed against the post. The French then produced some fine moves, with Simon getting round the English back four. But he was hurt in a nasty clash with Stiles and while he lay injured Hunt scored again with a header.

It was expected that Group 2 played at Sheffield (Hillsborough) and Birmingham (Villa Park), would produce West Germany and Argentina as qualifiers. The Germans, well managed by Helmut Schoen, began in fine style by beating group chopping-block Switzerland 5-0 at Hillsborough, while Argentina took a cautious line against Spain at Villa Park but won 2-1.

The Swiss made wholesale changes against Spain at Sheffield, and led after half an hour. With Spain in trouble, full-back Sanchis dribbled through to equalize and then Amancio—one of five Real Madrid players on duty—headed home Gento's cross for the winner. The next day West Germany were involved in an untidy 0-0 draw with Argentina at Villa Park. Both teams played defensively, tackling grew fierce, and

WORLD CUP GOALSCORING

Year	Ms	Total	Aver.
1930	18	70	3.88
1934	17	70	4.12
1938	18	84	4.67
1950	22	88	4.00
1954	26	140	5.38
1958	35	126	3.60
1962	32	89	2.78
1966	32	89	2.78
1970	32	95	2.97
1974	38	97	2.55
1978	38	102	2.68
1982	52	146	2.80
Total	360	1196	3.32

Albrecht, after a knee-high tackle on Weber, was sent off. Three days later, Argentina, without a suspended Albrecht, made heavy work of beating Switzerland 2-0.

For their next game at Villa Park West Germany rested Haller and had Emmerich in for the injured Brülls, while Spain dropped their three Italian exiles—Del Sol, Peiro, and Suarez. Spain had to win, and

England manager Alf Ramsey remains impassive at the fourth goal in 1966, his prediction realized. Jimmy Greaves can hardly believe his replacement, Geoff Hurst, has scored again to achieve a unique hat-trick.

their chances looked good when Fuste scored after 23 minutes. But Emmerich equalized before half-time with a superb shot from the by-line, and Seeler, playing in his third series, scored the winner with six minutes left.

Though Brazil were in the strongest group, they were still favoured. Against Bulgaria at Goodison Park Pelé scored from a free-kick after 14 minutes (the first goal of the competition) but for most of the match he was policed by Jetchev and took some rough treatment. A jaded Garrincha made it 2-0.

Hungary, after losing 3-1 to Portugal, produced stirring stuff for their second game and Brazil, with Pelé, suffered their first World Cup defeat since 1954, when their conquerers had been the very same country.

A desperate Brazil brought in nine new players and had an unfit Pelé in the line-up for the match with Portugal at Goodison. But with Manga unsafe in goal, Portugal took a 2-0 lead through Simoes and Eusebio. Vicente and Morais felled Pelé at every opportunity; eventually he had to limp off, and with him went Brazil's final hopes. Hungary qualified with a 3-1 win over Bulgaria at Old Trafford.

In Group 4 in the North-East, the tiny North Koreans illustrated their boundless enthusiasm and stamina against Russia at Middlesbrough, but still lost 3-0.

North Korea achieved a draw against Chile, much to the delight of the Ayresome Park crowd, who had by now 'adopted' them. Italy left out Gianni Rivera against Russia at Roker Park, and went down to a Chislenko goal.

North Korea v Italy: the biggest World Cup shock ever?

Then came the real surprise of the competition, when the confident North Koreans beat a petrified Italian side showing seven changes.

In the quarter-finals England, the only side not yet to concede a goal, faced Argentina in brilliant sunshine at Wembley. They brought in Hurst for the injured Greaves and Ball for Callaghan, while the Argentinians had Albrecht back after suspension. The match proved to be a microcosm of the tensions that existed between European and South American football and West German referee Kreitlein eventually sent off Antonio Rattin, the Argentina captain. Forced to open up, Argentina played some good attacking football, but in the 78th minute Hurst scored with a well-timed header from Peters' cross to decide it.

There was drama, too, between West Germany and Uruguay at Hillsborough, where two South Americans were sent off by Jim Finney and the Germans strolled into the last four.

Sensations of a different kind were happening at Goodison, where the North Koreans were running rings round Portugal

TOP: ***Geoff Hurst shoots, Willy Schulz lunges—and what followed was the most controversial goal in the history of the World Cup. Whether right or wrong, the decision gave the hosts a 3-2 extra-time lead.***
ABOVE: ***Saving here from Jack Charlton, Uruguay's Mazurkiewicz became the first foreign keeper to prevent England scoring at Wembley in the opening match of the tournament. For his part, England's Gordon Banks would not concede a goal until a semi-final penalty against Portugal's Eusebio, top scorer in the 1966 tournament.***
RIGHT: ***Alf Ramsey tries to prevent George Cohen exchanging shirts with an Argentinian player after the quarter-final in which Antonio Rattin was sent off. England won with a header from Hurst.***
FAR RIGHT: ***Bobby Moore and his merry men after the dramatic 4-2 victory over West Germany.***

8th WORLD CUP, ENGLAND, 1966

GROUP 1

England 0 Uruguay 0
France 1 Mexico 1
Uruguay 2 France 1
England 2 Mexico 0
Uruguay 0 Mexico 0
England 2 France 0

	P	W	D	L	F	A	P
England	3	2	1	0	4	0	5
Uruguay	3	1	2	0	2	1	4
Mexico	3	0	2	1	1	3	2
France	3	0	1	2	2	5	1

GROUP 2

West Germany 5 Switzerland 0
Argentina 2 Spain 1
Spain 2 Switzerland 1
West Germany 0 Argentina 0
Argentina 2 Switzerland 0
West Germany 2 Spain 1

	P	W	D	L	F	A	P
West Germany	3	2	1	0	7	1	5
Argentina	3	2	1	0	4	1	5
Spain	3	1	0	2	4	5	2
Switzerland	3	0	0	3	1	9	0

GROUP 3

Brazil 2 Bulgaria 0
Portugal 3 Hungary 1
Hungary 3 Brazil 1
Portugal 3 Bulgaria 0
Portugal 3 Brazil 1
Hungary 3 Bulgaria 1

	P	W	D	L	F	A	P
Portugal	3	3	0	0	9	2	6
Hungary	3	2	0	1	7	5	4
Brazil	3	1	0	2	4	6	2
Bulgaria	3	0	0	3	1	8	0

*at Wembley

GROUP 4

USSR 3 North Korea 0
Italy 2 Chile 0
Chile 1 North Korea 1
USSR 1 Italy 0
North Korea 1 Italy 0
USSR 2 Chile 1

	P	W	D	L	F	A	P
USSR	3	3	0	0	6	1	6
North Korea	3	1	1	1	2	4	3
Italy	3	1	0	2	2	2	2
Chile	3	0	1	2	2	5	1

QUARTER-FINALS

England 1 Argentina 0
Portugal 5 North Korea 3
USSR 2 Hungary 1
West Germany 4 Uruguay 0

SEMI-FINALS

England 2 Portugal 1
West Germany 2 USSR 1

THIRD PLACE MATCH

Portugal 2 USSR 1*

FINAL

England 4 West Germany 2 [aet]
(Wembley, 30.7.66, 93,000)

England: Banks, Cohen, Wilson, Stiles, J. Charlton, Moore, Ball, Hunt, Hurst, R. Charlton, Peters

West Germany: Tilkowski, Hottges, Schnellinger, Beckenbauer, Schultz, Weber, Held, Haller, Seeler, Overath, Emmerich

Scorers: Hurst 3, Peters; Haller, Weber

and led 3-0 after only 24 minutes. But instead of closing up, they continued to attack, and Eusebio took full advantage. He scored twice before half-time (the second from a penalty) and twice afterwards (again the second from a penalty) and Augusto scored the fifth. Hungary lost a game they should have won against Russia at Sunderland.

The hosts at last concede a goal—in their fifth game

It was the Russians' turn to be unlucky in the semi-final against West Germany at Goodison, where Chislenko was sent off just before half-time and nine fit men lost 2-1.

In the other semi-final, England met Portugal at Wembley. They kept an unchanged side, while Portugal replaced Vicente and Morais with Festa and Carlos. The expected Stiles-Eusebio clash never materialized, and in fact the game was 20 minutes old before referee Schwinte of France had to blow for a foul. Portugal played old-style attacking football, and Bobby Charlton, in his element, distributed with rare subtlety in one of his best ever internationals, scoring both England goals.

For the final—a dramatic, undulating affair—England and West Germany both fielded unchanged sides, in spite of speculation about the return of a fit Greaves to England's forward line. Germany marked man for man, detailing Beckenbauer to shadow Charlton—a move that wasted the German's talent in midfield. After 13 minutes, Ray Wilson miscued a header to the feet of Haller, who made no mistake. A few minutes later Moore took a quick free-kick on the left and West Ham club-mate Hurst headed past a stationary German defence to equalize. Ball was tireless in midfield, Moore immaculate at the back, while Banks made fine saves from Overath and Errmerich. In the second half, Germany appeared to tire and England, raised by the crowd, began to dominate. In the 78th minute Hurst's shot was half-cleared by Hottges, and Peters scored from close in. The match seemed won. But Germany counter-attacked and won several free-kicks. In injury time, Emmerich took one 10 yards outside the box, it ricochetted off the defensive wall, Held helped it on and Weber poked the ball past Banks. It was extra time.

England fulfil Alf Ramsey's prophecy

After 10 minutes Ball pulled the ball back to Hurst, whose shot hit the underside of the bar, and then bounced out for Weber to clear. Referee Dienst consulted linesman Bakhramov (who was no better placed to give an opinion), he nodded, and Dienst pointed to the middle. It is unfortunate that the match was decided by what must always be, despite all available evidence, a hotly disputed goal. Hurst's fine goal in the dying seconds, to complete the first hat-trick in a World Cup final, was almost irrelevant as the country set about celebrating the win with uncharacteristic virility.

Mexico, 1970

The ninth competition for the Jules Rimet Trophy promised so little and produced so much. It was widely believed that there would be a perpetration and even an extension of the tendencies that had bedevilled world football in the 1960s: negative play, low scores, ruthless tackling, and childish infringements leading to frayed tempers.

Instead it was an entertaining and intriguing affair. Brazil, with a forward line rivalled only by its predecessor in 1958 and Hungary's in 1954, made it perhaps the most memorable of all World Cups, and at the same time restored faith in the idea of international competition.

Mexico: a restoration of faith in football

The finals started at midday on Sunday 31 May, with Mexico and Russia playing a goalless Group 1 draw in the giant Aztec Stadium in Mexico City. The match was dominated by the zealous refereeing of West Germany's Tschenscher, who was acting to strict instructions from FIFA. It ruined this game, but probably had a beneficial effect in that during subsequent matches there was little trouble when referees relaxed the tight discipline.

The following Tuesday the other sections caught up. Group 2, playing at Puebla and Toluca, opened with Uruguay finding little difficulty in beating Israel.

At Guadalajara England took the field against Rumania to loud boos from the crowd, whose feelings had not been eased by a remark manager Alf Ramsey made about the pitch. The champions fielded the side that had beaten Colombia and Ecuador, and, playing slow, controlled football, got home against a tough defence with a 78th-minute goal from Hurst.

The game at León, between Bulgaria and Peru, made up for the others in both goals and drama, and was the first hint of a revival of attacking play in World Cup matches, Peru winning 3-2.

The next day involved all sections and produced widely varied matches. In Group 1 Belgium beat El Salvador 3-0 (including a late penalty) but should have scored a lot more. Meanwhile European champions Italy, leaving out Rivera, out-classed a ragged Sweden at Toluca in Group 2, but could manage only one goal, and that came from a goalkeeping error.

In Group 3 a superb attacking display, full of flair and individualism, gave Brazil a 4-1 win in their game against Czechoslovakia, with Pelé really at his best in front of a fiercely supportive Mexican crowd.

As in that game, the underdogs also scored first in the Group 4 match, with Houmane giving Morocco a surprise lead against West Germany before Seeler and then Müller relieved a very worried side.

With every team having played one match, only Group 1 had emerged without a clear division of points. For the next match there, on Saturday, the Russians made four changes and overpowered Belgium 4-1 with strong, simple football.

At Puebla, Uruguay and Italy were playing out what was probably the most uninspired match of the competition, a soulless, goalless draw in which what few chances arose were badly wasted. In Group 3 Rumania beat a Czech side that showed five changes, Dumitrache scoring the winner from a penalty. Peru, meantime, beat Morocco 3-0 at León to become—barring miracles—the first country to qualify for the quarter-finals.

The matches on the following day, Sunday, produced more goals (14) than any other qualifying day, despite being played at noon. In the Aztec Stadium, Mexico, roared on by a near-hysterical crowd, scored four against El Salvador.

Sweden were expected to atone for the Italian defeat in the match against Israel at Toluca, but could only draw an untidy affair witnessed, appropriately, by fewer than 3,000 people.

The Jalisco Stadium in Guadalajara, by contrast, was packed to its 75,000 capacity for the much-vaunted encounter between Brazil and England.

The result was decided by a second-half Jairzinho goal sparked by the genius of Tostao and Pelé, but England squandered several chances to earn a deserved draw.

For the game with Bulgaria at León, West Germany brought in two specialized wingers, Libuda and Löhr, for 1966 men Haller and Held, and it paid dividends, Müller netting a hat-trick in a 5-2 win.

On the Wednesday a solid performance by Russia took them into the last eight, while El Salvador went out without scoring a goal. Byshovets again scored two goals, both made by Muntian.

Müller chases Fontaine's World Cup goalscoring record

At Puebla, Uruguay were content to take it gently against Sweden, knowing they were almost guaranteed of qualification. They lost 1-0, but were almost certainly safe. In Group 3 Brazil registered maximum points by beating Rumania 3-2, Pelé scoring twice.

At León, West Germany beat Peru with Müller, beginning to look as though he might overhaul Just Fontaine's 1958 record of 13 goals, scoring another hat-trick before Cubillas replied.

The next day Mexico, Italy, and England joined the other qualifiers.

England had only to draw with Czechoslovakia at Guadalajara to qualify. If they lost by a goal, they would be equal on goal difference with Rumania and draw lots, while if they lost by two or more goals they would be eliminated. As it was, they won 1-0 with a controversial second-half penalty by Allan Clarke, playing in his first full international.

The quarter-finals were really the turning-point of the competition, producing 17 goals and one magnificent come-back. The highest score came at Guadalajara, where Brazil stayed on to meet Peru, and the two most adventurous sides in the competition produced a six-goal thriller.

Brazil were to play Uruguay, who had left it until the 27th minute of extra time before scoring against Russia in Mexico City and then with a disputed goal.

ABOVE: ***Carlos Alberto with the trophy that, after three successes, became the permanent property of Brazil in 1970.***
LEFT: ***Italians Facchetti and Burgnich (2) look suitably worried as Jairzinho (centre) and Pelé start to turn it on in the second half of the 1970 final. Both players scored in Brazil's emphatic 4-1 win.***
BELOW LEFT: ***De Sisti of Italy and Maneiro of Uruguay in contention during the 0-0 draw at Puebla. Both teams qualified from a group that produced only six goals in as many matches—and went on to finish second and fourth respectively.***

Mexico, trailed by thousands of supporters (many of whom could not get into the ground), travelled to Toluca to play Italy. The Italians won 4-1, Riva getting two, but the hosts held their own until well into the second half.

Meantime at León, England and West Germany met in a repeat of the 1966 final, and including the substitutes there were 11 survivors from that match. Like that game, the team that scored first lost; like that game, it went to extra time; like that game, England changed to red; but unlike that game, West Germany won. While Schoen fielded the side that played so well against Bulgaria and Peru, Ramsey reverted to his initial line-up, except that Bonetti was in goal in place of Banks, who had a severe stomach complaint.

The Germans were urged on by the thousands of their countrymen who had made León a temporary home, but it was England who went in front after half an hour through Mullery. Four minutes into the second-half Peters put England two up. It looked all over. Ramsey substituted Hunter and Bell for Peters and Charlton. But Germany pulled one back with a 20-yard shot from Beckenbauer in the 70th minute; eight minutes from time Schnellinger's lobbed pass was spectacularly back-headed over the hands of Bonetti by Seeler. In extra time it was Germany who threatened to score, and they did: five minutes into the second period Grabowski crossed to the far post, Löhr nodded back square, and Müller hit a waist-high winner from point-blank range. It was fitting recompense for 1966.

Italy win a 4-3 semi-final thriller

Against Brazil, Uruguay were in command early on, their hard defence deterring the ball-playing Brazilian forwards, and in the 18th minute they went ahead through Cubilla. Brazil were rescued, however, during first-half injury time, when Clodoaldo ran onto a perfect return pass from Tostao and beat Mazurkiewicz.

Brazil changed gear in the second half and first Tostao set up Jairzinho and then in the dying seconds Pelé laid one on for Rivelino to make it safe.

The Aztec Stadium, meanwhile, played hosts to Italy and West Germany. The Italians were unchanged, but Germany included the two substitutes who had played so well against England, Schulz and Grabowski, and also had Patzke in for Fichtel. The Germans equalized Boninsegna's 9th-minute goal through Schnellinger in the second minute of injury time, and then five goals came in a tense and exciting extra period, with Müller's two goals not enough to save his spirited side.

Exhibition football by Brazil in the Aztec Stadium

The match for third place on the same ground the following Saturday was expected to be the inevitable anti-climax. But with Uruguay attacking more and tackling less than usual, and West Germany surprisingly fresh after two successive extra-time matches, it produced some of the most skilful and polished soccer of the 1970 World Cup. With Beckenbauer absent, more duties fell on Wolfgang Overath in midfield, and he shouldered them supremely well. He had enjoyed a fine tournament and it was fitting that it was he who scored the only goal.

In the final, played on Sunday, 21 June, Brazil forged ahead in the 18th minute. Tostao's throw-in on the left was lobbed across by Rivelino, and up went Pelé to head past Albertosi.

But then, in the 37th minute Clodoaldo casually tried a clever back-pass, failed, and Boninsegna pounced on the chance, urging Riva out of the way and picking his spot to shoot past Felix. It was a Gerson goal in the 65th minute—a left-footer from the edge of the box that no goalkeeper in the world would have saved—which triggered of a display of Brazil's real talents. Five minutes later Gerson sent a high diagonal cross to the right-hand post and Pelé nodded down for Jairzinho to scramble the ball home. In doing so he became the first player ever to score in every round of a World Cup including the final. From then on it was exhibition football: Carlos Alberto's goal three minutes from time—a thundering shot after Pelé, apparently without even looking, had pushed the ball into his stride—was merely of statistical interest.

The scenes that followed were unprecedented at a World Cup final, with the Brazilians being mobbed as though they had won in Rio. The way they had played their football, they would have received a standing ovation anywhere in the world.

9th WORLD CUP, MEXICO, 1970

GROUP 1

Mexico 0 USSR 0
Belgium 3 El Salvador 0
USSR 4 Belgium 1
Mexico 4 El Salvador 0
USSR 2 El Salvador 0
Mexico 1 Belgium 0

	P	W	D	L	F	A	P
USSR	3	2	1	0	6	1	5
Mexico	3	2	1	0	5	0	5
Belgium	3	1	0	2	4	5	2
El Salvador	3	0	0	3	0	9	0

GROUP 2

Uruguay 2 Israel 0
Italy 1 Sweden 0
Italy 0 Uruguay 0
Israel 1 Sweden 1
Sweden 1 Uruguay 0
Italy 0 Israel 0

	P	W	D	L	F	A	P
Italy	3	1	2	0	1	0	4
Uruguay†	3	1	1	1	2	1	3
Sweden	3	1	1	1	2	2	3
Israel	3	0	2	1	1	3	2

GROUP 3

England 1 Rumania 0
Brazil 4 Czechoslovakia 1
Rumania 2 Czechoslovakia 1
Brazil 1 England 0
Brazil 3 Rumania 2
England 1 Czechoslovakia 0

	P	W	D	L	F	A	P
Brazil	3	3	0	0	8	3	6
England	3	2	0	1	2	1	4
Rumania	3	1	0	2	4	5	2
Czechoslovakia	3	0	0	3	2	7	0

*after extra time †qualified on goal difference ‡in Mexico City

GROUP 4

Peru 3 Bulgaria 2
West Germany 2 Morocco 1
Peru 3 Morocco 0
West Germany 5 Bulgaria 2
West Germany 3 Peru 1
Bulgaria 1 Morocco 1

	P	W	D	L	F	A	P
West Germany	3	3	0	0	10	4	6
Peru	3	2	0	1	7	5	4
Bulgaria	3	0	1	2	5	9	1
Morocco	3	0	1	2	2	6	1

QUARTER-FINALS

Brazil 4 Peru 2
Uruguay 1 USSR 0
West Germany *3 England 2
Italy 4 Mexico 1

SEMI-FINALS

Brazil 3 Uruguay 1
Italy *4 West Germany 3

THIRD PLACE MATCH

West Germany 1 Uruguay 0‡

FINAL

Brazil 4 Italy 1
(Mexico City, 21.6.70, 110,000)

Brazil: Felix, Carlos Alberto, Brito, Wilson Piazza, Everaldo, Clodoaldo, Gerson, Jairzinho, Tostao, Pele, Rivelino

Italy: Albertosi, Burgnich, Facchetti, Cera, Rosato, Bertini (Juliano), Domenghini, Mazzola, Boninsegna (Rivera), De Sisti, Riva

Scorers: Pele, Gerson, Jairzinho, Carlos Alberto; Boninsegna

Gerd Müller's extra-time winner in the quarter-final at León—the 8th of his 10 goals—extracted sweet revenge from the holders for West Germany's defeat in the 1966 final.

West Germany, 1974

A new trophy, a new-look competition, a new superstar. But the Brazil of 1970 (and Pelé) had gone, and in its place, to defend the world title if not the trophy, was a side more reliant on solid, uncompromising defence than on explosive attack. As it was, Brazil's challenge for the new World Cup ended in ignominy.

But if Brazil's demise came with regret, it came nonetheless on the world stage. England, for the first time since entering the competition in 1950, failed to qualify, losing to Poland in Chorzow and drawing with Poland and Wales at Wembley—while Scotland, by beating Denmark twice and the Czechs at Hampden Park, had made it for the first time in 16 years.

This World Cup was to have two further four-team groups following the initial four groups, instead of quarter-finals and semi-finals. The winners of the two groups were to meet in the final; the runners-up playing a somewhat meaningless third place match.

For the third successive World Cup finals, the opening match (at Frankfurt on 13 June) produced a goalless draw, Brazil and Yugoslavia sharing 90 minutes of missed chances. This result did not help the Scots, who were also in Group 2, especially when, the next day, they could put no more than two past an exhilarating but disorganized Zaire. The failure to exploit the Zairean weaknesses was to cost them dear, and there can be no excuses for the possession football the Scots indulged in late in the match.

Enter Johan Cruyff—inspired and inspiring

Earlier in the day, in Group 1, the West German challenge had begun with a 1-0 victory over Chile in Berlin; a performance far from worthy of the European champions.

Saturday saw Groups 3 and 4 in action and introduced the Dutch . . . plus Johan Cruyff; inspired, inspirational, and infuriating. Against Uruguay he was at his majestic best; seemingly indifferent to the scything tackles that aimed to maim, always prompting, stamping his personality on the match and the competition. Rep scored twice, and there could have been more.

After three days rest it was again the turn of Groups 1 and 2 and especially of Scotland, who met world champions Brazil in Frankfurt. Some truly brilliant goalkeeping by Harvey and a fine performance from skipper Bremner helped the Scots to a commendable goalless draw; but Brazil, still to meet Zaire, could afford the result, Scotland could not. The news of Yugoslavia's record-equalling 9-0 thrashing of the Africans meant Scotland had to beat Yugoslavia to qualify for the next round—or draw and hope Zaire could hold Brazil to two goals.

Scotland, undefeated, fail to qualify on goal difference

On the Saturday, the respective dramas unfolded simultaneously. In Frankfurt, Scotland pulled back to 1-1 through Jordan—but to no avail. A draw was not enough: Brazil had squeezed a vital third against the Africans.

In Group 1, the two Germanys, as expected, went through: the East convincingly, the West less so after a morale-sapping 1-0 defeat in a tense first-ever international between the two sides. Earlier in the week, West Germany had beaten Australia 3-0, beginning impressively but falling away.

The Dutch, as expected, qualified, but their group contained one of the two real surprises of the tournament. Sweden, after enjoying a goalless draw with the Dutch in Dortmund, hit three second-half goals past the Uruguayans in Dusseldorf to take the second qualifying place. That same day the Bulgarians scored against the Dutch; albeit through an own goal by Krol—the only time Jongbloed was beaten until the final.

The other surprise was Italy's

WORLD CUP ATTENDANCES

Year	Ms	Total	Aver.
1930	18	434,500	24,139
1934	17	395,000	23,235
1938	18	483,000	26,833
1950	22	1,337,000	60,772
1954	26	943,000	36,270
1958	35	868,000	24,800
1962	32	776,000	24,250
1966	32	1,614,677	50,458
1970	32	1,673,975	52,312
1974	38	1,774,022	46,685
1978	38	1,610,215	42,374
1982	52	1,766,277	33,967
Total	360	13,675,666	37,987

TOP: After a second place in 1966 and a third in 1970, Helmut Schoen had certainly earned the success his Bayern-based side gave him in Munich—even though most observers felt that Holland were the best side.
ABOVE: Grzegorz Lato of Poland gets his shot in despite the presence of Francisco Marinho during the third place match against Brazil. Lato scored in the 76th minute to top the list with seven goals—and complete an almost humiliating tournament for the former champions.

failure to qualify following a draw with Argentina and a telling defeat by the improving Poland.

If the Dutch thought they were in the harder group, it did not seem to worry them. They opened in Gelsenkirchen with a 4-0 win over Argentina, Cruyff again supreme with two goals. In Hanover, Brazil beat East Germany 1-0 with a Rivelino free-kick, while in Group B, Lato added to his tally to produce a similar score against Sweden.

In Dusseldorf the West Germans, now with Bonhof in midfield, showed they were getting it together at last with a 2-0 win against Yugoslavia and a 4-2 victory over Sweden. Poland's success against Yugoslavia meant their match with the Germans was virtually a semi-final: winner take all. In rain-soaked Frankfurt it took the reliable Müller to see the hosts through—after Hoeness had missed a penalty.

In Group A, the East Germans were no match for the ebullient Dutch, and Brazil suddenly flowered against Argentina in a thrilling game.

Brazil against Holland in Dortmund for the right to meet West Germany, a game that promised so much, produced two magnificent goals by Neeskens and Cruyff, and saw football at its worst. The Dutch, niggling, were by no means blameless, but Brazil's conduct

Holland score—before a West German touches the ball

was indefensible.

The third place match, the day before the final, was the inevitable anti-climax and had gone 76 minutes before Lato scored his seventh goal of the World Cup finals to win it for Poland.

Other World Cup finals have been more entertaining; none have begun so dramatically. From the Dutch kick-off, the ball was moved to Cruyff, whose burst into the penalty area ended when he was brought down by Hoeness. Penalty! The first ever in a World Cup final. English referee Jack Taylor's decision was as immediate as it was brave, in front of a Munich crowd with six of their own Bayern men in the German team. Neeskens' shot from the spot flashed to the centre of the goal as Maier dived to his right: 1-0, and no West German had touched the ball.

Feyenoord's Wim Rijsbergen was one of several talented young players who made Holland the team of the tournament in terms of skill and entertainment. In the final, however, despite a Dutch lead, it was the reliable Müller (right) who won the day.

Now the Dutch took charge, with Cruyff directing operations in magisterial style. But for all their monopoly of possession, they did not score and the West Germans, with Beckenbauer fully committed, recovered. With 24 minutes gone, Holzenbein was brought down by Jansen in the area. Perhaps he could have evaded the tackle; but down he went; and Jack Taylor awarded his second penalty. This time it was highly debatable but Breitner made no mistake.

The Dutch continued to attack with vigour, but after Rep squandered a good chance Müller showed him how it should be done, controlling a poor pass and putting the ball away to give West Germany the lead. And the FIFA World Cup. The second half, though full of incident, was goalless.

For Helmut Schoen, runner-up in 1966, third in 1970, it was the ultimate achievement. Experimenting throughout the tournament, on the day that mattered he produced the right blend. The Dutch might have been more adventurous, more attractive, but Schoen had a team with character to fight back from the shock of the early penalty. And he had Gerd Müller.

10th WORLD CUP, WEST GERMANY, 1974

GROUP 1

West Germany 1 Chile 0
East Germany 2 Australia 0
West Germany 3 Australia 0
East Germany 1 Chile 1
East Germany 1 West Germany 0
Chile 0 Australia 0

	P	W	D	L	F	A	P
East Germany	3	2	1	0	4	1	5
West Germany	3	2	0	1	4	1	4
Chile	3	0	2	1	1	2	2
Australia	3	0	1	2	0	5	1

GROUP 2

Brazil 0 Yugoslavia 0
Scotland 2 Zaire 0
Brazil 0 Scotland 0
Yugoslavia 9 Zaire 0
Yugoslavia 1 Scotland 1
Brazil 3 Zaire 0

	P	W	D	L	F	A	P
Yugoslavia*	3	1	2	0	10	1	4
Brazil*	3	1	2	0	3	0	4
Scotland	3	1	2	0	3	1	4
Zaire	3	0	0	3	0	14	0

GROUP 3

Holland 2 Uruguay 0
Sweden 0 Bulgaria 0
Holland 0 Sweden 0
Bulgaria 1 Uruguay 1
Holland 4 Bulgaria 1
Sweden 3 Uruguay 0

	P	W	D	L	F	A	P
Holland	3	2	1	0	6	1	5
Sweden	3	1	2	0	3	0	4
Bulgaria	3	0	2	1	2	5	2
Uruguay	3	0	1	2	1	6	1

GROUP 4

Italy 3 Haiti 1
Poland 3 Argentina 2
Argentina 1 Italy 1
Poland 7 Haiti 0
Argentina 4 Haiti 1
Poland 2 Italy 1

	P	W	D	L	F	A	P
Poland	3	3	0	0	12	3	6
Argentina*	3	1	1	1	7	5	3
Italy	3	1	1	1	5	4	3
Haiti	3	0	0	3	2	14	0

GROUP A

Holland 4 Argentina 0
Brazil 1 East Germany 0
Holland 2 East Germany 0
Brazil 2 Argentina 1
Holland 2 Brazil 0
East Germany 1 Argentina 1

	P	W	D	L	F	A	P
Holland	3	3	0	0	8	0	6
Brazil	3	2	0	1	3	3	4
East Germany	3	0	1	2	1	4	1
Argentina	3	0	1	2	2	7	1

GROUP B

West Germany 2 Yugoslavia 0
Poland 1 Sweden 0
Poland 2 Yugoslavia 1
West Germany 4 Sweden 2
Sweden 2 Yugoslavia 1
West Germany 1 Poland 0

	P	W	D	L	F	A	P
West Germany	3	3	0	0	7	2	6
Poland	3	2	0	1	3	2	4
Sweden	3	1	0	2	4	6	2
Yugoslavia	3	0	0	3	2	6	0

THIRD PLACE MATCH

Poland 1 Brazil 0†

FINAL

West Germany 2 Holland 1
(Munich, 7.7.74, 77,833)

West Germany: Maier, Vogts, Schwarzenbeck, Beckenbauer, Breitner, Bonhof, Hoeness, Grabowski, Muller, Overath, Holzenbein

Holland: Jongbloed, Suurbier, Rijsbergen (De Jong), Haan, Krol, Jansen, Van Hanegem, Neeskens, Rep, Cruyff, Resenbrink (R. van der Kerkhof)

Scorers: Breitner (pen), Muller; Neeskens (pen)

*qualified on goal difference †in Munich

Argentina, 1978

If there was any conclusion to be drawn by a betting man from the 1978 World Cup finals, it was that he should put his money on Spain in 1982. For the third time in four series, the home country won the tournament and, as with England in 1966 and West Germany in 1974, there was justifiable doubt that Argentina could have done as well elsewhere.

Having said that, they were an entertaining side, far more cultured and far less cynical than many Argentinian sides of the past, and they had in their ranks at least three of the true stars of 1978—goalkeeper Jaime Fillol, schemer Osvaldo Ardiles and striker Mario Kempes. Indeed Kempes, scorer of two goals in the final and the only Argentinian exile that manager Luis Cesar Menotti called home (from Valencia in Spain), was voted best player of the tournament as well as winning the Golden Boot award as top scorer.

The chain-smoking Menotti had caused something of a sensation throughout South America; not only by not calling on his exiles, but also by not using any players from the Argentinian champions Boca Juniors—and also deciding that the brilliant

Scotland's story—even more sad than in 1974

Diego Maradona, then 17, was too young to play.

Of all 16 finalists, perhaps only Argentina, Italy, France, Holland, Brazil and Austria really approached the heights that such a competition really demands, and the tragedy was that the first three were all in the same group. Of the rest Tunisia (in particular) and Iran performed the roles of rabbit well (though no rabbit have ever reappeared in a final series since the United States' two tries in 1930 and 1950); West Germany, Scotland and Hungary were public failures; Poland Spain, Sweden and Peru were also-rans; and Mexico hardly deserve being credited with making up the numbers.

To British eyes, of course, it was the failure of Scotland that was the most interesting feature of the whole tournament. Not since Franklin tried to find the North West Passage can an expedition have set out with such high hopes and returned in such disarray. The stage was set by the ludicrous optimism of Ally MacLeod, one-time manager of Ayr United and Aberdeen (and winner of only one trophy—the Scottish League Cup) and now successor to Willie Ormond after the latter had not lost a game in Scotland's ill-fated 1974 participation in West Germany.

The optimism should have been pricked a little by England's 1-0 win in Glasgow just before the party left, not to mention Wales and Northern Ireland achieving 1-1 draws, also at Hampden. Scotland scored twice and got just two points in their worst Home International Championship display in years. Still, one bright spark was the prolific Derek Johnstone of Rangers, who scored both those goals; MacLeod failed to play him once in Argentina and

Quiroga's quirks steal the show in Argentina

indeed brought Liverpool schemer Graeme Souness in only for the final game when all was virtually lost.

The Scottish expedition was a disaster from the start. Gordon McQueen had been injured against Wales and, though still unfit when the party left, was not replaced. His absence left a glaring hole at the heart of Scotland's defence, and it wasn't helped by Kenny Burns' distressingly poor displays.

The team's hotel and food were reputed to be poor, and there was misunderstanding and bitterness over the bonuses to be paid in the unlikely event of success (MacLeod thought that they were only half of what had been finally agreed by the Scottish FA). The recriminations started early on and hardly helped the atmosphere of the camp, and, to finish everything off, West Bromwich Albion's winger Willie Johnston was sent home after a dope test taken after the Peru game proved positive.

The Peru game had been a disaster in more than one way. Though they went ahead early on, Scotland allowed Peru to pull back and win 3-1, Cubillas scor-

Dutch captain Ruud Krol chases Mario Kempes. Like eight others, Krol faced a second final defeat.

WORLD CUP SUMMARY

Year	Venue	Winners		Runners-up		Third		Fourth	
1930	Uruguay	†Uruguay	4	Argentina	2	[USA & Yugoslavia]			
1934	Italy	†Italy	*2	Czechoslovakia	1	Germany	3	Austria	2
1938	France	Italy	4	Hungary	2	Brazil	4	Sweden	2
1950	Brazil	Uruguay	‡2	†Brazil	1	§Sweden		§Spain	
1954	Switzerland	W. Germany	3	Hungary	2	Austria	3	Uruguay	1
1958	Sweden	Brazil	5	†Sweden	2	France	6	W. Germany	3
1962	Chile	Brazil	3	Czechoslovakia	1	†Chile	1	Yugoslavia	0
1966	England	†England	*4	W. Germany	2	Portugal	2	USSR	1
1970	Mexico	Brazil	4	Italy	1	W. Gemany	1	Uruguay	0
1974	W. Germany	†W. Germany	2	Holland	1	Poland	1	Brazil	0
1978	Argentina	†Argentina	*3	Holland	1	Brazil	2	Italy	1
1982	Spain	Italy	3	W. Germany	1	Poland	3	France	2

*after extra time †host country ‡last match in final pool §placings in final pool

11th WORLD CUP, ARGENTINA, 1978

GROUP 1

Italy 2 France 1
Argentina 2 Hungary 1
Italy 3 Hungary 1
Argentina 2 France 1
France 3 Hungary 1
Italy 1 Argentina 0

	P	W	D	L	F	A	P
Italy	3	3	0	0	6	2	6
Argentina	3	2	0	1	4	3	4
France	3	1	0	2	5	5	2
Hungary	3	0	0	3	3	8	0

GROUP 2

Poland 0 West Germany 0
Tunisia 3 Mexico 1
Poland 1 Tunisia 0
West Germany 6 Mexico 0
Poland 3 Mexico 1
West Germany 0 Tunisia 0

	P	W	D	L	F	A	P
Poland	3	2	1	0	4	1	5
West Germany	3	1	2	0	6	0	4
Tunisia	3	1	1	1	3	2	3
Mexico	3	0	0	3	2	12	0

GROUP 3

Austria 2 Spain 1
Brazil 1 Sweden 1
Austria 1 Sweden 0
Brazil 0 Spain 0
Spain 1 Sweden 0
Brazil 1 Austria 0

	P	W	D	L	F	A	P
Austria	3	2	0	1	3	2	4
Brazil	3	1	2	0	2	1	4
Spain	3	1	1	1	2	2	3
Sweden	3	0	1	2	1	3	1

GROUP 4

Peru 3 Scotland 1
Holland 3 Iran 0
Scotland 1 Iran 1
Holland 0 Peru 0
Peru 4 Iran 1
Scotland 3 Holland 2

	P	W	D	L	F	A	P
Peru	3	2	1	0	7	2	5
Holland*	3	1	1	1	5	3	3
Scotland	3	1	1	1	5	6	3
Iran	3	0	1	2	2	8	1

GROUP A

Italy 0 West Germany 0
Holland 5 Austria 1
Italy 1 Austria 0
Holland 2 West Germany 2
Holland 2 Italy 1
Austria 3 West Germany 2

	P	W	D	L	F	A	P
Holland	3	2	1	0	9	4	5
Italy	3	1	1	1	2	2	3
West Germany	3	0	2	1	4	5	2
Austria	3	1	0	2	4	8	2

GROUP B

Argentina 2 Poland 0
Brazil 3 Peru 0
Poland 1 Peru 0
Argentina 0 Brazil 0
Brazil 3 Poland 1
Argentina 6 Peru 0

	P	W	D	L	F	A	P
Argentina†	3	2	1	0	8	0	5
Brazil	3	2	1	0	6	1	5
Poland	3	1	0	2	3	6	2
Peru	3	0	0	3	0	10	0

THIRD PLACE MATCH

Brazil 2 Italy 1‡

FINAL

Argentina 3 Holland 1 [aet]
(Buenos Aires, 25.6.78, 77,000)

Argentina: Fillol, Olguin, Galvan, Passarella, Tarantini, Ardiles (Larrosa), Gallego, Ortiz (Houseman), Bertoni, Luque, Kempes

Holland: Jongbloed, Jansen (Suurbier), Krol, Brandts, Poortvliet, Haan, Neeskens, W. van der Kerkhof, Rep (Nanninga), R. van der Kerkhof, Rensenbrink

Scorers: Kempes 2, Bertoni; Nanninga

*qualified for semi-final groups on goal difference †qualified for final on goal difference ‡in Buenos Aires

ing two excellent long-range goals. The critical moment in Scotland's whole bid for glory came in the second half, however, when Don Masson missed a penalty, placing the ball easily within reach of Peru goalkeeper Quiroga.

Argentine-born Quiroga was to distinguish himself later in a variety of ways—partially by letting in six goals against his homeland, partially by completely abandoning his goal in the game against Poland and ending up being booked for a rugby tackle on Lato in the Polish half of the field. It says a lot of Poland's poor displays in the series (they scored only six goals in as many games) that they could only beat Peru 1-0 even though the opposition keeper spent much of the game rampaging about outside his area.

Quiroga's save from Masson was, however, the turning point for Scotland and they went on to an even worse performance against Iran, drawing 1-1 only through the courtesy of an extremely silly own goal by Eskandarian.

In true Scottish fashion, they came back in glorious style by beating eventual runners-up Holland 3-2 (the only defeat the Dutch suffered apart from the final). Gemmill scored twice, once after a wonderful weaving run past four defenders, and the Scots were able to claim that, for the second consecutive World Cup, they went out only on goal difference.

Three of the best sides play in one group

It is unlikely that this was actually the case: had they finished above Holland with a 3-0 win it is almost certain that FIFA would have deducted two points from their total because of Johnston's indiscretions.

Italy's Paolo Rossi—here somewhat closely marked by Bernd Holzenbein of West Germany—was the best European player in 1978.

Both Poland and Scotland continued to decline after Argentina. Neither, for instance, reached the 1980 European Championship finals in Italy.

For West Germany, the other conspicuous failure in Argentina, however, 1978 was probably only a hiccup. As holders, much was expected of them, but their opening game, an appalling 0-0 draw with Poland (the fourth consecutive goalless opening game in a World final series) told of what was to come. They were to win only one of their six games, failing to score in three.

Helmut Schoen seemed thoroughly confused about his tactical line-up (he had lost several players since 1974, in particular Beckenbauer and Müller) and his best side. He chopped and changed to no good effect and the eventual result was splits and bitterness in the camp.

So much for the failures. Three of the best sides—France, Italy and Argentina—were placed together in Group 1 and played an excellent collection of games, after which none of the trio deserved to be eliminated. France scored against Italy through Bernard Lacombe within 31 seconds of the start of the first match, but Italy came back, arguably a shade luckily, to win 2-1.

The Italians, playing far more adventurously under Enzo Bearzot than had been expected of them, went on to beat Argentina 1-0 via a superb Rossi-Bettega one-two and goal. It meant later that Argentina became only the second country in history to lose a game and still win the World Cup.

France were one of the unluckiest sides in World Cup history in going out at this stage. The critical moment was when an absurd penalty was given against their black centre-back Tresor and Argentina thus beat them 2-1. Had the penalty not been converted, France would have gone through on goal difference and Argentina would have been eliminated.

Austria were to head the poorest of the groups, in which only eight goals were scored,

Kenny Dalglish powers the equalizer past Jan Jongbloed at Mendoza. After disasters against Peru and Iran, Scotland turned on a fine display against Holland to win 3-2 and salvage a little pride.

though they lost to Brazil. In the second series they were to prove a disappointment—losing 5-1 to a Dutch side which had finally found its confidence and 1-0 to Italy. They saved their greatest moment for the last, however, a 3-2 defeat of West Germany which was Austria's first over her neighbour for 47 years.

The Dutch had started a little uncertainly: they beat Iran 3-0 but could only draw with Peru. Then came that defeat by Scotland and a feeling in part of the Dutch camp that the team was probably not good enough, that

Argentina push Brazil into the background

it would do well to go further, and that their hard-won reputation was about to be permanently damaged.

Certainly their forwards were failing them; penalties apart, Rep and Rensenbrink (who, the Dutch had hoped, could partially compensate for Johan Cruyff's absence) scored only four goals.

But in the second final group, everything came right. After the defeat of Austria, a hard-fought 2-2 draw with Germany was some recompense for Munich four years before (Holland's four goal difference after Austria was worth a point) and Arie Haan's 30-yard spectacular goal was one of the highlights of the tournament. He was to cap it, though, with one from 35 yards against Italy and the great Dino Zoff which put the Dutch through 2-1 in what was effectively the semi-final.

Had the sides drawn, Italy would have won four games and drawn two, while Holland would have won two, drawn three and lost one; yet Holland would still have gone through to the final, a telling indictment of a poor system since quarter and semi-finals were dropped for 1974.

The other 'real' semi-final was between Brazil and Argentina, the traditional South American rivals who were meeting for the 57th time. It was a brutal game, scoreless and forgettable, and it left the other final place open until the last possible moment. Brazil, playing in Mendoza, kicked off at 4.15 and beat Poland 3-1 in an excellent game with two marvellous goals from Roberto. They then had to wait, listening on their transistor radios like everyone else in Argentina, for the home side to kick-off in Rosario at 7.15 against Peru.

No-one doubted that Argentina would win and would thus end with the same points total as Brazil—the question was by how many. They needed a four-goal victory to clinch their place in the final, and the Brazilians had embarked well before on a war of words over Argentina having the undoubted advantage of kicking-off later, of Peru having an Argentinian born goalkeeper (Quiroga) and throwing any other mud that they thought

might just stick to the hosts.

In the event, Peru's weakness was never Quiroga and their poor—some say suspiciously inept—performance was perhaps due more to a reserve full-back (Rojas) and a fanatical crowd. Argentina had gone two up at half-time, scored two more soon after the interval and ended the game 6-0 winners. One could understand Brazil's frustration—both of the eventual finalists had earlier suffered defeat while they had come back from terrible early tensions to play some good football and remain undefeated.

They stayed that way, winning the third place match against an Italy that, typically, retreated into its shell after taking a one-goal lead. Dirceu and Nelinho got the goals from long range.

The final, for the first time in 20 years, was bound to produce a new winner of the title. Both contenders had lost a final before—Argentina across the River Plate in Uruguay in 1930, Holland across the Rhine in 1974. And, while the Cruyff-less Dutch had not been as convincing as in 1974, it seemed inconceivable that they would finish the 1970s without a major national trophy.

They had improved as the tournament went on, and were arguably the tougher, certainly the more experienced side (10 of the team had played in the 1974 final). Against that, the Argentinians clearly had flair and that all-important home crowd. At the end, they also proved to have the luck that was going, surprisingly more stamina—and Mario Kempes.

Argentina started the game with some unpleasant gamesmanship—complaining about a plaster cast worn on his right wrist over the previous few games by Rene van der Kerkhof. Ruud Krol told his side to leave the field if referee Gonella persisted in taking it seriously and a solution was found.

That was Gonella's high point: gradually his control got less. After 38 minutes Argentina went ahead when Kempes, playing on the left slightly behind the front three and not being marked man-for-man, ripped through to score.

The rest of normal time belonged to the Dutch. They attacked incessantly but did not score until the 82nd minute when substitute Nanninga headed home. With 90 minutes up Rensenbrink hit the post, and the rebound bounced clear. It was as near as Holland came to winning the World Cup in the 1970s. The Dutch still appeared to have the game for their taking but, surprisingly, the Argentinians showed more stamina and, in the first period of extra time, Kempes broke clear again. The ball bounced back of Jongbloed—but this time Kempes was there to score.

The skills of Mario Kempes dominate the 1978 final

With just five minutes left it was Kempes again, creating an easy chance for Bertoni to score and make it, in the end, a relatively convincing 3-1. Rarely, if ever, can one man have had such an influence on the course of such a major game. As a result, Kempes was selected as the Best Player of the Series. He, plus the Argentinian crowd, had won the World Cup. And for the poor Dutch—just bitter disappointment, no magical Arie Haan shot this time—and a decade of fading memories. Perhaps 1980 in Italy and 1982 in Spain would bring something better.

Leopoldo Luque, Mario Kempes and Daniel Bertoni bask in the acclaim of the Buenos Aires crowd after Bertoni's extra-time goal had wrapped up the 1978 final for the hosts against Holland. These three players scored 12 of Argentina's 15 goals in the final series: six to Kempes, four to Luque and two to Bertoni.

LEADING SCORERS

Year	Player	(Ms)	Gls
1930	Guillermo Stabile *(Argentina)*	(4)	8
1934	Angelo Schiavio *(Italy)**	(3)	4
	Oldrich Nejedly *(Czech'vakia)*	(4)	4
	Edmund Conen *(Germany)*	(4)	4
1938	Leonidas *(Brazil)*	(3)	8
1950	Ademir *(Brazil)*	(6)	7
1954	Sandor Kocsis *(Hungary)*	(5)	11
1958	Just Fontaine *(France)*	(6)	13
1962	Drazen Jerkovic *(Yugoslavia)*	(6)	5
1966	Eusebio *(Portugal)*	(6)	9
1970	Gerd Muller *(W. Germany)*	(6)	10
1974	Grzegorz Lato *(Poland)*	(7)	7
1978	Mario Kempes *(Argentina)**	(7)	6
1982	Paolo Rossi *(Italy)**	(7)	6

* winners

Spain, 1982

The 1982 World Cup will be remembered more for the size than for the quality of the tournament. In Spain the finalists for the first time numbered 24; the competition almost spanned a calendar month from the opening game between Argentina the holders and Belgium on June 13 to the final, Italy versus West Germany, on July 11. In all 52 matches were staged.

England qualified for the finals for the first time for twenty years (in 1966 and 1970 the right of entry had been automatic as hosts and holders) though the process produced moments of extreme anxiety with defeats in Rumania, Norway and Switzerland. Ron Greenwood, the manager, was fond of referring to the style of qualification as 'by the back door.'

Scotland and Northern Ireland also won places to give the best representation of Home Countries since 1958. But for an unaccountable lapse at home to Iceland, Wales would also have been guests at the party. The Scots under the wise counsel of Jock Stein and the Ulstermen with the thoughtful Billy Bingham at the helm qualified from the same group, heading Portugal, Sweden and Israel.

Europe provided 14 nations: Austria, Belgium, Czechoslovakia, France, Hungary, Italy, Poland, Russia, West Germany, Yugoslavia, the three British teams and Spain as hosts. From South America Brazil, Chile and Peru joined Argentina. Algeria and the Cameroons represented Africa, Honduras and El Salvador won through from Central and North America, while Kuwait and New Zealand survived the Asia/Oceania section.

Argentina's defence of their crown began while the conflict between that nation and Great Britain over the sovereignty of the Falkland Islands was still casting a heavy shadow. If Argentine troops needed a morale boost from their football team, as was said at the time, that responsibility was too heavy a burden for the team which opened the tournament against Belgium in Barcelona. Nine of the 1978 winners remained, augmented by the youthful talents of Diego Maradona and Ramon Diaz. Belgium, though, gave the competition a sensational start winning through a goal from the predatory Erwin Vandenbergh.

Both countries, however, qualified for the second phase. Argentina with two-goal Maradona in full cry overcame Hungary 4-1, but the subsequent 2-0 victory over El Salvador was disappointing against the Central Americans who had been thrashed 10-1 by Hungary in their opening game. Belgium's margin against El Salvador was only one goal, from Ludo Coeck, but a 1-1 draw with Hungary saw the 1980 European Championship finalists head Group Three.

England, if not all the supporters, were popular visitors to their Group Four base in Bilbao. Deprived of Kevin Keegan and Trevor Brooking through injury Ron Greenwood's side gave their most impressive performance of the tournament in their first game against France. Bryan Robson struck the right

Spain, to be hosts in 1982, failed to enchance their poor World Cup record in Argentina in 1978. They played out a monstrously dull 0-0 draw with Brazil, who, in their turn, became only the second side ever to be eliminated undefeated.

vein with an opening goal after only 27 seconds. Soler equalised, the only time Peter Shilton was to be beaten in the finals, but Robson again and Paul Mariner quelled the passion of the exuberant French.

Subsequent victories over Czechoslovakia and Kuwait—with Trevor Francis on target in both games—were less substantial but England sat proudly on top of the Group with maximum points. France duly and deservedly took the crucial second place but not without a tussle. Kuwait's players wanted to leave the pitch during their 4-1 defeat by France, complaining that a whistle in the crowd has distracted their defenders at moments that had led to French goals. The World Cup saw the unusual spectable of Sheikh Fahid, head of Kuwait's delegation appearing on the touchline to repel the mutiny. Czechoslovakia, with good technique but poorer drive, might have stretched France more had not Vizek been sent off in the latter stages of the 1-1 draw that ensured France of further progress.

Scotland had become the victims of a cruel draw in Group Six, alongside the brilliance of Brazil and the strength of the Soviet Union. New Zealand could also have hoped for better reward after a memorable march through *fifteen* qualifying games, including a play-off against China and overall travelling of some 55,000 miles.

In the event Scotland came agonisingly close to overturning the odds, and but for lapses that turned what should have been a five-goal victory over New Zealand in Malaga into a three-goal success would have pipped Russia. Brazil went a goal behind to Russia but responded

England go out undefeated but largely uninspired

irrepressibly with thrilling shots from Socrates and Eder. Zico found the target in a 4-1 demolition of Scotland and contributed two of the four against New Zealand. Scotland had to beat Russia in their last match to accompany Brazil into the second phase. The recalled Joe Jordan contributed another important goal for his country in a World Cup context and Scotland led until the hour: then Chivadze and later Shengalia were allowed license to undermine Jock Stein's hopes. A goal from Souness that levelled the count just three minutes from time emphasised the frustration of elimination.

Northern Ireland, however, embarked on a crusade even more remarkable than that of 1958 when Bingham was a player. Spain and Yugoslavia were strong favourites in Group Five, but neither the Irish nor Honduras settled for making up the numbers. Spain needed a highly debatable penalty in Valencia to obtain a draw

12th WORLD CUP, SPAIN, 1982

GROUP 1

Italy 0 Poland 0
Peru 0 Cameroon 0
Italy 1 Peru 1
Poland 0 Cameroon 0
Poland 5 Peru 1
Italy 1 Cameroon 1

	P	W	D	L	F	A	P
Poland	3	1	2	0	5	1	4
Italy*	3	0	3	0	2	2	3
Cameroon	3	0	3	0	1	1	3
Peru	3	0	2	1	2	6	2

GROUP 2

Algeria 2 West Germany 1
Austria 1 Chile 0
West Germany 4 Chile 1
Austria 2 Algeria 0
Algeria 3 Chile 2
West Germany 1 Austria 0

	P	W	D	L	F	A	P
West Germany	3	2	0	1	6	3	4
Austria	3	2	0	1	3	1	4
Algeria	3	2	0	1	5	5	4
Chile	3	0	0	3	3	8	0

GROUP 3

Belgium 1 Argentina 0
Hungary 10 El Salvador 1
Argentina 4 Hungary 1
Belgium 1 El Salvador 0
Belgium 1 Hungary 1
Argentina 2 El Salvador 0

	P	W	D	L	F	A	P
Belgium	3	2	1	0	3	1	5
Argentina	3	2	0	1	6	2	4
Hungary	3	1	1	1	12	6	3
El Salvador	3	0	0	3	1	13	0

GROUP 4

England 3 France 1
Czechoslovakia 1 Kuwait 1
England 2 Czechoslovakia 0
France 4 Kuwait 1
France 1 Czechoslovakia 1
England 1 Kuwait 0

	P	W	D	L	F	A	P
England	3	3	0	0	6	1	6
France	3	1	1	1	6	5	3
Czechoslovakia	3	0	2	1	2	4	2
Kuwait	3	0	1	2	2	6	1

GROUP 5

Spain 1 Honduras 1
Northern Ireland 0 Yugoslavia 0
Spain 2 Yugoslavia 1
Honduras 1 Northern Ireland 1
Yugoslavia 1 Honduras 0
Northern Ireland 1 Spain 0

	P	W	D	L	F	A	P
Northern Ireland	3	1	2	0	2	1	4
Spain*	3	1	1	1	3	3	3
Yugoslavia	3	1	1	1	2	2	3
Honduras	3	0	2	1	2	3	2

GROUP 6

Brazil 2 USSR 1
Scotland 5 New Zealand 2
Brazil 4 Scotland 1
USSR 3 New Zealand 0
Scotland 2 USSR 2
Brazil 4 New Zealand 0

	P	W	D	L	F	A	P
Brazil	3	3	0	0	10	2	6
USSR*	3	1	1	1	6	4	3
Scotland	3	1	1	1	8	8	3
New Zealand	3	0	0	3	2	12	0

GROUP A

Poland 3 Belgium 0
USSR 1 Belgium 0
Poland 0 USSR 0

	P	W	D	L	F	A	P
Poland*	2	1	1	0	3	0	3
USSR	2	1	1	0	1	0	3
Belgium	2	0	0	2	0	4	0

GROUP B

West Germany 0 England 0
West Germany 2 Spain 1
Spain 0 England 0

	P	W	D	L	F	A	P
West Germany	2	1	1	0	2	1	3
England	2	0	2	0	0	0	2
Spain	2	0	1	1	1	2	1

GROUP C

Italy 2 Argentina 1
Brazil 3 Argentina 1
Italy 3 Brazil 2

	P	W	D	L	F	A	P
Italy	2	2	0	0	5	3	4
Brazil	2	1	0	1	5	4	2
Argentina	2	0	0	2	2	5	0

GROUP D

France 1 Austria 0
Northern Ireland 2 Austria 2
France 4 Northern Ireland 1

	P	W	D	L	F	A	P
France	2	2	0	0	5	1	4
Austria	2	0	1	1	2	3	1
Northern Ireland	2	0	1	1	3	6	1

SEMI-FINALS

Italy 2 Poland 0 *(in Barcelona)*
West Germany 3 France 3 (WG won 5-4 on penalties) *(in Seville)*

THIRD PLACE MATCH

Poland 3 France 2 *(in Alicante)*

FINAL

Italy 3 West Germany 1
(Madrid 11.7.82 92,000)
Italy: Zoff, Bergomi, Cabrini, Collavati, Scirea, Gentile, Oriali, Tardelli, Conti, Graziani (Altobelli) (Causio), Rossi
West Germany: Schumacher, Kaltz, K-H. Forster, Stielike, B. Forster, Breitner, Dremmler (Hrubesch), Littbarski, Briegel, Rummenigge (Muller), Fischer
Scorers: Rossi, Tardelli, Altobelli; Breitner

*qualified on goal difference

against a surprisingly fluent Honduras. The following night Northern Ireland and Yugoslavia played out a goalless draw in Zaragoza. The sequence of the matches unfolded with Spain, again unconvincing, creeping past Yugoslavia 2-1, and another draw for Bingham's side; Gerry Armstrong of Watford the scorer against Honduras.

When a Petrovic penalty beat Honduras in the penultimate match, only a Northern Ireland win could prevent Yugoslavia from reaching the second phase in tandem with the host nation. The Irish however defied logic, a Paraguayan referee who sent off Luton's Mal Donaghy for a mild infringement after 61 minutes, and the cacophony of a partisan 50,000 crowd who could hardly believe what they were seeing. Pat Jennings and a hugely courageous defence resist what Spain could muster and marvellously protected Armstrong's temerity at putting Northern Ireland in front after a powerful run from Billy Hamilton of Burnley. The file of World Cup upsets had a new entry.

TOP: ***Bryan Robson, soon to become England captain, takes a flier against hosts Spain in Madrid. England came into their second group having won a modern-day record of nine consecutive matches, but then completely lost their touch and failed to score against either West Germany or hosts Spain.***
LEFT: ***Trevor Francis receives a thigh tackle from West German Uli Stielike in the first of the second group games, drew 0-0.***

Oddly the dramas of these four Groups did not produce either finalist. Italy's progress was punctuated with stumbles in Group One. Five of the six matches—Poland, Peru and the Cameroons were the other participants—were drawn, including all three involving Italy who only surpassed the also unbeaten Cameroons on goals scored. Poland provided the sole decisive result, a 5-1 triumph over Peru that made them winners of a very disappointing group.

If Italy had been unappetising, West Germany and Austria offered tasteless fare in Group Two. A shameful final game which saw the Germans beat their supposedly bitter rivals by a solitary goal from Hrubesch became an indictment of the system of qualification. That one-goal scoreline meant that both teams would qualify and after Hrubesch had scored in the 11th minute neither side attempted to alter it. The farce was played out at the expense of a vibrant Algeria who had given the compeitition another sensation by beating West Germany 2-1 with goals from Madjer and the gifted Belloumi. Algeria also chalked up victory against Chile but in the end were the victims of cynicism.

For the second phase the twelve survivors were split into four further groups of three, the winner of each to take part in the first actual semi-finals since the 1970 World Cup.

England moved camp to Navacerrada, a picturesque village 25 miles from Madrid. One opponent, Spain, was based beyond the next hill. The other, West Germany, arrived at their more central hotel still smarting under criticism, from Franz Beckenbauer among many others, for the nature of their unpalatable victory over Austria.

England against West Germany opened the Group, a meeting lacking the drama and the goals of those in 1966 and 1970. German apprehension passed unrecognised and England's methodical play lacked a gambler's throw. It was a costly mistake. Even in their general uncertainty West Germany realised Spain's vulnerability. Littbarski, Cologne's burgeoning talent, and Fischer, his more experienced clubmate, struck in the second half. Spain's attempt at revival, a late goal by Zamora, was too late.

The Brazilian cavalry fails to come to the rescue

England, thus, had to beat Spain by two clear goals in the Bernabeu Stadium to pip West Germany for a semi-final place. The loss of Coppell led to a change of role for Francis; Keegan and Brooking, as substitutes finally intruded into the competition. Both with greater match practice might have turned immediate openings into goals, but England departed unbeaten in their five games with just one goal conceded and a feeling that a genuine opportunity to win the World Cup had been neglected.

That belief had become more intense because earlier that afternoon Brazil, inevitable winners it seemed, had self-destructed. In Group C in Barcelona Argentina had lost their crown—with some bad temper, Gallego being sent off in the 2-1 defeat by Italy and Maradona succumbing eventually to retaliation as Brazil beat the champions 3-1. Brazil's cavalier approach, epitomised by a marvellous sweeping move for Junior's goal against Argentina, seemed too overpowering for Italy. Yet Paolo Rossi, an alleged villain of a corruption scandal two years earlier, chose this moment to rebuild a tottering career.

Rossi had not scored in Italy's four previous games in Spain. Twice he had been substituted. Now he contributed a hat-trick; his third goal was decisive after first Socrates and then the excellent Falcao had equalised the other two in a match Brazil only needed to draw to take a place in the last four. While Rossi's finishing was impeccable Brazil's defending had been deplorable but with their departure went a piece of every football lover's heart.

The neutrals loved Northern Ireland, too, and particularly appreciated the direct attacking of Armstrong, voted the best British player in the tournament, and the seventeen year old Norman Whiteside of Manchester United, younger even than Pele when he first tiptoed onto the World Cup stage.

Two goals from Hamilton earned the Irish a creditable draw against Austria in Group D, but France beat Austria with a crafty free-kick from Genghini and then ended Northern Ireland's dream with Alain Giresse and Dominique Rocheteau, each with two goals, delivering the deadly thrusts.

Group A saw the eclipse of Belgium, less fervent competitors as the tournament lengthened, and Russia, whose team play, rather unusually for that nation, was less than the sum total of the individual talents. Poland marched into the semi-finals with Zbigniew Boniek scoring a rasping hat-trick against Belgium.

But Boniek was suspended when Poland met Italy in the first semi-final in Barcelona's Nou Camp stadium, where Rossi's change of fortune became even more remarkable. After 22 minutes he turned in Antognoni's free-kick, though six minutes later the provider limped off injured to miss the final. Conti's perceptive cross enabled Rossi to head a simple second goal eighteen minutes from time.

The West Germany-France semi-final in Seville produced the match of the tournament; indeed it was a match of many tournaments, the first World Cup tie to need penalties for a decision. The contest paraded the discipline and relentless competitiveness of the Germans against the buccaneering French whose flowing football had captured the imagination.

Littbarski drew first blood after 18 minutes, but in the 27th minute Michel Platini equalised with a penalty when Rochetau was held by Bernd Forster. Unpunished, however, went a ruthless bodycheck by Schumacher on Battiston whose shot rolled past the post as he was flattened by the onrushing German goalkeeper. Without Battiston the semi-final moved into extra time.

Within eight minutes France seemed safe when Marius Tresor, the veteran defender, and Giresse claimed goals that produced a 3-1 lead. Foolishly the French temperament desired an even greater margin of victory, and Karl-Heinz Rummenigge's introduction as a substitute—hamstring trouble had kept him from a starting role—gave West Germany greater penetration as gaps opened. Rummenigge reduced the deficit himself and then ten minutes from time Fischer twisted in mid-air to volley the Germans' equaliser.

France tossed aside one further opportunity to reach a World Cup final for the first time. Stielike was the first penalty taker to miss, but immediately Six allowed Schumacher to save his kick. The next failure was also French, Bossis, but Hrubesch did not waste his chance and West Germany had completed another remarkable comeback.

The absence of Brazil and the presence of two of the game's most calculating teams robbed the 1982 final of some of its glitter. Nevertheless the Bernabeu Stadium offered a fitting setting on July 11th, and if belatedly the match had moments that lived up to the billing. Italy had to manage without Antognoni; Guiseppe Bergomi, a tenderfoot 18-year-old, took his place. Rummenigge overruled Derwall's advice and played from the outset.

Arnold Cesar Coelho from Brazil was selected as the first South American to referee a World Cup final. In the 25th minute he rightly gave Italy a penalty when he spotted Briegel dragging Conti away from a deep cross. Cabrini, though, recorded the first miss on such a lofty occasion, rolling the ball tamely past Schumacher's left-hand post.

West Germany could not profit from the error. Eleven minutes into the second half Rossi just beat Cabrini to turn in a splendid low cross from Gentile; his sixth goal of the tournament brought the extra accolade of top scorer. Tardelli celebrated deliriously when his left-footed drive in the 72nd minute sped into the corner, and ten minutes from time Altobelli, an 18th minute substitute for Graziani, slotted in a third. Breitner responded with a late consolation goal, the only damp moment for the 40-year-old Dino Zoff who collected the World Cup for Italy from King Juan Carlos of Spain.

Northern Ireland—surprise team of the whole tournament

The crowning achievement in Irish football history was probably the 1-0 defeat of Spain in Valencia. Armstrong (9) and Hamilton were the heroes.

EUROPEAN CHAMPIONSHIP

Once shunned by the super-powers, the European Championship was the game's biggest event in 1980 . . .

Unlike its club-based cousin, the Champions Cup, which quickly won the affections of clubs and fans, Europe's national competition suffered a difficult and ill-supported childhood.

While South America had played a continental national championship since 1916, Europe had relied on regional competitions—like the Home Championship, the Scandinavian Cup, the Balkan Cup and so on. It was Henri Delaunay, secretary of the French Football Federation and the biggest champion of a European national tournament, who got the idea off the ground in the mid-1950s—though he didn't live to see the contest for the trophy which bore his name.

The first competition was in fact more notable for its absentees than for its participants. Italy, West Germany, Holland, Belgium and all four British sides refused the invitation, and the lack of quality in the field can be gauged by the fact that if the list is joined by Spain (they withdrew before the quarter-finals) it meant the homelands of six of the last eight in that year's European Cup were missing.

The big breakthrough came in 1966–68, when groups replaced the two-legged knock-out system. A superb display by West Germany in the 1972 final and an exhilarating series in Yugoslavia in 1976 helped lift the tournament as a spectacle, and by 1980 the competition had finally reached the position it should really enjoy in the world game.

The probing performances of double European Footballer of the Year Kevin Keegan—here under pressure from Republic of Ireland defender David O'Leary—helped England coast to the 1980 finals in Italy.

EUROPEAN CHAMPIONSHIP FINALS

Year	Venue	Winners		Runners-up		Third		Fourth	
1960	France	USSR	*2	Yugoslavia	1	Czechoslovakia	2	France	0
1964	Spain	Spain	2	USSR	1	Hungary	*3	Denmark	1
1968	Italy	Italy	*1:2	Yugoslavia	1:0	England	2	USSR	0
1972	Belgium	W. Germany	3	USSR	0	Belgium	2	Hungary	1
1976	Yugoslavia	Czechoslovakia	†*2	W. Germany	2	Holland	*3	Yugoslavia	2
1980	Italy	W. Germany	2	Belgium	1	Czechoslovakia	‡1	Italy	1

*after extra time †Czechoslovakia won 5-3 on penalties ‡Czechoslovakia won 9-8 on penalties

1958-60

Had Henri Delaunay lived to see the Nations Cup start, he may well have been disappointed: only 17 nations entered and the tournament—won by the Soviet Union—had something of an anti-climatic flavour.

Olympic champions Russia gave an impressive performance in the first round in beating Hungary both at home and away, but had an easy passage in the quarter-final when they received a walk-over against Spain, convincing conquerors of Poland in the previous round. The Spaniards withdrew after refusing to play in Russia for political reasons dating back to the Spanish Civil War.

The semi-finals and final were single-match deciders played in July 1960 in France. Russia beat Czechoslovakia 3-0 in Marseille, while Yugoslavia, who had reached the last four by beating Bulgaria and Portugal, won a high-scoring encounter against France in Paris.

The entertaining French, who had scored 23 goals in six matches in the 1958 World Cup in Sweden, had continued in similar vein with the Nations Cup, putting eight past Greece and nine past Austria before losing 5-4 to Yugoslavia. The hosts failed for once in the third place game, going down to the Czechs without scoring at Marseille.

In the final, also in Paris, Russia won 2-1 after extra time, Metreveli and Ponedelnik scoring for the Russians, Netto putting through his own goal to score for Yugoslavia. The crowd—it would certainly have been a sell-out had France been playing—was less than 18,000.

There was some consolation for the losing finalists that year: eight of that Yugoslavia side were in the team that beat Denmark 3-1 in Rome to take the Olympic title.

1962-64

The second competition, organized after the 1962 World Cup and on a similar knock-out basis, was better supported. Only Scotland of the home countries did not compete, and altogether 29 nations entered. England made a quick exit, however, held 1-1 at Hillsborough by the French and crushed 5-2 in Paris (their first game with Alf Ramsey as team manager). France lost to Hungary in the quarter-finals.

The final stages, held in Spain, involved Denmark, Russia, Hungary, and the host nation. The amateur Danes had been favoured with easy competition in Malta, Albania and Luxembourg, though the Duchy forced them into a play-off in the quarter-final.

Spain, who had defeated Rumania in the preliminary round, were hard pressed by Northern Ireland, a side boosted by a 4-0 aggregate win over Poland. Spain were held 1-1 at home and only just scraped through 1-0 away after recalling Del Sol and Suarez from Italy. They had a better time of it against Eire in the quarter-finals, winning both matches comfortably. Hungary beat Wales and survived a fright at home to East Germany, in a 3-3 draw, having won 2-1 away. In the quarter-finals they surprised France in Paris 3-1 and then won at home.

The semi-finals saw Russia achieve an easy 3-0 victory over Denmark in Barcelona, while in Madrid the hosts had more difficulty in beating Hungary 2-1.

The final, in front of 120,000, pitted the Soviet Union against Spain—this time with political animosity shelved. Spain had a fine start after five minutes from Pereda, but within two minutes Khusainov had levelled. It was not until six minutes from time that Spain's Marcelino scored an opportunist goal to produce Russia's first defeat in a competition which still lacked the prestige it should command.

EUROPEAN NATIONS CUP 1958-60

PRELIMINARY ROUND

Eire v Czechoslovakia (2-0, 0-4)	2-4

FIRST ROUND

USSR v Hungary (3-1, 0-1)	3-2
Poland v Spain (2-4, 0-3)	2-7
Denmark v C'slovakia (2-2, 1-5)	3-7
Rumania v Turkey (3-0, 0-2)	3-2
France v Greece (7-1, 1-1)	8-2
Norway v Austria (0-1, 2-5)	2-6
Portugal v E. Germany (3-2, 2-0)	5-2
Yugoslavia v Bulgaria (2-0, 1-1)	3-1

QUARTER-FINALS

USSR w.o. Spain (withdrew)	
Rumania v C'slovakia (0-2, 0-3)	0-5
France v Austria (5-2, 4-2)	9-4
Portugal v Yugoslavia (2-1, 1-5)	3-6

SEMI-FINALS

USSR 3 C'slovakia 0 *(Marseille)*
Yugoslavia 5 France 4 *(Paris)*

THIRD PLACE MATCH

C'vakia 2 France 0 *(Marseille)*

FINAL

USSR 2 Yugoslavia 1 [aet]
(Paris, 10.7.60, 17,966)

USSR: Yashin, Tchekeli, Kroutilov, Voinov, Maslenkin, Netto, Metreveli, Ivanov, Ponedelnik, Bubukin, Meshki

Yugoslavia: Vidinic, Durkovic, Jusufi, Zanetic, Miladinovic, Perusic, Sekularac, Jerkovic, Galic, Matus, Kostic

EUROPEAN NATIONS CUP 1962-64

FIRST ROUND

Spain v Rumania (6-0, 1-3)	7-3
Poland v N. Ireland (0-2, 0-2)	0-4
Eire v Iceland (4-2, 1-1)	5-3
B'garia v Portugal (3-1, 1-3, 1-0)	5-4
England v France (1-1, 2-5)	3-6
E. Germany v C'vakia (2-1, 1-0)	3-1
Hungary v Wales (3-1, 1-1)	4-2
Denmark v Malta (6-1, 3-1)	9-2
Albania w.o. Greece (withdrew)	
Holland v Switzerland (3-1, 1-1)	4-2
Norway v Sweden (0-2, 1-1)	1-3
Yugoslavia v Belgium (3-2, 1-0)	4-2
Italy v Turkey (6-0, 1-0)	7-0

[Austria, Luxembourg & USSR received byes]

SECOND ROUND

Spain v N. Ireland (1-1, 1-0)	2-1
Austria v Eire (0-0, 2-3)	2-3
Bulgaria v France (1-0, 1-3)	2-3
E. Germany v Hungary (1-2, 3-3)	4-5
Denmark v Albania (4-0, 0-1)	4-1
Holland v L'bourg (1-1, 1-2)	2-3
Yugoslavia v Sweden (0-0, 2-3)	2-3
USSR v Italy (2-0, 1-1)	3-1

QUARTER-FINALS

Spain v Eire (5-1, 2-0)	7-1
France v Hungary (1-3, 1-2)	2-5
L'bourg v Denmark (2-2, 3-3, 0-1)	5-6
Sweden v USSR (1-1, 1-3)	2-4

SEMI-FINALS

Spain 2 Hungary 1 *(Madrid)*
USSR 3 Denmark 0 *(Barcelona)*

THIRD PLACE MATCH

Hungary 3 Denmark 1* [aet]

FINAL

Spain 2 USSR 1
(Madrid, 21.6.64, 120,000)

Spain: Iribar, Rivilla, Calleja, Fuste, Olivella, Zoco, Amancio, Pereda, Marcelino, Suarez, Lapetra

USSR: Yashin, Chustikov, Mudrik, Voronin, Shesterniev, Anitchkin, Chislenko, Ivanov, Ponedelnik, Kornalev, Khusainov

Scorers: Pereda, Marcelino; Khusainov

*at Barcelona

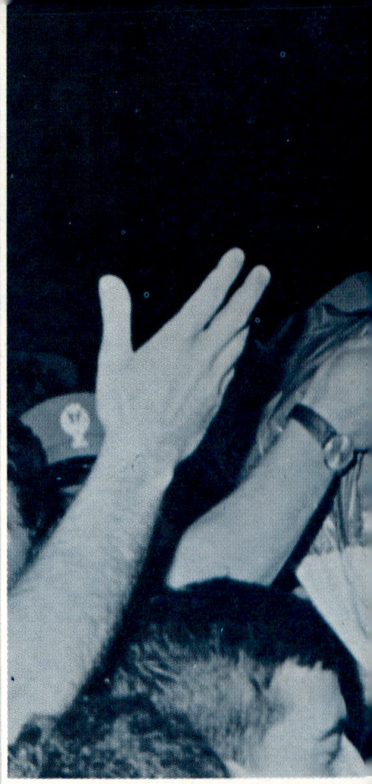

ABOVE: Jubilant Italian captain Giacinto Facchetti after Italy's 1968 success.
RIGHT: The semi-final defeat by Yugoslavia saw Alan Mullery become the first England player ever to be sent off in a full international.

1966-68

For the third competition, in 1966, which adopted the official title of European Championship, the 31 countries were split into eight groups.

The Home International Football Championship was used—over two seasons—to determine one group, and England emerged as the winners, one point ahead of Scotland. The Scots took three points out of four off England—including a memorable win over the World Champions at Wembley in 1967—but blew their chance with a draw in Cardiff and a defeat in Belfast.

Spain, Bulgaria, Russia, Yugoslavia, Hungary, Italy and France also qualified. The biggest shock was perhaps in Tirana, where Albania held West Germany 0-0 when the Germans needed only a single-goal win to go through.

At this stage the knock-out system on the home-and-away aggregate basis was used. England were the only team to win both matches, beating Spain 1-0 and 2-1. Italy reached the semi-finals by beating Bulgaria, Yugoslavia by beating France;

Russia recovered from a 2-0 defeat in Hungary to win 3-0 at home in front of 103,000.

The semi-finals were staged in Italy in June 1968. Yugoslavia beat England in Florence with a late goal by Dragan Dzajic, but in Naples Italy and Russia played a goalless draw, and a toss of the coin gave the Italians a lucky final place. England beat Russia 2-0 for third place.

In the final in Rome, the Italians were fortunate to hold a talented Yugoslav side to a 1-1 draw after extra time, Dzajic scoring for Yugoslavia and Domenghini replying. Italy made five changes for the replay two days later and were the fresher side, winning 2-0 with goals by Riva—one of the new boys—and Anastasi.

EUROPEAN CHAMPIONSHIP 1966-68

GROUP 1

Eire 0 Spain 0
Eire 2 Turkey 1
Spain 2 Eire 0
Turkey 0 Spain 0
Turkey 2 Eire 1
Eire 0 Czechoslovakia 2
Spain 2 Turkey 0
Czechoslovakia 1 Spain 0
Spain 2 Czechoslovakia 0
Czechoslovakia 3 Turkey 0
Turkey 0 Czechoslovakia 0
Czechoslovakia 1 Eire 2

	P	W	D	L	F	A	P
Spain	6	3	2	1	6	2	8
Czechoslovakia	6	3	1	2	8	4	7
Eire	6	2	1	3	5	8	5
Turkey	6	1	2	3	3	8	4

GROUP 2

Norway 0 Bulgaria 0
Portugal 1 Sweden 2
Bulgaria 4 Norway 2
Sweden 1 Portugal 1
Norway 1 Portugal 2
Sweden 0 Bulgaria 2
Norway 3 Sweden 1
Sweden 5 Norway 2
Bulgaria 3 Sweden 0
Portugal 2 Norway 1
Bulgaria 1 Portugal 0
Portugal 0 Bulgaria 0

	P	W	D	L	F	A	P
Bulgaria	6	4	2	0	10	2	10
Portugal	6	2	2	2	6	6	6
Sweden	6	2	1	3	9	12	5
Norway	6	1	1	4	9	14	3

GROUP 3

Finland 0 Austria 0
Greece 2 Finland 1
Finland 1 Greece 1
USSR 4 Austria 3
USSR 2 Finland 0
Finland 2 USSR 5
Austria 2 Finland 1
Greece 4 Austria 1
Austria 1 USSR 0
Greece 0 USSR 1
Austria 1 Greece 1
USSR 4 Greece 0

	P	W	D	L	F	A	P
USSR	6	5	0	1	16	6	10
Greece	6	2	2	2	8	9	6
Austria	6	2	2	2	8	10	6
Finland	6	0	2	4	5	12	2

GROUP 4

Albania 0 Yugoslavia 2
West Germany 6 Albania 0
Yugoslavia 1 West Germany 0
West Germany 3 Yugoslavia 1
Yugoslavia 4 Albania 0
Albania 0 West Germany 0

	P	W	D	L	F	A	P
Yugoslavia	4	3	0	1	8	3	6
West Germany	4	2	1	1	9	2	5
Albania	4	0	1	3	0	12	1

GROUP 5

Holland 2 Hungary 2
Hungary 6 Denmark 0
Holland 2 Denmark 0
East Germany 4 Holland 3
Hungary 2 Holland 1
Denmark 0 Hungary 2
Denmark 1 East Germany 1
Holland 1 East Germany 0
Hungary 3 East Germany 1
Denmark 3 Holland 2
East Germany 3 Denmark 2
East Germany 1 Hungary 0

	P	W	D	L	F	A	P
Hungary	6	4	1	1	15	5	9
East Germany	6	3	1	2	10	10	7
Holland	6	2	1	3	11	11	5
Denmark	6	1	1	4	6	16	3

GROUP 6

Cyprus 1 Rumania 5
Rumania 4 Switzerland 2
Italy 3 Rumania 1
Cyprus 0 Italy 2
Rumania 7 Cyprus 0
Switzerland 7 Rumania 1
Italy 5 Cyprus 0
Switzerland 5 Cyprus 0
Switzerland 2 Italy 2
Italy 4 Switzerland 0
Cyprus 2 Switzerland 1
Rumania 0 Italy 1

	P	W	D	L	F	A	P
Italy	6	5	1	0	17	3	11
Rumania	6	3	0	3	18	14	6
Switzerland	6	2	1	3	17	13	5
Cyprus	6	1	0	5	3	25	2

GROUP 7

Poland 4 Luxembourg 0
France 2 Poland 1
Luxembourg 0 France 3
Luxembourg 0 Belgium 5
Luxembourg 0 Poland 0
Poland 3 Belgium 1
Belgium 2 France 1
Poland 1 France 4
Belgium 2 Poland 4
France 1 Belgium 1
Belgium 3 Luxembourg 0
France 3 Luxembourg 1

	P	W	D	L	F	A	P
France	6	4	1	1	14	6	9
Belgium	6	3	1	2	14	9	7
Poland	6	3	1	2	13	9	7
Luxembourg	6	0	1	5	1	18	1

GROUP 8

Northern Ireland 0 England 2
Wales 1 Scotland 1
England 5 Wales 1
Scotland 2 Northern Ireland 1
Northern Ireland 0 Wales 0
England 2 Scotland 3
Wales 0 England 3
Northern Ireland 1 Scotland 0
England 2 Northern Ireland 0
Scotland 3 Wales 2
Wales 2 Northern Ireland 0
Scotland 1 England 1

	P	W	D	L	F	A	P
England	6	4	1	1	15	5	9
Scotland	6	3	2	1	10	8	8
Wales	6	1	2	3	6	12	4
N. Ireland	6	1	1	4	2	8	3

QUARTER-FINALS

Bulgaria v Italy (3-2, 0-2)	3-4
Hungary v USSR (2-0, 0-3)	2-3
England v Spain (1-0, 2-1)	3-1
France v Yugoslavia (1-1, 1-5)	2-6

SEMI-FINALS

Italy 0 USSR 0* *(Naples)*
Yugoslavia 1 England 0 *(Florence)*

THIRD PLACE MATCH

England 2 USSR 0 *(Rome)*

FINAL

Italy 1 Yugoslavia 1
(Rome, 8.6.68, 75,000)

Italy: Zoff, Burgnich, Facchetti, Ferrini, Guarneri, Castano, Domenghini, Juliano, Anastasi, Lodetti, Prati

Yugoslavia: Pantelic, Fazlagic, Damjanovic, Pavlovic, Paunovic, Holcer, Petkovic, Acimovic, Musemic, Trivic, Dzajic

Scorers: Domenghini; Dzajic

Replay (Rome, 10.6.68, 60,000)

Italy 2 Yugoslavia 0

Italy: Zoff, Burgnich, Facchetti, Rosato, Guarneri, Salvadore, Domenghini, Mazzola, Anastasi, De Sisti, Riva

Yugoslavia: Hosic for Petkovic

Scorers: Riva, Anastasi

*Italy won on toss of coin

Yugoslavia's brilliant winger Dragan Dzajic, whose late goal had put out England in Florence, was again the danger man in Rome, when he gave his side the lead against Italy. The struggling hosts, who had won their semi-final on the toss of a coin, replied through Domenghini and then won the replay two days later—thus restoring pride after their defeat by North Korea.

1970-72

A new star erupted on the fourth edition of the European Championships and stamped his personality through to the finals. That star was Gunter Netzer, a Viking general commanding the West German midfield whether with ball at toe or spraying immaculate passes the full dimension of the attack. England suffered from Netzer's magic in their quarter-final first leg at Wembley, omitting a ball-winning wing-half and so giving Netzer freedom to roam at will. Beckenbauer, in his new role of attacking sweeper, was as magisterial as ever; Müller, up front, as deadly.

For the first game at Wembley manager Sir Alf Ramsey experienced the familiar problems with clubs over player release. Roy McFarland was withdrawn on the grounds that he was injured—but not so badly that he could not play for Derby County and help them defeat Liverpool for the League title two days later. Ramsey hence played two stand-off centre-backs, Bobby Moore and Norman Hunter, and, unusually, failed to pick a ball-winner in midfield, Alan Mullery remaining on the bench. Moore made mistakes and gave away a penalty. Netzer ran free in midfield and Germany won 3-1 to virtually clinch a place in the last four.

For the return Ramsey picked his most cynical team ever. The picture of Peter Storey, arms round Müller's neck, became a symbol of the England side's tactical descent. A 0-0 draw in Berlin was, of course, of no use to anyone except the Germans.

Once again the competition was divided into eight groups, featuring 32 countries playing home-and-away ties. Belgium, qualifying at the expense of Portugal, were the surprise, while the adventurous Swiss had made England struggle (3-2 in Basle, 1-1 at Wembley). Next, the Belgians accounted for Italy in the quarter-finals, but lost Van Moer with a broken leg after Bertini's tackle. Elsewhere, Hungary needed a play-off in Belgrade to beat Rumania for a semi-final place, and Russia beat the other 1968 finalists, Yugoslavia—both teams having been undefeated in their group matches, conceding only six goals in 12 games between them.

In June 1972, the competition arrived in Belgium for the final stages. In Antwerp, the West Germans (with six Bayern Munich players in the side) beat the hosts 2-1 through Müller, while, with television covering that match live, a mere 3,500 in Brussels saw a dull Russia beat Hungary by the only goal to reach their third European final.

The Russians remained in Brussels for the final and played second fiddle to the combined talents of Beckenbauer, Müller, Netzer, Breitner, Hoeness and Wimmer—welded together by Helmut Schoen. Rudakov in the Russian goal was magnificent, but eventually the reliable Müller beat him. Wimmer added another in the second half, and finally Müller scored his 11th goal of the competition, having scored against every country West Germany played. It was a great victory for the Germans and for football, showing that attack, wingers and individualism can win major honours.

ABOVE: ***West Germany's impressive run to the 1972 final had been characterized as much by the superb midfield play of Gunter Netzer as by the scoring prowess of Gerd Müller—and both men were devastating in the 3-1 win over England at Wembley in the quarter-finals.*** *LEFT:* ***The victorious German side contained six Bayern Munich players. While all of them would appear against Holland in the 1974 World Cup final, none of the other five were retained by Schoen for that game.***

EUROPEAN CHAMPIONSHIP 1970-72

GROUP 1

Czechoslovakia 1 Finland 1
Rumania 3 Finland 0
Wales 0 Rumania 0
Wales 1 Czechoslovakia 3
Finland 0 Wales 1
Czechoslovakia 1 Rumania 0
Finland 0 Czechoslovakia 4
Finland 0 Rumania 4
Wales 3 Finland 0
Czechoslovakia 1 Wales 0
Rumania 2 Czechoslovakia 1
Rumania 2 Wales 0

	P	W	D	L	F	A	P
Rumania*	6	4	1	1	11	2	9
Czechoslovakia	6	4	1	1	11	4	9
Wales	6	2	1	3	5	6	5
Finland	6	0	1	5	1	16	1

GROUP 2

Norway 1 Hungary 3
France 3 Norway 1
Bulgaria 1 Norway 1
Hungary 1 France 1
Bulgaria 3 Hungary 0
Norway 1 Bulgaria 4
Norway 1 France 3
Hungary 2 Bulgaria 0
France 0 Hungary 2
Hungary 4 Norway 0
France 2 Bulgaria 1
Bulgaria 2 France 1

	P	W	D	L	F	A	P
Hungary	6	4	1	1	12	5	9
Bulgaria	6	3	1	2	11	7	7
France	6	3	1	2	10	8	7
Norway	6	0	1	5	5	18	1

GROUP 3

Greece 0 Switzerland 1
Malta 1 Switzerland 2
Malta 0 England 1
England 3 Greece 0
Switzerland 5 Malta 0
England 5 Malta 0
Malta 1 Greece 1
Switzerland 1 Greece 0
Greece 2 Malta 0
Switzerland 2 England 3
England 1 Switzerland 1
Greece 0 England 2

	P	W	D	L	F	A	P
England	6	5	1	0	15	3	11
Switzerland	6	4	1	1	12	5	9
Greece	6	1	1	4	3	8	3
Malta	6	0	1	5	2	16	1

GROUP 4

Spain 3 Northern Ireland 0
Cyprus 0 Northern Ireland 3
Northern Ireland 5 Cyprus 0
Cyprus 1 USSR 3
Cyprus 0 Spain 2
USSR 2 Spain 1
USSR 6 Cyprus 1
USSR 1 Northern Ireland 0
Northern Ireland 1 USSR 1
Spain 0 USSR 0
Spain 7 Cyprus 0
Northern Ireland 1 Spain 1

	P	W	D	L	F	A	P
USSR	6	4	2	0	13	4	10
Spain	6	3	2	1	14	3	8
N. Ireland	6	2	2	2	10	6	6
Cyprus	6	0	0	6	2	26	0

GROUP 5

Denmark 0 Portugal 1
Scotland 1 Denmark 0
Belgium 2 Denmark 0
Belgium 3 Scotland 0
Belgium 3 Portugal 0
Portugal 2 Scotland 0
Denmark 1 Scotland 0
Portugal 5 Denmark 0
Denmark 1 Belgium 2
Scotland 2 Portugal 1
Scotland 1 Belgium 0
Portugal 1 Belgium 1

	P	W	D	L	F	A	P
Belgium	6	4	1	1	11	3	9
Portugal	6	3	1	2	10	6	7
Scotland	6	3	0	3	4	7	6
Denmark	6	1	0	5	2	11	2

GROUP 6

Eire 1 Sweden 1
Sweden 1 Eire 0
Austria 1 Italy 2
Italy 3 Eire 0
Eire 1 Italy 2
Eire 1 Austria 4
Sweden 1 Austria 0
Sweden 0 Italy 0
Austria 1 Sweden 0
Italy 3 Sweden 0
Austria 6 Eire 0
Italy 2 Austria 2

	P	W	D	L	F	A	P
Italy	6	4	2	0	12	4	10
Austria	6	3	1	2	14	6	7
Sweden	6	2	2	2	3	5	6
Eire	6	0	1	5	3	17	1

GROUP 7

Holland 1 Yugoslavia 1
East Germany 1 Holland 0
Luxembourg 0 East Germany 5
Yugoslavia 2 Holland 0
East Germany 2 Luxembourg 1
Luxembourg 0 Yugoslavia 2
Holland 6 Luxembourg 0
East Germany 1 Yugoslavia 2
Holland 3 East Germany 2
Yugoslavia 0 East Germany 0
Yugoslavia 0 Luxembourg 0
Luxembourg 0 Holland 8

	P	W	D	L	F	A	P
Yugoslavia	6	3	3	0	7	2	9
Holland	6	3	1	2	18	6	7
East Germany	6	3	1	2	11	6	7
Luxembourg	6	0	1	5	1	23	1

GROUP 8

Poland 3 Albania 0
West Germany 1 Turkey 1
Turkey 2 Albania 1
Albania 0 West Germany 1
Turkey 0 West Germany 3
Albania 1 Poland 1
West Germany 2 Albania 0
Poland 5 Turkey 1
Poland 1 West Germany 3
Albania 3 Turkey 0
West Germany 0 Poland 0
Turkey 1 Poland 0

	P	W	D	L	F	A	P
West Germany	6	4	2	0	10	2	10
Poland	6	2	2	2	10	6	6
Turkey	6	2	1	3	5	13	5
Albania	6	1	1	4	5	9	3

QUARTER-FINALS

England v W. Germany (1-3, 0-0)	1-3
Italy v Belgium (0-0, 1-2)	1-2
H'ng'y v Rumania (1-1, 2-2, 2-1†)	5-4
Yugoslavia v USSR (0-0, 0-3)	0-3

SEMI-FINALS

West Germany 2 Belgium 1 *(Antwerp)*
USSR 1 Hungary 0 *(Brussels)*

THIRD PLACE MATCH

Belgium 2 Hungary 1 *(Liege)*

FINAL

West Germany 3 USSR 0
(Brussels, 18.6.72, 43,437)

West Germany: Maier, Hottges, Schwarzenbeck, Beckenbauer, Breitner, Hoeness, Wimmer, Netzer, Heynckes, Muller, Kremers

USSR: Rudakov, Dzodzuashvili, Khurtsilava, Kaplichny, Istomin, Troshkin, Kolotov, Baidachni, Konkov (Dolmatov), Banishevsky (Kozinkievits), Onishenko

Scorers: Muller 2, Wimmer

*qualified on goal difference †play-off in Belgrade

Herbert Wimmer's left-foot shot in the 52nd minute, making it 2-0, virtually sealed the 1972 final against the USSR in Brussels. Gerd Müller added a third five minutes later, his second, to take his tally for the competition to 11 in 10 matches. It was Russia's third final in four European Championships.

1974-76

The 1976 European Championship in Yugoslavia was to produce the best football ever seen in the competition and, many critics argued at the time and have done so since, the best concentrated series of games at international level ever played. There were still four finalists—hosts Yugoslavia, world champions West Germany, their opponents from two years before, Holland, and Czechoslovakia.

All four games went to extra time, the final was eventually decided on penalties, and 19 goals were scored in the four games. It was an intensely contested series, with more than its fair share of red and yellow cards, but it sent a surge of hope and pleasure through Europe.

Czechoslovakia beat Holland 3-1 in Zagreb and West Germany eventually overcame hosts Yugoslavia 4-2 in Belgrade, scoring twice in extra time. Unusually for this competition, the third place game was equally competitive, Holland coming out on top 3-2.

The final was a game of remarkably sustained excitement. Czechoslovakia went in 2-1 up at half-time but Holzenbein equalized and the game went to extra time—and then penalties. It was unfortunate that it had been agreed in advance not to play another game. Having reached this stage after so many matches, it struck an odd chord to award the trophy on the basis of five kicks per side. The good fortune went to Czechoslovakia, Uli Hoeness missing his penalty (West Germany's second) and Panenka chipping home an astonishingly casual shot to win the competition for the Czechs—their first ever major tournament success at international level. Previously they had been runners-up in two World Cups.

It is a remarkable illustration of how rapidly sides can decline, or how the chemistry of a successful team can disappear, that neither Yugoslavia (beaten by Spain both home and away) nor Czechoslovakia (bundled out by Scotland) were to appear in Argentina just two years later.

The home countries had again performed poorly in this championship. Only Wales, who took six points off Austria and Hungary, emerged in credit.

EUROPEAN CHAMPIONSHIP 1974-76

GROUP 1

England 3 Czechoslovakia 0
England 0 Portugal 0
England 5 Cyprus 0
Czechoslovakia 4 Cyprus 0
Czechoslovakia 5 Portugal 0
Cyprus 0 England 1
Cyprus 0 Portugal 2
Czechoslovakia 2 England 1
Portugal 1 Czechoslovakia 1
Portugal 1 England 1
Cyprus 0 Czechoslovakia 3
Portugal 1 Cyprus 0

	P	W	D	L	F	A	P
Czechoslovakia	6	4	1	1	15	5	9
England	6	3	2	1	11	3	8
Portugal	6	2	3	1	5	7	7
Cyprus	6	0	0	6	0	16	0

GROUP 2

Austria 2 Wales 1
Luxembourg 2 Hungary 4
Wales 2 Hungary 0
Wales 5 Luxembourg 0
Luxembourg 1 Austria 2
Austria 0 Hungary 0
Hungary 1 Wales 2
Luxembourg 1 Wales 3
Hungary 2 Austria 1
Austria 6 Luxembourg 2
Hungary 8 Luxembourg 1
Wales 1 Austria 0

	P	W	D	L	F	A	P
Wales	6	5	0	1	14	4	10
Hungary	6	3	1	2	15	8	7
Austria	6	3	1	2	11	7	7
Luxembourg	6	0	0	6	7	28	0

GROUP 3

Norway 2 Northern Ireland 1
Yugoslavia 3 Norway 1
Sweden 0 Northern Ireland 2
Northern Ireland 1 Yugoslavia 0
Sweden 1 Yugoslavia 2
Norway 1 Yugoslavia 3
Sweden 3 Norway 1
Norway 0 Sweden 2
Northern Ireland 1 Sweden 2
Yugoslavia 3 Sweden 0
Northern Ireland 3 Norway 0
Yugoslavia 1 Northern Ireland 0

	P	W	D	L	F	A	P
Yugoslavia	6	5	0	1	12	4	10
N. Ireland	6	3	0	3	8	5	6
Sweden	6	3	0	3	8	9	6
Norway	6	1	0	5	5	15	2

GROUP 4

Denmark 1 Spain 2
Denmark 0 Rumania 0
Scotland 1 Spain 2
Spain 1 Scotland 1
Spain 1 Rumania 1
Rumania 6 Denmark 1
Rumania 1 Scotland 1
Denmark 0 Scotland 1
Spain 2 Denmark 0
Scotland 3 Denmark 1
Rumania 2 Spain 2
Scotland 1 Rumania 1

	P	W	D	L	F	A	P
Spain	6	3	3	0	10	6	9
Rumania	6	1	5	0	11	6	7
Scotland	6	2	3	1	8	6	7
Denmark	6	0	1	5	3	14	1

GROUP 5

Finland 1 Poland 2
Finland 1 Holland 3
Poland 3 Finland 0
Holland 3 Italy 1
Italy 0 Poland 0
Finland 0 Italy 1
Holland 4 Finland 1
Poland 4 Holland 1
Italy 0 Finland 0
Holland 3 Poland 0
Poland 0 Italy 0
Italy 1 Holland 0

	P	W	D	L	F	A	P
Holland	6	4	0	2	14	8	8
Poland	6	3	2	1	9	5	8
Italy	6	2	3	1	3	3	7
Finland	6	0	1	5	3	13	1

GROUP 6

Eire 3 USSR 0
Turkey 1 Eire 1
Turkey 2 Switzerland 1
USSR 3 Turkey 0
Switzerland 1 Turkey 1
Eire 2 Switzerland 1
USSR 2 Eire 1
Switzerland 1 Eire 0
Switzerland 0 USSR 1
Eire 4 Turkey 0
USSR 4 Switzerland 1
Turkey 1 USSR 0

	P	W	D	L	F	A	P
USSR	6	4	0	2	10	6	8
Eire	6	3	1	2	11	5	7
Turkey	6	2	2	2	5	10	6
Switzerland	6	1	1	4	5	10	3

GROUP 7

Iceland 1 Belgium 2
East Germany 1 Iceland 1
Belgium 2 France 1
France 2 East Germany 2
East Germany 0 Belgium 0
Iceland 0 France 0
Iceland 2 East Germany 1
France 3 Iceland 0
Belgium 1 Iceland 0
Belgium 1 East Germany 2
East Germany 2 France 1
France 0 Belgium 0

	P	W	D	L	F	A	P
Belgium	6	3	2	1	6	3	8
East Germany	6	2	3	1	8	7	7
France	6	1	3	2	7	6	5
Iceland	6	1	2	3	3	8	4

GROUP 8

Bulgaria 3 Greece 3
Greece 2 West Germany 2
Greece 2 Bulgaria 1
Malta 0 West Germany 1
Malta 2 Greece 0
Bulgaria 1 West Germany 1
Greece 4 Malta 0
Bulgaria 5 Malta 0
West Germany 1 Greece 1
West Germany 1 Bulgaria 0
Malta 0 Bulgaria 2
West Germany 8 Malta 0

	P	W	D	L	F	A	P
West Germany	6	3	3	0	14	4	9
Greece	6	2	3	1	12	9	7
Bulgaria	6	2	2	2	12	7	6
Malta	6	1	0	5	2	20	2

QUARTER-FINALS

Czechoslovakia v USSR (2-0, 2-2) 4-2
Holland v Belgium (5-0, 2-1) 7-1
Yugoslavia v Wales (2-0, 1-1) 3-1
Spain v West Germany (1-1, 0-2) 1-3

SEMI-FINALS

Czechoslovakia 3 Holland 1*
(Zagreb)
West Germany 4 Yugoslavia 2*
(Belgrade)

THIRD PLACE MATCH

Holland 3 Yugoslavia 2* *(Zagreb)*

FINAL

Czechoslovakia 2 West Germany 2
[aet: Czechoslovakia won 5-3 on penalties]
(Belgrade, 20.6.76, 45,000)

Czechoslovakia: Viktor, Dobias, (F. Vesely), Pivarnik, Ondrus, Capkovic, Gogh, Moder, Panenka, Svehlik (Jurkemik), Masny, Nehoda

West Germany: Maier, Vogts, Beckenbauer, Schwarzenbeck, Dietz, Bonhof, Wimmer (Flohe), D. Muller, Beer (Bongartz), Hoeness, Holzenbein

Scorers: Svehlik, Dobias; Muller, Holzenbein

*after extra time

Nehoda clears from Malcolm Macdonald in Bratislava. The 2-1 defeat dashed England's high hopes of making the finals—where Czechoslovakia upset the odds, the Dutch and the Germans to win the title.

1978–80

If there was a day on which the destiny of the 1980 European Championship was decided, that date might well have been Sunday 23 March. The events that took place were nothing to do with the championships, but with a massive bribery scandal in domestic Italian football.

Among those implicated was Italy's golden boy, Paolo Rossi of Perugia and Lanerossi Vicenza, then still the most expensive player in the world. Though the scandal had been bubbling for two months, the shock waves were tremendous. The Italian FA had to formally announce the next day that the League season would continue, but, suddenly, Italy were anything but favourites.

As hosts, Italy had not needed to qualify for the finals and their recent performances had left something to be desired—a poor 1-0 win against Uruguay and a 2-2 draw at home to Poland being the worst—and the side was also jeered off the pitch in Udine after an uninspired 2-0 win against Switzerland. At home, though, they were bound to be difficult to beat and England's hopes therefore looked much brighter after the scandal had thrown into confusion the likely composition of Enzo Bearzot's team, and robbed him of Rossi, banned for three years by the FIGC on May 18, a few weeks before the finals.

Belgium were surprise qualifiers who went all the way

England, under Ron Greenwood, had steadily improved and impressed until, after their 2-0 win in Barcelona late in March, they suddenly became favourites to at least reach the final and even, according to several European commentators, to win the trophy. Such a prediction would have smacked of fantasy only but two years before, for this was the first time since 1968 that England had managed to qualify for the finals of a major international tournament.

Greenwood had lost only three games since taking over—2-1 in West Germany, 4-3 in Vienna and a shock 4-1 defeat in Wrexham—and had gone through his qualifying group undefeated. England had won seven group games, drawn only one, and produced two extremely impressive displays away from home in beating Bulgaria 3-0 and Northern Ireland 5-1.

Added to a magnificent win in Spain (to be opponents in Italy), England's chances did indeed seem rosy until, on 3 May, tragedy struck when Trevor Francis tore an Achilles tendon at the end of a Nottingham Forest game against Crystal Palace. He had finally emerged as a truly fine player on the international stage, scoring in all those games against Bulgaria, Northern Ireland and Spain.

Belgium make it—after drawing their first four games

England and Italy's group opponents appeared to have considerably less strength before the series began. Ladislao Kubala had been Spain's manager for 10 years at that stage, and was not a little conscious of the pressure on Spain for 1982, when she would be host to the first 24-team World Cup finals.

After their poor displays in Argentina, it was essential that a new team be built in time. The friendly against England came as a great shock to the Spanish. 'If you think this lot will be going to Italy you must need your head examined,' Kubala was supposed to have replied to a question asking how his side would fare in the European Championship after losing so badly to England in March.

Spain had really been very lucky to qualify for Italy and had lost a remarkable four home games in a year to Yugoslavia, England, Denmark and East Germany. The only bright spot was a 1-0 defeat of Holland on a poor pitch with failing floodlights at Vigo.

Belgium were perhaps the most surprising qualifiers, overcoming Austria and Scotland (both 1978 World Cup finalists) and Portugal. It was a tight group — and yet one in which Belgium did not win a game until their fifth match. Their qualifying performances really came against Scotland, whom they beat 2-0 at home and then 3-1 at Hampden.

François van der Elst scored twice in the away match and he and Wilfred van Moer, recalled to marshal them at the age of 35, emerged as the key players. Van der Elst's signing for Cosmos in April brought the usual howls of protest from Belgian fans and, although he was to be allowed to play in Italy, it was generally reckoned that the move must damage the side's morale. In a rather unsubtle piece of gamesmanship, manager Guy Thys began the finals by declaring that his side had no chance at all.

England's bleakest moment: Marco Tardelli wheels away after scoring Italy's goal in the grim group 2 game at Turin.

Showing so many poor games live on television proved a major mistake

Scotland's displays were anything but convincing; though her last, a 4-1 win over Portugal, might have produced a little hope for the future and gave them a bigger goal tally than any side in the group. Their inability to obtain a single win against Austria or Belgium did place question marks against Jock Stein's intentions to assemble a really good side.

The other home countries had a specially poor time. Wales were never in with a chance against West Germany (losing 2-0 in Wrexham and 5-1 away) and also lost in Turkey. Manager Mike Smith resigned to join Hull City soon afterwards, and Wales' brief spell of potential glory in international football had seemingly gone after that tragic penalty against Scotland in the World Cup at Liverpool. The two Irelands were drawn in England's group and they were never really in the running.

They did play each other twice, however, which was something of a political breakthrough, but only one goal was scored in the two games—by Gerry Armstrong for Northern Ireland in Belfast. Danny Blanchflower, Northern Ireland's manager, resigned after this game.

The experienced Czechs: everybody's favourite 'outsiders'

The other group in the championship finals was undoubtedly the stronger. Czechoslovakia, the holders, had a relatively easy time in overcoming France, Sweden and Luxembourg and lost only once—2-1 in Paris. Six players remained from the 1976 side—Ondrus, Gogh, Panenka (who scored the cheeky, chipped penalty that won the championship), Jurkemik, Masny and Nehoda, who missed the French game and was equally missed by his colleagues.

The team, managed by Josef Venglos, who remained a dedicated believer in team spirit over and above individual brilliance, was still heavily reliant on the Dukla Prague squad, and had also lost in Russia and Hungary during 1979. Czechoslovakia were by no means a favourite, but would equally not be underestimated by their opponents. As such, they were probably everyone's 'outsider' for the championship.

Their opponents in the 1976 final, West Germany, were to meet them again in the first match and were clear favourites to reach the final. Undoubtedly the strongest club nation in Europe—with all four of the UEFA Cup semi-finalists in 1980 plus SV Hamburg in the European Cup final—the international side had been carefully rebuilt from its old Bayern Munic core by new manager Jupp Derwall. Indeed, as Derwall approached Italy, he had still to be beaten during his 15-match spell as manager. Any side that could break this run was likely to win the whole competition—even with the Germans lacking key scorer Klaus Fischer and midfield general Rainer Bonhof, both injured.

Another of Czechoslovakia's conquests of 1976, Holland, were also back in their group. At the end of a remarkable decade the Dutch had still to win a major trophy—a remarkable fact in itself. They were perhaps losing their keenness to finally lay this bogey. Jan Zwartkruis, relegated to number two under Ernst Happel in Argentina, was now completely in charge and was certain to rely on most of the players who had gone as close as an Argentinian post in Buenos Aires.

Their crucial game was in November 1979 in Leipzig. East Germany had gone 2-0 up and appeared to be on their way to Italy. Then Konrad Weise of Germany and Tscheu La Ling were sent off for fighting and, seconds before the interval, Ipswich's Frans Thijssen got one goal back. After half-time substitute striker Kees Kist, European Golden Boot winner in 1979, equalized and René van der Kerkhof scored a third to give Holland the game and a place in the finals.

The Greeks sprang a surprise to knock out Russia

It was a recovery not unlike that they had produced in Argentina to go past Italy and West Germany to the final, and any side which could perform in such a way could never be discounted.

For the rank outsiders, Greece, it was little more than an opportunity just to enjoy an international stage. The 1979-80 season was the first in which the Greek First Division was fully professional, and their progress past Russia and Hungary was quite remarkable. Greece lost their first game 3-0 in Finland, their next 2-0 in Russia, but did take home wins against all the three sides in the group. This should not, in normal circumstances, have been anything like enough, but the Finns beat Hungary and drew twice with the USSR, the latter still not recovered from their Dynamo Kiev experiment of the mid-1970s.

The finals in Italy

After a massive build up of World Cup proportions, the finals themselves were a gross disappointment, pervaded by uninspired play, weak finishing, harsh tackling, poor refereeing, miserably low crowds and gamesmanship both on and off the field. Moments to treasure were indeed rare, and no great name or emerging star could break through the web of teamwork.

In Turin the English supporters begin their decline

The tone was set by the very first game, the Group 1 encounter between Czechoslovakia and West Germany at Rome on Wednesday 11 June, watched by a disgracefully small crowd of 15,000. This late afternoon match, a repeat of the 1976 final, was dominated by caution as both sides sought to avoid mistakes in a system where defeat in the first game virtually ensured absence from the final. It was left to Karl-Heinz Rummenigge, leading scorer in the 1979-80 Bundesliga with 26 goals for Bayern Munich, to break the deadlock with a brave header after skilful creative work by Hansi Müller.

Hamburg's Horst Hrubesch (9) lands after heading Rummenigge's 88th-minute corner past Pfaff and the Belgian defence to settle the 1980 final in Rome.

That evening the unfamiliar Greeks and a strangely out of touch Dutch side met in the other Group 1 match at Naples, and Greece were unlucky not to earn a point. Kees Kist's penalty after 65 minutes (a confused decision not untypical of the refereeing throughout the finals) scrambled Holland to safety.

The next day Group 2 kicked off in Turin with Belgium against England. The Belgian offside trap frustrated England all but once, when in the 25th minute Ray Wilkins chested down a poor headed clearance and picked his way through an advancing defence before lobbing the ball coolly over Pfaff.

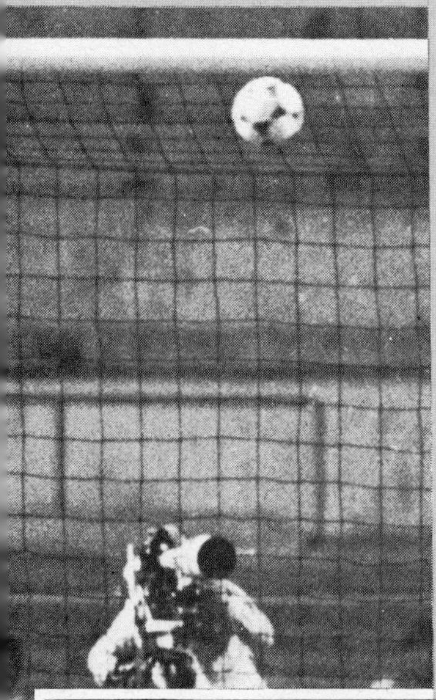

Belgium hit back only four minutes later when Ceulemans shot crisply past Clemence out of a ruck of players.

It was a goal that triggered a riot among a small section of English supporters. The Turin police were soon in there blasting teargas around and the match had to be stopped for five minutes just before half-time because chaos reigned at one end of the ground and several players—notably Clemence—had difficulty with their vision.

The whole incident not only ruined the match, of which the second half was curiously anticlimactic; it also set the image of the English supporter abroad back a decade and gave the Italian press powerful ammunition in the preamble to the game with England three days later on the same ground.

The papers on that Friday morning certainly needed another story, since Italy's debut in the championship, against

Yet again the Germans came good in the last minutes

Spain at Milan a few hours after the Belgium-England game, was hardly noteworthy. The result was 0-0, but the Spaniards surprised everyone with their fast aggressive play and the hosts were fortunate to hang on to rescue a point.

So the first round of games finished with four goals from as many games. The next activity, on the Saturday, proved a little more positive. The Germans moved up several gears at Naples and ripped Holland apart in the first competitive match between the countries since the World Cup final of 1974, with Klaus Allofs scoring three times to give his side a commanding lead by the 67th minute.

A Johnny Rep penalty looked mere compensation with a quarter of an hour to go, until Willy van der Kerkhof produced a fine shot against a casual defence in the 86th minute to make it 3-2

EUROPEAN CHAMPIONSHIP 1978-80

GROUP 1

Denmark 3 Eire 3
Eire 0 Northern Ireland 0
Denmark 3 England 4
Denmark 2 Bulgaria 2
Eire 1 England 1
Northern Ireland 2 Denmark 1
Bulgaria 0 Northern Ireland 2
England 4 Northern Ireland 0
Eire 2 Denmark 0
Northern Ireland 2 Bulgaria 0
Bulgaria 1 Eire 0
Denmark 4 Northern Ireland 0
Bulgaria 0 England 3
England 1 Denmark 0
Eire 3 Bulgaria 0
Northern Ireland 1 England 5
Bulgaria 3 Denmark 0
Northern Ireland 1 Eire 0
England 2 Bulgaria 0
England 2 Eire 0

	P	W	D	L	F	A	P
England	8	7	1	0	22	5	15
N. Ireland	8	4	1	3	8	14	9
Eire	8	2	3	3	9	8	7
Bulgaria	8	2	1	5	6	14	5
Denmark	8	1	2	5	13	17	4

GROUP 2

Norway 0 Austria 2
Belgium 1 Norway 1
Austria 3 Scotland 2
Portugal 1 Belgium 1
Scotland 3 Norway 2
Austria 1 Portugal 2
Portugal 1 Scotland 0
Belgium 1 Austria 1
Austria 0 Belgium 0
Norway 0 Portugal 1
Norway 0 Scotland 4
Austria 4 Norway 0
Norway 1 Belgium 2
Belgium 2 Portugal 0
Scotland 1 Austria 1
Portugal 3 Norway 1
Belgium 2 Scotland 0
Portugal 1 Austria 2
Scotland 1 Belgium 3
Scotland 4 Portugal 1

	P	W	D	L	F	A	P
Belgium	8	4	4	0	12	5	12
Austria	8	4	3	1	14	7	11
Portugal	8	4	1	3	10	11	9
Scotland	8	3	1	4	15	13	7
Norway	8	0	1	7	5	20	1

GROUP 3

Yugoslavia 1 Spain 2
Rumania 3 Yugoslavia 2
Spain 1 Rumania 0
Spain 5 Cyprus 0
Cyprus 0 Yugoslavia 3
Rumania 2 Spain 2
Cyprus 1 Rumania 1
Spain 0 Yugoslavia 1
Yugoslavia 2 Rumania 1
Yugoslavia 5 Cyprus 0
Rumania 2 Cyprus 0
Cyprus 1 Spain 3

	P	W	D	L	F	A	P
Spain	6	4	1	1	13	5	9
Yugoslavia	6	4	0	2	14	6	8
Rumania	6	2	2	2	9	8	6
Cyprus	6	0	1	5	2	19	1

GROUP 4

Iceland 0 Poland 2
Holland 3 Iceland 0
East Germany 3 Iceland 1
Switzerland 1 Holland 3
Holland 3 East Germany 0
Poland 2 Switzerland 0
Holland 3 Switzerland 0
East Germany 2 Poland 1
Poland 2 Holland 0
Switzerland 0 East Germany 2
Switzerland 2 Iceland 0
Iceland 1 Switzerland 2
Iceland 0 Holland 4
Switzerland 0 Poland 2
Iceland 0 East Germany 3
Poland 1 East Germany 1
Poland 2 Iceland 0
East Germany 5 Switzerland 2
Holland 1 Poland 1
East Germany 2 Holland 3

	P	W	D	L	F	A	P
Holland	8	6	1	1	20	6	13
Poland	8	5	2	1	13	4	12
East Germany	8	5	1	2	17	10	11
Switzerland	8	2	0	6	7	18	4
Iceland	8	0	0	8	2	21	0

GROUP 5

France 2 Sweden 2
Sweden 1 Czechoslovakia 3
Luxembourg 1 France 3
France 3 Luxembourg 0
Czechoslovakia 2 France 0
Luxembourg 0 Czechoslovakia 3
Sweden 3 Luxembourg 0
Sweden 1 France 3
Czechoslovakia 4 Sweden 1
Luxembourg 1 Sweden 1
France 2 Czechoslovakia 1
Czechoslovakia 4 Luxembourg 0

	P	W	D	L	F	A	P
Czechoslovakia	6	5	0	1	17	4	10
France	6	4	1	1	13	7	9
Sweden	6	1	2	3	9	13	4
Luxembourg	6	0	1	5	2	17	1

GROUP 6

Finland 3 Greece 0
Finland 2 Hungary 1
USSR 2 Greece 0
Hungary 2 USSR 0
Greece 8 Finland 1
Greece 4 Hungary 1
Hungary 0 Greece 0
USSR 2 Hungary 2
Finland 1 USSR 1
Greece 1 USSR 0
Hungary 3 Finland 1
USSR 2 Finland 2

	P	W	D	L	F	A	P
Greece	6	3	1	2	13	7	7
Hungary	6	2	2	2	9	9	6
Finland	6	2	2	2	10	15	6
USSR	6	1	3	2	7	8	5

GROUP 7

Wales 7 Malta 0
Wales 1 Turkey 0
Malta 0 West Germany 0
Turkey 2 Malta 1
Turkey 0 West Germany 0
Wales 0 West Germany 2
Malta 0 Wales 2
West Germany 5 Wales 1
Malta 1 Turkey 2
Turkey 1 Wales 0
West Germany 2 Turkey 0
West Germany 8 Malta 0

	P	W	D	L	F	A	P
West Germany	6	4	2	0	17	1	10
Turkey	6	3	1	2	5	5	7
Wales	6	3	0	3	11	8	6
Malta	6	0	1	5	2	21	1

FINAL GROUP 1

West Germany 1 Czechoslovakia 0
Holland 1 Greece 0
West Germany 3 Holland 2
Czechoslovakia 3 Greece 1
Czechoslovakia 1 Holland 1
Greece 0 West Germany 0

	P	W	D	L	F	A	P
West Germany	3	2	1	0	4	2	5
Czechoslovakia†	3	1	1	1	4	3	3
Holland	3	1	1	1	4	4	3
Greece	3	0	1	2	1	4	1

FINAL GROUP 2

Belgium 1 England 1
Italy 0 Spain 0
Belgium 2 Spain 1
Italy 1 England 0
England 2 Spain 1
Belgium 0 Italy 0

	P	W	D	L	F	A	P
Belgium*	3	1	2	0	3	2	4
Italy	3	1	2	0	1	0	4
England	3	1	1	1	3	3	3
Spain	3	0	1	2	2	4	1

THIRD PLACE MATCH

Czechoslovakia‡ 1 Italy 1 *(Naples)*

FINAL

West Germany 2 Belgium 1
(Rome, 22.6.80, 47,864)

West Germany: Schumacher, Kalz, K-H. Förster, Stielike, Dietz, Schuster, Briegel (Cullmann 55), H. Muller, Rummenigge, Hrubesch, Allofs

Belgium: Pfaff, Gerets, Millecamps, Meeuws, Renquin, Van Moer, Cools, Vandereycken, Van der Elst, Mommens, Ceulemans

Scorers: Hrubesch (10, 88); Vandereycken (pen-72)

Leading scorers: 7—Keegan *(England)*; 6—Fischer *(West Germany)*; 5—Allofs *(West Germany)*; Mavros *(Greece)*, Masny, Nehoda *(Czechoslovakia)*; 4—Latchford *(England)*, Kist *(Holland)*, Santillana *(Spain)*, Van der Elst *(Belgium)*, Vizek *(Czechoslovakia)*

*qualified for final on better goal record
†qualified for third place match on goal difference
‡Czechoslovakia won 9-8 on penalties

and put real pressure on. But the Germans held on fairly comfortably, and barring a colossal upset by Greece they were in the final for the third successive time.

That evening Czechoslovakia also improved, beating Greece at Rome with goals from Vizek and Nehoda after Anastopoulos had equalized Panenka's 6th-minute lead.

England 'fans'—part of a paltry crowd of 7,000—warm up before their side's first game, against Belgium in Turin. Trouble flared when the Belgians equalized and the England followers reacted to the taunts of Italian spectators. The local police, perhaps unnecessarily, went in with tear-gas blasting—a decision which quelled the riot but left many players (notably Ray Clemence, right, *being aided by physio Fred Street) with eyes streaming. Normal service was resumed after five minutes, but the match, like England's already ailing reputation, was virtually beyond repair.*

Italy win the battle of Turin with England—but lose the war

Three days later the West Germans, already requiring only a draw against Greece, had that pressure lifted as Czechoslovakia and Holland erased each other's hopes with a 1-1 draw in the afternoon game at Milan, Nehoda and Kist getting the goals.

Thus West Germany, sitting on four points, could afford to lose by any score to Greece and still play in the final. Jupp Derwall had already decided to rest three players who had received yellow cards, and his team went through the motions to register a goalless draw against a Greek side showing a curious lack of urgency.

While Group 1 produced a clear winner, Group 2 became bedevilled with statistical possibilities that baffled the average fan. In the second round of matches Belgium kept up their improvement with a 2-1 win over Spain at Milan, and in the evening a crowd of over 59,000 (almost four times that for the Belgium-England match on the same ground) turned up at the Stadio Communale in Turin to see Italy take on England.

It was not a pleasant game, with Garry Birtles (kicking off for the first time in a full international) and his former Forest colleague Tony Woodcock taking some fierce treatment from their Italian markers. Tardelli subdued Keegan too, but still found time to get in on the end of a cross from Graziani (Rossi's experienced replacement) to beat Shilton for the only time after 79 minutes.

England, for many the favourites at the start, were out of the final, but their hopes of salvaging something were boosted three days later in the final round of group games with a 2-1 win over Spain at Naples, where Clemence saved a second and twice-taken penalty from Dani, and where his opposite number Luis Arconada showed on a dozen occasions why he is rated by many as the best keeper in Europe.

For England to reach the third place game Belgium would have to win by 1-0 or more, or Italy by 2-0 or more, in the last group game that evening in Rome. As it turned out the now-confident Belgians played the Italians at their own containing game, knowing a draw would suffice because they had scored more goals than Italy, though the difference was the same.

While Italy's defence played well—they didn't concede a goal in three matches—their attack blew several good chances as Belgium squeezed into their first major final in 60 years. Their only other appearance of note had been in the Olympic final of 1920 at Antwerp.

The Italians were left with the scant compensation of the third place match against Czechoslovakia in Naples. There they managed to score their second goal of the tournament, through Graziani, after Jurkemik had become the first player to puncture their defensive record. A game usually devoid of tension acquired a little when it was still 1-1 after extra time, and penalties were required. As in Belgrade four years before the Czechs proved the masters, though on this occasion a second bout was needed when the scores were level after each side had taken five. Fulvio Collovati was the culprit, his kick being controversially saved by Netolicka at 8-8 before Barmos sealed it for Czechoslovakia.

Hamburg's Hrubesch delivers the vital goods for Germany

The West Germans, no doubt with the tragedy of 1976 still fresh in their minds, had refused the option of penalties should the final itself be level after extra time. In the event the matter didn't arise—but it was close.

When Vandereycken scored from the spot in the 72nd minute—following a Stielike trip on Van der Elst well outside the area—and continued with their fine second-half display, extra time loomed large. Then in the 88th minute Horst Hrubesch, the tall, ungainly Hamburg striker who had given the Germans the lead with a 20-yard shot in the 10th minute, rose above a packed defence to head home a Rummenigge corner and give his side a victory they just merited on points.

So Bernd Dietz, the only survivor from the side who had lost the 1976 final, led his side up the steps of the Olympic Stadium in Rome to collect the Henri Delaunay Cup. West Germany had become the first side to win the trophy for the second time, and they had done so in a final which, unlike the majority of the games in Italy, contained much to admire from both sides.

EUROPEAN CUP

In only a few years the European Champion Clubs' Cup established itself as the primary club competition in the world. For most players only a World Cup success could outstrip the thrill of a European Cup winner's medal. . .

Despite the success of the Latin Cup after 1950 and the revival of the Mitropa Cup, it took a friendly between Football League champions Wolves and Hungary's star-packed army side Honved in December 1954 to provide the real push for a European Cup: Wolves' 3-2 win over Puskas' men set the whole continent wondering just which was the best club side in Europe.

It was then that Gabriel Hanot, the much-respected journalist on *L'Equipe* and champion of such a competition for many years, set out detailed proposals for a European Cup.

There was, however, a constitutional problem to overcome before it could have official approval. FIFA, the world governing body, was concerned with national associations, as was the European body UEFA; FIFA agreed to authorize the cup on the condition that the participating clubs received approval from their own associations, and UEFA assumed the responsibility for its organization.

Ten years on for United: three survivors of the Munich crash—Bill Foulkes, Matt Busby and Bobby Charlton—after the 1968 final.

EUROPEAN CUP 1955-56

FIRST ROUND

Servette v Real Madrid (0-2, 0-5)	0-7
Sporting Lisbon v Partizan Belgrade (3-3, 2-5)	5-8
AC Milan v 1FC Saarbrucken (3-4, 4-1)	7-5
Rapid Vienna v PSV Eindhoven (6-1, 0-1)	6-2
Rot-Weiss v Hibernian (0-4, 1-1)	1-5
Djurgaarden v Gwardia Warsaw (0-0, 4-1)	4-1
Voros Lobogo v Anderlecht (6-3, 4-1)	10-4
Aarhus GF v Stade de Reims (0-2, 2-2)	2-4

QUARTER-FINALS

Real Madrid v Partizan Belgrade (4-0, 0-3)	4-3
Rapid Vienna v AC Milan (1-1, 2-7)	3-8
Hibernian v Djurgaarden (3-1, 1-0)	4-1
Stade de Reims v Voros Lobogo (4-2, 4-4)	8-6

SEMI-FINALS

Real Madrid v AC Milan (4-2, 1-2)	4-3
Stade de Reims v Hibernian (2-0, 1-0)	3-0

FINAL

Real Madrid 4 Stade de Reims 3
(Paris, 13.6.56, 38,239)

Real: Alonso, Atienza, Lesmes, Munoz, Marquitos, Zarraga, Joseito, Marsal, Di Stefano, Rial, Gento

Reims: Jacquet, Zimny, Giraudo, Leblond, Jonquet, Siatka, Hidalgo, Glovacki, Kopa, Bliard, Templin

Scorers: Di Stefano (14), Rial (30,79), Marquitos (67); Leblond (6), Templin (10), Hidalgo (62)

1955-56

The initial entry was not confined entirely to champion sides, and some invitations were extended to leading teams. The Football League, however, advised the English champions Chelsea against jeopardizing their domestic arrangements by overcrowding their fixture list, and they withdrew. Their place was taken by Gwardia Warsaw of Poland.

Eventually 16 teams assembled for the 1955-56 competition. The initial series was an instant success and could have been summed up in two words—Real Madrid. The Spanish club went on to win the first five competitions and matured into a peak of individual and collective ability rarely touched before or since.

The first European Cup tie was played on 4 September 1955, in Lisbon, between Sporting Club (Portugal) and Partizan Belgrade of Yugoslavia. The result was a 3-3 draw. Real Madrid, kicking off four days later, had a 7-0 aggregate win over Servette (Switzerland), and then built up a 4-0 lead over Partizan Belgrade in the home leg in the second round. It proved just enough—in Belgrade, Partizan scored three times without reply. Such were the fluctuating fortunes that the competition was to exhibit.

In the semi-final Real's 4-2 home win over AC Milan was sufficient to withstand a 2-1 defeat in Italy and to carry them into a final against Reims of France. Reims had accounted for Aarhus (Denmark), Voros Lobogo, or Red Banner (Hungary), and Hibernian without losing a match, and were confident that on French soil in Paris they could win the first European Cup final.

This confidence seemed amply justified when Leblond and Templin put Reims two up in 10 minutes, but goals from Di Stefano and Rial levelled the scores before half-time. Hidalgo gave Reims back their lead after the interval but within five minutes Marquitos had equalized and in the 79th minute Rial scored his second to give the Spaniards victory. Despite being behind for most of the match, Real had looked the more assured side, with Alfredo di Stefano outshining the Reims star Raymond Kopa. A year later Kopa was playing for Real in the second final, and in 1959 he would gain his third winner's medal—against Reims.

1956-57

Financially the first series had been a huge success, with big crowds at most of the matches and an aggregate attendance of 912,000—an average of 31,450. The goal tally of 127 from the 29 matches produced an astonishing average of 4.38 per game, a figure that has not been rivalled since.

It all served to confirm the interest and entertainment offered by the European Cup, and produced a clamour for entry into the 1956-57 competition, despite previous agreement that it should be open only to league champions. Clubs from England, Luxembourg, Czechoslovakia, Rumania, Bulgaria and Turkey boosted the entry to 22, a total that included Spanish champions Atlético Bilbao in addition to the holders Real Madrid.

From England came Manchester United, who declined to accept the unfortunate advice meted out to Chelsea a year earlier by the Football League. They had a fine start, winning 2-0 against Anderlecht in Brussels and scoring 10 goals without reply in the second leg at Maine Road—a European Cup record margin that was to stand for 12 years. Denis Viollet (4), Tommy Taylor (3), Billy Whelan (2) and John Berry got the goals. Viollet went on to score nine that season to head the list in Europe.

The next round provided more difficult opposition in Borussia Dortmund, and United won 3-2 at home and held the West German champions to a goalless draw away. This took them to the quarter-finals and a tie against Atlético Bilbao, who had knocked out Honved on a 6-5 aggregate and were fortunate enough to have met the Hungarians on neutral soil for the second leg because of the Hungarian uprising. Bilbao, three up at the interval against United, won 5-3 at home, but the Mancunians staged a dramatic recovery in the return to win 3-0 with goals from Viollet, Taylor and Berry.

Fellow Spaniards Real Madrid had been fortunate against Rapid Vienna in the previous round. Their Austrian opponents' liking for financial rewards led them to waive the right for a neutral play-off venue. They paid the penalty by losing 2-0 in Madrid and 7-5 on aggregate. Real then accounted for OGC Nice (France) and thus met Manchester United in the semi-final.

United were again two goals down in the away leg (Bobby Charlton's first European tie) but this time there was no recovery at Old Trafford. The 3-1 deficit increased to 5-1 by half-time and goals from Tommy Taylor and Charlton were not enough to save the English champions. With Rangers beaten by Nice in the first round, it began to dawn on British fans that winning the European Cup was going to be tough.

Opposing Real in the final were Fiorentina (Italy) who had beaten IFK Norrköping (Sweden), Grasshoppers Zurich (Switzerland), and Red Star Belgrade (Yugoslavia) without losing a match.

The Spaniards were favourites in front of 124,000 on their own Chamartin ground, but kept their fans waiting until well into the second half before Di Stefano put them ahead from the penalty spot in the 70th minute, a decision disputed by the Italians. Six minutes later Francisco Gento made sure of victory—deservedly so against a less adventurous Italian side who displayed signs of the defensive tactics that were to stunt the game in the next decade.

The overall attendance figures for 1956-57 nearly doubled to 1,786,000, and the average rose to more than 40,000 a game. The European Cup was here to stay.

EUROPEAN CUP 1956-57

PRELIMINARY ROUND

Aarhus GF v OGC Nice (1-1, 1-5)	2-6
Porto v Atletico Bilbao (1-2, 2-3)	3-5
Anderlecht v Manchester United (0-2, 0-10)	0-12
B. Dortmund v S. Luxembourg (4-3, 1-2, 7-0)	12-5
Dynamo Bucharest v Galatasaray (3-1, 1-2)	4-3
Slovan Bratislava v CWKS Warsaw (4-0, 0-2)	4-2

[Real Madrid (holders), Rapid Vienna, Rangers, Honved, Rapid JC Haarlem, Red Star Belgrade, CDNA Sofia, Grasshoppers Zurich, IFK Norrkoping and Fiorentina received byes]

FIRST-ROUND

Real Madrid v Rapid Vienna (4-2, 1-3, 2-0)	7-5
Rangers v OGC Nice (2-1, 1-2, 1-3)	4-6
Atletico Bilbao v Honved (3-2, 3-3)	6-5
Manchester U. v Bor. Dortmund (3-2, 0-0)	3-2
Rapid Haarlem v Red Star Belgrade (3-4, 0-2)	3-6
CDNA Sofia v Dynamo Bucharest (8-1, 2-3)	10-4
Slovan Bratislava v Grasshoppers (1-0, 0-2)	1-2
Fiorentina v IFK Norrkoping (1-1, 1-0)	2-1

QUARTER-FINALS

Real Madrid v Nice (3-0, 3-2)	6-2
Atletico Bilbao v Manchester United (5-3, 0-3)	5-6
Red Star Belgrade v CDNA Sofia (3-1, 1-2)	4-3
Fiorentina v Grasshoppers (3-1, 2-2)	5-3

SEMI-FINALS

Real Madrid v Manchester United (3-1, 2-2)	5-3
Red Star Belgrade v Fiorentina (0-1, 0-0)	0-1

FINAL

Real Madrid 2 Fiorentina 0
(Madrid, 30.5.57, 124,000)

Real: Alonso, Torres, Lesmes, Munoz, Marquitos, Zarraga, Kopa, Mateos, Di Stefano, Rial, Gento

Fiorentina: Sarti, Magnini, Cervato, Scaramucci, Orzan, Segato, Julinho, Gratton, Virgili, Montuori, Bizzarri

Scorers: Di Stefano (pen-70), Gento (76)

1957-58

For the 1957-58 competition Northern Ireland, Eire and East Germany entered clubs. Once again there were two from Spain, but Real Madrid accounted for their fellows from Seville in the quarter-final, after the latter had knocked out Benfica (Portugal) and Aarhus of Denmark. Real had already disposed of Royal Antwerp (Belgium) 8-1 on aggregate, and against Seville they had an 8-0 win in the first leg, Di Stefano scoring four, and eased to a 2-2 draw away.

The real drama of the round, and the biggest tragedy in the short history of the European Cup, came after the second leg of the tie between Manchester United and Red Star Belgrade. The young United side had already gained valuable experience and were being seriously considered as challengers for Real's title. They played confidently in disposing of Eire's Shamrock Rovers and Dukla Prague, the Czechoslovakian army side, and though not at their best in beating Red Star 2-1 at home, they came safely through the return game, and the quarter-final, with a fine 3-3 draw in Belgrade.

On 6 February 1958, the plane taking the United players back from Yugoslavia crashed on take-off at Munich airport. Among the fatal casualties were eight players, including England regulars Roger Byrne, Duncan Edwards and Tommy Taylor. Manager Matt Busby came close to death. Amazingly, United's strange mixture of survivors, reserves and hasty buys fought through three rounds of the FA Cup to reach Wembley.

Five days after a disappointing defeat by Bolton they faced Italian champions AC Milan, who had scored 21 goals in disposing of Rapid Vienna, Rangers and Borussia Dortmund, at Old Trafford. United held on 2-1, but in the return six days later they crashed 4-0 at San Siro. Charlton missed both games because England required his services; United needed him more. For the record, he scored both goals in a 2-1 win over Portugal at Wembley the day before the Old Trafford semi-final.

Real Madrid had come through on a 4-2 aggregate over Vasas Budapest, and met the Italians in the final at the Heysel Stadium, Brussels. Milan opened the score after an hour through their Uruguayan star Juan Schiaffino, and Di Stefano equalized after 74 minutes. Grillo re-established Milan's lead four minutes later only for Rial to level the scores again within 60 seconds. Gento scored Real's winner in extra time.

EUROPEAN CUP 1957-58

PRELIMINARY ROUND

Seville v Benfica (3-1, 0-0)	3-1
Aarhus GF v Glenavon (0-0, 3-0)	3-0
CDNA Sofia v Vasas Budapest (2-1, 1-6)	3-7
G. Warsaw v Karl-Marx-Stadt* (3-1, 1-3, 1-1)	*5-5
Shamrock Rovers v Manchester U. (0-6, 2-3)	2-9
Dudelange v Red Star Belgrade (0-5, 1-9)	1-14
Rangers v St Etienne (3-1, 1-2)	4-3
AC Milan v Rapid Vienna (4-1, 2-5, 4-2)	10-8

[Real Madrid (holders), Antwerp, Ajax, Young Boys Berne, Dukla Prague, IFK Norrkoping, Borussia Dortmund and CCA Bucharest received byes]

FIRST-ROUND

Antwerp v Real Madrid (1-2, 0-6)	1-8
Seville v Aarhus GF (4-0, 0-2)	4-2
Karl-Marx-Stadt v Ajax (1-3, 0-1)	1-4
Young Boys Berne v V. Budapest (1-1, 1-2)	2-3
Manchester United v Dukla Prague (3-0, 0-1)	3-1
IFK Norrkoping v Red Star Belgrade (2-2, 1-2)	3-4
B. Dortmund v CCA Bucharest (4-2, 1-3, 3-1)	8-6
Rangers v Milan (1-4, 0-2)	1-6

QUARTER-FINALS

Real Madrid v Seville (8-0, 2-2)	10-2
Ajax v Vasas Budapest (2-2, 0-4)	2-6
Manchester U. v Red Star Belgrade (2-1, 3-3)	5-4
Borussia Dortmund v AC Milan (1-1, 1-4)	2-5

SEMI-FINALS

Real Madrid v Vasas Budapest (4-0, 0-2)	4-2
Manchester United v AC Milan (2-1,0-4)	2-5

FINAL

Real Madrid 3 AC Milan 2 [aet]
(Brussels, 28.5.58, 67,000)

Real: Alonso, Atienza, Lesmes, Santisteban, Santamaria, Zarraga, Kopa, Joseito, Di Stefano, Rial, Gento

Milan: Soldan, Fontana, Beraldo, Bergamaschi, Maldini, Radice, Danova, Liedholm, Schiaffino, Grillo, Cucchaironi

Scorers: Di Stefano (74), Rial (79), Gento (107); Schiaffino (60), Grillo (78)

*won on toss of coin

LEFT: Duncan Edwards and Roger Byrne flank the Manchester United line-up before the 3-3 quarter-final draw with Red Star in Belgrade in February 1958. A few hours later eight players were dead at Munich.
BELOW: Alonso saves in the 1958 final—the toughest Real played in their run of five consecutive European Cup successes.

1958-59

Manchester United's heroism was recognized the following season when UEFA bent the rules to invite them to enter even though they had finished ninth in the Football League table. But pressure at home from the Football League and Football Association forced United to withdraw.

The 26 acceptors for the 1958-59 series were divided into three groups, but there was a mild surprise when the fancied Italians Juventus crashed to Wiener Sportklub 7-0 in Austria after winning 3-1 in Turin. Spain had both Madrid clubs, Real and Atlético, representing them. The former were strengthened by the inclusion of the self-exiled Honved and Hungarian star Ferenc Puskas. Though neither he nor Di Stefano were noted as physical players both were sent off in European ties that season: Di Stefano at Chamartin against Besiktas (Turkey), Puskas in Vienna against Wiener Sportklub.

Already the European stars were being more closely marked, and defensive inroads were being made into the free-scoring abandon that had characterized the earlier ties. The joy of its youthful beginnings was fading into the reality of adult life.

The semi-final draw pitched the Spanish clubs together, with Atlético led by Brazil's Vavà. Real won at home 2-1, lost away to a Collar goal and went to Zaragoza for the play-off. A capacity crowd, taking the total attendance for the tie to a quarter of a million, saw Real win 2-1.

With Reims defeating Young Boys Berne (Switzerland) in the other semi-final, the Stuttgart game was a repeat of the 1956 final, with 10 players surviving from that match, including the transferred Kopa. It took only two minutes for Real to break through, and Mateos scored. Di Stefano, later voted European Footballer of the Year for the second time in three years, clinched the tie with a goal after the interval.

EUROPEAN CUP 1958-59

PRELIMINARY ROUND

Besiktas w.o. Olympiakos Piraeus (withdrew)	
Juventus v Wiener SK (3-1, 0-7)	3-8
Dynamo Zagreb v Dukla Prague (2-2, 1-2)	3-4
KB Copenhagen v Schalke 04 (3-0, 2-5, 1-3)	6-8
Atletico Madrid v Drumcondra (8-0, 5-1)	13-1
Karl-Marx-Stadt v Petro Ploesti (4-2, 0-2, 5-0)	9-4
IFK Gothenburg v Jeun. Esch (2-1, 0-1, 5-1)	7-3
Polonia Bytom v MTK Budapest (0-3, 0-3)	0-6
DOS Utrecht v Sporting Lisbon (3-4, 1-2)	4-6
Young Boys w.o. Manchester U. (withdrew)	
Standard Liege v Hearts (5-1, 1-2)	6-3
Ards v Stade de Reims (1-4, 2-6)	3-10

[Real Madrid (holders) exempt until first round; CDNA Sofia, Wolverhampton Wanderers and Palloseura Helsinki received byes]

FIRST ROUND

Real Madrid v Besiktas (2-0, 1-1)	3-1
Wiener SK v Dukla Prague (3-1, 0-1)	3-2
Wolverhampton W. v Schalke 04 (2-2, 1-2)	3-4
Atletico Madrid v CDNA Sofia (2-1, 0-1, 3-1)	5-3
MTK Budapest v Young Boys Berne (1-2, 1-4)	2-6
IFK Gothenburg v Karl Marx Stadt (0-3, 2-2)	2-5
Sporting Lisbon v Standard Liege (2-3, 0-3)	2-6
Stade de Reims v PS Helsinki (4-0, 3-0)	7-0

QUARTER-FINALS

Wiener SK v Real Madrid (0-0, 1-7)	1-7
Atletico Madrid v Schalke 04 (3-0, 1-1)	4-1
Young Boys v Karl-Marx-Stadt (0-0, 2-2, 2-1*)	4-3
Standard Liege v Stade de Reims (2-0, 0-3)	2-3

SEMI-FINALS

Real Madrid v Atletico Madrid (2-1, 0-1, 2-1†)	4-3
Young Boys Berne v Stade de Reims (1-0, 1-3)	1-3

FINAL

Real Madrid: 2 Stade de Reims 0
(Stuttgart, 2.6.59, 80,000)

Real: Dominguez, Marquitos, Zarraga, Santisteban, Santamaria, Ruiz, Kopa, Mateos, Di Stefano, Rial, Gento

Reims: Colonna, Rodzik, Giraudo, Penverne, Jonquet, Leblond, Lamartine, Bliard, Fontaine, Piantoni, Vincent

Scorers: Mateos (2), Di Stefano (47)

*play-off in Amsterdam †play-off Zaragoza

LEFT: ***Reims' Just Fontaine is foiled by Dominguez in the 1959 game at Stuttgart—the second time in four years that Real had beaten the French side in the final.***
BELOW: ***Real maestro Alfredo di Stefano. His scoring record in the European Cup—49 goals, including six in seven finals—is unlikely ever to be beaten. Only one other player, 'Paco' Gento, figured in all five final sides from 1956 to 1960.***

EUROPEAN CUP 1959-60

PRELIMINARY ROUND

Jeunesse Esch v LKS Lodz (6-0, 1-2)	7-2
Fenerbahce v Vasas Csepel (1-1, 3-2)	4-3
OGC Nice v Shamrock Rovers (3-2, 1-1)	4-3
ASK Vorwaerts v Wolves (2-1, 0-2)	2-3
AC Milan v Olympiakos Piraeus (2-2, 3-1)	5-3
CDNA Sofia v Barcelona (2-2, 2-6)	4-8
Rangers v Anderlecht (5-2, 2-0)	7-2
Red Star Bratislava v Porto (2-1, 2-0)	4-1
Linfield v IFK Gothenburg (2-1, 1-6)	3-7
Petrolul Ploesti v Wiener SK (0-0, 1-2)	1-2
Eintracht Frankfurt w.o. PS Kuopion (withdrew)	

[Real Madrid (holders) exempt until first round; Red Star Belgrade, Sparta Rotterdam, Odense BK 09 and Young Boys Berne received byes]

FIRST ROUND

Real Madrid v Jeunesse Esch (7-0, 5-2)	12-2
Fenerbahce v OGC Nice (2-1, 1-2, 1-5)	4-8
Red Star Belgrade v Wolves (1-1, 0-3)	1-4
AC Milan v Barcelona (0-2, 1-5)	1-7
Rangers v Red Star Bratislava (4-3, 1-1)	5-4
Sp. Rotterdam v IFK Gothenb'g (3-1, 1-3, 3-1)	7-5
Odense BK 09 v Wiener SK (0-3, 2-2)	2-5
Young Boys v Eintracht Frankfurt (1-4, 1-1)	2-5

QUARTER-FINALS

OGC Nice v Real Madrid (3-2, 0-4)	3-6
Barcelona v Wolverhampton W. (4-0, 5-2)	9-2
Sparta Rotterdam v Rangers (2-3, 1-0, 2-3*)	5-6
Eintracht Frankfurt v Wiener SK (2-1, 1-1)	3-2

SEMI-FINALS

Real Madrid v Barcelona (3-1, 3-1)	6-2
Eintracht Frankfurt v Rangers (6-1, 6-3)	12-4

FINAL

Real Madrid 7 Eintracht Frankfurt 3
(Hampden Park, 18.5.60, 127,621)

Real: Dominguez, Marquitos, Pachin, Vidal, Santamaria, Zarraga, Canario, Del Sol, Di Stefano, Puskas, Gento

Eintracht: Loy, Lutz, Hoefer, Weilbacher, Eigenbrodt, Stinka, Kress, Lindner, Stein, Pfaff, Meier

Scorers: Di Stefano (27,30,75), Puskas (45,56-pen,60,71); Kress (10), Stein (72,74)
*play-off at Highbury

TOP: ***In typically dramatic fashion, Di Stefano beats the Eintracht Frankfurt defence to score one of his three goals in Real's 7-3 win over the West Germans in the 1960 final at Hampden Park. Real's reputation and Eintracht's 12-4 drubbing of Rangers in the semi-final produced a crowd of 127,621—a record for any European final—and they were not disappointed. The Hungarian master Ferenc Puskas scored all the four other goals, including a penalty.***
ABOVE: ***Real's deserved lap of honour after their fifth consecutive European Cup final win.***

1959-60

After its classic final, the 1959-60 campaign was notable for the quarter-final thrashing of Wolves, the club who had been one of the central figures in the move towards a European Cup, by Barcelona, the side who had lived so long under Real's shadow in Spain. Wolves, who had beaten ASK Vorwaerts of East Germany and Red Star Belgrade in previous rounds, were shattered by superior tactics. Barcelona, marshalled by Luis Suarez, won 4-0 at home in the first leg and then ran out 5-2 victors at Molineux, thanks mainly to four goals from Sandor Kocsis, another Hungarian exile. Having already conquered CSKA Sofia 8-4 on aggregate and AC Milan 7-1, Barcelona were revealed as no mean force, and the semi-final draw paired them with Real Madrid.

Real had a new manager in Miguel Munoz, the skipper of their 1956 and 1957 European sides, and Barcelona boss Helenio Herrera had dropped Ladislav Kubala. It proved a costly error: Real led 2-0 at the halfway mark and won 3-1—a score they repeated in Barcelona. Puskas scored three, Di Stefano two. It was the end of Herrera in Spain. Hounded by his critics, he resigned and went to Italy, where his greatest fame in the European Cup was yet to come.

Real's opposition in the final was to be Eintracht Frankfurt, a club with veteran star forwards in Pfaff and Kress. In the semi-final they had slammed Rangers 6-1 at home and then won 6-3 at Ibrox. This performance, coupled with the reputation of Real, produced a crowd of 127,621 at Hampden Park, and for once a cup final lived up to its pre-match publicity.

Eintracht went ahead through Kress after 10 minutes, but Di Stefano (twice) and Puskas sent Real into a comfortable lead towards half-time. A Puskas penalty after the break ended any hopes of a German revival and the Hungarian maestro added two more after dazzling passing movements with Di Stefano. Stein pulled one back for Eintracht, Di Stefano added Real's seventh, and then Stein closed the scoring with a consolation goal to make the final score 7-3.

Real were supreme in the European Cup, having won it for the first five years. Their strength lay in teamwork, which by 1960 had reached almost uncanny proportions. The terrible twins, Di Stefano and Puskas, dazzled defences with their artistry and finish, Gento was a fleet-footed winger, and the indefatigable Josê Santamaria was a pillar of resolution in defence. They had reached their peak in one of the finest exhibitions of attacking football ever witnessed.

In many ways 1959-60 was the finest ever season in the European Cup. Quite apart from the magnificent final itself—the attendance was a record and the aggregate score is easily a record for any single match European final—the series as a whole produced some very impressive figures.

The aggregate attendance, for example, was 2,780,000 from the 52 matches, giving a staggering average of 50,545. This includes home ties for Jeunesse Esch, Linfield and Odense. (For comparison the average for the 59 in 1977-78 was 25,584.)

EUROPEAN CUP 1960-61

PRELIMINARY ROUND

Heart of Midlothian v Benfica (1-2, 0-3)	1-5
Red Star Belgrade v Ujpest Dozsa (1-2, 0-3)	1-5
Fredrikstad v Ajax (4-3, 0-0)	4-3
Aarhus GF v Legia Warsaw (3-0, 0-1)	3-1
Juventus v CDNA Sofia (2-0, 1-4)	3-4
HJK Helsinki v IFK Malmo (1-3, 1-2)	2-5
Karl-Marx-Stadt w.o. Glenavon (withdrew)	
Rapid Vienna v Besiktas (4-0, 0-1)	4-1
Limerick v Young Boys Berne (0-5, 2-4)	2-9
Stade de Reims v Jeunesse Esch (6-1, 5-0)	11-1
CCA Bucharest* v Spartak Kralov (0-3)	0-3
Barcelona v Lierse SK (2-0, 3-0)	5-0

[Real Madrid (holders), SV Hamburg, Burnley and Panathinaikos received byes]

FIRST ROUND

Benfica v Ujpest Dozsa (6-2, 1-2)	7-4
Aarhus GF v Fredrikstad (3-0, 1-0)	4-0
IFK Malmo v CDNA Sofia (1-0, 1-1)	2-1
Rapid Vienna v Karl-Marx-Stadt (3-1, 0-2, 1-0)	4-3
Young Boys Berne v SV Hamburg (0-5, 3-3)	3-8
Burnley v Stade de Reims (2-0, 2-3)	4-3
Spartak Kralov v Panathinaikos (1-0, 0-0)	1-0
Real Madrid v Barcelona (2-2, 1-2)	3-4

QUARTER-FINALS

Benfica v Aarhus GF (3-1, 4-1)	7-2
Rapid Vienna v IFK Malmo (2-0, 2-0)	4-0
Burnley v SV Hamburg (3-1, 1-4)	4-5
Barcelona v Spartak Kralov (4-0, 1-1)	5-1

SEMI-FINALS

Benfica v Rapid Vienna (3-0, 1-1)	4-1
Barcelona v SV Hamburg (1-0, 1-2, 1-0†)	3-2

FINAL

Benfica 3 Barcelona 2
(Berne, 31.5.61, 33,000)

Benfica: Costa Pereira, Joao, Angelo, Neto, Germano, Cruz, Augusto, Santana, Aguas, Coluna, Cavem

Barcelona: Ramallets, Foncho, Gracia, Verges, Gensana, Garay, Kubala, Kocsis, Evaristo, Suarez, Czibor

Scorers: Aguas (30), Ramallets og (32), Coluna (55); Kocsis (20), Czibor (75)

*withdrew after first leg †play-off in Brussels

1960-61

In 1960-61 two Spanish clubs were on duty for the fifth successive year, although, as in 1959-60, Barcelona qualified as genuine champions. And they did not have to wait long for a chance to avenge their humiliating 6-2 aggregate defeat in the European Cup semi-final earlier in the year: fate drew them against their greatest rivals in the first round proper.

At Chamartin a disputed penalty near the end secured a draw for Barcelona and robbed Real of their record of winning every home European Cup tie. It was a bad omen—in Barcelona they were beaten 2-1 and knocked out of the cup for the first time. Barcelona made heavy weather of beating SV Hamburg after a play-off in Brussels in the semi-final and met Benfica, the Portuguese champions, in the final at Berne.

Under the very shrewd guidance of Hungarian-born Bela Guttmann, Benfica had kept their emphasis on attack and had outstanding individuals in strategic positions. Costa Pereira was a colossus in goal,

José Aguas (9), with his 11th goal of the competition, opened Benfica's account in the 1961 final against Barcelona at Berne.

Germano a fine stopper, Coluna a wily schemer, Augusto a clever winger, and Aguas a dynamic centre-forward. They had accounted for Hearts, Ujpest Dozsa (Hungary), Aarhus (Denmark), and Rapid Vienna (Austria), scoring 23 goals—10 of them to Aguas—and conceding only eight.

Barcelona, the favourites, led after 20 minutes through Sandor Kocsis, but goalkeeping errors gave Benfica a 2-1 lead through Aguas and Ramallets (own goal). A third goal from Coluna virtually clinched it, though Zoltan Czibor—like Kocsis and Puskas a self-exiled Hungarian—reduced the arrears. The European Cup left Spain for the first time and travelled across the Portuguese border to Lisbon.

This has been Barcelona's best season in the European Cup. Though they achieved notable success in the early years of the Fairs Cup with virtually the same side (and later in the Cup Winners Cup) the 'big one' has always eluded them, a burden they share with the likes of Juventus, Leeds, Rangers and Anderlecht.

1961-62

In 1961-62 Real Madrid, their forward line now ageing fast, made a brave effort to regain the trophy. In the preliminary round they beat Vasas Budapest 2-0 and 3-1 while Benfica were enjoying a bye. In the first round Real scored 12 in their two matches with Odense BK 1913 (Denmark). Benfica, strengthened now by the explosive skills of the 20-year-old Eusebio from Mozambique, were equally impressive in disposing of FK Austria 6-2 on aggregate.

There were shocks for both in the second round. Benfica were beaten 3-1 away by 1FC Nuremberg (West Germany) but hit their opponents for six in the return; Real were forced into a play-off in Paris by Juventus, after both sides had lost 1-0 at home, before emerging safely. In the semi-final Benfica had a tough time with England's double champions Tottenham Hotspur, going through 4-3, while Real coasted through 4-0 and 2-0 over Standard Liège (Belgium).

At Amsterdam in the final Real made an impressive opening against the holders, Puskas scoring twice in 23 minutes. Goals from Aguas and Cavem nullified them, but the amazing Puskas (he was now 36) completed his second European final hat-trick to give his side a 3-2 lead. After the interval, however, it was all Benfica; further goals—one from Coluna and two from Eusebio—finally wrecked Real. Di Stefano had an unusually ineffective game, and for the first time in his six European Cup finals he failed to score.

1962-63

With two titles under their belts, Benfica were now serious contenders for the crown once held by Real, and when the Spanish champions went out in the preliminary round of 1962-63 to Anderlecht, drawing 3-3 at home and falling to a Jeff Jurion goal in Brussels, Benfica were hot favourites for a European hat-trick in what was a relatively weak field.

EUROPEAN CUP 1961-62

PRELIMINARY ROUND

CCA Bucharest v FK Austria (0-0, 0-2)	0-2
1FC Nuremberg v Drumcondra (5-0, 4-1)	9-1
Servette v Hibernians Valletta (5-0, 2-1)	7-1
CDNA Sofia v Dukla Prague (4-4, 1-2)	5-6
FK Gothenburg v Feyenoord (0-3, 2-8)	2-11
Gornik Zabrze v Tottenham H. (4-2, 1-8)	5-10
Standard Liege v Fredrikstad (2-1, 2-0)	4-1
ASK Vorwaerts v Linfield (3-0)*	3-0
AS Monaco v Rangers (2-3, 2-3)	4-6
Sporting Lisbon v Par. Belgrade (1-1, 0-2)	1-3
Panathinaikos v Juventus (1-1, 1-2)	2-3
S. Luxembourg v Odense BK 1913 (0-6, 2-9)	2-15
Vasas Budapest v Real Madrid (0-2, 1-3)	1-5

[Benfica (holders) exempt until first round; Fenerbahce and Valkeakosken Haka received byes]

FIRST ROUND

FK Austria v Benfica (1-1, 1-5)	2-7
Fenerbahce v 1FC Nuremberg (1-2, 0-1)	1-3
Servette v Dukla Prague (4-3, 0-2)	4-5
Feyenoord v Tottenham Hotspur (1-3, 1-1)	2-4
ASK Vorwaerts v Rangers (1-2, 1-4)	2-6
Standard Liege v Valkeakosken (5-1, 2-0)	7-1
Partizan Belgrade v Juventus (1-2, 0-5)	1-7
Odense BK 1913 v Real Madrid (0-3, 0-9)	0-12

QUARTER-FINALS

1FC Nuremberg v Benfica (3-1, 0-6)	3-7
Dukla Prague v Tottenham Hotspur (1-0, 1-4)	2-4
Standard Liege v Rangers (4-1, 0-2)	4-3
Juventus v Real Madrid (0-1, 1-0, 1-3†)	2-4

SEMI-FINALS

Benfica v Tottenham Hotspur (3-1, 1-2)	4-3
Real Madrid v Standard Liege (4-0, 2-0)	6-0

FINAL

Benfica 5 Real Madrid 3
(Amsterdam, 2.5.62, 68,000)

Benfica: Costa Pereira, Joao, Angelo, Cavem, Germano, Cruz, Augusto, Eusebio, Aguas, Coluna, Simoes

Real: Araquistain, Cassado, Miera, Felo, Santamaria, Pachin, Tejada, Del Sol, Di Stefano, Puskas, Gento

Scorers: Aguas (25), Cavem (34), Coluna (51), Eusebio (65,68); Puskas (17,23,38)

*withdrew after first leg †play-off in Paris

Guttmann had left, and under the Chilean Fernando Riera a more defensive formula emerged. Benfica beat IFK Norrköping, Dukla Prague, and Feyenoord (Netherlands), in each case winning their home match and drawing away.

It was AC Milan, finalists in 1958, who emerged as the biggest threat. They had an impressive statistical journey to the final, beating Union Luxembourg by 14-0, then a record aggregate for the competition, and then Ipswich, who had themselves put 14 past Floriana of Malta in the previous round, with Ray Crawford accounting for half that haul. After trouncing the Turkish champions Galatasaray the Italians then beat Dundee to reach the final with a goal record of 31-5 in just eight games.

Dundee's performance deserves special mention, involving as it did three decisive victories over names far better known in European football. Only Hibs in 1956 (a small field) and Rangers in 1960 (beaten by a record semi-final score) had reached the last four, and it wasn't until Celtic went on to win the trophy in 1967 that another Scottish club reached that stage.

The final at Wembley attracted only 45,000, but Eusebio lived up to his increasing reputation as a marksman with a goal after 18 minutes. An injury to Coluna, however, disjointed a Benfica side already missing Germano and two goals by José Altafini in the second half—taking the Brazilian's tally for the tournament to an all-time record of 14—were sufficient to take the European Cup to Italy for the first time. The Italians, applying their league formula of safety first, made it clear that the era of prolific scoring in European Cup finals was on the wane.

The trophy would stay at the San Siro Stadium in Milan for three years—though not with the same club. It was to be AC's great rivals, the cleverly defensive Internazionale side of Helenio Herrera, who would dominate the next two seasons.

LEFT: Benfica keeper Costa Pereira offers a prayer after the holders had held on 4-3 on aggregate at White Hart Lane in the 1962 semi-final against Spurs.
BELOW: José Altafini beats Pereira for one of the two goals he scored for Milan in the 1963 final at Wembley, taking his tally to a record 14 for the series—and wrecking Benfica's dream of a hat-trick.

EUROPEAN CUP 1962-63

PRELIMINARY ROUND

AC Milan v Union Luxembourg (8-0, 6-0)	14-0
Floriana v Ipswich Town (1-4, 0-10)	1-14
Dynamo Bucharest v Galatasaray (1-1, 0-3)	1-4
Polonia Bytom v Panathinaikos (2-1, 4-1)	6-2
CDNA Sofia v Partizan Belgrade (2-1, 4-1)	6-2
Real Madrid v Anderlecht (3-3, 0-1)	3-4
Shelbourne v Sporting Lisbon (0-2, 1-5)	1-7
Dundee v 1FC Cologne (8-1, 0-4)	8-5
Servette Geneva v Feyenoord (1-3, 3-1, 1-3)	5-7
Fredrikstad v Vasas Budapest (1-4, 0-7)	1-11
FK Austria v IFK Helsinki (5-3, 2-0)	7-3
ASK Vorwaerts v Dukla Prague (0-3, 0-1)	0-4
Linfield v BK Esbjerg (1-2, 0-0)	1-2
IFK Norrkoping v Partizan Tirana (2-0, 1-1)	3-1

[Benfica (holders) exempt until first round; Stade de Reims received a bye]

FIRST ROUND

AC Milan v Ipswich Town (3-0, 1-2)	4-2
Galatasaray v Polonia Bytom (4-1, 0-1)	4-2
CDNA Sofia v Anderlecht (2-2, 0-2)	2-4
Sporting Lisbon v Dundee (1-0, 1-4)	2-4
Feyenoord v Vasas Budapest (1-1, 2-2, 1-0)	4-3
FK Austria v Stade de Reims (3-2, 0-5)	3-7
BK Esbjerg v Dukla Prague (0-0, 0-5)	0-5
IFK Norrkoping v Benfica (1-1, 1-5)	2-6

QUARTER-FINALS

Galatasaray v AC Milan (1-3, 0-5)	1-8
Anderlecht v Dundee (1-4, 1-2)	2-6
Stade de Reims v Feyenoord (0-1, 1-1)	1-2
Benfica v Dukla Prague (2-1, 0-0)	2-1

SEMI-FINALS

AC Milan v Dundee (5-1, 0-1)	5-2
Feyenoord v Benfica (0-0, 1-3)	1-3

FINAL

AC Milan 2 Benfica 1
(Wembley, 22.5.63, 45,000)

Milan: Ghezzi, David, Trebbi, Benitez, Maldini, Trapattoni, Pivatelli, Sani, Altafini, Rivera, Mora

Benfica: Costa Pereira, Cavem, Cruz, Humberto, Raul, Coluna, Augusto, Santana, Torres, Eusebio, Simoes

Scorers: Altafini (58,70); Eusebio (19)

EUROPEAN CUP 1963-64

PRELIMINARY ROUND

Everton v Inter-Milan (0-0, 0-1)	0-1
AS Monaco v AEK Athens (7-2, 1-1)	8-3
Valkeakosken v Jeunesse Esch (4-1, 0-4)	4-5
Par. Belgrade v Anorth. Famagusta (3-0, 3-1)	6-1
Distillery v Benfica (3-3, 0-5)	3-8
Lyn Oslo v Borussia Dortmund (2-4, 1-3)	3-7
Gornik Zabrze v FK Austria (1-0, 2-1)	3-1
Dukla Prague v Valletta (6-0, 2-0)	8-0
Dundalk v FC Zurich (0-3, 2-1)	2-4
Galatasaray v Ferencvaros (4-0, 0-2)	4-2
Partizan Tirana v Spartak Plovdiv (1-0, 1-3)	2-3
BK Esbjerg v PSV Eindhoven (3-4, 1-7)	4-11
Standard Liege v IFK Norrkoping (1-0, 0-2)	1-2
Dynamo Bucharest v Motor Jena (2-0, 1-0)	3-0
Rangers v Real Madrid (0-1, 0-6)	0-7

[AC Milan (holders) exempt until first round]

FIRST ROUND

Inter-Milan v AS Monaco (1-0, 3-1)	4-1
Jeunesse Esch v Partizan Belgrade (2-1, 2-6)	4-7
Benfica v Borussia Dortmund (2-1, 0-5)	2-6
Gornik Zabrze v Dukla Prague (2-0, 1-4)	3-4
FC Zurich* v Galatasaray (2-0, 0-2, 2-2)	4-4
Spartak Plovdiv v PSV Eindhoven (0-1, 0-0)	0-1
IFK Norrkoping v AC Milan (1-1, 2-5)	3-6
Dynamo Bucharest v Real Madrid (1-3, 3-5)	4-8

QUARTER-FINALS

Partizan Belgrade v Inter-Milan (0-2, 1-2)	1-4
Dukla Prague v Borussia Dortmund (0-4, 3-1)	3-5
PSV Eindhoven v FC Zurich (1-0, 1-3)	2-3
Real Madrid v AC Milan (4-1, 0-2)	4-3

SEMI-FINALS

Borussia Dortmund v Inter-Milan (2-2, 0-2)	2-4
FC Zurich v Real Madrid (1-2, 0-6)	1-8

FINAL

Inter-Milan 3 Real Madrid 1
(Vienna, 27.5.64, 72,000)

Inter: Sarti, Burgnich, Facchetti, Tagnin, Guarneri, Picchi, Jair, Mazzola, Milani, Suarez, Corso

Real: Vicente, Isidro, Pachin, Zoco, Santamaria, Muller, Amancio, Felo, Di Stefano, Puskas, Gento

Scorers: Mazzola (43,76), Milani (61); Felo (70)
*won on toss of a coin

1963-64

In 1963-64 Benfica went out in the first round, beaten in Dortmund by Borussia. AC Milan were eliminated in the last eight 4-3 by a somewhat rejuvenated Real Madrid, and their mantle was taken on by San Siro stable companions Internazionale, with Helenio Herrera at the helm. Inter removed Everton, AS Monaco, Partizan Belgrade, and Borussia Dortmund without losing a game, and with Real humiliating Zurich 8-1 to reach their seventh final the stage was set for an interesting match in Vienna.

Herrera was seeking personal revenge against Real for his Barcelona days, and Inter punished their ageing opponents for their mistakes. Mazzola gave them an interval lead, and Milani added a second before Felo gave Real a theoretical chance of staying in the game. Mazzola, however, clinched it for the Italians in the 76th minute. Inter, successful at their first attempt, became the first club to win without losing a match.

Sandro Mazzola, who like Sarti, Burgnich, Facchetti, Guarneri and Corso played in all three of Inter-Milan's European Cup finals, scored twice in the win over Real Madrid at Vienna in 1964. It was Mazzola who scored from the spot against Celtic in the 1967 final.

1964-65

Italy now appeared to be the home of the trophy, and in 1964-65 this was confirmed, if with less conviction than before. Internazionale began in high-scoring mood by putting six past Dynamo Bucharest in Milan. Benfica, with Torres prominent, also piled on the goals against Aris (Luxembourg) and Chaux-de-Fonds (Switzerland), scoring 16 in four matches.

In the quarter-final Inter's 3-1 advantage over Rangers just saw them through after a 1-0 reverse in Scotland, their first defeat in the cup. Benfica merely confirmed the decline of Real Madrid by rapping them 5-1 in Lisbon, and a 2-1 defeat in Madrid was of little consequence. Benfica also cruised through the semi-final over Vasas Györ (Hungary) 1-0 and 4-0. Inter had a tougher time with Liverpool: the Merseysiders, in what proved to be the first season of their great consecutive run in Europe, built up a formidable 3-1 lead at home with goals from

St John, Strong and Yeats pressurize the Inter-Milan defence during Liverpool's 3-1 semi-final win in 1965. The holders went through after a controversial second leg.

EUROPEAN CUP 1964-65

PRELIMINARY ROUND

Sliema W. v Dynamo Bucharest (0-2, 0-5)	0-7
Rangers v Red Star Belgrade (3-1, 2-4, 3-1)	8-6
Rapid Vienna v Shamrock Rovers (3-0, 2-0)	5-0
Glentoran v Panathinaikos (2-2, 2-3)	4-5
Partizan Tirana v 1FC Cologne (0-0, 0-2)	0-2
Anderlecht* v Bologna (1-0, 1-2, 0-0)	2-2
KR Reykjavik v Liverpool (0-5, 1-6)	1-11
Chemie Leipzig v Vasas Gyor (0-2, 2-4)	2-6
Lokomotiv Sofia v Malmo FF (8-3, 0-2)	8-5
DWS Amsterdam v Fenerbahce (3-1, 1-0)	4-1
Lahden Reipas v Lyn Oslo (2-1, 0-3)	2-4
Odense BK 09 v Real Madrid (2-5, 0-4)	2-9
Dukla Prague* v Gornik Zabrze (4-1, 0-3, 0-0)	4-4
St Etienne v La Chaux de Fonds (2-2, 1-2)	3-4
Aris Bonnevoie v Benfica (1-5, 1-5)	2-10

[Inter-Milan (holders) exempt until first round]

FIRST ROUND

Inter-Milan v Dynamo Bucharest (6-0, 1-0)	7-0
Rangers v Rapid Vienna (1-0, 2-0)	3-0
Panathinaikos v 1FC Cologne (1-1, 1-2)	2-3
Liverpool v Anderlecht (3-0, 1-0)	4-0
Vasas Gyor v Lokomotiv Sofia (5-3, 3-4)	8-7
DWS Amsterdam v Lyn Oslo (5-0, 3-1)	8-1
Real Madrid v Dukla Prague (4-0, 2-2)	6-2
La Chaux de Fonds v Benfica (1-1, 0-5)	1-6

QUARTER-FINALS

Inter-Milan v Rangers (3-1, 0-1)	3-2
1FC Cologne v Liverpool* (0-0, 0-0, 2-2†)	2-2
DWS Amsterdam v Vasas Gyor (1-1, 0-1)	1-2
Benfica v Real Madrid (5-1, 1-2)	6-3

SEMI-FINALS

Liverpool v Inter-Milan (3-1, 0-3)	3-4
Vasas Gyor v Benfica (0-1, 0-4)	0-5

FINAL

Inter-Milan 1 Benfica 0
(Milan, 28.5.65, 85,000)

Inter: Sarti, Burgnich, Facchetti, Bedin, Guarneri, Picchi, Jair, Mazzola, Peiro, Suarez, Corso

Benfica: Costa Pereira, Cavern, Cruz, Neto, Germano, Raul, Augusto, Eusebio, Torres, Coluna, Simoes

Scorer: Jair (42)
*won on toss of coin †play-off in Rotterdam

Hunt, Callaghan and St John, but with more than a little luck on their side, and a vital goal by full-back Facchetti, Inter won the return with some dubious decisions by 3–0.

The final, played on Inter's own San Siro in heavy rain in front of 85,000, was settled by a goal from Jair in the 42nd minute. Benfica, with nine of the 1963 side playing, were hit by injuries and Germano took over from Costa Pereira in goal in the second half. Although the victors achieved little glory, there was no doubt about the talent of a side masterfully guided in midfield by Luis Suarez, formerly with Barcelona. While the explosive Eusebio took the European Footballer of the Year award for 1965 it was two Internazionale players, Suarez and the elegant full-back Giacinto Facchetti, who took the runners-up slots.

1965-66

In the preliminary round of 1965-66 Real Madrid were beaten 2-1 in Holland by Feyenoord, and it seemed that the younger Spanish side was to go the way of its immediate predecessor. But with Puskas scoring four goals they won the return 5-0. They went on to beat Kilmarnock 7-3 on aggregate, revenged their 1962-63 defeat by taking Anderlecht by exactly the same score, and disposed of Inter, the holders, in the semi-final, winning 1-0 at home and holding the Italians 1-1 in Milan.

Benfica, with an 18-0 win over the unfortunate Stade Dudelange of Luxembourg under their belts from the preliminary round (still a European Cup record) appeared to have done well when they held Manchester United to 3-2 in the first leg of their quarter-final at Old Trafford. But five weeks later United achieved one of their greatest triumphs with a remarkable 5-1 victory in Lisbon, with goals from Best (2), Connelly, Crerand and Charlton. United, however, failed in the semi-final, losing 2-0 in Belgrade to Partizan and only managing to pull one back at home, and that an own goal.

Thus, in Brussels, Real Madrid appeared in their eighth European Cup final. Partizan proved dour opponents, and scored first through Vasovic, later to play in two European Cup finals for Ajax. But the stronger Spaniards, with only Gento remaining from the old days, had goals from Amancio and Serena to see them home. It was Real's cup for the sixth time, but it was not won as convincingly as in former years.

Ironically, the same season saw Atlético Madrid oust Real from the top of the Spanish League, the only time in nine seasons (1961-9) that the great side did not win their domestic competition.

So after three years the European Cup left Milan, destined for a place it knew only too well. It would be back at San Siro, this time under the auspices of AC, in 1969, after a trip to unfamiliar territory. Celtic (1967) and Manchester United (1968) both beat experienced finalists to signal the end of the Latin domination that had characterized the competition since its inception.

EUROPEAN CUP 1965-66

PRELIMINARY ROUND

Feyenoord v Real Madrid (2-1, 0-5)	2-6
Nendori Tirana v Kilmarnock (0-0, 0-1)	0-1
Fenerbahce v Anderlecht (0-0, 1-5)	1-5
Lyn Oslo v Derry City (5-3, 1-5)	6-8
Dynamo Bucharest v Odense BK 09 (3-2, 4-0)	7-2
Panathinaikos v Sliema Wanderers (4-1, 0-1)	4-2
IB Keflavik v Ferencvaros (1-4, 1-9)	1-13
HJK Helsinki v Manchester United (2-3, 0-6)	2-9
Drumcondra v ASK Vorwaerts (1-0, 0-3)	1-3
Stade Dudelange v Benfica (0-8, 0-10)	0-18
Djurdaarden v Levski Sofia (2-1, 0-6)	2-7
Lausanne v Sparta Prague (0-0, 0-4)	0-4
ASK Linz v Gornik Zabrze (1-3, 1-2)	2-5
Apoel Nicosia v Werder Bremen (0-5, 0-5)	0-10
Partizan Belgrade v Nantes (2-0, 2-2)	4-2

[Inter-Milan (holders) exempt until first round]

FIRST ROUND

Kilmarnock v Real Madrid (2-2, 1-5)	3-7
Anderlecht v Derry City (9-0*)	9-0
Dynamo Bucharest v Inter-Milan (2-1, 0-2)	2-3
Ferencvaros v Panathinaikos (0-0, 3-1)	3-1
ASK Vorwaerts v Manchester U. (0-2, 1-3)	1-5
Levski Sofia v Benfica (2-2, 2-3)	4-5
Sparta Prague v Gornik Zabrze (3-0, 2-1)	5-1
Partizan Belgrade v Werder Bremen (3-0, 0-1)	3-1

QUARTER-FINALS

Anderlecht v Real Madrid (1-0, 2-4)	3-4
Inter-Milan v Ferencvaros (4-0, 1-1)	5-1
Manchester United v Benfica (3-2, 5-1)	8-3
Sparta Prague v Partizan Belgrade (4-1, 0-5)	4-6

SEMI-FINALS

Real Madrid v Inter-Milan (1-0, 1-1)	2-1
Partizan Belgrade v Manchester U. (2-0, 0-1)	2-1

FINAL

Real Madrid 2 Partizan Belgrade 1
(Brussels, 11.5.66, 55,000)

Real: Araquistain, Pachin, Sanchis, Pirri, De Felipe, Zoco, Serena, Amancio, Grosso, Velasquez, Gento

Partizan: Soskic, Jusufi, Milhailovic, Becejac, Rasovic, Vasovic, Bajic, Kovacevic, Hasanagic, Galic, Pirmajer

Scorers: Amancio (70), Serena (75); Vasovic (55)

*Derry withdrew after first leg

ABOVE: ***Paco Gento, still only 33, holds the European Cup aloft after Real's 2-1 win over Partizan Belgrade at Brussels in 1966. It was his eighth final—the sixth on the winning side. In 1971, aged 38, he appeared in the Real side that lost the Cup Winners Cup final to Chelsea after a replay in Athens.***

LEFT: ***Partizan go close in the 1966 final—Yugoslavia's only appearance in a European decider until Red Star's defeat in the 1979 UEFA Cup by Moenchengladbach. Velibor Vasovic, later to play in two finals for Ajax, was their scorer.***

1966-67

The 1966-67 series was destined, at last, to see the trophy leave the preserve of the Latins, snatched by Jock Stein's Celtic, a club competing for the first time. Real went out to Inter (who had narrowly beaten Moscow Torpedo, Russia's first entrant, in the first round). They thus gained swift revenge for their semi-final defeat the previous year.

The Italians, however, were given a rough passage in the last four by CSKA Sofia, trying for the cup for the eighth time. The Bulgarian champions took Inter to a play-off in Bologna before going down to a Cappellini goal.

Celtic, on the other hand, had quietly reached the semi-finals with Zurich (Switzerland), Nantes (France), and Vojvodina (Yugoslavia) tucked comfortably away behind them. European veterans Dukla Prague provided a sterner test, but their 3-1 lead from home saw them through.

The Lisbon final was a fascinating contest. Celtic had gained a name for their attacking football—though at the same time the defence, with the veteran Ronnie Simpson between the posts, had conceded only five goals in eight games—while Inter were past masters of the cat and mouse game that characterized the Italian style. Inter certainly had the experience, with seven players who had figured in the successful 1964 and 1965 finals on duty.

It seemed everything was going their way when Mazzola, whose father had played his last game in the very same stadium before dying in the Turin air disaster of 1949, scored from a penalty after only eight minutes. But Inter, without Suarez, appeared jaded. Celtic began to apply themselves to the relentless task of breaking down the Italian wall, and twice in the second half they succeeded, first through the adventurous full-back Gemmell and then again five minutes from the end when Chalmers ensured Britain's first victory in the competition. This was, nevertheless, essentially a Scottish honour and not one to be shared by those south of the border.

Celtic's victory proved to be a watershed in the European Cup. All 11 competitions before 1966-67 had been won by 'Latin' sides, and then (with the exception of AC Milan in 1969) the trophy became the firm preserve of the northern European sides. Throughout the 1970s the three countries which had dominated the event before Celtic's win—Spain, Portugal and Italy—managed only three finalists, and all lost.

EUROPEAN CUP 1966-67

EXTRA PRELIMINARY ROUND	
Sliema Wanderers v CSKA Sofia (1-2, 0-4)	1-6
Waterford v ASK Vorwaerts (1-6, 0-6)	1-12
PRELIMINARY ROUND	
Celtic v FC Zurich (2-0, 3-0)	5-0
KR Reykjavik v Nantes (2-3, 2-5)	4-8
Admira Vienna v Vojvodina N. Sad (0-1, 0-0)	0-1
Malmo FF v Atletico Madrid (0-2, 1-3)	1-5
Liverpool v Petrolul Ploesti (2-0, 1-3, 2-0*)	5-3
Ajax v Besiktas (2-0, 2-1)	4-1
Valkeakosken Haka v Anderlecht (1-10, 0-2)	1-12
BK Esbjerg v Dukla Prague (0-2, 0-4)	0-6
Aris Bonnevoie v Linfield (3-3, 1-6)	4-9
Valerengen v Nendori Tirana (withdrew)	
G. Zabrze v ASK Vorwaerts (2-1, 1-2, 3-1†)	6-4
CSKA Sofia v Olympiakos Piraeus (3-1, 0-1)	3-2
Munich 1860 v Omonia Nicosia (8-0, 2-1)	10-1
Vasas Budapest v Sporting Lisbon (5-0, 2-0)	7-0
Inter-Milan v Torpedo Moscow (1-0, 0-0)	1-0
[Real Madrid (holders) exempt until first round]	
FIRST ROUND	
Nantes v Celtic (1-3, 1-3)	2-6
Vojvodina v Atletico Madrid (3-1, 0-2, 3-2‡)	6-5
Ajax v Liverpool (5-1, 2-2)	7-3
Dukla Prague v Anderlecht (4-1, 2-1)	6-2
Valerengen v Linfield (1-4, 1-1)	2-5
CSKA Sofia v Gornik Zabrze (4-0, 0-3)	4-3
TSV Munich 1860 v Real Madrid (1-0, 1-3)	2-3
Inter-Milan v Vasas Budapest (2-1, 2-0)	4-1
QUARTER-FINALS	
Vojvodina Novi Sad v Celtic (1-0, 0-2)	1-2
Ajax v Dukla Prague (1-1, 1-2)	2-3
Linfield v CSKA Sofia (2-2, 0-1)	2-3
Inter-Milan v Real Madrid (1-0, 2-0)	3-0
SEMI-FINALS	
Celtic v Dukla Prague (3-1, 0-0)	3-1
Inter-Milan v CSKA Sofia (1-1, 1-1, 1-0§)	3-2

FINAL

Celtic 2 Inter-Milan 1
(Lisbon, 25.5.67, 45,000)

Celtic: Simpson, Craig, Gemmell, Murdoch, McNeill, Clark, Johnstone, Wallace, Chalmers, Auld, Lennox

Inter: Sarti, Burgnich, Facchetti, Bedin, Guarneri, Picchi, Domenghini, Mazzola, Cappellini, Bicicli, Corso

Scorers: Gemmell (63), Chalmers (85); Mazzola (pen-8)

*play-off in Brussels †play-off in Budapest
‡play-off in Madrid §play-off in Bologna

LEFT: *Bobby Murdoch fails to cut out Mario Corso's cross in the 1967 final in Lisbon, when the European Cup left the preserve of the 'Latin' nations after 11 years.*
BELOW: *Scottish delight after Steve Chalmers (9) had deflected Murdoch's shot past Sarti in the 85th minute to put Celtic 2-1 up. Left-back Tommy Gemmell (right) had scored the equalizer.*

EUROPEAN CUP 1967-68

FIRST ROUND

Manchester U. v Hibernians Valletta (4-0, 0-0)	4-0
Olympiakos Nicosia v Sarajevo (2-2, 1-3)	3-5
Gornik Zabrze v Djurgaarden (1-0, 3-0)	4-0
Celtic v Dynamo Kiev (1-2, 1-1)	2-3
Ajax v Real Madrid (1-1, 1-2)	2-3
Basle v Hvivdovre Copenhagen (1-2, 3-3)	4-5
Skeid Oslo v Sparta Prague (0-1, 1-1)	1-2
Karl-Marx-Stadt v Anderlecht (1-3,1-2)	2-5
Olympiakos Piraeus v Juventus (0-0, 0-2)	0-2
Botev Plovdiv v Rapid Bucharest (2-0, 0-3)	2-3
Eintracht Brunswick v Dynamo Tirana (w'drew)	
Besiktas v Rapid Vienna (0-1, 0-3)	0-4
Dundalk v Vasas Budapest (0-1, 1-8)	1-9
Valur Reykjavik* v Jeunesse Esch (1-1, 3-3)	4-4
St Etienne v PS Kuopion (2-0, 3-0)	5-0
Glentoran v Benfica* (1-1, 0-0)	1-1

SECOND ROUND

Sarajevo v Manchester United (0-0, 1-2)	1-2
Dynamo Kiev v Gornik Zabrze (1-2, 1-1)	2-3
Hvivdovre v Real Madrid (2-2, 1-4)	3-6
Sparta Prague v Anderlecht (3-2, 3-3)	6-5
Juventus v Rapid Bucharest (1-0, 0-0)	1-0
Rapid Vienna v Eintracht Brunswick (1-0, 0-2)	1-2
Vasas Budapest v Valur Reykjavik (6-0, 5-1)	11-1
Benfica v St Etienne (2-0, 0-1)	2-1

QUARTER-FINALS

Manchester United v Gornik Zabrze (2-0, 0-1)	2-1
Real Madrid v Sparta Prague (3-0, 1-2)	4-2
E. Brunswick v Juventus (3-2, 0-1, 0-1†)	3-4
Vasas Budapest v Benfica (0-0, 0-3)	0-3

SEMI-FINALS

Manchester United v Real Madrid (1-0, 3-3)	4-3
Benfica v Juventus (2-0, 1-0)	3-0

FINAL

Manchester United 4 Benfica 1 [aet] (Wembley, 29.5.68, 100,000)

United: Stepney, Brennan, Dunne, Crerand, Foulkes, Stiles, Best, Kidd, Charlton, Sadler, Aston

Benfica: Henrique, Adolfo, Humberto, Jacinto, Cruz, Graca, Coluna, Augusto, Eusebio, Torres, Simoes

Scorers: Charlton (53,99), Best (93), Kidd (94); Graca (75)

*won on away goals rule †play-off in Berne

Manchester United's best performance in 1967-68 was probably in Madrid, where they held Real 3-3 to reach the final. This goal by David Sadler (10) was followed by scores from Brian Kidd and Bill Foulkes—like Bobby Charlton a survivor from the 1957 semi-final with Real.

1967-68

The following season saw the hordes south of Hadrian's Wall appeased by Manchester United, a club who had long battled for the honour. Each of their three previous attempts—in 1957, 1958 and 1966—had ended in the semi-finals.

United showed nothing spectacular against Hibernians (Malta) and Sarajevo (Yugoslavia), but did well to beat the strong Polish side Gornik Zabrze in the quarter-finals. In the semi-finals a George Best goal against Real Madrid seemed scant advantage, but in a remarkable display in a torrid atmosphere they drew 3-3 in Madrid, after trailing 3-1, to book a Wembley place. The crucial goal that night was scored by none other than defender Bill Foulkes, along with Bobby Charlton a survivor from the semi-final against Real back in 1957.

Their opponents, Benfica, were old European campaigners too, appearing in their fifth final and their second at Wembley. Three players, Cruz, Coluna and Augusto, appeared in all five of them.

Apart from the first round, when the away-goals rule helped them through against Glentoran of Northern Ireland, Benfica had a convincing passage to the final, accounting for St Etienne (France), Vasas and Juventus with increasing ease. Eusebio was still scoring well, and the defence had been tightened up, the carefree abandon of earlier times giving way to the modern essentials. The cup holders, Celtic, had been eliminated in the first round by Dynamo Kiev of Russia, who lost in turn to Gornik.

On 29 May millions of sympathetic viewers waited as Matt Busby's side set out to finish a journey that had traversed that Munich runway just over 10 years before.

The signs were good. The final had been scheduled for Wembley; United enjoyed the knowledge of a 5-1 win over the Portuguese in Lisbon two years earlier; if they could beat Real Madrid, then they could beat Benfica; and if Denis Law was injured, George Best, the League's joint leading scorer that season, was at his peak.

The first half was stale anti-climax, but after Charlton had glanced home a rare header eight minutes into the second period, United relaxed and played well. Then Graça equalized. In the dying seconds Stepney made a fine save from Eusebio. It was a coolly taken goal by Best—later the first Irishman to be voted European Footballer of the Year—that really settled it three minutes into extra time. Brian Kidd, on his 19th birthday, added another a minute later, and Charlton gave United a flattering scoreline when he curled home a fourth.

EUROPEAN CUP LEADING SCORERS

Season	Player	Gls	Season	Player	Gls
1955-56	Milutinovic *(Partizan Belgrade)*	7	1967-68	Eusebio *(Benfica)*	7
1956-57	Viollet *(Manchester United)*	9	1968-69	Law *(Manchester United)*	9
1957-58	Di Stefano *(Real Madrid)**	10	1969-70	Jones *(Leeds United)*	8
1958-59	Fontaine *(Stade de Reims)*	10	1970-71	Antoniadis *(Panathinaikos)*	10
1959-60	Puskas *(Real Madrid)*	12	1971-72	Cruyff *(Ajax)**	5
1960-61	Aguas *(Benfica)**	11		Macari *(Celtic)*	5
1961-62	Di Stafano *(Real Madrid)*	7		Takac *(Standard Liege)*	5
	Puskas *(Real Madrid)*	7	1972-73	Muller *(Bayern Munich)**	12
	Tejada *(Real Madrid)*	7	1973-74	Muller *(Bayern Munich)**	9
1962-63	Altafini *(AC Milan)**	14	1974-75	Markarov *(Ararat Erevan)*	7
1963-64	Kovacevic *(Partizan Belgrade)*	7	1975-76	Heynckes *(Borussia M'gladbach)*	6
	Mazzola *(Inter-Milan)**	7	1976-77	Cucinotta *(FC Zurich)*	5
	Puskas *(Real Madrid)*	7		Muller *(Bayern Munich)*	5
	Wosab *(Borussia Dortmund)*	7	1977-78	Simonsen *(Borussia M'gladbach)*	5
1964-65	Torres *(Benfica)*	9	1978-79	Sulser *(Grasshoppers Zurich)*	11
1965-66	Albert *(Ferencvaros)*	7	1979-80	Lerby *(Ajax)*	10
	Eusebio *(Benfica)*	7	1980-81	Rummenigge *(Bayern Munich)*	6
1966-67	Piepenburg *(ASK Vorwaerts)*	7		Souness & McDermott *(Liverpool)*	6
	Van Himst *(Anderlecht)*	7	1981-82	Hoeness *(Bayern Munich)*	7
			1982-83	Rossi *(Juventus)*	6

*winners

EUROPEAN CUP 1968-69

FIRST ROUND

Malmo FF v AC Milan (2-1, 1-4)	3-5
Red Star w.o. Carl Zeiss Jena (withdrew)	
St Etienne v Celtic (2-0, 0-4)	2-4
Anderlecht v Glentoran (3-0, 2-2)	5-2
Waterford v Manchester United (1-3, 1-7)	2-10
Rosenborg v Rapid Vienna (1-3, 3-3)	4-6
Real Madrid v Union Limassol (6-0, 6-0)	12-0
Steaua Bucharest v Spartak Trnava (3-1, 0-4)	3-5
Floriana v Lahden Reipas (1-1, 0-2)	1-3
AEK Athens v Jeunesse Esch (3-0, 2-3)	5-3
FC Zurich v AB Copenhagen (1-3, 2-1)	3-4
Valur Reykjavik v Benfica (0-0, 1-8)	1-8
Manchester City v Fenerbahce (0-0, 1-2)	1-2
1FC Nuremberg v Ajax (1-1, 0-4)	1-5

SECOND ROUND

Celtic v Red Star Belgrade (5-1, 1-1)	6-2
Manchester United v Anderlecht (3-0, 1-3)	4-3
Rapid Vienna* v Real Madrid (1-0, 1-2)	2-2
Lahden Reipas v Spartak Trnava (1-9, 1-7)	2-16
AEK Athens v AB Copenhagen (0-0, 2-0)	2-0
Ajax v Fenerbahce (2-0, 2-0)	4-0

[AC Milan and Benfica received byes]

QUARTER-FINALS

AC Milan v Celtic (0-0, 1-0)	1-0
Manchester United v Rapid Vienna (3-0, 0-0)	3-0
Spartak Trnava v AEK Athens (2-1, 1-1)	3-2
Ajax v Benfica (1-3, 3-1, 3-0†)	7-4

SEMI-FINALS

AC Milan v Manchester United (2-0, 0-1)	2-1
Ajax v Spartak Trnava (3-0, 0-2)	3-2

FINAL

AC Milan 4 Ajax 1
(Madrid, 28.5.69, 31,782)

Milan: Cudicini, Anquilletti, Schnellinger, Rosato, Maldera, Trapattoni, Hamrin, Lodetti, Sormani, Rivera, Prati

Ajax: Bals, Suurbier (Muller), Hulshoff, Pronk, Van Duivenbode, Vasovic, Groot (Nuninga), Swart, Cruyff, Danielsson, Keizer

Scorers: Prati (7,40,75), Sormani (67); Vasovic (pen-60)

*won on away goals rule †play-off in Paris

A far-from-fit Johan Cruyff and a youthful Ajax side found the experience of AC Milan too much to handle in the 1969 final, when Pierino Prati scored a hat-trick in Madrid.

1968-69

Manchester United's win did much to revive the theory that a more vigorous approach in style and method, traditional traits of the English game, could win further honours for the home country. But the 1968-69 season was disappointing: League champions Manchester City lost to Fenerbahce of Turkey in the first round, and United, after wins over Waterford (Eire), Anderlecht, and Rapid Vienna, again went out to AC Milan—who were, incidentally, holders of the Cup Winners Cup—in the semi-final.

The cup returned to Italy, and to San Siro, where once again it was AC Milan's turn to hold it. They were totally different in style from their final opponents Ajax Amsterdam from Holland. The Italians were schooled in the art of the thrusting counter-attack and massed defence, while Ajax relied on open play.

Milan had started the series none too brightly by losing 2-1 in Malmö, but came through at home 4-1. A re-draw of the competition by UEFA (after protests from some Western countries against playing Eastern Europeans who had been involved in the invasion of Czechoslovakia) led to mass withdrawals from the Eastern bloc and gave Milan a bye. In the quarter-finals they drew Celtic, and seemed out of it when the Scots held them to a goalless draw at San Siro. But Celtic were completely baffled by Milan's defence at home and succumbed to a goal by outside-left Pierino Prati.

Ajax had beaten 1FC Nuremberg 5-1, and then beat Fenerbahce of Turkey before meeting Benfica in the new draw. The Portuguese were in command in Amsterdam, winning 3-1, but were never within sight of Ajax in Lisbon as the Dutch built up a 3-0 lead before half-time with goals by Cruyff (2) and Danielsson. Only a late goal by Torres forced a play-off in Paris. That went into extra time before any goals were scored, but then Benfica collapsed and Ajax pumped in three.

Milan were in command from the start in the Madrid final. Prati netted the first after seven minutes, and scored another before the break, just when Ajax were gaining some territorial advantage. Vasovic, Partizan Belgrade's scorer in the 1966 European final, reduced the arrears with a penalty, but five minutes later Sormani made certain with Milan's third, and Prati completed an excellent hat-trick before the end to make it a convincing 4-1 victory. Ajax, however, would be back—in style.

Bertie Auld conveys Celtic's feelings only too well after their double semi-final win over Leeds in 1970—but the Scots would lose to Feyenoord in extra time at Milan.

1969-70

If Ajax had failed to lift the prize in 1969, their great rivals, Feyenoord of Rotterdam, did just that in 1970. And in showing that the Dutch emergence was no passing phase, they avenged Ajax by eliminating 2-1 an AC Milan side still shell-shocked from their abrasive clashes with Estudiantes in the World Club Championship. Earlier,

EUROPEAN CUP 1969-70

PRELIMINARY ROUND

Turun PS Turku v KB Copenhagen (0-1, 0-4)	0-5

FIRST ROUND

Feyenoord v KR Reykjavik (12-2, 4-0)	16-2
AC Milan v Avenir Beggen (5-0, 3-0)	8-0
Red Star Belgrade v Linfield (8-0, 4-2)	12-2
ASK Vorwaerts v Panathinaikos (1-1, 2-0)	3-1
Galatasaray v Waterford (2-0, 3-2)	5-2
Hibs Valletta v Spartak Trnava (2-2, 0-4)	2-6
Bayern Munich v St Etienne (2-0, 0-3)	2-3
UT Arad v Legia Warsaw (1-2, 0-8)	1-10
Leeds United v Lyn Oslo (10-0, 6-0)	16-0
CSKA Sofia v Ferencvaros (2-1, 1-4)	3-5
Real Madrid v Olympiakos Nicosia (8-0, 6-1)	14-1
Standard Liege v Nendori Tirana (1-1, 3-0)	4-1
Fiorentina v Oster Vaxjo (2-1, 1-0)	3-1
FK Austria v Dynamo Kiev (1-2, 1-3)	2-5
Benfica v KB Copenhagen (2-0, 3-2)	5-2
Basle v Celtic (0-0, 0-2)	0-2

SECOND ROUND

AC Milan v Feyenoord (1-0, 0-2)	1-2
ASK Vorwaerts* v Red S. Belgrade (2-1, 2-3)	4-4
Galatasaray† v Spartak Trnava (1-0, 0-1)	1-1
Legia Warsaw v St Etienne (2-1, 1-0)	3-1
Leeds United v Ferencvaros (3-0, 3-0)	6-0
Standard Liege v Real Madrid (1-0, 3-2)	4-2
Dynamo Kiev v Fiorentina (1-2, 0-0)	1-2
Celtic† v Benfica (3-0, 0-3)	3-3

QUARTER-FINALS

ASK Vorwaerts v Feyenoord (1-0, 0-2)	1-2
Galatasaray v Legia Warsaw (1-1, 0-2)	1-3
Standard Liege v Leeds United (0-1, 0-1)	0-2
Celtic v Fiorentina (3-0, 0-1)	3-1

SEMI-FINALS

Legia Warsaw v Feyenoord (0-0, 0-2)	0-2
Leeds United v Celtic (0-1, 1-2)	1-3

FINAL

Feyenoord 2 Celtic 1 [aet]
(Milan, 6.5.70, 53,187)

Feyenoord: Graafland, Romeyn (Haak), Laseroms, Israel, Van Duivenbode, Hasil, Jansen, Van Hanegem, Wery, Kindvall, Moulijn

Celtic: Williams, Hay, Gemmell, Murdoch, McNeill, Brogan, Johnstone, Lennox, Wallace, Auld (Connelly), Hughes

Scorers: Israel (31), Kindvall (117); Gemmell (29)

Feyenoord had hammered Reykjavik (Iceland) by a record 12-2 and then 4-0 in two Rotterdam ties, and later they accounted for Vorwaerts Berlin and Legia Warsaw.

For the first time, two British clubs reached the semi-finals—and had the misfortune to be drawn against each other. Leeds, chasing the League Championship, FA Cup and European Cup, had shown impressive strength in getting to the last four in their first European Cup: 16-0 over Lyn Oslo, 6-0 over Ferencvaros and 2-0 over Standard Liège, themselves surprise conquerors of Real Madrid. Celtic, after a 2-0 win over Basle, needed the right side of the coin to remove Benfica after both had 3-0 wins at home. They were more composed against Fiorentina, and then met a Leeds side exhausted by a three-game FA Cup semi-final against Manchester United. There was really only one team in it and the Scots, with a 1-0 win in Yorkshire and a 2-1 victory at home, moved on to their second European final.

In Milan, playing 4-2-4, a Celtic team containing seven 'Lisbon Lions' came up against Feyenoord's attacking brand of catenaccio and had no real answer. Israel, the sweeper, immediately answered Gemmell's tremendous free-kick goal, heading in from a free-kick, and the Dutch took over the midfield. The only surprise was that they could not affirm their control in the 90 minutes. But in extra time, Kindvall, the elegant Swedish centre-forward, chased a high lob on the left, McNeill tried to handle, missed, and Kindvall gave the Dutch horns something to honk about.

1970-71

This European Cup tournament was notable for the return of an old hero—Ferenc Puskas, the galloping major of Real Madrid. Now, however, he was manager of Greek club Panathinaikos, and true to form he reached the finals—at the expense, among others, of English champions Everton, beaten by their own ineptitude and the away goals rule. Everton's second round game against Borussia Moenchengladbach had been reduced to penalties. Of all the major English clubs, they have by far the worst record in Europe—and the quarter-final against the Greeks remains their best attempt in nine entries in the three competitions.

Holders Feyenoord went out on away goals to Arad (Rumania), but Ajax kept up the Dutch interest with wins over Nendori (Albania), Basle, Celtic, and, in the semi-finals, Atlético Madrid. Under the authoritarian control of Rinus Michels, Ajax's obvious promise had come to fruition. Cruyff was already the orchestrator—an emerging Di Stefano—Keizer was fast and dangerous on the left, Hulshoff a strong centre-half, and Vasovic an intelligent attacking sweeper. Against Atlético, there was a sign of another star: one of the three goals came from the young midfield player Johan Neeskens.

EUROPEAN CUP 1970-71

PRELIMINARY ROUND

Levski Spartak v FK Austria (3-1, 0-3)	3-4

FIRST ROUND

Nendori Tirana v Ajax (2-2, 0-2)	2-4
Spartak Moscow v Basle* (3-2, 1-2)	4-4
Glentoran v Waterford (1-3, 0-1)	1-4
Celtic v Kokkolan PV (9-0, 5-0)	14-0
IFK Gothenburg v Legia Warsaw (0-4, 1-2)	1-6
Rosenborg v Standard Liege (0-2, 0-5)	0-7
Cagliari v St Etienne (3-0, 0-1)	3-1
Atletico Madrid v FK Austria (2-0, 2-1)	4-1
Ujpest Dozsa v Red Star Belgrade (2-0, 0-4)	2-4
Feyenoord v UT Arad* (1-1, 0-0)	1-1
Sporting Lisbon v Floriana (5-0, 4-0)	9-0
Fenerbahce v Carl Zeiss Jena (0-4, 0-1)	0-5
Everton v KB Keflavik (6-2, 3-0)	9-2
Bor. M'gladbach v EPA Larnaca (6-0, 10-0)	16-0
Sl. Bratislava v Copenhagen BK 03 (2-1, 2-2)	4-3
Jeunesse Esch v Panathinaikos (1-2, 0-5)	1-7

SECOND ROUND

Ajax v Basle (3-0, 2-1)	5-1
Waterford v Celtic (0-7, 2-3)	2-10
Standard Liege v Legia Warsaw (1-0, 0-2)	1-2
Cagliari v Atletico Madrid (2-1, 0-3)	2-4
Red Star Belgrade v UT Arad (3-0, 3-1)	6-1
Carl Zeiss Jena v Sporting Lisbon (2-1, 2-1)	4-2
Borussia M'gladbach v Everton† (1-1, 1-1)	2-2
Panathinaikos v Slovan Bratislava (3-0, 1-2)	4-2

QUARTER-FINALS

Ajax v Celtic (3-0, 0-1)	3-1
Atletico Madrid* v Legia Warsaw (1-0, 1-2)	2-2
C. Zeiss Jena v Red Star Belgrade (3-2, 0-4)	3-6
Everton v Panathinaikos* (1-1, 0-0)	1-1

SEMI-FINALS

Atletico Madrid v Ajax (1-0, 0-3)	1-3
Red Star Belgrade v Panathinaikos* (4-1, 0-3)	4-4

FINAL

Ajax 2 Panathinaikos 0
Wembley, 2.6.71, 83,179)

Ajax: Stuy, Neeskens, Vasovic, Suurbier, Hulshoff, Rijnders (Blankenburg), Swart (Haan), G. Muhren, Cruyff, Van Dijk, Keizer

Panathinaikos: Oconomopoulos, Tomaras, Vlahos, Elefterakis, Kamaras, Sourpis, Grammos, Filakouris, Antoniadis, Domazos, Kapsis

Scorers: Van Dijk (5), Kapsis og (87)
*won on away goals rule †won on penalties

In the other semi-final, Panathinaikos did the seemingly impossible, beating Red Star Belgrade, coming back magnificently from 4-1 down in the away leg to tie 4-4 and go through on away goals.

Unfortunately Wembley (holding its third European Cup final in nine years) dwarfed the Greeks and Ajax, with only five survivors from the Madrid final two seasons before, were able to dictate at will after Van Dijk had headed in Keizer's cross after five minutes. As they were to show in the next two seasons, Ajax rarely let the scoreline reflect their superiority and it was not until the very end that substitute Haan added the second via Kapsis after a dazzling run by Cruyff.

After this triumph, Michels went to Spain and Barcelona, but he left behind an attractive, multi-talented side that was to grace the European Cup final for another two years.

EUROPEAN CUP 1971-72

PRELIMINARY ROUND

Valencia v US Luxembourg (3-1, 1-0)	4-1

FIRST ROUND

Ajax v Dynamo Dresden (2-0, 0-0)	2-0
Olym. Marseille v Gornik Zabrze (2-1, 1-1)	3-2
Lahden Reipas v Grasshoppers (1-1, 0-8)	1-9
Stromsgodset Drammen v Arsenal (1-3, 0-4)	1-7
Feyenoord v Olympiakos Nicosia (8-0, 9-0)	17-0
Dynamo Bucharest* v Sp. Trnava (0-0, 2-2)	2-2
CSKA Sofia v Partizan Tirana (3-0, 1-0)	4-0
Wacker Innsbruck v Benfica (0-4, 1-3)	1-7
Copenhagen BK 03 v Celtic (2-1, 0-3)	2-4
IA Akranes v Sliema Wanderers (0-4, 0-0)	0-4
Valencia* v Hajduk Split (0-0, 1-1)	1-1
Ujpest Dozsa v Malmo FF (4-0, 0-1)	4-1
Standard Liege v Linfield (2-0, 3-2)	5-2
Galatasaray v CSKA Moscow (1-1, 0-3)	1-4
Cork Hibernians v B. M'gladbach (0-5, 1-2)	1-7
Inter-Milan v AEK Athens (4-1, 2-3)	6-4

SECOND ROUND

Olympique Marseille v Ajax (1-2, 1-4)	2-6
Grasshoppers Zurich v Arsenal (0-2, 0-3)	0-5
Dynamo Bucharest v Feyenoord (0-3, 0-2)	0-5
Benfica v CSKA Sofia (2-1, 0-0)	2-1
Celtic v Sliema Wanderers (5-0, 2-1)	7-1
Valencia v Ujpest Dozsa (0-1, 1-2)	1-3
CSKA Sofia v Standard Liege (1-0, 1-2)	1-2
Inter-Milan v B. M'gladbach (4-2, 0-0)	‡4-2

QUARTER-FINALS

Ajax v Arsenal (2-1, 1-0)	3-1
Feyenoord v Benfica (1-0, 1-5)	2-5
Ujpest Dozsa v Celtic (1-2, 1-1)	2-3
Inter-Milan* v Standard Liege (1-0, 1-2)	2-2

SEMI-FINALS

Ajax v Benfica (1-0, 0-0)	1-0
Inter-Milan† v Celtic (0-0, 0-0)	0-0

FINAL

Ajax 2 Inter-Milan 0
(Rotterdam, 31.5.72, 61,354)

Ajax: Stuy, Suurbier, Blankenburg, Hulshoff, Krol, Neeskens, Haan, G. Muhren, Swart, Cruyff, Keizer

Inter: Bordon, Burgnich, Facchetti, Bellugi, Oriali, Bedin, Jair (Pellizzarro), Mazzola, Giubertoni (Bertini), Boninsenga, Frustalupi

Scorer: Cruyff (47,78)

*won on away goals rule †won on penalties after extra time ‡Borussia won first leg 7-1; replay ordered due to spectator violence (second leg played before replayed first leg) and played in West Berlin

Decked in Juventus shirts, Heinz Stuy, Johan Cruyff, Johnny Rep (with cup), Ruud Krol and Piet Keizer parade in front of the massive Belgrade crowd after completing Ajax's hat-trick in 1973.

1971-72

With a new manager, Stefan Kovacs, and a more self-expressive policy, Ajax flowed through to their third final in four years, though not without moments of anxiety for their supporters. Dynamo Dresden and Olympique Marseille were easily accounted for, but Arsenal, against the run of the game, could have held them to a 1-1 draw in Amsterdam but for a dubious penalty, and a Graham own goal was the only one at Highbury. Nor were Benfica, who had put out fellow countrymen Feyenoord in the previous round, any walkover in the semi-finals.

Elsewhere there were problems on and off the field, most notably in Moenchengladbach, where Inter's Boninsegna, having just made it 2-1, was knocked out by a can of Coca-Cola. Later, Corso was sent off for kicking the referee and Inter tumbled 7-1. UEFA's answer to Inter's protest was to annul the tie, and after winning 4-2 at San Siro, Inter packed their defence to draw the replayed leg in Berlin. Not content with that, the Italians then ran the gamut of escapologist possibilities: away goals against Standard Liège in the quarter-finals, penalties against Celtic in the semis.

In the Rotterdam final, Cruyff was having no nonsense. Ajax, now with Krol and Haan in their line-up, went on the attack from the start and it was only a matter of time before a tentative Inter, missing regular keeper Vieri and losing stopper Giubertoni, gave way. Cruyff himself scored both goals, taking advantage of a defensive muddle for the first and heading Keizer's free-kick for the second to give Holland a hat-trick.

1972-73

Another Dutch-Italian final saw Ajax back for the third consecutive time and the Italians represented by the multi-million lira Juventus, for whom Altafini, AC Milan's goalscorer in the 1963 final, had joined the expensive Pietro Anastasi in attack. Zoff was rejuvenated in goal.

Juventus, with 3-1 and 2-0 wins over Marseille and Magdeburg respectively, had quarter-final trouble with Ujpest Dozsa, who had beaten Celtic 4-2 in the previous round. Two goals from Anastasi in Hungary put the Italians into the semi-finals on away goals. There they met Brian Clough's Derby County who, beginning with a comfortable 4-1 win over Zeljeznicar (Yugoslavia), were most impressive, beating Benfica 3-0 at home and drawing 0-0 away. In Turin,

EUROPEAN CUP 1972-73

FIRST ROUND

CSKA Sofia v Panathinaikos (2-1, 2-0)	4-1
Waterford v Omonia Nicosia (2-1, 0-2)	2-3
Galatasaray v Bayern Munich (1-1, 0-6)	1-7
T-S Innsbruck v Dynamo Kiev (0-1, 0-2)	0-3
Sliema W. v Gornik Zabrze (0-5, 0-5)	0-10
Aris Bonnevoie v Arges Pitesti (0-2, 0-4)	0-6
Real Madrid v IB Keflavik (3-0, 1-0)	4-0
Derby County v Zeljeznicar (2-0, 2-1)	4-1
Malmo FF v Benfica (1-0, 1-4)	2-4
Anderlecht v Vejle BK (4-2, 3-0)	7-2
Ujpest Dozsa v Basle (2-0, 2-3)	4-3
Celtic v Rosenborg Trondheim (2-1, 3-1)	5-2
FC Magdeburg v Turun PS Turku (6-0, 3-1)	9-1
Olympique Marseille v Juventus (1-0, 0-3)	1-3

[Ajax (holders) and Spartak Trnava received byes]

SECOND ROUND

CSKA Sofia v Ajax (1-3, 0-3)	1-6
Omonia Nicosia v Bayern Munich (0-9, 0-4)	0-13
Dynamo Kiev v Gornik Zabrze (2-0, 1-2)	3-2
Arges Pitesti v Real Madrid (2-1, 1-3)	3-4
Derby County v Benfica (3-0, 0-0)	3-0
Spartak Trnava v Anderlecht (1-0, 1-0)	2-0
Celtic v Ujpest Dozsa (2-1, 0-3)	2-4
Juventus v FC Magdeburg (1-0, 1-0)	2-0

QUARTER-FINALS

Ajax v Bayern Munich (4-0, 1-2)	5-2
Dynamo Kiev v Real Madrid (0-0, 0-3)	0-3
Spartak Trnava v Derby County (1-0, 0-2)	1-2
Juventus* v Ujpest Dozsa (0-0, 2-2)	2-2

SEMI-FINALS

Ajax v Real Madrid (2-1, 1-0)	3-1
Juventus v Derby County (3-1, 0-0)	3-1

FINAL

Ajax 1 Juventus 0
(Belgrade, 30.5.73, 89,484)

Ajax: Stuy, Suurbier, Krol, Hulshoff, Blankenburg, Neeskens, Rep, Haan, Cruyff, G. Muhren, Keizer

Juventus: Zoff, Longobucco, Marchetti, Furino, Salvadore, Morini, Causio (Cuccureddu), Altafini, Anastasi, Bettega (Haller), Capello

Scorer: Rep (4)

*won on away goals rule

though, they allowed Altafini and Anastasi too much freedom and went down 3-1. Additionally they lost McFarland and Gemmill for the return, both receiving second bookings for the tournament. Worse was to come in Derby: Hinton missed a penalty and Davies was sent off in a goalless draw.

Ajax, meanwhile, had been putting down their pretenders. A bye and 3-1, 3-0 victories over CSKA Sofia brought them up against Bayern Munich, the nucleus of West Germany's great European Championship side. But in Amsterdam, goalkeeper Sepp Maier had one of his really bad days, and with four goals under their belt Ajax could afford to lose 2-1 in Munich. Real Madrid were no match for the highly tuned Dutch in the semi-finals and indeed were flattered by the 3-1 aggregate.

In Belgrade, Ajax fielded a virtually unchanged side from the one that beat Inter in 1972. Rep came in for Swart, and with less than five minutes gone he headed in Blankenburg's cross. And that was it. The Dutch dominated, delighted, infuriated; Cruyff, with his acceleration and control, baffled the Juventus defence but Muhren and Rep failed to exploit his openings. Juventus occasionally broke dangerously, but Stuy held firm in goal and Ajax, by no means at their most attractive, completed the first hat-trick since Real Madrid in the 1950s, winning 19 of their 26 games over the three seasons.

1973-74

It is said that one man doesn't make a team. But when Johan Cruyff went off to join Michels at Barcelona—for a then world record £922,300—Ajax went out of the European Cup in their first tie, losing 2-1 to CSKA Sofia.

For the first time in the competition's history, the final went to a replay: in the last seconds of the final, Schwarzenbeck stormed upfield to equalize from 30 yards out and give a lifeless Bayern Munich another shot at an Atlético Madrid who had shown a Jekyll and Hyde character in earlier rounds, and for whom victory would have been a travesty of football justice.

In the semi-finals, the Spanish side had gone to Celtic determined to draw—by any means. Three players sent off and three others cautioned reflects their cynical approach. All six were suspended for the return, where Atlético showed their other side, winning in style with excellent goals from Garate and Adelardo. Earlier victims had been Galatasaray (1-0), Dynamo Bucharest (4-2), and Red Star Belgrade (2-0). Red Star, in one of the finest exhibitions of attacking football seen in Britain, had beaten Liverpool 2-1 at Anfield for a 4-2 aggregate.

Bayern's campaign began intriguingly enough, needing penalties to remove Atvidaberg (Sweden) after winning the home leg 3-1. A missile from the crowd broke Breitner's shin, and Bayern claimed their own kind of compensation by luring away Torstensson, who had scored twice against them. He scored two for them in the quarter-final against CSKA Sofia and another in the semi-final with Ujpest Dozsa. A high-scoring second round tie had seen East meet West (a forerunner of the 1974 World Cup encounter) with Bayern beating Dynamo Dresden 7-6 on aggregate.

The final, the third in Brussels, was in extra time when Luis curled his free-kick past Maier, and it seemed the cup was going to Madrid again before Schwarzenbeck intervened. The replay two days later was all Bayern Munich: Hoeness and Müller dissected the Atlético defence, sharing four goals equally, while behind them Beckenbauer strolled supreme with aloof control.

Six of the Bayern side—Maier, Breitner, Beckenbauer, Schwarzenbeck, Hoeness and Müller—won World Cup winners' medals for West Germany a few weeks later.

EUROPEAN CUP 1973-74

FIRST ROUND

Bayern Munich* v Atvidaberg (3-1, 1-3)	4-4
Dynamo Dresden v Juventus (2-0, 2-3)	4-3
CSKA Sofia v T-S Innsbruck (3-0, 1-0)	4-0
Viking Stavanger v Sp. Trnava (1-2, 0-1)	1-3
Voroshilovgrad v Apoel Nicosia (2-0, 1-0)	3-0
Benfica v Olympiakos Piraeus (1-0, 1-0)	2-0
Waterford v Ujpest Dozsa (2-3, 0-3)	2-6
Turun PS Turku v Celtic (1-6, 0-3)	1-9
Vejle BK v Nantes (2-2, 1-0)	3-2
FC Bruges v Floriana (8-0, 2-0)	10-0
Fram Reykjavik v Basle (0-5, 2-6)	2-11
Red Star Belgrade v Stal Mielec (2-1, 1-0)	3-1
Jeunesse Esch v Liverpool (1-1, 0-2)	1-3
Crusaders v Dynamo Bucharest (0-1, 0-11)	0-12
Atletico Madrid v Galatasaray (0-0, 1-0)	1-0

[Ajax (holders) received bye]

SECOND ROUND

Bayern Munich v Dynamo Dresden (4-3, 3-3)	7-6
Ajax v CSKA Sofia (1-0, 0-2)	1-2
Spartak Trnava v Voroshilovgrad (0-0, 1-0)	1-0
Benfica v Ujpest Dozsa (1-1, 0-2)	1-3
Celtic v Vejle BK (0-0, 1-0)	1-0
FC Bruges v Basle (2-1, 4-6)	6-7
Red Star Belgrade v Liverpool (2-1, 2-1)	4-2
Dynamo Bucharest v A. Madrid (0-2, 2-2)	2-4

QUARTER-FINALS

Bayern Munich v CSKA Sofia (4-1, 1-2)	5-3
Spartak Trnava* v Ujpest Dozsa (1-1, 1-1)	2-2
Basle v Celtic (3-2, 2-4)	5-6
Red Star Belgrade v A. Madrid (0-2, 0-0)	0-2

SEMI-FINALS

Ujpest Dozsa v Bayern Munich (1-1, 0-3)	1-4
Celtic v Atletico Madrid (0-0, 0-2)	0-2

FINAL

Bayern Munich 1 Atletico Madrid 1
(Brussels, 15.5.74, 49,000)

Bayern: Maier, Hansen, Breitner, Schwarzenbeck, Beckenbauer, Roth, Torstensson (Durnberger), Zobel, Muller, Hoeness, Kapellmann

Atletico: Reina, Melo, Capon, Adelardo, Heredia, Eusebio, Ufarte (Becerra), Luis, Garate, Irueta, Salcedo (Alberto)

Scorers: Schwarzenbeck (120); Luis (95)

Replay (Brussels, 17.5.74, 40,000)

Bayern Munich 4 Atletico Madrid 0

Bayern: Unchanged
Atletico: Alberto for Irueta; Benegas and Becerra came on for Adelardo and Ufarte

Scorers: Hoeness (28,83), Muller (58,71)

*won on penalties

BELOW: ***The Bayern Munich players must have been as much relieved as jubilant after their replay victory over Atlético Madrid in the 1974 final; only a last-minute goal from Schwarzenbeck had saved the first game.***
BOTTOM: ***Atlético's Capon and Bayern's Kapellmann competing in Brussels.***

EUROPEAN CUP 1974-75

FIRST ROUND

Cork Celtic w.o. Omonia Nicosia (withdrew)	
Viking Stavanger v Ararat Erevan (0-2, 0-4)	0-6
Hvidovre v Ruch Chorzow (0-0, 1-2)	1-2
Jeunesse Esch v Fenerbahce (2-3, 0-2)	2-5
Hajduk Split v IB Keflavik (7-1, 2-0)†	9-1
St Etienne v Sporting Lisbon (2-0, 1-1)	3-1
VOEST Linz v Barcelona (0-0, 0-5)	0-5
Feyenoord v Coleraine (7-0, 4-1)	11-1
Valletta v HJK Helsinki (1-0, 1-4)	2-4
Univ. Craiova v Atvidaberg (2-1, 1-3)	3-4
Slovan Bratislava v Anderlecht* (4-2, 1-3)	5-5
Celtic v Olympiakos Piraeus (1-1, 0-2)	1-3
Levski Spartak v Ujpest Dozsa (0-3, 1-4)	1-7
Leeds United v FC Zurich (4-1, 1-2)	5-3

[Bayern Munich (holders) and FC Magdeburg received byes]

SECOND ROUND

Bayern Munich v FC Magdeburg (3-2, 2-1)	5-3
Cork Celtic v Ararat Erevan (1-2, 0-5)	1-7
Ruch Chorzow v Fenerbahce (2-1, 2-0)	4-1
Hajduk Split v St Etienne (4-1, 1-5)	5-6
Feyenoord v Barcelona (0-0, 0-3)	0-3
HJK Helsinki v Atvidaberg (0-3, 0-1)	0-4
Anderlecht v Olympiakos Piraeus (5-1, 0-3)	5-4
Ujpest Dozsa v Leeds United (1-2, 0-3)	1-5

QUARTER-FINALS

Bayern Munich v Ararat Erevan (2-0, 0-1)	2-1
Ruch Chorzow v St Etienne (3-2, 0-2)	3-4
Barcelona v Atvidaberg (2-0, 3-0)	5-0
Leeds United v Anderlecht (3-0, 1-0)	4-0

SEMI-FINALS

St Etienne v Bayern Munich (0-0, 0-2)	0-2
Leeds United v Barcelona (2-1, 1-1)	3-2

FINAL

Bayern Munich 2 Leeds United 0
(Paris, 28.5.75, 48,374)

Bayern: Maier, Durnberger, Andersson (Weiss), Schwarzenbeck, Beckenbauer, Roth, Torstensson, Zobel, Muller, Hoeness (Wunder), Kapellmann

Leeds: Stewart, Reaney, F. Gray, Bremner, Madeley, Hunter, Lorimer, Clarke, Jordan, Giles, Yorath (E. Gray)

Scorers: Roth (71), Muller (81)

*won on away goals rule †both legs played in Split

1974-75

The 1974-75 European Cup was to be remembered almost entirely for its final. After a decade of slowly building ambition Leeds United finally reached the pinnacle on 28 May in Paris, attempting to become only the second English club to win the European Cup. Only Manchester United had appeared in a final before them after nearly 20 years of Europe's premier competition.

But by the end of that evening they had experienced another of those terrible disasters which dogged Don Revie's teams. It was another runners-up spot to add to the array they had already accumulated in the previous decade in the League (five), the FA Cup (three), the Fairs Cup (one) and the Cup Winners Cup (one).

And yet again there seemed an element of unfairness. Lorimer scored what appeared to be a perfectly good goal only for the referee to disallow it as another Leeds player was in an offside position, a seemingly obvious penalty was turned down, and then Bayern scored two relatively late goals through Roth and the almost inevitable Müller to retain their hard-won trophy.

Memories of Chelsea, Sunderland, Arsenal and other disappointments gone by came back to the players and their fans and, in the aftermath, the Yorkshire side's supporters wrecked parts of the stadium and its environs. The incident was made much worse than it might have been by the zealous response of the French police, but it represented the absolute nadir of British soccer in Europe. It wasn't until Liverpool won in Rome and Forest in Munich that European police forces began to relax if their local sides were drawn against English clubs. The result for Leeds was a hefty ban from any European competition.

The final apart, it was an unmemorable series. Leeds had struggled against Zurich (losing in Switzerland) but then won every game but one against worthy opponents in Ujpest Dozsa, Anderlecht and Barcelona; the exception was a 1-1 draw in Spain. Bayern struggled, not finding fellow Germans Magdeburg easy, then losing in Russia to Ararat Erevan. A preview of the following year's final saw them squeeze past St Etienne in the semis and then return to Paris for a game which most who saw it would prefer to forget.

Frank Gray looks on as Johan Neeskens gets in a header for Barcelona in the first leg of the 1975 semi-final at Elland Road. Leeds, having put 14 goals past three good sides (Zurich, Ujpest Dozsa and Anderlecht) won 2-1 at home and drew in Spain to reach the final in Paris, where they were unlucky to lose to a below-par Bayern Munich.

EUROPEAN CUP FINALS

Year	Venue	Winners		Runners-up	
1956	Paris	Real Madrid	4	Stade de Reims	3
1957	Madrid	Real Madrid	2	Fiorentina	0
1958	Brussels	Real Madrid	*3	AC Milan	2
1959	Stuttgart	Real Madrid	2	Stade de Reims	0
1960	Glasgow	Real Madrid	7	Eintracht Frankfurt	3
1961	Berne	Benfica	3	Barcelona	2
1962	Amsterdam	Benfica	5	Real Madrid	3
1963	Wembley	AC Milan	2	Benfica	1
1964	Vienna	Inter-Milan	3	Real Madrid	1
1965	Milan	Inter-Milan	1	Benfica	0
1966	Brussels	Real Madrid	2	Partizan Belgrade	1
1967	Lisbon	Celtic	2	Inter-Milan	1
1968	Wembley	Manchester United	*4	Benfica	1
1969	Madrid	AC Milan	4	Ajax	1
1970	Milan	Feyenoord	*2	Celtic	1
1971	Wembley	Ajax	2	Panathinaikos	0
1972	Rotterdam	Ajax	2	Inter-Milan	0
1973	Belgrade	Ajax	1	Juventus	0
1974	Brussels	Bayern Munich	†4	Atletico Madrid	0
1975	Paris	Bayern Munich	2	Leeds United	0
1976	Glasgow	Bayern Munich	1	St Etienne	0
1977	Rome	Liverpool	3	Borussia M'gladbach	1
1978	Wembley	Liverpool	1	FC Bruges	0
1979	Munich	Nottingham Forest	1	Malmo FF	0
1980	Madrid	Nottingham Forest	1	SV Hamburg	0
1981	Paris	Liverpool	1	Real Madrid	0
1982	Rotterdam	Aston Villa	1	Bayern Munich	0
1983	Athens	SV Hamburg	1	Juventus	0

*after extra time †after 1-1 draw in Brussels

Franz Roth's free-kick beats St Etienne keeper Ivan Curkovic to settle the 1976 final at Hampden—and give a jaded Bayern their third consecutive success. Roth had also scored against Leeds in the 1975 final.

1975-76

The big question to be answered in the 1976 European Cup was whether Bayern Munich could emulate Real Madrid and Ajax and make it a hat-trick.

The core of their side had been together a long time now, and Maier, Schwarzenbeck, Beckenbauer, Hoeness and Müller had all played their parts in the European Championship win of 1972 and the World Cup victory of 1974.

Indeed, by 1976 Bayern were roundly being accused of losing interest in the domestic Bundesliga, concentrating on retaining their European club prize and, perhaps, on the European Championship.

In fact, Bayern had already handed over their Bundesliga title after three successive wins to Borussia Moenchengladbach, themselves now on the road to a League hat-trick. It is interesting to note that between Nuremberg in 1968 and Cologne in 1978 these two shared the West German championship, but although Borussia came out on top (five titles to Bayern's four) they never won the European Cup and reached only one final.

This season they went out in the quarter-finals, on the away goals rule, to Real Madrid, after beating Juventus in the previous round. West German pride was restored when Bayern, having scraped through the second round against Malmö with some dubious refereeing after losing away, emulated the quarter-final performance against Benfica by drawing away in Madrid and winning comfortably in Munich, with Gerd Müller scoring all three goals against Real.

St Etienne were the first French finalists in any European competition since Reims second appearance in the European Cup in 1959. Capturing the continent with their 'Allez Les Verts' car stickers, banners and flags their team took the impressive scalps of Rangers, Dynamo Kiev and PSV Eindhoven, coming back from a 2-0 defeat in Russia to win at home with an extra-time goal by golden boy Dominique Rocheteau.

Like Reims before them, St Etienne attacked, played well, and lost. Perhaps Rocheteau, not fully fit, should have been brought on earlier than the 83rd minute, when he replaced a player who had blown several good chances. But one had a feeling that Bayern, playing an extremely cautious and boring game, were going to get their hat-trick.

The deciding goal, in the 57th minute, followed a free-kick given when Janvion brought down Müller. Beckenbauer, restrained all night, touched the ball on to Roth, whose well placed shot beat the unfortunate Curkovic.

Bayern's side quickly broke up following this final and just four years later, as they contested the leadership of the West German League with SV Hamburg, only Horsmann, Durnberger and Rummenigge of the Hampden side were still playing.

England's representatives, Derby County, went out 6-5 on aggregate to Real Madrid despite a fine 4-1 win at home. This will always be remembered as Charlie George's game, when he scored a hat-trick of two penalties and a glorious left-footed volley. He also scored in the return, when Derby collapsed in the Bernabeu and lost 5-1.

By now the manager who had built that Derby side was 15 miles down the road, fashioning a new dream. That any East Midlands side should begin the next decade as holders of the European Super Cup—and that one Charlie George should score a crucial goal—would then have been thought just a little fanciful.

EUROPEAN CUP 1975-76

FIRST ROUND

Jeunesse Esch v Bayern Munich (0-5, 1-3)	1-8
Malmo FF† v FC Magdeburg (2-1, 1-2)	3-3
Ujpest Dozsa* v FC Zurich (4-0, 1-5)	5-5
Benfica v Fenerbahce (7-0, 0-1)	7-1
Bor. M'gladbach v T-S Innsbruck (1-1, 6-1)	7-2
CSKA Sofia v Juventus (2-1, 0-2)	2-3
Slovan Bratislava v Derby County (1-0, 0-3)	1-3
Real Madrid v Dynamo Bucharest (4-1, 0-1)	4-2
Linfield v PSV Eindhoven (1-2, 0-8)	1-10
Ruch Chorzow v PS Kuopion (5-0, 2-2)	7-2
RWD Molenbeek v Viking Stavanger (3-2, 1-0)	4-2
Valletta v Hajduk Split (0-5, 0-3)	0-8
Olympiakos Piraeus v Dynamo Kiev (2-2, 0-1)	2-3
Omonia Nicosia v Akranes (2-1, 0-4)	2-5
Rangers v Bohemians (4-1, 1-1)	5-2
KB Copenhagen v St Etienne (0-2, 1-3)	1-5

SECOND ROUND

Malmo FF v Bayern Munich (1-0, 0-2)	1-2
Benfica v Ujpest Dozsa (5-2, 1-3)	6-5
Borussia M'gladbach v Juventus (2-0, 2-2)	4-2
Derby County v Real Madrid (4-1, 1-5)	5-6
Ruch Chorzow v PSV Eindhoven (1-3, 0-4)	1-7
Hajduk Split v RWD Molenbeek (4-0, 3-2)	7-2
Dynamo Kiev v Akranes (3-0, 2-0)	5-0
St Etienne v Rangers (2-0, 2-1)	4-1

QUARTER-FINALS

Benfica v Bayern Munich (0-0, 1-5)	1-5
Bor. M'gladbach v Real Madrid* (2-2, 1-1)	3-3
Hajduk Split v PSV Eindhoven (2-0, 0-3)	2-3
Dynamo Kiev v St Etienne (2-0, 0-3)	2-3

SEMI-FINALS

Real Madrid v Bayern Munich (1-1, 0-2)	1-3
St Etienne v PSV Eindhoven (1-0, 0-0)	1-0

FINAL

Bayern Munich 1 St Etienne 0
(Hampden Park, 12.5.76, 63,279)

Bayern: Maier, Hansen, Schwarzenbeck, Beckenbauer, Horsmann, Roth, Durnberger, Kapellmann, Rummenigge, Muller, Hoeness

St Etienne: Curkovic, Repellini, Piazza, Lopez, Janvion, Bathenay, Santini, Larque, P. Revelli, H. Revelli, Sarramagna (Rocheteau)

Scorer: Roth (57)

*won on away goals rule †won on penalties

1976-77

At last England were to have another European champion—and in truly dramatic circumstances, with Liverpool coming within a whisker of bringing off an unprecedented treble of League, FA Cup and European Cup.

The final, against the club Liverpool had beaten in the 1973 UEFA Cup final, was a magnificent match. Twelve players survived from that encounter, and among them was Kevin Keegan, scourge of Borussia in the 1973 first leg and now wanting to make a real impression in his last match before joining SV Hamburg. It was also supposed to be farewell for Tommy Smith, but he stayed on for another fine season—having scored with a superb header to turn the game—and then only missed the 1978 European Cup final because of a foot injury.

Liverpool's performance in Rome was a wonderful response to the events of the previous Saturday, when they had lost the FA Cup final to Manchester United through a strange Jimmy Greenhoff goal, despite largely dominating the match. As Brian James of the *Daily Mail* observed in the dressing-room after that game: 'Other sides have lost a game, a chance, a bonus, a final. Liverpool have lost their place in history. One day some side may do this treble. Maybe even a side from Liverpool. But not these men. No-one even mentions how close they have just come to being only the fifth side in history to do the double.

'The silence is appalling. What *are* they thinking? Keegan stares across the room . . . looking into the past hour? Or his future? You sense the mood—self-accusation. All of them have done what they could, but a few have not done what they were capable of.'

Five days later they certainly did more than enough, shrugging off that massive Wembley disappointment to win one of the

best of all European finals. McDermott put Liverpool ahead with a superbly taken goal after one of his characteristic long runs into space, but early in the second half a mistake by Jimmy Case let in Danish star Allan Simonsen to score a well-taken goal.

The equalizer seemed to gee up Liverpool. They changed gear, and from a corner following several minutes of pressure Smith headed home. With five minutes left Bertie Vogts brought down the slippery Keegan and Phil Neal sent Kneib the wrong way to wrap it all up.

Keegan had enjoyed a glorious game against the man-for-man marking, even against one of the best in the world. and gave the Germans in the crowd—and millions more on television—a taste of what was to come as he took Hamburg to the Bundesliga title and succeeded Simonsen to become European Footballer of the Year two years running.

Liverpool's passage to the final had not been overly difficult, though they lost 1-0 away to Turkish champions Trabzonspor, and they met only one really class team. They were the previous year's runners-up St Etienne, already with two wins over tricky opposition and a clean sheet to their credit, in the quarter-finals. Liverpool played well in France, but they returned trailing to a Bathenay goal. At Anfield Keegan scored early with a strange curling cross from near the corner-flag, but Bathenay struck again with a fine 30-yarder; suddenly Liverpool, because of the away-goals rule, had to score twice in half-an-hour. They did it with goals from Ray Kennedy and David Fairclough, who so often over these two seasons of Liverpool dominance in Europe was to come on and score the vital goal, earning the nick-name 'super-sub'. It was these 30 minutes, in a sense, that more than any period decided it would be Liverpool to face Borussia in Rome.

Liverpool's semi-final against FC Zurich, conquerors of Rangers in the first round, was almost anti-climax. A 3-1 win in Switzerland made the return virtually a formality, and British fans were treated to the arrogant sight of an English club saving themselves for a crucial domestic game on the Saturday (in this case the FA Cup semi-final against neighbours Everton). In this context it's worth remembering that before this game English clubs had reached the same stage on no less than ten occasions—and only twice, with Manchester United in 1968 and Leeds in 1975—had they gone further.

Borussia Moenchengladbach, packed with internationals and on their way to a third successive German championship, left little to spare in reaching the final, relying on away wins against Torino and Bruges because of weaker form at home. Their relative lack of form, and certainly lack of conviction—it was rumoured that several players, including scoring machine Jupp Heynckes, were injured—appeared to follow them to the final.

Nevertheless they provided tough enough opposition; and in that Liverpool won in Italy, won in style after a real body blow five days before, and that their fans were magnificent in every sense, it was perhaps the best performance of any British side in the first 25 years of European competition.

EUROPEAN CUP 1976-77

FIRST ROUND	
Liverpool v Crusaders (2-0, 5-0)	7-0
Akranes v Trabzonspor (1-3, 2-3)	3-6
Dundalk v PSV Eindhoven (1-1, 0-6)	1-7
CSKA Sofia v St Etienne (0-0, 0-1)	0-1
Dynamo Dresden v Benfica (2-0, 0-0)	2-0
Ferencvaros v Jeunesse Esch (5-1, 6-2)	11-3
Sliema W. v Turun PS Turku* (2-1, 0-1)	2-2
Rangers v FC Zurich (1-1, 0-1)	1-2
Dynamo Kiev v Partizan Belgrade (3-0, 2-0)	5-0
Omonia Nicosia v PAOK Salonika (0-2, 1-1)	1-3
Viking Stavanger v Banik Ostrava (2-1, 0-2)	2-3
Koge BK v Bayern Munich (0-5, 1-2)	1-7
FC Bruges v Steaua Bucharest (2-1, 1-1)	3-2
Stal Mielec v Real Madrid (1-2, 0-1)	1-3
Torino v Malmo FF (2-1, 1-1)	3-2
Austria/WAC v Borussia M'gladbach (1-0, 0-3)	1-3
SECOND ROUND	
Trabzonspor v Liverpool (1-0, 0-3)	1-3
St Etienne v PSV Eindoven (1-0, 0-0)	1-0
Ferencvaros v Dynamo Dresden (1-0, 0-4)	1-4
FC Zurich v Turun PS Turku (2-0, 1-0)	3-0
Dynamo Kiev v PAOK Salonika (4-0, 2-0)	6-0
Banik Ostrava v Bayern Munich (2-1, 0-5)	2-6
Real Madrid v FC Bruges (0-0, 0-2)	0-2
Torino v Borussia M'gladbach (1-2, 0-0)	1-2
QUARTER-FINALS	
St Etienne v Liverpool (1-0, 1-3)	2-3
FC Zurich* v Dynamo Dresden (2-1, 2-3)	4-4
Bayern Munich v Dynamo Kiev (1-0, 0-2)	1-2
Borussia M'gladbach v FC Bruges (2-2, 1-0)	3-2
SEMI-FINALS	
FC Zurich v Liverpool (1-3, 0-3)	1-6
Dynamo Kiev v Bor. M'gladbach (1-0, 0-2)	1-2

FINAL

Liverpool 3 Borussia Moenchengladbach 1
(Rome, 25.5.77, 52,078)

Liverpool: Clemence, Neal, Jones, Smith, R. Kennedy, Hughes, Keegan, Case, Heighway, Callaghan, McDermott

Borussia: Kneib, Vogts, Klinkhammer, Wittkamp, Bonhof, Wohlers, (Hannes), Wimmer (Kulik), Stielike, Simonsen, Schaffer, Heynckes

Scorers: McDermott (29), Smith (67), Neal (pen-85); Simonsen (50)

*won on away goals rule

FAR LEFT: ***Tommy Smith, whose fine header restored Liverpool's lead, gets a lift after the 1977 final with Borussia Moenchengladbach in Rome—one of the finest in the history of the competition.***

LEFT: ***Terry McDermott had put the Football League champions ahead in the 29th minute when after a long run he converted Steve Heighway's pass into space (see diagram).***

1977-78

After the heady wine of Rome the cold beer of Wembley a year later was poor fare indeed. Champions Liverpool had home advantage and, like all teams who have enjoyed it in the final (with the exception of Reims in the first competition in 1956) they made it work to their advantage.

Later voted European Footballer of the Year, Allan Simonsen gave Borussia hope in Rome with a 50th-minute goal, but Liverpool—as they were to do in the 1978 semi-final—proved the tougher side. The same could be said of the 1973 UEFA Cup final.

For the second consecutive year, their opponents were a side they had already beaten recently in a UEFA Cup final, but despite the tight score this was not the dynamic Bruges of 1976, who had gone two goals up at Anfield. Much more of a threat were Borussia Moenchengladbach, who won the first leg of their semi-final 2-1 before going down, as they had done in the 1973 UEFA Cup final, 3-0 at Anfield. Five of the Borussia side—Vogts, Bonhof, Wimmer, Kulik and Heynckes—had played in all five European games against Liverpool, and by this stage must have been fairly sick of the sight of the red strip.

Unlike the West Germans, who took the UEFA Cup in both 1975 and 1979, Bruges would finish the decade without their name on a European trophy. Ernst Happel, their Austrian manager, was also the Dutch national boss, and it was to be a disappointing year for him, coming second in what must rank as the world's two most prestigious tournaments.

Bruges had played extremely well to get to Wembley, scoring twice in Madrid to thwart Atlético and holding talented Juventus to a single goal in Turin to win the semi-final with goals by Bastijns and Vandereycken. Happel was to come across ten of that Juventus side three months later in what was effectively a World Cup semi-final, when Holland met Italy in Buenos Aires, and he again outwitted them to reach another final.

But at least his Dutch side deserved to win, attacking for most of the match. Had it not been for the dismal display by Malmö a year later, Bruges would probably have gone down as the least memorable finalists of the

EUROPEAN CUP 1977-78

FIRST ROUND

Dynamo Dresden v Halmstad BK (2-0, 1-2)	3-2
Trabzonspor v Copenhagen BK 03 (1-0, 0-2)	1-2
Benfica† v Torpedo Moscow (0-0, 0-0)	0-0
Basle v T-S Innsbruck (1-3, 1-0)	2-3
Celtic v Jeunesse Esch (5-0, 6-1)	11-1
Red Star Belgrade v Sligo Rovers (3-0, 3-0)	6-0
Vasas Budapest v Bor. M'gladbach (0-3, 1-1)	1-4
Omonia Nicosia v Juventus (0-3, 0-2)	0-5
Valur Reykjavik v Glentoran (1-0, 0-2)	1-2
Levski Spartak v Slask Wroclaw (3-0, 2-2)	5-2
Lillestrom SK v Ajax (2-0, 0-4)	2-4
Dyn. Bucharest v Atletico Madrid (2-1, 0-2)	2-3
Dukla Prague v Nantes* (1-1, 0-0)	1-1
Floriana v Panathinaikos (1-1, 0-4)	1-5
PS Kuopion v FC Bruges (0-4, 2-5)	2-9

[Liverpool (holders) received bye]

SECOND ROUND

Liverpool v Dynamo Dresden (5-1, 1-2)	6-3
Benfica v Copenhagen BK 03 (1-0, 1-0)	2-0
Celtic v T-S Innsbruck (2-1, 0-3)	2-4
Red S. Belgrade v Bor. M'gladbach (0-3, 1-5)	1-8
Glentoran v Juventus (0-1, 0-5)	0-6
Levski Spartak v Ajax (1-2, 1-2)	2-4
Nantes v Atletico Madrid (1-1, 1-2)	2-3
FC Bruges v Panathinaikos (2-0, 0-1)	2-1

QUARTER-FINALS

Benfica v Liverpool (1-2, 1-4)	2-6
T-S Innsbruck v Bor. M'gladbach* (3-1, 0-2)	3-3
Ajax v Juventus† (1-1, 1-1)	2-2
FC Bruges v Atletico Madrid (2-0, 2-3)	4-3

SEMI-FINALS

Borussia M'gladbach v Liverpool (2-1, 0-3)	2-4
Juventus v FC Bruges (1-0, 0-2)	1-2

FINAL

Liverpool 1 FC Bruges 0
(Wembley, 10.5.78, 92,000)

Liverpool: Clemence, Neal, Hansen, Thompson, R. Kennedy, Hughes, Dalglish, Case (Heighway), Fairclough, McDermott, Souness

Bruges: Jensen, Bastijns, Krieger, Leekens, Maes (Volders), Cools, De Cubber, Vandereycken, Ku (Sanders), Simoen, Sorensen

Scorer: Dalglish (64)

*won on away goals rule †won on penalties

One good goal decided the disappointing 1978 final at Wembley, and it came via Liverpool's two new stars. Graeme Souness, chesting down a headed clearance, found time under pressure to push a neat ball through to fellow-Scot Kenny Dalglish. The £440,000 signing from Celtic accelerated a few yards and, as Jensen came out to close him down, clipped the ball over the advancing keeper (bottom picture) and inside the far post. It was the second time in three years that Liverpool had beaten Bruges in a European final; they had also met in the 1976 UEFA Cup.

decade. It took a lack-lustre Liverpool most of the match to break down a resolute Bruges defence inspired by the goalkeeping form of Danish international Jensen. After 64 minutes Kenny Dalglish, Keegan's successor as Liverpool's superstar and the sharpest forward playing in the Football League, settled it with a cool chip after being put through by another 'new boy', fellow Scot Graeme Souness.

If manager Bob Paisley had been unsuccessful in enticing Dalglish south to Anfield—the £440,000 fee was a record between British clubs—the Scottish international may well have had a very different season in Europe as Celtic, after hammering Jeunesse Esch of Luxembourg, lost 4-2 to Innsbruck in the second round. The previous appearance of Celtic in the competition had also seen them fail against poor opposition, when they lost 3-1 to Olympiakos of Greece in 1974-75.

Liverpool's progress to the 1978 final had relied on superb form at home, where their goal record was 12-2. They lost in both East Germany, to old enemies Dynamo Dresden, and in West Germany, to Borussia, and as they enjoyed a bye through the first round that left only one other opponent—a Benfica side that was but a shadow of the great team of the 1960s.

Their goal tally against the Portuguese champions began a sequence that brought 16 in six games up to the final, and the club's all-round strength is reflected in the fact that in those matches eight different names appeared on the scoresheet.

Nevertheless it was something of an anti-climatic affair, and the atmosphere was strangely subdued—not at all like that remarkable night 10 years before in the same stadium.

There was an uncertainty about Liverpool. Forest had just taken their League title and beaten them in the League Cup final. So both would be in the European Cup next year, with Liverpool going for the hat-trick. . . .

1978-79

This was the season of the unexpected: England duly won their third consecutive final, equalling the feats of Holland and West Germany and making the 1970s the total preserve of those three countries, but they did it with the 'wrong' club'.

Neither of the finalists had ever remotely approached such exalted heights in European competition, and yet between them they lost just one game on the way to Munich. Nottingham Forest became the first team for a dozen years to win the European Cup at the first attempt (Celtic and Inter-Milan were their only predecessors) and the first since Ajax in 1972 to win it without losing a match.

If you add to this the fact that just two years before Forest were a Second Division side, one that squeezed into the First in third place, and that their home town is by far the smallest ever to spawn the European champions, then the achievement ranks as one of the most remarkable, and certainly the least predicted, in the competition's history.

The fact that Forest would succeed where the likes of Arsenal, Everton, Leeds, Manchester City and Spurs had failed was surely beyond conjecture in the mid-1970s, when the club was bumping along the bottom of the Second Division.

Now they were in the European Cup. And the first round draw was amazing, the one game millions of Englishmen were hoping would be a classic final, or perhaps a heart-stopping semi-final: Forest v Liverpool.

For the first of what were really three European finals for Forest that season, they were in peak form, engaged in a run of 63 matches that saw just one defeat. Liverpool, for their remarkable part, had not been knocked out of Europe since Ferencvaros beat them on the away goals rule in the Cup Winners Cup second round in 1974-75—nearly four years before.

But 13 September 1978 was to be Forest's night. And it was a very special night for a 19-year-old called Garry Birtles, playing only his second first-class match, as he scored the first and, in the dying seconds, made a second for full-back Colin Barrett. Their goals proved more than enough; the tactics that Forest evolved to hold Bob Paisley's sides saw them through to a 0-0 draw, and Liverpool's dreams of emulating the hat-tricks of Ajax and Bayern were over.

By this stage the competition had a rather strange look about it: of the 16 sides left in the second round only one, Real Madrid, had ever even reached the final before, and they were soon to be eliminated by Grasshoppers—thanks mainly to three goals by Claudio Sulser.

Heavy going for John Robertson and Cologne's Harald Konopka at Nottingham in the 1979 semi-final. Forest went behind 2-0, pulled it round to 3-2, and then let the West Germans equalize. In the second leg, needing a victory, they won 1-0 through Ian Bowyer.

EUROPEAN CUP 1978-79

FIRST ROUND

Nottingham Forest v Liverpool (2-0, 0-0)	2-0
AEK Athens v Porto (6-1, 1-4)	7-5
Real Madrid v Progres Niedercorn (5-0, 7-0)	12-0
Grasshoppers Zurich v Valletta (8-0, 5-3)	13-3
Juventus v Rangers (1-0, 0-2)	1-2
Fenerbahce v PSV Eindhoven (2-1, 1-6)	3-7
Odense BK 09 v Lokomotiv Sofia (2-2, 1-2)	3-4
1FC Cologne v Akranes (4-1, 1-1)	5-2
Vlaznia v Austria/WAC (2-0, 1-4)	3-4
Linfield v Lillestrom SK (0-0, 0-1)	0-1
Omonia Nicosia v Bohemians* (2-1, 0-1)	2-2
Par. Belgrade v Dynamo Dresden† (2-0, 0-2)	2-2
FC Bruges v Wisla Krakow (2-1, 1-3)	3-4
Zbrojovka Brno v Ujpest Dozsa (2-2, 2-0)	4-2
Valkeakosken Haka v Dynamo Kiev (0-1, 1-3)	1-4
Malmo FF v AS Monaco (0-0, 1-0)	1-0

SECOND ROUND

AEK Athens v Nottingham Forest (1-2, 1-5)	2-7
Real Madrid v Grasshoppers* (3-1, 0-2)	3-3
Rangers v PSV Eindhoven (0-0, 3-2)	3-2
Lokomotiv Sofia v 1FC Cologne (0-1, 0-4)	0-5
Austria/WAC v Lillestrom SK (4-1, 0-0)	4-1
Bohemians v Dynamo Dresden (0-0, 0-6)	0-6
Zbrojovka Brno v Wisla Krakow* (2-2, 1-1)	3-3
Dynamo Kiev v Malmo FF (0-0, 0-2)	0-2

QUARTER-FINALS

Nottingham Forest v Grasshoppers (4-1, 1-1)	5-2
1FC Cologne v Rangers (1-0, 1-1)	2-1
Austria/WAC v Dynamo Dresden (3-1, 0-1)	3-2
Wisla Krakow v Malmo FF (2-1, 1-4)	3-5

SEMI-FINALS

Nottingham Forest v 1FC Cologne (3-3, 1-0)	4-3
Austria/WAC v Malmo FF (0-0, 0-1)	0-1

FINAL

Nottingham Forest 1 Malmo FF 0
(Munich, 30.5.79, 57,500)

Forest: Shilton, Anderson, Clark, McGovern, Lloyd, Burns, Francis, Bowyer, Birtles, Woodcock, Robertson

Malmo: Moller, R. Andersson, Jonsson, M. Andersson, Erlandsson, Tapper (Malmberg), Lungberg, Prytz, Kinnvall, Hansson (T. Andersson), Cervin

Scorer: Francis (45)

*won on away goals rule †won on penalties

Rangers were effectively acting as a brush for Forest, clearing their path to the final by first removing Juventus, UEFA Cup winners in 1977 and then PSV Eindhoven, UEFA Cup winners in 1978. The second success was particularly notable, the Scots winning 3-2 in Holland after a goalless draw at Ibrox to inflict the Dutch club's first home defeat in 23 years of European competition.

Meanwhile Forest moved easily past AEK Athens, Birtles picking up three more as Forest's fast, first-time style brought victory in Greece and a runaway win in Nottingham. The score against Grasshoppers now looks comfortable, too, but Forest went 1-0 down at the City Ground to a Sulser goal, saw Peter Shilton make a super save from the same player at 2-1, and really only made it safe with two goals in the dying minutes.

The real tie of the whole competition—and, given the last four, what most neutral observers were hoping would be the final—was the clash between Forest and West Germany's double winners 1FC Cologne. At Nottingham, Forest attacked with their usual energy, but were caught on the break twice inside 20 minutes, with Van Gool and Dieter Müller doing the damage.

Only ardent fans would have given Forest a prayer: 2-0 down to the West German double champions at home. But a tremendous fightback in the mud, bringing goals from Birtles, Bowyer and Robertson (a rare diving header superbly engineered by Birtles) gave Forest the lead, only for the hero of the previous round, Shilton, to make a hash of Japanese substitute Okudera's first kick of the match.

Cologne only had to draw in the Mungersdorf Stadion to go through, and with FK Austria/WAC favourites to beat Malmö in the other semi-final, the choice of Munich as the venue for the final looked perfect. But the best laid schemes of UEFA organizing committees can go astray: Malmö made it with the rather predictable scorelines of 0-0 and 1-0, and Forest played arguably the best football of their revival to not only hold Cologne but win 1-0, Birtles flicking on a corner for Ian Bowyer to head home.

The final was, to say the least, a disappointing one. The tactics of Malmö, with two key central defenders injured, were even more negative than usual, relying almost entirely on an offside trap and containment.

Forest, for their part, looked tired and frustrated by the continuous tight decisions against front runners Birtles and Woodcock (who would join Cologne later that year), as they tried to break the trap. It was left to Trevor Francis, Britain's first million pound player and appearing in his first European tie, to score the only goal.

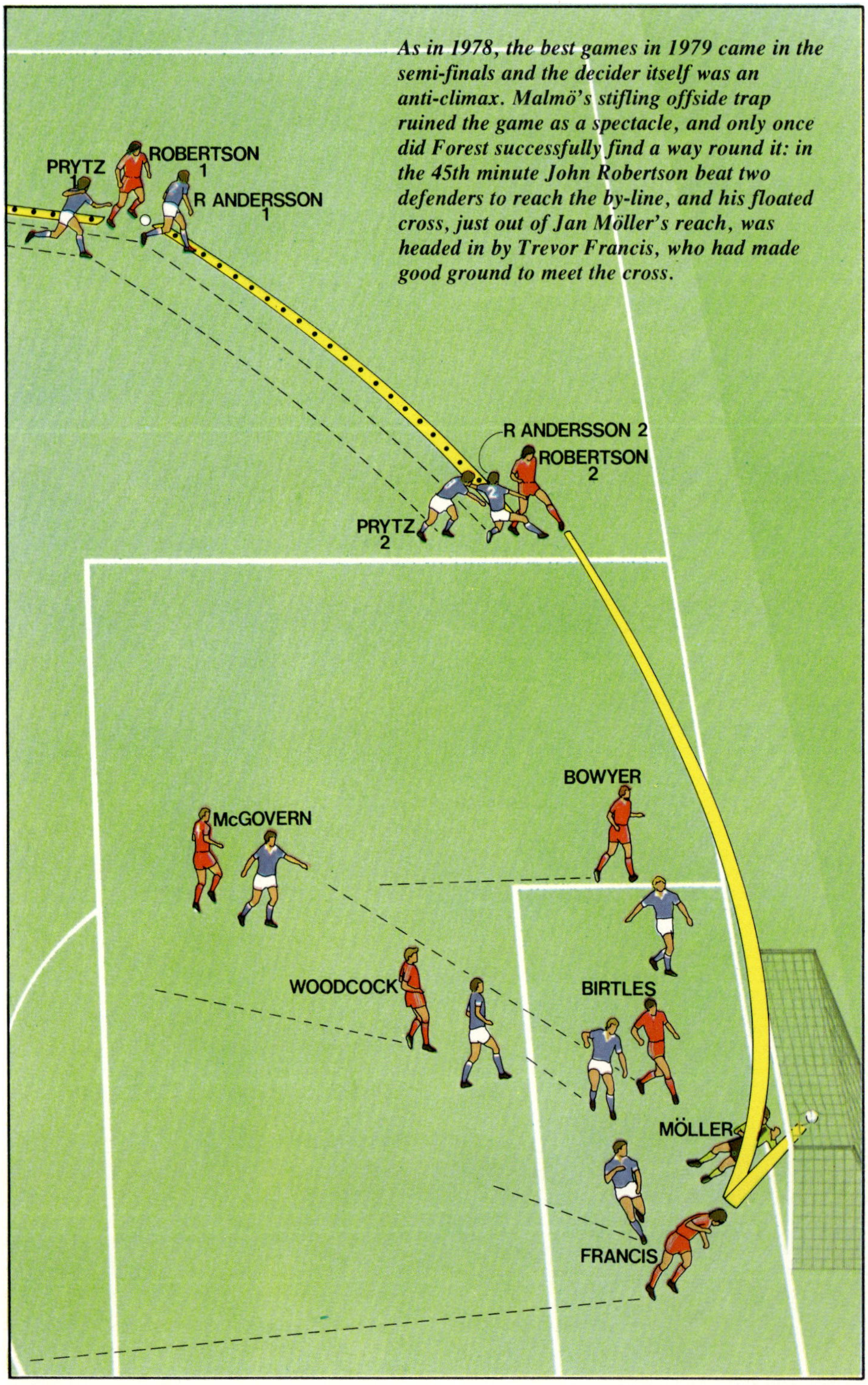

As in 1978, the best games in 1979 came in the semi-finals and the decider itself was an anti-climax. Malmö's stifling offside trap ruined the game as a spectacle, and only once did Forest successfully find a way round it: in the 45th minute John Robertson beat two defenders to reach the by-line, and his floated cross, just out of Jan Möller's reach, was headed in by Trevor Francis, who had made good ground to meet the cross.

Trevor Francis, the £1 million Forest signing playing his first European game, celebrates the goal that took the cup to Nottingham.

1979–80

Nottingham Forest gave the expression defending a trophy' a new dimension with their performance in the 1980 final against SV Hamburg, packing a retreating midfield with five players in a latter-day form of catennacio that set the European Cup back 15 years.

Then, the Inter-Milan sides of Helenio Herrera employed a sweeper and skilful players capable of breaking quickly and menacingly from midfield. Brian Clough and Peter Taylor, their thin resources already stretched to the limit by the tragic injury to Trevor Francis and the sad absence of Stan Bowles, were forced to rely on application, determination and stamina. And it worked.

Their defence played as well as any in the history of the competition, their midfield toiled as hard. Garry Birtles, marooned up front, wore himself into the ground. Peter Shilton was spectacularly secure in goal. And on a rare excursion into German territory John Robertson, shaking off Manny Kaltz and taking a well-won return pass from Birtles, steered his shot neatly to beat Rudi Kargus after 20 minutes and score the goal that would settle it.

Hamburg, endlessly probing, lacked the invention and flair that had characterized their semi-final win at home over Real Madrid. They had a Willi Reimann 'goal' disallowed only seconds after Forest had taken the lead (Kevin Keegan was just offside), but for the most part a superbly organized defence allowed them only long-range shots, the two best being from Peter Nogly (magnificently saved by Shilton) and Kaltz (struck the angle of bar and post).

Forest's strategy turns up trumps—and fuels a new European soccer debate

The confident Kaltz, a truly attacking full-back, always looked Hamburg's main danger once Kenny Burns had blotted out the menace of Keegan, playing his penultimate game for the club before leaving for Southampton.

While instant euphoria swept through the English media—after all it was the Football League's fourth success in four years—the press in Europe were as damning of Forest as they had been of Malmö, Forest's dour opponents in the final of 1979. Grudging acknowledgement of their resourcefulness and spirit was their only acclaim, and there was an understandable fear expressed of the nature of European club football in the 1980s. Only two weeks before, the continent had witnessed a dull, goalless 90 minutes in the Cup Winners Cup final, again with an English club involved.

The Madrid match was the third successive European Cup final won by an English club with a score of 1-0. The British sides—the distinction is largely irrelevant in Europe's eyes, and Forest began with four Scots and an Ulsterman in their line-up—once the liberators from Latin negativity with Celtic and Manchester United, were now accused of purveying the very stuff they had fought to conquer.

Forest's tactics were predictable, and there is more than a suspicion that they would have adopted the same basic pattern even with Francis fit, as they had done in the second leg of the semi-final against Ajax. Clough and Taylor claimed then they had been forced to play that way in defence of the 2-0 lead won in Nottingham with the help of a dubious penalty. But, quite apart from the basic psychological factors involved, they were under relatively little pressure in the first half. In the second, as they were to do in Madrid, they often just seemed to let their opponents dictate and come at them. This was not the team that had romped through Europe the previous season. Forest were to receive considerable criticism after both their wins, much of it misplaced. What was easily forgotten was that Nottingham was by far the smallest city ever to host a European Cup finalist. It was remarkable that a team, and one of two in the League, from a city less than one fifth the size of Manchester should have got so far.

The great awakening came in the quarter-finals. Forest's record in the European Cup to that date—nine wins, four draws, no defeats, 26 goals for and nine against—surpassed any run from the great days of Real Madrid. Dynamo Berlin's visit to Nottingham hardly seemed the likely moment for the unbeaten sequence to end, but after 63 minutes East German international star Reideger scored on a break and Forest, despite nearly all the play, could not claw their way back.

Skipper John McGovern holds the European Cup aloft after Forest had retained it with a controversial performance in Madrid.

They certainly missed Tony Woodcock in that task—this was their first European Cup tie without his services—but it may be that the sight of the East Germans jumping for joy at the end, having played nine men in defence and had perhaps 30% of the possession, had a profound effect on Forest's continually changing managerial strategy.

In the event it took a marvellous response by Francis to a typically adroit piece of Clough chastisement to see the holders home in Berlin, where through his two goals and a Robertson penalty they went 3-0 up in 38 minutes.

Liverpool and AC Milan crash but the other 'big four' all make the semi-finals

By this stage the competition had sifted the fancied clubs, and of the semi-finalists only SV Hamburg (though successful in the Cup Winners Cup) had never appeared in a Champions Cup decider. A notable absentee, however, was the Liverpool side leading the Football League. For the second successive season the 1977 and 1978 European champions had gone out in the first round, this time to a Dynamo Tbilisi team who deserved their passage with a fine win in Russia—despite the help of a crucial penalty from Chivadze, the man who had scored at Anfield to keep them in with a fair chance. In the next round Hamburg showed how it

EUROPEAN CUP 1979-80

PRELIMINARY ROUND

Dundalk v Linfield (1-1, 2-0)	3-1

FIRST ROUND

Nottingham Forest v Oester Vaxjo (2-0, 1-1)	3-1
Arges Pitesti v AEK Athens (3-0, 0-2)	3-2
Servette Geneva v Beveren-Waas (3-1, 1-1)	4-2
Dynamo Berlin v Ruch Chorzow (4-1, 0-0)	4-1
Start Kristiansand v R. Strasbourg (1-2, 0-4)	1-6
Ujpest Dozsa v Dukla Prague (3-2, 0-2)	3-4
Red Boys Differdange v O. Nicosia (2-1, 1-6)	3-7
HJK Helsinki v Ajax (1-8, 1-8)	2-16
Levski-Spartak v Real Madrid (0-1, 0-2)	0-3
Porto v AC Milan (0-0, 1-0)	1-0
Dundalk v Hibernians Valletta (2-0, 0-1)	2-1
Partizan Tirana v Celtic (1-0, 1-4)	2-4
Hajduk Split v Trabzonspor (1-0, 1-0)	2-0
Vejle BK v FK Austria/WAC (3-2, 1-1)	4-3
Liverpool v Dynamo Tbilisi (2-1, 0-3)	2-4
Valur Reykjavik v SV Hamburg (0-3, 1-2)	1-5

SECOND ROUND

Nottingham Forest v Arges Pitesti (2-0, 2-1)	4-1
Dynamo Berlin v Servette (2-1, 2-2)	4-3
Dukla Prague v Racing Strasbourg (1-0, 0-2)	1-2
Ajax v Omonia Nicosia (10-0, 0-4)	10-4
Porto v Real Madrid* (2-1, 0-1)	2-2
Celtic v Dundalk (3-2, 0-0)	3-2
Vejle BK v Hajduk Split (0-3, 2-1)	2-4
SV Hamburg v Dynamo Tbilisi (3-1, 3-2)	6-3

QUARTER-FINALS

Nottingham F. v Dynamo Berlin (1-0, 2-3)	3-2
Racing Strasbourg v Ajax (0-0, 0-4)	0-4
Celtic v Real Madrid (2-0, 0-3)	2-3
SV Hamburg* v Hajduk Split (1-0, 2-3)	3-3

SEMI-FINALS

Nottingham Forest v Ajax (2-0, 0-1)	2-1
Real Madrid v SV Hamburg (2-0, 1-5)	3-5

FINAL

Nottingham Forest 1 SV Hamburg 0
(Madrid, 28.5.80, 50,000)

Forest: Shilton, Anderson, Gray (Gunn 83), McGovern, Lloyd, Burns, O'Neill, Bowyer, Birtles, Mills (O'Hare 67), Robertson

Hamburg: Kargus, Kaltz, Nogly, Jakobs, Buljan, Memering, Keegan, Hieronymous (Hrubesch 46), Milewski, Magath, Reimann

Scorer: Robertson (20)

Leading scorers: 10— Lerby *(Ajax)*; 7— Blanker *(Ajax)*, Hrubesch *(Hamburg)*; 6— Kajafas *(Omonia Nicosia)*; 4— Arnesen, Krol *(Ajax)*, Robertson *(Nottingham Forest)*

*won on away goals rule

should be done with victories in both legs, Keegan scoring in each.

Another famous name to come a cropper at the first hurdle was AC Milan, beaten by a Duda goal for Porto at the Giuseppe Meazza stadium at the beginning of a miserable season that would see them relegated from Serie A after the bribery scandal that rocked Italy.

In a tournament littered with home leads thrown away, perhaps the biggest culprits were Celtic. After surviving a shock defeat in Albania and struggling through by the odd goal in five against Dundalk, the Scottish champions seemed to have at last struck form with a 2-0 win over Real Madrid in Glasgow, McCluskey and Doyle getting the goals. But at Chamartin a woeful defensive display let in Santillana, Stielike and, just five minutes from extra time, Juanito.

In their turn Real, with two Santillana goals in Madrid against Hamburg, looked to have booked a place in a final on their own ground against Ajax or Forest. In the second leg, however, the West German champions turned on what was probably the best display of the series. Over 61,000 (still less than half the first leg crowd) saw Keegan shake off Perez Garcia, so effective as his marker in Madrid, and the Englishman tormented Real—so much so that Vincente Del Bosque was sent off for punching him five minutes from time.

Two goals from Kaltz, the first a penalty after the frustrated Garcia brought down Keegan, two from the giant striker Horst Hrubesch (taking his competition tally to seven) and one from Caspar Memering ruined Real's dream of repeating the club's 1957 success with a final appearance at home, Laurie Cunningham's beautifully lobbed goal being scant compensation.

The Bernabeu Stadium is less than half full for Europe's club football showpiece

When the Hamburg players returned to Madrid five weeks later it was to a Bernabeu Stadium less than half full. Perhaps the Spanish capital's football public were peeved. Perhaps they knew that after two dreary 1-0 results it was unlikely to be third time lucky. The few thousand who did go were left to mourn the passing of Di Stefano and Gento, Puskas and Kopa—in their more generous moments of Eusebio, Best, Beckenbauer and Cruyff—while for England it was left to Ron Greenwood to try to add admiration to the considerable if begrudging respect earned by Brian Clough.

The goal that decided the 1980 final: Ian Bowyer holds off as John Robertson lets fly from the edge of the Hamburg area.

Kevin Keegan after being awarded his second consecutive European Footballer of the Year trophy at the end of 1979. The award is actually made in December each year and, five months later, Keegan was to be in the Hamburg side which lost the 1980 European Cup final.

1980-81

Nottingham Forest's two year reign as European champions came to an abrupt end in the first round, but the re-emergence of Liverpool as a force in the tournament ensured that the trophy remained in England for a fifth successive season.

Forest had been quite content to return from a first leg in Bulgaria trailing to a solitary goal from Yonchev for CSKA Sofia. At the City Ground, however, Kerimov added to that lead and in a puzzling performance from Brian Clough's side the holders could not redress the balance.

Liverpool exacted substantial revenge in the quarter-final. Graeme Souness, who had already claimed one hat-trick in a 10-1 first round, second leg annihilation of Oulun Palloseura of Finland, contributed another as CSKA were overwhelmed 5-1 at Anfield. A typically thorough Liverpool away display, and a goal from David Johnson,

EUROPEAN CUP 1980-81

PRELIMINARY ROUND

Honved v Valletta (8-0, 3-0)	11-0

FIRST ROUND

Linfield v Nantes (0-1, 0-2)	0-3
Aberdeen v Austria Vienna (1-0, 0-0)	1-0
Bruges v Basel (0-1, 1-4)	1-5
CSKA Sofia v Nottingham Forest (1-0, 1-0)	2-0
Dynamo Berlin v Apoel (3-0, 1-2)	4-2
Dynamo Tirana v Ajax (0-2, 0-1)	0-3
Inter-Milan v Uni Craiova (2-0, 1-1)	3-1
Jeunesse Esch v Moscow Spartak (0-5, 0-4)	0-9
Limerick v Real Madrid (1-2, 1-5)	2-7
Olympiakos v Bayern Munich (2-4, 0-3)	2-7
OPS Oulu v Liverpool (1-1, 1-10)	2-11
Sporting Lisbon v Honved (0-2, 0-1)	0-3
Trabzonspor v Szombierki Bytom (2-1, 0-3)	2-4
Viking Stavanger v Red Star Belgrade (2-3, 1-4)	3-7
IBV Vestmannayjar v Banik Ostrava (1-1, 0-1)	1-2
Halmstad v Esbjerg (0-0, 2-3)	2-3

SECOND ROUND

Nantes v Inter-Milan (1-2, 1-1)	2-3
Aberdeen v Liverpool (0-1, 0-4)	0-5
Basel v Red Star Belgrade (1-0, 0-2)	1-2
CSKA Sofia v Szombierki Bytom (4-0, 1-0)	5-0
Banik Ostrava* v Dynamo Berlin (0-0, 1-1)	1-1
Bayern Munich v Ajax (5-1, 1-2)	6-3
Real Madrid v Honved (1-0, 2-0)	3-0
Moscow Spartak v Esbjerg (3-0, 0-2)	3-2

QUARTER-FINALS

Liverpool v CSKA Sofia (5-1, 1-0)	6-1
Bayern Munich v Banik Ostrava (2-0, 4-2)	6-2
Inter-Milan v Red Star Belgrade (1-1, 1-0)	2-1
Moscow Spartak v Real Madrid (0-0, 2-0)	2-0

SEMI-FINALS

Liverpool* v Bayern Munich (0-0, 1-1)	1-1
Real Madrid v Inter-Milan (2-0, 0-1)	2-1

FINAL

Liverpool 1 Real Madrid 0
(Paris 27.5.81, 48,360)

Liverpool: Clemence, Neal, A. Kennedy, Thompson, R. Kennedy, Hansen, Dalglish (Case), Lee, Johnson, McDermott, Souness

Real Madrid: Rodriguez, Garcia Cortes, Camacho, Stielike, Sabido (Pineda), Del Bosque, Juanito, De Los Santos, Santillana, Navajas, Cunningham

Scorer: A. Kennedy

*won on away goals rule

LEFT: ***Liverpool skipper Phil Thompson holds the European Cup aloft for the third time in five years at Paris's Parc des Princes.***

ABOVE: ***David Johnson is beaten by a Real challenge. Full-back Alan Kennedy scored the game's only goal with just 8 minutes left.***

EUROPEAN CUP 1981-82

PRELIMINARY ROUND

St. Etienne v Dynamo Berlin (1-1, 0-2)	1-3

FIRST ROUND

Oster v Bayern Munich (0-1, 0-5)	0-6
Widzew Lodz v Anderlecht (1-4, 1-2)	2-6
Dynamo Berlin* v Zurich (2-0, 1-3)	3-3
Ferencvaros v Banik Ostrava (3-2, 0-3)	3-5
Celtic v Juventus (1-0, 0-2)	1-2
Hibernians v Red Star Belgrade (1-2, 1-8)	2-10
OPS Oulu v Liverpool (0-1, 0-7)	0-8
Benfica v Omonia Nicosia (3-0, 1-0)	4-0
Austria Vienna v Partizani (3-1, 0-1)	3-2
Dynamo Kiev v Trabzonspor (1-0, 1-1)	2-1
Start v AZ'67 Alkmaar (1-3, 0-1)	1-4
Progres Niedercorn v Glentoran (1-1, 0-4)	1-5
KB Copenhagen* v Athlone Town (1-1, 2-2)	3-3
CSKA Sofia v Real Sociedad (1-0, 0-0)	1-0
Uni. Craiova v Olympiakos (3-0, 0-2)	3-2
Aston Villa v Valur (5-0, 2-0)	7-0

SECOND ROUND

Benfica v Bayern Munich (0-0, 1-4)	1-4
Anderlecht v Juventus (3-1, 1-1)	4-2
AZ'67 Alkmaar v Liverpool (2-2, 2-3)	4-5
CSKA Sofia v Glentoran (2-0, 1-2)	3-2
KB Copenhagen v Uni. Craiova (1-0, 1-4)	2-4
Banik Ostrava v Red Star Belgrade (3-1, 0-3)	3-4
Austria Vienna v Dynamo Kiev (0-1, 1-1)	1-2
Dynamo Berlin v Aston Villa* (1-2, 1-0)	2-2

QUARTER FINALS

Uni. Craiova v Bayern Munich (0-2, 1-1)	1-3
Anderlecht v Red Star Belgrade (2-1, 2-1)	4-2
Liverpool v CSKA Sofia (1-0, 0-2)	1-2
Dynamo Kiev v Aston Villa (0-0, 0-2)	0-2

SEMI-FINALS

CSKA Sofia v Bayern Munich (4-1, 0-4)	4-5
Aston Villa v Anderlecht (1-0, 0-0)	1-0

FINAL

Aston Villa 1 Bayern Munich 0
(Rotterdam, 26.5.82, 46,000)

Aston Villa: Rimmer (Spink), Swain, Williams, Evans, McNaught, Mortimer, Bremner, Shaw, Withe, Cowans, Morley

Bayern Munich: Muller, Dremmler, Horsmann, Weiner, Augenthaler, Kraus (Niedermayer), Durnburger, Breitner, Hoeness, Mathy (Guttler), Rummenigge

Scorer: Withe

*won on away goals

made certain that there would be no fall from grace in the return.

Liverpool had already announced their intentions with a masterful victory over Aberdeen in the second round, five goals overall without reply. In the semi-final they were paired with Bayern Munich, whose pedigree had been aptly illustrated by 19 goals in their six matches to reach the last four, with Karl-

Liverpool are back and a full-back's goal beats mighty Real Madrid

Heinz Rummenigge and Dieter Hoeneṣs, brother of Uli, a formidable strike force.

Neither could score at Anfield, but nor could Liverpool. But in the Olympic Stadium in Munich, the lessons of 17 consecutive European seasons were firmly on show from Bob Paisley's team. Ray Kennedy gave Liverpool the lead in a breakaway in the second half, and though Rummenigge equalised close to time, the away goal put out Bayern.

A sense of history was added to the final by the appearance of Real Madrid, conquerors of Europe for the first five years of the competition and now in their first Champions Cup final for fifteen years. They included a West German, Stielike, a black Londoner, Cunningham and a sprinkling of experienced Spanish internationals, Camacho, Del Bosque, Juanito and Santillana.

In the splendid theatre of the Parc des Princes in Paris, the match itself lacked spectacle. Both sides plotted a cautious path until 8 minutes from extra time, one of Liverpool's unsung heroes produced the winning goal. Left-back Alan Kennedy had not convinced all on Merseyside that his bustling style was suited to Anfield, but with a typical show of enterprise his angled drive ensured his place in Liverpool's history.

1981-82

On May 26th 1982 Aston Villa, in their first tilt at the European Cup, overcame Bayern Munich in Rotterdam and wrote a fairytale for their manager Tony Barton.

At 44, Barton had been Villa's chief scout the previous February when Ron Saunders, who had guided the club to their first Football League title for 71 years, resigned. Barton, one of the game's most likeable servants, had been asked to hold the reins. To all, including himself, it was to be a temporary post. Three and a half months later, and with a three year contract to his name,

Barton was holding the European Cup.

Villa passed through the first two rounds under Saunders, despite a hiccough at home to Dynamo Berlin. In the quarter-final, which to cynical minds saw more than a quirk of fate in a draw which for the second season ensured that none of the four Eastern European qualifiers met another, Villa were solid in a 0-0 draw away to Dynamo Kiev. Goals at Villa Park from the young, blond Gary Shaw and the strong central defender Ken McNaught took the side now run by Barton into the last four.

The semi-final did leave a mark which scarred Villa's later triumph. Anderlecht, the Belgian champions, had looked the better side in Birmingham though losing to a Tony Morley goal. In Brussels lack of segregation in the crowd produced fighting

Villa survive a fan on the pitch to draw 0-0 in Brussels

on the terraces which spilt on to the pitch. The delay did not disturb Villa's concentration in a disciplined performance which kept the second leg goalless. In defeat, however, Anderlecht demanded that, because of the behaviour of some of their followers, Villa should be expelled from the competition. A week later UEFA fined Villa £14,500, Anderlecht £4,375, but the result was confirmed.

While Villa were making progress, Celtic had not been able to overcome a difficult first round draw against Juventus, the veteran Roberto Bettega claiming the winning goal in Turin. Liverpool, too, had lost their grip on the trophy. Maybe the signs had been there in the second round, when a late goal from Alan Hansen was required to put out AZ'67 from Alkmaar in Holland. In the quarter-final, however, there was no redress from mistakes by their new goalkeeper Bruce Grobbelaar in Sofia against CSKA. Mark Lawrenson was sent off in Liverpool's unavailing attempt to stay in the competition.

CSKA should have reached the final when they led Bayern 3-0 after just 17 minutes of the first leg. The West Germans battled back to a 4-3 defeat and then scored four goals—two each from Breitner and Rummenigge—without reply in Múnich.

A twenty-three year old goalkeeper in only his second senior game made sure that Bayern would not capture tht scoring touch in the final in Rotterdam. Called on after only eight minutes because of injury to Jimmy Rimmer, Nigel Spink made a number of critical saves to add to the unreal feeling about Villa's success. Peter Withe, the battering-ram centre-forward, sliced in the winning goal in the 67th minute. Jimmy Rimmer's was the oddest story, for he had now won two European Cup winners' medals for playing 8 minutes—the first was on the substitutes' bench for Manchester United 14 years before in 1968 at Wembley.

1982-83

After six consecutive years of triumph the European Cup finally slipped out of English hands to be collected by those of West Germany. Hamburg reclaiming the trophy that last went to that country in 1976.

The two-pronged challenge of Aston Villa

Jimmy Rimmer wins a second European Cup medal for 8 minutes play

and Liverpool did not survive the quarter-final. Villa's attempts to retain the title had begun in the strange setting of a home leg behind closed doors against Besiktas from Turkey—part of the UEFA punishment for the crowd trouble the previous season against Anderlecht in Brussels. A 6-2 aggregate success against Dynamo Bucharest in

EUROPEAN CUP 1982-83

PRELIMINARY ROUND	
Dynamo Bucharest v Valerengen (3-1, 1-2)	4-3
FIRST ROUND	
Dynamo Berlin v Hamburg (1-1, 0-2)	1-3
Dundalk v Liverpool (1-4, 0-1)	1-5
Aston Villa v Beziktas (3-1, 0-0)	3-1
Avenir Beggen v Rapid Vienna (0-5, 0-8)	0-13
Celtic v Ajax (2-2, 2-1)	4-3
Dynamo Bucharest v Dukla Prague (2-0, 1-2)	3-2
Dynamo Zagreb v Sporting Lisbon (1-0, 0-3)	1-3
Grasshoppers v Dynamo Kiev (0-1, 0-3)	0-4
Hibernians v Widzew Lodz (1-4, 1-3)	2-7
Monaco v CSKA Sofia (0-0, 0-2)	0-2
Nendori Tirana* v Linfield (1-0, 1-2)	2-2
Omonia Nicosia v JK Helsinki (2-0, 0-3)	2-3
Vikingur v Real Sociedad (0-1, 2-3)	2-4
Standard Liege v Raba Gyor (5-0, 0-3)	5-3
Olympiakos v Oster (2-0, 0-1)	2-1
Hvidore v Juventus (1-4, 3-3)	4-7
SECOND ROUND	
Hamburg v Olympiakos (1-0, 4-0)	5-0
JK Helsinki v Liverpool (1-0, 0-5)	1-5
CSKA Sofia v Sporting Lisbon* (2-2, 0-0)	2-2
Dynamo Bucharest v Aston Villa (0-2, 2-4)	2-6
Rapid Vienna v Widzew Lodz (2-1, 3-5)	5-6
Real Sociedad v Celtic (2-0, 1-2)	3-2
Dynamo Kiev v Nendori Tirana (walk-over)	
Standard Liege v Juventus (1-1, 0-2)	1-3
QUARTER-FINALS	
Dynamo Kiev v Hamburg (0-3, 2-1)	2-4
Sporting Lisbon v Real Sociedad (1-0, 0-2)	1-2
Widzew Lodz v Liverpool (2-0, 2-3)	4-3
Aston Villa v Juventus (1-2, 1-3)	2-5
SEMI-FINALS	
Real Sociedad v Hamburg (1-1, 1-2)	2-3
Juventus v Widzew Lodz (2-0, 2-2)	4-2

FINAL

Hamburg 1 Juventus 0
(Athens, 25.5.83, 80,000)

Hamburg: Stein, Kaltz, Wehmeyer, Jakobs, Hieronymus, Rolff, Milewski, Groh, Hrubesch, Magath, Bastrup (Von Heesen)

Juventus: Zoff, Gentile, Cabrini, Bonini, Brio, Scirea, Bettega, Tardelli, Rossi (Marocchino), Platini, Boniek

Scorer: Magath

*won on away goals

ABOVE: ***Peter Withe pokes the ball over the line in the 67th minute of the 1982 European Cup final to give Aston Villa their surprising success. Withe's shot has to be reckoned a lucky one—with an empty goal it still went in off the post. Villa's win over Bayern Munich was largely due to 23-year-old Nigel Spink's excellent keeping in only his second senior game; he came on after Rimmer was forced to retire.***
LEFT: ***A joyous Villa throng surrounds goalscorer Withe.***

the second round gave signs that their momentum was undisturbed, but Juventus fashioned a deadly blow in the opening moments of the first leg of the quarter-final at Villa Park. Villa never recovered from that early strike by Paolo Rossi, and 5-2 was the eventual margin of victory for Juventus.

Liverpool's path to the quarter-final was untroubled against Dundalk and JK Helsinki, but unhappily another error by Grobbelaar against Widzew Lodz brought the Polish champions back to Anfield with a two-goal advantage. After Phil Neal's penalty had lifted hopes of a recovery, Grobbelaar conceded a penalty, and Liverpool could find no route to safety. Smolarek, the Polish international forward,

Hamburg win at long last with the sixth consecutive 1-0 score

was outstanding in both matches.

Nor were Scotland's representative, Celtic, around to take up the slack. A splendid win in Amsterdam against Ajax—with goals from the prolific Charlie Nicholas and George McCluskey—had been followed by defeat at the hands of Real Sociedad in a tight contest.

Juventus—with their former Widzew player Zbigniew Boniek—made first leg home advantage count against the Poles in the semi-final. Hamburg built their platform with a 1-1 draw in San Sebastian against Real Sociedad, and scraped through at home.

The new Olympic Stadium in Athens provided a perfect setting for the final. With six members of Italy's World Cup, winning side plus Boniek and the gifted Frenchman Michel Platini, Juventus were well fancied. Hamburg could boast the influence of Manny Kaltz, Felix Magath, the strength of Horst Hrubesch and most significantly the inspiration of their coach Ernst Happel.

Happel's sad face belies the nature of a man who enjoys life to the full and has a gambler's instincts. His side did not betray him. Magath's goal arrived after only 9 minutes—a wickedly curling shot which totally deceived Dino Zoff—but for the sixth year in a row one goal was enough to win the European Cup. Yet again, Europe was not really treated to a spectacle worthy of the occasion and it was one that would probably be remembered in the history books as the game Juventus were expected to win and didn't.

Carlos Rexach (number 7) hits Barcelona's third goal in their famous 4-3 defeat of Fortuna Dusseldorf in the 1979 European Cup Winners' Cup final, played in Basle. It was one of the better European finals and came exactly ten years to the week after Barcelona had lost 3-2 to Slovan Bratislava in the same final in the same stadium.

EUROPEAN CUP WINNERS CUP 1965-66

FIRST ROUND

Floriana v Borussia Dortmund (1-5, 0-8)	1-13
Limerick v CSKA Sofia (1-2, 0-2)	1-4
Wiener Neustadt v Stinta Cluj (0-1, 0-2)	0-3
Atletico Madrid v Dynamo Zagreb (1-0, 4-0)	5-0
Sion v Galatasaray (5-1, 1-2)	6-3
Magdeburg Auf. v Spora Luxemb'g (1-0, 2-0)	3-0
Omonia Nicosia v Olym. Piraeus (0-1, 1-1)	1-2
Go Ahead Deventer v Celtic (0-6, 0-1)	0-7
GF Aarhus v Vitoria Setubal (2-1, 2-1)	4-2
KR Reykjavik v Rosenborg Trond. (1-3, 1-3)	2-6
Coleraine v Dynamo Kiev (1-6, 0-4)	1-10
Lahden Reipas v Honved (2-10, 0-6)	2-16
Dukla Prague v Stade Rennes (2-0, 0-0)	2-0
Cardiff City v Standard Liege (1-2, 0-1)	1-3
Juventus v Liverpool (1-0, 0-2)	1-2

[West Ham United (holders) received bye]

SECOND ROUND

Borussia Dortmund v CSKA Sofia (3-0, 2-4)	5-4
Stinta Cluj v Atletico Madrid (0-2, 0-4)	0-6
Magdeburg Aufbau v Sion (8-1, 2-2)	10-3
West Ham U. v Olympiakos Piraeus (4-0, 2-2)	6-2
GF Aarhus v Celtic (0-1, 0-2)	0-3
Rosenborg Trond. v Dynamo Kiev (1-4, 0-2)	1-6
Dukla Prague v Honved* (3-2, 1-2)	4-4
Liverpool v Standard Liege (3-1, 2-1)	5-2

QUARTER-FINALS

Atletico Madrid v Bor. Dortmund (1-1, 1-0)	2-1
West Ham U. v Magdeburg Aufbau (1-0, 1-1)	2-1
Celtic v Dynamo Kiev (3-0, 1-1)	4-1
Honved v Liverpool (0-0, 0-2)	0-2

SEMI-FINALS

West Ham U. v Borussia Dortmund (1-2, 1-3)	2-5
Celtic v Liverpool (1-0, 0-2)	1-2

FINAL

Borussia Dortmund 2 Liverpool 1 [aet]
(Hampden Park, 5.5.66, 41,657)

Borussia: Tilkowski, Cyliax, Redder, Kurrat, Paul, Assauer, Libuda, Schmidt, Held, Sturm, Emmerich

Liverpool: Lawrence, Lawler, Byrne, Milne, Yeats, Stevenson, Callaghan, Hunt, St John, Smith, Thompson

Scorers: Held, Yeats (og); Hunt

*won on away goals rule

1964-65

This was a year of some glory for the British clubs. Holders Sporting Lisbon were put out by Second Division Cardiff City, competing in the first of their numerous Cup Winners Cup ventures, thanks to a fine 2-1 win in Portugal with goals from Farrell and Tapscott. Cardiff were then only just beaten by Fairs Cup holders Real Zaragoza after drawing 2-2 in Spain. Zaragoza, firm favourites to win the trophy, met their match in Ron Greenwood's West Ham in the semi-final, able only to draw 1-1 at home after losing 2-1 at Upton Park.

Until that stage the London side—like Cardiff competing in Europe for the first time—had hardly been convincing, beating the Belgian side La Gantoise only by the odd goal and losing to Sparta in Prague. They had the good fortune to play the final at Wembley, however, and Alan Sealey played the game of his life in scoring both West Ham goals in a 2-0 win over TSV Munich 1860—a fast-flowing, open match worthy of a European final. It was the second of three remarkable Wembley appearances in consecutive years for the West Ham captain Bobby Moore: in 1964 he had carried off the FA Cup, and in 1966, of course, he would climb the steps to receive the World Cup; some hat-trick.

1965-66

West Ham survived in the 1965-66 series until the semi-finals, where they lost both legs to Borussia Dortmund—the only non-British club to reach that stage of the competition. The Germans had floored Floriana 5-1 in Malta and 8-0 at home, but had been given a fright by CSKA Sofia in the second leg, when a 3-0 lead was almost swallowed up by a 4-2 defeat in Bulgaria.

In the quarter-finals they drew 1-1 in Madrid with Atlético and won 1-0 at home. Lothar Emmerich scored 14 goals up to the semi-finals, along with Altafini's haul for AC Milan in the 1962-63 Champions Cup still a record for any one season in any European club competition. His six goals in Borussia's home leg against Floriana of Malta has been equalled only by Milanov of Levski Spartak (against Lahden Reipas in the 1976-77 Cup Winners) as a record for any single European game. In the final, once again at Hampden, Borussia faced Liverpool, a side conditioned to continental competition the previous season when they reached the semi-finals of the European Cup.

The Merseysiders had done well against strong opposition, beating Juventus 2-1, Standard Liège (Belgium) 5-2, Honved (Hungary) 2-0, and Celtic 2-1, recovering from 1-0 deficits against both the Italians and the Scots, and on both occasions with goals from Chris Lawler and Ian St John.

But in the final the Germans were stronger all round, with a particularly formidable defence, and were tactically more sound. Sigi Held—who along with Emmerich and keeper Tilkowski would figure against England in the World Cup final two months later—put them ahead only for Roger Hunt to equalize from a controversial centre that might have upset less resilient teams. Yet Libuda's cross in extra time was a winner, going in off Liverpool centre-half Ron Yeats. Liverpool were to have their rewards in the years to come, with four victories in four European finals.

1966-67

West Germany did well again in the 1966-67 contest, producing the winners, Bayern Munich, though Dortmund went out in the second round to Rangers on a 2-1 aggregate. From this series onwards, in the event of the teams being level on aggregate, away goals counted double.

Rangers improved on rivals Celtic a year before. In the first round they beat Glentoran of Northern Ireland 1-1 and 4-0, and, after removing Borussia, they beat Real Zaragoza, the side which had eliminated Everton. It was ironic that, with the new away goals rule, the deadlock that resulted when both teams won 2-0 at home had to be removed by the toss of a coin. It said much for Rangers' performance that year that the game in Zaragoza was the only one they lost before the final. In the semi-finals the Scots defeated Slavia Sofia 2-0, winning narrowly in each leg with goals by Davie Wilson and Willie Henderson.

Bayern, with Maier, Beckenbauer and Müller (leading scorer in the competition) already fixtures in the side, reached the final with three odd-goal victories—against Tatran Presov (Czechoslovakia) 4-3, Shamrock Rovers (Eire) 4-3 and Rapid Vienna 2-1—and wins over Standard Liège in both legs in the last four. The Germans were fortunate that the final was held in neighbouring Nuremberg, but although they

EUROPEAN CUP WINNERS CUP 1966-67

PRELIMINARY ROUND

Valur Reykjavik v Standard Liege (1-1, 1-8)	2-9

FIRST ROUND

Tatran Presov v Bayern Munich (1-1, 2-3)	3-4
Shamrock R. v Spora Luxembourg (4-1, 4-1)	8-2
OFK Belgrade v Spartak Moscow (1-3, 0-3)	1-6
Rapid Vienna v Galatasaray (4-0, 5-3)	9-3
Fiorentina v Vasas Gyor (1-0, 2-4)	3-4
AEK Athens v Sporting Braga (0-1, 2-3)	2-4
Chemie Leipzig v Legia Warsaw (3-0, 2-2)	5-2
Standard Liege v Apollon Limassol (5-1, 1-0)	6-1
Swansea Town v Slavia Sofia (1-1, 0-4)	1-5
R. Strasbourg v Steaua Bucharest (1-0, 1-1)	2-1
Floriana v Sparta Rotterdam (1-1, 0-6)	1-7
Servette v IF Finstroms Kamreterna (1-1, 2-1)	3-2
Skeid Oslo v Real Zaragoza (3-2, 1-3)	4-5
Aalborg BK 85 v Everton (0-0, 1-2)	1-2
Glentoran v Rangers (1-1, 0-4)	1-5

[Borussia Dortmund (holders) received bye]

SECOND ROUND

Shamrock Rovers v Bayern Munich (1-1, 2-3)	3-4
Spartak Moscow v Rapid Vienna (1-1, 0-1)	1-2
Vasas Gyor v Sporting Braga (3-0, 0-2)	3-2
Chemie Leipzig v Standard Liege* (2-1, 0-1)	2-2
Racing Strasbourg v Slavia Sofia (1-0, 0-2)	1-2
Servette v Sparta Rotterdam (2-0, 0-1)	2-1
Real Zaragoza v Everton (2-0, 0-1)	2-1
Rangers v Borussia Dortmund (2-1, 0-0)	2-1

QUARTER-FINALS

Rapid Vienna v Bayern Munich (1-0, 0-2)	1-2
Vasas Gyor v Standard Liege (2-1, 0-2)	2-3
Servette Geneva v Slavia Sofia (1-0, 0-3)	1-3
Rangers† v Real Zaragoza (2-0, 0-2)	2-2

SEMI-FINALS

Bayern Munich v Standard Liege (2-0, 3-1)	5-1
Slavia Sofia v Rangers (0-1, 0-1)	0-2

FINAL

Bayern Munich 1 Rangers 0 [aet]
(Nuremberg, 31.5.67, 69,480)

Bayern: Maier, Nowak, Kupferschmidt, Roth, Beckenbauer, Olk, Nafziger, Ohlhauser, Muller, Koulmann, Brenninger

Rangers: Martin, Johansen, Provan, Jardine, McKinnon, Greig, Henderson, A. Smith, Hynd, D. Smith, Johnston

Scorer: Roth

*won on away goals rule †won on toss of coin

In a poor game it took an extra-time goal by Franz Roth—later to score in two European Cup finals, including the only goal at Hampden Park against St Etienne in 1976—to settle the 1967 Cup Winners Cup final in Bayern Munich's favour at nearby Nuremberg. John Greig (second left) would captain Rangers to victory in 1972, but the Scottish side remain the only club to lose two finals in the competition.

always had the edge on their Scottish opponents, they still needed extra time to win a rather boring final 1-0 with a goal by Franz Roth. Rather overshadowed by his more famous colleagues, Roth went on to score in successive European Cup finals, including the only goal of the 1976 decider.

Just six days before Nuremberg Celtic had won the European Cup in Lisbon, and it was a great disappointment to Glasgow that Rangers had not made it a unique double. As it is, that remains the closest a single city, or even one country, has got to taking the two major titles in one year. Italy did well in 1973, with AC Milan taking the Cup Winners Cup and Juventus losing the European Cup by a single goal to Ajax. Belgium matched this in 1978 with Anderlecht's second Cup Winners Cup success and Bruges' Wembley defeat by Liverpool, but the Glasgow performance of 1967 is surely the most creditable of the three.

1967-68

Holders Bayern lasted until the semi-finals in 1967-68, but there they were beaten 2-0 on aggregate by AC Milan. The Italians, who had gained earlier success in the Champions Cup, made this a happy first entry. In round one they had accounted for Bulgaria's Levski Sofia 6-2, then went through on the away goals rule against Vasas Györ (Hungary) after a 3-3 tie.

In the quarter-finals, Standard Liège forced Milan into a play-off before they emerged 4-2 winners overall. The organizers had changed the rules again, introducing play-offs in the quarter- and semi-finals rather than the away goals rule. By coincidence, three of the four quarter-finals had to be replayed, only Bayern going through unscathed.

By far the most interesting tie of the series was between Cardiff City and Moscow Torpedo, Cardiff having to travel some 3,000 miles to play the away game in Tashkent, Georgia, because the Moscow grounds were unplayable in mid-winter. They lost 1-0 to cancel out a similar win at Ninian Park. The result was a play-off in Augsburg, and despite having to field five reserves the Welshmen pulled off an excellent 1-0 victory. Sadly, another fine result in Germany—1-1 at Hamburg, with Augsburg hero Dean again the scorer—was followed by a 3-2 defeat at home to take SV through to the finals. It remains the best ever performance in Europe by a Welsh club in terms of the stage reached.

So for the fourth successive year a German side reached the final. Hamburg had beaten Randers Freja (Denmark), Wislaw Krakow (Poland), and Olympique Lyon (conquerors of Spurs on the away goals rule) after a play-off.

The final at Rotterdam proved considerably easier for Milan than many of their earlier matches, and a two-goal win from a Kurt Hamrin first-half double did not really reflect their superiority over Hamburg. Hamrin, star of Sweden's 1958 World Cup final side, was no stranger to Cup Winners Cup finals. He had appeared for Fiorentina in the first two. The following year he won a European Cup winner's medal in the 4-1 victory over Ajax at Madrid.

EUROPEAN CUP WINNERS CUP 1967-68

FIRST ROUND

AC Milan v Levski Sofia (5-1, 1-1)	6-2
Vasas Gyor v Apollon Limassol (5-0, 4-0)	9-0
Aberdeen v KR Reykjavik (10-0, 4-1)	14-1
Altay Izmir v Standard Liege (2-3, 0-0)	2-3
Valencia v Crusaders (4-0, 4-2)	8-2
FK Austria v Steaua Bucharest (0-2, 1-2)	1-4
Fredrikstad v Vitoria Setubal (1-5, 1-2)	2-7
Bayern Munich v Panathinaikos (5-0, 2-1)	7-1
Shamrock Rovers v Cardiff City (1-1, 0-2)	1-3
Floriana v NAC Breda (1-2, 0-1)	1-3
Lausanne v Spartak Trnava (3-2, 0-2)	3-4
Torpedo Moscow v Motor Zwickau (0-0, 1-0)	1-0
Aris Bonnevoie v Olympique Lyon (0-3, 1-2)	1-5
Hajduk Split v Tottenham Hotspur (0-2, 3-4)	3-6
HJK Helsinki v Wisla Krakow (1-4, 0-4)	1-8
SV Hamburg v Randers Freja (5-3, 2-0)	7-3

SECOND ROUND

Vasas Gyor v AC Milan* (2-2, 1-1)	3-3
Standard Liege v Aberdeen (3-0, 0-2)	3-2
Valencia v Steaua Bucharest (3-0, 0-1)	3-1
Bayern Munich v Vitoria Setubal (6-2, 1-1)	7-3
NAC Breda v Cardiff City (1-1, 1-4)	2-5
Torpedo Moscow v Spartak Trnava (3-0, 3-1)	6-1
Olympique Lyon* v Tottenham H. (1-0, 3-4)	4-4
Wisla Krakow v SV Hamburg (0-1, 0-4)	0-5

QUARTER-FINALS

Standard Liege v AC Milan (1-1, 1-1, 0-2†)	2-4
Valencia v Bayern Munich (1-1, 0-1)	1-2
Cardiff City v Torpedo Moscow (1-0, 0-1, 1-0‡)	2-1
SV Hamburg v Olym. Lyon (2-0, 0-2, 2-0§)	4-2

SEMI-FINALS

AC Milan v Bayern Munich (2-0, 0-0)	2-0
SV Hamburg v Cardiff City (1-1, 3-2)	4-3

FINAL

AC Milan 2 SV Hamburg 0
(Rotterdam, 23.5.68, 53,276)

Milan: Cudicini, Anquilletti, Schnellinger, Rosato, Scala, Trapattoni, Hamrin, Lodetti, Sormani, Rivera, Prati

Hamburg: Ozcan, Sondemann, Kurbjuhn, Dieckemann, Horst, Schulz, B. Dorfel, Kramer, Seeler, Hornig, G. Dorfel

Scorer: Hamrin 2

*won on away goals rule †play-off in Milan ‡play-off in Augsburg §play-off in Hamburg

1968-69

The 1968-69 version, like the European Cup, was affected by the re-draw of the first round to keep the Eastern European and Western countries apart because of the Russian invasion of Czechoslovakia. Several of the Eastern representatives withdrew, leaving only 27 rather than the usual 32 or 33

EUROPEAN CUP WINNERS CUP 1968-69

FIRST ROUND

Slovan Bratislava v Bor (3-0, 2-0)	5-0
Cardiff City v Porto (2-2, 1-2)	3-4
Partizan Tirana v Torino (1-3, 1-0)	2-3
FC Bruges v West Bromwich A.* (3-1, 0-2)	3-3
Dynamo Bucharest w.o. Vasas Gyor (withdrew)	
Olym. Piraeus v Fram Reykjavik (2-0, 2-0)	4-0
Dunfermline Ath. v Apoel Nicosia (10-1, 2-0)	12-1
Girondins Bordeaux v 1FC Cologne (2-1, 0-3)	2-4
Altay Izmir v Lyn Oslo (3-1, 1-4)	4-5
US Rumelange v Sliema Wands.* (2-1, 0-1)	2-2
Randers Freja v Shamrock Rovers (1-0, 2-1)	3-1
AK Graz v ADO Den Haag (1-4, 0-2)	1-6
Crusaders v IFK Norrkoping (2-2, 1-4)	3-6
Lugano v Barcelona (0-1, 0-3)	0-4

SECOND ROUND

Porto v Slovan Bratislava (1-0, 0-4)	1-4
Dynamo Bucharest v WBA (1-1, 0-4)	1-5
Dunfermline v Olympiakos Piraeus (4-0, 0-3)	4-3
ADO Den Haag v 1FC Cologne (0-1, 0-3)	0-4
Randers Freja v Sliema Wanderers (6-0, 2-0)	8-0
Lyn Oslo v IFK Norrkoping (2-0, 2-3)	4-3

[Barcelona & Torino received byes]

QUARTER-FINALS

Torino v Slovan Bratislava (1-0, 1-2)	1-3
Dunfermline Athletic v WBA (0-0, 1-0)	1-0
1FC Cologne v Randers Freja (2-1, 3-0)	5-1
Barcelona v Lyn Oslo (3-2, 2-2)	5-4

SEMI-FINALS

Dunfermline v Slovan Bratislava (1-1, 0-1)	1-2
1FC Cologne v Barcelona (2-2, 1-4)	3-6

FINAL

Slovan Bratislava 3 Barcelona 2
(Basle, 21.5.69, 19,478)

Slovan: Vencel, Filo, Hrivnak, Zlocha, Horvath, Hrdlicka, Cvetler, Moder (Macar), Josef Capkovîc, Jokl, Jan Capkovic

Barcelona: Sadurni, Franch (Pereda), Eladio, Rife, Olivella, Zabalza, Pellicer, Castro (Mendoza), Zaldua, Fuste, Rexach

Scorers: Cvetler, Hrivnak, Jan Capkovic; Zaldua, Rexach

*won on away goals rule

entries. In rather fairy-tale fashion, justice was seen to be done and it was the Czech entrants, Slovan Bratislava, who emerged as winners. They were the first club from behind the iron curtain to win a European competition and remain the only Czech side to have won one of the major club prizes despite many stirring performances from the national as well as their club teams over the years.

Slovan started slowly by beating the unknown Yugoslavian side Bor 3-2, but looked a better team when they accounted for Porto 4-1. Torino were their quarter-final victims, 1-0 and 2-1, and in the semi-finals they drew 1-1 in Scotland against Dunfermline Athletic and won 1-0 at home. Dunfermline had removed West Bromwich Albion in the quarter-finals with a Gardner goal to go one better than their performance in the Cup Winners Cup in 1962.

Barcelona, experienced campaigners in Europe, ploughed through Lugano (Switzerland) 4-0, Lyn Oslo (Norway) 5-4—luckily, playing both legs at home—and Cologne 6-3, to line up in Basle for the final with Slovan.

The Czechs were off to a fine start with a goal from Cvetler in the second minute. Further goals from full-back Hrivnak and winger Jan Capkovic, to one by Zaldua for Barcelona, put Slovan well on the road to success. Though Rexach added a second for Barcelona, direct from a corner, their destiny was to lose another European final in the same country where their hopes had faded eight years earlier against Benfica in the Champions Cup. All three of Barcelona's single-match European finals, in fact, have been played in Switzerland, including their victory in this competition in 1979.

EUROPEAN CUP WINNERS CUP 1969-70

PRELIMINARY ROUND

Rapid Vienna* v Torpedo Moscow (0-0, 1-1)	1-1

FIRST ROUND

Atletico Bilbao v Manchester City (3-3, 0-3)	3-6
Lierse SK v Apoel Nicosia (10-1, 1-0)	11-1
FC Magdeburg v MTK Budapest (1-1, 1-0)	2-1
Academica Coimbra v Kuopion PS (0-0, 1-0)	1-0
Dynamo Zagreb v Slovan Bratislava (3-0, 0-0)	3-0
Dukla Prague v Olym. Marseille (1-0, 0-2)	1-2
IFK Norrkoping v Sliema Wanderers (5-1, 0-1)	5-2
Shamrock Rovers v Schalke 04 (2-1, 0-3)	2-4
Ards v AS Roma (0-0, 1-3)	1-3
Rapid Vienna v PSV Eindhoven (2-4, 1-2)	3-6
Mjoendalen JF v Cardiff City (1-7, 1-5)	2-12
Goztepe Izmir v US Luxembourg (3-0, 3-2)	6-2
IB Vestmannaey v Levski Sofia (0-4, 0-4)	0-8
Frem Copenhagen v St Gallen* (2-1, 0-1)	2-2
Rangers v Steaua Bucharest (2-0, 0-0)	2-0
Olympiakos Piraeus v Gornik Zabrze (2-2, 0-5)	2-7

SECOND ROUND

Lierse SK v Manchester City (0-3, 0-5)	0-8
FC Magdeburg v Acad. Coimbra (1-0, 0-2)	1-2
Olym. Marseille v Dynamo Zagreb (1-1, 0-2)	1-3
IFK Norrkoping v Schalke 04 (0-0, 0-1)	0-1
AS Roma† v PSV Eindhoven (1-0, 0-1)	1-1
Goztepe Izmir v Cardiff City (3-0, 0-1)	3-1
Levski Sofia v St Gallen (4-0, 0-0)	4-0
Gornik Zabrze v Rangers (3-1, 3-1)	6-2

QUARTER-FINALS

Acad. Coimbra v Manchester City (0-0, 0-1)	0-1
Dynamo Zagreb v Schalke 04 (1-3, 0-1)	1-4
AS Roma v Goztepe Izmir (2-0, 0-0)	2-0
Levski Sofia v Gornik Zabrze (3-2, 1-2)	4-4

SEMI-FINALS

Schalke 04 v Manchester City (1-0, 1-5)	2-5
AS Roma v Gornik Zabrze‡ (1-1, 2-2, 1-1)	4-4

FINAL

Manchester City 2 Gornik Zabrze 1
(Vienna, 29.4.70, 7,968)

City: Corrigan, Book, Pardoe, Doyle (Bowyer), Booth, Oakes, Heslop, Bell, Lee, Young, Towers

Gornik: Kostka, Oslizlo, Florenski (Deja), Gorgon, Olek, Latogha, Szoltysik, Wilczek (Skowronek), Szarinski, Banas, Lubanski

Scorers: Young, Lee (pen); Oslizlo

*won on away goals rule †won on toss of coin
‡play-off in Strasbourg: Gornik won on toss of coin

Neil Young about to put Manchester City ahead in the 1970 final against Gornik Zabrze at Vienna. City also beat the Polish side in the quarter-finals the following season before losing to Chelsea.

EUROPEAN CUP WINNERS CUP 1970-71

PRELIMINARY ROUND

Bohemians v TJ Gottwaldov (1-2, 2-2)	3-4
Atvidaberg v Partizan Tirana (0-2, 1-1)	1-3

FIRST ROUND

Aris Salonika v Chelsea (1-1, 1-5)	2-6
CSKA Sofia v Valkeakosken Haka (9-0, 2-1)	11-1
Akureyri v FC Zurich (1-7, 0-7)	1-14
Offenbach Kickers v FC Bruges (2-1, 0-2)	2-3
Aalborg BK 85 v Gornik Zabrze (0-1, 1-8)	1-9
Goztepe Izmir v US Luxembourg (5-0, 0-1)	5-1
Aberdeen v Honved† (1-3, 3-1)	4-4
Manchester City* v Linfield (1-0, 1-2)	2-2
TJ Gottwaldov v PSV Eindhoven* (2-1, 0-1)	2-2
Steaua Bucharest v Karpaty Lvov (3-3, 1-0)	4-3
Olympija Ljubljana v Benfica (1-1, 1-8)	2-9
ASK Vorwaerts* v Bologna (0-0, 1-1)	1-1
Cardiff City v Pezoporikos Larnaca (8-0, 0-0)	8-0
Stromsgodset Drammen v Nantes (0-5, 3-2)	3-7
Wacker Innsbruck v Partizan Tirana (3-2, 2-1)	5-3
Hibernians Valletta v Real Madrid (0-0, 0-5)	0-5

SECOND ROUND

CSKA Sofia v Chelsea (0-1, 0-1)	0-2
FC Bruges v FC Zurich (2-0, 2-3)	4-3
Goztepe Izmir v Gornik Zabrze (0-1, 0-3)	0-4
Honved v Manchester City (0-1, 0-2)	0-3
PSV Eindhoven v Steaua Bucharest (4-0, 3-0)	7-0
Benfica v ASK Vorwaerts† (2-0, 0-2)	2-2
Cardiff City v Nantes (5-1, 2-1)	7-2
Real Madrid v Wacker Innsbruck (0-1, 2-0)	2-1

QUARTER-FINALS

FC Bruges v Chelsea (2-0, 0-4)	2-4
Manchester C. v Gornik Zabrze (2-0, 0-2, 3-1‡)	5-3
PSV Eindhoven v ASK Vorwaerts (2-0, 0-1)	2-1
Cardiff City v Real Madrid (1-0, 0-2)	1-2

SEMI-FINALS

Chelsea v Manchester City (1-0, 1-0)	2-0
PSV Eindhoven v Real Madrid (0-0, 1-2)	1-2

FINAL

Chelsea 1 Real Madrid 1 [aet]
(Athens, 19.5.71, 43,000)

Chelsea: Bonetti, Boyle, Harris, Hollins (Mulligan), Dempsey, Webb, Weller, Hudson, Osgood (Baldwin), Cooke, Houseman

Real: Borja, Luis, Zunzunegui, Pirri, Benito, Zoco, Perez (Fleitas), Amancio, Grosso, Velasquez, Gento (Grande)

Scorers: Osgood; Zoco

Replay (Athens, 21.5.71, 35,000)

Chelsea 2 Real Madrid 1

Chelsea: Bonetti, Boyle, Harris, Cooke, Dempsey, Webb; Weller, Baldwin, Osgood (Smethurst), Hudson, Houseman

Real: Borja, Luis, Zunzunegui, Pirri, Benito, Zoco, Fleitas, Amancio, Grosso, Velasquez (Gento), Bueno (Grande)

Scorers: Dempsey, Osgood; Fleitas

*won on away goals rule †won on penalties
‡play-off in Copenhagen

1969-70

With the Eastern Bloc back after the previous season's walkout, the competition continued at full strength. The holders soon fell by the wayside, beaten 3-0 in the first round by Dynamo Zagreb who then moved on to the quarter-finals at the expense of Olympique Marseille. There they were joined by Manchester City, Britain's only representative after Rangers (to Gornik Zabrze) and Cardiff (to Goztepe Izmir) had been eliminated in the second round.

Manchester's wins over Atlético Bilbao of Spain (6-3) and Belgium's Lierse (8-0, Lee scoring four goals) suggested real form, but Academica, from the Portuguese university city of Coimbra, held them to a solitary goal in the quarter-final, and in the semi-final Schalke 04 of Gelsenkirkchen took a typically individual goal by Libuda to Maine Road. There, however, they met City in irrepressible mood, and lost 5-1.

City's opponents in the Vienna final, Gornik, had experienced stumbling blocks along the way. Away goals took them past Levski Sofia, the right side of the coin past Roma after a third match. Lubanski, one of Poland's great players, spearheaded Gornik's attack, and with a solid defence around the raw but giant Gorgon, they were expected to give City a difficult time in the Prater Stadium.

In the event, Manchester's flair proved decisive. Young, from close in, opened the scoring; Lee, when Young was fouled, converted a penalty for the second. Lubanski set Oslizlo up to reduce the margin, but it was too late; City added the Cup Winners Cup to the League Cup won earlier in the season. It was in fact their fourth major triumph in a brief three seasons (after the League Championship in 1968, the FA Cup in 1969 and the League Cup in 1970), though one of the least remembered of England's European successes.

It was a rather poor spectacle; watched by less than 8,000 people in driving rain in Vienna, and City fans at home did not even have the satisfaction of seeing the game on television. By chance, all eyes that evening were elsewhere in Manchester—on Old Trafford, where Chelsea were defeating Leeds in the only game to be replayed since the FA Cup final moved to Wembley.

The scene in the Chelsea dressing-room after the Londoners had beaten Real Madrid in the replayed 1971 final in Athens. Peter Osgood (back, by cup) scored in both games to keep the trophy in England.

1970-71

But for the draw, Britain might have had both finalists in 1971. They might even have had three semi-finalists, had Cardiff City, cup fighters extraordinary, sustained their challenge. An 8-0 win over Pesoporikos of Cyprus was followed by a 7-2 defeat of French Cup runners-up Nantes, with John Toshack picking up five goals on the way. Then they beat Real Madrid (with the evergreen Gento a still-formidable reminder of the glorious past) 1-0 at home, only to slump 2-0 in Madrid.

Scotland's entry, Aberdeen, lost their first-round tie on penalties to Honved, both games ending 3-1. Honved, in their turn, were beaten 3-0 by Manchester City. The holders were lucky to have reached the second round at all, having lost 2-1 to Linfield in Belfast to two Millen goals in what may still be reasonably regarded as the best performance in Europe by an Ulster club. That away goal from Lee let City through and then, after Honved, they met Gornik in a repeat of the 1970 final and found themselves in Copenhagen for a replay after shared 2-0 home wins. Goals from Young, Booth and Lee put them through. Lubanski replied for the Poles, making him the competition's top scorer for the second successive season, again with eight goals.

The semi-finals pitted City against FA Cup holders Chelsea, who had done their familiar Houdini act in the quarter-finals to come back from a 2-0 defeat to beat Bruges 4-2. Aris Salonika of Greece and CSKA Sofia were earlier scalps. Lacking Doyle, Oakes and Bell, City lost by Derek Smethurst's goal at Stamford Bridge; and at Maine Road a reserve-laden side never recovered from an early own goal by goalkeeper Healey. After a goalless draw in Holland, Real beat PSV Eindhoven 2-1 in Madrid to reach their ninth European final, their first outside the Champions Cup.

EUROPEAN CUP WINNERS CUP 1971-72

PRELIMINARY ROUND

Odense BK 09 v FK Austria* (4-2, 0-2)	4-4
Hibs Valletta v Fram Reykjavik (3-0, 0-2)	3-2

FIRST ROUND

Stade Rennes v Rangers (1-1, 0-1)	1-2
Sporting Lisbon v Lyn Oslo (3-0, 4-0)	7-0
Dynamo Tirana v FK Austria (1-1, 0-1)	1-2
Limerick v Torino (0-1, 0-4)	0-5
Hibs Valletta v Steaua Bucharest (0-0, 0-1)	0-1
Distillery v Barcelona (1-3, 0-4)	1-7
Servette Geneva v Liverpool (2-1, 0-2)	2-3
Skoda Pilzen v Bayern Munich (0-1, 1-6)	1-7
Dynamo Berlin† v Cardiff City (1-1, 1-1)	2-2
Beerschot v Anorthosis Famagusta (7-0, 1-0)	8-0
Jeunesse Hautcharage v Chelsea (0-8, 0-13)	0-21
Zaglebie Sosnowiec v Atvidaberg (3-4, 1-1)	4-5
Komlo Banyasi v Red Star Belgrade (2-7, 2-1)	4-8
Levski Spartak v Sparta Rotterdam (1-1, 0-2)	1-3
Mikkelin Pallokissat v Eskisehirspor (0-0, 0-4)	0-4
Olym. Piraeus v Dynamo Moscow (0-2, 2-1)	2-3

SECOND ROUND

Rangers* v Sporting Lisbon (3-2, 3-4)	6-6
Torino v FK Austria (1-0, 0-0)	1-0
Barcelona v Steaua Bucharest (0-1, 1-2)	1-3
Liverpool v Bayern Munich (0-0, 1-3)	1-3
Beerschot v Dynamo Berlin (1-3, 1-3)	2-6
Atvidaberg* v Chelsea (0-0, 1-1)	1-1
Sp. Rotterdam v Red Star Belgrade (1-1, 1-2)	2-3
Eskisehirspor v Dynamo Moscow (0-1, 0-1)	0-2

QUARTER-FINALS

Torino v Rangers (1-1, 0-1)	1-2
Steaua Bucharest v Bayern Munich* (1-1, 0-0)	1-1
Atvidaberg v Dynamo Berlin (0-2, 2-2)	2-4
Red Star Belgrade v Dyn. Moscow (1-2, 1-1)	2-3

SEMI-FINALS

Bayern Munich v Rangers (1-1, 0-2)	1-3
Dynamo Berlin v Dynamo Moscow† (1-1, 1-1)	2-2

FINAL

Rangers 3 Moscow Dynamo 2
(Barcelona, 24.5.72, 24,701)

Rangers: McCloy, Jardine, Mathieson, Greig, Johnstone, Smith, McLean, Conn, Stein, MacDonald, Johnston

Dynamo: Pilgui, Bassaliev, Dolmatov, Dolbonosov (Jerochkovich), Zhukov, Baidatchini, Yakubik (Estrekov), Sabo, Makovikov, Evryuzhikin

Scorers: Stein, Johnstone 2; Estrekov, Greig (og)

*won on away goals rule †won on penalties

Chelsea returned to Greece for the final, and in Athens Peter Osgood's goal looked to have given them the cup, only for Dempsey's mis-kicked clearance to let Zoco in during injury time. Bonetti kept a rejuvenated Real at bay throughout extra time, and did enough to keep thousands of Londoners, unprepared for such an eventuality, sleeping rough for the two nights until the replay—and in many cases for much longer. But for those fans it was well worth it, and a crowd almost as large as that at the first game saw Chelsea sweep Real aside with a great first-half display of attacking football that brought goals from the central characters of the first match, Dempsey and Osgood. Fleitas' goal 15 minutes from time was more consolation than threat.

1971-72

For the first time in European club competition a Russian club contested a final—a piece of history lost in the orgy of violence before, during and (particularly) after the match between Dynamo Moscow and Rangers in Barcelona. Such was the conduct of Rangers fans that the club were in danger of losing the trophy after winning it with a fine performance on the field. Eventually, UEFA allowed them to keep it but a two-year ban, commuted to a year, ensured they could not defend it. Rangers' next appearance in Europe, in fact, was in this competition in 1973-74, when they lost to Borussia Moenchengladbach in the second round.

For Rangers, it was a sordid end to an impressive campaign, one that produced wins over Rennes, Sporting Lisbon (with Colin Stein scoring four of their six goals), Torino and, even more convincingly, the Bayern Munich of Beckenbauer, Müller and the nucleus of the side which went on to win the European Championship for West Germany later that year. The goals at Ibrox from Sandy Jardine and Derek Parlane also provided sweet revenge for the narrow defeat in the final of 1967.

In the second round, Müller and Hoeness had knocked out Liverpool (in for double-

ABOVE: *John Greig, like Davie Smith and Willie Johnston a survivor from the 1967 final, gives chase to Dynamo Moscow's Sabo during the 1972 final in Barcelona.*
BELOW: *The disgusting behaviour of some Rangers supporters both on and off the field led to a two-year European ban on the club, later commuted to a year.*

A free-kick from Chiarugi, scorer of the game's only goal, tests a precarious wall of Jordan (8), Bates, Yorath and Lorimer in the 1973 final at Salonika. Leeds, missing four key players, were further punished by the outrageously biased refereeing of Greek referee Michas, whose actions led to his suspension by both UEFA and his national FA. But the result stood.

EUROPEAN CUP WINNERS CUP 1972-73

FIRST ROUND

Red Boys Differdange v AC Milan (1-4, 0-3)	1-7
Viking. Reykjavik v Legia Warsaw (0-2, 0-9)	0-11
Bastia v Atletico Madrid (0-0, 1-2)	1-2
Spartak Moscow v ADO Den Haag (1-0, 0-0)	1-0
Schalke 04 v Slavia Sofia (2-1, 3-1)	5-2
Pezoporikos Larnaca v Cork Hibs (1-2, 1-4)	2-6
Floriana v Ferencvaros (1-0, 0-6)	1-6
Standard Liege v Sparta Prague (1-0, 2-4)	3-4
Hajduk Split v Fredrikstad (1-0, 1-0)	2-0
FC Zurich v Wrexham (1-1, 1-2)	2-3
Fremad Amager v Besa* (1-1, 0-0)	1-1
Sporting Lisbon v Hibernian (2-1, 1-6)	3-7
Rapid Bucharest v Landskrona (3-0, 0-1)	3-1
Rapid Vienna* v PAOK Salonika (0-0, 2-2)	2-2
Carl Zeiss Jena v Mikkelin Pallo. (6-1, 2-3)	8-4
Ankåragucu v Leeds United (1-1, 0-1)	1-2

SECOND ROUND

Legia Warsaw v AC Milan (1-1, 1-2)	2-3
Atletico Madrid v Spartak Moscow* (3-4, 2-1)	5-5
Cork Hibernians v Schalke 04 (0-0, 0-3)	0-3
Ferencvaros v Sparta Prague (2-0, 1-4)	3-4
Wrexham v Hajduk Split* (3-1, 0-2)	3-3
Hibernian v Besa (7-1, 1-1)	8-2
Rapid Vienna v Rapid Bucharest (1-1, 1-3)	2-4
Carl Zeiss Jena v Leeds United (0-0, 0-2)	0-2

QUARTER-FINALS

Spartak Moscow v AC Milan (0-1, 1-1)	1-2
Schalke 04 v Sparta Prague (2-1, 0-3)	2-4
Hibernian v Hajduk Split (4-2, 0-3)	4-5
Leeds United v Rapid Bucharest (5-0, 3-1)	8-1

SEMI-FINALS

AC Milan v Sparta Prague (1-0, 1-0)	2-0
Leeds United v Hajduk Split (1-0, 0-0)	1-0

FINAL

AC Milan 1 Leeds United 0
(Salonika, 16.5.73, 45,000)

Milan: Vecchi, Sabadini, Zignoli, Anquilletti, Turone, Benetti, Rosato (Dolci), Sogliano, Bigon, Rivera, Chiarugi

Leeds: Harvey, Reaney, Cherry, Bates, Madeley, Hunter, Lorimer, Jordan, Jones, E. Gray, Yorath (McQueen)

Scorer: Chiarugi

*won on away goals rule

winners Arsenal), the Merseysiders still being in their relatively poor European phase during which they were regularly outplayed by the better continental sides, notably Red Star Belgrade and Ajax.

Meanwhile Chelsea were establishing a record by beating the tiny Luxembourg side Jeunesse Hautcharage 21-0, still the record aggregate score for any European tie. Peter Osgood's eight goals, three in the Duchy and five at Stamford Bridge, were enough to give him the top scorer slot for the whole competition. Tommy Baldwin picked up four, Peter Houseman, David Webb and John Hollins two each. The holders were brought down to earth with a mighty bump in the next round, however, when Sweden's Atvidaberg drew 0-0 at home and then sneaked a goal to make it 1-1 at Stamford Bridge and go through on the away goals rule.

This was the first year that all rounds were decided on this rule or on penalties, play-offs being abandoned except in the final. One result was that the two Dynamos, Moscow and Berlin, decided their semi on penalties—with the Russians going through to Barcelona for a game they are unlikely to forget any more quickly than the British Consulate there.

In the final itself Rangers, fast and skilful, emphasized their class with good goals by Stein and Willie Johnston (2). Then, overconfident or perhaps upset by their fans' behaviour, they fell away, giving Estrekov a goal and letting through Mahovikov for a second. Skipper John Greig, one of four survivors from the 1967 final with Bayern, made sure it would be third time lucky for the Scots—and football reeled from a match that left one dead and hundreds injured and arrested.

1972-73

A competition still recovering from the adverse publicity of the previous season could hardly afford the scandal attached to the 1973 final. Disgracefully biased decisions by the Greek referee, Michas, in favour of AC Milan led to his suspension by UEFA and his own national association; it was little consolation for Leeds, who conceded a goal after three minutes and spent the rest of the match frustrated by the Italians' spoiling tactics and by the referee. Even two penalties would have been sparse justice: instead, Hunter was sent off for retaliating, as was Sogliano for attacking Hunter. An altogether shabby affair, and little wonder the Greek crowd at Salonika jeered the winners off the pitch.

Earlier, Third Division Wrexham showed cup-fighting spirit, beating Zurich in the first round before losing on away goals (3-1, 0-2) to Hajduk Split from Yugoslavia. But Britain's best hopes lay with Leeds and Hibernian. The Scots, helped by two hat-tricks from John O'Rourke, beat Sporting Lisbon 7-3 and Besa (Albania) 8-2 before Hajduk stopped them in a high-scoring quarter-final. Leeds' wins over Ankaragucu (Turkey) and Carl Zeiss Jena of East Germany were more conservative, but an 8-1 aggregate against Rapid Bucharest reflected some adventurous form for the only time in this competition. Clarke's goal at Elland Road took them through the semi-final with Hajduk. In the other semi-final, Milan beat Sparta Prague 1-0 in both legs, having accounted for Red Boys Differdange, Legia Warsaw (3-2 after extra time) and Spartak Moscow 2-1.

So to Salonika, and a referee that even members of the Greek federation opposed because of his Italian connections. Leeds, missing Giles and Eddie Gray (injured) and Bremner and Clarke (suspended), went down to a goal from Chiarugi (his seventh of the competition), and could be excused wondering why they bothered to turn up. It was the worst incident of its kind in European football, and was to draw attention to Italian political tactics in international circles. But, while it certainly quelled similar incidents, UEFA steadfastly refused a genuine investigation.

1973-74

AC Milan's defence of their dubiously won trophy took them past Rapid Vienna (4-0), PAOK Salonika (5-2) and Borussia Moenchengladbach (2-1) to their second consecutive final. There they met and lost to FC Magdeburg, who thus became the second iron curtain country to win the trophy and the first from East Germany.

British hopes foundered early. Second Division Sunderland, with Dennis Tueart prominent, excelled in beating Vasas 2-0 in Budapest and 1-0 at Roker, but found a 2-1 lead insufficient in Lisbon and lost 2-3 on aggregate to Sporting. Rangers, back again, crashed 5-3 to an exuberant Moenchengladbach in the second round, and with Cardiff being Sporting's first-round victims only little Glentoran reached the quarter-finals, where the West Germans beat them home and away. Tragically, the Irishmen lost centre-half Walker with a broken leg in the home match and that night midfield man Roy Stewart died from a heart attack.

Magdeburg, with World Cup men Sparwasser, Hoffmann and Pommerenke to the fore, had a relatively easy passage to the semi-finals, beating NAC Breda (Holland) 2-0, Banik Ostrava (Czechoslovakia) 3-2 and Beroe Stara Zagora (Bulgaria) 3-1. Against Sporting they built on their 1-1 draw in Lisbon with a 2-1 home win, and their strong confident running looked sufficient to carry them past a crisis-ridden Milan who had lost two managers—Rocco and Maldini—and had striker Chiarugi suspended. So it proved before less than 5,000 in Rotterdam. Lanzi put the ball into his own goal trying to stop Raugust's cross reaching Sparwasser; in the second half Hoffmann broke away, split the defence with his cross, and Seguin, slipping Sabadini, put the issue beyond doubt.

The United Kingdom's most successful entrants, Glentoran, had beaten Chimia Ramnicu Vilcea of Rumania 4-2 and Brann

Boris Onischenko scored seven goals in helping Dynamo Kiev to win Russia's only European club honour in 1974-75, including two in the final against Ferencvaros. Dynamo's superb displays, prompted by Oleg Blokhin (later European Footballer of the Year), led the Soviet authorities to adopt the side as the national team.

EUROPEAN CUP WINNERS CUP 1973-74

FIRST ROUND

NAC Breda v FC Magdeburg (0-0, 0-2)	0-2
Banik Ostrava v Cork Hibernians (1-0, 2-1)	3-1
Torpedo Moscow v Atletico Bilbao (0-0, 0-2)	0-2
Fola Esch v Beroe Stara Zagora (0-7, 1-4)	1-11
Anderlecht v FC Zurich* (3-2, 0-1)	3-3
Pezoporikos Larnaca v Malmo FF (0-0, 0-11)	0-11
Vasas Budapest v Sunderland (0-2, 0-1)	0-3
Cardiff City v Sporting Lisbon (0-0, 1-2)	1-2
IB Vestmannaey v Bor. M'gladbach (0-7, 1-9)	1-16
Ankaragucu v Rangers (0-2, 0-4)	0-6
Gzira United v SK Brann Bergen (0-2, 0-7)	0-9
Chimia Ramnicu Vilcea v Glentoran (2-2, 0-2)	2-4
Legia Warsaw v PAOK Salonika (1-1, 0-1)	1-2
Lahden Reipas v Olympique Lyon (0-0, 0-2)	0-2
Randers Freja v Rapid Vienna (0-0, 1-2)	1-2
AC Milan v Dynamo Zagreb (3-1, 1-0)	4-1

SECOND ROUND

Banik Ostrava v FC Magdeburg (2-0, 0-3)	2-3
Beroe Stara Zagora v At. Bilbao (3-0, 0-1)	3-1
FC Zurich* v Malmo FF (0-0, 1-1)	1-1
Sunderland v Sporting Lisbon (2-1, 0-2)	2-3
Borussia M'gladbach v Rangers (3-0, 2-3)	5-3
SK Brann Bergen v Glentoran (1-1, 1-3)	2-4
Olympique Lyon v PAOK Salonika (3-3, 0-4)	3-7
AC Milan v Rapid Vienna (0-0, 2-0)	2-0

QUARTER-FINALS

FC Magdeburg v B. Stara Zagora (2-0, 1-1)	3-1
Glentoran v Borussia M'gladbach (0-2, 0-5)	0-7
Sporting Lisbon v FC Zurich (3-0, 1-1)	4-1
AC Milan v PAOK Salonika (3-0, 2-2)	5-2

SEMI-FINALS

Sporting Lisbon v FC Magdeburg (1-1, 1-2)	2-3
AC Milan v Borussia M'gladbach (2-0, 0-1)	2-1

FINAL

FC Magdeburg 2 AC Milan 0
(Rotterdam, 8.5.74, 4,641)

Magdeburg: Schultz, Tyll, Enge, Zapf, Caube, Abraham, Seguin, Pommerenke, Raugust, Sparwasser, Hoffman

Milan: Pizzabella, Sabadini, Anquilletti, Lanzi, Schnellinger, Benetti, Maldera, Tresoldi, Bigon, Rivera, Bergamaschi (Turini)

Scorers: Lanzi (og), Seguin

*won on away goals rule

EUROPEAN CUP WINNERS CUP 1974-75

FIRST ROUND

Dynamo Kiev v CSKA Sofia (1-0, 1-0)	2-0
Eintracht Frankfurt v AS Monaco (3-0, 2-2)	5-2
Dundee United v Jiul Petrosani (3-0, 0-2)	3-2
Bursaspor v Finn Harps (4-2, 0-0)	4-2
Benfica v Vanlose IF (4-0, 4-1)	8-1
Slavia Prague v Carl Zeiss Jena† (1-0, 0-1)	1-1
Gwardia Warsaw† v Bologna (2-1, 1-2)	3-3
PSV Eindhoven v Ards (10-0, 4-1)	14-1
PAOK Salonika v Red Star Belgrade (1-0, 0-2)	1-2
Avenir Beggen w.o. Paralimni (withdrew)	
SV Waregem v FK Austria/WAC (2-1, 1-4)	3-5
Fram Reykjavik v Real Madrid (0-2, 0-6)	0-8
Malmo FF† v Sion (1-0, 0-1)	1-1
Sliema Wanderers v Lahden Reipas (2-0, 4-1)	6-1
Liverpool v Stromsgodset (11-0, 1-0)	12-0
Ferencvaros v Cardiff City (2-0, 4-1)	6-1

SECOND ROUND

Eintracht Frankfurt v Dynamo Kiev (2-3, 1-2)	3-5
Dundee United v Bursaspor (0-0, 0-1)	0-1
Carl Zeiss Jena v Benfica* (1-1, 0-0)	1-1
Gwardia Warsaw v PSV Eindhoven (1-5, 0-3)	1-8
Avenir Beggen v Red Star Belgrade (1-6, 0-5)	1-11
Real Madrid v FK Austria/WAC (3-0, 2-2)	5-2
Malmo FF v Lahden Reipas (3-1, 0-0)	3-1
Liverpool v Ferencvaros* (1-1, 0-0)	1-1

QUARTER-FINALS

Bursaspor v Dynamo Kiev (0-1, 0-2)	0-3
PSV Eindhoven v Benfica (0-0, 2-1)	2-1
Real Madrid v Red Star Belgrade† (2-0, 0-2)	2-2
Malmo FF v Ferencvaros (1-3, 1-1)	2-4

SEMI-FINALS

Dynamo Kiev v PSV Eindhoven (3-0, 1-2)	4-2
Ferencvaros v Red Star Belgrade (2-1, 2-2)	4-3

FINAL

Dynamo Kiev 3 Ferencvaros 0
(Basle, 14.5.75, 10,897)

Dynamo: Rudakov, Troshkin, Matvienko, Reshko, Fomenko, Muntian, Konkov, Burjak, Kolotov, Onischenko, Blokhin

Ferencvaros: Geczi, Martos, Megyesi, Pataki, Rab, Nyilasi (Onhaus), Juhasz, Mucha, Szabo, Mate, Magyar

Scorers: Onischenko 2, Blokhin

*won on away goals rule †won on penalties

LEADING SCORERS

Season	Player	Gls
1965-66	Emmerich *(Borussia Dortmund)**	14
1966-67	Muller *(Bayern Munich)*	9
1967-68	Seeler *(SV Hamburg)*	6
1968-69	Ruhl *(1FC Cologne)*	6
1969-70	Lubanski *(Gornik Zabrze)*	8
1970-71	Lubanski *(Gornik Zabrze)*	8
1971-72	Osgood *(Chelsea)**	8
1972-73	Chiarugi *(AC Milan)**	7
1973-74	Heynckes *(Borussia M'gladbach)*	10
1974-75	Onischenko *(Dynamo Kiev)**	7
1975-76	Rensenbrink *(Anderlecht)**	8
1976-77	Milanov *(Levski Spartak)*	13
1977-78	Keller *(SV Hamburg)*	6
	Van der Elst *(Anderlecht)**	6
1978-79	Altobelli *(Inter-Milan)*	7
1979-80	Kempes *(Valencia)**	9
1980-81	Cross *(West Ham)*	6
1981-82	Shengelia *(Dynamo Tbilisi)*	6
	Voordeckers *(Standard Liege)*	6
1982-83	Santillana *(Real Madrid)*	9

*winners

EUROPEAN CUP WINNERS CUP 1975-76

FIRST ROUND

Rapid Bucharest v Anderlecht (1-0, 0-2)	1-2
Borac Banja Luka v US Rumelange (9-0, 5-1)	14-1
Skeid Oslo v Stal Rzeszow (1-4, 0-4)	1-8
Wrexham v Djurgaarden (2-1, 1-1)	3-2
Valur Reykjavik v Celtic (0-2, 0-7)	0-9
Spartak Trnava v Boavista Porto (0-0, 0-3)	0-3
Besiktas v Fiorentina (0-3, 0-3)	0-6
Panathinaikos v Sach. Zwickau (0-0, 0-2)	0-2
Eintracht Frankfurt v Coleraine (5-1, 6-2)	11-3
Basle v Atletico Madrid (1-2, 1-1)	2-3
Haladas Szombathely v Valletta (7-0, 1-1)	8-1
Sturm Graz v Slavia Sofia (3-1, 0-1)	3-2
Vejle BK v FC Den Haag (0-2, 0-2)	0-4
Home Farm v RC Lens (1-1, 0-6)	1-7
Ararat Erevan v Anor. Famagusta (9-0, 1-1)	10-1
Lahden Reipas v West Ham United (2-2, 0-3)	2-5

SECOND-ROUND

Anderlecht v Borac Banja Luka (3-0, 0-1)	3-1
Wrexham v Stal Rzeszow (2-0, 1-1)	3-1
Boavisto Porto v Celtic (0-0, 1-3)	1-3
Fiorentina v Sachsenring Zwickau† (1-0, 0-1)	1-1
Atletico Madrid v Ein. Frankfurt (1-2, 0-1)	1-3
Sturm Graz v Haladas Szombathely (2-0, 1-1)	3-1
FC Den Haag v RC Lens (3-2, 3-1)	6-3
Ararat Erevan v West Ham United (1-1, 1-3)	2-4

QUARTER-FINALS

Anderlecht v Wrexham (1-0, 1-1)	2-1
Celtic v Sachsenring Zwickau (1-1, 0-1)	1-2
Sturm Graz v Eintracht Frankfurt (0-2, 0-1)	0-3
FC Den Haag v West Ham United* (4-2, 1-3)	5-5

SEMI-FINALS

Sachsenring Zwickau v Anderlecht (0-3, 0-2)	0-5
Eintracht Frankfurt v West Ham U. (2-1, 1-3)	3-4

FINAL

Anderlecht 4 West Ham United 2
(Brussels, 5.5.76, 58,000)

Anderlecht: Ruiter, Lomme, Broos, Van Binst, Thissen, Dockx, Coeck (Vercauteren), Van der Elst, Haan, Ressel, Rensenbrink

West Ham: Day, Coleman, Lampard (A. Taylor), Bonds, T. Taylor, McDowell, Brooking, Paddon, Holland, Jennings, Robson

Scorers: Rensenbrink 2 (1 pen), Van der Elst 2; Holland, Robson

*won on away goals rule †won on penalties

Anderlecht's Van Binst climbs above Broos to clear from Robson in the 1976 final with West Ham in Brussels. The Belgians won 4-2 in the first of their three consecutive Cup Winners Cup finals: these two players, plus Thissen, Dockx, Coeck, Van der Elst and Dutch stars Haan and Rensenbrink appeared in all three matches.

Bergen of Norway by the same score, drawing away and then winning at home in both cases. That they should have progressed further than their English or Scottish counterparts was surprising but somehow indicative of the way Britain was losing her grip on a competition she had effectively created with her age-old domestic cup competitions. Having provided finalists in as many as nine of the first 13 tournaments, with four winners, the British effort was to fall away to the point that only twice in the next eight years did British clubs reach the final—West Ham (1976) and Arsenal (1980)—and both lost.

1974-75

The competition surprisingly continued its Eastern European way in 1975, with both finalists coming from the Communist bloc and the winners, Dynamo Kiev, actually being the same as the USSR national side at the time. With the excellent Oleg Blokhin their undisputed star (he was later voted European Footballer of the Year), Kiev had a steady if unexciting run to the final past CSKA Sofia, Eintracht Frankfurt, Bursaspor (Turkey) and PSV Eindhoven.

Their opponents in the final, Ferencvaros, had their revenge for the defeat by Leeds in the 1968 Fairs Cup final with a display of British bashing past Cardiff City and then Liverpool. The latter could only draw 1-1 on Merseyside and were then held to a goalless draw in Hungary. In the first round Liverpool had established a record in beating the Norwegian side Stromsgodset 11-0 at Anfield, with nine of the side scoring: Lindsay (penalty), Boersma (2), Heighway, Peter Thompson (2), Smith, Cormack, Hughes, Callaghan and Kennedy. The exceptions were keeper Ray Clemence and Brian Hall. By way of sublime contrast, Liverpool managed only one in the second leg, from Ray Kennedy.

In the Basle final Blokhin, ably supported in midfield by Muntian, was devastating, and it was fitting that he should add the finishing touch to a great team performance after two goals from Onischenko, taking his season's tally to seven, had wrapped it up. Thus Kiev became the only Soviet team, before or since, to win a European title.

1975-76

The 1975-76 series produced the first of Anderlecht's run of three consecutive finals. It was not a great year for the competition, however, with neither finalist, Anderlecht nor West Ham, distinguishing themselves before the final. Anderlecht lost to Rapid in Bucharest and to Borac Banja Luka in Yugoslavia and only drew 1-1 in Wrexham, who were a little unlucky to go out in the quarter-finals by the odd goal in three. After a good performance against the powerful

EUROPEAN CUP WINNERS CUP 1976-77

PRELIMINARY ROUND

Cardiff City* v Servette Geneva (1-0, 1-2)	2-2

FIRST ROUND

SV Hamburg v IB Keflavik (3-0, 1-1)	4-1
Lokomotiv Leipzig v Hearts (2-0, 1-5)	3-5
Cardiff City v Dynamo Tbilisi (1-0, 0-3)	1-3
MTK Budapest v Sparta Prague (3-1, 1-1)	4-2
Levski Spartak v Lahden Reipas (12-2, 7-1)	19-3
CSU Galati v Boavista Porto (2-3, 0-2)	2-5
Lierse SK v Hajduk Split (1-0, 0-3)	1-3
Rapid Vienna v Atletico Madrid (1-2, 1-1)	2-3
Bodo Glimt v Napoli (0-2, 0-1)	0-3
Iraklis Salonika v Apoel Nicosia (0-0, 0-2)	0-2
Bohemians v BK Esbjerg (2-1, 1-0)	3-1
Floriana v Slask Wroclaw (1-4, 0-2)	1-6
Southampton v Olym. Marseille (4-0, 1-2)	5-2
Carrick Rangers v Aris Bonnevoie (3-1, 1-2)	4-3
AIK Stockholm v Galatasaray (1-2, 1-1)	2-3
Anderlecht v Roda JC (2-1, 3-2)	5-3

SECOND ROUND

SV Hamburg v Heart of Midlothian (4-2, 4-1)	8-3
Dynamo Tbilisi v MKT Budapest (1-4, 0-1)	1-5
Boavisto Porto v Levski Spartak* (3-1, 0-2)	3-3
Atletico Madrid v Hajduk Split (1-0, 2-1)	3-1
Apoel Nicosia v Napoli (1-1, 0-2)	1-3
Slask Wroclaw v Bohemians (3-0, 1-0)	4-0
Carrick Rangers v Southampton (2-5, 1-4)	3-9
Anderlecht v Galatasaray (5-1, 5-1)	10-2

QUARTER-FINALS

MTK Budapest v SV Hamburg (1-1, 1-4)	2-5
Levski Spartak v Atletico Madrid (2-1, 0-2)	2-3
Slask Wroclaw v Napoli (0-0, 0-2)	0-2
Anderlecht v Southampton (2-0, 1-2)	3-2

SEMI-FINALS

Atletico Madrid v SV Hamburg (3-1, 0-3)	3-4
Napoli v Anderlecht (1-0, 0-2)	1-2

FINAL

SV Hamburg 2 Anderlecht 0
(Amsterdam, 11.5.77, 66,000)

Hamburg: Kargus, Kaltz, Ripp, Nogly, Hidien, Steffenhagen, Keller, Reimann, Memering, Magath, Volkert

Anderlecht: Ruiter, Van Binst, Broos, Vandendaele, Thissen, Dockx (Van Poucke), Van der Elst, Coeck, Haan, Ressel, Rensenbrink

Scorers: Volkert (pen), Magath

*won on away goals rule

Russians Ararat Erevan West Ham were fortunate to survive a 4-2 defeat in The Hague, going through on away goals after winning 3-1 at home, and then beat poor Eintracht Frankfurt, who seem destined to be the bridesmaids of European football. The artistic Trevor Brooking, noted more for making goals than for scoring them, produced two to send the Hammers on the way to a 3-1 win over the West Germans at Upton Park, and to a 4-3 aggregate victory.

The final in Brussels, with Anderlecht playing 'at home', at last drew a crowd worthy of the event, following two finals whose total together barely topped 15,000. And they were not disappointed, either with the value or the result. In the end Anderlecht's fast running style overpowered West Ham, with Dutch international Robbie Rensenbrink and François van der Elst sharing four goals.

1976-77

Holders Anderlecht reached the final again, looking more convincing this year until the quarter-finals, when they won through by the odd goal in five against Southampton. They squeezed through the semis by the same margin against Italian Cup winners Napoli, again losing away, but were well beaten in the final by SV Hamburg, West Germany's first victory in the competition for 10 years.

Hamburg had had an easy passage until meeting Atlético Madrid in the semi-finals. They scored once in Spain to keep their deficit to a manageable 3-1, but the return leg, a 3-0 victory in Hamburg led by a Capon own goal, was in a sense more of a key game for them than the actual final. For that game, in Amsterdam, Anderlecht showed only one change from the 1977 final, but for all their experience the holders just could not get going, and after a goalless first half a penalty from Volkert virtually settled the issue.

1977-78

Although this was to be Anderlecht's season again, it was Spain's Betis from Seville who caused the talking point of the first round by knocking out AC Milan. The Italian club were still a feared force in Europe, although their great period 1963-73, in which they won four major trophies, was well behind them. English representatives Manchester United had to play their first round home leg against St Etienne in Plymouth—after UEFA had initially threatened to ban them altogether following the now traditional behaviour from United fans in the first, away leg, drawn 1-1. UEFA had clearly lost patience with British soccer fans and United, though guilty, seemed set to suffer for the sins of the many. As it happened this was probably the watershed. The following three seasons saw a dramatic improvement in the behaviour of British fans abroad, notably during and after the Rome and Munich European Cup finals of 1977 and 1979, which helped to erase the bad old days.

United won in Plymouth, but then lost 4-0 in Porto and were unable to make up the gap in the return—winning an exciting match 5-2 with the unlikely help of two separate own goals by Murca. Porto went on to beat Anderlecht 1-0 in the home leg of the

EUROPEAN CUP WINNERS CUP 1977-78

PRELIMINARY ROUND

Rangers v Young Boys Berne (1-0, 2-2)	3-2

FIRST ROUND

Lokomotiv Sofia v Anderlecht (1-6, 0-2)	1-8
SV Hamburg v Lahden Reipas (8-1, 5-2)	13-3
St Etienne v Manchester United (1-1, 0-2)	1-3
1FC Cologne v Porto (2-2, 0-1)	2-3
Progres Niedercorn v Vejle BK (0-1, 0-9)	0-10
PAOK Salonika v Zag. Sosnowiec (2-0, 2-0)	4-0
SK Brann Bergen v IA Akranes (1-0, 4-0)	5-0
Rangers v Twente Enschede (0-0, 0-3)	0-3
Valletta v Dynamo Moscow (0-2, 0-5)	0-7
Olympiakos Nicosia v Uni. Craiova (1-6, 2-0)	3-6
Coleraine v Lokomotiv Leipzig (1-4, 2-2)	3-6
Betis Seville v AC Milan (2-0, 1-2)	3-2
Dundalk v Hajduk Split (1-0, 0-4)	1-4
Besiktas v Diosgyor (2-0, 0-5)	2-5
Lokomotiv Kosice* v Oster Vaxjo (0-0, 2-2)	2-2
Cardiff City v FK Austria/WAC (0-0, 0-1)	0-1

SECOND ROUND

SV Hamburg v Anderlecht (1-2, 1-1)	2-3
Porto v Manchester United (4-0, 2-5)	6-5
Vejle BK v PAOK Salonika (3-0, 1-2)	4-2
Twente Enschede v SK B. Bergen (2-0, 2-1)	4-1
Dynamo Moscow† v Uni. Craiova (2-0, 0-2)	2-2
Lokomotiv Leipzig v Betis Seville (1-1, 1-2)	2-3
Diosgyor v Hajduk Split† (2-1, 1-2)	3-3
FK Austria/WAC* v Lok. Kosice (0-0, 1-1)	1-1

QUARTER-FINALS

Porto v Anderlecht (1-0, 0-3)	1-3
Vejle BK v Twente Enschede (0-3, 0-4)	0-7
Betis Seville v Dynamo Moscow (0-0, 0-3)	0-3
FK Austria/WAC† v Hajduk Split (1-1, 1-1)	2-2

SEMI-FINALS

Twente Enschede v Anderdecht (0-1, 0-2)	0-3
Dyn. Moscow v FK Austria/WAC† (2-1, 1-2)	3-3

FINAL

Anderlecht 4 FK Austria/WAC 0
(Paris, 3.5.78, 48,769)

Anderlecht: De Bree, Van Binst, Broos, Dusbaba, Thissen, Vercauteren (Dockx), Coeck, Haan, Van der Elst, Nielsen, Rensenbrink

Austria/WAC: Baumgartner, R. Sara, Baumeister, Obermeyer, J. Sara, Prohaska, Daxbacher (Martinez), Gasselich, Morales (Drazan), Pirkner, Parits

Scorers: Rensenbrink 2, Van Binst 2

*won on away goals rule †won on penalties

FAR LEFT: ***Double goalscorers François van der Elst and Robbie Rensenbrink parade the cup in front of their 'home' fans after the 1976 win over West Ham.***
LEFT: ***Van der Elst led the series scorers in 1976-77, but the holders lost the final to SV Hamburg.***

EUROPEAN CUP WINNERS CUP 1978-79

FIRST ROUND

Barcelona v Shaktor Donetz (3-0, 1-1)	4-1
Zaglebie Sosnowiec v SW Innsbruck (2-3, 1-1)	3-4
AZ 67 Alkmaar v Ipswich Town (0-0, 0-2)	0-2
Floriana v Inter-Milan (1-3, 0-5)	1-8
Bodo Glimt v Union Luxembourg (4-1, 0-1)	4-2
NK Rijeka v Wrexham (3-0, 0-2)	3-2
Beveren-Waas v Ballymena (3-0, 3-0)	6-0
Sporting Lisbon v Banik Ostrava (0-1, 0-1)	0-2
Apoel Nicosia v Shamrock Rovers (0-2, 0-1)	0-3
Ferencvaros v Kalmar FF (2-0, 2-2)	4-2
Valur Reykjavik v FC Magdeburg (1-1, 0-4)	1-5
PAOK Salonika v Servette Geneva (2-0, 0-4)	2-4
Frem Copenhagen v AS Nancy (2-0, 0-4)	2-4
Marek Stanke Dimitrov v Aberdeen (3-2, 0-3)	3-5
Uni. Craiova v Fortuna Dusseldorf (3-4, 1-1)	4-5

[Anderlecht (holders) received bye]

SECOND ROUND

Anderlecht v Barcelona† (3-0, 0-3)	3-3
Ipswich Town v SW Innsbruck (1-0, 1-1)	2-1
Inter-Milan v Bodo Glimt (5-0, 2-1)	7-1
NK Rijeka v Beveren-Waas (0-0, 0-2)	0-2
Banik Ostrava v Shamrock Rovers (3-0, 3-1)	6-1
FC Magdeburg* v Ferencvaros (1-0, 1-2)	2-2
Servette Geneva v AS Nancy (2-1, 2-2)	4-3
Fortuna Dusseldorf v Aberdeen (3-0, 0-2)	3-2

QUARTER-FINALS

Ipswich Town v Barcelona† (2-1, 0-1)	2-2
Inter-Milan v Beveren-Waas (0-0, 0-1)	0-1
FC Magdeburg v Banik Ostrava (2-1, 2-4)	4-5
Fortuna Dusseldorf* v Servette (0-0, 1-1)	1-1

SEMI-FINALS

Barcelona v Beveren-Waas (1-0, 1-0)	2-0
Fortuna Dusseldorf v Banik Ostrava (3-1, 1-2)	4-3

FINAL

Barcelona 4 Fortuna Dusseldorf 3 [aet] (Basle, 16.5.79, 50,000)

Barcelona: Artola, Zuviria, Migueli, Costas (Martinez), Albaladejo (De la Cruz), Neeskens, Sanchez, Asensi, Rexach, Krankl, Carrasco

Fortuna: Daniel, Baltes, Brei (Weike), Zewe, Zimmermann (Lumb), Kohnen, Bommer, Schmitz, T. Allofs, K. Allofs, Seel

Scorers: Sanchez, Asensi, Rexach, Krankl; K. Allofs, Seel 2

*won on away goals rule †won on penalties

A shot from Barcelona captain Carlos Rexach (7) gives his side a 3-2 extra-time lead in the 1979 final against Fortuna Dusseldorf in Basle. The Spaniards eventually won a pulsating if technically naïve match 4-3—in a game which helped to lift the Cup Winners Cup back towards second place in the European hierarchy. It was Barcelona's seventh European final, and 10 years since they lost to Slovan Bratislava in the Cup Winners Cup on the same ground. Rexach, the sole survivor from that game, had also scored against the Czechs.

EUROPEAN CUP WINNERS CUP FINALS

Year	Venue	Winners		Runners-up	
1961	*(two legs)*	Fiorentina	2:2	Rangers	0:1
1962	Stuttgart	Atletico Madrid	†3	Fiorentina	0
1963	Rotterdam	Tottenham Hotspur	5	Atletico Madrid	1
1964	Antwerp	Sporting Lisbon	‡1	MTK Budapest	0
1965	Wembley	West Ham United	2	TSV Munich 1860	0
1966	Glasgow	Borussia Dortmund	*2	Liverpool	1
1967	Nuremberg	Bayern Munich	*1	Rangers	0
1968	Rotterdam	AC Milan	2	SV Hamburg	0
1969	Basle	Slovan Bratislava	3	Barcelona	2
1970	Vienna	Manchester City	2	Gornik Zabrze	1
1971	Athens	Chelsea	§2	Real Madrid	1
1972	Barcelona	Rangers	3	Dynamo Moscow	2
1973	Salonika	AC Milan	1	Leeds United	0
1974	Rotterdam	FC Magdeburg	2	AC Milan	0
1975	Basle	Dynamo Kiev	3	Ferencvaros	0
1976	Brussels	Anderlecht	4	West Ham United	2
1977	Amsterdam	SV Hamburg	2	Anderlecht	0
1978	Paris	Anderlecht	4	FK Austria WAC	0
1979	Basle	Barcelona	4	Fortuna Dusseldorf	3
1980	Brussels	Valencia**	0	Arsenal	0
1981	Dusseldorf	Dynamo Tbilisi	2	Carl Zeiss Jena	1
1982	Barcelona	Barcelona	2	Standard Liege	1
1983	Gothenburg	Aberdeen	2	Real Madrid	1

*after extra time †after 1-1 draw at Hampden Park ‡after 3-3 draw in Brussels §after 1-1 draw in Athens **won 5-4 on penalties after extra-time

quarter-finals, not nearly enough, and from here on in Anderlecht went all the way without conceding a goal. No doubt their most satisfying moment came in the second round in Hamburg—where they won 2-1 to gain revenge for the previous season's final. Kevin Keegan's goal in the return could only equal Van der Elst's effort and Anderlecht were through.

Their opponents FK Austria/WAC must be among the most dubious finalists ever. Their 1-0 aggregate win over Cardiff (competing for the 11th time in 14 seasons) was followed by an away goal scrape against Locomotiv Kosice of Czechoslovakia and then victories on penalties against Hajduk Split and Dynamo Moscow. Despite the presence of stars like Robert and Josef Sara, Prohaska and Pirkner they lived up to their pre-match billing and crashed 4-0. Again Rensenbrink scored twice, this time sharing the spoils with Van Binst.

1978-79

It is one of those strange inconsistencies of the game that while Anderlecht reached three successive Cup Winners Cup finals, winning two in style, they managed nothing at home. They only qualified for the 1977-78 series, in fact, as losing Belgian Cup finalists to double winners Bruges. In 1978-79 the holders, after a bye, were to fall at the first fence, but even then only on penalties, and against the eventual winners at that.

Barcelona then went all the way, being fortunate to defeat Ipswich in the quarter-finals with some debatable tactics. The FA Cup holders won the first game 2-1, with Eric Gates scoring twice, but they should never have let Krankl get free to create Barcelona's goal for Esteban and suffered from that inevitable European complaint—a certain penalty which only the referee failed to see. The Spanish side really struggled against Anderlecht's countrymen Beveren in the semi-finals, relying on a penalty in each leg to get through.

Fortuna Dusseldorf did not have an easy passage to the final, either, going through with odd-goal victories after losing the away legs in three ties (including the one against Aberdeen), and beating Servette on the away goals rule in the quarter-finals thanks to Bommer's effort in Geneva. But in their first European final they certainly contributed to 120 minutes of non-stop action in Basle. The teams were level at 2-2 at the end of full-time but Barcelona always had the edge, never actually going behind and finally winning 4-3 with extra-time goals by Rexach and Krankl. It was 10 years to the very month since Barcelona had last been on the Basle pitch—losing a European Cup Winners Cup final by the odd goal in five. Spanish international Carlos Rexach was the only survivor from that 3-2 defeat.

1979–80

When the UEFA organizing committee decided that penalties would be used in the 1980 European club finals if the scores were level after extra time they hardly expected their ruling to be employed at the very first opportunity. After all, replays had been required only four times before in 45 single-match finals.

But it came to pass that at the Heysel Stadium on 14 May Arsenal and Valencia were still goalless after 120 minutes of frustrating stalemate; and if the controversial decision had one factor in its favour, it was that the contest contained more tension and goalmouth action than the entire match which it followed—a match that produced just five on-target attempts at scoring.

History will record that it was Graham Rix, taking Arsenal's sixth spot-kick, who cost his side the trophy. But it could have been so different if Liam Brady, the Irish star then under the microscope of several top European clubs, had converted his, Arsenal's first. Mario Kempes, averaging a goal a game in the competition, had failed with Valencia's first kick, Pat Jennings diving to his right to save; had Brady then scored, he would have given Arsenal not only a 1-0 lead but also a massive psychological advantage as the tension mounted.

As it was, with Pereira saving his weak shot, it was back to square one with Arsenal under more pressure as the side going second. Solsona, Pablo, substitute Castellanos (off the bar) and Bonhof survived the ordeal for Valencia; Stapleton, Sunderland, Talbot and substitute Hollins made it for Arsenal.

After yet more confusion and delay the order was sorted out for the next 10 candidates, though sudden death now applied. Arias' shot just squeezed under Jennings falling body, and then poor Rix saw his unconvincing shot gathered by Carlos Pereira in much the same place as the one from Brady.

The Spanish side celebrated as though they had won 5-0 in the 90 minutes, and the Arsenal squad trudged wearily to their supporters in a noble attempt to thank them for coming to their 70th competitive game of the season, their fifth in 15 days.

It was an unsatisfactory conclusion to a disappointing match that had promised intriguing confrontation between a side which had scored 20 goals in eight games—with three ties against top-class opponents in Rangers (three out of their four goals coming from Kempes), Barcelona and Nantes—and one which had conceded only five goals in their eight games. On the day both defences played well, with their youngest members—O'Leary and Tendillo—the outstanding players in each. Chances were few, and when they did come along both keepers produced good saves to make the threat of deciding penalties increasingly real.

With the exception of holders Barcelona—eliminated by fellow Spanish Leaguers Valencia in the quarter-finals with Pablo's goal at Campo Nuevo and then contributions by Saura (2), Bonhof and Kempes in Valencia making it an impressive double—the last four could have been the seeds. All arrived in the semi-finals without too much trouble, though Dynamo Moscow's 3-2 win in Nantes came perilously close to wiping out the Frenchmen's fine 2-0 victory in Russia in the previous round.

Nantes fell to a rampant Valencia in the semi-final leg in Spain, Kempes adding two goals (including his second penalty of the series!) to those from Bonhof and Suburats. Arsenal, meanwhile, were chalking up an even more impressive performance against a Juventus side composed almost entirely of current Italian internationals. After a controversial game at Highbury which saw the near-blameless Tardelli sent off and the real culprit, Bettega, score at the wrong end five minutes from time to equalize Cabrini's penalty, the London side pulled off one of the really great European results.

Only two sides—Ferencvaros in the 1965 Fairs Cup final and Twente Enschede in the semi-final of the UEFA Cup in 1975—had ever won a match in Turin's Stadio Comunale in more than 20 years of European competition, and few people gave Arsenal much chance of making it three. But they did, Paul Vaessen nodding in a Rix cross in the 87th minute to put his seniors in the Brussels final.

The final in Brussels was to be poor reward and it was also the end of a very good cup sequence for Arsenal as they had just become the first side for a century to appear in three consecutive FA Cup finals. Their record of not losing a single game in Europe, reaching the final and still remaining undefeated while not winning the trophy remains, not surprisingly, unique.

Penalty number six: Pereira saves Graham Rix's softly struck spot-kick, and Valencia take the Cup Winners Cup.

EUROPEAN CUP WINNERS CUP 1979-80

PRELIMINARY ROUND

Copenhagen BK 1903 v A. Nicosia (6-0, 1-0)	7-0
Rangers v Lillestrom SK (1-0, 2-0)	3-0

FIRST ROUND

Copenhagen BK 1903 v Valencia (2-2, 0-4)	2-6
Rangers v Fortuna Dusseldorf (2-1, 0-0)	2-1
Lahden Reipas v Aris Bonnevoie (0-1, 0-1)	0-2
IA Akranes v Barcelona (0-1, 0-5)	0-6
Dynamo Moscow w.o. Vlaznia (withdrew)	
Sliema Wanderers v Boavista (2-1, 0-8)	2-9
Young Boys Berne v S. Bucharest (2-2, 0-6)	2-8
Cliftonville v Nantes (0-1, 0-7)	0-8
Juventus v Raba ETO Gyor (2-0, 1-2)	3-2
Arka Gdynia v Beroe S. Zagora (3-2, 0-2)	3-4
SW Innsbruck v Lokomotiv Kosice (1-2, 0-1)	1-3
Beerschot v NK Rijeką (0-0, 1-2)	1-2
IFK Gothenburg v Waterford (1-0, 1-1)	2-1
Panionios v Twente Enschede (4-0, 1-3)	5-3
Wrexham v FC Magdeburg (3-2, 2-5)	5-7
Arsenal v Fenerbahce (2-0, 0-0)	2-0

SECOND ROUND

Valencia v Rangers (1-1, 3-1)	4-2
Aris Bonnevoie v Barcelona (1-4, 1-7)	2-11
Dynamo Moscow* v Boavista (0-0, 1-1)	1-1
Nantes v Steaua Bucharest (3-2, 2-1)	5-3
Beroe S. Zagora v Juventus (1-0, 1-3)	1-3
Lokomotiv Kosice v NK Rijeka (2-0, 0-3)	2-3
Panionios v IFK Gothenburg (1-0, 0-2)	1-2
Arsenal v FC Magdeburg (2-1, 2-2)	4-3

QUARTER-FINALS

Barcelona v Valencia (0-1, 3-4)	3-5
Dynamo Moscow v Nantes (0-2, 3-2)	3-4
NK Rijeka v Juventus (0-0, 0-2)	0-2
Arsenal v IFK Gothenburg (5-1, 0-0)	5-1

SEMI-FINALS

Nantes v Valencia (2-1, 0-4)	2-5
Arsenal v Juventus (1-1, 1-0)	2-1

FINAL

Valencia† 0 Arsenal 0 [aet]
(Brussels, 14.5.80, 40,000)

Valencia: Pereira, Carrete, Botubot, Arias, Tendillo, Solsona, Saura, Bonhof, Kempes, Suburats (Castellanos 111), Pablo

Arsenal: Jennings, Rice, Nelson, Talbot, O'Leary, Young, Brady, Sunderland, Stapleton, Price, (Hollins 106), Rix

Leading scorers: 9—Kempes *(Valencia)*; 7—Pecout *(Nantes)*; 4—Krankl, Simonsen *(Barcelona)*, Sunderland *(Arsenal)*

*won on away goals rule †Valencia won 5-4 on penalties

EUROPEAN CUP WINNERS CUP 1980-81

PRELIMINARY ROUND	
Celtic v Diosgyor (6-0, 1-2)	7-2
Altay Izmir v Benfica (0-0, 0-4)	0-4
FIRST ROUND	
Kastoria v Dynamo Tbilisi (0-0, 0-2)	0-2
Newport County v Crusaders (4-0, 0-0)	4-0
Spora Luxembourg v Sparta Prague (0-6, 0-6)	0-12
Slavia Sofia v Legia Warsaw (3-1, 0-1)	3-2
Castilla v West Ham United (3-1, 1-5)	4-6
Celtic v Poli Timisoara (2-1, 0-1)	2-2
Dynamo Zagreb v Benfica (0-0, 0-2)	0-2
Fortuna Dusseldorf v Austria Salzburg (5-0, 3-0)	8-0
Hibernians v Waterford (1-0, 0-4)	1-4
Ilves Tampere v Feyenoord (1-3, 2-4)	3-7
Hvidovre v Fram (1-0, 2-0)	3-0
Malmo FF v Partizan Tirana (1-0, 0-0)	1-0
Omonia Nicosia v Waterschei (1-3, 0-4)	1-7
Sion v Haugar (1-1, 0-2)	1-3
Valencia v Monaco (2-0, 3-3)	5-3
AS Roma v Carl Zeiss Jena (3-0, 0-4)	3-4
SECOND ROUND	
Waterford v Dynamo Tbilisi (0-1, 0-4)	0-5
Malmo FF v Benfica (1-0, 0-2)	1-2
Waterschei v Fortuna Dusseldorf (0-0, 0-1)	0-1
Feyenoord v Hvidovre (2-1, 1-0)	3-1
Sparta Prague v Slavia Sofia (2-0, 0-3)	2-3
Haugar v Newport County (0-0, 0-6)	0-6
West Ham United v Poli Timisoara (4-0, 0-1)	4-1
Carl Zeiss Jena v Valencia (3-1, 0-1)	3-2
QUARTER FINALS	
West Ham United v Dynamo Tbilisi (1-4, 1-0)	2-4
Slavia Sofia v Feyenoord (3-2, 0-4)	3-6
Fortuna Dusseldorf v Benfica (2-2, 0-1)	2-3
Carl Zeiss Jena v Newport County (2-2, 1-0)	3-2
SEMI-FINALS	
Dynamo Tbilisi v Feyenoord (3-0, 0-2)	3-2
Carl Zeiss Jena v Benfica (2-0, 0-1)	2-1

FINAL

Dynamo Tbilisi 2 Carl Zeiss Jena 1
(Dusseldorf, 13.5.81, 9,000)

Dynamo Tbilisi: Gabelia, Kostava, Chivadze, Khisanishvili, Tavadze, Svanadze (Kakilashvili) Sulakvelidze, Daraselia, Gutsayev, Kipiani, Shengelia

Carl Zeiss Jena: Grapenthin, Brauer, Kurbjuweit, Schnuphase, Schilling, Hoppe (Overmann), Krause, Lindemann, Bieleau (Topfer), Raab, Vogel

Scorers: Gutsayev, Daraselia: Hoppe

1980-81

A crowd of only nine thousand watched the 1981 Cup Winners Cup final in Dusseldorf, an inappropriate venue for two Eastern European finalists. The economic shortcomings of their success tended to obscure the genuine merit of Dynamo Tbilisi, from Georgia, who came from behind to win the trophy against East Germany's Carl Zeiss Jena.

West Ham United certainly felt the quality in Tbilisi's football in the quarter-final. The English Cup holders had already overcome first round difficulties; crowd trouble in Spain in the first leg against Castilla, Real Madrid's reserve team, had been blamed on London supporters. The second leg was staged behind closed doors and despite the lack of atmosphere West Ham overturned a 3-1 deficit with David Cross completing a hat-trick in extra time.

Poli Timisoara, conquerors of Celtic, were also swept aside by West Ham, but not Tbilisi, who won 4-1 at Upton Park. Chivadze, a sweeper who used his freedom to provide a regular supply of goals, Kipriani, the balding English-speaking creator, and two short mobile forwards, Shengelia and Gutsayev, all revealed the class that marked Tbilisi as eventual winners.

The heroics from the British standpoint came from Third Division Newport County who like West Ham reached the last eight. Then two goals in Jena by Tommy Tynan in a 2-2 draw gave County a marvellous opportunity to progress even further at Somerton Park. Though Newport dominated the second leg, the only goal came from Kurbjuweit for Carl Zeiss.

In the semi-final the East German club surprisingly beat Benfica while Tbilisi battled past Feyenoord. Goals from Sulakvelidze (2) and Gutsaev established a commanding lead in the home leg, but Tbilisi had three more controversially disallowed in Rotterdam, and only just hung on as Feijenoord pulled back two.

The small crowd lent disenchantment to the final where Tbilisi again revealed an appetite for victory to go with their flair. The goals all came in the second half, with Hoppe edging Carl Zeiss Jena into the lead. Gutsayev contributed again with the equaliser and with extra time beckoning Daraselia darted into the penalty area to give Dynamo Tbilisi the victory they deserved.

1981-82

The 1982 final could have hardly provided a more stark contrast in atmosphere to the preceding year. In front of one hundred thousand spectators in their own Nou Camp stadium Barcelona beat Standard Liege 2-1 to reclaim the trophy won only three seasons

Graham Roberts expresses everyone's views of the Barcelona team during Spurs' brutal 1982 semi-final at White Hart Lane.

EUROPEAN CUP WINNERS CUP 1981-82

PRELIMINARY ROUND

Poli Timisoara v Lokomotiv Leipzig (2-0, 0-5)	2-5

FIRST ROUND

Barcelona v Trakia Plovdiv (4-1, 0-1)	4-2
Ajax v Tottenham Hotspur (1-3, 0-3)	1-6
KTP v Bastia (0-0, 0-5)	0-5
Eintracht Frankfurt v PAOK Salonika (2-0, 0-2)	2-2
Dynamo Tbilisi v Grazer AK (2-0, 2-2)	4-2
Swansea City v Lokomotiv Leipzig (0-1, 1-2)	1-3
Valerengen v Legia Warsaw (2-2, 1-4)	3-6
SKA Rostov v Ankaragucu (3-0, 2-0)	5-0
Paralimni v Vasas (1-0, 0-8)	1-8
Ballymena United v AS Roma (0-2, 0-4)	0-6
Lausanne v Kalmar (2-1, 2-3)	4-4
Jeunesse Esch v Velez Mostar (1-1, 1-6)	2-7
Fram v Dundalk (2-1, 0-4)	2-5
Dukla Prague v Rangers (3-0, 1-2)	4-2
Veijle v Porto (2-1, 0-3)	2-4
Floriana v Standard Liege (1-3, 0-9)	1-12

SECOND ROUND

Dukla Prague v Barcelona (1-0, 0-4)	1-4
Legia Warsaw v Lausanne (2-1, 1-1)	3-2
SKA Rostov v Eintracht Frankfurt (1-0, 0-2)	1-2
Porto v AS Roma (2-0, 0-0)	2-0
Dundalk v Tottenham Hotspur (1-1, 0-1)	1-2
Lokomotiv Leipzig* v Velez Mostar (1-1, 1-1)	2-2
Bastia v Dynamo Tbilisi (1-1, 1-3)	2-4
Vasas v Standard Liege (0-2, 0-2)	0-4

QUARTER FINALS

Lokomotiv Leipzig v Barcelona (0-3, 2-1)	2-4
Legia Warsaw v Dynamo Tbilisi (0-1, 0-1)	0-2
Tottenham Hotspur v Eintracht Frankfurt (2-0, 1-2)	3-2
Standard Liege v Porto (2-0, 2-2)	4-2

SEMI-FINALS

Tottenham Hotspur v Barcelona (1-1, 0-1)	1-2
Dynamo Tbilisi v Standard Liege (0-1, 0-1)	0-2

FINAL

Barcelona 2 Standard Liege 1
(Barcelona, 12.5.82, 100,000)

Barcelona: Urruti, Gerado, Migueli, Alesanco, Manolo, Sanchez, Moratalla, Esteban, Simonsen, Quini, Carrasco

Standard Liege: Preud'homme, Gerets, Poel, Meeuws, Plessers, Vandersmissen, Daerden, Haan, Botteron, Tahamata, Wendt

Scorers: Simonsen, Quini: Vandersmissen

*on penalties

earlier against Fortuna Dusseldorf in Basle.

Yet it was a success more than tinged with adverse reaction, particularly in London where Barcelona disgraced their semi-final first leg against Tottenham with a cynical display of violence on the field. Spurs reacted by meeting fire with fire and subsequently both clubs—Barcelona £7,000 and Tottenham £2,500—were fined by UEFA. Oddly the key moment in the match had nothing to do with its shameful character. Ray Clemence, in his first season at White Hart Lane, fumbled most uncharacteristically a soft shot from Olmo and Barcelona were presented with an away goal that eased their eventual passage into the final. In all a disappointing end to a run in the competition that had seen the English Cup holders past Ajax, Dundalk and Eintracht Frankfurt in some style; other British hopes, Rangers and Swansea City had both departed in the first round.

Dynamo Tbilisi made a creditable attempt to retain the trophy, eventually losing to two 1-0 defeats to Standard Liege in the semi-final. The Belgian club fielded a cosmopolitan side with two Dutchmen, the World Cup veteran Arie Haan and Simon Tahamata, Rene Botteron, the Swiss international and a Swedish striker, Benny Wendt. In defence Standard were particularly well served by two battle-hardened performers for Belgium, Eric Gerets and Walter Meeuws, the latter to be sent off in the last minute of a distasteful final.

Despite the misfortune of meeting Barcelona on their own territory, Liege started the final with scant regard for the hostile environment. Guy Vandermissen, playing his way into the Belgian World Cup 22, opened the scoring. On half-time though they allowed the tiny Dane Allan Simonsen to head Barcelona level.

The winning goal heaped even more controversy on Barcelona's success. Referee Walter Eshweiler from West Germany allowed Quini to take and score from a free-kick without apparently indicating for the kick to be taken. So quickly did it happen that the Spanish television director in charge of the match coverage was totally caught out and Quini's triumphant moment was not witnessed by the cameras and the millions of viewers watching throughout Europe.

1982-83

The 1983 Cup Winners Cup represented a glorious march to success from Aberdeen, providing Scotland with their first taste of European success for eleven years. From the humble beginnings of a start in the preliminary round, Aberdeen swept all aside including a victory in the final against none other than Real Madrid.

Alex Ferguson had brought to the managers office at Pittodrie not only an in-

Eric Black puts Aberdeen 1-0 up in the 1983 final against Real Madrid in a nearly empty and rain-sodden Gothenburg stadium.

spiring personality but also a firm belief in creating a squad with a depth of talent that was perfectly suited to the demands of European competition. Most of his players were regularly collecting representative recognition; none though could be absolutely sure that they would retain their place in Aberdeen's side week in week out. No complacency at Pittodrie.

That preliminary round began with a warning that few in Europe would have heeded, eleven goals in total past Sion of Switzerland. The least attractive draw—a trip to Albania against Dynamo Tirana—did not hinder Aberdeen's progress. Nor Poland's Lech Poznan who were beaten home and away in the second round.

Bayern Munich provided the next test which Aberdeen passed with flying colours by drawing in the Olympic Stdium—where Spurs had been trounced 4-1 in the previous round. At Pittodrie Aberdeen stumbled and Bayern led 2-1, but Scotland's centre-half Alex McLeish equalised from Gordon Strachan's subtle free-kick; in the next minute John Hewitt, talented but a reserve for much of the campaign, popped in the winner. Hewitt's flair for the dramatic would reappear later in even more important circumstances.

Ferguson's clever use of his forces was perfectly illustrated again in the semi-final against Waterschei of Belgium. Doug Bell, a free running midfield player had taken something of a back seat after a match-winning goal and performance in Poznan. Now Ferguson picked Bell as the significant weapon to take Aberdeen into the final. Waterschei were demolished, 5-1, Bell the architect of their downfall.

Incessant rain and a soggy pitch could neither dampen nor clog up Aberdeen's talents in the final in Gothenburg. Eric Black, another of Ferguson's gifted teenagers, contributed an early lead. Juanito equalised with a penalty before half-time after Santillana had been fouled. The stalemate continued into extra time even though Aberdeen always looked the more impressive side. With just six minutes left the setting was perfect for John Hewitt to make another of his impressive intrusions. On as substitute for Black, Hewitt's diving header wrote the perfect ending for Ferguson's fairytale. Sad to relate, the following season's expected repeat performance was to be halted by clever Porto.

EUROPEAN CUP WINNERS CUP 1982-83

PRELIMINARY ROUND

Aberdeen v Sion (7-0, 4-1)	11-1
Swansea City v Braga (3-0, 0-1)	3-1

FIRST ROUND

Aberdeen v Dynamo Tirana (1-0, 0-0)	1-0
IBV Vestmannayjar v Lech Poznan (0-1, 0-3)	0-4
Barcelona v Apollo Limassol (8-0, 1-1)	9-1
Coleraine v Tottenham Hotspur (0-3, 0-4)	0-7
Dynamo Dresden v BK Copenhagen (3-2, 1-2)	4-4
Austria Vienna v Panathinaikos (2-0, 1-2)	3-2
Galataseray v Kuuysi-69 (2-1, 1-1)	3-2
IFK Gothenburg v Ujpest Dozsa (1-1, 1-3)	4-2
Inter-Milan v Slovan Bratislava (2-0, 1-2)	3-2
Lillestroem v Red Star Belgrade (0-4, 0-3)	0-7
Limerick v AZ'67 Alkmaar (1-1, 0-1)	1-2
Lokomotiv Sofia v Paris St. Germain (1-0, 1-5)	2-5
Swansea City v Sliema Wanderers (12-0, 5-0)	17-0
Moscow Torpedo v Bayern Munich (1-1, 0-0)	1-1
Waterschei v Red Boys Differdange (7-1, 1-0)	8-1
Baia Mare v Real Madrid (0-0, 2-5)	2-5

SECOND ROUND

Aberdeen v Lech Poznan (2-0, 1-0)	3-0
AZ'67 Alkmaar v Inter-Milan (1-0, 0-2)	1-2
BK Copenhagen v Waterschei (0-2, 1-4)	1-6
Galataseray v Austria Vienna (2-4, 1-0)	3-4
Red Star Belgrade v Barcelona (2-4, 0-2)	2-6
Swansea City v Paris St. Germain (0-1, 0-2)	0-3
Tottenham Hotspur v Bayern Munich (1-1, 1-4)	2-5
Real Madrid v Ujpest Dozsa (3-1, 1-0)	4-1

QUARTER-FINALS

Bayern Munich v Aberdeen (0-0, 2-3)	2-3
Austria Vienna v Barcelona (0-0, 1-1)	1-1
Paris St. Germain v Waterschei (2-0, 0-3)	2-3
Inter-Milan v Real Madrid (1-1, 1-3)	2-4

SEMI-FINALS

Aberdeen v Waterschei (5-1, 0-1)	5-2
Austria Vienna v Real Madrid (2-2, 1-3)	3-5

FINAL

Aberdeen 2 Real Madrid 1
(Gothenburg, 11.5.83, 17,804)

Aberdeen: Leighton, Rouvie, Miller, McLeish, McMaster, Cooper, Strachan, Simpson, McGhee, Black (Hewitt), Weir

Real Madrid: Augustin, Juan Jose, Camacho (San Jose), Metgod, Bonet, Gallego, Angel, Stielike, Juanito, Santillana, Isidro (Salguero)

Scorers: Black, Hewitt: Juanito (pen)

RIGHT: John Hewitt wheels away after scoring the winning goal against Real Madrid in the 1983 European Cup Winners Cup final in Gothenburg. After Real had scored from a penalty by Juanito before half-time, Alfredo di Stefano's team were clearly hoping that they could win the match on penalty kicks at the end —a sad commentary on the decline of the great Real Madrid. Aberdeen came back with an excellent extra-time display to secure their victory with just six minutes left and allow (ABOVE) Willie Miller to lift the hard-won Cup.

FAIRS CUP & UEFA CUP

Now called the UEFA Cup, Europe's third major club competition has been dominated by Spain, England and West Germany . . .

Given its rather complicated history, its rather random method of selecting its entrants, its multiplicity of names and its domination by Spain and England, it is rather surprising that the Fairs/UEFA Cup has managed to reach adulthood in such a healthy state.

The Fairs Cup can actually claim to be the first of the four major European competitions. A vice-president of FIFA, Ernst Thommen, suggested a competition between cities which regularly held industrial and trade fairs as early as 1950, but as UEFA was not formed until 1954, it was only then that an organizing committee got to work. Since 1954 it has passed through a remarkable variety of nomenclatures—the International Inter-City Industrial Fairs Cup, the Inter-City Fairs Cup, European Fairs Cup, plain Fairs Cup, then, finally, the UEFA Cup.

It soon came to be regarded as an opportunity for also-ran clubs to compete in Europe, and the entrants were eventually

Mick Jones scores from close in against Ferencvaros to give Leeds a 1-0 lead to take to Hungary in the 1968 Fairs final. It proved just enough.

expanded to 64—twice as many as the other two club competitions and hence requiring an extra round. One other important difference from the Champions Cup and Cup Winners Cup is that the final is played over two legs (the only exceptions were in 1964 and 1965). While this has some financial logic, it robs the competition of an appropriate climax and has probably tended to lessen the significance of the whole affair. Indeed, Leeds only attracted 35,604 and 25,268 for the home legs of their 1967 and 1968 finals.

FAIRS CUP 1955-58

GROUP A

Barcelona 6 KB Copenhagen 2
KB Copenhagen 1 Barcelona 1
[Vienna withdrew]

	P	W	D	L	F	A	P
Barcelona	2	1	1	0	7	3	3
KB Copenhagen	2	0	1	1	3	7	1

GROUP B

Inter-Milan 0 Birmingham City 0
Zagreb 0 Birmingham City 1
Zagreb 0 Inter-Milan 1
Birmingham City 3 Zagreb 0
Inter-Milan 4 Zagreb 0
Birmingham City 2 Inter-Milan 1

	P	W	D	L	F	A	P
Birmingham City	4	3	1	0	6	1	7
Inter-Milan	4	2	1	1	6	2	5
Zagreb	4	0	0	4	0	9	0

GROUP C

Leipzig 6 Lausanne 3
Lausanne 7 Leipzig 3
[Cologne withdrew]

	P	W	D	L	F	A	P
Lausanne†	2	1	0	1	10	9	2
Leipzig	2	1	0	1	9	10	2

GROUP D

Basle 0 London 5
London 3 Frankfurt 2
London 1 Basle 0
Frankfurt 5 Basle 1
Frankfurt 1 London 0
Basle 6 Frankfurt 2

	P	W	D	L	F	A	P
London*	4	3	0	1	9	3	6
Frankfurt*	4	2	0	2	10	10	4
Basle	4	1	0	3	7	13	2

SEMI-FINALS

Birmingham City v Barcelona (4-3, 0-1, 1-2‡)	5-6
Lausanne v London (2-1, 0-2)	2-3

FINAL

London 2 Barcelona 2
(Stamford Bridge, 5.3.58, 45,466)

London: Kelsey *(Arsenal)*, P. Sillett *(Chelsea)*, Langley *(Fulham)*, Blanchflower *(Spurs)*, Norman *(Spurs)*, Coote *(Brentford)*, Groves *(Arsenal)*, Greaves *(Chelsea)*, Smith *(Spurs)*, Haynes *(Fulham)*, Robb *(Spurs)*

Barcelona: Estrems, Olivella, Segarra, Gracia, Gensana, Ribelles, Vasora, Evaristo, Martinez, Villaverde, Tejada

Scorers: Greaves, Langley (pen); Tejada, Martinez

Barcelona 6 London 0
(Barcelona, 1.5.58, 62,000)

Barcelona: Ramallets, Olivella, Segarra, Verges, Brugue, Gensana, Tejada, Evaristo, Martinez, Suarez, Vasora

London: Kelsey *(Arsenal)*, Wright *(West Ham)*, Cantwell *(West Ham)*, Blanchflower *(Spurs)*, Brown *(West Ham)*, Bowen *(Arsenal)*, Medwin *(Spurs)*, Groves *(Arsenal)*, Smith *(Spurs)*, Bloomfield *(Arsenal)*, Lewis *(Chelsea)*

Scorers: Suarez 2, Evaristo 2, Martinez, Verges

*composite side †qualified on goal record
‡play-off in Basle

1955-58

Representatives of 12 cities from 10 countries met in Basle in April 1955 to draw up regulations. They decided that the competition should be played over two years and that a maximum of two cities from each nation could enter. Teams should try, wherever possible, to arrange fixtures to coincide with industrial fairs.

Some cities entered composite teams (London, Frankfurt), while others preferred to nominate a club side (CF Barcelona, Birmingham City). The entries were divided into four groups of three, but the withdrawals of Vienna and Cologne left two groups of two. Considering that only 10 clubs were left to compete, it is remarkable that it took three years to complete the competition.

London secured a draw in the first leg of the final at Stamford Bridge, with the help of a Jim Langley penalty. The return, however, was a different story. The London side, showing eight changes and without Jimmy Greaves and Johnny Haynes, went down 6-0 at the Gran Estadio to a Barcelona team strengthened by Luis Suarez. London, being a composite side, were at a great disadvantage and their heavy defeat was effectively the end of the 'city club' idea.

FAIRS CUP 1958-60

FIRST ROUND

Basle v Barcelona (1-2, 2-5)	3-7
Inter-Milan v Olympique Lyon (7-0, 1-1)	8-1
Frem Copenhagen v Chelsea (1-3, 1-4)	2-7
Belgrade v Lausanne (6-1, 5-3)	11-4
Union St Gilloise v Leipzig (6-0, 0-1)	6-1
Hanover 96 v AS Roma (1-3, 1-1)	2-4
Zagreb v Ujpest Dozsa (4-2, 0-1)	4-3
1FC Cologne v Birmingham City (2-2,0-2)	2-4

QUARTER-FINALS

Barcelona v Inter-Milan (4-0, 4-2)	8-2
Chelsea v Belgrade (1-0, 1-4)	2-4
Union St Gilloise v AS Roma (2-0, 1-1)	3-1
Birmingham City v Zagreb (1-0, 3-3)	4-3

SEMI-FINALS

Belgrade v Barcelona (1-1, 1-3)	2-4
St Gilloise v Birmingham City (2-4, 2-4)	4-8

FINAL

Birmingham City 0 Barcelona 0
(Birmingham, 29.3.60, 40,500)

Birmingham: Schofield, Farmer, Allen, Watts, Smith, Neal, Astall, Gordon, Weston, Orritt, Hooper

Barcelona: Ramallets, Olivella, Gracia, Segarra, Rodri, Gensana, Coll, Kocsis, Martinez, Ribelles, Villaverde

Barcelona 4 Birmingham City 1
(Barcelona, 4.5.60, 70,000)

Barcelona: Verges for Gensana, Kubala for Kocsis, Czibor for Villaverde

Birmingham: Murphy for Orritt

Scorers: Martinez, Czibor 2, Coll; Hooper

1958-60

There were 16 entries for the second competition and most cities chose to nominate a club side. This time the sides were drawn in a straight knock-out tournament on a home-and-away basis, but for the second time it produced an Anglo-Spanish final.

Barcelona, now with three famous Hungarians and destined to win without losing a game, began well by beating Basle 2-1 away and then 5-2 at home. They defeated Inter-Milan 4-0 and 4-2 in the next round. Birmingham City, Barcelona's victims in the previous season's semi-final, held the West German side 1FC Cologne to a 2-2 draw away and won at home, then took a one-goal lead to Zagreb and successfully held the Yugoslavs, playing hard on President Tito's birthday, to a 3-3 draw.

In the semi-finals, Barcelona beat Belgrade, conquerors of Chelsea, on aggregate 4-2, while Birmingham were even more convincing in their 8-4 overall win against Union St Gilloise of Belgium, who had previously produced a surprise by beating AS Roma. Barcelona and Birmingham played a goalless draw in the St Andrews' mud in the first leg of the final (held, like that of 1958, in March); and, with Ramallets in splendid form in goal and Hungarian exile Zoltan Czibor scoring twice, the Spanish side beat the Midlanders 4-1 at home to retain the trophy.

ABOVE: ***Fontana challenges Birmingham's Orritt—a scorer in the first leg—in the 1961 final second leg in Rome. It was City's second final.*** *LEFT:* ***Joe Baker's record of six goals in five games for Hibs in the 1960-61 Fairs Cup led to his move to Torino—here playing Man. City.***

FAIRS CUP 1960-61

FIRST ROUND

Union St Gilloise v AS Roma (0-0, 1-4)	1-4
Olympique Lyon v 1FC Cologne (1-3, 2-1)	3-4
Zagreb v Barcelona (1-1, 3-4)	4-5
Lausanne v Hibernian (0-2*)	0-2
Inter-Milan v Hanover 96 (8-2, 6-1)	14-3
Leipzig v Belgrade (5-2, 1-4, 0-2†)	6-8
KB Copenhagen v Basle (8-1, 3-3)	11-4
Birmingham City v Ujpest Dozsa (3-2, 2-1)	5-3

QUARTER-FINALS

1FC Cologne v AS Roma (0-2, 2-0, 1-4‡)	3-6
Barcelona v Hibernian (4-4, 2-3)	6-7
Inter-Milan v Belgrade (5-0, 0-1)	5-1
KB Copenhagen v Birmingham City (4-4, 0-5)	4-9

SEMI-FINALS

Hibernian v AS Roma (2-2, 3-3, 0-6‡)	5-11
Inter-Milan v Birmingham City (1-2, 1-2)	2-4

FINAL

Birmingham City 2 AS Roma 2
(Birmingham, 27.9.61, 21,005)

Birmingham: Schofield, Farmer, Sissons, Hennessey, Foster, Beard, Hellawell, Bloomfield, Harris, Orritt, Auld

Roma: Cudicini, Fontana, Corsini, Guiliana, Losi, Carpanesi, Orlando, Da Costa, Manfredini, Angelillo, Menichelli

Scorers: Hellawell, Orritt; Manfredini 2

AS Roma 2 Birmingham City 0
(Rome, 11.10.61, 60,000)

Roma: Pestrin for Guiliana, Lojacono for Da Costa

Birmingham: Smith for Foster, Singer for Auld

Scorers: Farmer (og), Pestrin

*Lausanne withdrew after first leg †play-off in Budapest ‡play-off in Rome

FAIRS CUP 1961-62

FIRST ROUND

Valencia v Nottingham Forest (2-0, 5-1)	7-1
Union St Gilloise v Hearts (1-3, 0-2)	1-5
1FC Cologne v Inter-Milan (4-2, 0-2, 3-5*)	7-9
Spartak Brno v Leipzig (2-2, 1-4)	3-6
AC Milan v Vojvodina Novi Sad (0-0, 0-2)	0-2
R. Strasbourg v MTK Budapest (1-3, 2-10)	3-13
Basle v Red Star Belgrade (1-1, 1-4)	2-5
Hibernian v Belenenses (3-3, 3-1)	6-4
Hanover 96 v Espanol Barcelona (0-1, 0-2)	0-3
Olympique Lyon v Sheffield Wed. (4-2, 2-5)	6-7
KB Copenhagen v Dynamo Zagreb (2-7, 2-2)	4-9
West Berlin v Barcelona (1-0, 0-3)	1-3

[AS Roma (holders), Lausanne, Iraklis Salonika & Birmingham City received byes]

SECOND ROUND

Lausanne v Valencia (3-4†)	3-4
Heart of Midlothian v Inter-Milan (0-1, 0-4)	0-5
Iraklis Salonika v Vojvodina (2-1, 1-9)	3-10
MTK Budapest v Leipzig (3-0, 0-3, 2-0)	5-3
Red Star Belgrade v Hibernian (4-0, 1-0)	5-0
Espanol v Birmingham City (5-2, 0-1)	5-3
Sheffield Wednesday v AS Roma (4-0, 0-1)	4-1
Barcelona v Dynamo Zagreb (5-1, 2-2)	7-3

QUARTER-FINALS

Valencia v Inter-Milan (2-0, 3-3)	5-3
Vojvodina v MTK Budapest (1-4, 1-2)	2-6
Espanol v Red Star Belgrade (2-1, 0-5)	2-6
Sheffield Wednesday v Barcelona (3-2, 0-2)	3-4

SEMI-FINALS

Valencia v MTK Budapest (3-0, 7-3)	10-3
Red Star Belgrade v Barcelona (0-2, 1-4)	1-6

FINAL

Valencia 6 Barcelona 2
(Valencia 8.9.62, 65,000)

Valencia: Zamora, Verdu, Chicao, Piquer, Mestre, Sastre, Ficha, Ribebe, Waldo, Guillot, Coll

Barcelona: Pesudo, Benitez, Rodri, Olivella, Verges, Gracia, Cubilla, Kocsis, Re, Villaverde, Camps

Scorers: Waldo 2, Guillot 3, Ribebe; Kocsis 2

Barcelona 1 Valencia 1
(Barcelona, 12.9.62, 60,000)

Barcelona: Garay for Rodri, Fuste for Olivella, Goyvaerts for Re

Valencia: Urtiaga for Ribebe

Scorers: Kocsis; Guillot

*play-off in Milan †second leg not played

1960-61

The third series was shortened to one season but kept its 16 entries and previous formula. There were plenty of high scores, with Inter-Milan hitting 14 on aggregate against Hanover 96 of West Germany and BK Copenhagen putting 11 past Basle. But Birmingham City accounted for the Danish side, drawing 4-4 away and winning 5-0 at home. Inter-Milan, too, succeeded in getting to the semi-finals, having disposed of Belgrade 5-1 overall, but Birmingham beat the Italians (as they had in the first competition), winning both legs 2-1. Harris scored three of the four goals.

In the other half of the draw AS Roma beat Union St Gilloise to meet 1FC Cologne, but were taken to a play-off in Rome by the Germans. Hibernian received a walkover against Lausanne after the Swiss withdrew having lost their home leg (the cash involved would prevent such a thing happening nowadays but it was then very common with Swiss clubs if they lost the first leg), and joined the holders, Barcelona, in the quarter-finals. The Scots, though beaten 5-1 by Barcelona in a pre-season friendly, became the first side to hold the Spaniards to a draw at home in the Fairs Cup, and, in a dramatic game at Easter Road, with Barcelona losing their heads, won 3-2 to go through to the semi-finals.

At this time, it was possible for clubs to be involved in more than one competition, and the finals were not necessarily held at the end of the usual season. Only a few weeks after their defeat by Hibs, Spanish League champions Barcelona were to eliminate Real Madrid from the European Cup—the latter's first defeat in the senior competition after five consecutive years of success. (Barcelona went on to reach the final, where they lost 3-2 to Benfica.)

In the semi-final AS Roma were taken to a play-off by Hibernian, with Joe Baker taking his total to six goals in four games. But having drawn 2-2 and 3-3 the Scots surprisingly slumped by six goals in the play-off, four of them coming from the new Argentine signing Manfredini. The length of this tie delayed the final until the September, when Birmingham held a Roma side bulging with recent transfers to a 2-2 draw at home but lost 2-0 to the Italians in Rome. The Fairs Cup, like the European Cup, was proving a Latin preserve.

Later that season Birmingham were knocked out at their next attempt by Espanol and so ended a remarkably creditable spell of European football by the Midlands club, a period which they have never since had a chance to emulate. In three competitions, over a period of six years, they lost just four out of 23 games, being beaten only by Barcelona and Roma in that whole period and accounting, undefeated, for the likes of Inter-Milan, Cologne and Ujpest Dozsa.

1961-62

Though only two teams had been eligible from any one national association before 1961, Spain succeeded in getting the allocation increased to three per country and, significantly perhaps, had two teams in the final, while their third entry (Espanol) reached the quarter-finals by beating Birmingham City. With the entry almost doubled to 28 clubs, an extra round was included.

Valencia proved high-scoring finalists in a prolific competition: from the start they were among the goals, defeating Nottingham Forest 7-1, Lausanne 4-3 (only one match played), Inter-Milan 5-3, and MTK Budapest 10-3 in the semi-final. With a 6-2 lead on their home leg, Valencia were content to draw in Barcelona 1-1 in the final.

FAIRS CUP 1962-63

FIRST ROUND

Valencia v Celtic (4-2, 2-2)	6-4
Everton v Dunfermline Athletic (1-0, 0-2)	1-2
DOS Utrecht v Tasmania Berlin (3-2, 2-1)	5-3
Hibernian v KB Copenhagen (4-0, 3-2)	7-2
Rapid Vienna v Red Star Belgrade (1-1, 0-1)	1-2
Barcelona v Belenenses (1-1, 1-1, 3-2)*	5-4
Glentoran v Real Zaragoza (0-2, 2-6)	2-8
Altay Izmir v AS Roma (2-3, 1-10†)	3-13
Viktoria Cologne v Ferencvaros (4-3, 1-4)	5-7
Sampdoria v Aris Bonnevoie (1-0, 2-0)	3-0
Vojvodina Novi Sad v Leipzig (1-0, 0-2)	1-2
Petrolul Ploesti v Spartak Brno (4-2, 0-1)	4-3
Basle v Bayern Munich (0-3‡)	0-3
Drumcondra v Odense BK 09 (4-1, 2-4)	6-5
Olym. Marseille v Union St Gilloise (1-0, 2-4)	3-4
Porto v Dynamo Zagreb (1-2, 0-0)	1-2

SECOND ROUND

Valencia v Dunfermline Ath. (4-0, 2-6, 1-0)	7-6
DOS Utrecht v Hibernian (0-1, 1-2)	1-3
Red Star Belgrade v Barcelona (3-2, 0-1, 1-0)	4-3
Real Zaragoza v AS Roma (2-4, 1-2)	3-6
Sampdoria v Ferencvaros (1-0, 0-6)	1-6
Petrolul Ploesti v Leipzig (1-0, 0-1, 1-0)	2-1
Bayern Munich v Drumcondra (6-0, 0-1)	6-1
Dynamo Zagreb v St Gilloise (2-1, 0-1, 3-2)	5-4

QUARTER-FINALS

Valencia v Hibernian (5-0, 1-2)	6-2
AS Roma v Red Star Belgrade (3-0, 0-2)	3-2
Ferencvaros v Petrolul Ploesti (2-0, 0-1)	2-1
Bayern Munich v Dynamo Zagreb (1-4, 0-0)	1-4

SEMI-FINALS

Valencia v AS Roma (3-0, 0-1)	3-1
Ferencvaros v Dynamo Zagreb (0-1, 1-2)	1-3

FINAL

Dynamo Zagreb 1 Valencia 2
(Zagreb, 12.6.63, 40,000)

Zagreb: Skoric, Belin, Braun, Biscam, Markovic, Perusic, Kobsnac, Zambata, Knez, Matus, Lamza

Valencia: Zamora, Piquer, Chicao, Paquito, Quinocis, Sastre, Mano, Sanchez-Lage, Waldo, Ribelles, Urtiaga

Scorers: Zambata; Waldo, Urtiaga

Valencia 2 Dynamo Zagreb 0
(Valencia: 26.6.63, 55,000)

Valencia: Nunez for Urtiaga

Zagreb: Raus for Biscam

Scorers: Mano, Nunez

*all matches in Barcelona †second leg in Istanbul
‡second leg not played

1962-63

Thirty-two teams entered the 1962-63 series and, apart from a big fright against Dunfermline Athletic, Valencia again proved well suited to the competition. In their second round encounter Dunfermline, managed by Jock Stein, lost 4-0 in Valencia but made a spectacular recovery at East End Park to win 6-2, only to go out 1-0 in the play-off in Lisbon. In fact Valencia took on Scotland single-handed, defeating Celtic 6-4, Dunfermline 7-6 and Hibernian 6-2.

In the semi-final Valencia beat AS Roma and qualified to meet Dynamo Zagreb, the first Eastern European side to reach a European final. The Yugoslavs had accounted for Porto, Union St Gilloise, Bayern Munich (who had lost an academic away leg to Drumcondra) and Ferencvaros.

Valencia had the edge in both matches in the June final.

FAIRS CUP 1963-64

FIRST ROUND

Real Zaragoza v Iraklis Salonika (3-0, 6-1)	9-1
Lausanne v Hearts (2-2, 4-4, 3-2*)	9-8
Atletico Madrid v Porto (2-1, 0-0)	2-1
Juventus v OFK Belgrade (2-1, 1-2, 1-0)	4-3
Spartak Brno v Servette Geneva (5-0, 2-1)	7-1
Glentoran v Partick Thistle (1-4, 0-3)	1-7
Staevnet Copenhagen v Arsenal (1-7, 3-2)	4-9
Aris Bonnevoie v FC Liege (0-2, 0-0)	0-2
1FC Cologne v La Gantoise (3-1, 1-1)	4-2
DOS Utrecht v Sheffield Wednesday (1-4, 1-4)	2-8
Tresnjevka Zagreb v Belenenses (0-2, 1-2)	1-4
Hertha Berlin v AS Roma (1-3, 0-2)	1-5
Ujpest Dozsa v Lokomotiv Leipzig (0-0, 3-2)	3-2
Red Flag Brasov v Loko. Plovdiv (1-3, 1-2)	2-5
Rapid Vienna v Racing Club Paris (1-0, 3-2)	4-2
Shamrock Rovers v Valencia (0-1, 2-2)	2-3

SECOND ROUND

Lausanne v Real Zaragoza (1-2, 0-3)	1-5
Juventus v Atletico Madrid (1-0, 2-1)	3-1
Partick Thistle v Spartak Brno (3-2, 0-4)	3-6
Arsenal v FC Liege (1-1, 1-3)	2-4
1FC Cologne v Sheffield Wednesday (3-2, 2-1)	5-3
AS Roma v Belenenses (2-1, 1-0)	3-1
Ujpest Dozsa v Lokomotiv Plovdiv (0-0, 3-1)	3-1
Rapid Vienna v Valencia (0-0, 2-3)	2-3

QUARTER-FINALS

Real Zaragoza v Juventus (3-2, 0-0)	3-2
FC Liege v Spartak Brno (2-0, 0-2, 1-0†)	3-2
AS Roma v 1FC Cologne (3-1, 0-4)	3-5
Valencia v Ujpest Dozsa (5-2, 1-3)	6-5

SEMI-FINALS

FC Liege v Real Zaragoza (1-0, 1-2, 0-2‡)	2-4
Valencia v 1FC Cologne (4-1, 0-2)	4-3

FINAL

Real Zaragoza 2 Valencia 1
(Barcelona, 24.6.64; 50,000)

Zaragoza: Yarza, Cortizo, Reija, Isasi, Santamaria, Pepin, Canario, Duca, Marcelino, Villa, Lapetra

Valencia: Zamora, Arnal, Videgany, Paquito, Quincoces, Roberto, Suco, Guillot, Waldo, Urtiaga, Ficha

Scorers: Villa, Marcelino; Urtiaga

*play-off in Lausanne †play-off in Liege ‡play-off in Zaragoza

1963-64

Valencia came within an ace of scoring a hat-trick in 1963-64 in a competition that again had an all-Spanish final. For this series it was decided to play a one-match final on a neutral ground.

The British clubs among the 32 entrants fared miserably. Hearts lost to Lausanne in the first round after a play-off and Arsenal, Sheffield Wednesday, and Partick Thistle all went out in the second round—to Liège, Cologne and Spartak Brno respectively.

Real Zaragoza, who accompanied Valencia to the final, started off by cantering past Iraklis Salonika (Greece) 9-1 and Lausanne 5-1, before running into stronger opposition in Juventus (3-2) and Liège, who went down 4-2 only after a play-off in Zaragoza. For their part, Valencia defeated Shamrock Rovers 3-2, Rapid Vienna 3-2, Ujpest Dozsa 6-5, and then Cologne 4-3 in the semi-final. Continuous odd-goal victories in the tournament had done little for Valencia's confidence, and on 24 June they came up against a Zaragoza side that had just beaten Atlético Madrid in the Spanish Cup final. With a team full of experienced players Zaragoza won 2-1 in the final at Barcelona. Whichever side had won it meant five Fairs Cup wins out of six for Spain.

FAIRS CUP 1964-65

FIRST ROUND

Ferencvaros v Spartak Brno (2-0, 0-1)	2-1
Wiener SK v Lokomotiv Leipzig (2-1, 1-0)	3-1
Aris Salonika v AS Roma (0-0, 0-3)	0-3
Dynamo Zagreb v Graz AK (3-2, 6-0)	9-2
Dunfermline Athletic v Oergryte (4-2, 0-0)	4-2
Odense BK 13 v VfB Stuttgart (1-3, 0-1)	1-4
Hertha Berlin v Antwerp (2-1, 0-2)	2-3
Atletico Bilbao v OFK Belgrade (2-2, 2-0)	4-2
Valerengen v Everton (2-5, 2-4)	4-9
Eintracht Frankfurt v Kilmarnock (3-0, 1-5)	4-5
Manchester United v Djurgaarden (1-1, 6-1)	7-2
Borussia Dortmund v Bordeaux (4-1, 0-2)	4-3
Leixoes Porto v Celtic (1-1, 0-3)	1-4
Barcelona v Fiorentina (0-1, 2-0)	2-1
Racing Strasbourg v AC Milan (2-0, 0-1)	2-1
Basle v Spora Luxembourg (2-0, 0-1)	2-1
Servette Geneva v Atletico Madrid (2-2, 1-6)	3-8
Belenenses v Shelbourne (1-1, 0-0, 1-2)	2-3
Valencia v FC Liege (1-1, 1-3)	2-4
KB Copenhagen v DOS Utrecht (3-4, 1-2)	4-6
Vojvodina v Lokomotiv Plovdiv (1-1, 1-1, 0-2)	2-4
Goztepe Izmir v Petrolul Ploesti (1-2, 0-1)	1-3
Betis Seville v Stade Francais (1-1, 0-2)	1-3
Union St Gilloise v Juventus (0-1, 0-1)	0-2

SECOND ROUND

Ferencvaros v Wiener SK (0-1, 2-1, 2-0)	4-2
Dynamo Zagreb v AS Roma (1-1, 0-1)	1-2
Dunfermline Ath. v VfB Stuttgart (1-0, 0-0)	1-0
Atletico Bilbao v Antwerp (2-0, 1-0)	3-0
Kilmarnock v Everton (0-2, 1-4)	1-6
Bor. Dortmund v Manchester U. (1-6, 0-4)	1-10
Barcelona v Celtic (3-1, 0-0)	3-1
Basle v Racing Strasbourg (0-1, 2-5)	2-6
Shelbourne v Atletico Madrid (0-1, 0-1)	0-2
DOS Utrecht v FC Liege (0-2, 0-2)	0-4
Pet. Ploesti v Lokomotiv Plovdiv (1-0, 0-2)	1-2
Stade Francais v Juventus (0-0, 0-1)	0-1

THIRD ROUND

AS Roma v Ferencvaros (1-2, 0-1)	1-3
At. Bilbao v Dunfermline Ath. (1-0, 0-1, 2-1)	3-2
Racing Strasbourg* v Barcelona (0-0, 2-2, 0-0)	2-2
FC Liege v Atletico Madrid (1-0, 0-2)	1-2
Juventus v Lokomotiv Plovdiv (1-1, 1-1, 2-1)	4-3

QUARTER-FINALS

Ferencvaros v Atletico Bilbao (1-0, 1-2, 3-0†)	5-2
Racing Strasbourg v Manchester U. (0-5, 0-0)	0-5

[Juventus & Atletico Madrid received byes]

SEMI-FINALS

Manchester U. v Ferencvaros (3-2, 0-1, 1-2†)	4-5
Atletico Madrid v Juventus (3-1, 1-3, 1-3‡)	5-7

FINAL

Ferencvaros 1 Juventus 0
(Turin, 23.6.65, 25,000)

Ferencvaros: Geczi, Novak, Horvath, Juhasz, Matrai, Orosz, Karaba, Varga, Albert, Rakosi, Fenyvesi

Juventus: Anzolin, Gori, Sarti, Bercellino, Castano, Leoncini, Stachini, Del Sol, Combin, Mazzia, Menichelli

Scorer: Fenyvesi

*won on toss of coin after play-off in Barcelona †play-off in Budapest ‡play-off in Turin

TOP: ***A nervous Manchester United wall faces Horvath (3) and Albert of Ferencvaros in the 1965 semi-final second leg. The Hungarians forced a play-off, won it at home 2-1, and then stunned Juventus on their own ground.***
ABOVE: ***Denis Law, top scorer in the European Cup four seasons later, led the Fairs Cup list with eight goals in 1964—65.***

1964-65

For the 1964-65 competition the number of entries had spiralled to 48, a situation that produced a bye for two clubs from the quarter- into the semi-finals—not the happiest of circumstances. The two lucky ones, Juventus and Atlético Madrid, were then drawn together and fought out a stern battle, with the Italians getting the verdict on the third match, played at Turin. In the other semi-final Manchester United were beaten by Ferencvaros, again after a play-off which proved a success for the home side.

Juventus' early trail of scores—1-0, 1-0, 0-0, 1-0, 1-1, 1-1, 2-1, plus a bye—indicated a dismal defensive strategy, and that may have been partly to blame for the small crowd that turned up to see a game which by chance had been allocated in Turin. The fans who stayed away showed good sense: it was a predictably dull affair played at the height (or depth) of the Italian period of European soccer influence. The only surprise was that it was Ferencvaros who scored to produce the almost inevitable scoreline.

1965-66

With another massive entry of 48 UEFA took the wise precaution of drawing the byes in the first round, but the number of matches in which there was violence grew to alarming proportions.

At the semi-final stage the competition had resolved itself into a battle between England, represented by Chelsea and Leeds, and Spain, with the old campaigners Barcelona and Zaragoza as their ambassadors. Of the quartet only Zaragoza had been given a bye, after which they beat Shamrock Rovers, Hearts (after a play-off) and the adventurous Dunfermline. Against Leeds, who had earlier knocked out Valencia after a rough-house affair, Zaragoza needed an extra match, though their clinching victory was achieved at Elland Road with three goals in 13 minutes.

The other semi-final pitted Barcelona against Chelsea. The latter, after the Rome debacle, had done well to eliminate Wiener SK, AC Milan, and Munich 1860, though the matches produced some incidents best forgotten, and they needed the luck of the toss against AC Milan. Barcelona were taken to a play-off by Hanover 96 in the third round, and the coin also favoured them. In the last eight they beat neighbours Espanol, who had Alfredo di Stefano at centre-forward. Barcelona also needed a third game against Tommy Docherty's side, but they showed their class with a 5-0 win.

In the third all-Spanish final Zaragoza seemed to have it wrapped up in Barcelona with a Canario goal, but the return proved a sensational affair. Though Marcelino headed two goals for Zaragoza, Barcelona stormed back to lead 3-2 after 90 minutes and so force extra time. With 30 seconds left, new boy Pujol completed his hat-trick to give Barcelona their third Fairs Cup victory. This remains the only occasion in international club competition history that a team has lost the home leg of a two-legged final and yet still gone on to win the trophy.

FAIRS CUP 1965-66

FIRST ROUND

DOS Utrecht v Barcelona (0-0, 1-7)	1-7
Antwerp v Glentoran (1-0, 3-3)	4-3
Stade Francais v Porto (0-0, 0-1)	0-1
Bordeaux v Sporting Lisbon (0-4, 1-6)	1-10
FC Liege v Dynamo Zagreb (1-0, 0-2)	1-2
TSV Munich 1860 v Malmo FF (4-0, 3-0)	7-0
AIK Stockholm v Daring Brussels (3-1, 0-0)	3-1
AC Milan* v Racing Strasbourg (1-0, 1-2, 1-1)	3-3
Wiener SK v PAOK Salonika (6-0, 1-2)	7-2
Chelsea v AS Roma (4-1, 0-0)	4-1
Leeds United v Torino (2-1, 0-0)	2-1
Hibernian v Valencia (2-0, 0-2, 0-3)	2-5
US Luxembourg v 1FC Cologne (0-4, 0-13)	0-17
1FC Nuremberg v Everton (1-1, 0-1)	1-2
Red Star Belgrade v Fiorentina (0-4, 1-3)	1-7
Spartak Brno v Lokomotiv Plovdiv (2-0, 0-1)	2-1

[Hanover 96, Espanol Barcelona, Red Flag Brasov, Goztepe Izmir, Servette Geneva, CUF, Lokomotiv Leipzig, Basle, Aris Salonika, Ujpest Dozsa, Dunfermline Athletic, KB Copenhagen, Heart of Midlothian, Valerengen, Shamrock Rovers & Real Zaragoza received byes]

SECOND ROUND

Antwerp v Barcelona (2-1, 0-2)	2-3
Hanover 96 v Porto (5-0, 1-2)	6-2
Dynamo Zagreb v Red Flag Brasov (2-2, 0-1)	2-3
Sporting Lisbon v Espanol (2-1, 3-4, 1-2)	6-7
Goztepe Izmir v TSV Munich 1860 (2-1, 1-9)	3-10
AIK Stockholm v Servette Geneva (2-1, 1-4)	3-5
CUF v AC Milan (2-0, 0-2, 0-1)	2-3
Wiener SK v Chelsea (1-0, 0-2)	1-2
Lokomotiv Leipzig v Leeds United (1-2, 0-0)	1-2
Basle v Valencia (1-3, 1-5)	2-8
Aris Salonika v 1FC Cologne (2-1, 0-2)	2-3
Ujpest Dozsa v Everton (3-0, 1-2)	4-2
Dunfermline A. v KB Copenhagen (5-0, 4-2)	9-2
Fiorentina v Spartak Brno (2-0, 0-4)	2-4
Heart of Midlothian v Valerengen (1-0, 3-1)	4-1
Shamrock Rovers v Real Zaragoza (1-1, 1-2)	2-3

THIRD ROUND

Hanover 96 v Barcelona* (2-1, 0-1, 1-1)	3-3
Espanol v Red Flag Brasov (3-1, 2-4, 1-0)	6-5
Servette Geneva v TSV Munich 1860 (1-1, 1-4)	2-5
AC Milan v Chelsea* (2-1, 1-2, 1-1)	4-4
Leeds United v Valencia (1-1, 1-0)	2-1
1FC Cologne v Ujpest Dozsa (3-2, 0-4)	3-6
Dunfermline Ath. v Spartak Brno (2-0, 0-0)	2-0
Hearts v Real Zaragoza (3-3, 2-2, 0-1)	5-6

QUARTER-FINALS

Barcelona v Espanol Barcelona (1-0, 1-0)	2-0
TSV Munich 1860 v Chelsea (2-2, 0-1)	2-3
Leeds United v Ujpest Dozsa (4-1, 1-1)	5-2
Dunfermline Ath. v Real Zaragoza (1-0, 2-4)	3-4

SEMI-FINALS

Barcelona v Chelsea (2-0, 0-2, 5-0†)	7-2
Real Zaragoza v Leeds United (1-0, 1-2, 3-1‡)	5-3

FINAL

Barcelona 0 Real Zaragoza 1
(Barcelona, 14.9.66, 70,000)

Barcelona: Sadurni, Benitez, Eladio, Montesinos, Gallego, Torres, Zaballa, Muller, Zaldua, Fuste, Vidal

Zaragoza: Yarza, Irusquieta, Reija, Pais, Santamaria, Violeta, Canario, Santos, Marcelino, Villa, Lapetra

Scorer: Canario

Real Zaragoza 2 Barcelona 4 [aet]
(Zaragoza, 21.9.66, 35,000)

Zaragoza: Unchanged

Barcelona: Foncho for Benitez, Mas for Muller, Pujol for Vidal

Scorers: Marcelino 2; Pujol 3, Zaballa

*won on toss of coin after drawn play-off †play-off in Barcelona ‡play-off in Leeds

FAIRS CUP 1966-67

FIRST ROUND

Spartak Brno v Dynamo Zagreb* (0-2, 2-0)	2-2
Frigg Oslo v Dunfermline Athletic (1-3, 1-3)	2-6
Dynamo Pitesti v Seville (2-0, 2-2)	4-2
Juventus v Aris Salonika (5-0, 2-0)	7-0
Wiener SK v Napoli (1-2, 1-3)	2-5
VfB Stuttgart v Burnley (1-1, 0-2)	1-3
Olympija Ljubljana v Ferencvaros (3-3, 0-3)	3-6
OGC Nice v Oergryte (2-2, 1-2)	3-4
Drumcondra v Eintracht Frankfurt (0-2, 1-6)	1-8
Porto v Girondins Bordeaux* (2-1, 1-2)	3-3
US Luxembourg v Antwerp (0-1, 0-1)	0-2
Djurgaarden v Lokomotiv Leipzig (1-3, 1-2)	2-5
Bologna v Goztepe Izmir (2-1, 3-1)	5-2
DOS Utrecht v Basle (2-1, 2-2)	4-3
Red Star Belgrade v At. Bilbao (5-0, 0-2)	5-2
1FC Nuremberg v Valencia (1-2, 0-2)	1-4

[Barcelona (holders), Toulouse, Dundee United, Vitoria Setubal, Odense BK 09, Lausanne, Hvidovre Copenhagen, La Gantoise, Kilmarnock, Spartak Plovdiv, Benfica, FC Liege, Sparta Prague, West Bromwich Albion, DWS Amsterdam & Leeds United received byes]

SECOND ROUND

Dunfermline Ath. v Dynamo Zag.† (4-2, 0-2)	4-4
Toulouse v Dynamo Pitesti (3-0, 1-5)	4-5
Barcelona v Dundee United (1-2, 0-2)	1-4
Juventus v Vitoria Setubal (3-1, 2-0)	5-1
Lausanne v Burnley (1-3, 0-5)	1-8
Odense BK 09 v Napoli (1-4, 1-2)	2-6
Oergryte v Ferencvaros (0-0, 1-7)	1-7
Eintracht Frankfurt v Hvidovre (5-1, 2-2)	7-3
Antwerp v Kilmarnock (0-1, 2-7)	2-8
La Gantoise v Girondins Bordeaux (1-0, 0-0)	1-0
Spartak Plovdiv v Benfica (1-1, 0-3)	1-4
FC Liege v Lokomotiv Leipzig (0-0, 1-2)	1-2
Sparta Prague v Bologna (2-2, 1-2)	3-4
WBA v DOS Utrecht (5-2, 1-1)	6-3
Valencia v Red Star Belgrade (1-0, 2-1)	3-1
DWS Amsterdam v Leeds United (1-3, 1-5)	2-8

THIRD ROUND

Dynamo Pitesti v Dynamo Zagreb (0-1, 0-0)	0-1
Juventus v Dundee United (3-0, 0-1)	3-1
Burnley v Napoli (3-0, 0-0)	3-0
Eintracht Frankfurt v Ferencvaros (4-1, 1-2)	5-3
Kilmarnock v La Gantoise (1-0, 2-1)	3-1
Lokomotiv Leipzig v Benfica (3-1, 1-2)	4-3
Bologna v West Bromwich Albion (3-0, 3-1)	6-1
Leeds United v Valencia (1-1, 2-0)	3-1

QUARTER-FINALS

Juventus v Dynamo Zagreb (2-2, 0-3)	2-5
Eintracht Frankfurt v Burnley (1-1, 2-1)	3-2
Lokomotiv Leipzig v Kilmarnock (1-0, 0-2)	1-2
Bologna v Leeds United* (1-0, 0-1)	1-1

SEMI-FINALS

Eintracht Frankfurt v Dyn. Zagreb (3-0, 0-4)	3-4
Leeds United v Kilmarnock (4-2, 0-0)	4-2

FINAL

Dynamo Zagreb 2 Leeds United 0
(Zagreb, 30.8.67, 40,000)

Zagreb: Skoric, Gracacin, Brnic, Belin, Ramljak, Blaskovic, Cercer, Piric, Zambata, Guomirtl, Rota

Leeds: Sprake, Reaney, Cooper, Bremner, Charlton, Hunter, Lorimer, Bates, Belfitt, Gray, O'Grady

Scorer: Cercer 2

Leeds United 0 Dynamo Zagreb 0
(Leeds, 6.9.67, 35,604)

Leeds: Sprake, Bell, Cooper, Bremner, Charlton, Hunter, Reaney, Belfitt, Greenhoff, Giles, O'Grady

Zagreb: Unchanged

*won on toss of coin †won on away goals rule

FAIRS CUP 1967-68

FIRST ROUND

Spora Luxembourg v Leeds United (0-9, 0-7)	0-16
Partizan Belgrade v Loko. Plovdiv (5-1, 1-1)	6-2
Hibernian v Porto (3-0, 1-3)	4-3
Napoli v Hanover 96 (4-0, 1-1)	5-1
OGC Nice v Fiorentina (0-1, 0-4)	0-5
FC Bruges v Sporting Lisbon (0-0, 1-2)	1-2
1FC Cologne v Slavia Prague (2-0, 2-2)	4-2
Dynamo Dresden v Rangers (1-1, 1-2)	2-3
FC Zurich v Barcelona (3-1, 0-1)	3-2
Eintracht Frankfurt v Nottingham F. (0-1, 0-4)	0-5
PAOK Salonika v FC Liege (0-2, 2-3)	2-5
DWS Amsterdam v Dundee (2-1, 0-3)	2-4
Bologna v Lyn Oslo (2-0, 0-0)	2-0
Dynamo Zagreb v Petrolul Ploesti (5-0, 0-2)	5-2
Wiener SK v Atletico Madrid (2-5, 1-2)	3-7
Antwerp v Goztepe Izmir (1-2, 0-0)	1-2
Lokomotiv Leipzig v Linfield (5-1, 0-1)	5-2
Vojvodina Novi Sad v CUF (1-0, 3-1)	4-1
Frem Copenhagen v Atletico Bilbao (0-1, 2-3)	2-4
St Patrick's Athletic v Bordeaux (1-3, 3-6)	4-9
Malmo FF v Liverpool (0-2, 1-2)	1-4
Servette Geneva v TSV Munich 1860 (2-2, 0-4)	2-6
DOS Utrecht v Real Zaragoza (3-2, 1-3)	4-5
Arges Pitesti v Ferencvaros (3-1, 0-4)	3-5

SECOND ROUND

Partizan Belgrade v Leeds United (1-2, 1-1)	2-3
Napoli v Hibernian (4-1, 0-5)	4-6
Fiorentina v Sporting Lisbon (1-1, 1-2)	2-3
Rangers v 1FC Cologne (3-0, 1-3)	4-3
Nottingham Forest v FC Zurich* (2-1, 0-1)	2-2
Dundee v FC Liege (3-1, 4-1)	7-2
Bologna v Dynamo Zagreb (0-0, 2-1)	2-1
Vojvodina v Lokomotiv Leipzig (0-0, 2-0)	2-0
Atletico Madrid v Goztepe Izmir (2-0, 0-3)	2-3
Bordeaux v Atletico Bilbao (1-3, 0-1)	1-4
Liverpool v TSV Munich 1860 (8-0, 1-2)	9-2
Real Zaragoza v Ferencvaros (2-1, 0-3)	2-4

THIRD ROUND

Leeds United v Hibernian (1-0, 1-1)	2-1
FC Zurich v Sporting Lisbon (3-0, 0-1)	3-1
Vojvodina v Goztepe Izmir (1-0, 1-0)	2-0
Ferencvaros v Liverpool (1-0, 1-0)	2-0

[Rangers, Dundee, Bologna & Atletico Bilbao received byes]

QUARTER-FINALS

Rangers v Leeds United (0-0, 0-2)	0-2
Dundee v FC Zurich (1-0, 1-0)	2-0
Bologna v Vojvodina Novi Sad (0-0, 2-0)	2-0
Ferencvaros v Atletico Bilbao (2-1, 2-1)	4-2

SEMI-FINALS

Dundee v Leeds United (1-1, 0-1)	1-2
Ferencvaros v Bologna (3-2, 2-2)	5-4

FINAL

Leeds United 1 Ferencvaros 0
(Leeds, 7.8.68, 25,268)

Leeds: Sprake, Reaney, Cooper, Bremner, Charlton, Hunter, Lorimer, Madeley, Jones (Belfitt), Giles (Greenhoff), Gray

Ferencvaros: Geczi, Novak, Pancsics, Havasi, Juhasz, Szucs, Szoke, Varga, Albert, Rakosi, Fenyvesi (Balint)

Scorer: Jones

Ferencvaros 0 Leeds United 0
(Budapest, 11.9.68, 76,000)

Ferencvaros: Katona for Fenyvesi; Karaba came on for Szoke

Leeds: Hibbitt (Bates) for Giles, O'Grady for Gray

*won on away goals rule

1966-67

Barcelona did not last long as champions. Less than two months after the 1966 final they met European newcomers Dundee United and lost both legs; 2-1 at home and 2-0 away. It was a disastrous series for Spain: Seville and Atlético Bilbao went out in the first round, Barcelona in the second after a bye, and Valencia in the third.

Dundee United, after their triumph, were beaten 3-1 by Juventus, but the Italians went out in turn to Dynamo Zagreb on a 5-2 aggregate. Zagreb then beat Eintracht Frankfurt 4-3 in the semi-final, having lost the first leg 3-0. The Yugoslavs' opponents in the final were Leeds United, who in the semi-final had defeated Kilmarnock 4-2.

Leeds had strolled through DWS Amsterdam 8-2 and Valencia, but only the toss of a coin saved them against Bologna after the teams had deadlocked 1-1. Once again the tournament lapped over into the next season and the final was postponed. In Zagreb Dynamo won by two clear goals, and at Elland Road they secured a goalless draw.

1967-68

There was consolation for Leeds the following season. Getting off to a prolific start, they swamped luckless Spora Luxembourg 16-0, before putting up a fine display against Partizan Belgrade (2-1 away, 1-1 home), and finding stiff resistance in Hibs (2-1). They then held Rangers scoreless at Ibrox and won the home leg by two clear goals. In the semi-finals they met Dundee, who had knocked out DWS Amsterdam 4-2, Liège 7-2, and Zurich, who had knocked out Nottingham Forest on the away goals rule, by 2-0. But Leeds held the Scots 1-1 at Dens Park and then won by the only goal at Elland Road to reach their second final.

The other semi-final was between Ferencvaros, winners in 1965, whose victims had included Liverpool (2-0) and Bologna, who, thanks to West Germany's Haller, had accounted for the holders Dynamo Zagreb in the second round.

Newcastle manager Joe Harvey, no stranger to cup success as a player with United, enjoys the taste of victory after his side had produced two fine displays in the 1969 final.

FAIRS CUP 1968-69

FIRST ROUND

Newcastle United v Feyenoord (4-0, 0-2)	4-2
Sporting Lisbon v Valencia (4-0, 1-4)	5-4
Slavia Sofia v Aberdeen (0-0, 0-2)	0-2
Trakia Plovdiv v Real Zaragoza* (3-1, 0-2)	3-3
Dynamo Zagreb v Fiorentina (1-1, 1-2)	2-3
Hansa Rostock v OGC Nice (3-0, 1-2)	4-2
Olym. Lyon† v Academica Coimbra (1-0, 0-1)	1-1
Vitoria Setubal v Linfield (3-0, 3-1)	6-1
Atletico Bilbao† v Liverpool (2-1, 1-2)	3-3
Daring Brussels v Panathinaikos (2-1, 0-2)	2-3
Lausanne v Juventus (0-2, 0-2)	0-4
Wacker Innsbruck v E. Frankfurt (2-2, 0-3)	2-5
Beerschot v DWS Amsterdam (1-1, 1-2)	2-3
Chelsea v Morton (5-0, 4-3)	9-3
DOS Utrecht v Dundalk (1-1, 1-2)	2-3
Rangers v Vojvodina Novi Sad (2-0, 0-1)	2-1
Goztepe Izmir† v Olym. Marseille (2-0, 0-2)	2-2
Bologna v Basle (4-1, 2-1)	6-2
Rapid Bucharest v OFK Belgrade (3-1, 1-6)	4-7
Ljubljana v Hibernian (0-3, 1-2)	1-5
Wiener SK v Slavia Prague (1-0, 0-5)	1-5
Metz v SV Hamburg (1-4, 2-3)	3-7
Standard Liege v Leeds United (0-0, 2-3)	2-3
Napoli v Grasshoppers Zurich (3-1, 0-1)	3-2
Skeid Oslo v AIK Stockholm (1-1, 1-2)	2-3
Hanover 96 v Odense BK 09 (3-2, 1-0)	4-2
Legia Warsaw v TSV Munich 1860 (6-0, 3-2)	9-2
Atletico Madrid v SV Waragem* (2-1, 0-1)	2-2
Aris Salonika v Hibs Valletta (1-0, 6-0)	7-0

[Arges Pitesti, Lokomotiv Leipzig & Ujpest Dozsa received byes]

SECOND ROUND

Sporting Lisbon v Newcastle U. (1-1, 0-1)	1-2
Aberdeen v Real Zaragoza (2-1, 0-3)	2-4
Hansa Rostock v Fiorentina* (3-2, 1-2)	4-4
Vitoria Setubal v Olympique Lyon (5-0, 2-1)	7-1
Panathinaikos v Atletico Bilbao (0-0, 0-1)	0-1
Juventus v Eintracht Frankfurt (0-0, 0-1)	0-1
Chelsea v DWS Amsterdam† (0-0, 0-0)	0-0
Rangers v Dundalk (6-1, 3-0)	9-1
Goztepe Izmir v Arges Pitesti (3-0, 2-3)	5-3
OFK Belgrade v Bologna (1-0, 1-1)	2-1
Hibernian v Lokomotiv Leipzig (3-1, 1-0)	4-1
SV Hamburg v Slavia Prague (4-1, 1-3)	5-4
Leeds United† v Napoli (2-0, 0-2)	2-2
AIK Stockholm v Hanover 96 (4-2, 2-5)	6-7
SV Waregem v Legia Warsaw (1-0, 0-2)	1-2
Aris Salonika v Ujpest Dozsa (1-2, 1-9)	2-11

THIRD ROUND

Real Zaragoza v Newcastle United* (3-2, 1-2)	4-4
Vitoria Setubal v Fiorentina (3-0, 1-2)	4-2
Eintracht Frankfurt v Atletico Bilbao (1-1, 0-1)	1-2
DWS Amsterdam v Rangers (0-2, 1-2)	1-4
OFK Belgrade v Goztepe Izmir* (3-1, 0-2)	3-3
SV Hamburg* v Hibernian (1-0, 1-2)	2-2
Leeds United v Hanover 96 (5-1, 2-1)	7-2
Legia Warsaw v Ujpest Dozsa (0-1, 2-2)	2-3

QUARTER-FINALS

Newcastle United v Vitoria Setubal (5-1, 1-3)	6-4
Rangers v Atletico Bilbao (4-1, 0-2)	4-3
Goztepe Izmir w.o. SV Hamburg (withdrew)	
Leeds United v Ujpest Dozsa (0-1, 0-2)	0-3

SEMI-FINALS

Rangers v Newcastle United (0-0, 0-2)	0-2
Goztepe Izmir v Ujpest Dozsa (1-4, 0-4)	1-8

FINAL

Newcastle United 3 Ujpest Dozsa 0
(Newcastle, 29.5.69, 60,000)

Newcastle: McFaul, Craig, Clark, Gibb, Burton, Moncur, Scott, Robson, Davies, Arentoft, Sinclair (Foggon)

Ujpest: Szentimihalyi, Kaposza, Solymosi, Bankuti, Nosko, E. Dunai, Fazekas, Gorocs, Bene, A. Dunai, Zambo

Scorers: Moncur 2, Scott

Ujpest Dosza 2 Newcastle United 3
(Budapest, 11.6.69, 37,000)

Ujpest: Unchanged

Newcastle: Unchanged; Foggon came on for Scott

Scorers: Bene, Gorocs; Moncur, Arentoft, Foggon

*won on away goals rule †won on toss of a coin

Yet again the final had to be held over to the following season. Leeds took a slender 1-0 lead to Hungary in September but produced a strong rearguard action to keep the scoreline clean and take the trophy. It was a dour final, very much in keeping with the Leeds of the late 1960s, but it was some consolation to them after a semi-final play-off defeat in 1966 and a losing final in 1967. As it happened, they were to have many more disappointments in semi-finals and finals to face in the decade that followed.

1968-69

Once again the finalists were drawn from England and Hungary, but from different towns. Leeds, the holders, survived a close call against Standard Liège to win 3-2 in the first round and then squeaked through against Naples thanks to the right side of the coin after the teams had been level 2-2.

Leeds went on to beat Hanover 96 by a 7-2 aggregate before bowing out in the quarter-finals to Ujpest Dozsa without scoring. It was sweet revenge to Ujpest, who had lost to Leeds at the same stage in 1966. The Hungarians then squashed Goztepe Izmir (Turkey) while the other semi-final was an Anglo-Scottish affair between Rangers and Newcastle United.

Rangers were held goalless at home by Newcastle and then lost 2-0 to United at St James' Park, where late in the game frantic Rangers supporters invaded the pitch and threatened to stop the match. Rangers had already beaten Vojvodina (Yugoslavia) 2-1, Dundalk 9-1, Amsterdam 4-1, and Atlético Bilbao 4-3. Newcastle's passage had started off with an impressive victory against Feyenoord: a four-goal lead from the home leg was sufficient to see them through.

In the second round Newcastle drew 1-1 away to Sporting Lisbon and won the return 1-0. There was just a little to spare against Real Zaragoza, the Tynesiders proceeding on the away goals rule, now universal in European club competitions if applicable. In the quarter-finals United again blessed their good lead from the home leg.

Their opponents in the final, Ujpest Dozsa, had beaten Aris Salonika and Legia Warsaw before disposing of Leeds, but in the final they found Newcastle's home standards still high. Two goals from their captain, Bobby Moncur, virtually the first he had ever scored for the club, and one from Jim Scott gave Newcastle a 3-0 home lead, but it looked to be in jeopardy in the return in Budapest when Ujpest led by two goals at half-time. A storming rally by Newcastle, however, produced three goals (including another from Moncur) and an impressive unexpected away victory.

Rod Belfitt (8) and a youthful Jimmy Greenhoff are thwarted by Dynamo Zagreb keeper Skoric in the second leg of the 1967 final. The Yugoslavs, with Skoric, midfielder Belin and striker Zambata outstanding, played well to keep their 2-0 lead intact. Leeds would have ample compensation, taking the trophy in both 1968 and 1971, and starring in a run of six consecutive English successes in the competition.

1969-70

Newcastle's fine win was the last under the old title of Inter-Cities Fairs Cup: for 1969-70 it became the European Fairs Cup, a nomenclature to go with its much-enhanced reputation as a tournament worthy, at that point, of second place in Europe to the Champions Cup.

The newly-named competition produced a new name to add to the list of winners—Arsenal, for whom the Fairs Cup was the first major honour for 17 years. Their progress in part reflected their growing belief in themselves, as the side built up to a 9-1 hammering of Dynamo Bacau before taking a 3-0 semi-final lead against Ajax.

Their opponents in the final were Anderlecht, victors by away goals over both Dunfermline and holders Newcastle. Newcastle, in turn, had beaten Southampton the same way, while the rule also put paid to Liverpool, having a poor spell in Europe, against Vitoria Setubal in the second round.

Anderlecht certainly looked useful. Not only had they scored 29 goals in reaching the final; but also, in beating the powerful Inter-Milan, they became the only team in the history of *all* European club competitions to reach a final after losing the home leg of the semi-final. That remarkable feat remains unique.

In Brussels a late goal from substitute Kennedy kept Arsenal's hopes barely alive with the Gunners showing the form that was to bring the double the next season, but at Highbury, the Belgians were never given a chance. Kelly, with a tremendous shot, and Radford wiped out Anderlecht's lead, then Sammels scored the certain winner. For the third year running, with three different clubs, the Fairs Cup remained in England.

FAIRS CUP 1969-70

FIRST ROUND

Arsenal v Glentoran (3-0, 0-1)	3-1
Sporting Lisbon v ASK Linz (4-0, 2-2)	6-2
SC Charleroi v ZNK Zagreb (2-1, 3-1)	5-2
Rouen v Twente Enschede (2-0, 0-1)	2-1
FC Zurich v Kilmarnock (3-2, 1-3)	4-5
Slavia Sofia v Valencia (2-0, 1-1)	3-1
TSV Munich 1860 v Skeid Oslo (2-2, 1-2)	3-4
Dynamo Bacau v Floriana (6-0, 1-0)	7-0
Carl Zeiss Jena v Altay Izmir (1-0, 0-0)	1-0
Aris Salonika v Cagliari (1-1, 0-3)	1-4
Partizan Belgrade v Ujpest Dozsa (2-1, 0-2)	2-3
Metz v Napoli (1-1, 1-2)	2-3
VfB Stuttgart v Malmo FF (3-0, 1-1)	4-1
Sabadell v FC Bruges (2-0, 1-5)	3-5
Wiener SK v Ruch Chorzow (4-2, 1-4)	5-6
Hanover 96 v Ajax (2-1, 0-3)	2-4
Inter-Milan v Sparta Prague (3-0, 1-0)	4-0
Hansa Rostock v Panionios Athens (3-0, 0-2)	3-2
Lausanne v Vasas Gyor (1-2, 1-2)	2-4
Barcelona v Odense BK 09 (4-0, 2-0)	6-0
Vitoria Setubal v Rapid Bucharest (3-1, 4-1)	7-2
Liverpool v Dundalk (10-0, 4-0)	14-0
Juventus v Lokomotiv Plovdiv (3-1, 2-1)	5-2
Las Palmas v Hertha Berlin (0-0, 0-1)	0-1
Dundee United v Newcastle United (1-2, 0-1)	1-3
Hvidovre Copenhagen v Porto (1-2, 0-2)	1-4
Vitoria Guimaraes v Banik Ostrava (1-0, 1-1)	2-1
Rosen. Trondheim v Southampton (1-0, 0-2)	1-2
Dunfermline Athletic v Bordeaux (4-0, 0-2)	4-2
Gwardia Warsaw v Vojvodina N. Sad (1-0, 1-1)	2-1
Jeunesse Esch v Coleraine (3-2, 0-4)	3-6
Valur Reykjavik v Anderlecht (0-6, 0-2)	0-8

SECOND ROUND

Sporting Lisbon v Arsenal (0-0, 0-3)	0-3
SC Charleroi v Rouen* (3-1, 0-2)	3-3
Kilmarnock v Slavia Sofia (4-1, 0-2)	4-3
Skeid Oslo v Dynamo Bacau (0-0, 0-2)	0-2
Carl Zeiss Jena v Cagliari (2-0, 1-0)	3-0
FC Bruges v Ujpest Dozsa* (5-2, 0-3)	5-5
VfB Stuttgart v Napoli (0-0, 0-1)	0-1
Ajax v Ruch Chorzow (7-0, 2-1)	9-1
Hansa Rostock v Inter-Milan (2-1, 0-3)	2-4
Vasas Gyor v Barcelona (2-3, 0-2)	2-5
Vitoria Setubal* v Liverpool (1-0, 2-3)	3-3
Hertha Berlin v Juventus (3-1, 0-0)	3-1
Porto v Newcastle United (0-0, 0-1)	0-1
Vitoria Guimaraes v Southampton (3-3, 1-5)	4-8
Dunfermline Ath. v Gwardia Warsaw (2-1, 1-0)	3-1
Anderlecht v Coleraine (6-1, 7-3)	13-4

THIRD ROUND

Rouen v Arsenal (0-0, 0-1)	0-1
Kilmarnock v Dynamo Bacau (1-1, 0-2)	1-3
Carl Zeiss Jena v Ujpest Dozsa (1-0, 3-0)	4-0
Napoli v Ajax (1-0, 0-4)	1-4
Barcelona v Inter-Milan (1-2, 1-1)	2-3
Vitoria Setubal v Hertha Berlin (1-1, 0-1)	1-2
Newcastle United* v Southampton (0-0, 1-1)	1-1
Anderlecht* v Dunfermline Athletic (1-0, 2-3)	3-3

QUARTER-FINALS

Dynamo Bacau v Arsenal (0-2, 1-7)	1-9
Carl Zeiss Jena v Ajax (3-1, 1-5)	4-6
Hertha Berlin v Inter-Milan (1-0, 0-2)	1-2
Anderlecht* v Newcastle United (2-0, 1-3)	3-3

SEMI-FINALS

Arsenal v Ajax (3-0, 0-1)	3-1
Anderlecht v Inter-Milan (0-1, 2-0)	2-1

FINAL

Anderlecht 3 Arsenal 1
(Brussels, 22.4.70, 37,000)

Anderlecht: Trappaniers, Heylens, Velkeneers, Nordahl, Kialunda, Cornelis (Peeters), Desanghere, Devrindt, Mulder, Van Himst, Puis

Arsenal: Wilson, Storey, McNab, Kelly, McLintock, Simpson, Armstrong, Sammels, Radford, George (Kennedy), Graham

Scorers: Devrindt, Mulder 2; Kennedy

Arsenal 3 Anderlecht 0
(Highbury, 28.4.70, 51,612)

Arsenal: Unchanged

Anderlecht: Maartens for Cornelis

Scorers: Kelly, Radford, Sammels

*won on away goals rule

FAIRS CUP 1970-71

FIRST ROUND

Sarpsborg v Leeds United (0-1, 0-5)	0-6
Partizan Belgrade v Dynamo Dresden (0-0, 0-6)	0-6
Dundee United v Grasshoppers (3-2, 0-0)	3-2
Sparta Prague v Atletico Bilbao (2-0, 1-1)	3-1
Zeljeznicar v Anderlecht (4-5, 3-4)	7-9
KB Copenhagen v Sliema Wanderers (7-0, 3-2)	10-2
Hajduk Split v Slavia Sofia (3-0, 0-1)	3-1
Lausanne v Vitoria Setubal (0-2, 1-2)	1-4
Bayern Munich v Rangers (1-0, 1-1)	2-1
Trakia Plovdiv v Coventry City (1-4, 0-2)	1-6
Coleraine v Kilmarnock (1-1, 3-2)	4-3
Sparta Rotterdam v IA Akranes (6-0, 9-0)	15-0
Hibernian v Malmo FF (6-0, 3-2)	9-2
Vitoria Guimaraes v Angouleme (3-0, 1-3)	4-3
Dynamo Bucharest v PAOK Salonika (5-0, 0-1)	5-1
Liverpool v Ferencvaros (1-0, 1-1)	2-1
1FC Cologne v Sedan-Torcy (5-1, 0-1)	5-2
Ruch Chorzow v Fiorentina (1-1, 0-2)	1-3
Nykoping v Hertha Berlin (2-4, 1-4)	3-8
Spartak Trnava† v Olym. Marseille (2-0, 0-2)	2-2
Wiener SK v Beveren-Wass (0-2, 0-3)	0-5
Cork Hibernians v Valencia (0-3, 1-3)	1-6
Ilves Kissat v Sturm Graz (4-2, 0-3)	4-5
Lazio v Arsenal (2-2, 0-2)	2-4
AEK Athens v Twente Enschede (0-1, 0-3)	0-4
Seville v Eskisehirspor (1-0, 1-3)	2-3
La Gantoise v SV Hamburg (0-1, 1-7)	1-8
Barreirense v Dynamo Zagreb (2-0, 1-6)	3-6
Universitatea Craiova v Pecs Dozsa (2-1, 0-3)	2-4
Inter-Milan v Newcastle United (1-1, 0-2)	1-3
GKS Katowice v Barcelona (0-1, 2-3)	2-4
Juventus v US Luxembourg (7-0, 4-0)	11-0

SECOND ROUND

Leeds United* v Dynamo Dresden (1-0, 1-2)	2-2
Sparta Prague v Dundee United (3-1, 0-1)	3-2
KB Copenhagen v Anderlecht (1-3, 0-4)	1-7
Bayern Munich v Coventry City (6-1, 1-2)	7-3
Vitoria Setubal v Hajduk Split (2-0, 1-2)	3-2
Sparta Rotterdam v Coleraine (2-0, 2-1)	4-1
Hibernian v Vitoria Guimaraes (2-0, 1-2)	3-2
Liverpool v Dynamo Bucharest (3-0, 1-1)	4-1
Fiorentina v 1FC Cologne (1-2, 0-1)	1-3
Hertha Berlin v Spartak Trnava (1-0, 1-3)	2-3
Valencia v Beveren-Waas (0-1, 1-1)	1-2
Sturm Graz v Arsenal (1-0, 0-2)	1-2
Eskisehirspor v Twente Enschede (3-2, 1-6)	4-8
Dynamo Zagreb v SV Hamburg (4-0, 0-1)	4-1
Newcastle United v Pecsi Dozsa† (2-0, 0-2)	2-2
Barcelona v Juventus (1-2, 1-2)	2-4

THIRD ROUND

Leeds United v Sparta Prague (6-0, 3-2)	9-2
Anderlecht v Vitoria Setubal (2-1, 1-3)	3-4
Bayern Munich v Sparta Rotterdam (2-1, 3-1)	5-2
Hibernian v Liverpool (0-1, 0-2)	0-3
Spartak Trnava v 1FC Cologne (0-1, 0-3)	0-4
Arsenal v Beveren-Waas (4-0, 0-0)	4-0
Dynamo Zagreb v Twente Enschede (2-2, 0-1)	2-3
Pecsi Dozsa v Juventus (0-1, 0-2)	0-3

QUARTER-FINALS

Leeds United v Vitoria Setubal (2-1, 1-1)	3-2
Liverpool v Bayern Munich (3-0, 1-1)	4-1
Arsenal v 1FC Cologne* (2-1, 0-1)	2-2
Juventus v Twente Enschede (2-0, 2-2)	4-2

SEMI-FINALS

Liverpool v Leeds United (0-1, 0-0)	0-1
1FC Cologne v Juventus (1-1, 0-2)	1-3

FINAL

Juventus‡ 2 Leeds United 2
(Turin, 29.5.71, 45,000)

Juventus: Piloni, Spinosi, Marchetti, Furino, Morini, Salvadore, Haller, Causio, Anastasi, (Novellini), Capello, Bettega

Leeds: Sprake, Reaney, Cooper, Bremner, Charlton, Hunter, Lorimer, Clarke, Jones (Bates), Giles, Madeley

Scorers: Bettega, Capello; Madeley, Bates

Leeds United* 1 Juventus 1 [aet]
(Leeds, 2.6.71, 42,483)

Leeds: Unchanged; Bates came on for Madeley

Juventus: Tancredi for Piloni

Scorers: Clarke; Anastasi

*won on away goals rule †won on penalties ‡replayed first leg: initial game abandoned after 60 minutes because of waterlogged pitch (0-0)

Goalscorer Allan Clarke and substitute Mick Bates chair skipper Billy Bremner after Leeds had drawn 1-1 with Juventus at Elland Road in June 1971 to win the last Fairs Cup final—the fourth year in succession that a Football League side had taken the trophy. While the Italians were a little unlucky to lose the tie on the away goals rule, they would in turn benefit from that format in the 1977 final against Atlético Bilbao.
For Don Revie's Leeds, it completed a fine spell in the Fairs Cup, following a semi-final play-off defeat in 1967, a winning final in 1968, and a losing quarter-final in 1969. The 'missing' year, 1970, saw them beaten by Celtic in the semi-final of the European Cup.
Leeds' 1971 victory meant they became the first British club to win two European titles. The following season Spurs won the new UEFA Cup competition to become the first British club (and only the second in all) to win two different European tournaments—while Leeds crashed 4-0 at home to Lierse SK of Belgium in what is easily their record defeat in any European match.

1970-71

Yet again England kept the trophy—but only just. For the first time the final was decided on away goals—an iniquitous way of concluding a six-round, season-long competition. Juventus, for once, deserved sympathy, while Leeds, just for once, were the lucky ones.

Goals from Madeley and Bates answered those from Bettega and Capello in Turin, and a goal apiece from Clarke and Anastasi failed to settle the matter satisfactorily at Elland Road. Paradoxically, both teams gave their best away from home. Leeds had a sort of claim to victory, however, in that they actually played 150 minutes in Italy: the first game was abandoned after an hour with no score and the 2-2 draw was a replay two days later. The same thing was to happen in 1973, at Liverpool.

Britain's challenge, for what was to be the last Fairs Cup, was a strong one: Liverpool, Arsenal, Coventry, Newcastle, Rangers, Hibs and Dundee United as well as Leeds. Newcastle beat Inter-Milan before losing on away goals to Ujpest's namesakes Pecsi; Liverpool gave notice of their European intentions by removing Ferencvaros, Dynamo Bucharest, Hibs and Bayern Munich (conquerors of both Rangers and Coventry) without losing a game, but gave away the only goal—at Anfield!—to Leeds captain Billy Bremner in the semi-final. Holders Arsenal went out on away goals to Cologne in the previous round, having survived a disgusting exhibition by Lazio both during and after the match in Rome.

The West Germans were well beaten in the semi-final by Juventus, whose record had been not only impressive but uncharacteristically prolific, their 24-goal total including four against the powerful threat of Barcelona in the second round. But for the Italians it would be a six-year wait for another final—when they themselves would benefit from the away goals rule against Atlético Bilbao to win the UEFA Cup.

Meanwhile, England had taken over Spain's mantle with four wins in four years—and the monopoly would continue.

It was fitting that the two nations who had dominated the Fairs Cups, with 10 out of 13 wins between them, should fight it out for permanent possession of the old trophy. Thus Barcelona, original and three times winners, met Leeds, last and twice winners, in Barcelona in September 1971. Lacking Jones, Clarke, Gray and Cooper, United went down 2-1 to goals from new star Duenas—a youngster called Joe Jordan giving them some hope with an equalizer.

FAIRS CUP FINALS

Year	Winners	Runners-up		Score
1958	Barcelona	§*London	(2-2, 6-0)	8-2
1960	Barcelona	*Birmingham City	(0-0, 4-1)	4-1
1961	AS Roma	*Birminham City	(2-2, 2-0)	4-2
1962	*Valencia	Barcelona	(6-2, 1-1)	7-3
1963	Valencia	*Dynamo Zagreb	(2-1, 2-0)	4-1
1964‡	Real Zaragoza	Valencia	(in Barcelona)	2-1
1965‡	Ferencvaros	Juventus	(in Turin)	1-0
1966	*Barcelona	Real Zaragoza	(0-1, 4-2)	4-3
1967	*Dynamo Zagreb	Leeds United	(2-0, 0-0)	2-0
1968	*Leeds United	Ferencvaros	(1-0, 0-0)	1-0
1969	*Newcastle United	Ujpest Dozsa	(3-0, 3-2)	6-2
1970	Arsenal	*Anderlecht	(1-3, 3-0)	4-3
1971	†Leeds United	*Juventus	(2-2, 1-1)	3-3

*home team in first leg †won on away goals rule ‡one-match final
§composite team

UEFA CUP

1971-72

For the 1971-72 season there was a new trophy, the UEFA Cup, presented by the European association, while the old one took up permanent residence in Barcelona's boardroom after the special play-off with Leeds. The format remained the same—and so, as it turned out, did the balance of power in the competition, with England not only retaining her hold on what was then Europe's second most important club competition, but also reinforcing her domination by providing both finalists.

Tottenham had beaten Iceland's Keflavik (15-1), Nantes of France, Rapid Bucharest and UT Arad (both of Rumania) and a defensive AC Milan with the help of a magnificent goal at San Siro by Alan Mullery. Wolves' travels had taken them past Academica Coimbra of Portugal and Den Haag of Holland (both 7-1 on aggregate), Carl Zeiss Jena, Juventus and Ferencvaros, the last two successes coming from solid draws away and well-won odd-goal victories at home against vastly experienced European sides. The old warhorse Derek Dougan was in fine fettle, his nine goals making him the series' leading scorer. Leeds, however, had gone out in the first round, giving away four goals against Lierse in Belgium and pulling only two back at home.

England regular Martin Chivers scored twice at Molineux to give Spurs a 2-1 advantage at White Hart Lane, where Wagstaffe's goal encouraged Wolves in a fast, hard second leg. But Mullery, recalled to the side before the semi-finals, scored with a brave diving header to give Spurs their second European trophy.

It was England's fifth success in five years—with more to come.

Nine goals from the veteran Derek Dougan put him top of the UEFA Cup list for 1971-72 and helped Wolves to their only European final. In his first game in Europe, against Coimbra, Dougan scored a hat-trick.

Spurs' Alan Mullery and Wolves' Jim McCalliog go through the motions before the second leg of the all-England final at White Hart Lane. A draw saw the London side to victory.

UEFA CUP 1971-72

FIRST ROUND

IB Keflavik v Tottenham Hotspur (1-6, 0-9)	1-15
Porto v Nantes (0-2, 1-1)	1-3
Lugano v Legia Warsaw (1-3, 0-0)	1-3
Napoli v Rapid Bucharest (1-0, 0-2)	1-2
Vitoria Setubal* v Nimes (1-0, 1-2)	2-2
Spartak Moscow v VSS Kosice (1-2, 2-0)	3-2
Zaglebie Walbrzych v Union Teplice (1-0, 3-2)	4-2
UT Arad v Austria Salzburg (4-1, 1-3)	5-4
Lierse SK v Leeds United (0-2, 4-0)	4-2
Rosenborg Trondheim v HJK Helsinki (3-0, 1-0)	4-0
Basle v Real Madrid (1-2, 1-2)	2-4
Chemie Halle v PSV Eindhoven (0-0‡)	0-0
Dundee v AB Copenhagen (4-2, 1-0)	5-2
St Etienne v 1FC Cologne (1-1, 1-2)	2-3
Hertha Berlin v Elfsborg Boras (4-1, 3-1)	7-2
AC Milan v Dighenis Morphou (4-0, 3-0)	7-0
Fenerbahce v Ferencvaros (1-1, 1-3)	2-4
Atletico Madrid v Panionios Athens* (2-1, 0-1)	2-2
Southampton v Atletico Bilbao (2-1, 0-2)	2-3
Glentoran v Eintracht Brunswick (0-1, 1-6)	1-7
SV Hamburg v St Johnstone (2-1, 0-3)	2-4
Vasas Budapest v Shelbourne (1-0, 1-1)	2-1
Bologna v Anderlecht (2-0, 1-1)	3-1
Zeljeznicar v FC Bruges (3-0, 1-3)	4-3
Marsa v Juventus (0-6, 0-5)	0-11
Celta Vigo v Aberdeen (0-2, 0-1)	0-3
Dynamo Zagreb v Botev Vratza (6-1, 2-1)	8-2
Rapid Vienna w.o. Vlaznia (withdrew)	
Carl Zeiss Jena v Lokomotiv Plovdiv (3-0, 1-3)	4-3
OFK Belgrade v Djurgaarden (2-2, 4-1)	6-3
FC Den Haag v Aris Bonnevoie (5-0, 1-1)	6-1
Wolves v Academica Coimbra (3-0, 4-1)	7-1

SECOND ROUND

Nantes v Tottenham Hotspur (0-0, 0-1)	0-1
Rapid Bucharest v Legia Warsaw (4-0, 0-2)	4-2
Spartak Moscow v Vitoria Setubal (0-0, 0-4)	0-4
Zaglebie Walbrzych v UT Arad (1-1, 1-2)	2-3
Rosenborg Trondheim v Lierse SK* (4-1, 0-3)	4-4
Real Madrid v PSV Eindhoven* (3-1, 0-2)	3-3
1FC Cologne v Dundee (2-1, 2-4)	4-5
AC Milan v Hertha Berlin (4-2, 1-2)	5-4
Ferencvaros v Panionios Athens (6-0§)	6-0
Eintracht Brunswick v At. Bilbao (2-1, 2-2)	4-3
St Johnstone v Vasas Budapest (2-0, 0-1)	2-1
Zeljeznicar* v Bologna (1-1, 2-2)	3-3
Juventus v Aberdeen (2-0, 1-1)	3-1
Dynamo Zagreb v Rapid Vienna* (2-2, 0-0)	2-2
OFK Belgrade v Carl Zeiss Jena (1-1, 0-4)	1-5
FC Den Haag v Wolverhampton W. (1-3, 0-4)	1-7

THIRD ROUND

Tottenham H. v Rapid Bucharest (3-0, 2-0)	5-0
UT Arad v Votoria Setubal (3-0, 0-1)	3-1
PSV Eindhoven v Lierse SK (1-0, 0-4)	1-4
AC Milan v Dundee (3-0, 0-2)	3-2
Eintracht Brunswick v Ferencvaros (1-1, 2-5)	3-6
St Johnstone v Zeljeznicar (1-0, 1-5)	2-5
Rapid Vienna v Juventus (0-1, 1-4)	1-5
Carl Zeiss Jena v Wolverhampton W. (0-1, 0-3)	0-4

QUARTER-FINALS

UT Arad v Tottenham Hotspur (0-2, 1-1)	1-3
AC Milan v Lierse SK (2-0, 1-1)	3-1
Ferencvaros† v Zeljeznicar (1-2, 2-1)	3-3
Juventus v Wolverhampton W. (1-1, 1-2)	2-3

SEMI-FINALS

Tottenham Hotspur v AC Milan (2-1, 1-1)	3-2
Ferencvaros v Wolverhampton W. (2-2, 1-2)	3-4

FINAL

Wolverhampton W. 1 Tottenham Hotspur 2
(Wolverhampton, 2.5.72, 45,000)

Wolves: Parkes, Shaw, Taylor, Hegan, Munro, McAlle, McCalliog, Hibbitt, Richards, Dougan, Wagstaffe

Spurs: Jennings, Kinnear, Knowles, Mullery, England, Beal, Gilzean, Perryman, Chivers, Peters, Coates (Pratt)

Scorers: McCalliog; Chivers 2

Tottenham Hotspur 1 Wolverhampton W. 1
(Tottenham, 17.5.72, 54,303)

Spurs: Unchanged

Wolves: Unchanged; Bailey came on for Hibbitt, Curran came on for Dougan

Scorers: Mullery; Wagstaffe

*won on away goals rule †won on penalties ‡Halle withdrew after first leg §Panionios disqualified after first leg

1972-73

Tottenham's defence of the trophy was brought to an end in the semi-finals by Liverpool and the away goals rule, Heighway's goal at White Hart Lane proving better value than Peters' two. There was some justice: Spurs had survived Vitoria Setubal on the same rule in the previous round.

Manchester City, Stoke, and Aberdeen all failed to reach the second round, the Scots going down 9-5 to Borussia Moenchengladbach. The West Germans had an impressive march to the finals, during which they rattled up an amazing 35 goals in 10 games.

The first leg of the final was abandoned after 27 minutes through torrential rain, time enough for manager Bill Shankly to see the German's weakness in the air and bring in Toshack for the replay. Feeding off the big Welshman, Keegan scored twice; Lloyd added a third. Clemence saved a penalty (vitally, as it proved), as did Kleff. Netzer was strangely subdued, and wasted, as sweeper. In Moenchengladbach, with Netzer restored to midfield, it was a different story. Heynckes got two in the first half, but Liverpool, newly crowned League champions, held firm.

UEFA CUP 1972-73

FIRST ROUND

Liverpool v Eintracht Frankfurt (2-0, 0-0)	2-0
AEK Athens v Salgotarjan (3-1, 1-1)	4-2
Universitatea Cluj v Levski Spartak (4-1, 1-5)	5-6
Angers v Dynamo Berlin (1-1, 1-2)	2-3
Porto v Barcelona (3-1, 1-0)	4-1
Atvidaberg v FC Bruges (3-5, 2-1)	5-6
Ruch Chorzow v Fenerbahce (3-0, 0-1)	3-1
Dynamo Dresden v VOEST Linz (2-0, 2-2)	4-2
Vitoria Setubal v Zaglebie Sosnowiec (6-1, 0-1)	6-2
Eskisehirspor v Fiorentina (1-2, 0-3)	1-5
UT Arad v IFK Norrkoping (1-2, 0-2)	1-4
Inter-Milan v Valletta (6-1, 1-0)	7-1
Red Star Belgrade v Lausanne (5-1, 2-3)	7-4
Manchester City v Valencia (2-2, 1-2)	3-4
Olympiakos Piraeus v Cagliari (2-1, 1-0)	3-1
Lyn Oslo v Tottenham Hotspur (3-6, 0-6)	3-12
Dynamo Tbilisi v Twente Enschede (3-2, 0-2)	3-4
Sochaux v Frem Copenhagen (1-3, 1-2)	2-5
Slovan Bratislava v Vojvodina N. Sad (6-0, 2-1)	8-1
Torino v Las Palmas (2-0, 0-4)	2-4
Beroe Stara Zagora v FK Austria (7-0, 3-1)	10-1
Honved v Partick Thistle (1-0, 3-0)	4-0
Feyenoord v US Luxembourg (9-0, 12-0)	21-0
Dukla Prague v OFK Belgrade (2-2, 1-3)	3-5
Stoke City v 1FC Kaiserslautern (3-1, 0-4)	3-5
Racing White v CUF Barrierense (0-1, 0-2)	0-3
Grasshoppers Zurich v Nimes (2-1, 2-1)	4-2
EPA Larnaca v Ararat Erevan (0-1, 0-1)	0-2
1FC Cologne v Bohemians (2-1, 3-0)	5-1
Viking Stavanger v IB Vestmannaey (1-0, 0-0)	1-0
Hvidovre w.o. IFK Helsinki (withdrew)	
Aberdeen v Borussia M'gladbach (2-3, 3-6‡)	5-9

SECOND ROUND

Liverpool v AEK Athens (3-0, 3-1)	6-1
Dynamo Berlin v Levski Spartak (3-0, 0-2)	3-2
Porto v FC Bruges (3-0, 2-3)	5-3
Ruch Chorzow v Dynamo Dresden (0-1, 0-3)	0-4
Vitoria Setubal* v Fiorentina (1-0, 1-2)	2-2
Inter-Milan v IFK Norrkoping (2-2, 2-0)	4-2
Red Star Belgrade v Valencia (3-1, 1-0)	4-1
Tottenham H. v Olympiakos Piraeus (4-0, 0-1)	4-1
Frem Copenhagen v Twente Enschede (0-5, 0-4)	0-9
Las Palmas v Slovan Bratislava (2-2, 1-0)	3-2
Beroe Stara Zagora v Honved (3-0, 0-1)	3-1
Feyenoord v OFK Belgrade* (4-3, 1-2)	5-5
CUF Barrierense v 1FC Kaiserslautern (1-3, 1-0)	2-3
Grasshoppers v Ararat Erevan (1-3, 2-4)	3-7
Viking Stavanger v 1FC Cologne (1-0, 1-9)	2-9
Borussia M'gladbach v Hvidovre (3-0‡, 3-1)	6-1

THIRD ROUND

Dynamo Berlin v Liverpool (0-0, 1-3)	1-3
Porto v Dynamo Dresden (1-2, 0-1)	1-3
Vitoria Setubal v Inter-Milan (2-0, 0-1)	2-1
Tottenham H. v Red Star Belgrade (2-0, 0-1)	2-1
Twente Enschede v Las Palmas (3-0, 1-2)	4-2
OFK Belgrade v Beroe Stara Zagora (0-0, 3-1)	3-1
Ararat Erevan v 1FC Kaiserslautern† (2-0, 0-2)	2-2
1FC Cologne v Borussia M'gladbach (0-0, 0-5)	0-5

QUARTER-FINALS

Liverpool v Dynamo Dresden (2-0, 1-0)	3-0
Tottenham Hotspur* v Vitoria Setubal (1-0, 1-2)	2-2
OFK Belgrade v Twente Enschede (3-2, 0-2)	3-4
1FC Kaiserslautern v Bor. M'gladbach (1-2, 1-7)	2-9

SEMI-FINALS

Liverpool* v Tottenham Hotspur (1-0, 1-2)	2-2
Bor. M'gladbach v Twente Enschede (3-0, 2-1)	5-1

FINAL

Liverpool §3 Borussia Moenchengladbach 0
(Liverpool, 10.5.73, 41,169)

Liverpool: Clemence, Lawler, Lindsay, Smith, Lloyd, Hughes, Keegan, Cormack, Toshack, Heighway (Hall), Callaghan

Borussia: Kleff, Vogts, Michalik, Danner, Bonhof, Kulik, Jensen, Wimmer, Rupp (Simonsen), Netzer, Heynckes

Scorers: Keegan 2, Lloyd

Borussia Moenchengladbach 2 Liverpool 0
(Moenchengladbach, 23.5.73, 35,000)

Borussia: Surau for Michalik

Liverpool: Unchanged; Boersma came on for Heighway

Scorer: Heynckes 2

*won on away goals rule †won on penalties ‡at Nuremberg §replayed first leg: initial game abandoned after 27 minutes because of waterlogged pitch

Liverpool boss Bill Shankly brought in John Toshack after seeing the Borussia defence in action in the abandoned 1973 game and, as here, the Welshman caused havoc, creating two goals for Kevin Keegan in a 3-0 win.

1973-74

The freewheeling exuberance of Dutch football, epitomized by Ajax in the European Cup over the previous three seasons, took over the UEFA Cup to the detriment of Spurs and England's long tenure of the trophy. More detrimental to English football, though, was the disgraceful behaviour of the Spurs fans, who ran riot before and during the second leg of the final with Feyenoord in Rotterdam. Level at 2-2 after the White Hart Lane leg, Spurs never looked like getting back in the game against a side attacking from all quarters. Van Hanegem (suspended for the second leg), Rijsbergen, De Jong and Jansen were all to play in the World Cup final six weeks later in Munich.

A progressive young Ipswich side looked good value against Real Madrid, Lazio (with yet more Italian brawling), and Twente Enschede of Holland before going out on the away goal to Lokomotiv Leipzig in the quarter-finals. Leeds, suffering a Cup Winners Cup final hangover from Salonika, got through after a goalless second round with Hibs only on penalties before bowing out to Vitoria Setubal in Portugal.

Spurs, poor in the League, always seemed to pull something special out for UEFA Cup ties and ended the aspirations of Grasshoppers Zurich (9-2), Aberdeen (5-2), Dynamo Tbilisi (6-2), Cologne (5-1) and Leipzig, away goals conquerors of Wolves as well as Ipswich.

Against Feyenoord, though, despite fielding eight of the 12 players who had won the trophy two years before, they ran out of magic and came up against their own shortcomings. And their fans knew it.

RIGHT: ***A rare moment of Tottenham progress with Ralph Coates in the second leg of the 1974 final with Feyenoord. Spurs, level from White Hart Lane, went out 4-2 to the Dutchmen—and England's six-year hold on the competition was over.***
BELOW: ***Disgruntled Spurs fans ran riot when their side went behind, adding to Britain's already poor reputation in Europe.***

UEFA CUP 1973-74

FIRST ROUND

Oester Vaxjo v Feyenoord (1-3, 1-2)	2-5
Ferencvaros v Gwardia Warsaw (0-1, 1-2)	1-3
Fiorentina v Universitatea Craiova (0-0, 0-1)	0-1
Ards v Standard Liege (3-2, 1-6)	4-8
Sliema W. v Lokomotiv Plovdiv (0-2, 0-1)	0-3
VSS Kosice v Honved (1-0, 2-5)	3-5
Carl Zeiss Jena v Mikkelin Pallokissat (3-0, 3-0)	6-0
Ruch Chorzow v SV Wuppertal (4-1, 4-5)	8-6
Vitoria Setubal v Beerschot (2-0, 2-0)	4-0
Espanol v RWD Molenbeek (0-3, 2-1)	2-4
Hibernian v IB Keflavik (2-0, 1-1)	3-1
Stromsgodset Drammen v Leeds U. (1-1, 1-6)	2-7
Fredrikstad v Dynamo Kiev (0-1, 0-4)	0-5
Copenh'g'n BK 1903 v AIK Stockholm (2-1, 1-1)	3-2
Tatran Presov v Velez Mostar (4-2, 1-1)	5-3
VfB Stuttgart v Olympiakos Nicosia (9-0, 4-0)	13-0
Torino v Lokomotiv Leipzig (1-2, 1-2)	2-4
Belenenses v Wolverhampton W. (0-2, 1-2)	1-4
Fortuna Dusseldorf v Naetsved IF (1-0, 2-2)	3-2
Admira Wacker* v Inter-Milan (1-0, 1-2)	2-2
Panachaiki Patras v Graz AK (2-1, 1-0)	3-1
Dundee v Twente Enschede (1-3, 2-4)	3-7
Lazio v Sion (3-0, 1-3)	4-3
Ipswich Town v Real Madrid (1-0, 0-0)	1-0
US Luxembourg v Olym. Marseille (0-5, 1-7)	1-12
Eskisehirspor v 1FC Cologne (0-0, 0-2)	0-2
Fenerbahce v Arges Pitesti (5-1, 1-1)	6-2
OGC Nice v Barcelona (3-0, 0-2)	3-2
Dynamo Tbilisi v Slavia Sofia (4-1, 0-2)	4-3
Panathinaikos v OFK Belgrade* (1-2, 1-0)	2-2
Aberdeen v Finn Harps (4-1, 3-1)	7-2
Grasshoppers v Tottenham Hotspur (1-5, 1-4)	2-9

SECOND ROUND

Feyenoord v Gwardia Warsaw (3-1, 0-1)	3-2
Standard Liege v Univ. Craiova (2-0, 1-1)	3-1
Lokomotiv Plovdiv v Honved (3-4, 2-3)	5-7
Ruch Chorzow v Carl Zeiss Jena (3-0, 0-1)	3-1
Vitoria Setubal* v RWD Molenbeek (1-0, 1-2)	2-2
Leeds United† v Hibernian (0-0, 0-0)	0-0
Dynamo Kiev v Copenhagen BK 1903 (1-0, 2-1)	3-1
VfB Stuttgart v Tatran Presov (3-1, 5-3)	8-4
Lokomotiv Leipzig* v Wolves (3-0, 1-4)	4-4
Admira Wacker v Fortuna Dusseldorf (2-1, 0-3)	2-4
Panachaiki Patras v Twente Enschede (1-1, 0-7)	1-8
Ipswich Town v Lazio (4-0, 2-4)	6-4
Olympique Marseille v 1FC Cologne (2-0, 0-6)	2-6
OGC Nice v Fenerbahce (4-0, 0-2)	4-2
Dynamo Tbilisi v OFK Belgrade (3-0, 5-1)	8-1
Aberdeen v Tottenham Hotspur (1-1, 1-4)	2-5

THIRD ROUND

Standard Liege v Feyenoord* (3-1, 0-2)	3-3
Honved v Ruch Chorzow (2-0, 0-5)	2-5
Leeds United v Vitoria Setubal (1-0, 1-3)	2-3
Dynamo Kiev v VfB Stuttgart (2-0, 0-3)	2-3
F. Dusseldorf v Lokomotiv Leipzig (2-1, 0-3)	2-4
Ipswich Town v Twente Enschede (1-0, 2-1)	3-1
OGC Nice v 1FC Cologne (1-0, 0-4)	1-4
Dynamo Tbilisi v Tottenham Hotspur (1-1, 1-5)	2-6

QUARTER-FINALS

Ruch Chorzow v Feyenoord (1-1, 1-3)	2-4
VfB Stuttgart v Vitoria Setubal (1-0, 2-2)	3-2
Ipswich Town v Lokomotiv Leipzig† (1-0, 0-1)	1-1
1FC Cologne v Tottenham Hotspur (1-2, 0-3)	1-5

SEMI-FINALS

Feyenoord v VfB Stuttgart (2-1, 2-2)	4-3
Lokomotiv Leipzig v Tottenham H. (1-2, 0-2)	1-4

FINAL

Tottenham Hotspur 2 Feyenoord 2
(Tottenham, 21.5.74, 46,281)

Spurs: Jennings, Evans, Naylor, Pratt, England, Beal, McGrath, Perryman, Chivers, Peters, Coates

Feyenoord: Treytel, Rijsbergen, Van Daele, Israel, Vos, De Jong, Jansen, Van Hanegem, Ressel, Schoenmaker, Kristensen

Scorers: England, Van Daele (og); Van Hanegem, De Jong

Feyenoord 2 Tottenham Hotspur 0
(Rotterdam, 29.5.74, 68,000)

Feyenoord: Ramljak for Van Hanegem; Boskamp came on for Kristensen

Spurs: Unchanged; Holder came on for Pratt

Scorers: Rijsbergen, Ressel

*won on away goals rule †won on penalties

UEFA CUP 1974-75

FIRST ROUND

TS Innsbruck v Borussia M'gladbach (2-1, 0-3)	2-4
O. Lyon v Red Boys Differdange (7-0, 4-1)	11-1
Grasshoppers v Panathinaikos (2-0, 1-2)	3-2
Vitoria Setubal v Real Zaragoza (1-1, 0-4)	1-5
Napoli v Videoton (2-0, 1-1)	3-1
Porto v Wolverhampton Wanderers (4-1, 1-3)	5-4
Nantes v Legia Warsaw (2-2, 1-0)	3-2
Real Sociedad v Banik Ostrava (0-1, 0-4)	0-5
FC Amsterdam v Hibernians Valletta (5-0, 7-0)	12-0
Etar Tirnovo v Inter-Milan (0-0, 0-3)	0-3
Lokomotiv Plovdiv v Vasas Gyor† (3-1, 1-3)	4-4
Torino v Fortuna Dusseldorf (1-1, 1-3)	2-4
Gornik Zabrze v Partizan Belgrade (2-2, 0-3)	2-5
Valur Reykjavik v Portadown (0-0, 1-2)	1-2
Boluspor v Dynamo Bucharest (0-1, 0-3)	0-4
1FC Cologne v Kokkolan PV (5-1, 4-1)	9-2
Vorwaerts Frankfurt v Juventus (2-1, 0-3)	2-4
Rosenborg Trondheim v Hibernian (2-3, 1-9)	3-12
Sturm Graz v Antwerp* (2-1, 0-1)	2-2
Stoke City v Ajax* (1-1, 0-0)	1-1
Randers Freja v Dynamo Dresden* (1-1, 0-0)	1-1
Oster Vaxjo v Dynamo Moscow* (3-2, 1-2)	4-4
Besiktas v Steagul Rosu Brasov (2-0, 0-3)	2-3
SV Hamburg v Bohemians (3-0, 1-0)	4-0
Spartak Moscow v Velez Mostar* (3-1, 0-2)	3-3
Rapid Vienna v Aris Salonika (3-1, 0-1)	3-2
KB Copenhagen v Atletico Madrid (3-2, 0-4)	3-6
Derby County v Servette Geneva (4-1, 2-1)	6-2
Dukla w.o. Peoporikis Larnaca (withdrew)	
Start Kristiansand v Djurgaarden (1-2, 1-5)	2-7
RWD Molenbeek v Dundee (1-0, 4-2)	5-2
Ipswich Town v Twente Enschede* (2-2, 1-1)	3-3

SECOND ROUND

Borussia M'gladbach v Olym. Lyon (1-0, 5-2)	6-2
Grasshoppers v Real Zaragoza (2-1, 0-5)	2-6
Napoli v Porto (1-0, 1-0)	2-0
Nantes v Banik Ostrava (1-0, 0-2)	1-2
Inter-Milan v FC Amsterdam (1-2, 0-0)	1-2
Vasas Gyor v Fortuna Dusseldorf (2-0, 0-3)	2-3
Partizan Belgrade v Portadown (5-0, 1-1)	6-1
Dynamo Bucharest v 1FC Cologne (1-1, 2-3)	3-4
Hibernian v Juventus (2-4, 0-4)	2-8
Ajax* v Antwerp (1-0, 1-2)	2-2
Dyn. Dresden† v Dyn. Moscow (1-0, 0-1)	1-1
SV Hamburg v Steagul Rosu Brasov (8-0, 2-1)	10-1
Rapid Vienna v Velez Mostar (1-1, 0-1)	1-2
Derby County† v Atletico Madrid (2-2, 2-2)	4-4
Djurgaarden v Dukla Prague (0-2, 1-3)	1-5
Twente Enschede v RWD Molenbeek (2-1, 1-0)	3-1

THIRD ROUND

Borussia M'gladbach v Real Zaragoza (5-0, 4-2)	9-2
Napoli v Banik Ostrava (0-2, 1-1)	1-3
FC Amsterdam v Fortuna Dusseldorf (3-0, 2-1)	5-1
Partizan Belgrade v 1FC Cologne (1-0, 1-5)	2-5
Juventus* v Ajax (1-0, 1-2)	2-2
SV Hamburg v Dynamo Dresden (4-1, 2-2)	6-3
Derby County v Velez Mostar (3-1, 1-4)	4-5
Dukla Prague v Twente Enschede (3-1, 0-5)	3-6

QUARTER-FINALS

Banik Ostrava v Borussia M'gladbach (0-1, 1-3)	1-4
1FC Cologne v FC Amsterdam (5-1, 3-2)	8-3
Juventus v SV Hamburg (2-0, 0-0)	2-0
Velez Mostar v Twente Enschede (1-0, 0-2)	1-2

SEMI-FINALS

1FC Cologne v Borussia M'gladbach (1-3, 0-1)	1-4
Twente Enschede v Juventus (3-1, 1-0)	4-1

FINAL

Borussia M'gladbach 0 Twente Enschede 0
(Dusseldorf, 7.5.75, 42,368)

Borussia: Kleff, Wittkamp, Stielike, Vogts, Surau, Bonhof, Wimmer, Danner (Del Haye), Kulik (Schaffer), Simonsen, Jensen

Twente: Gross, Drost, Van Ierssel, Overweg, Oranen, Thijssen, Pahlplatz, Van der Vall, Bos, Jeurig (Achterberg), Zuidema

Twente Enschede 1 Borussia M'gladbach 5
(Enschede, 21.5.75, 21,767)

Twente: Unchanged: Muhren came on for Bos, Achterberg came on for Pahlplatz

Borussia: Kleff, Wittkamp, Vogts, Surau (Schaffer), Klinkhammer, Bonhof, Wimmer (Koppel), Danner, Simonsen, Jensen, Heynckes

Scorers: Drost; Heynckes 3, Simonsen 2 (1 pen)

*won on away goals rule †won on penalties

England stars Martin Chivers (9) and Martin Peters pressure the Dutch defence in the first leg.

1974-75

That England's domination of the UEFA Cup was well and truly over was well illustrated by the fact that only one Football League side reached the last 16. That was Derby County, who had performed well to eliminate Servette of Geneva and Atlético Madrid, the previous season's European Cup finalists. In the third round, however, Derby could not recover from a 4-1 deficit away to the obscure Velez Mostar of Yugoslavia. Ipswich, Stoke and Wolves had all disappeared at the first hurdle—the latter well beaten by Porto but the first two had gone down on away goals to Dutch sides.

Twente stars Muhren and Thijssen would later become Ipswich players, but this season they were to go all the way; and their home town is the smallest ever to provide a European finalist. Their other victims were Molenbeek, Dukla Prague (including a 5-0 win at home), Velez Mostar and then, their best performance of all, two wins against Juventus.

Remarkably, they held Borussia Moenchengladbach in Dusseldorf and looked set for victory, but the Germans hit form in Holland and won 5-1, with Heynckes' hat-trick taking his haul to 11 for the series.

Substitute Jimmy Case is feted after scoring the second of Liverpool's three comeback goals at Anfield against Bruges in the 1976 final.

The preliminaries before the second leg in Belgium, where Keegan's goal secured Liverpool's second UEFA Cup success.

UEFA CUP 1975-76

FIRST ROUND

Hibernian v Liverpool (1-0, 1-3)	1-3
Grasshoppers v Real Sociedad* (3-3, 1-1)	4-4
Antwerp v Aston Villa (4-1, 1-0)	5-1
GAIS Gothenburg v Slask Wroclaw (2-1, 2-4)	4-5
Torpedo Moscow v Napoli (4-1, 1-1)	5-2
Rapid Vienna v Galatasaray (1-0, 1-3)	2-3
Bohemians Prague v Honved (1-2, 1-1)	2-3
Tirgu Mures v Dynamo Dresden (2-2, 1-4)	3-6
Levski Spartak v Eskisehirspor (3-0, 4-1)	7-1
MSV Duisburg v Paralimni (7-1, 3-2)	10-4
Hertha Berlin v HJK Helsinki (4-1, 2-1)	6-2
Glentoran v Ajax (1-6, 0-8)	1-14
VOEST Linz v Vasas Budapest (2-0, 0-4)	2-4
Sliema Wanderers v Sporting Lisbon (1-2, 1-3)	2-5
Chernomonretz Odessa v Lazio (1-0, 0-3)	1-3
PAOK Salonika v Barcelona (1-0, 1-6)	2-6
Young Boys Berne v SV Hamburg (0-0, 2-4)	2-4
Univ. Craiova v Red Star Belgrade (1-3, 1-1)	2-4
IB Keflavik v Dundee United (0-2, 0-4)	0-6
Porto v Avenir Beggen (7-0, 3-0)	10-0
Inter Bratislava v Real Zaragoza (5-0, 3-2)	8-2
Vojvodina Novi Sad v AEK Athens (0-0, 1-3)	1-3
Carl Zeiss Jena v Olym. Marseille (3-0, 1-0)	4-0
Holbaek IF v Stal Mielec (0-1, 1-2)	1-3
Everton v AC Milan (0-0, 0-1)	0-1
Athlone Town v Valerengen (3-1, 1-1)	4-2
1FC Cologne v Copenhagen BK 03 (2-0, 3-2)	5-2
AIK Stockholm v Spartak Moscow (1-1, 0-1)	1-2
AS Roma v Dounav Russe (2-0, 0-1)	2-1
Molde SK v Oster Vaxjo (1-0, 0-6)	1-6
Feyenoord v Ipswich Town (1-2, 0-2)	1-4
Olympique Lyon v FC Bruges (4-3, 0-3)	4-6

SECOND ROUND

Real Sociedad v Liverpool (1-3, 0-6)	1-9
Slask Wroclaw v Antwerp (1-1, 2-1)	3-2
Galatasaray v Torpedo Moscow (2-4, 0-3)	2-7
Honved v Dynamo Dresden (2-2, 0-1)	2-3
MSV Duisburg v Levski Spartak* (3-2, 1-2)	4-4
Hertha Berlin v Ajax (1-0, 1-4)	2-4
Vasas Budapest v Sporting Lisbon (3-1, 1-2)	4-3
Lazio v Barcelona (0-3‡)	0-3
Red Star Belgrade v SV Hamburg (1-1, 0-4)	1-5
Dundee United v Porto (1-2, 1-1)	2-3
Inter Bratislava* v AEK Athens (2-0, 1-3)	3-3
Carl Zeiss Jena v Stal Mielec† (1-0, 0-1)	1-1
Athlone Town v AC Milan (0-0, 0-3)	0-3
Spartak Moscow v 1FC Cologne (2-0, 1-0)	3-0
Oster Vaxjo v AS Roma (1-0, 0-2)	1-2
Ipswich Town v FC Bruges (3-0, 0-4)	3-4

THIRD ROUND

Slask Wroclaw v Liverpool (1-2, 0-3)	1-5
Dynamo Dresden v Torpedo Moscow (3-0, 1-3)	4-3
Ajax v Levski Spartak† (2-1, 1-2)	3-3
Barcelona v Vasas Budapest (3-1, 1-0)	4-1
SV Hamburg v Porto (2-0, 1-2)	3-2
Inter Bratislava v Stal Mielec (1-0, 0-2)	1-2
AC Milan v Spartak Moscow (4-0, 0-2)	4-2
FC Bruges v AS Roma (1-0, 1-0)	2-0

QUARTER-FINALS

Dynamo Dresden v Liverpool (0-0, 1-2)	1-2
Barcelona v Levski Spartak (4-0, 4-5)	8-5
SV Hamburg v Stal Mielec (1-1, 1-0)	2-1
FC Bruges v AC Milan (2-0, 1-2)	3-2

SEMI-FINALS

Barcelona v Liverpool (0-1, 1-1)	1-2
SV Hamburg v FC Bruges (1-1, 0-1)	1-2

FINAL

Liverpool 3 FC Bruges 2
(Liverpool, 28.4.76, 56,000)

Liverpool: Clemence, Smith, Neal, Thompson, Kennedy, Hughes, Keegan, Fairclough, Heighway, Toshack (Case), Callaghan

Bruges: Jensen, Bastyns, Krieger, Leekens, Volders, Cools, Van der Eycken, De Cubber, Van Gool, Lambert, Le Fevre

Scorers: Kennedy, Case, Keegan (pen); Lambert, Cools

FC Bruges 1 Liverpool 1
(Bruges, 19.5.76, 32,000)

Bruges: Unchanged; Sanders came on for Lambert, Hinderyckx came on for De Cubber

Liverpool: Case for Fairclough; Fairclough came on for Toshack

Scorers: Lambert (pen); Keegan

*won on away goals rule †won on penalties ‡Lazio refused to play fearing demonstrations; FIFA awarded game 3-0 to Barcelona

1975-76

The 1975-76 series saw the first of the two European finals which have been repeated in another tournament—Liverpool versus Bruges. It is an odd coincidence that Liverpool's four European successes should have brought them together with just two final opponents—twice against Borussia Moenchengladbach, twice against Bruges. And, just as they did at Wembley in 1978, Liverpool were to win by the odd goal.

Liverpool actually lost their first game—at Hibernian—but came back with a Toshack hat-trick at Anfield. Meanwhile, rivals Everton couldn't manage a goal against AC Milan and went out, while Antwerp beat Aston Villa twice. Ipswich, however, did better in beating Feyenoord but then, amazingly, squandered a three-goal lead to Bruges and ended up losing 4-3.

Elsewhere Lazio, not normally noted for their sensitivity, refused to play Barcelona because they claimed to fear political demonstrations against the Spaniards and Barcelona were awarded a 3-0 away victory. Little Athlone Town held AC Milan to a goalless draw on their tiny League of Ireland ground and Liverpool plodded gamely on through Real Sociedad, Slask Wroclaw and Dynamo Dresden.

In the semi-finals Liverpool put out Barcelona by the odd goal and Bruges did the same to SV Hamburg. In the first leg of the final Bruges, and in particular Cools, provided some early apprehensive moments for the Kop, but Liverpool came back from 2-0 down for a slim 3-2 lead. All three goals were scored in a hectic five-minute spell in the second half. Liverpool played better in the second leg, however, and a competent 1-1 draw in Belgium gave them victory.

UEFA CUP 1976-77

FIRST ROUND

Manchester City v Juventus (1-0, 0-2)	1-2
Ajax v Manchester United (1-0, 0-2)	1-2
Inter-Milan v Honved (0-1, 1-1)	1-2
Shaktor Donetz v Dynamo Berlin (3-0, 1-1)	4-1
Fenerbahce v Videoton (2-1, 0-4)	2-5
TS Innsbruck v Start Kristiansand (2-1, 5-0)	7-1
Tirgu Mures v Dynamo Zagreb (0-1, 0-3)	0-4
FC Magdeburg v Cesena (3-0, 1-3)	4-3
Queen's Park Rangers v SK Brann (4-0, 7-0)	11-0
Fram Reykjavik v Slovan Bratislava (0-3, 0-5)	0-8
Grasshoppers v Hibernians Valletta (7-0, 2-0)	9-0
1FC Cologne v GKS Tychy (2-0, 1-1)	3-1
Loko. Plovdiv v Red Star Belgrade (2-1, 1-4)	3-5
Austria Salzburg v Adanaspor (5-0, 0-2)	5-2
Derby County v Finn Harps (12-0, 4-1)	16-1
AEK Athens v Dynamo Moscow (2-0, 1-2)	3-2
Naestved IF v RWD Molenbeek (0-3, 0-4)	0-7
Celtic v Wisla Krakow (2-2, 0-2)	2-4
Sportul Studentes v Olym. Piraeus (3-0, 1-2)	4-2
Porto v Schalke 04 (2-2, 2-3)	4-5
Espanol Barcelona v OGC Nice (3-1, 1-2)	4-3
Eintracht Brunswick v Holbaek IF (7-0, 0-1)	7-1
Paralimni v 1FC Kaiserslautern (1-3, 0-8*)	1-11
Feyenoord v Djurgaarden (3-0, 1-2)	4-2
Belenenses v Barcelona (2-2, 2-3)	4-5
Red Boys Differdange v SC Lokeren (0-3, 1-3)	1-6
Hibernian v Sochaux (1-0, 0-0)	1-0
PS Kuopion v Oster Vaxjo (3-2, 0-2)	3-4
Dynamo Bucharest v AC Milan (0-0, 1-2)	1-2
Slavia Prague v Akademik Sofia (2-0, 0-3)	2-3
Glentoran v Basle (3-2, 0-3)	3-5
Ujpest Dozsa v Atletico Bilbao (1-0, 0-5)	1-5

SECOND ROUND

Manchester United v Juventus (1-0, 0-3)	1-3
Shaktor Donetz v Honved (3-0, 3-2)	6-2
TS Innsbruck v Videoton (1-1, 0-1)	1-2
FC Magdeburg v Dynamo Zagreb (2-0, 2-2)	4-2
Slovan Bratislava v QPR (3-3, 2-5)	5-8
1FC Cologne v Grasshoppers (2-0, 3-2)	5-2
A. Salzburg v Red Star Belgrade* (2-1, 0-1)	2-2
AEK Athens v Derby County (2-0, 3-2)	5-2
Wisla Krakow v RWD Molenbeek† (1-1, 1-1)	2-2
Sportul Studentes v Schalke 04 (0-1, 0-4)	0-5
Eintracht Brunswick v Espanol (2-1, 0-2)	2-3
1FC Kaiserslautern v Feyenoord (2-2, 0-5)	2-7
Barcelona v SC Lokeren (2-0, 1-2)	3-2
Hibernian v Oster Vaxjo (2-0, 1-4)	3-4
Akademik Sofia v AC Milan (4-3, 0-2)	4-5
Basle v Atletico Bilbao (1-1, 1-3)	2-4

THIRD ROUND

Juventus v Shaktor Donetz (3-0, 0-1)	3-1
FC Magdeburg v Videoton (5-0, 0-1)	5-1
QPR* v 1FC Cologne (3-0, 1-4)	4-4
AEK Athens* v Red Star Belgrade (2-0, 1-3)	3-3
RWD Molenbeek v Schalke 04 (1-0, 1-1)	2-1
Espanol v Feyenoord (0-1, 0-2)	0-3
Oster Vaxjo v Barcelona (0-3, 1-5*)	1-8
Atletico Bilbao v AC Milan (4-1, 1-3)	5-4

QUARTER-FINALS

FC Magdeburg v Juventus (1-3, 0-1)	1-4
QPR v AEK Athens† (3-0, 0-3)	3-3
Feyenoord v RWD Molenbeek (0-0, 1-2)	1-2
Atletico Bilbao v Barcelona (2-1, 2-2)	4-3

SEMI-FINALS

Juventus v AEK Athens (4-1, 1-0)	5-1
RWD Molenbeek v Atletico Bilbao* (1-1, 0-0)	1-1

FINAL

Juventus 1 Atletico Bilbao 0
(Turin, 4.5.77, 75,000)

Juventus: Zoff, Cuccureddu, Gentile, Scirea, Morini, Tardelli, Furino, Benetti, Causio, Boninsegna (Gori), Bettega

Bilbao: Iribar, Villar, Escalza, Guoicoechea, Guisasola, Quaderra, Irureta, M. Rojo, Dani, Churruca, J. Rojo

Scorer: Tardelli

Atletico Bilbao 2 Juventus 1
(Bilbao, 18.5.77, 43,000)

Bilbao: Iribar, Lasa (Carlos), Guisasola, Alesanco, Escalza, Villar, Churruca, Irureta, Amarrortu, Dani, J. Rojo

Juventus: Unchanged; Spinosi came on for Boninsegna

Scorers: Irureta, Carlos; Bettega
[Juventus won on away goals rule]

*won on away goals rule †won on penalties

1976-77

A somewhat unsatisfactory year's competition ended with Juventus winning on the basis of away goals. By a quirk of chance, they had been the sufferers on the only other occasion this had happened in European history—when Leeds had 'beaten' them 3-3 in 1971. Their opponents were Atlético Bilbao, who had looked to have done enough when they came back with only a 1-0 deficit from Turin. Juventus, however, held on to a 1-1 half-time score in Spain until late in the game and that one away goal was enough to nullify Bilbao's extra goal and prevent a fourth Spanish club winning the trophy.

The English sides had mixed fortunes. Manchester United knocked out Ajax, but City fell to the old enemy Juventus, who then beat United. Queen's Park Rangers, fresh from their magnificent failure to win the League Championship the season before (despite taking 27 points from their last 15 games) ran riot, scoring 23 goals in the first three rounds (10 of them to Stan Bowles) and disposing of Slovan Bratislava and Cologne in the process. Sadly for them, AEK Athens proved the stumbling block, just as they had for Derby County.

Bilbao were really a little unlucky: they had consistently met fine opposition in the likes of Ujpest Dozsa and AC Milan and had won their own personal cup final in the quarter-finals with a 2-2 draw in Barcelona to add to a 2-1 win at home. But Bettega's goal in Spain gave Juventus the UEFA Cup.

ABOVE: The Juventus line-up that won the Italian League title in 1977—and the UEFA Cup. The team formed the basis of the Italy side that put England out of the World Cup.
RIGHT: It was a goal by Roberto Bettega in Bilbao that enabled Juventus, who had eliminated both Manchester clubs, to win the UEFA Cup—their first European trophy.

1977-78

For the first time since it began, the UEFA Cup produced two finalists who had never previously appeared in a European final. Bastia of Corsica were the great surprise—the first team from any Mediterranean island to make any impact on European football—and their route was quite remarkable. In the first three rounds, all against class opposition, they managed just a one-goal lead from the home leg, and then won away each time.

The other finalists were PSV Eindhoven, the fourth club from Holland to reach a European final—after Ajax, Feyenoord and Twente—during this golden era of Dutch football. Their passage had been impressive with 29 goals scored and just two defeats, away to experienced East Germans Magdeburg and, in the semi-final, in Barcelona.

The final was a disappointment. PSV, packed with future World Cup names, easily held Bastia in Corsica before a tiny 15,000 crowd. Ironically, Bastia's star attraction was another Dutch World Cup Star, Johnny Rep. Two weeks later in Eindhoven, the result was something of a formality, PSV winning 3-0. So, for the fourth time, a French team had lost a European final.

1978-79

The last tournament of the 1970s was important in that UEFA had devised a points system which would determine how many clubs each country had in the competition in future years. This depended on performances in the three major competitions over the previous few years when, oddly, English teams had come to monopolize the European Cup but fared badly in the second-rank

UEFA CUP 1977-78

FIRST ROUND

Glenavon v PSV Eindhoven (2-6, 0-5)	2-11
Manchester City v Widzew Lodz* (2-2, 0-0)	2-2
Start Kristiansand v Fram Reykjavik (6-0, 2-0)	8-0
Dyn. Kiev v Eintracht Brunswick* (1-1, 0-0)	1-1
Boavisto v Lazio (1-0, 0-5)	1-5
RC Lens v Malmo FF (4-1, 0-2)	4-3
Fiorentina v Schalke 04 (0-0, 1-2)	‡1-2
Odra Opole v FC Magdeburg (1-2, 1-1)	2-3
Aston Villa v Fenerbahce (4-0, 2-0)	6-0
Gornik Zabrze v Valkeakosken Haka (5-3, 0-0)	5-3
Linz ASK v Ujpest Dozsa (3-2, 0-7)	3-9
Servette Geneva v Atletico Bilbao (1-0, 0-2)	1-2
Landskrona BOIS v Ipswich Town (0-1, 0-5)	0-6
Las Palmas v Sloboda Tuzla (5-0, 3-4)	8-4
AZ 67 v Red Boys Differdange (11-1, 5-0)	16-1
Barcelona v Steaua Bucharest (5-1, 3-1)	8-2
Frem Copenhagen v Grasshoppers (0-2, 1-6)	1-8
Rapid Vienna v Inter Bratislava (1-0, 0-3)	1-3
Dundee United v KB Copenhagen (1-0, 0-3)	1-3
Inter-Milan v Dynamo Tbilisi (0-1, 0-0)	0-1
Bayern Munich v Mjoendalen JF (8-0, 4-0)	12-0
Marek S. Dimitrov v Ferencvaros (3-0, 0-2)	3-2
FC Zurich v CSKA Sofia (5-1, 3-1)	8-2
Eintracht Frankfurt v Sliema W. (5-0, 0-0)	5-0
RWD Molenbeek v Aberdeen (0-0, 2-1)	2-1
Carl Zeiss Jena v Altay Izmir (5-1, 1-4)	6-5
Standard Liege* v Slavia Prague (1-0, 2-3)	3-3
ASA Tirgu Mures v AEK Athens (1-0, 0-3)	1-3
Torino v Apoel Nicosia (3-0, 1-1)	4-1
Olym. Piraeus v Dynamo Zagreb (3-1, 1-5)	4-6
Bohemians v Newcastle United (0-0, 0-4)	0-4
Bastia v Sporting Lisbon (3-2, 2-1)	5-3

SECOND ROUND

Widzew Lodz v PSV Eindhoven (3-5, 0-1)	3-6
S. Kristiansand v Eint. Brunswick (1-0, 0-4)	1-4
Lazio v RC Lens (2-0, 0-6)	2-6
FC Magdeburg v Schalke 04 (4-3, 3-1)	7-3
Aston Villa v Gornik Zabrze (2-0, 1-1)	3-1
Ujpest Dozsa v Atletico Bilbao (2-0, 0-3)	2-3
Ipswich Town v Las Palmas (1-0, 3-3)	4-3
AZ 67 Alkmaar v Barcelona† (1-1, 1-1)	2-2
Inter Bratislava v Grasshoppers (1-0, 1-5)	2-5
KB Copenhagen v Dynamo Tbilisi (1-4, 1-2)	2-6
Bayern Munich v Marek Stanke (3-0, 0-2)	3-2
FC Zurich v Eintracht Frankfurt (0-3, 3-4)	3-7
RWD Molenbeek v Carl Zeiss Jena† (1-1, 1-1)	2-2
AEK Athens v Standard Liege (2-2, 1-4)	3-6
Torino v Dynamo Zagreb (3-1, 0-1)	3-2
Bastia v Newcastle United (2-1, 3-1)	5-2

THIRD ROUND

PSV Eindhoven v Ein. Brunswick (2-0, 2-1)	4-1
FC Magdeburg v RC Lens (4-0, 0-2)	4-2
Aston Villa v Atletico Bilbao (2-0, 1-1)	3-1
Ipswich Town v Barcelona† (1-1, 1-1)	2-2
Dynamo Tbilisi v Grasshoppers (1-0, 0-4)	1-4
Eintracht Frankfurt v Bayern Munich (4-0, 2-1)	6-1
Carl Zeiss Jena v Standard Liege (2-0, 2-1)	4-1
Bastia v Torino (2-1, 3-2)	5-3

QUARTER-FINALS

FC Magdeburg v PSV Eindhoven (1-0, 2-4)	3-4
Aston Villa v Barcelona (2-2, 1-2)	3-4
Ein. Frankfurt v Grasshoppers* (3-2, 0-1)	3-3
Bastia v Carl Zeiss Jena (7-2, 2-4)	9-6

SEMI-FINALS

PSV Eindhoven v Barcelona (3-0, 1-3)	4-3
Grasshoppers Zurich v Bastia* (3-2, 0-1)	3-3

FINAL

Bastia 0 PSV Eindhoven 0
(Bastia, 26.4.78, 15,000)

Bastia: Hiard, Burkhard, Guesdon, Orlanducci, Cazes, Papi, Lacuesta (Felix), Larios, Rep, Krimau, Mariot

PSV: Van Beveren, Van Kraay, Krijgh, Stevens, Brandts, Poortvliet, Van der Kuylen, W. Van der Kerkhof, Deijkers, R. Van der Kerkhof, Lubse

PSV Eindhoven 3 Bastia 0
(Eindhoven, 9.5.78, 27,000)

PSV: Unchanged; Deacy came on for Van Kraay

Bastia: Marchioni for Burkhard; Weller came on for Hiard, De Zerbi came on for Mariot

Scorers: W. Van der Kerkhof, Deijkers, Van der Kuylen

*won on away goals rule †won on penalties ‡first leg awarded 3-0 to Schalke after Fiorentina used ineligible player; aggregate score 1-5

The goalscoring of Dusan Savic, including this well-constructed away-goals winner against Arsenal in the quarter-finals, helped Red Star Belgrade to their first ever European final in 1979.

events. Sadly, this season proved no better and England was relegated to three UEFA Cup entrants rather than four in future seasons. West Germany, Holland and Belgium were still able to enter four clubs.

Nonetheless, West Brom and Manchester City both reached the quarter-finals, where they went out respectively to the eventual finalists, Red Star Belgrade and Borussia Moenchengladbach. Red Star had crept past Arsenal in the previous round with a goal by Savic in the very last minute at Highbury. Everton had gone out on away goals to Dukla Prague in the second round and hence completed a thoroughly undistinguished two decades of European competition—particularly when compared with the red shirts across Stanley Park. Only twice had Everton ever managed to get beyond the second round of any European competition. The final was a rather dour affair—being Borussia's fourth European final of the 1970s but Yugoslavia's first appearance in a final since Dynamo Zagreb won the Fairs Cup in 1967.

Borussia didn't lose a game during the whole competition—the first time a team had managed this feat since Tottenham in 1971-72. Three of the teams in the semi-finals were German, Borussia defeating local rivals Duisburg and Red Star taking Hertha Berlin, again on away goals. (In 1980 all four would be West German.)

The first leg of the 1979 final, in Belgrade, resulted in a rather lucky 1-1 draw for Borussia, Jurisic scoring an own goal. Back in Dusseldorf (where Borussia play their big games in preference to the smaller ground in their home town) their Danish European Footballer of the Year Allan Simonsen scored the only goal with a penalty.

It was no great spectacle and only served to confirm that the rather cumbersome UEFA Cup, with its six rounds, its constant victories on away goals and its two-legged final was heading once again for third place in the hierarchy of European competition.

Allan Simonsen's penalty—his ninth goal in the series—decides the 1979 final with Red Star.

UEFA CUP 1978-79

FIRST ROUND

Borussia M'gladbach v Sturm Graz (5-1, 1-2)	6-3
Nantes v Benfica (0-2, 0-0)	0-2
Glentoran* v IB Vestmannaey (0-0, 1-1)	1-1
Pezoporikos v Slask Wroclaw (2-2, 1-5)	3-7
AC Milan† v Lokomotiv Kosice (1-0, 0-1)	1-1
Olympiakos v Levski Spartak (2-1, 1-3)	3-4
Standard Liege v Dundee United (1-0, 0-0)	1-0
Twente Enschede v Manchester City (1-1, 2-3)	3-4
Honved v Adanaspor (6-0, 2-2)	8-2
Timisoara v MTK Budapest (2-0, 1-2)	3-2
Jeunesse Esch v Lausanne (0-0, 0-2)	0-2
Atletico Bilbao v Ajax (2-0, 0-3)	2-3
Elfsborg v Racing Strasbourg (2-0, 1-4)	3-4
Sporting Braga v Hibernian (5-0, 2-3)	7-3
Carl Zeiss Jena v Lierse SK (1-0, 2-2)	3-2
MSV Duisburg v Lech Poznan (5-0, 5-2)	10-2
Hertha Berlin v Trakia Plovdiv (0-0, 2-1)	2-1
Dynamo Tbilisi v Napoli (2-0, 1-1)	3-1
Kuopion PS v Copenhagen BK 1913 (2-1, 4-4)	6-5
Start Kristiansand v BK Esbjerg (0-0, 0-1)	0-1
Basle v VfB Stuttgart (2-3, 1-4)	3-7
Torpedo Moscow v Molde SK (4-0, 3-3)	7-3
Everton v Finn Harps (5-0, 5-0)	10-0
Dukla Prague v Lanerossi Vicenza (1-0, 1-1)	2-1
Galatasaray v WBA (1-3, 1-3)	2-6
Hibernian v IFK Norrkoping (3-2, 0-0)	3-2
Arges Pitesti v Panathinaikos (3-0, 2-1)	5-1
CSKA Sofia v Valencia (2-1, 1-4)	3-5
Hajduk Split v Rapid Vienna (2-0, 1-2)	3-2
Arsenal v Lokomotiv Leipzig (3-0, 4-1)	7-1
Sporting Gijon v Torino (3-0, 0-1)	3-1
Dyn. Berlin v Red Star Belgrade* (5-2, 1-4)	6-6

SECOND ROUND

Benfica v Borussia M'gladbach (0-0, 0-2)	0-2
IB Vestmannaey v Slask Wroclaw (0-2, 1-2)	1-4
Levski Spartak v AC Milan (1-1, 0-3)	1-4
Manchester City v Standard Liege (4-0, 0-2)	4-2
Honved v Timisoara (4-0, 0-2)	4-2
Ajax v Lausanne (1-0, 4-0)	5-0
Racing Strasbourg v Hibernian (2-0, 0-1)	2-1
Carl Zeiss Jena v MSV Duisburg (0-0, 0-3)	0-3
Hertha Berlin v Dynamo Tbilisi (2-0, 0-1)	2-1
Kuopion PS v BK Esbjerg (0-2, 1-4)	1-6
Torpedo Moscow v VfB Stuttgart (2-1, 0-2)	2-3
Everton v Dukla Prague* (2-1, 0-1)	2-2
Sporting Braga v WBA (0-2, 0-1)	0-3
Arges Pitesti v Valencia (2-1, 2-5)	3-6
Hajduk Split v Arsenal* (2-1, 0-1)	2-2
Sporting Gijon v Red Star Belgrade (0-1, 1-1)	1-2

THIRD ROUND

Bor. M'gladbach v Slask Wroclaw (1-1, 4-2)	5-3
AC Milan v Manchester City (2-2, 0-3)	2-5
Honved v Ajax (4-1, 0-2)	4-3
Racing Strasbourg v MSV Duisburg (0-0, 0-4)	0-4
BK Esbjerg v Hertha Berlin (2-1, 0-4)	2-5
VfB Stuttgart v Dukla Prague (4-1, 0-4)	4-5
Valencia v West Bromwich Albion (1-1, 2-0)	3-1
Red Star Belgrade v Arsenal (1-0, 1-1)	2-1

QUARTER-FINALS

Manchester City v Bor. M'gladbach (1-1, 1-3)	2-4
Honved v MSV Duisburg* (2-3, 2-1)	4-4
Hertha Berlin v Dukla Prague (1-1, 2-1)	3-2
Red Star Belgrade v WBA (1-0, 1-1)	2-1

SEMI-FINALS

MSV Duisburg v Bor. M'gladbach (2-2, 1-4)	3-6
Red Star Belgrade* v Hertha Berlin (1-0, 1-2)	2-2

FINAL

Red Star Belgrade 1 Borussia M'gladbach 1
(Belgrade, 9.5.79, 87,500)

Red Star: Stojanovic, Jovanovic, Miletovic, Jurisic, Jovin, Muslin (Krmpotic), Petrovic, Blagojevic, Milosavljevic (Milovanovic), Savic, Sestic

Borussia: Kneib, Vogts, Hannes, Schaffer, Ringles, Schafer, Kulik, Nielsen (Danner), Wohlers (Gores), Simonsen, Lienen

Scorers: Sestic; Jurisic (og)

Borussia M'gladbach 1 Red Star Belgrade 0
(Dusseldorf, 23.5.79, 45,000)

Borussia: Gores for Nielsen; Koppel came on for Kulik

Red Star: Milovanovic for Sestic, who later substituted for him

Scorer: Simonsen (pen)

*won on away goals rule †won on penalties

UEFA CUP FINALS

Year	Winners	Runners-up	Score
1972	Tottenham Hotspur	*Wolverhampton W.	(2-1, 1-1) 3-2
1973	*Liverpool	Borussia M'gladbach	(3-0, 0-2) 3-2
1974	Feyenoord	*Tottenham Hotspur	(2-2, 2-0) 4-2
1975	*Borussia M'gladbach	Twente Enschede	(0-0, 5-1) 5-1
1976	*Liverpool	FC Bruges	(3-2, 1-1) 4-3
1977	†*Juventus	Athletic Bilbao	(1-0, 1-2) 2-2
1978	PSV Eindhoven	*Bastia	(0-0, 3-0) 3-0
1979	Borussia M'gladbach	*Red Star Belgrade	(1-1, 1-0) 2-1
1980	†Eintracht Frankfurt	*Borussia M'gladbach	(2-3, 1-0) 3-3
1981	*Ipswich Town	AZ 67 Alkmaar	(3-0, 2-4) 5-4
1982	*IFK Gothenburg	SV Hamburg	(1-0, 3-0) 4-0
1983	*Anderlecht	Benfica	(1-0, 1-1) 2-1

*home team in first leg †won on away goals rule

While the Fairs Cup was dominated by Spain—six wins and nine finalists in the first eight years—the Latin influence in the UEFA Cup, apart from the 1977 final, has been negligible, and all the clear winners have been from northern Europe—a fact mirrored in the European Cup in recent years.

1979–80

It was obvious after the quarter-finals in March that the UEFA Cup would stay in West Germany in 1980; the only question was in which city. The domination of 1979—four clubs in the last eight, three in the semi-finals—became a monopoly, with all five of the Bundesliga's quota making the quarter-finals, and then four of them taking full advantage of a kindly draw to produce a totally Germanic affair.

There was little in the earlier rounds to suggest that the traditional sources of competition for West Germany in the UEFA Cup during the 1970s—England and Holland—would threaten their hold in 1980.

Everton produced their usual tame performance in Europe, losing to Feyenoord in the first round, while Leeds also lost both legs of a tie, against the Rumanians Craiova in the second round. Ipswich, having put 10 goals past Skeid Oslo, lost on the away goals rule to Grasshoppers, with the impressive Claudio Sulser the scorer at Portman Road.

The year's best performance was at St. Etienne by Borussia. Nielsen (2), Nickel and Lienen put the holders four up in 37 minutes. Platini's second-half goal was irrelevant, and Borussia finished the job with another early blitz in Germany, Tychosen and Hännes making it 2-0 inside a quarter of an hour.

The semi-final draw kept the two favourites apart, and most people expected the giants of West German football in the 1970s—Borussia and Bayern—to fight out the final in May. The holders made it, with goals from Matthaus and Schäfer after losing 2-1 to a late flourish by VfB in Stuttgart; but Bundesliga leaders Bayern, travelling to Frankfurt with a 2-0 lead provided by Dieter Hoeness and Paul Breitner, were run ragged by Eintracht in extra time after two goals from Austrian star Bruno Pezzey (under suspension in the League) had levelled the aggregate score after 90 minutes. Substitute Harald Karger then scored each side of a Dremmler reply, and Werner Lorant wrapped it all up with a late penalty.

The first leg of the final was a pulsating affair, full of flair, pace and skill. Eintracht, despite missing their skipper and inspiration Jurgen Grabowski (ironically he was injured in a League game with Borussia) threw caution to the wind and were rewarded in the 37th minute, when Karger headed in a Bernd Nickel corner.

It was a poor goal compared to the four that followed—a superbly constructed effort from Christian Kulik to level just before the break, a spectacular diving header by the veteran Bernd Holzenbein, another fine equalizer by Lothar Matthaus and, two minutes from time, a flying header from Kulik, the only survivor from the Borussia side who played Liverpool in the 1973 final.

Though leading only 3-2 Jupp Heynckes' side made the trip to Frankfurt still favourites. And for 81 minutes they held on to their lead and their title. But then came another inspired piece of substitution by Eintracht coach Friedel Rausch; on went the almost unknown 19-year-old youth international Freddy Schaub, and after only four minutes he squeezed past two tackles before slipping the ball past Kneib. The away goals rule meant that the one score had been enough.

For Borussia, it meant no record third UEFA Cup win. For Eintracht, fondly remembered as 'the other team' in Real Madrid's 7–3 win at Hampden Park in the European Cup final almost exactly 20 years before, it was a very special anniversary that would give them something more tangible to hold on to. It was also evidence of the massive strength of the German Bundesliga.

EUROPEAN NATIONAL MERIT TABLE (1955-56 to 1982-83 inc)	Champions Cup winners	Cup Winners Cup winners	Fairs/UEFA Cup winners	Champions Cup runners-up	Cup Winners Cup runners-up	Fairs/UEFA Cup runners-up
England	7	4	8	1	4	6
Spain	6	4	6	5	4	4
West Germany	4	3	3	4	3	3
Italy	4	3	2	6	2	2
Holland	4	—	2	1	—	2
Portugal	2	1	—	3	—	1
Scotland	1	2	—	1	2	—
Belgium	—	2	1	1	2	2
USSR	—	2	—	—	1	—
East Germany	—	1	—	—	1	—
Czechoslovakia	—	1	—	—	—	—
Hungary	—	—	1	—	2	2
Yugoslavia	—	—	1	1	—	2
Sweden	—	—	1	1	—	—
France	—	—	—	3	—	1
Greece	—	—	—	1	—	—
Austria	—	—	—	—	1	—
Poland	—	—	—	—	1	—

UEFA CUP 1979-80

FIRST ROUND

Aberdeen v Eintracht Frankfurt (1-1, 0-1) 1-2
Dynamo Bucharest v Alki Larnaca (3-0, 9-0) 12-0
Kuopion Palloseura v Malmo FF (1-2, 0-2) 1-4
Feyenoord v Everton (1-0, 1-0) 2-0
Glenavon v Standard Liege (0-1,0-1) 2-0
Napoli v Olympiakos Piraeus (2-0, 0-1) 2-1
Kalmar v IB Keflavik* (2-1, 0-1) 2-2
Zbrojovka Brno v BK Esbjerg (6-0, 1-1) 7-1
FC Zurich v 1FC Kaiserslautern (1-3, 1-5) 2-8
Sporting Lisbon v Bohemians Dublin (2-0, 0-0) 2-0
Dundee United* v Anderlecht (0-0, 1-1) 1-1
Rapid Vienna v Diosgyor Miskoic (0-1, 2-3) 2-4
Galatasaray v Red Star Belgrade (0-0, 1-3) 1-3
Carl Zeiss Jena v WBA (2-0, 2-1) 4-1
Aarhus GF v Stal Mielec (1-1, 1-0) 2-1
Bohemians Prague v Bayern Munich (0-2, 2-2) 2-4
VfB Stuttgart* v Torino (1-0, 1-2) 2-2
Atletico Madrid v Dynamo Dresden (1-2, 0-3) 1-5
Skeid Oslo v Ipswich Town (1-3, 0-7) 1-10
Progres Niedercorn v Grasshoppers (0-2, 0-4) 0-6
Dynamo Kiev v CSKA Sofia (2-1, 1-1) 3-2
Orduspor v Banik Ostrava (2-0, 0-6) 2-6
Shaktor Donetz v AS Monaco (2-1, 0-2) 2-3
Lokomotiv Sofia v Ferencvaros (3-0, 0-2) 3-2
Widzew Lodz v St Etienne (2-1, 0-3) 2-4
Gijon v PSV Eindhoven (0-0, 0-1) 0-1
Perugia v Dynamo Zagreb (1-0, 0-0) 1-0
Aris Salonika v Benfica (3-1, 1-2) 4-3
Wiener SK v Universitatea Craiova (0-0, 1-3) 1-3
Valletta v Leeds United (0-4, 0-3) 0-7
Inter-Milan v Real Sociedad (3-0, 0-2) 3-2
Bor. M'gladbach v Viking Stavanger (3-0, 1-1) 4-1

SECOND ROUND

Dynamo Bucharest v E. Frankfurt (2-0, 0-3) 2-3
Feyenoord v Malmo FF (4-0, 1-1) 5-1
Standard Liege v Napoli (2-1, 1-1) 3-2
Zbrojovka Brno v IB Keflavik (3-1, 2-1) 5-2
Sp. Lisbon v 1FC Kaiserslautern (1-1, 0-2) 1-3
Dundee United v Diosgyor Miskoic (0-1, 1-3) 1-4
Red Star Belgrade v C. Zeiss Jena (3-2, 3-2) 6-4
Aarhus GF v Bayern Munich (1-2, 1-3) 2-5
Dynamo Dresden v VfB Stuttgart* (1-1, 0-0) 1-1
Grasshoppers Zurich* v Ipswich T. (0-0, 1-1) 1-1
Banik Ostrava v Dynamo Kiev (1-0, 0-2) 1-2
Lokomotiv Sofia v AS Monaco (4-2, 1-2) 5-4
PSV Eindhoven v St Etienne (2-0, 0-6) 2-6
Aris Salonika v Perugia (1-1, 3-0) 4-1
Univ. Craiova v Leeds United (2-0, 2-0) 4-0
Borussia M'gladbach v Inter-Milan (1-1, 3-2) 4-3

*won on away goals rule

THIRD ROUND

Eintracht Frankfurt v Feyenoord (4-1, 0-1) 4-2
Standard Liege v Zbrojovka Brno (1-2, 2-3) 3-5
Diosgyor v 1FC Kaiserslautern (0-2, 1-6) 1-8
Bayern Munich v Red Star Belgrade (2-0, 2-3) 4-3
Grasshoppers v VfB Stuttgart (0-2, 0-3) 0-5
Lokomotiv Sofia* v Dynamo Kiev (1-0, 1-2) 2-2
St Etienne v Aris Salonika (4-1, 3-3) 7-4
Bor. M'gladbach v Univ. Craiova (2-0, 0-1) 2-1

QUARTER-FINALS

Eintracht Frankfurt v Z. Brno (4-1, 2-3) 6-4
1FC Kaiserslautern v Bay. Munich (1-0, 1-4) 2-4
VfB Stuttgart v Lokomotiv Sofia (3-1, 1-0) 4-1
St Etienne v Borussia M'gladbach (1-4, 0-2) 1-6

SEMI-FINALS

Bay. Munich v Eintracht Frankfurt (2-0, 1-5) 3-5
VfB Stuttgart v Bor. M'gladbach (2-1, 0-2) 2-3

FINAL

Borussia M'gladbach 3 Eintracht Frankfurt 2 (Boekelberg, 7.5.80, 25,000)

Borussia: Kneib, Schaffer, Schafer, Hannes, Ringels, Matthaus, Kulik, Nielsen (Tychosen 85), Del Haye, H. Nickel, Lienen

Eintracht: Pahl, Ehrmanntraut, Neuberger, Korbel, Pezzey, Lorant, Holzenbein, Karger, Borchers, B. Nickel, Cha

Scorers: Kulik (44, 88), Matthaus (76); Karger (37), Holzenbein (71)

Eintracht Frankfurt* 1 Borussia M'gladbach 0 (Frankfurt, 21.5.80, 60,000)

Eintracht: Pahl, Neuberger, Pezzey, Korbel, Ehrmanntraut, Lorant, Holzenbein, Borchers, B. Nickel, Cha, Nachtweih (Schaub 77)

Borussia: Kneib, Bodecker, Hannes, Schafer, Ringels, Matthaus (Tychosen 85), Fleer, Kulik, Nielsen (Del Haye 68), H. Nickel

Scorer: Schaub (81)

[Eintracht won on away goals rule after 3-3 aggregate]

Leading scorers: 7—D. Hoeness *(Bayern Munich)*, H. Nickel *(Borussia M'gladbach)*; 6—Mihailov *(Lokomotiv Sofia)*; 5—Bongartz *(Kaiserslautern)*, Platini, Rep *(St Etienne)*, Rummenigge *(Bayern Munich)*

1980-81

Ipswich Town under Bobby Robson returned the UEFA Cup to England after a five-year gap, bringing to the homely Suffolk club another major trophy to add to their FA Cup victory in 1978.

The tournament had begun unpromisingly for English clubs. Manchester United went out in the first round to Widzew Lodz on away goals. On the same night Wolverhampton Wanderers were eliminated by PSV Eindhoven. For Scotland Dundee United and St. Mirren fell at the second fence, and Ipswich apart the only Briton for whom the competition stayed meaningful was Tony Woodcock, now a striker for Cologne after leaving Nottingham Forest.

To augment a long-passing philosophy Ipswich had turned to Europe for more subtlety in midfield. Bobby Robson brough to Portman Road two Dutch internationals, Frans Thijssen and Arnold Muhren. Both were at the hub of Ipswich's eventual victory.

The midfield department also produced the goals that mattered. John Wark began his career with Ipswich as a central defender, but from the centre of midfield he showed a marvellous sense of timing when arriving in opposing penalty areas—and an unerring touch from the penalty spot. Wark began with a hat-trick of penalties, and four goals in all, at home to Aris Salonika. In the second round he scored twice at Portman Road in a 3-0 win against Bohemians from Prague, a margin of victory that was almost lost in the second leg. For an encore there was another Wark hat-trick to admire in the third round as Widzew Lodz failed to reproduce the form that had toppled Manchester United.

Ipswich's strength was best illustrated in the quarter-final when two goals from Paul Mariner spearheaded a magnificent 4-1 triumph against St. Etienne in France; the aggregate score, 7-2, included the inevitable goal in each leg from the insatiable Wark.

In the semi-final Ipswich were drawn against Cologne—and Woodcock—whose sense of brinkmanship had just kept them alive. A home defeat in the second round by Barcelona had marked the West Germans, seemingly, for an early exit. Cologne went to Nou Camp and won the return match 4-0! In the third round a 3-1 deficit to Stuttgart had been overturned by a 4-1 victory in Cologne which included an important goal from Woodcock.

At Portman Road Ipswich kept Cologne at bay but could only score once; the marksman of course was Wark. In the second leg Robson's side were superbly resilient and won again when the tall defender Terry Butcher provided the goal. In many ways the final came as less of a test. AZ'67 Alkmaar, a developing Dutch club, were built around Jan Peters, famous for his two Wembley goals for Holland, and the prolific Kees Kist. A penalty from Wark. Thijssen against his fellow countrymen and Mariner struck three goals without reply at home, and though AZ'67 beat Paul Cooper four times in Amsterdam, away goals from Thijssen and Wark's record 14th in the competition always retained Ipswich's advantage.

UEFA CUP 1980-81

FIRST ROUND

Ipswich Town v Aris Salonika (5-1, 1-3)	6-4
AZ'67 Alkmaar v Red Boys Diff'dange (6-0, 4-0)	10-0
IA Akranes v Cologne (0-4, 0-6)	0-10
Sliema Wanderers v Barcelona (0-2, 0-1)	0-3
Ujpest Dozsa v Real Sociedad (1-1, 0-1)	1-2
Arges Pitesti v Utrecht (0-0, 0-2)	0-2
Ballymena United v Vorwaerts (2-1, 0-3)	2-4
Bohemians Prague v Gijon (3-1, 1-2)	4-3
Dynamo Dresden v Napredak (1-0, 1-0)	2-0
Elfsborg v St. Mirren (1-2, 0-0)	1-2
Grasshoppers v KB Copenhagen (3-1, 5-2)	8-3
Hamburg v Sarajevo (4-2, 3-3)	7-5
Juventus v Panathinaikos (4-0, 2-4)	6-4
Kaiserslautern v Anderlecht (1-0, 2-3)	3-3
Dynamo Kiev v Levski Spartak (1-1, 0-0)	1-1
PSV Eindhoven v Wolverhampton W. (3-1, 0-1)	3-2
Kuopion Paloseura v St. Etienne (0-7, 0-7)	0-14
ASK Linz v Radnicki Nis (1-2, 1-4)	2-6
Lokeren v Moscow Dynamo (1-1, 1-0)	2-1
Magdeburg v Moss (2-1, 3-2)	5-3
Manchester United v Widzew Lodz (1-1, 0-0)	1-1
Porto v Dundalk (1-0, 0-0)	1-0
RWD Molenbeek v Torino (1-2, 2-2)	3-4
Shakhtor Donetsk v Eintracht Frankfurt (1-0, 0-3)	1-3
Slask Wroclaw v Dundee United (0-0, 2-7)	2-7
Sochaux v Servette (2-0, 1-2)	3-2
Standard Liege v Steau Bucharest (1-1, 2-1)	3-2
Stuttgart v Pezoporikos (6-0, 4-1)	10-1
Twente Enschede v IFK Gothenburg (5-1, 0-2)	5-3
Vasas v Boavista (0-2, 1-0)	1-2
Zbrojovka Brno v Voest Linz (3-1, 2-0)	5-1
Fenerbahce v Beroe Stara Zagora (0-1, 1-2)	1-3

SECOND ROUND

Ipswich Town v Bohemians Prague (3-0, 0-2)	3-2
Sochaux v Boavista (2-2, 1-0)	3-2
St. Mirren v St. Etienne (0-0, 0-2)	0-2
Torino v Magdeburg (3-1, 0-1)	3-2
Twente Enschede v Dynamo Dresden (1-1, 0-0)	1-1
Widzew Lodz v Juventus (3-1, 1-3)	4-4
Dundee United v Lokeren (1-1, 0-0)	1-1
Utrecht v Eintracht Frankfurt (2-1, 1-3)	3-4
PSV Eindhoven v Hamburg (1-1, 1-2)	2-3
Cologne v Barcelona (0-1, 4-0)	4-1
Stuttgart v Vorwaerts (5-1, 2-1)	7-2
Kaiserslautern v Standard Liege (1-2, 1-2)	2-4
Beroe Stara Zagora v Radnicki Nis (0-1, 1-2)	1-3
Zbrojovka Brno v Real Sociedad (1-1, 1-2)	2-3
Porto v Grasshoppers (2-0, 0-3)	2-3
Levski Spartak v AZ'67 Alkmaar (1-1, 0-5)	1-6

THIRD ROUND

Ipswich Town v Widzew Lodz (5-0, 0-1)	5-1
Hamburg v St. Etienne (2-1, 0-5)	2-6
Eintracht Frankfurt v Sochaux (4-2, 0-2)	4-4
Stuttgart v Cologne (3-1, 1-4)	4-5
Lokeren v Real Sociedad (1-0, 2-2)	3-2
Grasshoppers v Torino (2-1, 1-2)	3-3
Standard Liege v Dynamo Dresden (1-1, 4-1)	5-2
Radnicki Nis v AZ'67 Alkmaar (2-2, 0-5)	2-7

QUARTER FINALS

St. Etienne v Ipswich Town (1-4, 1-3)	2-7
Standard Liege v Cologne (0-0, 2-3)	2-3
Grasshoppers v Sochaux (0-0, 1-2)	1-2
AZ'67 Alkmaar v Lokeren (2-0, 0-1)	2-1

SEMI-FINALS

Ipswich Town v Cologne (1-0, 1-0)	2-0
Sochaux v AZ'67 Alkmaar (1-1, 2-3)	3-4

FINAL

Ipswich Town 3 AZ'67 Alkmaar 0
(Ipswich, 6.5.81, 27,532)

Ipswich Town: Cooper, Mills, McCall, Thijssen, Osman, Butcher, Wark, Muhren, Mariner, Brazil, Gates

AZ'67 Alkmaar: Treytel, Van der Meer, Spelbos, Metgod, Hovenkamp, Peters, Jonker, Arntz, Nygaard (Welzl), Kist, Tol

Scorers: Wark (pen), Thijssen, Mariner

AZ'67 Alkmaar 4 Ipswich Town 2
(Amsterdam, 20.5.81, 28,500)

AZ'67 Alkmaar: Treytel, Reynders, Spelbos, Metgod, Hovenkamp, Peters, Welzl (Kist), Arntz, Jonker, Nygaard, Tol

Ipswich Town: Unchanged

Scorers: Welzl, Metgod, Tol, Jonkers: Thijssen, Wark

1981-82

In the highly combative world of European club football, the 1981-82 UEFA tournament showed that there was still room for a sprinkling of romance. Unheralded and unsung IFK Gothenburg, part-time players who trained in the evenings after a working-day in other occupations, brought Sweden a first success.

At the outset it seemed inconceivable that Gothenburg could go all the way. With their domestic League finishing in the autumn they suffered the grave disadvantage of playing in the latter stages of the competition out of competitive practice. Yet their young, thoughtful coach, Sven-Goran Eriksson, constructed a squad of players who made light of their hardship.

Out of their path quickly went the holders; Ipswich fell to the fast-improving Aberdeen in the first round. Indeed the stronger British showing came from Scotland. Aberdeen reached the third round and Dundee United the quarter-final, both giving early indication of the force they would later become domestically and abroad. By contrast England lost West Bromwich Albion to Grasshoppers of Switzerland in the first round; Albion in some disarray after the departure of manager Ron Atkinson to Manchester United soon to be followed by Bryan Robson their best player. Southampton went out by dint of some poor defending against Malcolm Allison's Sporting Lisbon in round two. At the same stage Arsenal surprisingly were beaten by Winterslag, one of Belgium's lesser lights.

Gothenburg's early successes against Haka from Finland and Austria's Sturm Graz did not elevate them to the stature of favourites. Not with Real Madrid, Valencia and Hamburg still in the running. The flair that Eriksson had brought to augment traditional Swedish competitiveness was more apparent in the the third round. Gothenburg went to Bucharest and won after beating Dynamo 3-1 at home. A 2-2 draw in Valencia in the quarter-final was further evidence with the Spaniards seen off 2-0 in the Ullevi Stadium. Kaiserslautern were also held in

UEFA CUP 1981-82

FIRST ROUND

Haka v IFK Gothenburg (2-3, 0-4)	2-7
Adanasporv v Inter-Milan (1-3, 1-4)	2-7
Napoli v Radnicki Nis (2-2, 0-0)	2-2
Bohemians v Valencia (0-1, 0-1)	0-2
Nantes v Lokeren (1-1, 2-4)	3-5
Limerick v Southampton (0-3, 1-1)	1-4
Sporting Lisbon v Red Boys Diff'dange (4-0, 7-0)	11-0
PSV Eindhoven v Naestved (7-0, 1-2)	8-2
Boavista v Atletico Madrid (4-1, 1-3)	5-4
Rapid Vienna v Videoton (2-2, 2-0)	4-2
Neuchatel Xamax v Sparta Prague (4-0, 2-3)	6-3
Dynamo Tirana v Carl Zeiss Jena (1-0, 0-4)	1-4
Tatabanya v Real Madrid (2-1, 0-1)	2-2
Aris Salonika v Sliema Wanderers (4-0, 4-2)	8-2
Malmo FF v Wisla Krakow (2-0, 3-1)	5-1
Grasshoppers v West Bromwich Albion (1-0, 3-1)	4-1
Vikingur v Bordeaux (0-4, 0-4)	0-8
Feyenoord v Szombierki Bytom (2-0, 1-1)	3-1
Ipswich Town v Aberdeen (1-1, 1-3)	2-4
Bryne v Winterslag (0-2, 2-1)	2-3
Zenit Leningrad v Dynamo Dresden (1-2, 1-4)	2-6
Magdeburg v Borussia M'Gladbach (3-1, 0-2)	3-3
Beveren v Linfield (3-0, 5-0)	8-0
Monaco v Dundee United (2-5, 2-1)	4-6
Panathinaikos v Arsenal (0-2, 0-1)	0-3
Spartak Moscow v Bruges (3-1, 3-1)	6-2
Kaiserslautern v Akademik (1-0, 2-1)	3-1
Apoel v Arges Pitesti (1-1, 0-4)	1-5
Hadjuk Split v Stuttgart (3-1, 2-2)	5-3
Dynamo Bucharest v Levski Spartak (3-0, 1-2)	4-2
Sturm Graz v CSKA Moscow (1-0, 1-2)	2-2
Hamburg v Utrecht (0-1, 6-3)	6-4

SECOND ROUND

Sturm Graz v IFK Gothenburg (2-2, 2-3)	4-5
Southampton v Sporting Lisbon (2-4, 0-0)	2-4
Real Madrid v Carl Zeiss Jena (3-2, 0-0)	3-2
Grasshoppers v Radnicki Nis (2-0, 0-2)	2-2
Aris Salonika v Lokeren (1-1, 0-4)	1-5
Rapid Vienna v PSV Eindhoven (1-0, 1-2)	2-2
Valencia v Boavista (2-0, 0-1)	2-1
Malmo FF V Neuchatel Xamax (0-1, 0-1)	0-2
Spartak Moscow v Kaiserslautern (2-1, 0-4)	2-5
Winterslag v Arsenal (1-0, 1-2)	2-2
Aberdeen v Arges Pitesti (3-0, 2-2)	5-2
Feyenoord v Dynamo Dresden (2-1, 1-1)	3-2
Inter-Milan v Dynamo Bucharest (1-1, 2-3)	3-4
Borussia M'Gladbach v Dundee United (2-0, 0-5)	2-5
Beveren v Hajduk Split (2-3, 2-1)	4-4
Bordeaux v Hamburg (2-1, 0-2)	2-3

THIRD ROUND

IFK Gothenburg v Dynamo Bucharest (3-1, 1-0)	4-1
Lokeren v Kaiserslautern (1-0, 1-4)	2-4
Rapid Vienna v Real Madrid (0-1, 0-0)	0-1
Sporting Lisbon v Neuchatel Xamax (0-0, 0-1)	0-1
Winterslag v Dundee United (0-0, 0-5)	0-5
Radnicki Nis v Feyenoord (2-0, 0-1)	2-1
Valencia v Hajduk Split (5-1, 1-4)	6-5
Aberdeen v Hamburg (3-2, 1-3)	4-5

QUARTER-FINALS

Valencia v IFK Gothenburg (2-2, 0-2)	2-4
Real Madrid v Kaiserslautern (3-1, 0-5)	3-6
Dundee United v Radnicki Nis (2-0, 0-3)	2-3
Hamburg v Neuchatel Xamax (3-2, 0-0)	3-2

SEMI-FINALS

Kaiserslautern v IFK Gothenburg (1-1, 1-2)	2-3
Radnicki Nis v Hamburg (2-1, 1-5)	3-6

FINAL

IFK Gothenburg 1 Hamburg 0
(Gothenburg, 5.5.82, 42,548)

IFK Gothenburg: Wernersson, Svensson, Hysen, C. Karlsson, Frederiksson, Tord Holmgren, J. Karlsson, Stromberg, Corneliusson, Nilsson (Sandberg), Tommy Holgren (Schiller)

Hamburg: Stein, Kaltz, Groh, Jakobs, Hieronymus, Hartwig, Wehmeyer, Magath, Von Heesen (Memering), Bastrup, Hrubesch

Scorer: Tord Holmgren

Hamburg 0 IFK Gothenburg 3
(Hamburg, 19.5.82, 60,000)

Hamburg: Memering for Jakobs; Hidien came on for Kaltz

IFK Gothenburg: Unchanged; Schiller came on for Hysen; Sandberg came on for Corneliusson

Scorers: Corneliusson, Nilsson, Fredriksson (pen)

the away leg of the semi-final, though it needed an extra-time penalty from Stig Fredriksson to clinch victory in Gothenburg.

Above all Eriksson's side could score goals, especially at home. Torbjorn Nilsson, a tall if temperamental striker, possessed delicate touch for a big man. Alongside him 20-year-old Dan Corneliusson was less sophisticated, but another regular marksman. Tommy Holmgren provided exciting wing play, while his elder brother Tord, a plumber in the daytime, gave him service from midfield. The team also included non-identical twins Conny and Jerry Carlsson.

The last giants awaiting to be slain were Hamburg, arch-professionals under the wise counsel of Ernst Happel. As in all the best fairytales there was pain to be endured before the happy ending, particularly by Tommy Holmgren and Nilsson who were both substituted in the first half of the first leg in Sweden, victims of crude, cynical tackles. Hamburg, contrary, apparently, to Happel's instructions, adopted a policy of containment. It was only in the final seconds that Tord Holmgren breached their defences; it seemed a shallow advantage.

But with their two injured forwards happily restored, Gothenburg gave a masterful display in Hamburg, silencing the majority of the 60,000 crowd. Goals from Coneliusson, Nilsson and Fredriksson (penalty) sealed one of the UEFA Cup's biggest surprises.

1982-83

In 1983 Sven-Goran Eriksson came within touching distance of a remarkable UEFA Cup double. The Swedish coach who had guided Gothenburg to win the competition almost repeated the feat in his first season in charge of Benfica. His new club reached the final but lost to Anderlecht.

No English club survived the opening round. Manchester United were subjected to the roughhouse style of Valencia in a goalless draw at Old Trafford. Yet after taking the lead in Spain United only had themselves to blame for conceding two goals in quick succession in the second half. Arsenal were pleased to return from Moscow Spartak trailing only by three goals to two; the Russians though struck five at Highbury in an exhilarating display. Ipswich faced formidable opponents in AS Roma and at Portman Road performed gallantly but in vain in their efforts to recover from a three-goal deficit in the Olympic Stadium. Southampton's exit was less proud. Norkopping's two away goals at the Dell took them through and police accusations against two Southampton players after the second leg in Sweden only added to the misery of defeat.

Dundee United could hold their heads high after winning in Eindhoven to put out PSV, and Rangers overcame Borussia Dortmund, only to fall to more West German opposition, Cologne. United reached the quarter-final but a solitary goal from the Czech international Pavel Chaloupka clinched the tie for Bohemians.

The Prague club were joined in the semi-

finals by Uni.Craiova of Rumania but both Eastern European sides were beaten by Western opposition. Ironically it was a Yugoslav, Zoran Filipovie, whose goal in Craiova took Benfica into the final on the away goals rule. Anderlecht—with Erwin Vandenbergh scoring in both legs—carried too much firepower for Bohemians.

Foreigners extended their influence into the final. One of Anderlecht's Danish contingent, Kenneth Brylle, struck the only goal of the first leg in Brussels to give the tie a delicate balance. When the spotlight switched to Benfica's marvellous Stadium of Light, the ground was packed two hours before the kick off. Eusebio was present to see whether the 1983 Benfica side could recapture the glories of the sixties, but Anderlecht, now coached by their own former star Paul Van Himst, proved too strong.

Han Sheu gave Benfica hope with a goal after 36 minutes that levelled the aggregate scores. Three minutes later Anderlecht replied with a superb move finished by their Spanish-born midfield player Juan Lozano. Needing two goals now for victory Benfica could not penetrate again, and after two marvellous UEFA Cup campaigns Sven-Goran Eriksson was a loser at last.

BELOW and LEFT: Dutch delight for the player but not for his fellow countrymen in the crowd as Frans Thijssen turns away after scoring Ipswich's first goal in the second leg of the 1981 UEFA Cup final. The game between Alkmaar AZ'67 and the East Anglians was won 4-2 by the Dutch team but Ipswich won the final 5-4 on aggregate. Thijssen was also elected English Footballer of the Year that season.

UEFA CUP 1982-83

FIRST ROUND

Anderlecht v Kuopion Palloseura (3-0, 3-1)	6-1
Spartak Moscow v Arsenal (3-2, 5-2)	8-4
Slavia Sofia v Sarajevo (2-2, 2-4)	4-6
Bohemians Prague v Admira-Wacker (5-0, 2-1)	7-1
Borussia Dortmund v Rangers (0-0, 0-2)	0-2
Carl Zeiss Jena v Bordeaux (3-1, 0-5)	3-6
Dundee United v PSV Eindhoven (1-1, 2-0)	3-1
Dynamo Tbilisi v Napoli (2-1, 0-1)	2-2
Ferencvaros v Athletic Bilbao (2-1, 1-1)	3-2
Glentoran v Banik Ostrava (1-3, 0-1)	1-4
Grazer AK v Corvinul (1-1, 0-3)	1-4
Haarlem v La Gantoise (2-1, 3-3)	5-4
Kaiserslautern v Trabzonspor (3-0, 3-0)	6-0
Manchester United v Valencia (0-0, 1-2)	1-2
PAOK Salonika v Sochaux (1-0, 1-2)	2-2
Pezporikos v Zurich (2-2, 0-1)	2-3
AS Roma v Ipswich Town (3-0, 1-3)	4-3
St. Etienne v Tatabanya (4-1, 0-0)	4-1
Sevilla v Levski Spartak (3-1, 3-0)	6-1
Slask Wroclaw v Dynamo Moscow (2-2, 1-0)	3-2
Southampton v Norrkopping (2-2, 0-0)	2-2
Stal Mielec v Lokeren (1-1, 0-0)	1-1
Uni. Craiova v Fiorentina (3-1, 0-1)	3-2
Utrecht v Porto (0-1, 0-2)	0-3
Viking Stavanger v Lokomotiv Leipzig (1-0, 2-3)	3-3
Vorwaerts v Werder Bremen (1-3, 2-0)	3-3
Progres Niedercorn v Servette (0-1, 0-3)	0-4
Lyngsby v Brage (1-2, 2-2)	3-4
Zurrieq v Hajduk Split (1-4, 0-4)	1-8
Fram v Shamrock Rovers (0-3, 0-4)	0-7
AEK Athens v Cologne (0-1, 0-5)	0-6
Benfica v Real Betis (2-1, 2-1)	4-2

SECOND ROUND

Anderlecht v Porto (4-0, 2-3)	6-3
Corvinul v Sarajevo (4-5, 0-4)	4-9
Ferencvaros v Zurich (1-1, 0-1)	1-2
Hajduk Split v Bordeaux (4-1, 0-4)	4-5
Napoli v Kaiserslautern (1-2, 0-2)	1-4
POAK Salonika v Sevilla (2-0, 0-4)	2-4
Rangers v Cologne (2-1, 0-5)	2-6
AS Roma v Norrkopping (1-0, 0-1)	1-1
Shamrock Rovers v Uni. Craiova (2-1, 0-3)	2-4
St. Etienne v Bohemians Prague (0-0, 0-4)	0-4
Slask Wroclaw v Servette (0-2, 1-5)	1-7
Spartak Moscow v Haarlem (2-0, 3-1)	5-1
Valencia v Banik Ostrava (1-0, 0-0)	1-0
Viking Stavanger v Dundee United (1-3, 0-0)	1-3
Werder Bremen v Brage (2-0, 6-2)	8-2
Benfica v Lokeren (2-0, 2-1)	4-1

THIRD ROUND

Anderlecht v Sarajevo (6-1, 0-1)	6-2
Bordeaux v Uni. Craiova (1-0, 0-2)	1-2
Dundee United v Werder Bremen (2-1, 1-1)	3-2
Cologne v AS Roma (1-0, 0-2)	1-2
Servette v Bohemians Prague (2-2, 1-2)	3-4
Sevilla v Kaiserslautern (1-0, 0-4)	1-4
Spartak Moscow v Valencia (0-0, 0-2)	0-2
Zurich v Benfica (1-1, 0-4)	1-5

QUARTER-FINALS

Valencia v Anderlecht (1-2, 1-3)	2-5
Bohemians Prague v Dundee United (1-0, 0-0)	1-0
Kaiserslautern v Uni. Craiova (3-2, 0-1)	3-3
AS Roma v Benfica (1-2, 1-1)	2-3

SEMI-FINALS

Bohemians Prague v Anderlecht (0-1, 1-3)	1-4
Benfica v Uni. Craiova (0-0, 1-1)	1-1

FINAL

Anderlecht 1 Benfica 0
(Brussels, 4.5.83, 60,000)

Anderlecht: Munaron, Olsen, Hofkens, Peruzovic, De Groote, Frimann, Lozano, Coeck, Vercauteren, Vandenbergh (Czerniatynski), Brylle

Benfica: Bento, Pietra, Humberto, Alvaro, Frederico (Bastos Lopes II), Chalana, Jose Luis, Carlos Manuel, Diamantino, Filipovic (Nene), Sheu

Scorer: Brylle

Benfica 1 Anderlecht 1
(Lisbon, 18.5.83, 80,000)

Benfica: Bento, Pietra, Humberto, Bastos Lopes II, Veloso, Chalana, Nene, Carlos Manuel, Diamantino (Alves), Stromberg, Sheu (Filipovic)

Anderlecht: De Groote for Hofkens; Broos for Brylle; Brylle came on for Vandenbergh

Scorers: Sheu; Lozano

SOUTH AMERICAN CHAMPIONSHIP

After a history which is turbulent as well as long—it pre-dates the European equivalent by more than 40 years—the South American Championship has abandoned the one-venue format and settled for a home-and-away basis . . .

The South American Championships, by far the longest-running international tournament outside the British Isles, has finally reversed the decline in popularity and prestige that threatened its existence in the 1960s.

The competition was first contested in Buenos Aires in 1916. Since then, the Copa America trophy has been awarded only 27 times, though a further four tournaments—known as 'extraordinarios'—are usually included in lists of past results.

Midway through the two weeks of that first competition, the four participants—Argentina, Brazil, Chile and the winners, Uruguay—announced the formation of the Confederación Sudamericana de Fútbol, the body that remains responsible for competition today.

Argentina and Uruguay dominate the tournament for 25 years

Each of the founder members played host to the tournament in turn, but Argentina did not gain the first of their record number of championship wins until they were hosts again in 1921.

Paraguay took Brazil to a play-off for the 1922 championship, held in Rio. It was to be Brazil's last trophy win for some time, as jurisdictional disputes and other problems restricted them to just one tournament between 1923 and 1936.

Not surprisingly, this era was dominated by Argentina and by Uruguay, whose great world-conquering side was built around a number of prolific forwards and a half-back line known as 'la costilla metallica' (the iron curtain)—José Andrade, Lorenzo Fernandez and Alvaro Gestide.

Brazil, building a formidable squad for the coming World Cup, won the 1949 tournament at home, hammering Paraguay 7-0 in a play-off. The same two countries had to play off for the next title in 1953. This time Paraguay, utilizing an innovatory 4-2-4 system, triumphed 3-2.

Argentina, who had withdrawn from international competition in pique at being passed over for the 1950 World Cup, returned in Santiago in 1955, going undefeated once again to win the trophy.

They were to win the next official tournament two years later in Peru with a young inside-forward trio that so enchanted South American supporters that they were named 'el trio de la muerte' (the trio of death). The three youngsters—Humberto Maschio, Antonio Angelillo and Omar Sivori—also enchanted European scouts, and all three were soon signed by Italian clubs.

Bolivia won its first and only Copa America in 1963, in the thin air of La Paz.

Interest in the competition was waning. Brazil, who had fielded a far from full-strength side in La Paz, neglected to enter in 1967.

Uruguay overcame the problems set by suspensions imposed during the previous year's World Cup in England to win the tournament, getting the victory they needed in a dull, defensive final game against Argentina thanks to a mis-hit goal from Pedro Rocha. Despite the host nation's success, attendances were tiny. Reforms were evidently needed if the competition was to survive.

They were finally effected eight years later, when the present formula was adopted. Nine national teams were divided into three qualifying groups, the winners of which joined the holders in two-game knock-out semi-finals.

Group one was decided by the games between Brazil, fielding a Minas Gerais state selection based round Cruzeiro, and Argentina, fielding a Santa Fé state selection that included Mario Kempes, Leopoldo Luque and Ossie Ardiles. Nelinho scored the goals that gave Brazil a 2-1 win in Belo Horizonte, then the Argentinians spent the week before the return in Rosario on strike. Brazil broke out for the game's only goal just on half-time when Danival outwitted the advancing Hugo Gatti.

Surprise finalists of the new-look competition: Peru and Colombia

Colombia gained maximum points in their group, though their game in Asuncion was abandoned at half-time. Paraguayan dissent over the game's only goal five minutes before the break boiled over into a free-for-all as the referee ended the half. When the local police joined in, cracking heads, the game was prudently called off.

Colombia shocked Uruguay in the semi-finals, building a

SOUTH AMERICAN CHAMPIONSHIP

Year	Venue	Teams	Winners	Pts	Runners-up	Pts
1916	Buenos Aires	4	Uruguay	5	*Argentina	4
1917	Montevideo	4	*Uruguay	6	Argentina	4
1919	Rio de Janeiro	4	*Brazil†	5	Uruguay	5
1920	Valparaiso	4	Uruguay	5	Argentina	4
1921	Buenos Aires	4	*Argentina	6	Brazil	2
1922	Rio de Janeiro	5	*Brazil†	5	Paraguay	5
1923	Montevideo	4	*Uruguay	6	Argentina	4
1924	Montevideo	4	*Uruguay	5	Argentina	4
1925	Buenos Aires	3	*Argentina	7	Brazil	5
1926	Santiago	5	Uruguay	8	Argentina	5
1927	Lima	4	Argentina	6	Uruguay	4
1929	Buenos Aires	4	*Argentina	6	Paraguay	4
1935	Lima	4	Uruguay	6	Argentina	4
1937	Buenos Aires	6	*Argentina†	8	Brazil	8
1939	Lima	5	*Peru	8	Uruguay	6
1941§	Santiago	5	Argentina	8	Uruguay	6
1942	Montevideo	7	*Uruguay	12	Argentina	9
1945	Santiago	7	Argentina	11	Brazil	10
1946§	Buenos Aires	6	*Argentina	10	Brazil	7
1947	Guayaquil	8	Argentina	13	Paraguay	11
1949	Rio de Janeiro	8	*Brazil†	12	Paraguay	12
1953	Lima	7	Paraguay†	8	Brazil	8
1955	Santiago	6	Argentina	9	*Chile	7
1956§	Montevideo	6	*Uruguay	9	Brazil	8
1957	Lima	7	Argentina	10	Brazil	8
1959	Buenos Aires	7	*Argentina	11	Brazil	10
1959§	Guayaquil	5	Uruguay	7	Argentina	5
1963	La Paz	7	*Bolivia	11	Paraguay	9
1967	Montevideo	6	*Uruguay	9	Argentina	8
1975	‡	10	Peru	0:2:1	Colombia	1:0:0
1979	‡	10	Paraguay	3:0:1	Chile	0:1:0
1983	‡	10	Uruguay	2:1	Brazil	0:1

*Host nation †after play-off ‡played on basis of group, elimination and two legged final; 1975 play off in Caracas, 1979 play off in Buenos Aires §'extraordinary' unofficial tournaments three-goal home-leg lead against a Uruguayan side reduced to 10 men by a 17th-minute sending off, then holding on for a 1-0 defeat in Montevideo.

Peru caused an even bigger upset by beating Brazil in Belo Horizonte, astonishing the confident home crowd by seizing and holding the initiative. They took the lead through Cassaretto, survived a 54th-minute equalizer from Roberto Batata and finally saw their verve and audacity rewarded with two goals in the last seven minutes—from Teofilo Cubillas, the game's outstanding player, and from Cassaretto. Brazil responded with a 2-0 win in Lima, but Peru went through on the 'drawing of cards', South America's equivalent to the toss of a coin.

Paraguay win in 1979 to keep the 'big three' on the sidelines

The final, which went to a play-off in Caracas, was disappointing. Hugo Sotil's first-half goal was enough to give Peru their first title since 1939.

Paraguay then caused the upset of the 1979 tournament by putting Brazil out in the semi-finals, a result that sealed the sacking of Brazil manager Claudio Coutinho. In Asuncion, superb goals from Eugenio Morel and Hugo Talavera set the seal on an excellent Paraguayan first-half display, before Brazil pulled a goal back through Palinha. In Rio, Falcao and Socrates twice gave Brazil the lead, only for Milciades Morel and Julio Cesar Romero to equalize each time.

The other semi-final was settled by Chile's 2-1 away win over Peru. Carlos Caszely headed both their goals.

The final was again a disappointment. Romero (2) and Milciades Morel scored the goals for Paraguay that set them on course for their second title.

LEFT: ***Even eight goals from Pelé (seen here scoring against Chile) could not prevent Argentina pushing Brazil into second place in 1959—the ninth time they had been runners-up. Despite Brazil's great World Cup exploits, they have managed only three South American titles—all of them won in Rio.***
BELOW: ***The Olimpia Asuncion line-up in 1979—South American Cup winners and the backbone of the Paraguay side that beat Brazil on the way to a surprise success in the South American Championship.***

LEADING SCORERS

Year	Player	Gls
1916	Oradin *(Uruguay)**	3
1917	Romano *(Uruguay)**	4
1919	Neco *(Brazil)**	4
1920	Perez *(Uruguay)**	4
1921	*not available*	
1922	Francia *(Argentina)*	4
1923	Aguirre *(Argentina)*	4
	Petrone *(Uruguay)**	4
1924	Petrone *(Uruguay)**	4
1925	Seoane *(Argentina)**	6
1926	Castro *(Uruguay)**	6
	Scarone *(Uruguay)**	6
1927	Figueroa *(Uruguay)**	3
	Luna *(Argentina)**	3
	Petrone *(Uruguay)*	3
	Scarone *(Uruguay)*	3
1929	Gonzalez *(Paraguay)*	5
1935	Massantonio *(Argentina)*	4
1937	Roro *(Chile)*	7
1939	Fernandez *(Peru)**	7
1941	Marvezzi *(Argentina)**	5
1942	Moreno *(Argentina)*	5
1945	Menendez *(Argentina)**	7
1946	Medina *(Uruguay)*	7
1947	Fallero *(Uruguay)*	6
	Menendez *(Argentina)**	6
1949	Pinto *(Brazil)**	6
1953	Molina *(Chile)*	7
1955	Micheli *(Argentina)**	7
1956	Hormazabel *(Chile)*	4
1957	Ambrosis *(Uruguay)*	9
	Maschio *(Argentina)**	9
1959	Pele *(Brazil)*	8
1963	Sanfilippo *(Argentina)*	6
1967	Raffo *(Ecuador)*	5
	Rodriguez *(Argentina)*	5
	Zarate *(Paraguay)*	5
1975	Artime *(Argentina)*	5
1979	Romero *(Paraguay)*	4

*winners

SOUTH AMERICAN CUP

To many Europeans the 'Copa Libertadores' is merely the device that produced so many bruising teams in the World Club Championship. But that's a narrow view of what has become South America's premier event . . .

Launched in 1960 as South America's answer to the European Cup, the Copa Libertadores de America has survived a testing time to emerge as the most stable and popular South American international competition. Because of the amount of prestige and money at stake, the few moments of pure pleasure and superlative skill have tended to be swamped by fearful violence, the worst excesses of anti-football and incompetent and occasionally corrupt refereeing.

The first two competitions were won by the Uruguayan champions Penarol. Although neither Brazilian nor Argentinian clubs were as yet whole-heartedly committed to the new cup, there was still no doubt that Penarol were an outstanding side. Their forward line contained such players as the clever, stocky winger Luis Cubilla—the outstanding Uruguayan forward of recent times—the gifted José Sasia, the powerful Peruvian winger Luis Joya and centre-forward Alberto Spencer from Ecuador.

It took an even more outstanding side to take the trophy from them. With the recently-signed Gilmar in goal and Coutinho the ideal foil for a Pelé at the height of his powers, Santos won the competition in 1962, scoring 29 goals in nine games.

Argentina are represented in 17 successive finals, winning 12 Libertadores titles

Santos triumphed again in 1963, winning both legs of the final against a Boca Juniors side whose major stars—Silvio Marzolini, Antonio Rattin and goalkeeper Antonio Roma—appeared in defence. Boca had nevertheless begun a remarkable run of success for Argentinian clubs, who placed one of their number in every Libertadores final to 1980. This included two wins for Independente in 1964 and 1965 over Uruguay's two giants.

The Libertadores had by now grown to an almost impractical size. The 1966 tournament was the first to include two clubs from each country and the proliferation of qualifying groups meant that River Plate, for instance, were required to play 21 games (10 in the first round, six in the semi-final round, a semi-final play-off and a three-game final). The prospect of a programme like this, with its attendant unprofitable trips to the continent's backwaters, discouraged any Brazilian clubs from entering in 1966 and

Penarol's Aendro flies at Universidad of Chile's Aranguiz in the semi-final of the first South American Cup in 1960. The Uruguayan side won this series, and again in 1961 and 1966.

Boca Juniors beat Colombia's first finalists Deportivo Cali in 1978 to hold on to their title and maintain the Argentinian domination built by Independiente and Estudiantes.

helped keep Santos out again in 1967.

Brazil's one entrant was Cruzeiro, who, inspired by the 20-year-old Tostao, cruised into the semi-final round only to lose twice in Montevideo, putting Nacional into the final against the Racing side who would later play Celtic in the World Club Championship.

The final in 1968 went to a play-off for a fourth successive year and Palmeiras succumbed to two goals from Juan 'la Bruja' Veron, Estudiantes' one player of undoubted individual talent.

Reforms in the 1971 competition brought about a fairer and less demanding schedule and encouraged Brazilian clubs back into the fold. The year also saw the virtual demise of Estudiantes, despite reaching the final. Manager Zubeldia resigned, taking Poletti with him to Huracan, and the club president shot himself.

Nacional went out in unfortunate circumstances in the semi-final group the following year. Four goals from Artime were enough to give them three points against Penarol, but they slipped at home to Universitario of Peru, for whom Oscar Ramirez hit a hat-

River Plate's World Cup star Leopoldo Luque is outnumbered by Boca players in the Buenos Aires derby. While Boca have reached four Libertadores finals and won two, River Plate have lost both their finals after play-offs.

trick. The 'U' went into the final on goal difference, but lost the final to Independiente, and two Maglioni goals, after a play-off in Avellaneda.

Independiente went on to win four Libertadores in succession, beating teams from Chile (Colo Colo and Union Española) in the 1973 and 1975 finals. Their reign ended in the 1976 semi-final play-off with River Plate, in which they had Ruben Galvan sent off before conceding the decisive goal. But the outstanding team of the competition was Cruzeiro, who finally came good after several near misses. Under former Brazilian World Cup coach Zeze Moreira, they scored 46 goals (Jairzinho 14, Palinha 12) in 13 games to win the trophy.

The 1977 competition was marred by some of the worst excesses of the Libertadores' unsavoury history, culminating in a semi-final feud between Juan Carlos Lorenzo's Boca Juniors and Colombia's Deportivo Cali, coached by the former Estudiantes midfielder Carlos Bilardo. Lorenzo steered his team to the final against a Cruzeiro side that had deprived themselves of both Jairzinho (to Venezuela) and Palinha (to Corinthians). Cruzeiro could only penetrate the malicious Boca defence with a 40-yard free-kick from the inevitable Nelinho. In the Montevideo play-off, on a fog-shrouded mud-heap, Raul saved Cruzeiro with two spectacular extra-time saves from Dario Felman, but it was the Boca keeper, Hugo Gatti, who had the last word, saving Cruzeiro's final attempt in the penalty show-down.

The Lorenzo-Bilardo feud had its sequel in the final the following year. Lacking their outstanding midfielder Diego Umana, Cali went down in two games.

Boca scraped through a rough semi-final group in 1979, winning a play-off with injury-stricken Independiente thanks to an extra-time goal from Ernesto Mastrangelo. Their opponents in the final were Olimpia of Asuncion—coached by Luis Cubilla—who had barely survived a riot in Cochabamba in the opening round. Boca's poverty of attacking ideas was exposed when they went two down in the first half of the first leg in Asuncion and Paraguay took the cup for the first time ever—with the club who had been the first losing finalists back in 1960.

SOUTH AMERICAN CUP FINALS

Year	Teams	Winners	Runners-up	Scores
1960	7	*Penarol *(Uruguay)*	Olimpia Asuncion *(Paraguay)*	1-0, 0-0
1961	9	*Penarol *(Uruguay)*	Palmeiras *(Brazil)*	1-0, 1-1
1962	10	*Santos *(Brazil)*	Penarol *(Uruguay)*	2-1, 2-3, 3-0
1963	9	*Santos *(Brazil)*	Boca Juniors *(Argentina)*	3-2, 2-1
1964	10	Independiente *(Argentina)*	*Nacional *(Uruguay)*	0-0, 1-0
1965	10	*Independiente *(Argentina)*	Penarol *(Uruguay)*	1-0, 1-3, 4-1
1966	17	*Penarol *(Uruguay)*	River Plate *(Argentina)*	2-0, 2-3, 4-2
1967	19	*Racing Club *(Argentina)*	Nacional *(Uruguay)*	0-0, 0-0, 2-1
1968	21	*Estudiantes *(Argentina)*	Palmeiras *(Brazil)*	2-1, 1-3, 2-0
1969	17	Estudiantes *(Argentina)*	*Nacional *(Uruguay)*	1-0, 2-0
1970	19	*Estudiantes *(Argentina)*	Penarol *(Uruguay)*	1-0, 0-0
1971	21	Nacional *(Uruguay)*	*Estudiantes *(Argentina)*	0-1, 1-0, 2-0
1972	20	Independiente*(Argentina)*	*Universitario *(Peru)*	0-0, 2-1
1973	19	*Independiente *(Argentina)*	Colo Colo *(Chile)*	1-1, 0-0, 2-1
1974	21	Independiente *(Argentina)*	*Sao Paulo *(Brazil)*	1-2, 2-0
1975	21	Independiente *(Argentina)*	*Union Espanola *(Chile)*	0-1, 3-1, 2-0
1976	21	*Cruzeiro *(Brazil)*	River Plate *(Argentina)*	4-1, 1-2, 3-2
1977	21	*Boca Juniors *(Argentina)*	Cruzeiro *(Brazil)*	1-0, 0-1, †0-0
1978	21	Boca Juniors *(Argentina)*	*Deportivo Cali *(Colombia)*	0-0, 4-0
1979	21	*Olimpia Asuncion *(Paraguay)*	Boca Juniors *(Argentina)*	2-0, 0-0
1980	20	Nacional *(Uruguay)*	*Internacional *(Brazil)*	0-0, 1-0
1981	20	*Flamengo *(Brazil)*	Cobreloa *(Chile)*	2-1, 0-1, ‡2-0
1982	20	*Penarol *(Uruguay)*	Cobreloa *(Chile)*	0-0, 1-0
1983	20	Gremio *(Brazil)*	*Penarol *(Uruguay)*	1-1, 2-1

*home team in first leg †Boca won on penalties after goalless play-off in Montevideo ‡play-off in Montevideo

SOCCER IN THE USA

In 1984 the North American Soccer League again faced the crisis days last encountered in the late sixties. This trough has followed a boom period when Pele was wooed to the New York Cosmos and other international stars followed his example. Yet while the professional game struggles to survive and the United States make little impact internationally, millions of young Americans have been entranced by a game their fathers never knew; the future of soccer in the States lies with them.

On January 1 1984 the North American Soccer League numbered just nine clubs under its auspices, a far cry from the heady days of the expansion programme and 24 franchises first created in 1979.

Seemingly solid organisations like Seattle Sounders, Minnesota Kicks and Portland Timbers had dropped into oblivion, and the desperation was most graphically illustrated by an offer—thankfully rejected—to bring the 43-year-old Pele out of retirement.

At the start of 1984 seven of the nine clubs were contesting the Indoor Championship, to greater public interest where the easy comparison with ice hockey created better understanding.

The League had suffered particularly from a lack of patience along financial backers, many of whom sought a quick return rather than held at heart soccer's longer-term interests. The Americanisation policy—each club had to field five North American citizens in 1984—had not produced immediate local heroes; most notably the concept of fielding a club of Americans —Team America based in Washington for the 1983 season—had not stimulated a rise in standards or more fervent support.

The NASL had not benefitted either from its uneasy relationship with FIFA. The much-vaunted 35-yard line was finally abolished because of consistent protest.

The individualistic points scoring system in 1983 remained six for a win (four for a shootout victory) and a point per goal up to three in the regulation 90-minute play.

For all the NASL's disappointments, soccer's popularity continues to increase among the young Americans. What is lacking is a structure at grass roots level after high school and college to give them a chance to play.

Early days—home and abroad

Association football became formalized in the United States in 1913, when the United

Training proves to be thirsty work for Aztecs' Jim Millinder. The American season runs from March to October, and even with evening kick-offs playing in high summer can mean temperatures rarely encountered in the European season.

Even a veteran Pelé commands a good deal of

States Football Association was recognized by FIFA as an authorized governing body. Yet the game captured no national interest, being played almost exclusively by ethnic groups as a reminder of the days before emigration. The influence of rugby held more appeal to the developing nation, and its handling code had already been gradually adapted into the American grid-iron game—what is meant there by 'football'.

The American Soccer League, still in existence today, offered part-time professional football from 1933, and the German-American League in New York typified the sport for first-generation Americans. But on a major level, the grid-iron game became the major winter sport in the United States. Only in St Louis did soccer find an oasis through a Catholic Youth Council programme, and local players formed the core of the 1950 United States World Cup squad. In the mid-1970s St Louis continued to beat the American soccer drum when, under British coach John Sewell, the St Louis Stars fought an NASL campaign with a team comprised mainly of Americans.

attention, this time from Dallas Tornado. It was Cosmos' $4.5 million signing of the Brazilian in 1975 that triggered the US soccer boom.

Sadly the gamble failed—despite the NASL Championship runners-up slot in 1972—and the franchise was moved to Anaheim near Los Angeles as the California Surf.

By the end of the Second World War the USFA made a public statement of its failure to keep pace with American football by changing its name to the United States Soccer Football Association.

United States 1 England 0: could that shock result ever occur again?

Yet despite their minor-league status the United States took part in the final stages of three of the first four World Cups, and in two series gained conspicuous success. In 1930 their squad was reinforced by a number of British-born players who had been enticed abroad in the previous decade in one of several abortive attempts to promote professional soccer in America. When they arrived in Uruguay for the finals, the French players took one look at the sturdy frames of the 'Americans' and unkindly nicknamed them the 'shot-putters'.

Posted in Group 4 with Paraguay and Belgium, the United States beat both opponents by three clear goals for a comfortable passage to the semi-finals. But their success proved their undoing. Drawn against Argentina, their manager Wilfred Cummings began to make public utterances about the final; indeed Argentina went into the semi-finals as underdogs. Over-confident and out-skilled, and according to some reports out-kicked, the United States conceded five goals in the second half and were beaten 6-1.

An even heavier beating followed in 1934 when, in a competition run on straight knock-out lines, the United States were paired with Italy, the host nation, in the first round. Schiavio, who would not score again in the tournament until his extra-time winner in the final, claimed three of Italy's seven goals. The solitary reply came from Donelli, whose Italian background enabled him to stay on and play League football in Italy.

In 1950 the United States made their third, and to date last, foray into the World Cup finals—and left their mark on the legends of the competition. Once more the team had a British influence: it was captained by Eddie McIlvenny, whose domestic career had finished with a free transfer from Wrexham, then of the Third Division North. For McIlvenny, and America's Scottish-born coach Bill Jeffrey, the fabled events that took place in Belo Horizonte held special meaning.

History records that United States beat England 1-0 with a 37th-minute goal from Larry Gaetjens, a reflex header that deflected the ball past Bert Williams. What the chronicles of 29 June 1950 can never explain is how England's stars, including Billy Wright, Alf Ramsey, Stan Mortensen, Wilf Mannion and Tom Finney could lose to a team so sure they were facing annihilation that they sat up drinking late into the night before the game. A rutted pitch, a partisan crowd, and a goal not allowed when Mullen's header appeared to cross the line hardly amounted to an explanation of defeat, let alone excuses for it.

The result effectively ended England's

NASL CHAMPIONSHIP

Year	Winners	Runners-up	Score
1967	Los Angeles Wolves (USA)† Oakland Clippers (NPSL‡)		
1968	Atlanta Chiefs	San Diego Toros	0-0, 3-0
1969	Kansas City Spurs	Atlanta Chiefs	*
1970	Rochester Lancers	Washington Darts	3-0, 1-3
1971	Dallas Tornado	Atlanta Chiefs	1-2, 4-1, 2-0
1972	New York Cosmos	St Louis Stars	2-1
1973	Philadelphia Atoms	Dallas Tornado	2-0
1974	Los Angeles Aztecs	Miami Toros	4-3
1975	Tampa Bay Rowdies	Portland Timbers	2-0
1976	Toronto Metros	Minnesota Kicks	3-0
1977	New York Cosmos	Seattle Sounders	2-1
1978	New York Cosmos	Tampa Bay Rowdies	3-1
1979	Vancouver Whitecaps	Tampa Bay Rowdies	2-1
1980	New York Cosmos	Fort Lauderdale Strikers	3-0
1981	Chicago Sting	New York Cosmos	1-0
1982	New York Cosmos	Seattle Sounders	1-0
1983	Tulsa Roughnecks	Toronto Blizzard	2-0

*no play-off †United Soccer Association ‡National Professional Soccer League

University graduate and former Welsh international inside-forward Phil Woosnam signs as general manager and player/coach to Atlanta Chiefs in 1968. At times reduced to working from the visitors' locker-room at Atlanta Stadium, Woosnam and ex-*Daily Express *man Clive Toye, backed by the resources of Lamar Hunt, ran the infant NASL. After enormous initial problems—and a number of set-backs—the organization gradually grew in the early 1970s, laying the base for the subsequent success. Woosnam, following two years as executive director, became NASL commissioner in 1971.

challenge in their first World Cup finals, and the United States lost both their other group games, to Spain 3-1 after scoring first through John Souza, and to Chile 5-2—a result which emphasized both the lack of calibre of the American side and the magnitude of their remarkable shock victory against England.

Yet though the rest of the world marvelled at the triumph over England, the event passed almost without record in the States. To the American sports fan soccer was still merely a game played in parks and sandlots by immigrants, a part of the culture that had been left behind, like going to the appropriate church on Sundays.

The great American disaster of '67 and '68
Ironically it was another World Cup, that of 1966, that convinced American sports entrepreneurs to think again about the potential of soccer as a major-league sport. England's 4-2 defeat of West Germany at Wembley was beamed live via satellite all over North America—and if the audience watched initially out of curiosity they were soon captured by the drama of West Germany's fight-back, the controversy over England's third goal and Geoff Hurst's eventual hat-trick.

The businessmen so essential to the promotion of the professional game had already witnessed with interest the growth of the International Soccer League, which for six seasons from 1960 invited top clubs from around the globe to participate in an American tournament. Everton, West Ham United, Dukla Prague, Monaco and Gornik Zabrze were among many who embarked on the series as a longer, more competitive version of a close-season tour.

Regular crowds of 15,000 attracted for the first time American sports promoters who saw nothing enthralling about soccer except the lure of the dollar. What followed almost destroyed any possibility of soccer getting a foothold in the US sports calendar: oversell was so nearly overkill.

In 1966 three separate groups of entrepreneurs approached the USSFA to start full-time professional leagues. The governing body, wisely, felt that at very best one league alone would struggle to get off the ground; moreover they suspected the intentions of the promoters, who were urged to pool their resources. One amalgamation reduced the number of factions to two, but the USSFA was still faced with a choice.

A franchise war nearly wrecks any hopes of soccer success

Finally they ratified a consortium including Lamar Hunt and Jack Kent Cooke, leading figures in other American pro sports, and each newly formed club paid the USSFA $25,000 for its franchise. After originally calling itself the NASL the reorganized league retitled itself the United Soccer Association, and began plans for a first operating year in 1968.

Meanwhile the rival group did not accept defeat. In August 1966 came the announcement that the National Professional Soccer League would begin operations—in 1967. Even though it was officially outlawed by FIFA and its players therefore subject to suspension, the NPSL brandished a television contract (from CBS) which is considered crucial to the development of sports in America. Moreover by starting in 1967 it would have the field to itself.

At the very time the game needed a concerted effort from all those wishing to elevate soccer to major-league status, it faced a war. The USA responded quickly to the threat and rapidly made plans to start their league, also in 1967, with 12 clubs to the NPSL's planned 10; thus there were 22 franchises hoping to cash in on a market that had never before guaranteed success.

The two leagues both agreed on one factor: there were not enough home-grown players to stimulate interest. Even the untutored eye of the American fan would spot the difference between the sandlot players and what many had seen in the World Cup telecasts. But they attacked the problem in different ways. The NPSL sought out individuals who were prepared to risk the wrath of FIFA for a good wage—players like Cesar Luis Menotti, who linked up with the much-travelled English striker George Kirby for the New York Generals; like Phil Woosnam and Peter McParland, Welsh and Irish internationals who signed for the the Atlanta Chiefs; like Ladislav Kubala, capped for Hungary, Czechoslovakia and Spain, who played for Toronto Falcons; like Denis Viollet, once of Manchester United, who threw in his lot with the Baltimore Bays. But many of the recruits were less distinguished, even though the clubs' press officers did their best to obscure the fact.

The USA League, however, extended the principle on which the International League had been based, and imported entire teams to represent cities: a League which began on 26 May and finished on 14 July, and fitted comfortably into Europe's summer break. The following teams took part: Shamrock Rovers (representing Boston), Cagliari (Chicago), Stoke City (Cleveland), Dundee United (Dallas), Glentoran (Detroit),

Bangu of Brazil (Houston), Wolverhampton Wanderers (Los Angeles), Cerro of Uruguay (New York), ADO Den Haag of Holland (San Francisco), Hibernian (Toronto), Sunderland (Vancouver) and Aberdeen (Washington).

At the same time the 10 NPSL clubs took shape: Atlanta Chiefs, Baltimore Bays, Chicago Spurs, Los Angeles Toros, New York Generals, Oakland Clippers, Philadelphia Spartans, Pittsburgh Phantoms, St Louis Stars and. Toronto Falcons. Thus Chicago, Los Angeles, New York, Toronto and San Francisco/Oakland were asked to support *two* new teams, with further complications that in Los Angeles, New York and Toronto both teams used the same stadium. The American fan would face his problems simply by learning the rules of the new sport set before him; trying to work out which team was in which league could only impair his potential support.

While 9,500 people attended the USA's opening game in Washington, where the home-town Whips were beaten 2-1 by Cleveland's Stokers, the following day just under 35,000 (the biggest crowd of the season) were attracted to Houston, where the Stars drew 1-1 with the Los Angeles Wolves. Los Angeles in the Western Division and Cleveland in the Eastern made much of the early running, but while the Wolves made sure of reaching the final by losing only two games, the Stokers were pipped by Washington. The play-off took place in Los Angeles' Memorial Stadium on 14 July—and produced a remarkable dénouement in front of 17,824 paying customers.

Only one club averages more than 10,000 in the first season

Peter Knowles shot Wolves in front in the third minute before Jimmy Smith, later to become a Scottish international and join Newcastle United, took the stage. Smith equalized for Washington only to be sent off after 34 minutes for kicking an opponent. Washington withstood their handicap until the 63rd minute and then overcame it, taking the lead through Frank Munro. David Burnside levelled two minutes later, only for Jim Storrie to put Washington's Scottish side in front again in the next attack. Within 30 seconds Wolves found another equalizer, again from Burnside.

Only eight minutes remained when Burnside completed his hat-trick to inch Wolves ahead 4–3. Enough to finish most depleted teams. But in the last minute Munro headed in Petersen's free-kick to send the match into a conventional extra time of 15 minutes play each way.

At the end of the extra period, the scores remained level, but now 5-5 as the drama continued unabated. Derek Dougan finally got on the scoresheet to put Wolves in front yet again, and with just a minute to play Terry Wharton squandered the chance of certain victory when Bobby Clark saved his penalty. Washington immediately mounted one desperate attack and won a penalty for themselves, with which the gallant Munro, whose performance surely influenced Wolves to sign him a few months later, completed his hat-trick from the spot.

The final solution to this extraordinary spectacle came in an extra period of sudden-death overtime. Six minutes had elapsed, making the total time of the match two hours and six minutes, when defender Ally Shewan helped a Bobby Thomson cross into his own net to give Wolves a 6-5 triumph—and a $3,000 bonus for winning the USA championship. Attendances throughout the League had varied from Houston, just under 20,000 per game and the only club to average more than 10,000, to Chicago and Boston, who drew slightly over 4,000.

The NPSL fared even worse through the turnstiles over a much longer season, from 16 April to 9 September. Only 775,846 spectators watched 159 games in the regular season for an average of around 4,500, much less than the entrepreneurs had anticipated.

ABOVE: Dennis Tueart (bottom left) scores his second goal to give Cosmos their 3-1 win over Tampa Bay Rowdies in the Soccer Bowl '78. Cosmos, playing the final in their own Giants Stadium, thus remained NASL champions.
LEFT: NASL commissioner Phil Woosnam looks on as Sir Stanley Rous, then president of FIFA, presents the trophy to the Cosmos' Yugoslavian-born captain Werner Roth. The relationship between the world's governing body and the NASL remains a little ambiguous and a point of confusion.

Baltimore Bays and Oakland Clippers won the two divisions on a points system that produced six for a win, three for a draw and one point for each goal scored up to a maximum of three (a similar system to that now in use in the NASL except that there are no drawn matches).

In a two-legged final Viollet's goal gave the Bays an uncertain advantage in the first game in Baltimore. But at Oakland a hat-trick by Yugoslav Dragan Djukic sealed a 4-2 aggregate triumph with Baltimore suffering the added indignity of their Spanish defender Santisteban being sent off. In the Oakland squad were Mel Scott, formerly an England Under-23 international centre-half, Roy Lunnis, once of Crystal Palace and Portsmouth, and Barry Rowan, a forward who played for Millwall.

But the lack of financial stability immediately finished Pittsburgh and Philadelphia, who along with all 10 NPSL clubs had lost money. Even the much-cherished television coverage had caused problems. Danny Blanchflower's honest comment as expert analyst had been out of keeping with the prevailing style in American television, which is to boost every aspect of the play. Blanchflower would not compromise; what he so often saw on the field was mediocrity and he said so. He was not retained for a second season.

Even more disquieting was the media's

The marketing men tamper with the game—to get their ads on TV

inability to come to terms with the very nature of the game. Non-stop action was its strong selling point, yet television needed breaks in the play to insert the advertisements, which recur much more regularly than on English commercial television. For a time referees were primed to delay treatments for injuries and any other stoppages so that the television director could safely switch to the advertisements. The result was angry crowds at the stadia who sensed tampering with the essence of the game. To this day US television coverage of live soccer is always likely to miss a goal because of a commercial break, but all the missed action is recorded and inserted as soon as the commercial is over. Pelé scored his first NASL goal, against Dallas in 1975, during a 'natural break'.

Midway through this saturated season of 1967, the NPSL officials offered to fall into line with the USSFA. After lengthy negotiations involving FIFA (who plainly wanted the matter settled without offending either party) an announcement was made from New York's Waldorf Astoria in January 1968 confirming a new league, the Professional Soccer League, comprising 17 clubs. The next day an amendment was declared renaming the venture the North American Soccer League. Whatever the billing the 1968 season would prove even more disastrous than its predecessor.

Coaching camps and schools for soccer-mad youngsters of both sexes—like this one in Los Angeles run by former Football League players Paul Taylor (left) and Jim Hinch (right), sprung up all over the States in the late 1970s. The appeal for parents and educational authorities is partly financial—the cost of gear is a fraction of that for American football—and partly the fact that the risk of injury is so small. For the kids, so many of whom are ruled out of major sports on the grounds of size, it means a new and continually active medium of sporting expression. The country's governing body, the USSF, estimate that through the state associations alone there will be five million children playing the game by 1985.

Of the 17 clubs who started the year, a mere five survived to take part in the 1969 competition: Kansas City Spurs, Atlanta Chiefs, St Louis Stars, Baltimore Bays and Dallas Tornado. Dallas' existence was the more remarkable because they had won only two of 32 matches in 1968, following a world tour that was designed to establish an international stature for the club. Chicago set another unenviable record in 1968—the lowest attendance, a meagre 336. Phil Woosnam's Atlanta won this first NASL Championship, beating San Diego 3-0 on aggregate, an event which made sure that one pioneering spirit would not diminish.

Elsewhere those whose priorities were to bank balances rather than any love for the game were discarding what had been an expensive new plaything. The promoters blamed their burnt fingers on soccer itself; the game, they were sure, was not suited to the American mentality. In reality their attempts to build a structure for the professional game had been naïve. CBS needed only one glance at an apparently sinking ship to make another decision which crippled the League's hopes. They did not renew their contract for 1969.

Al Miller, who remains the only man to have been voted NASL Coach of the Year on two occasions, and the only native American to receive that award, took the Philadelphia Atoms to a surprise championship success in 1973 with a side composed mostly of Americans. That year, too, Kyle Rote Jr became the first American-born player to head the NASL goalscoring list in a season which seemed to herald a healthy Americanization of the League. Since then, however, the competition has again been dominated by foreign-born players and imported coaches, particularly from Britain, with only two US coaches in charge in 1980.

NASL COACH OF THE YEAR

Year	Coach
1968	Phil Woosnam *(Atlanta Chiefs)* *
1969	*(no selection)*
1970	*(no selection)*
1971	*(no selection)*
1972	Casey Frankiewicz *(St Louis Stars)*
1973	Al Miller *(Philadelphia Atoms)* *
1974	Al Miller *(Philadelphia Atoms)*
1975	John Sewell *(St Louis Stars)*
1976	Eddie Firmani *(New York Cosmos)*
1977	Ron Newman *(Fort Lauderdale Strikers)*
1978	Tony Waiters *(Vancouver Whitecaps)*
1979	Timo Liekoski *(Houston Hurricane)*
1980	Alan Hinton *(Seattle Sounders)*
1981	Willie Roy *(Chicago Sting)* *
1982	Johnny Giles *(Vancouver Whitecaps)*
1983	Don Popovic *(Golden Bay Earthquakes)*

*NASL Championship winners

The art of soccer survival

Had the NASL been allowed to fold at the end of the 1968 season, full-time professional soccer might never have become established in the United States. Of the millionaire backers only Lamar Hunt, owner of the Dallas Tornado, remained optimistic, alongside the two British visionaries, Toye and Woosnam. For a while they controlled the League's bureaucratic business from the dressing-room at the Atlanta club.

Yet if professional soccer was hanging on to its life by a thread, other factors at youth level were bringing the game to parental attention. American football continued its popularity as a spectator sport, but there were problems for youngsters wanting to play it. The risk of serious injury was much greater than in most sports; the expense of kitting out youngsters with the helmet and other protective equipment was continually rising; and successful American footballers rely greatly on enormous physiques. Soccer was far less open to criticism on all three counts, from parents, schools—and kids.

Lucy's simplistic view of soccer may help to explain its appeal.

The soccer snowball gradually gathers momentum

Despite its five-team division the NASL stayed alive in 1969, the only concession to the abbreviated format being the absence of a play-off. Each team played its rivals four times and Kansas City pipped Atlanta by one point. In a League now bereft of star names the top scorer was Atlanta's South African striker, Kaizer Motaung.

But gradually the role of the professional soccer ball gained momentum. The five clubs became six in 1970, though Baltimore fell by the wayside; Rochester and Washington were the additions, and both proved their worth by reaching the play-off, Rochester winning the two-legged affair 4-3 on aggregate. Eight teams contested the championship in 1971 and 1972.

In 1971 Dallas, who had finished only second in the Southern Division, eliminated Rochester, the holders and the most successful team in regular-season play, and then Atlanta in a best of three final series, two of the games taking place in Atlanta. Mirko Stojanovic, the Yugoslavia international goalkeeper who had starred for Oakland Clippers in their USA triumph in 1967, was the Dallas hero. That season also marked the return of a franchise to New York, a symbol of the League's progress. And in 1972 New York Cosmos, with their Bermudan striker Randy Horton the top marksman in the NASL, took the championship.

The 1973 season belonged to an expansion team and to a striker from Dallas Tornado. Kyle Rote Jr, son of a grid-iron star, finished League top scorer with 10 goals and 10 assists, a shot in the arm for the Americanization of the League. Moreover Dallas, on the back of Rote's goals, reached the final of the play-offs. There they were

NASL MOST VALUABLE PLAYER

Year	Player
1967	†Ruben Navarro *(Philadelphia Spartans)*
1968	John Kowalik *(Chicago Mustangs)*
1969	Cirilio Fernandez *(Kansas City Spurs)*
1970	Carlos Metidieri *(Rochester Lancers)**
1971	Carlos Metidieri *(Rochester Lancers)*
1972	Randy Horton *(New York Cosmos)**
1973	Warren Archibald *(Miami Toros)*
1974	Peter Silvester *(Baltimore Comets)*
1975	Steve David *(Miami Toros)*
1976	Pele *(New York Cosmos)*
1977	Franz Beckenbauer *(Cosmos)**
1978	Mike Flanagan *(New England Tea Men)*
1979	Johan Cruyff *(Los Angeles Aztecs)*
1980	Roger Davies *(Seattle Sounders)*
1981	Giorgio Chinaglia *(New York Cosmos)*
1982	Peter Ward *(Seattle Sounders)*
1983	Roberto Cabanas *(New York Cosmos)*

*NASL Championship winners †NPSL

ABOVE: ***The change above from little-known players in the early years to international superstars in the late 1970s is a fair indication of the way NASL teams were able to lure big names to the US after the boom began in 1975. A trio of winners—Pelé, Beckenbauer and Cruyff—are arguably the three greatest players of modern times. Mike Flanagan won his place for 30 goals and eight 'assists' (68 points) in his 28 games—a total bettered only by Giorgio Chinaglia's massive record haul of 79 points.***

RIGHT: ***Johan Cruyff came out of retirement and followed his former Ajax and Barcelona boss Rinus Michels to Los Angeles Aztecs, where his performances in revitalizing a struggling franchise won him the 1979 award, before he moved on to Washington.***

beaten 2-0 by the Philadelphia Atoms, in their first season in the League, whose starting line-up in the championship decider included *six* American-born players. Atoms trainer Al Miller became the first American to be coach of the year.

But the Philadelphia experience illustrates the tenuous nature of all sports in the United States, and especially within the growth of the NASL. After their triumph in 1973 Miller echoed the feelings of the League's administrators when he proclaimed: 'We are the greatest thing that ever happened to soccer in America.' The fans in Philly certainly agreed: for the first home game of 1974 an NASL record crowd of 24,093 flocked to Veterans Stadium.

But that season, and in 1975, the Atoms failed to make the play-offs and at the end of the 1975 campaign the club was sold to the

'The greatest thing that ever happened to American soccer' folds

United Clubs of Jalisco, Mexico, who fielded unknown, unsupported Mexicans in 1976. With the crowds down to 3,000 'the best thing in American soccer' folded.

The continual changing of playing personnel within the League, heavily reliant at this time on lower-division British players—some of whom did their profession less than justice by treating the experience as a

The fans at the Meadowlands for the crunch match between Cosmos and arch rivals Tampa Bay Rowdies are able to see an action replay of the goal which gives Cosmos the lead on a massive television screen. This American spectator refinement was taken to its logical conclusion in the Seattle King Dome, an indoor stadium where the Sounders played. Sitting on the main side of the pitch it was possible to watch the game and a simultaneous live televised version. A massive screen hung from the ceiling, on which the players could even watch themselves.

paid holiday—led to a lack of consistency around the League. The 1974 season saw yet another new team head the NASL. Los Angeles Aztecs were one of eight new clubs in the League which, with the loss of Atlanta and Montreal, raised the numbers to 15, split for the first time since 1968 into four divisions.

At this time the Aztecs had still to be taken over by Elton John and the arrival of George Best was two seasons away; their humble stadium was at East Los Angeles College. Yet they topped the Western Division, and in the final at Miami they beat the home side 4-3 in a tie-breaker. The match was televised—the first NASL game to be on national television since 1968—and it marked the end of a successful season.

The coming of Pelé

The NASL began 1975 with the first Indoor Championship, another small indication that soccer was at last beginning to make a worthwhile impact. Yet though the League was making steady progress, allied to considerable development at schools and youth level, that progress was still not quick enough to ensure that those who had invested money in the sport would keep it there. Around the world the prevailing view of the NASL was still one of a rest-home for ageing pros, looking for a last meal-ticket. One swooping, sensational stroke of business was to change that.

Toye and Woosnam had courted Pelé since 1971. The great Brazilian declined, preferring to spend his retirement in Santos with his family. Three years later he took the field, supposedly for the last time, but his genuine intentions were heavily compromized by a disastrous business deal. To ensure his family's future he had to play again and, in both financial and footballing terms, the offer from New York held the most attractions. For $4.5 million the man who had scored a thousand goals put his signature on a three-year contract with the Cosmos.

The money, a colossal amount for any league in the world, let alone one that walked an economic tightrope, brought an immediate return. Soccer had always struggled for space at the bottom of the sports section; now it was front page news. Pelé, the one name that transcended the ignorance of the game in the United States, had come to town. And alongside internal recognition from the NASL came worldwide respect. If Pelé was to play in America no other player could scoff at a similar opportunity. If the NASL was built on any one particular day, it was 11 June 1975.

At 34 the Brazilian was no spent force on the field. In 56 regular-season games over his three seasons he would score 31 goals—as well as embroidering most performances with touches of authentic world-class play. That in itself would have justified the outlay on his services. But even more significantly he became the game's perfect ambassador. Well-schooled from his many years of non-stop publicity all over the world, he performed to marvellous effect off the field. His endearing, stumbling English, with the accompaniment of the ever-present smile, mastered coaching clinic, press conference and every conceivable public engagement that the marketing men could create for him. And wherever he played gate records tumbled.

Yet even Pelé's mid-season arrival could not help New York into the play-offs in 1975. Eddie Firmani's Tampa Bay Rowdies, another franchise in its first season, beat Portland Timbers in the first Soccer Bowl final, staged in San Jose, which had become the most enthusiastic soccer outpost in California with average crowds for the local Earthquakes in excess of 17,000. Pelé's presence set a new individual League record when 35,620 crammed inside RFK Stadium in Washington for the visit of the Cosmos.

In 1976 the NASL attracted other 'star' names in the wake of Pelé. Bobby Moore signed for San Antonio Thunder, yet another new club in a League now 20-strong; George Best declared a new contentment after his move to the Aztecs; Rodney Marsh's flamboyant style fitted easily into a new career with Tampa; and Giorgio Chinaglia defected from Lazio to line up alongside Pelé in a Cosmos shirt, and eventually become a United States citizen.

But the biggest star on the horizon came from Canada, via Mozambique and Lisbon. The 34-year old Eusebio had played half a dozen games for Boston the previous season, but in 1976 he appeared regularly for Toronto whose club title, Metros–Croatia, indicated their strong Slavic core. After coming through three rounds of play-offs, Toronto were very much the underdogs

NASL ROOKIE OF THE YEAR

Year	Player
1967	†Willie Roy *Chicago Spurs)*
1968	Kaizer Motaung *(Atlanta Chiefs)**
1969	Siggy Stritzl *(Baltimore Bays)*
1970	Jim Leeker *(St Louis Stars)*
1971	Randy Horton *(New York Cosmos)*
1972	Mike Winter *(St Louis Stars)*
1973	Kyle Rote Jr *(Dallas Tornado)*
1974	Doug McMillan *(Los Angeles Aztecs)**
1975	Chris Bahr *(Philadelphia Atoms)*
1976	Steve Pecher *(Dallas Tornado)*
1977	Jim McAlister *(Seattle Sounders)*
1978	Gary Etherington *(New York Cosmos)**
1979	Larry Hulcer *(Los Angeles Aztecs)*
1980	Jeff Durgan *(New York Cosmos)**
1981	Joe Morrone *(Tulsa Roughnecks)*
1982	Pedro DeBrito *(Tampa Bay Rowdies)*
1983	Gregg Thompson *(Tampa Bay Rowdies)*

*NASL Championship winners †NPSL

against Freddie Goodwin's Minnesota Kicks in the 1976 Soccer Bowl. But Eusebio added to his list of honours by inspiring a 3-0 win in the Seattle final.

At the end of the 1977 season optimism had reached its highest point thus far in the NASL. Attendances escalated to more than 3½ million, with average gates at 13,555. At the splendid new Giants Stadium in New Jersey, Cosmos attracted 77,691 converts to their divisional play-off tie against Fort Lauderdale Strikers. Plans to expand the League to 24 were announced. And Pelé took his tearful leave from the enthusiasm he had done so much to stimulate as a champion, playing a half for each side in his farewell friendly against his old club, Santos, in front of 70,000.

In the previous Bicentennial summer Pelé had even become an 'American', representing a hybrid Team America, along with Moore, Chinaglia, Tommy Smith and Mike England, in a four-cornered tournament with England, Brazil and Italy. In the face of his retirement Cosmos imported Franz Beckenbauer to wear his mantle. It was another boost for the NASL: at 32 the supremely elegant West German opted for New York instead of leading his country in its defence of the World Cup in Argentina.

Pelé's sense of style remained to the last, his final competitive game being the 1977 Soccer Bowl against Seattle. Yet as though another generation was announcing its willingness to take over, 21-year-old Steve Hunt, transported from the obscurity of Aston Villa's reserves, produced the killing moments. First he pilfered the ball from Sounders goalkeeper Chursky to give Cosmos the lead; then his cross was headed in by Chinaglia for the winner.

Cosmos money buys international stars—and the Soccer Bowl

Consolidating the gains

By now Cosmos was owned by the giant Warner Communications group whose massive financial resources enabled them to compete for any player in the world. Dennis Tueart, then a current England international forward, and in his prime at 28, was successfully wooed to New York. Later Johan Neeskens would reject more meaningful offers from European clubs to accept lucrative terms from the Cosmos. Security meant more than ambition.

In 1978 their spending again paid dividends when Cosmos retained their title, beating Tampa 3-1 in Giants Stadium with Tueart scoring twice. Yet in any other country in the world they would have lost their two-legged semi-final. In Minnesota in the first leg Cosmos crashed to a 9-2 defeat but under NASL rules they needed only to win the second leg to send the tie into an extra time decider. A 4-0 win only reduced the deficit to 9-6 but in extra time Cosmos won on a shoot-out to go into the final.

Though other large consortia like the Lipton Tea Company, owners of the New England Teamen, put their money into the NASL, many franchises lacked such backing. Thus in some ways it was good for the League's democracy that Cosmos did not pay their way to automatic success in 1979. They failed, however, in controversial circumstances. In the first leg of their semi-final in Vancouver, the Iran World Cup full-back Eskandarian and Carlos Alberto, captain of Brazil in the 1970 World Cup, were both

Every gimmick and form of entertainment imaginable have been used to help soccer in its fight to capture the loyalty of the American sporting public—with limited success. The cheerleaders, mascots (middle left, Washington Diplomats' 'bear', left, Warner-backed Cosmos' Bugs Bunny), and complex electronic scoreboards with instant replays are only a fraction of the huge promotional apparatus involved. For the crowds—largely American-born, middle-class and attending as a family—it is what they would expect; but its intensity usually surprises even the most visionary of visitors from other parts of the world.

sent off. Cosmos protested to the League but both players were suspended from the second leg, which saw New York's elimination.

The Whitecaps had to return to New York for Soccer Bowl '79, but in the face of great hostility from Cosmos' fans they showed their resilience to beat Tampa 2-1, both goals coming from Trevor Whymark. Even the ultimate moment of triumph, the presentation of the trophy, was marred by the continual booing of the New York fans directed at Woosnam, now the League's Commissioner and representative of the decision to uphold the suspensions.

Vancouver's success confirmed the continuing British influence in the League, even though its overlapping season still caused problems in shipping Football League players to and fro across the Atlantic; even though, too, players from other European countries, notably Holland and Yugoslavia, were available at cheaper prices in less complex deals. Tony Waiters, once an England goalkeeper, masterminded the Whitecaps' triumph with a side that included nine Britons—Whymark, Alan Ball, Kevin Hector, Willie Johnston, Roger Kenyon, John Craven, Ray Lewington, Phil Parkes (from Wolves) and Carl Valentine. Another, Canadian Bob Lenarduzzi, also played in the Football League with Reading.

It was a result that yet again questioned the Americanization of the League. In October 1977 it had been agreed that in 1980 each team must have three non-North Americans on the field at all times, rising to four in 1982 and five in 1984. At the same time the number of foreigners on the 30-man club rosters must decrease to 13 in 1980, 12 in 1982 and 11 in 1984. Yet the use of Canadians and the citizency switches like that by Chinaglia still combined to restrict the opportunity of United States products.

In 1979 the Cosmos roster read like a gathering of the United Nations: Yasin from Turkey; Eskandarian—Iran; Marinho and

The second-class status of the American player in the NASL

Carlos Alberto—Brazil; Beckenbauer and Birkenmeier—West Germany; Bogicevic—Yugoslavia; Seninho—Angola; Neeskens and Rijsbergen—Holland; Carbognani—Argentina; Razak—Ghana; Tueart and Ingram—England. Not much scope for home-grown talent with only the promising Rick Davis a regular in the starting line-up, with Chinaglia counting as the second American. Some other teams are just as dominated by foreigners.

Curtis Leeper's experience in 1979 epitomized the frustrations facing the young, low-paid American footballer. Leeper was the first youngster from Miami's youth programme to obtain a contract with Fort Lauderdale Strikers. In his first two seasons he played in total a dozen games. By mid-season in 1979 he had added only another six appearances, four of which were as a substitute, yet he was chosen to captain the United States team in the Pan-American Games and for the qualifying rounds for the Olympic Games.

Beset by injuries, Strikers' English coach Ron Newman pulled Leeper out of the national squad back to Fort Lauderdale. Even then Leeper was only used as a substitute. The 23-year old utility player complained so bitterly that he was sold to the Philadelphia Fury. 'If you're an American in Fort Lauderdale you don't have a chance,' he explained. 'They give you no confidence. There's no training. I was captain of the Pan-Am team and I had an obligation to be there. What a big deal, to call me back and

NASL LEADING GOALKEEPER

Year	Player	Min.	SV	G	SH	GAA
1967	†Mirko Stojanovic *(Oakland Clippers)*	‡29	§	29	10	1.00
1968	Ataulfo Sanchez *(San Diego Toros)*	‡22	130	19	§	0.93
1969	Manfred Kammerer *(Atlanta Chiefs)*	‡14	56	15	4	1.07
1970	Lincoln Phillips *(Washington Darts)*	‡22	96	21	12	0.95
1971	Mirko Stojanovic *(Dallas Tornado)**	1359	91	11	8	0.79
1972	Ken Cooper *(Dallas Tornado)*	1260	107	12	6	0.86
1973	Bob Rigby *(Philadelphia Atoms)**	1157	78	8	6	0.62
1974	Barry Watling *(Seattle Sounders)*	1800	132	16	8	0.80
1975	Shep Messing *(Boston Minutemen)*	1639	140	17	6	0.93
1976	Tony Chursky *(Seattle Sounders)*	1981	135	20	9	0.91
1977	Ken Cooper *(Dallas Tornado)*	2100	120	21	8	0.90
1978	Phil Parkes *(Vancouver Whitecaps)*	2650	133	28	10	0.95
1979	Phil Parkes *(Vancouver Whitecaps)**	2704	99	29	7	0.96
1980	Jack Brand *(Seattle Sounders)*	2975	170	30	15	0.91
1981	Arnie Mausser *(Jacksonville Tea Men)*	2906	177	39	3	1.21
1982	Tino Lettieri *(Vancouver Whitecaps)*	2506	130	34	4	1.23
1983	Tino Lettieri *(Vancouver Whitecaps)*	2594	159	28	11	0.84

*NASL Championship winners †NPSL ‡play assessed by games until 1971
Min. – minutes played; SV – saves; G – goals conceded; SH – shutouts;
GAA – goals against average §records not available

Nowhere is the American passion for statistics more in evidence in soccer than in goalkeeping. It is also an area where the United States seems most likely to produce a high standard in large numbers, possibly because handling skills are an integral part of their three major sports. For a comparison, Ray Clemence's League record for Liverpool in 1978-79 would have an average of 0.38, with 28 shut-outs.

just use me as a reserve.' They were similar sentiments to those put in print by the US national team goalkeeper Shep Messing, who has continually referred disparagingly to the British 'mafia' in the NASL.

The professional coaches would counter-argue that American players, with the exception of goalkeepers like Messing, Alan Mayer and Arnie Mausser, have not yet reached sufficient standards to merit regular inclusion. Coaches have to protect their own interests in the hire-and-fire environment of the NASL. Winning is paramount and the experience of Eddie Firmani, fired from the Cosmos after his title wins in 1977 and 1978, and after winning nine of his first 11 games in 1979, was a reminder that it pays to think only in the short-term. Moreover, as the standard of foreign imports has increased it has highlighted the rawness of the American players.

Johan Cruyff, like Pelé prised from 'retirement', became the latest jewel in the NASL crown in 1979, immediately forcing up the attendances and the level of performance at the previously recalcitrant Aztecs before moving across country to Washington for 1980. By then football had taken a much firmer grip on its American audience because of intense, well-directed marketing, and because the standard of play has greatly improved. It remains, however, still something of a foreign circus.

A different ball-game . . .

The history of American sports reveals a willingness to tinker with the rules and structure to fine down the product for the local market. Their treatment of soccer has been no exception. Watching a match in the United States reveals significant differences both on and off the field from Europe.

The constant visits of executives from professional clubs around the world confirms that the off-the-field expertise in the NASL has much to offer the game's more senior organizations. Soccer in the United States is, of course, a summer sport, and the contentment of a shirt-sleeved crowd in all-seater stadia has been a basis behind similar schools of thought in Britain.

'That's Entertainment' approach to keep the family fans happy

There is far less hooliganism in the NASL, partly because it's a family affair and partly because distances between teams preclude travel by visiting supporters. But it would be wrong to presume a total absence of violence; in a 1979 visit to Tampa this writer saw a middle-aged woman start a small affray and it took three muscular policemen to escort her from the ground. Nevertheless soccer in the States is middle-class family entertainment with the much-pictured 'tailgate', picnic parties before the games, and post-match revelries in which the fans are encouraged to mingle with the players.

The good weather enables the club to stage various entertainments around the matches. Youth games are a regular feature —between teams of girls as well as boys— while circus acts and firework displays typify the desire to hold the spectators' attention during the intervals. Match preliminaries take longer with each player, including the substitutes, introduced individually and if the usual running commentary over the speakers is an irritant to a foreign spectator it is a helpful guide to the majority, who are often learning about the game from scratch. The 40-yard headed clearance is still likely to bring a more admiring cheer than a subtle touch in midfield.

But it is on the field that the game differs most drastically from that which is known to the rest of the world, and two basic differences stem from the fact that the NASL clubs have had to use stadia which are not designed for soccer. In 1978 that meant that almost half the League games were played on synthetic surfaces, including the Soccer Bowl, when the players' first gesture, at the final whistle, in triumph or defeat was to rip off their boots to relieve their aching feet. Astroturf's all-weather properties are hardly required for a summer season, and though it provides a true surface it is unpopular with the players. Whatever the pros and cons it is an anomaly that half the clubs should play on grass and the others on a type of carpet.

The dimension of many of the stadia has influenced the second significant difference. The grid-iron pitch is some 10 yards narrower than the average soccer field; this had the effect of reducing width that could be used in attack, spoiling elements of the game's spectacle. Gordon Jago, wanting to play a 4-2-4 formation with Tampa in 1979, found that the width of his Tampa Stadium (68 yards) did not give his four forwards enough room. The width at the Rose Bowl, the hallowed grid-iron stadium used by Los Angeles, is a mere 63 yards, with the length much the same as for soccer.

The introduction of the 35-yard offside line was partly influenced by this particular problem. Now in the NASL an attacker cannot be offside unless he is within 35 yards of his opponents' goal. The effect of the rule is to open the game up in midfield and it is claimed that it produces more goals: in 1978 the NASL averaged just under four per

What is this stuff, man? Sporting the new title of Blizzard, Toronto's first home game of the 1979 season was played in a snowstorm. Their Brazilian midfield player Ivair Ferreira, in his fifth season with the club, and Fort Lauderdale Strikers' Colin Fowles, Jamaica-born but now a US citizen, just can't believe it. Two weeks later just 653 fans braved rising waters to see New England Tea Men take on Houston Hurricane in flood conditions. It's all a far cry from the norm in American soccer, where matches are usually played in very warm conditions, and often inside. More than half the NASL venues boast artificial grass, which requires studless footwear—and virtually rules out the sliding tackle beloved by so many British fans.

LEFT: ***A Dutchman, a Yugoslav, a Brazilian and two Englishmen line up in a Cosmos wall. Despite the laws increasing the ratio of American-born players in a side each year, foreign imports still dominate. The list of leading scorers (below left) comprises players from England, Poland, Greece, Italy, Czechoslovakia, South Africa, Argentina, Brazil, Trinidad, Bermuda and just one native American—Kyle Rote Jr.***

BELOW: ***The impact of Italian international Giorgio Chinaglia from Lazio in 1976 was stunning, and despite missing a month of the season he finished top NASL scorer. The former Swansea player repeated the feat with a record haul in 1978, was fourth in 1977 and second to Tampa's Argentinian find Oscar Fabbiani in 1979. He won the title again in 1980, 1981 and 1982 before returning to Roma and Lazio.***

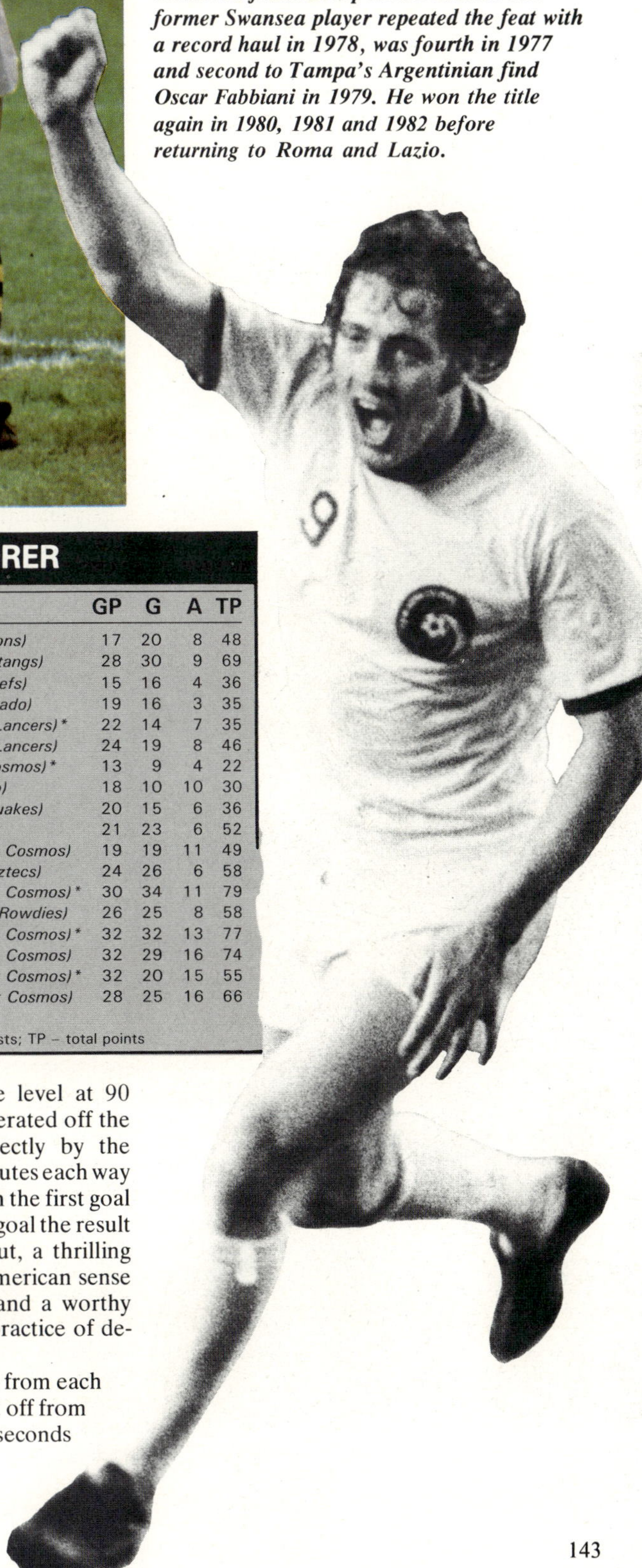

game. But other factors are surely involved, like the concentration by each club on acquiring top-level strikers rather than less marketable solid defenders.

What the new offside law does mean is that soccer in the NASL is a different game. Forwards are protected by the rule to the extent that they can 'goal hang' around the 35-yard line with impunity from the lines-

You'll always get a result with the NASL system

man's flag. Consequently, defenders stay back to mark them, often with the insurance of a genuine sweeper. The area between the two 35-yard lines is left for midfield players to patrol without the congestion seen there so much in British football, where both sets of defenders can push up towards the halfway line.

The result is much more room for manoeuvre for midfield players when they are on the ball, but much less opportunity for them to make a telling tackle when they are not in possession. The end product is akin to basketball, with the defending team conceding ground until they are grouped around their own 35-yard line. If they then win possession they will find relatively little resistance until they have worked the ball up to the other offside line.

The other main difference is that soccer has been tailored to suit the American desire for a definite result; draws were stricken from the rules at the end of the 1974 season.

NASL LEADING SCORER

Year	Player	GP	G	A	TP
1967	†Yanko Daucik *(Toronto Falcons)*	17	20	8	48
1968	John Kowalik *(Chicago Mustangs)*	28	30	9	69
1969	Kaizer Motaung *(Atlanta Chiefs)*	15	16	4	36
1970	Kirk Apostolidis *(Dallas Tornado)*	19	16	3	35
	Carlos Metidieri *(Rochester Lancers)**	22	14	7	35
1971	Carlos Metidieri *(Rochester Lancers)*	24	19	8	46
1972	Randy Horton *(New York Cosmos)**	13	9	4	22
1973	Kyle Rote Jr *(Dallas Tornado)*	18	10	10	30
1974	Paul Child *(San Jose Earthquakes)*	20	15	6	36
1975	Steve David *(Miami Toros)*	21	23	6	52
1976	Giorgio Chinaglia *(New York Cosmos)*	19	19	11	49
1977	Steve David *(Los Angeles Aztecs)*	24	26	6	58
1978	Giorgio Chinaglia *(New York Cosmos)**	30	34	11	79
1979	Oscar Fabbiani *(Tampa Bay Rowdies)*	26	25	8	58
1980	Giorgio Chinaglia *(New York Cosmos)**	32	32	13	77
1981	Giorgio Chinaglia *(New York Cosmos)*	32	29	16	74
1982	Giorgio Chinaglia *(New York Cosmos)**	32	20	15	55
1983	Roberto Cabanas *(New York Cosmos)*	28	25	16	66

*NASL Championship winners †NPSL
GP – games played; G – goals; A – assists; TP – total points

Instead, if the two teams are level at 90 minutes—timed by a clock operated off the field and not controlled directly by the referee—the teams play 7½ minutes each way of sudden-death overtime, with the first goal ending the game. If there is no goal the result is determined by the shoot-out, a thrilling invention conceived by the American sense of tension and razzamatazz, and a worthy successor to the more sober practice of decision by penalties.

In the shoot-out five players from each side, taking alternate turns, set off from the 35-yard line, and have five seconds before they must shoot. It is surely, also, a greater test of skill than taking penalties.

Edmonton Drillers
Vancouver Whitecaps
Seattle Sounders
Portland Timbers
Minnesota Kicks
San Jose Earthquakes
California Surf
Los Angeles Aztecs
San Diego Sockers
Tulsa Roughnecks
Dallas Tornado
Houston Hurricane

THE NAME GAME

The NASL is modelled on the same pattern as other major league sports in North America, and particularly on the very successful National Football League. The member clubs are franchise operations licensed by the League. Franchises can change name, stadium and—with the agreement of other members of the League—city and ownership. Thus the Edmonton Drillers entered the League in 1979 through the efforts of Peter Pocklington, who bought a controlling share in the Oakland Stompers and relocated them.

Of the NASL's 17 founder members of 1968, only the Dallas Tornado survived under their original name through to 1980 and by 1984 none of the original sides remained in existence. In that year the very existence of soccer as a professional sport was understandably being questioned and only nine sides began the season—the New York Cosmos, the Tampa Bay Rowdies (traditionally the two most durable and best supported sides), the Toronto Blizzard, the Chicago Sting, the San Diego Sockers, Golden Bay Earthquakes, NASL Champions Tulsa Roughnecks, the Vancouver Whitecaps and the Minnesota Strikers, newly transported from the sun of Fort Lauderdale. The map on the left shows the League at its height, with the 24 sides which competed in both 1979 and 1980. Those were the years of optimism when the ABC Television network regularly screened games on Sundays and there were far more bidders for franchises than there were places in the set-up. In retrospect, the League expanded too fast and allowed in too many owners who liked the idea of owning a major sporting team but knew nothing about soccer.

The League has always been run on a strange (to European eyes) combination of league and knock-out. Teams are grouped into artificial geographical sets, the winners of each going into a series of play-offs with the best performing losers. Eventually two sides meet in the equivalent of a combined Cup final and Championship play-off, the Soccer Bowl.

SOCCER IN AUSTRALIA

Australian soccer celebrated its centenary in 1980 with a series of matches against major national teams. Throughout its history the game down under has had to take a back seat to no less than three other footballing codes: Rugby League, Rugby Union and Australian Rules. But there are signs that soccer is on the up . . .

The highlight of 100 years of Australian soccer came with the 1974 World Cup finals in West Germany, for which the national team—known as the 'Socceroos'—qualified for the first time.

Not that Australia achieved anything dramatic in West Germany. Although they gained a draw with Chile, they failed to score a goal in any of their three games.

Nevertheless, qualification was a major achievement. After winning their preliminary group, the Socceroos qualified for the finals by winning a tournament in Hong Kong. The final victory, over a skilful South Korea, made a hero out of midfielder Jim Mackay, the former Scots junior whose shot from 25 yards proved to be the winning goal. His boot was plated with gold and now goes on annual display, like some holy relic.

After the disappointments of the two previous World Cups this at least was a sign of some progress. After the heavy defeats at the hands of North Korea in the 1966 qualifying games, some steps were taken to effect much-needed reforms. The game remained divided: nationally, by inter-state bickering, and locally, by feuding ethnic groups.

But Yugoslav coaches Frank Arok and Rale Rasic did pioneering work in Sydney, traditionally the stronghold of soccer in Australia. Both men had spells in charge of St George-Budapest, the club that was to provide most of the Socceroos' defence in the 1974 World Cup—including the aboriginal Harry Williams. George Yardley, who made his name in Australia before becoming a prolific goalscorer in the lower divisions of the Football League, was a member of Arok's side, as was Johnny Warren, a busy, inventive midfielder whose career as the key player in the

World Cup groups —from Rhodesia to Tel Aviv

Australian national team was slowed by a bad injury before the 1974 World Cup.

Then, in 1969, South Coast United, from Woonoma, 50 miles south of Sydney, won the New South Wales State championship, breaking the hegemony of the ethnic-based Sydney clubs—APIA, Hakoah and St George. Adrian Alston and Peter Wilson, key figures in the 1974 Socceroos, were members of that side.

But 1969 also put an end to Australian hopes of qualifying for the World Cup in Mexico. After a series of matches in which they were required to cross Asia several times, the national team were sent to Africa to play the politically embarrassing Rhodesians. After three hard games—the last in Mozambique—the Australians advanced to play Israel in the decider. The journey from Lourenço Marques to Tel Aviv—via Angola, Lisbon, Rome and Athens—took a further 38 exhausting hours and the team succumbed to a deflected Israeli goal.

Finally the Australian Soccer Federation was persuaded to effect the most urgently needed

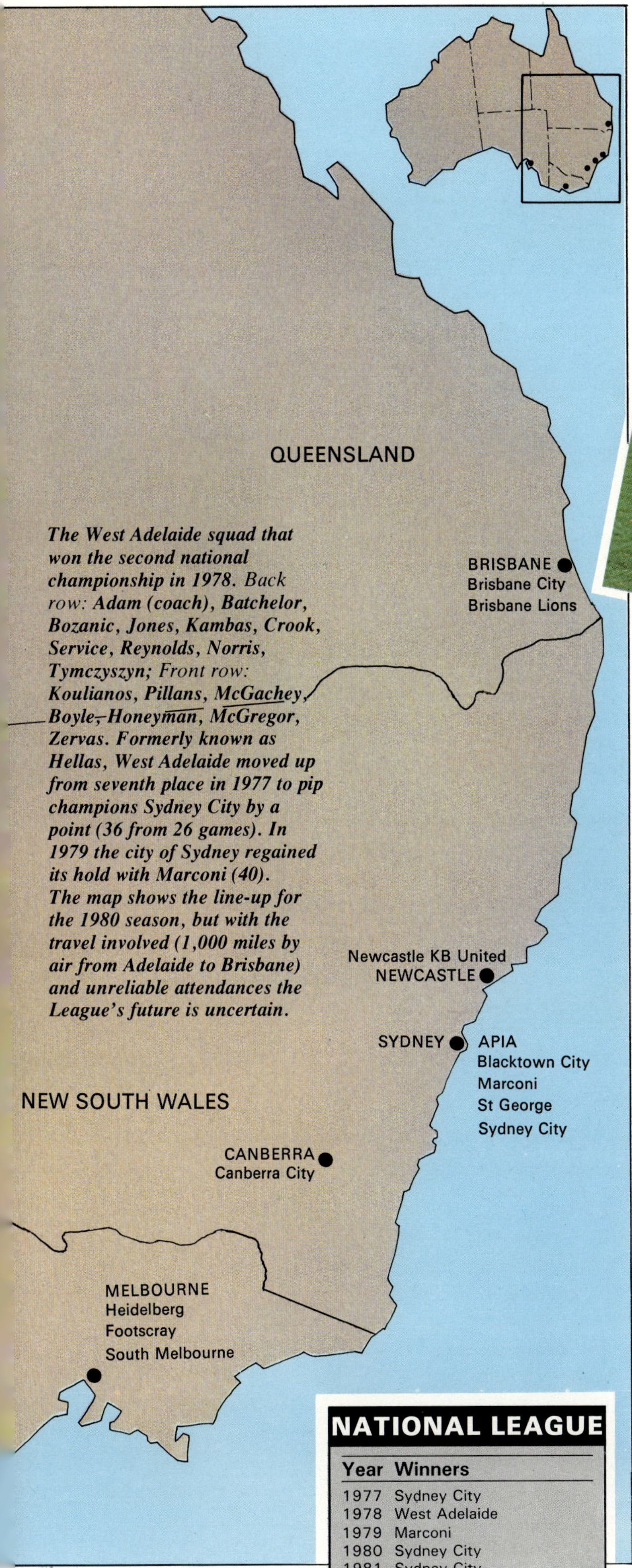

The West Adelaide squad that won the second national championship in 1978. *Back row:* ***Adam (coach), Batchelor, Bozanic, Jones, Kambas, Crook, Service, Reynolds, Norris, Tymczyszyn;*** *Front row:* ***Koulianos, Pillans, McGachey, Boyle, Honeyman, McGregor, Zervas. Formerly known as Hellas, West Adelaide moved up from seventh place in 1977 to pip champions Sydney City by a point (36 from 26 games). In 1979 the city of Sydney regained its hold with Marconi (40). The map shows the line-up for the 1980 season, but with the travel involved (1,000 miles by air from Adelaide to Brisbane) and unreliable attendances the League's future is uncertain.***

NATIONAL LEAGUE

Year	Winners
1977	Sydney City
1978	West Adelaide
1979	Marconi
1980	Sydney City
1981	Sydney City
1982	Sydney City
1983	Sydney St George

South Melbourne keeper Peter Laumets saves from 'Dixie' Deans of Adelaide City in a 1979 Philips League game.

reform. For the qualifying games of the 1974 World Cup they appointed a national team coach—Rale Rasic, a Yugoslav with an FA coaching badge.

Rasic's early games did not promise much. With a team that had apparently been picked as much for its strength and stamina as for its technique, Australia laboured through a preliminary tournament against a frail Indonesia, a poor New Zealand and an Iraqi team playing its first ever games on grass. Only in the last match—with Attila Abonyi, a Hungarian-born winger who had been the object of some interest from Manchester United, playing his first full game of the tournament—did they look at all convincing. Abonyi scored twice, and they beat Indonesia 6-0.

Australia go to the World Cup while the Pommies stay at home

Abonyi scored again in the next match—an encouraging 3-0 win over Iran in Sydney—but the second leg proved an uncomfortable experience. In front of 75,000 fans in Tehran, Australia were soon 2-0 down to a doubtful penalty and a superb 25-yard drive from Parviz 'Sultan' Gheleechkhani. But Rasic switched the team around at half-time and they hung on for a narrow aggregate victory.

The sole remaining barrier to qualification was South Korea. At this late stage the Australians' nerve faltered. The home leg in Sydney attracted unprecedented interest and a 32,000 crowd. Australia should have lost to a Korean side that dominated the game but failed to take its chances.

In Seoul, though, the South Koreans were less diffident, punishing Australian defensive errors to go 2-0 up within half-an-hour. It should have been all over, but Branko Buljevic, with an excellent header, and Ray Baartz, who was to be seriously injured by a Uruguayan karate chop in a pre-World Cup 'friendly', brought Australia level again and took the series to a third game in Hong Kong.

This time the Socceroos, looking impressive against a Korean side apparently still suffering the after-effects of the game in Seoul three days earlier, made no mistake. Mackay's goal was the only one of the match and it arrived in the 70th minute, or just after half past midnight for those who had stayed up to watch the live television broadcast back home.

Australia were going to the World Cup finals, England were not. For a brief while at least, soccer held the centre of the Australian sporting arena.

Despite his achievements, Rasic was dismissed after the World Cup—a decision that apparently caused him little or no dismay. In his place the ASF astonishingly engaged a man whose previous job had been as a coach with Fourth Division Chester. Brian Green's first recorded announcement on arrival in Australia was 'I'm a winner'. He fairly promptly disappeared into oblivion when he was dismissed after committing a minor police offence.

England can only manage two draws and a doubtful win on tour

Late in 1976 another Englishman was appointed: the 28-year-old Jimmy Shoulder, who, strangely enough, had never coached a senior team. Shoulder lasted until Australia were eliminated from the 1978 World Cup; home defeats against Iran and Kuwait—Australia's first ever in World Cup play—were particularly damaging.

The ASF at last appointed someone whose reputation matched their ambition. Rudi Gutendorf had already gained experience as a national team manager (with Chile, among others) and as a club coach in his native West Germany and elsewhere (Australia was his 18th job and his fourth continent). Gutendorf was introduced to Australians as 'the man who signed Kevin Keegan' for Hamburg, where he had been team coach until the shake-up that brought in Gunter Netzer and Branko Zebec.

Gutendorf, as he admits, is no diplomat. He has been named 'rude Rudi' by his critics. Already there are said to be several officials who would like to see him out of his £30,000-a-year job. But other factors are apparently working in his favour.

Past Australian teams have had to rely heavily on imports—European immigrants who failed to make the grade in their own countries. Peter Wilson, team captain and holder of a record number of Australian caps, had a brief and undistinguished career with Middlesbrough. Jim Mackay, the hero of Hong Kong, was a Scot. Even Adrian Alston, who made a respectable career for himself in the Football League and the NASL after the 1974 World Cup, only came to Australia after being freed by Preston North End and playing semi-professionally with Fleetwood Town.

Although Australians have for some time played junior soccer in surprisingly high numbers, especially in and around Sydney, clubs have until recently lacked the will and often the resources to develop local talent. It was always easier to import ready-made players, largely from Britain, where footballers were plentiful, English-speaking and inexpensive. To take the most extreme examples: for the 1967 season the Sydney club Pan-Hellenic signed 16 British players; the Victorian State League at about that time featured only one native-born Australian.

Sponsorship triggers a soccer breakthrough 'down under'

The success of the 1974 Socceroos and the popularity of English television programmes such as 'Match of the Day' and 'The Big Match', which are shown throughout Australia, attracted sponsorship to the game. And sponsorship brought money, coaching schemes and a league that, for the first time, brought together Australia's leading clubs.

Up until 1977 the highest level Australian clubs could aspire to was the top division of their state league. Britain's summer pools coupons still give some idea of these leagues: a multitude of

Between them Adrian Alston (left) and Peter Wilson have won over 100 caps for Australia, national captain Wilson being his country's most experienced international. Alston once played for Luton Town and Cardiff City.

divisions, each consisting of about 12 teams.

The top leagues were the New South Wales (Sydney) and Victoria (Melbourne). Other semi-professional leagues are the Western Australia (Perth and Freemantle), South Australia (Adelaide), Queensland (Brisbane), Capital Territory (Canberra) and Northern New South Wales (Newcastle). The Tasmanian Leagues—North (Launceston) and South (Hobart)—were amateur. Thanks to sponsorship there is now a state league embracing clubs from both areas.

BELOW: Iran's Ali Parvin and Peter Wilson shake hands before the World Cup qualifier at Melbourne in 1977.
CENTRE: A good performance gave Iran a 1-0 win—later repeated in Tehran—and dashed Australia's hopes of a second finals appearance.

The clubs' names testify to their identification with immigrant communities. Every major ethnic group had its own clubs. Among the leading teams in the Victorian League, for instance, were South Melbourne Hellas (Greek), Croatia (Yugoslavian), Slavia (Yugoslavian), Hungaria (Hungarian), Juventus (Italian), Ringwood City (Dutch), George Cross (Maltese), Polonia (Polish), Hakoah (Jewish), Box Hill (British), Lions (Ukranian), and Fitzroy-Alexander (Greek).

The ethnic nature of these clubs might give comparatively humdrum local games a flavour of international rivalry, but it also had the less welcome effect of excluding non-immigrants from the game.

A far-sighted Sydney club—St George-Budapest—was the first to act on the implication that if soccer was ever to be anything other than a minority sport it would have to abandon its ethnic base. The club moved out into the suburbs, where it built a new club-house, began work on a modern stadium and dropped 'Budapest' from its name. It was always likely to be a difficult transition and so far the results have not been very encouraging.

At least now they are not alone. With backing from Philips, the giant Dutch electronics firm, a national league was set up in 1977. Ethnic names were to be abandoned.

Philips retained their sponsorship until, dissatisfied with the game's progress, they pulled out in October 1982. With a few exceptions, attendances are disappointing. Many of the 16 teams are based in Sydney and Melbourne—a proportion that is considered too high. The League's election and re-election procedure has been criticized.

The picture is not entirely gloomy. Philips provided a much-needed stimulus for a long-ailing game, especially in the smaller centres of Adelaide and Newcastle.

In Adelaide, Adelaide City (formerly Juventus) and West Adelaide (formerly Hellas) both cultivated reasonable crowds at their impressive facilities. West Adelaide won the PSL championship in 1978. Adelaide City, with former Scotland international centre forward Dixie Deans prominent, lifted the Philips Cup in 1979.

The Philips League: foundation or a five-year wonder?

Newcastle United, from the New South Wales town 100 miles north of Sydney, also produced a rise in attendance figures—18,376 attended their home game against Sydney Olympic in 1979.

An ambitious new club, founded in 1978, their most audacious move was to sign Bobby Charlton for a brief spell as a guest player.

The heart of the national league lies in Sydney but success has proved to be a costly afair. The Jewish-backed club, Sydney City (formerly Hakoah) won the first Philips title in 1977, and followed on with a hat-trick of triumphs 1980-82. Early in 1983, however, Sydney City folded after losses estimated at £200,000 per season. The national league championship stayed in the city with Sydney St. George carrying off the honours under the coaching skills of Yugoslavian-born Frank Arok.

In 1983 Arok took charge of the national team for a series of three internationals against Bobby Robson's England.

There had been some resentment in Australia three years earlier that England had sent out a less than full-strength squad for a long-awaited first full international arranged as part of the celebration of 100 years of Australian soccer.

For the then England supremo, Ron Greenwood, the timing of the fixture could hardly have been more awkward, only days before the start of the European Championship finals. Greenwood protected his first choice players from the travelling and England's 2-1 victory was more comfortable than the scoreline suggests. Glenn Hoddle and Paul Mariner contributed England's goals.

Northern Ireland played a more substantial part in the celebrations; a series of three internationals against Australia in Sydney, Melbourne and Adelaide ended in two Irish victories and a draw.

In 1983 Robson's England found the going tough against determined opposition on pitches that drastically reduced the gap in skill. Ron Greenwood helped in the Australian preparation and took on the role of television commentator for the three inernationals. Arok even scored a verbal point of two when he was caught 'spying' on an England training session that was supposed to be 'behind closed doors.'

The first international in Sydney ended goalless, a moral triumph for Arok's side even though England lacked their Liverpool and Manchester United contingent because of club tours. Three days later in Brisbane England scraped home 1-0 though television replays later confirmed that the ball had gone behind for a goal-kick before John Gregory of Queens Park Rangers turned it back for Luton's Paul Walsh to score.

The third match in Melbourne only added to Australia's delight. Their goal was put into his own net by Phil Neal and Trevor Francis did miss a penalty but a 1-1 draw at least gave the Aussie Rules and Rugby League followers a reminder that soccer could have a meaningful place in Australia's sporting calendar.

Peter Jackson, a 22-year-old central defender, performed heroically throughout the series. But his background—Yorkshire born with a couple of seasons of League football with Bradford City behind him—emphasised again that imported skills are still needed.

A look at the 1983 coaches in the National League confirmed that impression. Only one of the sixteen in charge of the top clubs

Craig Johnston —Australia's best known soccer export

was Australian born, Ken Kaiser at Newcastle United.

In 1981 Australia staged the World Youth Championship which West Germany won by beating Qatar in the final. The nature of such a competition—and the example of Liverpool's Craig Johnston (South Africa born but raised in Australia) gave young Australians soccer heroes and helped in the development at school level. Australia's youth team helped that growth by finishing third in the Joao Havelange tournament in Mexico in January 1983.

Clive Walker in the uniform of the Fort Lauderdale Strikers. The Florida team abandoned the sun and the sand in 1984 to find a new home in an indoor stadium in cold and windy Minneapolis-St Paul.

SOCCER IN NEW ZEALAND

While rugby still rules in New Zealand, soccer received a memorable boost when a place in the 1982 World Cup finals was clinched in dramatic style . . .

Until the World Cup campaign of 1982 the most satisfying result for New Zealand football had been a 1-0 win over Australia in 1979, the first ever in 25 years of competition between the two countries.

All that changed in a nine-month charge to a place in Spain which began with a 3-3 home draw with Australia and ended fifteen matches and 55,000 miles later with a play-off in Bangkok.

With two Englishmen, John Adshead and Kevin Fallon at the helm, New Zealand's progress included a 2-0 victory in Australia, a record 13-0 demolition of Fiji and a recovery of stupendous proportions after a last-minute goal by Kuwait seemed to have put them out.

New Zealand then needed to win by six goals away to Saudi Arabia to qualify! In an extraordinary match, in Riyadh they struck five before half-time—two from the teenage Wynton Rufer, two from Brian Turner once of Brentford, and another from Steve Wooddin, a former striker with Tranmere Rovers.

Incredibly New Zealand could not score again in the second half, but the story had a happy ending. Wooddin and Rufer contributed the two goals in the play-off which took their side into the finals for the first time at the expense of China.

A new national league shows the way

In Spain New Zealand did score twice against Scotland before losing as expected to all three games in a difficult group which also included Brazil and Russia. The adventure had been in getting there.

Unhappily Adshead lost his job in the aftermath in a dispute over money, and Allan Jones, well-known in the North-East of England for inspiring giant-killing acts by Blyth Spartans, took over the position.

The structure of soccer in New Zealand had improved in the sixties when League football became more formalised.

The first Southern League was also formed in 1968, consisting of five Christchurch clubs, four from Dunedin and Queen's Park of Invercargill.

Two years later the National League became a reality. It was formed by the top three clubs from the Northern League (Eastern Suburbs, Blockhouse Bay and Mount Wellington—all from Auckland), the top three clubs from the Central League (Stop Out and Western Suburbs of Wellington and Gisborne City), a newly-formed club from the south island (Christchurch United) and the winners of a play-off between the fourth-placed clubs of the Northern and Central Leagues (Hungaria, who were later renamed Wellington City). The three regional leagues became, in effect, a second division.

The National League expanded and attracted sponsorship from a multi-national tobacco company. By the end of the decade there were 12 clubs in the competition. Courier Rangers and Manurewa from Franklin, 25 miles south of Auckland, had gained admission. Nelson (Newmans United), Dunedin (Dunedin City) and Palmerston North (Manawatu United) each claimed a representative.

The Chatham Cup, New Zealand's long-established national knock-out competition, had also found a sponsor.

Wellington's Clem Winter looks on as John Ritchie outjumps John Coe at the Basin Reserve during Stoke City's tour of 1977. The visitors' 5-1 victory gives a fair indication of the soccer standards in New Zealand, where rugby union still reigns supreme.

A-Z OF EUROPE

No country is a stranger to football in the continent where the organized game was born and developed. This chapter looks at the fortunes and problems of UEFA's 34 member nations . . .

Albania

Participation by Albania in international football has been sporadic because of the country's political secrecy. In September 1979 Celtic chose to fulfil their European Cup tie with Partizan Tirana despite the restrictions placed by the Albanian authorities on who was allowed to travel in the Scottish party. Northern Ireland, 4-1 winners in Belfast, achieved a 1-1 draw in the return leg in the qualifying rounds for the 1966 World Cup, and remain the only home country to have played Albania at full international level in any competition.

Albania's most profitable years occurred immediately after the Second World War. In 1946 they hosted and won the Balkan Cup, and in the years that followed they achieved respectable victories over Rumania, Poland, Bulgaria and Czechoslovakia, before the change in Albania's political climate made them virtual exiles from world football.

The domestic game had been boosted by British occupation during the First World War, but it was not until 1932 that the governing body became affiliated to FIFA. The championship began two years earlier, and has been supported by a cup competition since 1938. The 1978-79 league contained 14 clubs and as usual was dominated by the Tirana teams—Partizan (Albania's first European Cup entry in 1962), Dynamo and 17 Nendori.

ALBANIA

Year	Champions	Cup winners
1930	SC Tirana	....
1931	SC Tirana	....
1932	SC Tirana	....
1933	Scanderbeu Korca	....
1934	SC Tirana	....
1935	*No competition*	....
1936	SC Tirana	....
1937-44	*No competition*	....
1945	Vlaznia	....
1946	Vlaznia	....
1947	Partizan Tirana	....
1948	Partizan Tirana	Partizan Tirana
1949	Partizan Tirana	Partizan Tirana
1950	Dynamo Tirana	Dynamo Tirana
1951	Dynamo Tirana	Dynamo Tirana
1952	Dynamo Tirana	Dynamo Tirana
1953	Dynamo Tirana	Dynamo Tirana
1954	Partizan Tirana	Dynamo Tirana
1955	Dynamo Tirana	*No competition*
1956	Dynamo Tirana	*No competition*
1957	Partizan Tirana	Partizan Tirana
1958	Partizan Tirana	Partizan Tirana
1959	Partizan Tirana	*No competition*
1960	Partizan Tirana	Dynamo Tirana
1961	Partizan Tirana	Partizan Tirana
1962	*No competition*	*No competition*
1963	Dynamo Tirana	17 Nendori Tirana
1964	Partizan Tirana	Partizan Tirana
1965	17 Nendori Tirana	Dynamo Tirana
1966	17 Nendori Tirana	Dynamo Tirana
1967	Dynamo Tirana	Vlaznia
1968	17 Nendori Tirana	Dynamo Tirana
1969	17 Nendori Tirana	17 Nendori Tirana
1970	17 Nendori Tirana	Partizan Tirana
1971	Partizan Tirana	Dynamo Tirana
1972	Vlaznia	Besa
1973	Dynamo Tirana	Partizan Tirana
1974	Vlaznia	Dynamo Tirana
1975	Dynamo Tirana	Labinota
1976	Dynamo Tirana	17 Nendori Tirana
1977	Dynamo Tirana	Nendori Tirana
1978	Dynamo Tirana	Dynamo Tirana
1979	Partizan Tirana	Vlaznia
1980	Dynamo Tirana	Partizan Tirana
1981	Partizan Tirana	Vlaznia
1982	17 Nendori Tirana	Dynamo Tirana
1983	Vlaznia	17 Nendori Tirana

Austria

Austria's failure to qualify for the finals of the 1980 European Championship came as one of the tournament's great surprises. Two years earlier a famous victory over West Germany in the World Cup finals in Argentina had revived memories of the days when Austria were formidable in world football.

In 1902, in Vienna, Austria beat Hungary in the first full international between two non-British nations. Three years later Austria joined FIFA, though they declined to enter the first World Cup in 1930. Fostered by Hugo Meisl and the coaching skills of Jimmy Hogan, Austria produced the Wunderteam in the 1930s. In 1932 they lost a memorable international at Stamford Bridge, 4-3, but four years later they beat England 2-1 in Vienna. In the interim Austria had reached the semi-final of the 1934 World Cup, with Matthias Sindelar a majestic figure in attack, but they went down to Italy.

In 1954 a new Austria, with Ernst Ocwirk, Ernst Happel and Gerd Hanappi in key roles, again made an impact on the World Cup. Austria's power in attack brought a 5-0 win over Czechoslovakia and a remarkable 7-5 success over Switzerland, before the aggression of Germany reversed the tide; Austria lost 6-1 in the semi-final, but recovered to beat Uruguay to win third place.

AUSTRIA

Year	Champions	Cup winners
1912	Rapid Vienna	....
1913	Rapid Vienna	....
1914	WAF	....
1915	WAC	....
1916	Rapid Vienna	....
1917	Rapid Vienna	....
1918	Florisdorfer AC	....
1919	Rapid Vienna	Rapid Vienna
1920	Rapid Vienna	Rapid Vienna
1921	Rapid Vienna	Amateure
1922	Wiener Sportklub	WAF
1923	Rapid Vienna	Sportklub
1924	Amateure	Amateure
1925	Hakoah Vienna	FK Austria
1926	FK Austria	FK Austria
1927	SK Admira	Rapid Vienna
1928	SK Admira	SK Admira
1929	Rapid Vienna	First Vienna
1930	Rapid Vienna	First Vienna
1931	First Vienna	WAC
1932	SK Admira	SK Admira
1933	First Vienna	FK Austria
1934	SK Admira	SK Admira
1935	Rapid Vienna	FK Austria
1936	SK Admira	FK Austria
1937	SK Admira	First Vienna
1938	Rapid Vienna	WAC
1939	SK Admira	....
1940	Rapid Vienna	....
1941	Rapid Vienna	....
1942	First Vienna	....
1943	First Vienna	....
1944	First Vienna	....
1945	*Not completed*	....
1946	Rapid Vienna	Rapid Vienna
1947	Wacker Vienna	Wacker Austria

Though Austria qualified again for the finals in 1958, it was 20 years before they reappeared on the world stage in Argentina.

Austria's club football has suffered from financial insecurity. The country continues to produce quality players but cannot pay them enough to stay in the Austrian League. Of the 1978 side Krankl, Kreuz and Jara were all lost to Austrian football for various periods. In 1974 the First Division was reduced to 10 clubs to form a super-league, a process of concentration already helped by regular amalgamation between clubs to make ends meet. But attendances continue to decline, and the regular departure of the best players to more lucrative work in West Germany and Holland restricts the appeal of even a super-league. FK Austria/WAC, who lost to Anderlecht in the Cup Winners Cup in 1978, remain the only Austrian club to reach a major European final.

Hans Krankl, Austria's World Cup star.

Year	Champions	Cup winners
1948	Rapid Vienna	FK Austria
1949	FK Austria	FK Austria
1950	FK Austria	....
1951	Rapid Vienna	....
1952	Rapid Vienna	....
1953	FK Austria	....
1954	Rapid Vienna	....
1955	FK Austria	....
1956	Rapid Vienna	....
1957	Rapid Vienna	....
1958	Wiener Sportklub	....
1959	Wiener Sportklub	Wiener Sportklub
1960	Rapid Vienna	FK Austria
1961	FK Austria	Rapid Vienna
1962	FK Austria	FK Austria
1963	FK Austria	FK Austria
1964	Rapid Vienna	SK Admira
1965	Linz ASK	Linz ASK
1966	Admira-Energie	Admira-Energie
1967	Rapid Vienna	FK Austria
1968	Rapid Vienna	Rapid Vienna
1969	FK Austria	Rapid Vienna
1970	FK Austria	Wacker Innsbruck
1971	Wacker Innsbruck	FK Austria
1972	T-S Innsbruck	Rapid Vienna
1973	T-S Innsbruck	T-S Innsbruck
1974	VOEST Linz	FK Austria
1975	T-S Innsbruck	T-S Innsbruck
1976	FK Austria/WAC	Rapid Vienna
1977	T-S Innsbruck	FK Austria/WAC
1978	FK Austria/WAC	T-S Innsbruck
1979	FK Austria/WAC	T-S Innsbruck
1980	FK Austria/WAC	FK Austria/WAC
1981	Austria Vienna	Graz AK
1982	Rapid Vienna	Austria Vienna
1983	Rapid Vienna	Rapid Vienna

Belgium

Two superb goals by François van der Elst gave Belgium a splendid end to the 1970s. Scored against Scotland at Hampden Park, they confirmed Belgium as qualifiers for the 1980 European Championship finals. In that successful side 35-year-old Wilfred van Moer organized the midfield just as skilfully as he had 10 years before when Belgium qualified for the 1970 World Cup finals in Mexico. A broken leg kept him out of the final stages of the 1972 European Championship, but Belgium still finished third.

Though Belgium's inability to overcome Holland in crucial internationals restricted the progress of the national team through much of the 1970s, Anderlecht, in particular, made a great impact at club level. With Van der Elst and Rob Rensenbrink in their attack, the Brussels side won the Cup Winners Cup in 1976 and 1978, and in 1983 beat Benfica to win the UEFA Cup. In 1970 another Belgian-Dutch strike force of Paul van Himst and Jan Mulder took Anderlecht to the Fairs Cup final, where they narrowly lost to Arsenal. Bruges, while gaining a hat-trick of Belgian league titles, came runners-up in the 1976 UEFA Cup and the 1978 European Cup, on both occasions to Liverpool.

Belgium, traditionally drawing their players from the Flemish rather than French-speaking population, developed football in the middle of the 19th century; the Belgian FA was founded in 1895. In 1920 the Olympic Games was staged in Antwerp and Belgium won the football gold medal when Czechoslovakia walked off in the final in protest after a player had been sent off. Belgium also enjoyed a period of success after the Second World War with Mermans and Coppens two formidable strikers. They reached the finals of the 1954 World Cup where they held England to a 4-4 draw after trailing 3-1.

BELGIUM

Year	Champions	Cup winners
1896	FC Liege	....
1897	RC Brussels	....
1898	FC Liege	....
1899	FC Liege	....
1900	RC Brussels	....
1901	RC Brussels	....
1902	RC Brussels	....
1903	RC Brussels	....
1904	Union St Gilloise	....
1905	Union St Gilloise	....
1906	Union St Gilloise	....
1907	Union St Gilloise	....
1908	RC Brussels	....
1909	Union St Gilloise	....
1910	Union St Gilloise	....
1911	CS Bruges	....
1912	Daring Brussels	RC Brussels
1913	Union St Gilloise	Union St Gilloise
1914	Daring Brussels	Union St Gilloise
1915-19	*No competition*	....
1920	FC Bruges	....
1921	Daring Brussels	....
1922	Beerschot	....
1923	Union St Gilloise	....
1924	Beerschot	....
1925	Beerschot	....
1926	Beerschot	....
1927	CS Bruges	CS Bruges
1928	Beerschot	....
1929	Antwerp	....
1930	CS Bruges	....
1931	Antwerp	....
1932	Lierse SK	....
1933	Union St Gilloise	....
1934	Union St Gilloise	....
1935	Union St Gilloise	....
1936	Daring Brussels	....
1937	Daring Brussels	....
1938	Beerschot	....
1939	Beerschot	....
1940	*No competition*	....
1941	*No competition*	....
1942	Lierse SK	....
1943	Malines	....
1944	Antwerp	....
1945	*No competition*	....
1946	Malines	....
1947	Anderlecht	....
1948	Malines	....
1949	Anderlecht	....
1950	Anderlecht	....
1951	Anderlecht	....
1952	FC Liege	....
1953	FC Liege	....
1954	Anderlecht	Standard Liege
1955	Anderlecht	Antwerp
1956	Anderlecht	Racing de Tournai
1957	Antwerp	....
1958	Standard Liege	....
1959	Anderlecht	....
1960	Lierske SK	....
1961	Standard Liege	....
1962	Anderlecht	....
1963	Standard Liege	....
1964	Anderlecht	La Gantoise
1965	Anderlecht	Anderlecht
1966	Anderlecht	Standard Liege
1967	Anderlecht	Standard Liege
1968	Anderlecht	FC Bruges
1969	Standard Liege	Lierse SK
1970	Standard Liege	FC Bruges
1971	Standard Liege	Beerschot
1972	Anderlecht	Anderlecht
1973	FC Bruges	Anderlecht
1974	Anderlecht	SV Waregem
1975	RWD Molenbeek	Anderlecht
1976	FC Bruges	Anderlecht
1977	FC Bruges	FC Bruges
1978	FC Bruges	Beveren-Waas
1979	Beveren-Waas	Beerschot
1980	FC Bruges	Waterschei
1981	Anderlecht	Standard Liege
1982	Standard Liege	Waterschei
1983	Standard Liege	Beveren-Waas

Flying action from Anderlecht's Paul van Himst, Belgium's most capped player.

BULGARIA

Year	Champions	Cup winners
1925	Vladislav Varna	....
1926	Vladislav Varna	....
1927	*No competition*	....
1928	Slavia Sofia	....
1929	Botev Plovdiv	....
1930	Slavia Sofia	....
1931	AS 23 Sofia	....
1932	Sokol Varna	....
1933	Levski Sofia	....
1934	Vladislav Varna	....
1935	SC Sofia	....
1936	Slavia Sofia	....
1937	Levski Sofia	....
1938	Tichka Varna	....
1939	Slavia Sofia	....
1940	ZSK Sofia	....
1941	Slavia Sofia	....
1942	Levski Sofia	....
1943	Slavia Sofia	....
1944	*No competition*	....
1945	Lokomotiv Sofia	....
1946	Levski Sofia	Levski Sofia
1947	Levski Sofia	Levski Sofia
1948	CDNA Sofia	Lokomotiv Sofia
1949	Levski Sofia	Levski Sofia
1950	Levski Sofia	Levski Sofia
1951	CDNA Sofia	CDNA Sofia
1952	CDNA Sofia	Slavia Sofia
1953	Levski Sofia	Lokomotiv Sofia
1954	CDNA Sofia	CDNA Sofia
1955	CDNA Sofia	CDNA Sofia
1956	CDNA Sofia	Levski Sofia
1957	CDNA Sofia	Levski Sofia
1958	CDNA Sofia	Spartak Plovdiv
1959	CDNA Sofia	Levski Sofia
1960	CDNA Sofia	CDNA Sofia
1961	CDNA Sofia	CDNA Sofia
1962	CDNA Sofia	Botev Plovdiv
1963	Botev Plovdiv	Slavia Sofia
1964	Lokomotiv Sofia	Slavia Sofia
1965	Levski Sofia	CSKA Sofia
1966	CSKA Sofia	Slavia Sofia
1967	Trakia Plovdiv	Levski Sofia
1968	Levski Sofia	Spartak Sofia
1969	CSKA Sofia	CSKA Sofia
1970	Levski-Spartak	Levski-Spartak
1971	CSKA Sofia	Levski-Spartak
1972	CSKA Sofia	CSKA Sofia
1973	CSKA Sofia	CSKA Sofia
1974	Levski-Spartak	CSKA Sofia
1975	CSKA Sofia	Slavia Sofia
1976	CSKA Sofia	Levski-Spartak
1977	Levski-Spartak	Levski-Spartak
1978	Lokomotiv Sofia	Marek Stanke
1979	Levski-Spartak	Levski-Spartak
1980	CSKA Sofia	Slavia Sofia
1981	CSKA Sofia	Trakia Plovdiv
1982	CSKA Sofia	Lokomotiv Sofia
1983	CSKA Sofia	Spartak Varna

Bulgaria

Three successes in the Balkan Cup represent the only trophies won by Bulgaria. Yet Bulgaria qualified for all World Cup final series between 1962 and 1974, and in CSKA Sofia the country has had one of the most regular qualifiers for the European Cup. Even in the Olympic Games, traditionally a happy hunting ground for Eastern European countries, Bulgaria has been able to do no better than finish third in 1956 and runners-up in 1968; even then the silver medal was tainted by three Bulgarians being sent off in the final against Hungary.

Bulgarian football has its roots in Turkey from where a group of students returning home spread the gospel of the game. In 1925 Bulgaria were admitted to FIFA and the first championship was completed. The first international resulted in a 6-0 defeat in Vienna against the already mighty Austrians, and in 1934 and 1938 Bulgaria were eliminated from the World Cup in the qualifying rounds.

In 1945, however, the Bulgarian FA fell under governmental control and eventually all players became employees of the state. The new regime heralded the growth of CSKA Sofia (formerly CDNA) the Army representative side, and Levski Sofia. In 1969 Levski merged with Spartak Sofia to become Levski-Spartak.

Bulgaria has produced a number of outstanding players, like Ivan Kolev, whose creative skills provided the fulcrum of the 1956 Olympic and the 1962 World Cup sides. Dimitar Yakimov of CSKA and Christo Bonev, an impressive midfield player in the 1974 side in Munich, both came from the same mould. But Bulgaria, sadly, never drew the full benefit from Georgi Asparoukhov, the superb striker who scored a marvellous solo goal at Wembley in 1968, but who was injured during both the 1966 and 1970 World Cup finals, and was tragically killed in a car crash in 1971.

Cyprus

On 14 February 1973 Cyprus shook off its mantle as one of the poorest of relations in international football to beat Northern Ireland in a World Cup qualifying match in Nicosia. The goalscorer, Antoniou, immediately became a hero on an island which follows the game with fanaticism.

In 1972-73 Omonia of Nicosia also scored a victory that lives in annals of Cypriot football when they overcame Waterford in the first round of the European Cup. More typical of the experience of the amateur sides from this small country—one which is regularly troubled by political unrest—came in the next round when Omonia lost 13-0 on aggregate to Bayern Munich.

Ten years earlier Apoel had suffered a similar experience in the Cup Winners Cup. In the first round they had produced a splendid 6-0 victory (6-1 on aggregate) over Gjoevik Lyn from Norway. That result was put into context in the next round when Apoel's visit to Sporting Lisbon resulted in a 16-1 defeat!

Cyprus football is controlled by the Greek community—until 1975 a Cypriot club competed in the Greek First Division—and traditionally the Greek League clubs cream off the best Cypriot players. Chetin Kaya, champions in 1951 and cup winners in 1952 and 1954, are the only Turkish-based club to have won honours in Cyprus. The occupation of part of the island by Turkey in 1974 resulted in a rival FA being established which was not recognized by FIFA. Consequently Anorthosis and Salamis, both First Division clubs, had to move their headquarters back into Greek-occupied territory to continue their existence. The Nicosia-based clubs have been the most successful in Cyprus, while the international side remains among the least successful in the world—their only point in the 1980 European Championship was a 1-1 draw with Rumania.

Czechoslovakia

England's elimination from the 1976 European Championships at the hands of Czechoslovakia, at the time an occasion for domestic soul-searching, was put into context when the Czechs went on to win the European title. The quality in their play overcame Holland in a bad-tempered semi-final; their temperament survived the loss of a two-goal lead, including a last-minute equalizer, to outmanoeuvre West Germany in the penalty competition that determined the outcome of the final. Panenka's icily-chipped winning kick typified their resilience.

Twice before Czechoslovakia had faltered on the brink of success—in the World Cup. In 1934 a goal from Puc gave them the lead in the final against Italy in Rome, but a freak equalizer and the passion of the home crowd finally deprived the Czechs of football's ultimate prize. In 1962 Josef Masopust struck the first blow again in the World Cup final in Chile, but disappointing goalkeeping from the usually excellent Schroif allowed Brazil to retain the Jules Rimet Trophy.

The nation made its early marks on international football as Bohemia. As Czechoslovakia, the possibility of a gold medal in the 1920 Olympic Games was surrendered when the team walked off in the final against

CYPRUS

Year	Champions	Cup winners
1935	Trust	Trust
1936	Apoel	Trust
1937	Apoel	Apoel
1938	Apoel	Trust
1939	Apoel	AEL Limassol
1940	Apoel	AEL Limassol
1941	AEL Limassol	Apoel
1942-44	*No competition*	*No competition*
1945	EPA Larnaca	EPA Larnaca
1946	EPA Larnaca	EPA Larnaca
1947	Apoel	Apoel
1948	Apoel	EPA Larnaca
1949	Apoel	Anorthosis
1950	Anorthosis	EPA Larnaca
1951	Chetin Kaya	Apoel
1952	Apoel	Chetin Kaya
1953	AEL Limassol	EPA Larnaca
1954	Pezoporikas	EPA Larnaca
1955	AEL Limassol	EPA Larnaca
1956	AEL Limassol	*No competition*
1957	Anorthosis	*No competition*
1958	Anorthosis	*No competition*
1959	*No competition*	*No competition*
1960	Anorthosis	*No competition*
1961	Omonia	*No competition*
1962	Anorthosis	Anorthosis
1963	Anorthosis	Apoel
1964	*No competition*	*No competition*
1965	Apoel	Omonia
1966	Omonia	Apollon
1967	Olympiakos	Apollon
1968	AEL Limassol	Apoel
1969	Olympiakos	Apoel
1970	EPA Larnaca	Pezoporikas
1971	Olympiakos	Anorthosis
1972	Omonia	Omonia
1973	Apoel	Apoel
1974	Omonia	Omonia
1975	Omonia	Anorthosis
1976	Omonia	Apoel
1977	Omonia	Olympiakos
1978	Omonia	Apoel
1979	Omonia	Apoel
1980	Apoel	Omonia
1981	Omonia	Omonia
1982	Omonia	Omonia
1983	Omonia	Omonia

Belgium in protest against the decisions of the referee. Czechoslovakia also reached the final of the Olympic football tournament in 1964, but were beaten 2-1 by Hungary in Tokyo. In 1960 they had beaten Hungary by a point to win what proved to be the last (six-year) series of the Dr Gero Cup.

Before the Second World War football in Czechoslovakia operated on a professional basis, but in 1948 it came directly under the government, and as in other Eastern European countries the players became employees of the state.

Army side Dukla Prague became the first club to carry the Czech flag regularly into Europe (they also made an impact in the United States in the early 1960s in the International Soccer League) but it was Slovan Bratislava who became the first club to win a major title. And they took the 1969 European Cup Winners Cup in rather ironic circumstances.

It was the year after Russia's invasion of Czechoslovakia, and the political ramifications forced UEFA to redraw the opening round of the competition. In protest most Eastern European countries withdrew their entries but the Czechs remained in the tournament. Though Slovan were total outsiders they won through to the final in Basle, where their 3-2 win over Barcelona was a most popular success.

Slovan Bratislava and Spartak Trnava dominated Czech football in the late 1960s and early 1970s, but in 1977 Dukla re-emerged to lift the championship for the first time in 11 years.

In the 1970s the competitiveness of the international side that led to the European championship win in 1976 misfired in the two World Cups on either side, and in both 1974 and 1978 Czechoslovakia were drawn in qualifying groups that were won by Scotland. At Hampden Park the ferocity of the home support plus physical Scottish tactics overcame the Czech resistance in key games.

Czechoslovakia were back to more convincing form as they finished third in the 1980 European Championship. They qualified for those finals in good style, overcoming both France and Sweden. Ivo Viktor's long tenure in goal had ended, but coach Josef Venglos was able to call on an experienced core including Ondrus, Masny and Nehoda as survivors of 1976. To that the Czechs could ally the youthful promise of players like Stambacher and Vizek, who both played in the 1980 Olympic triumph and who helped Czechoslovakia qualify for the 1982 World Cup finals.

CZECHOSLOVAKIA

Year	Champions	Cup winners
1912	Sparta Prague	....
1913	Slavia Prague	....
1914-18	*No competition*	....
1919	Sparta Prague	....
1920	Sparta Prague	....
1921	Sparta Prague	....
1922	Sparta Prague	....
1923	Sparta Prague	....
1924	Slavia Prague	....
1925	Sparta Prague	....
1926	Sparta Prague	....
1927	Sparta Prague	....
1928	Viktoria Zizkov	....
1929	Slavia Prague	....
1930	Slavia Prague	....
1931	Slavia Prague	....
1932	Sparta Prague	....
1933	Slavia Prague	....
1934	Slavia Prague	....
1935	Slavia Prague	....
1936	Sparta Prague	....
1937	Slavia Prague	....
1938	Sparta Prague	....
1939	Sparta Prague	....
1940	Slavia Prague	....
1941	Slavia Prague	....
1942	Slavia Prague	....
1943	Slavia Prague	....
1944	Slavia Prague	....
1945	*No competition*	....
1946	Sparta Prague	....
1947	Slavia Prague	....
1948	Sparta Prague	....
1949	Slovan Bratislava	....
1950	Slovan Bratislava	....
1951	Slovan Bratislava	....
1952	Sparta Prague	....
1953	Dukla Prague	....
1954	Sparta Prague	....
1955	Slovan Bratislava	....
1956	Dukla Prague	....
1957	*No competition*	....
1958	Dukla Prague	....
1959	Inter Bratislava	....
1960	Hradec Kralove	....
1961	Dukla Prague	Dukla Prague
1962	Dukla Prague	Slovan Bratislava
1963	Dukla Prague	Slovan Bratislava
1964	Dukla Prague	Sparta Prague
1965	Sparta Prague	Dukla Prague
1966	Dukla Prague	Dukla Prague
1967	Sparta Prague	Sparta Trnava
1968	Sparta Trnava	Slovan Bratislava
1969	Sparta Trnava	Dukla Prague
1970	Slovan Bratislava	TJ Gottwaldov
1971	Slovan Bratislava	Spartak Trnava
1972	Spartak Trnava	Sparta Prague
1973	Spartak Trnava	Banik Ostrava
1974	Slovan Bratislava	Slovan Bratislava
1975	Slovan Bratislava	Spartak Trnava
1976	Banik Ostrava	Sparta Prague
1977	Dukla Prague	Lokomotiv Kosice
1978	Zbrojovka Brno	Banik Ostrava
1979	Dukla Prague	Lokomotiv Kosice
1980	Banik Ostrava	Sparta Prague
1981	Banik Ostrava	Dukla Prague
1982	Dukla Prague	Slovan Bratislava
1983	Bohemians	Dukla Prague

Midfielder Koloman Gogh, here taking on Luxembourg's Niro Wagner in a 1979 European Championship qualifier, was one of Czechoslovakia's heroes in the 1976 final.

Denmark

On three occasions—in 1908, 1912 and 1960—Denmark, who only adopted professionalism in 1978, were runners-up in the Olympic Games. Considering the size of the country, that impact and the continual supply of players good enough to become professionals in other European countries represents a remarkable achievement.

Nils Middelboe, who became captain of Chelsea around the time of the First World War, was the first Danish player to make a great impact abroad. More recently, Henning Jensen played for Borussia Moenchengladbach, Real Madrid and Ajax while Soren Lerby and Frank Arnesen were also key figures in Ajax's European Cup campaign of 1979-80. Above all there is Allan Simonsen, with Barcelona after Borussia, and European Footballer of the Year in 1977.

It was the British influence at the end of the 19th century that helped to develop the game in Denmark, and a Danish side played Greece in an exhibition match at the first modern Olympics in 1896. Also in Greece in 1906, Denmark won the gold medal at the unofficial intermediate games.

Most of Denmark's early internationals, however, were played against their northern neighbours, and they won the now-defunct Scandinavian Championship in 1929.

In 1972 Denmark proved to be a major stumbling block to the Eastern European nations who totally dominate the Olympic Games, and in a group match they drew 1-1 with Poland—who went on to win the gold medal with virtually the same set of players who came third in the World Cup in Munich in 1974. But the absence of professionalism has always hindered Denmark in the World Cup—they have never qualified for the finals—and in the major European club tournaments.

The clubs from Copenhagen have dominated the League Championship which began in 1913, though the Cup has had a wider range of winners. Even with professionalism it is hard to envisage that the standard of play and the limited economic resources will ever be enough to keep the best players in Denmark. But as England discovered in two close games in the European Championship, Denmark's national side can still compete with the best when they are able to call regularly on all their exported stars. Despite finishing bottom of the group they scored 13 goals—more than Northern Ireland, Eire or Bulgaria.

DENMARK

Year	Champions	Cup winners
1913	KB Copenhagen	....
1914	KB Copenhagen	....
1915	*No competition*	....
1916	BK 93	....
1917	KB Copenhagen	....
1918	KB Copenhagen	....
1918	Akademisk	....
1920	BK 1903	....
1921	Akademisk	....
1922	KB Copenhagen	....
1923	Frem	....
1924	BK 1903	....
1925	KB Copenhagen	....
1926	BK 1903	....
1927	BK 93	....
1928	*No competition*	....
1929	BK 93	....
1930	BK 93	....
1931	Frem	....
1932	KB Copenhagen	....
1933	Frem	....
1934	BK 93	....
1935	BK 93	....
1936	Frem	....
1937	Akademisk	....
1938	1903	....
1939	BK 93	....
1940	KB Copenhagen	KB Copenhagen
1941	Frem	....
1942	BK 93	....
1943	Akademisk	....
1944	Frem	....
1945	Akademisk	....
1946	BK 93	....
1947	Akademisk	....
1948	KB Copenhagen	....
1949	KB Copenhagen	....
1950	KB Copenhagen	....
1951	Akademisk	....
1952	Akademisk	....
1953	KB Copenhagen	....
1954	Koge BK	....
1955	Aarhus GF	Aarhus GF
1956	Aarhus GF	Frem
1957	Aarhus GF	Aarhus GF
1958	Vejle BK	Vejle BK
1959	Odense BK 09	Vejle BK
1960	Aarhus GF	Aarhus GF
1961	Esbjerg	Aarhus GF
1962	Esbjerg	Odense BK 09
1963	Esbjerg	Odense BK 09
1964	Odense BK 09	Esbjerg
1965	Esbjerg	Aarhus GF
1966	Hvidovre	Aalborg BK 85
1967	Akademisk	Randers Freja
1968	KB Copenhagen	Randers Freja
1969	BK 1903	Aalborg BK 85
1970	BK 1903	Aalborg BK 85
1971	Vejle BK	Odense BK 09
1972	Vejle BK	Vejle BK
1973	Hvidovre	Randers Freja
1974	KB Copenhagen	Vanlose 1F
1975	Koge BK	Vejle BK
1976	BK 1903	Esbjerg
1977	Odense BK 09	Vejle BK
1978	Vejle BK	Frem
1979	Esbjerg	BK 1903
1980	KB Copenhagen	Hvidovre
1981	Hvidovre	Vejle BK
1982	Odense BK 09	BK 93 Copenhagen
1983	Lyngby	B1901 Nykobing

England

For the first six decades of organized competition, the story of the game is largely that of the English (and, to a lesser extent, Scottish) Football Association, Cup and League. It was not until 1929 that the England team (professional, not amateur) was defeated by foreign opposition (in Spain), though actually after only 24 matches against non-UK opposition in fully 66 years.

Another 20 years elapsed before England's first home defeat by a non-UK side—Eire at Goodison Park on 21 September 1949. It can fairly be argued that this hardly counted as a foreign team as nine of its 11 members played in the Football League. Certainly a far more significant defeat was England's next at home four years later when Hungary cast their spells at Wembley and humiliated England 6-3. In Budapest the following year England suffered her heaviest ever defeat—7-1.

While these games are generally taken to signify the coming home to roost of various tactical and insular pigeons, such an analysis does scant justice to the Hungarians.

England, since that time, have certainly fallen from grace to the role of mere also-ran in international competition—with just one brief if glorious exception. That was the World Cup win of 1966, engineered by a man whose last international appearance had been in that game against the Hungarians at Wembley—Alf Ramsey.

Apart from that lone success, English football has never even been moderately successful in international competition. It is worth remembering that England did not qualify once for the World Cup finals in the 1970s (the side were in Mexico as holders), a dreadful record for the fourth largest of all the recognized footballing nations, though Ron Greenwood took this squad to the 1980 European finals and the 1982 World Cup.

Other World Cup and European Championship accounts have been little better than mediocre, and it was not until the performances of Liverpool and Nottingham Forest in the late 1970s that England finally had club sides to match any in the European Cup, despite massive success in the two less prestigious European competitions.

English football has provided the world

ENGLAND

Year	Champions	Cup winners
1872	....	Wanderers
1873	....	Wanderers
1874	....	Oxford University
1875	....	Royal Engineers
1876	....	Wanderers
1877	....	Wanderers
1878	....	Wanderers
1879	....	Old Etonians
1880	....	Clapham Rovers
1881	....	Old Carthusians
1882	....	Old Etonians
1883	....	Blackburn Olympic
1884	....	Blackburn Rovers
1885	....	Blackburn Rovers
1886	....	Blackburn Rovers
1887	....	Aston Villa
1888	....	West Brom. Alb.
1889	Preston North End	Preston North End
1890	Preston North End	Blackburn Rovers
1891	Everton	Blackburn Rovers
1892	Sunderland	West Brom. Alb.
1893	Sunderland	Wolverhampton W.
1894	Aston Villa	Notts County
1895	Sunderland	Aston Villa
1896	Aston Villa	The Wednesday
1897	Aston Villa	Aston Villa
1898	Sheffield United	Nottingham Forest
1899	Aston Villa	Sheffield United
1900	Aston Villa	Bury
1901	Liverpool	Tottenham Hotspur
1902	Sunderland	Sheffield United
1903	The Wednesday	Bury
1904	The Wednesday	Manchester City
1905	Newcastle United	Aston Villa
1906	Liverpool	Everton
1907	Newcastle United	The Wednesday
1908	Manchester United	Wolverhampton W.
1909	Newcastle United	Manchester United
1910	Aston Villa	Newcastle United
1911	Manchester United	Bradford City
1912	Blackburn Rovers	Barnsley
1913	Sunderland	Aston Villa
1914	Blackburn Rovers	Burnley
1915	Everton	Sheffield United
1916-19	*No competition*	*No competition*
1920	West Brom. Alb.	Aston Villa
1921	Burnley	Tottenham Hotspur
1922	Liverpool	Huddersfield Town
1923	Liverpool	Bolton Wanderers
1924	Huddersfield Town	Newcastle United
1925	Huddersfield Town	Sheffield United
1926	Huddersfield Town	Bolton Wanderers

Bobby Moore led England to World Cup success at Wembley in 1966.

Year	Champions	Cup winners
1927	Newcastle United	Cardiff City
1928	Everton	Blackburn Rovers
1929	Sheffield Wednesday	Bolton Wanderers
1930	Sheffield Wednesday	Arsenal
1931	Arsenal	West Brom. Alb.
1932	Everton	Newcastle United
1933	Arsenal	Everton
1934	Arsenal	Manchester City
1935	Arsenal	Sheffield Wednesday
1936	Sunderland	Arsenal
1937	Manchester City	Sunderland
1938	Arsenal	Preston North End
1939	Everton	Portsmouth
1940-45	*No competition*	*No competition*
1946	*No competition*	Derby County
1947	Liverpool	Charlton Athletic
1948	Arsenal	Manchester United
1949	Portsmouth	Wolverhampton W.
1950	Portsmouth	Arsenal
1951	Tottenham Hotspur	Newcastle United
1952	Manchester United	Newcastle United
1953	Arsenal	Blackpool
1954	Wolverhampton W.	West Brom. Alb.
1955	Chelsea	Newcastle United
1956	Manchester United	Manchester City
1957	Manchester United	Aston Villa
1958	Wolverhampton W.	Bolton Wanderers
1959	Wolverhampton W.	Nottingham Forest
1960	Burnley	Wolverhampton W.
1961	Tottenham Hotspur	Tottenham Hotspur
1962	Ipswich Town	Tottenham Hotspur
1963	Everton	Manchester United
1964	Liverpool	West Ham United
1965	Manchester United	Liverpool
1966	Liverpool	Everton
1967	Manchester United	Tottenham Hotspur
1968	Manchester United	West Brom. Alb.
1969	Leeds United	Manchester City
1970	Everton	Chelsea
1971	Arsenal	Arsenal
1972	Derby County	Leeds United
1973	Liverpool	Sunderland
1974	Leeds United	Liverpool
1975	Derby County	West Ham United
1976	Liverpool	Southampton
1977	Liverpool	Manchester United
1978	Nottingham Forest	Ipswich Town
1979	Liverpool	Arsenal
1980	Liverpool	West Ham United
1981	Aston Villa	Tottenham Hotspur
1982	Liverpool	Tottenham Hotspur
1983	Liverpool	Manchester United

After failure to qualify for the 1974 and 1978 World Cups, Ron Greenwood moulded an enterprising side that turned in impressive performances in making the 1980 European finals in Rome one short of maximum points.

with perhaps three internationally renowned clubs—Arsenal, Manchester United and Liverpool—plus Aston Villa and Newcastle United, who have claims to have been the best club sides in the world for a period of considerable domestic eminence, Villa in the last decade of the 19th century and Newcastle in the first of the 20th.

Liverpool, given their successes of the 1960s and 1970s in the face of tougher competition, are the greatest of the three. In 1983 they won their 14th League Championship (their seventh since 1973) to complement their three European Cups and two UEFA Cups.

Only Arsenal, next in line with eight League titles, have ever really matched that dominance with their five Championships (including one of only two hat-tricks) and two FA Cup wins in the 1930s. Manchester United have, however, probably the most famous name internationally, largely due to the Munich air crash of 1958 which wiped out most of a side which had become favourites to be the first club to defeat mighty Real Madrid in the European Cup. In the subsequent decade they took two Championships, the FA Cup and the European Cup but their reputation was based on their style and stars—notably Best, Law and Charlton, who were all elected European Footballer of the Year—rather than on their results. In the 1970s, for instance, they won just one trophy—the FA Cup that denied Liverpool their ambitious double and treble in 1977.

Finland

The absence of full-time professionalism in Finland has restricted the development of football in a country that has nevertheless produced competitive teams. England's failure to beat Finland by more than 2-1 at Wembley in the World Cup qualifiers in 1976 was partly responsible for Italy's superior goal difference at the end of the group.

The fact that the Finnish season runs from April to October because of the weather has proved to be another handicap, with important international and club matches sometimes having to be played in the close season.

FINLAND

Year	Champions	Cup winners
1908	Unitas Helsinki	....
1909	PUS Helsinki	....
1910	Abo IFK	....
1911	JK Helsinki	....
1912	JK Helsinki	....
1913	KJF Turku	....
1914	*No competition*	....
1915	KFJ Helsinki	....
1916	KFJ Helsinki	....
1917	JK Helsinki	....
1918	JK Helsinki	....
1919	JK Helsinki	....
1920	Abo IFK	....
1921	PS Helsinki	....
1922	PS Helsinki	....
1923	JK Helsinki	....
1924	Abo IFK	....
1925	JK Helsinki	....
1926	PS Helsinki	....
1927	PS Helsinki	....
1928	Turun PS Turku	....
1929	PS Helsinki	....
1930	IFK Helsinki	....
1931	IFK Helsinki	....
1932	PS Helsinki	....
1933	IFK Helsinki	....
1934	PS Helsinki	....
1935	PS Helsinki	....
1936	JK Helsinki	....
1937	IFK Helsinki	....
1938	JK Helsinki	....
1939	Turun PS Turku	....
1940	Sudet Helsinki	....
1941	Turun PS Turku	....
1942	HT Helsinki	....
1943	*No competition*	....
1944	IFK Vaasa	....
1945	Turun PS Turku	....
1946	IFK Vaasa	....
1947	IFK Helsinki	....
1948	PS Vaasa	....
1949	Turun PS Turku	....
1950	Ilves-Kisset	....
1951	Kotkan TP	....
1952	Kotkan TP	....
1953	IFK Vaasa	....
1954	Pentterit Helsinki	....
1955	IFK Helsinki	Valkeakosken Haka
1956	PS Kuopion	Pall-Peikot
1957	PS Helsinki	IF Drott
1958	PS Kuopion	Kotkan TP
1959	IFK Helsinki	Valkeakosken Haka
1960	Valkeakosken Haka	Valkeakosken Haka
1961	IFK Helsinki	Kotkan TP
1962	Valkeakosken Haka	PS Helsinki
1963	Lahden Reipas	Valkeakosken Haka
1964	JK Helsinki	Lahden Reipas
1965	Valkeakosken Haka	Abo IFK
1966	PS Kuopion	HJK Helsinki
1967	Lahden Reipas	Kotkan TP
1968	Turun PS Turku	PS Kuopion
1969	Kokkolan PV	Valkeakosken Haka
1970	Lahden Reipas	Mikkelin Pallokissat
1971	Turun PS Turku	Mikkelin Pallokissat
1972	Turun PS Turku	Lahden Reipas
1973	HJK Helsinki	Lahden Reipas
1974	PS Kuopion	Lahden Reipas
1975	Turun PS Turku	Lahden Reipas
1976	PS Kuopion	Lahden Reipas
1977	Valkeakosken Haka	Valkeakosken Haka
1978	HJK Helsinki	Lahden Reipas
1979	Oulun Palloseura	Ilves Tampere
1980	Oulun Palloseura	Kotkan TP
1981	JK Helsinki	JK Helsinki
1982	Kuuysi	Valkeakosken Haka
1983	Ilves Tampere	Kuuysi

Internationally Finland's record is poor, and judges them the weakest of the Scandinavian countries—though they won the Scandinavian Championship in 1963. The First Division comprises 12 clubs, none of whom has established a consistent domination. Lahden Reipas, however, won the cup competition five years in succession from 1972-76.

In 1979 St Etienne bought French football's golden boy Michel Platini—seen here in action against FK Austria—in a bid to regain their dominance of the recent past.

FRANCE

Year	Champions	Cup winners
1918	....	Olympique de Pantin
1919	....	CAS Genereaux
1920	....	CA Paris
1921	....	Red Star Paris
1922	....	Red Star Paris
1923	....	Red Star Paris
1924	....	Olympique M'seille
1925	....	CAS Genereaux
1926	....	Olympique M'seille
1927	....	Olympique M'seille
1928	....	Red Star Paris
1929	....	SO Montpelier
1930	....	Sete
1931	....	Club Francais
1932	....	Cannes
1933	Lille OSC	Excelsior Roubaix
1934	Sete	Sete
1935	Sochaux	Olympique M'seille
1936	Racing Club Paris	Racing Club Paris
1937	Olympique M'seille	Sochaux
1938	Sochaux	Olympique M'seille
1939	Sete	Racing Club Paris
1940	*No competition*	Racing Club Paris
1941	*No competition*	Girondins Bordeaux
1942	*No competition*	Red Star Paris
1943	*No competition*	Olympique M'seille
1944	*No competition*	Nancy-Lorraine
1945	*No competition*	Racing Club Paris
1946	Lille OSC	Lille OSC
1947	CO Roubaix-T'coing	Lille OSC
1948	Olympique M'seille	Lille OSC
1949	Stade de Reims	Racing Club Paris
1950	Girondins Bordeaux	Stade de Reims
1951	OGC Nice	RC Strasbourg
1952	OGC Nice	OGC Nice
1953	Stade de Reims	Lille OSC
1954	Lille OSC	OGC Nice
1955	Stade de Reims	Lille OSC
1956	OGC Nice	UA Sedan-Torcy
1957	Saint Etienne	Toulouse
1958	Stade de Reims	Stade de Reims
1959	OGC Nice	Le Havre AC
1960	Stade de Reims	AS Monaco
1961	AS Monaco	UA Sedan-Torcy
1962	Stade de Reims	Saint Etienne
1963	AS Monaco	AS Monaco
1964	Saint Etienne	Olympique Lyon
1965	Nantes	Stade Rennais
1966	Nantes	RC Strasbourg
1967	Saint Etienne	Olympique Lyon
1968	Saint Etienne	Saint Etienne
1969	Saint Etienne	Olympique M'seille
1970	Saint Etienne	Saint Etienne
1971	Olympique M'seille	Stade Rennais
1972	Olympique M'seille	Olympique M'seille
1973	Nantes	Olympique Lyon
1974	Saint Etienne	Saint Etienne
1975	Saint Etienne	Saint Etienne
1976	Saint Etienne	Olympique M'seille
1977	Nantes	Saint Etienne
1978	AS Monaco	Nancy-Lorraine
1979	RC Strasbourg	Nantes
1980	Nantes	AS Monaco
1981	Saint Etienne	Bastia
1982	AS Monaco	Paris St Germain
1983	Nantes	Paris St Germain

France

Though France's influence on football has been enormous, the nation has not yet been able to capitalize, on the field, on the inventiveness of its administrators. Jules Rimet saw his own concept of a World Cup become reality; Robert Guerin became the first president of FIFA. Gabriel Hanot, a former French international, used his position as editor of the sports paper *L'Equipe* to outline an idea for a competition between the champion clubs of each European nation; Henri Delaunay was the founding father of the European Nations Cup, later the European Championship.

Yet France have never won any of the trophies that their thinking created. In the World Cup their most impressive year came in 1958, when an attack inspired by Raymond Kopa produced a goalscorer of deadly instincts in Just Fontaine. His 13 goals in the finals remain a record and he scored in every game including the semi-final defeat by an irresistible Brazil.

Hopes were high for France in the 1978 finals with Michel Platini now in the Kopa role, but a much-disputed penalty cost them dear against Argentina in the tough group which also included Italy.

In the European Championship, England were decisively defeated over two legs in the qualifying rounds in the 1962–64 tournament, and France went on to reach the quarter-final, a stage also attained in 1968.

At club level the coaching of Albert Batteux, the trainer for France in the 1958 World Cup campaign, elevated Reims to the status of a top continental side in the late 1950s, when they were twice beaten by Real Madrid in European Cup finals. In 1976 St Etienne exhibited the same silky touch in their play to reach the final in Glasgow, but Bayern Munich's more functional approach brought the game's only goal. In the other French final appearance, Bastia of Corsica lost the 1978 UEFA Cup to Eindhoven.

Football in France has to fight a never-ending battle with rugby for popularity, a battle which is not helped by the lack of feeling for the game in the capital city. The famed Racing Club de Paris, who used to play regularly against the great Arsenal side of the 1930s, became a victim of Parisian soccer apathy, and though Paris St Germain have retained an interest in the first division for the capital they lack top level support.

The French League enjoys a reputation for open football and is prepared to add to its glamour by introducing foreign players like Johnny Rep, the Dutch international, who linked up with Platini at St Etienne in 1979. But the failure to qualify for the finals of the 1980 European Championship was a great blow to a nation which has given so much to the game.

EAST GERMANY

Year	Champions	Cup winners
1948	SG Planitz	....
1949	Union Halle	Wag'nbau N-Dessau
1950	Horch Zwickau	EHW Thale
1951	Chemie Leipzig	*No competition*
1952	Turbine Halle	VP Dresden
1953	Dynamo Dresden	*No competition*
1954	Turbine Erfurt	ASK Vorwaerts
1955	Turbine Erfurt	Karl-Max-Stadt
1956	Karl-Marx-Stadt	Chemie Halle-Leuna
1957	Karl-Marx-Stadt	Lokomotiv Leipzig
1958	ASK Vorwaerts	Einheit Dresden
1959	Karl-Marx-Stadt	Dynamo Berlin
1960	ASK Vorwaerts	Motor Jena
1961	Empor Rostock	Motor Jena
1962	ASK Vorwaerts	Chemie Halle
1963	Motor Jena	Motor Zwickau
1964	Chemie Leipzig	Aufbau Magdeburg
1965	ASK Vorwaerts	Aufbau Magdeburg
1966	ASK Vorwaerts	Chemie Leipzig
1967	Karl-Marx-Stadt	Motor Zwickau
1968	Carl Zeiss Jena	Union Berlin
1969	ASK Vorwaerts	FC Magdeburg
1970	Carl Zeiss Jena	ASK Vorwaerts
1971	Dynamo Dresden	Dynamo Dresden
1972	FC Magdeburg	Carl Zeiss Jena
1973	Dynamo Dresden	FC Magdeburg
1974	FC Magdeburg	Carl Zeiss Jena
1975	FC Magdeburg	Sachsenr'g Zwickau
1976	Dynamo Dresden	Lokomotiv Leipzig
1977	Dynamo Dresden	Dynamo Dresden
1978	Dynamo Dresden	FC Magdeburg
1979	Dynamo Berlin	FC Magdeburg
1980	Dynamo Berlin	Carl Zeiss Jena
1981	Dynamo Berlin	Lokomotiv Leipzig
1982	Dynamo Berlin	Dynamo Dresden
1983	Dynamo Berlin	FC Magdeburg

East Germany

East Germany's introduction into world football, after the nation's formation, was treated with suspicion. Between 1948, when the Football Federation was formed, and 1960, only World Cup and European Championship internationals were played. East Germany's first World Cup tie took place in 1958 against Wales in Leipzig, a match which produced a 2-1 victory but was not a stepping-stone to qualification.

The East Germans had to wait until 1974 to reach the finals, and in West Germany they reached the last eight, enjoying an historic win in their first ever meeting with the hosts and eventual winners. In Berlin, Jurgen Sparwasser's winning goal was joyously greeted by specially chosen supporters who had been allowed to cross the border to watch the match.

In common with other Eastern European countries, East Germany have also profited from being able to field their best players in Olympic tournaments. Bronze medallists in 1964 and 1972, they won gold in Montreal, earning a distinguished victory.

FC Magdeburg and Dynamo Dresden have been impressive competitors in European competitions, having dominated the East German League, and in 1974 Magdeburg won the Cup Winners Cup, beating holders AC Milan 2-0 in the final.

The events of the mid-1970s appeared to herald a great East German impact on the game, but with failure to reach the finals of the 1978 World Cup and the 1980 European Championships the country has not yet made the real transition from producing sides that are hard to beat rather than outright winners.

West Germany

In international football, at both club and national level, West Germany have a proud record as serious and successful competitors. Right from the outset—the German Football Association was founded in 1900, becoming affiliated as West Germany in 1954—their teams have always been renowned for their fitness, physical prowess and spirit; in more recent times, those qualities have been splendidly harnessed to a high degree of application and skill.

West Germany have won every honour in football—though surprisingly the first success in the Champions Cup (Bayern Munich in 1974) did not arrive until the competition was 19 years old. In the World Cup Germany's is a splendid record, under Sepp Herberger, his former assistant, Helmut Schoen, and in turn Jupp Derwall.

In 1954 it was Herberger who out-thought the mighty Hungary by fielding virtually a reserve side when the two teams met in a group match—and lost 8-3. When both reached the final Herberger still held his best cards and Germany overcame a two-goal deficit to win 3-2, a match which elevated the name of Helmut Rahn into history.

Twenty years later West Germany beat the world again—two years after a dominant performance in winning the European Championship. Gunter Netzer had pulled the strings in midfield in that success but by 1974 Wolfgang Overath had been recalled. Once more West Germany's competitive spirit made light of a stuttering start which included that pride-denting defeat by East Germany. In the final they again trailed, to Holland's first-minute penalty, but found that winning extra gear. For Schoen it was a fitting triumph, coming after his squad had finished second to England in 1966 and third in Mexico in 1970. West Germany were also beaten semi-finalists in 1958.

Bayern Munich's hat-trick of European Cup wins between 1974 and 1976 is the highlight of the impact of West German clubs in Europe—a rise in standards that dates back to the belated formation of the national Bundesliga in 1963, now fed by a National Second Division. Borussia Dortmund, Borussia Moenchengladbach (twice) and Hamburg (twice) have also won in Europe for West Germany, and the events of the 1979-80 UEFA Cup epitomized the strengths in depth in the Bundesliga. The four semi-finalists, Eintracht Frankfurt, VfB Stuttgart, Bayern Munich and Borussia Moenchengladbach made the competition an all West German affair.

The manner of such success, and the high wages and lower taxes of the country have lured top British players and though Dave Watson spent an unhappy short period with Werder Bremen, the rewarding experiences of Kevin Keegan with Hamburg and Tony Woodcock with Cologne offered an attractive alternative to the best players in the Football League.

WEST GERMANY

Year	Champions*	Cup winners
1903	VfB Leipzig	....
1904	*No competition*	....
1905	Union 92 Berlin	....
1906	VfB Leipzig	....
1907	Freiburger FC	....
1908	Viktoria 89 Berlin	....
1909	Phoenix Karlsruhe	....
1910	Karlsruhe FV	....
1911	Viktoria 89 Berlin	....
1912	Holstein Kiel	....
1913	VfB Leipzig	....
1914	SpV Furth	....
1915-19	*No competition*	....
1920	1FC Nurnberg	....
1921	1FC Nurnberg	....
1922	*Not decided*	....
1923	SV Hamburg	....
1924	1FC Nurnberg	....
1925	1FC Nurnberg	....
1926	SpV Furth	....
1927	1FC Nurnberg	....
1928	SV Hamburg	....
1929	SpV Furth	....
1930	Hertha-BSC-Berlin	....
1931	Hertha-BSC-Berlin	....
1932	Bayern Munich	....
1933	Fortuna Dusseldorf	....
1934	Schalke 04	....
1935	Schalke 04	1FC Nurnberg
1936	1FC Nurnberg	VfB Leipzig
1937	Schalke 04	Schalke 04
1938	Hanover 96	Rapid Vienna
1939	Schalke 04	1FC Nurnberg
1940	Schalke 04	Dresden SC
1941	Rapid Vienna	Dresden SC
1942	Schalke 04	TSV Munich 1860
1943	Dresden SC	First Vienna
1944	Dresden SC	*No competition*
1945-47	*No competition*	*No competition*
1948	1FC Nurnberg	*No competition*
1949	VfR Mannheim	*No competition*
1950	VfB Stuttgart	*No competition*
1951	1FC Kaiserslautern	*No competition*
1952	VfB Stuttgart	*No competition*
1953	VfB Kaiserslautern	Rot-Weiss Essen
1954	Hanover 96	VfB Stuttgart
1955	Rot-Weiss Essen	Karlsruhe SC
1956	Borussia Dortmund	Karlsruhe SC
1957	Borussia Dortmund	Bayern Munich
1958	Schalke 04	VfB Stuttgart
1959	Eintracht Frankfurt	Schwarz-W's Essen
1960	SV Hamburg	Bor'sia M'gladbach
1961	1FC Nurnberg	Werder Bremen
1962	1FC Cologne	1FC Nurnberg
1963	Borussia Dortmund	SV Hamburg
1964†	1FC Cologne	TSV Munich 1860
1965	Werder Bremen	Borussia Dortmund
1966	TSV Munich1860	Bayern Munich
1967	Eintracht Brunswick	Bayern Munich
1968	1FC Nurnberg	1FC Cologne
1969	Bayern Munich	Bayern Munich
1970	Bor'sia M'gladbach	Offenbach Kickers
1971	Bor'sia M'gladbach	Bayern Munich
1972	Bayern Munich	Schalke 04
1973	Bayern Munich	Bor'sia M'gladbach
1974	Bayern Munich	Eintracht Frankfurt
1975	Bor'sia M'gladbach	Eintracht Frankfurt
1976	Bor'sia M'gladbach	SV Hamburg
1977	Bor'sia M'gladbach	1FC Cologne
1978	1FC Cologne	1FC Cologne
1979	SV Hamburg	Fortuna Dusseldorf
1980	Bayern Munich	Fortuna Dusseldorf
1981	Bayern Munich	Eintracht Frankfurt
1982	SV Hamburg	Bayern Munich
1983	SV Hamburg	1FC Cologne

*German League until 1944 †first Bundesliga winners

After leading West Germany to the European title in 1972, Franz Beckenbauer took his side to World Cup success in 1974 on Bayern's ground.

Greece

On 12 September 1979 a goal from Nikoloudis revamped the history of Greek football. It was enough to beat Russia in Athens and make Greece qualifiers for the finals of the 1980 European Championship—even though they had not scored a single goal in their three away games in a group that also contained Hungary, Finland and the USSR.

Greater emphasis on professionalism and the import of experienced British coaching has increased the standards in the Greek League despite difficult pitches and a lack of discipline on the field.

The success in the European Championship evoked memories of Greece's only other taste of genuine triumph. In 1971 Panathinaikos, along with Olympiakos the most traditional of Greek clubs, reached the final of the European Cup. Under the guidance of Ferenc Puskas, Panathinaikos eliminated Everton and Red Star Belgrade, both on away goals, in the quarter- and semi-finals. At Wembley Puskas's side lost 2-0 to Ajax but when the Dutch declined to participate in the World Club Championship, Panathinaikos eagerly took their place, losing narrowly to Nacional.

Panathinaikos continue to play an important part in the Greek League which is now composed of 18 clubs. The feeder system for a time allowed a representative from Cyprus and now both Crete and Rhodes are represented. Olympiakos Piraeus, however, with 24 championships and 18 cup wins up to 1983, are the country's most successful club.

GREECE

Year	Champions	Cup winners
1928	Aris Salonika	....
1929	*No competition*	....
1930	Panathinaikos	....
1931	Olympiakos	....
1932	Aris Salonika	AEK Athens
1933	Olympiakos	Ethnikos
1934	Olympiakos	*No competition*
1935	*No competition*	*No competition*
1936	Olympiakos	*No competition*
1937	Olympiakos	*No competition*
1938	Olympiakos	*No competition*
1939	AEK Athens	AEK Athens
1940	AEK Athens	Panathinaikos
1941-45	*No competition*	*No competition*
1946	Aris Salonika	*No competition*
1947	Olympiakos	Olympiakos
1948	Olympiakos	Panathinaikos
1949	Panathinaikos	AEK Athens
1950	*No competition*	AEK Athens
1951	Olympiakos	Olympiakos
1952	*No competition*	Olympiakos
1953	Panathinaikos	Olympiakos
1954	Olympiakos	Olympiakos
1955	Olympiakos	Panathinaikos
1956	Olympiakos	AEK Athens
1957	Olympiakos	Olympiakos
1958	Olympiakos	Olympiakos
1959	Olympiakos	Olympiakos
1960	Panathinaikos	Olympiakos
1961	Panathinaikos	Olympiakos
1962	Panathinaikos	Olympiakos
1963	AEK Athens	Olympiakos
1964	Panathinaikos	AEK Athens
1965	Panathinaikos	Olympiakos
1966	Olympiakos	AEK Athens
1967	Olympiakos	Panathinaikos
1968	AEK Athens	Olympiakos
1969	Panathinaikos	Panathinaikos
1970	Panathinaikos	Aris Salonika
1971	AEK Athens	Olympiakos
1972	Panathinaikos	PAOK Salonika
1973	Olympiakos	Olympiakos
1974	Olympiakos	PAOK Salonika
1975	Olympiakos	Olympiakos
1976	PAOK Salonika	Heraklis Salonika
1977	Panathinaikos	Panathinaikos
1978	AEK Athens	AEK Athens
1979	AEK Athens	Panionios
1980	Olympiakos	Kastoria
1981	Olympiakos	Olympiakos
1982	Olympiakos	Panathinaikos
1983	Olympiakos	AEK Athens

Holland

Holland's rise from a country which had no professional football until 1954 to a major soccer nation has been both spectacular and swift. At the core of the growth was a supremely talented generation of players who first lifted Ajax to become the best club in Europe and then made Dutch football a real force in the world game.

Johan Cruyff, Piet Keizer, Ruud Krol, Wim Suurbier, Johan Neeskens, Arie Haan and Johnny Rep matured together in Amsterdam with Ajax. As all but Krol sought fortune to go with their fame in other European countries most of the group were reunited for two marvellous World Cup campaigns which surely would have brought success had they not twice had the misfortune of meeting the host nation in the final.

Cruyff, Suurbier and Keizer had all been in the young Ajax team which surprisingly reached the European Cup final in 1969. Though their naïve approach cost them dear in a 4-1 defeat by AC Milan in Madrid, Ajax were mature and battle-hardened by the time they swept aside Europe's best in their hat-trick of triumphs from 1971.

In 1970 Feyenoord, Ajax's principal rival in the Dutch League, had become the first winners from Holland of a major club trophy. Superbly marshalled by their sweeper Rinus Israel and their Swedish international forward, Ove Kindvall, Feyenoord took the European Cup to Rotterdam.

Dutch football, however, has been more than merely successful. Its free-flowing 'total' style, exemplified by the genius of Cruyff, offered an exciting innovation in world football, and the nature of Holland's displays in the 1974 World Cup lives in the memory more strongly than the success of West Germany. Though the independent spirit of the Dutch players, which causes regular disputes about money and availability, was in evidence again in Argentina, Holland timed their challenge almost to perfection. Even without Cruyff they came within a post (Rensenbrink's shot) of winning the final before losing to the hosts in extra time.

Holland's present place in the higher echelons of world football is in stark contrast to the amateur thinking that governed the game for so long after English textile workers had planted the first seeds in the 1860s. The game grew quickly and the Dutch won three successive Olympic bronze medals in 1908, 1912 and 1920.

As founder members of FIFA Holland competed regularly in international football,

The only player from Ajax's heyday to survive the 1980s with the club, Ruud Krol became Holland's most capped player.

but with less success as professionalism grew elsewhere. Holland reached the final stages of the World Cups of 1934 and 1938 but were eliminated in the first round on both occasions. Puck van Heel of Feyenoord was the mainspring of the national team at this time, winning 64 caps, a record until overtaken by Krol in 1979.

Even after professionalism Holland took some time to shrug off the amateur philosophy, and in 1963 were still capable of suffering a humiliating defeat in the European Championship qualifying rounds by Luxembourg. Two years later Rinus Michels began his reign as manager of Ajax, fostered the talent of the young Cruyff, and the evolution began in Dutch football.

Hungary

Hungary's football will always be most remembered for producing what was possibly the world's greatest team. Between 1950 and 1954 Hungary played 34 international matches undefeated, a run which included winning the Olympic gold medal in 1952 and the utter and double destruction of England.

In November 1953, Hungary became the first team outside the British Isles to beat England on her own soil. The margin of victory, 6-3, flattered England as the skills and, especially, the tactics of the 'Magic

HOLLAND

Year	Champions	Cup winners
1898	RAP	....
1899	RAP	RAP
1900	HVV Den Haag	Velocitas Breda
1901	HVV Den Haag	HBS Den Haag
1902	HVV Den Haag	Haarlem
1903	HVV Den Haag	HVV Den Haag
1904	HBS Den Haag	HFC
1905	HVV Den Haag	VOC
1906	HBS Den Haag	Concordia Rot'dam
1907	HVV Den Haag	VOC
1908	Quick Den Haag	HBS Den Haag
1909	Sparta Rotterdam	Quick Den Haag
1910	HVV Den Haag	Quick Den Haag
1911	Sparta Rotterdam	Quick Den Haag
1912	Sparta Rotterdam	Haarlem
1913	Sparta Rotterdam	HFC
1914	HVV Den Haag	DFC
1915	Sparta Rotterdam	HFC
1916	Willem II Tilburg	Quick Den Haag
1917	Go Ahead Deventer	Ajax
1918	Ajax	RCH Haarlem
1919	Ajax	*No competition*
1920	Be Quick Groningen	CVV
1921	NAC Breda	Schoten
1922	Go Ahead Deventer	*No competition*
1923	RCH Haarlem	*No competition*
1924	Feyenoord	*No competition*
1925	HBS Den Haag	ZFC
1926	Enschede	Longa
1927	Heracles	VUC
1928	Feyenoord	RCH Haarlem
1929	PSV Eindhoven	*No competition*
1930	Go Ahead Deventer	Feyenoord
1931	Ajax	*No competition*
1932	Ajax	DFC
1933	Go Head Deventer	*No competition*
1934	Ajax	Velocitas Gron'gen
1935	PSV Eindhoven	Feyenoord
1936	Feyenoord	Roermond
1937	Ajax	Eindhoven
1938	Feyenoord	VSV
1939	Ajax	Wageningen
1940	Feyenoord	*No competition*
1941	Heracles	*No competition*
1942	ADO Den Haag	*No competition*
1943	ADO Den Haag	Ajax
1944	Volewijckers	Willem II Tilburg
1945	*No competition*	*No competition*
1946	Haarlem	*No competition*
1947	Ajax	*No competition*
1948	SVV Scheidam	Wageningen
1949	SVV Scheidam	Quick Nijmegen
1950	Limburgia	PSV Eindhoven
1951	PSV Eindhoven	*No competition*
1952	Willem II Tilburg	*No competition*
1953	RCH Haarlem	*No competition*
1954	Eindhoven	*No competition*
1955	Willem II Tilburg	*No competition*
1956	Rapid JC Haarlem	*No competition*
1957	Ajax	Fortuna Geleen
1958	DOS Utrecht	Sparta Rotterdam
1959	Sparta Rotterdam	VVV Groningen
1960	Ajax	*No competition*
1961	Feyenoord	Ajax
1962	Feyenoord	Sparta Rotterdam
1963	PSV Eindhoven	Willem II Tilburg
1964	DWS Amsterdam	Fortuna Geleen
1965	Feyenoord	Feyenoord
1966	Ajax	Sparta Rotterdam
1967	Ajax	Ajax
1968	Ajax	ADO Den Haag
1969	Feyenoord	Ajax
1970	Ajax	Ajax
1971	Feyenoord	Ajax
1972	Ajax	Ajax
1973	Ajax	NAC Breda
1974	Feyenoord	PSV Eindhoven
1975	PSV Eindhoven	FC Den Haag
1976	PSV Eindhoven	PSV Eindhoven
1977	Ajax	Twente Enschede
1978	PSV Eindhoven	AZ 67 Alkmaar
1979	Ajax	Ajax
1980	Ajax	Feyenoord
1981	AZ 67 Alkmaar	AZ 67 Alkmaar
1982	Ajax	AZ 67 Alkmaar
1983	Ajax	Ajax

HUNGARY

Year	Champions	Cup winners
1901	BTC	....
1902	BTC	....
1903	FTC	....
1904	MTK	....
1905	FTC	....
1906	*No competition*	....
1907	FTC	....
1908	MTK	....
1909	FTC	....
1910	FTC	MTK
1911	FTC	MTK
1912	FTC	MTK
1913	FTC	FTC
1914	MTK	MTK
1915-19	*No competition*	*No competition*
1920	MTK	*No competition*
1921	MTK	*No competition*
1922	MTK	FTC
1923	MTK	MTK
1924	MTK	*No competition*
1925	MTK	MTK
1926	FTC	Kispest
1927	Ferencvaros	Ferencvaros
1928	Ferencvaros	Ferencvaros
1929	Hungaria	*No competition*
1930	Ujpest Dozsa	Bocskai
1931	Ujpest Dozsa	III Ker
1932	Ferencvaros	Hungaria
1933	Ujpest Dozsa	Ferencvaros
1934	Ferencvaros	Soroksar
1935	Ujpest Dozsa	Ferencvaros
1936	Hungaria	*No competition*
1937	Hungaria	*No competition*
1938	Ferencvaros	*No competition*
1939	Ujpest Dozsa	*No competition*
1940	Ferencvaros	*No competition*
1941	Ferencvaros	Szolnok
1942	Vasas Csepel	Ferencvaros
1943	Vasas Csepel	Ferencvaros
1943-44	Nagyvarad	Ferencvaros
1944	Ferencvaros	*No competition*
1945	Ujpest Dozsa	*No competition*
1946	Ujpest Dozsa	*No competition*
1947	Ujpest Dozsa	*No competition*
1948	Vasas Csepel	*No competition*
1949-50	Honved	*No competition*
1950	Honved	*No competition*
1951	Bastya	*No competition*
1952	Honved	Bastya
1953	Voros Lobogo	*No competition*
1954	Honved	*No competition*
1955	Honved	Vasas Budapest
1956	*Abandoned*	Ferencvaros
1957	Vasas Budapest	Ferencvaros
1958	MTK	Ferencvaros
1959	Vasas Csepel	*No competition*
1960	Ujpest Dozsa	*No competition*
1961	Vasas Budapest	*No competition*
1962	Vasas Budapest	*No competition*
1962-63	Ferencvaros	*No competition*
1963	Vasas Gyor	*No competition*
1964	Ferencvaros	Honved
1965	Vasas Budapest	Vasas Gyor
1966	Vasas Budapest	Vasas Gyor
1967	Ferencvaros	Vasas Gyor
1968	Ferencvaros	MTK
1969	Ujpest Dozsa	Ujpest Dozsa
1970	Ujpest Dozsa	Ujpest Dozsa
1971	Ujpest Dozsa	Ujpest Dozsa
1972	Ujpest Dozsa	Ferencvaros
1973	Ujpest Dozsa	Vasas Budapest
1974	Ujpest Dozsa	Ferencvaros
1975	Ujpest Dozsa	Ujpest Dozsa
1976	Ferencvaros	Ferencvaros
1977	Vasas Budapest	Diosgyor
1978	Ujpest Dozsa	Ferencvaros
1979	Ujpest Dozsa	Raba Eto Gyor
1980	Honved	Diosgyor
1981	Ferencvaros	Vasas Budapest
1982	Raba Eto Gyor	Ujpest Dozsa
1983	Raba Eto Gyor	Ujpest Dozsa

Magyars' wrought havoc. By the time of the return the following May, which Hungary won 7-1, the likes of Ferenc Puskas, Nandor Hidegkuti and Sandor Kocsis had become household names.

The end of the unbeaten run still seems inexplicable today. Hungary duly reached the 1954 World Cup final and established a two-goal lead—only to be beaten by West Germany.

They then went another 18 games without defeat before the uprising of 1956 broke up their marvellous side. Honved were on tour in Western Europe when the political upheaval took place: Puskas, Kocsis and Czibor chose not to return home.

Hungary's football history stretches back well into the 19th century, and Ferencvaros, the major club in Budapest, was founded in 1899. Jimmy Hogan, the Scottish coach who deeply influenced football thinking in Austria, was appointed to MTK in 1916 and helped lay the foundations for the skill which is traditionally part of the Hungarian game.

In 1934 the rivalry with Austria reached a new peak when the teams were paired the second round of the World Cup finals: Austria won 2-1. Four years later Hungary, with a forward line that included Sarosi and Titkos, reached the final. Both star attackers scored but Italy still rampaged to a 4-2 win.

As well as 1952, Hungary also reached the Olympic final in 1964, 1968 and 1972—winning the gold medal again on the first two occasions—but their teams have made little impact in recent years at full international level.

Ferencvaros (twice) and Ujpest Dozsa have both reached the finals of major European competitions—Ferencvaros winning the Fairs Cup in 1965—but the country has yet to provide a Champions Cup finalist.

Ujpest's seven successive championships from 1969 reflected their consistency, but without any real international success it remains the fate of every player in Hungary to be ill-compared with the days of Puskas and Kocsis.

Ferenc Puskas and Billy Wright lead out the sides before Hungary's 6-3 humbling of England at Wembley in 1953. Six months later they won 7-1 in Budapest.

ICELAND

Year	Champions	Cup winners
1912	KR Reykjavik	....
1913	IA Fram	....
1914	IA Fram	....
1915	IA Fram	....
1916	IA Fram	....
1917	IA Fram	....
1918	IA Fram	....
1919	KR Reykjavik	....
1920	Vikingur	....
1921	IA Fram	....
1922	IA Fram	....
1923	IA Fram	....
1924	Vikingur	....
1925	IA Fram	....
1926	KR Reykjavik	....
1927	KR Reykjavik	....
1928	KR Reykjavik	....
1929	KR Reykjavik	....
1930	Valur	....
1931	KR Reykjavik	....
1932	KR Reykjavik	....
1933	Valur	....
1934	KR Reykjavik	....
1935	Valur	....
1936	Valur	....
1937	Valur	....
1938	Valur	....
1939	IA Fram	....
1940	Valur	....
1941	KR Reykjavik	....
1942	Valur	....
1943	Valur	....
1944	Valur	....
1945	Valur	....
1946	IA Fram	....
1947	IA Fram	....
1948	KR Reykjavik	....
1949	KR Reykjavik	....
1950	KR Reykjavik	....
1951	IA Akranes	....
1952	KR Reykjavik	....
1953	IA Akranes	....
1954	IA Akranes	....
1955	KR Reykjavik	....
1956	Valur	....
1957	IA Akranes	....
1958	IA Akranes	....
1959	KR Reykjavik	....
1960	IA Akranes	KR Reykjavik
1961	KR Reykjavik	KR Reykjavik
1962	IA Fram	KR Reykjavik
1963	KR Reykjavik	KR Reykjavik
1964	IB Keflavik	KR Reykjavik
1965	KR Reykjavik	Valur
1966	Valur	KR Reykjavik
1967	Valur	KR Reykjavik
1968	KR Reykjavik	IB Vestmannaey
1969	IB Keflavik	IB Akureyri
1970	IA Akranes	IA Fram
1971	IB Keflavik	Vikingur
1972	IA Fram	IB Vestmannaey
1973	IB Keflavik	IA Fram
1974	IA Akranes	Valur
1975	IA Akranes	Valur
1976	Valur	Valur
1977	IA Akranes	Valur
1978	Valur	IA Akranes
1979	IB Vestmannaey	IA Fram
1980	Valur	IA Fram
1981	Vikingur	IB Vestmannaey
1982	Vikingur	IA Akranes
1983	IA Akranes	IA Akranes

Iceland

In the 1970s Iceland showed that despite their short season (May to October) and a small number of top-class players they could still influence international football. With strong British coaching, notably from Tony Knapp, the former Leicester and Southampton centre-half, Iceland beat East Germany, Norway, Luxembourg and also Northern Ireland.

Domestically the players are restricted by the paucity of grass pitches and by a small first division of only eight clubs. Albert Gudmundsson, who played for Arsenal and AC Milan amongst other clubs, set a trend of the better players moving into Europe, and more recently Ausgei Sigurvinsson (Standard Liège) and also Petur Petursson (Feyenoord) had successful spells in more competitive leagues. The capital city of Reykjavik has produced the most successful clubs—Fram, KR and Valur—challenged particularly by IB Keflavik and IA Akranes.

Northern Ireland

Like the history of the Republic of Ireland, the soccer story of what is now known as Northern Ireland has come to be dominated by political rather than sporting considerations. From October 1971 through to March 1975 no internationals were played in the province and European Championship and World Cup qualifying games took place in places as unlikely as Hull, Coventry and Sheffield.

Not only was this a blow to Irish pride; it also hurt the purse, as there was little incentive for the good people of Coventry to watch Ireland play Portugal at Highfield Road. Eventually soccer returned to Windsor Park but it was hard for the team and fans to regain the atmosphere of earlier, happier, times—until Billy Bingham's side beat Scotland 1-0 in 1980 to set them on the road to only their second outright success in the Home International Championship. A draw at Wembley was followed by a 1-0 win over Wales in Cardiff.

The previous Irish success was just before the First World War, in 1913–14. Wins against Wales at Wrexham and England at Middlesbrough gave Ireland the trophy, with a home draw against Scotland to finish matters off. It was the last time a single Irish side could be chosen; as soon as the war finished, the country was plunged into civil conflict. It was not for nine years that the Irish FA had another victory to celebrate, and by this time it controlled only a third of the players and a quarter of the territory that it had previously held sway over. In fact Northern Ireland (a title not actually adopted until 1954) won only 11 internationals between the wars. It was during that small number, however (against Wales in Belfast on 1 February 1930), that Linfield's Joe Bambrick, playing on his home ground, set up the scoring record for any UK international in a single game by grabbing six goals—a remarkable achievement considering Ireland's almost total lack of international success.

But the team's purple patch undoubtedly came at the end of the 1950s. A great 3-2 win at Wembley in 1957, on only their second visit, led to the World Cup finals in Sweden in 1958—the only time an Irish side had ever competed. Two wins against Czechoslovakia (including a dramatic play-off) and a draw against then World champions West Germany put them through to the quarter-finals, but by that stage injuries had played havoc

NORTHERN IRELAND

Year	Champions	Cup winners
1881	....	Moyola Park
1882	....	Queen's Island
1883	....	Cliftonville
1884	....	Distillery
1885	....	Distillery
1886	....	Distillery
1887	....	Ulster
1888	....	Cliftonville
1889	....	Distillery
1890	....	Gordon Highlanders
1891	Linfield	Linfield
1892	Linfield	Linfield
1893	Linfield	Linfield
1894	Glentoran	Distillery
1895	Linfield	Linfield
1896	Distillery	Distillery
1897	Glentoran	Cliftonville
1898	Linfield	Linfield
1899	Distillery	Linfield
1900	Belfast Celtic	Cliftonville
1901	Distillery	Cliftonville
1902	Linfield	Linfield
1903	Distillery	Distillery
1904	Linfield	Linfield
1905	Glentoran	Distillery
1906	Cliftonville/Distillery	Shelbourne
1907	Linfield	Cliftonville
1908	Linfield	Bohemians
1909	Linfield	Cliftonville
1910	Cliftonville	Distillery
1911	Linfield	Shelbourne
1912	Glentoran	Linfield
1913	Glentoran	Linfield
1914	Linfield	Glentoran
1915	Belfast Celtic	Linfield
1916	*No competition*	Linfield
1917	*No competition*	Glentoran
1918	*No competition*	Belfast Celtic
1919	*No competition*	Linfield
1920	Belfast Celtic	Shelbourne
1921	Glentoran	Glentoran
1922	Linfield	Linfield
1923	Linfield	Linfield
1924	Queen's Island	Queen's Island
1925	Glentoran	Distillery
1926	Belfast Celtic	Belfast Celtic
1927	Belfast Celtic	Ards
1928	Belfast Celtic	Willowfield
1929	Belfast Celtic	Ballymena
1930	Linfield	Linfield
1931	Glentoran	Linfield
1932	Linfield	Glentoran
1933	Belfast Celtic	Glentoran
1934	Linfield	Linfield
1935	Linfield	Glentoran
1936	Belfast Celtic	Linfield
1937	Belfast Celtic	Belfast Celtic
1938	Belfast Celtic	Belfast Celtic
1939	Belfast Celtic	Linfield
1940	Belfast Celtic	Ballymena
1941	*No competition*	Belfast Celtic
1942	*No competition*	Linfield
1943	*No competition*	Belfast Celtic
1944	*No competition*	Belfast Celtic
1945	*No competition*	Linfield
1946	*No competition*	Linfield
1947	*No competition*	Belfast Celtic
1948	Belfast Celtic	Linfield
1949	Linfield	Derry City
1950	Linfield	Linfield

Terry Neill's goal at Wembley in 1972 gave Northern Ireland their first victory over England since 1957—and only their second success against England in 45 years.

and a very good French side won easily by 4-0. Nonetheless the team of Danny Blanchflower and Jimmy McIlroy had been one of the delights of the series and—like Wales—had gone a round further than either England or Scotland.

Republic of Ireland

It is unfortunately impossible to separate politics from football in assessing the international record of Irish football over the years. Unlike rugby, which manages quite capably to operate with a combined side, this small island has to split its resources and, arguably as a result, has never achieved anything of great importance in international competition.

Year	Champions	Cup winners
1951	Glentoran	Glentoran
1952	Glenavon	Ards
1953	Glentoran	Linfield
1954	Linfield	Derry City
1955	Linfield	Dundela
1956	Linfield	Distillery
1957	Glentoran	Glenavon
1958	Ards	Ballymena
1959	Linfield	Glenavon
1960	Glenavon	Linfield
1961	Linfield	Glenavon
1962	Linfield	Linfield
1963	Distillery	Linfield
1964	Glentoran	Derry City
1965	Derry City	Coleraine
1966	Linfield	Glentoran
1967	Glentoran	Crusaders
1968	Glentoran	Crusaders
1969	Linfield	Ards
1970	Glentoran	Linfield
1971	Linfield	Distillery
1972	Glentoran	Coleraine
1973	Crusaders	Glentoran
1974	Coleraine	Ards
1975	Linfield	Coleraine
1976	Crusaders	Carrick Rangers
1977	Glentoran	Coleraine
1978	Linfield	Linfield
1979	Linfield	Cliftonville
1980	Linfield	Linfield
1981	Glentoran	Ballymena
1982	Linfield	Linfield
1983	Linfield	Glentoran

The split effectively came in 1921, a time of civil war in Ireland though Westminster had effectively conceded the principle of Home Rule. The 1920 Irish League and Cup were the last competitions which were realistically open to sides from all over the island, and that year a near riot at a Cup semi-final between Belfast Celtic (Ulster's premier Catholic side) and Glentoran eventually led to both being eliminated and Dublin's Shelbourne being awarded the Cup.

The following year Shelbourne again reached the semi-finals, drew with the Lurgan (Ulster) club Glenavon in Belfast, but were then ordered to replay the game in Belfast. Because of the political situation, Shelbourne understandably refused to travel north again and Glenavon went through. This particular incident was the trigger for the southern clubs to get together and form a separate association and, with the Irish Free State established in June 1921, the Football Association of Ireland was created on 1 September that year.

Catholic teams from Belfast continued to enter the Dublin-based competitions for several years—indeed Alton United actually won the FA of Ireland Cup in 1923.

Two years later the new association was accepted by the home countries on condition that they changed the name to FA of the Irish Free State. FIFA also accepted this nomenclature, but the matter was raised again 30 years later when the Belfast-based association was finally persuaded to stop calling itself Ireland and adopt the title Northern Ireland. At that stage the Dublin association became the 'Republic of Ireland'.

Up to the time that the South declared itself a completely autonomous republic (in 1949) it had been quite common for players to appear for both countries (the most celebrated case being Johnny Carey, who played for both teams against England in the space of three days in 1946) but after this stage the two became totally independent. The Republic of Ireland celebrated in fine style with what remains their most celebrated victory: on 21 September 1949 they defeated England at Goodison and so inflicted on the mother of football her first home defeat by a foreign side. Not that the team was strictly 'foreign'—all but two had played in the Football League.

REPUBLIC OF IRELAND

Year	Champions	Cup winners
1922	St James Gate	St James Gate
1923	Shamrock Rovers	Alton United
1924	Bohemians	Athlone Town
1925	Shamrock Rovers	Shamrock Rovers
1926	Shelbourne	Fordsons
1927	Shamrock Rovers	Drumcondra
1928	Bohemians	Bohemians
1929	Shelbourne	Shamrock Rovers
1930	Bohemians	Shamrock Rovers
1931	Shelbourne	Shamrock Rovers
1932	Shamrock Rovers	Shamrock Rovers
1933	Dundalk	Shamrock Rovers
1934	Bohemians	Cork
1935	Dolphin	Bohemians
1936	Bohemians	Shamrock Rovers
1937	Sligo Rovers	Waterford
1938	Shamrock Rovers	St James Gate
1939	Shamrock Rovers	Shelbourne
1940	St James Gate	Shamrock Rovers
1941	Cork United	Cork United
1942	Cork United	Dundalk
1943	Cork United	Drumcondra
1944	Shelbourne	Shamrock Rovers
1945	Cork United	Shamrock Rovers
1946	Cork United	Drumcondra
1947	Shelbourne	Cork United
1948	Drumcondra	Shamrock Rovers
1949	Drumcondra	Dundalk
1950	Cork Athletic	Transport
1951	Cork Athletic	Cork Athletic
1952	St Patrick's Ath.	Dundalk
1953	Shelbourne	Cork Athletic
1954	Shamrock Rovers	Drumcondra
1955	St Patrick's Ath.	Shamrock Rovers
1956	St Patrick's Ath.	Shamrock Rovers
1957	Shamrock Rovers	Drumcondra
1958	Drumcondra	Dundalk
1959	Shamrock Rovers	St Patrick's Ath.
1960	Limerick	Shelbourne
1961	Drumcondra	St Patrick's Ath.
1962	Shelbourne	Shamrock Rovers
1963	Dundalk	Shelbourne
1964	Shamrock Rovers	Shamrock Rovers
1965	Drumcondra	Shamrock Rovers
1966	Waterford	Shamrock Rovers
1967	Dundalk	Shamrock Rovers
1968	Waterford	Shamrock Rovers
1969	Waterford	Shamrock Rovers
1970	Waterford	Bohemians
1971	Cork Hibernian	Limerick
1972	Waterford	Cork Hibernian
1973	Waterford	Cork Hibernian
1974	Cork Celtic	Finn Harps
1975	Bohemians	Home Farm
1976	Dundalk	Bohemians
1977	Sligo Rovers	Dundalk
1978	Bohemians	Shamrock Rovers
1979	Dundalk	Dundalk
1980	Limerick	Waterford
1981	Athlone Town	Dundalk
1982	Dundalk	Limerick
1983	Athlone Town	Sligo Rovers

Sadly, since then Eire have had little to celebrate. Some good wins in the 1970s under Johnny Giles—against Poland in Poznan and 3-0 against Russia for instance—are little consolation for never having reached the final stages of any major competition.

As with Northern Ireland, nearly all the best players from the Republic find their way to English clubs, leaving the domestic scene one of dubious quality.

ITALY

Year	Champions	Cup winners
1898	Genoa	....
1899	Genoa	....
1900	Genoa	....
1901	AC Milan	....
1902	Genoa	....
1903	Genoa	....
1904	Genoa	....
1905	Juventus	....
1906	AC Milan	....
1907	AC Milan	....
1908	Pro Vercelli	....
1909	Pro Vercelli	....
1910	Inter-Milan	....
1911	Pro Vercelli	....
1912	Pro Vercelli	....
1913	Pro Vercelli	....
1914	Casale	....
1915	Genoa	....
1916-19	*No competition*	....
1920	Inter-Milan	....
1921	Pro Vercelli	....
1922	Novese (FIGC)	Vado
1922	Pro Vercelli (CGI)	....
1923	Genoa	....
1924	Genoa	....
1925	Bologna	....
1926	Juventus	....
1927	Torino	....
1928	Torino	....
1929	Bologna	....
1930	Ambrosiani-Inter	....
1931	Juventus	....
1932	Juventus	....
1933	Juventus	....
1934	Juventus	....
1935	Juventus	....
1936	Bologna	Torino
1937	Bologna	Genoa
1938	Ambrosiani-Inter	Juventus
1939	Bologna	Ambrosiani-Inter
1940	Ambrosiani-Inter	Fiorentina
1941	Bologna	Venezia
1942	AS Roma	Juventus
1943	Torino	Torino
1944	*No competition*	....
1945	*No competition*	....
1946	Torino	....
1947	Torino	....
1948	Torino	....
1949	Torino	....
1950	Juventus	....
1951	AC Milan	....
1952	Juventus	....
1953	Inter-Milan	....
1954	Inter-Milan	....
1955	AC Milan	....
1956	Fiorentina	....
1957	AC Milan	....
1958	Juventus	Lazio
1959	AC Milan	Juventus
1960	Juventus	Juventus
1961	Juventus	Fiorentina
1962	AC Milan	Napoli
1963	Inter-Milan	Atalanta
1964	Bologna	AS Roma
1965	Inter-Milan	Juventus
1966	Inter-Milan	Fiorentina
1967	Juventus	AC Milan
1968	AC Milan	Torino
1969	Fiorentina	AS Roma
1970	Cagliari	Bologna
1971	Inter-Milan	Torino
1972	Juventus	AC Milan
1973	Juventus	AC Milan
1974	Lazio	Bologna
1975	Juventus	Fiorentina
1976	Torino	Napoli
1977	Juventus	AC Milan
1978	Juventus	Inter-Milan
1979	AC Milan	Juventus
1980	Inter-Milan	AS Roma
1981	Juventus	AS Roma
1982	Juventus	Inter-Milan
1983	AS Roma	Juventus

Italy

Twice winners of the World Cup, European Champions and with five clubs on the roll of European honours, Italy remains without doubt one of football's major powers.

Its domestic game retains a unique flavour, backed by big business and thus at times vulnerable to scandal. The distinctive style of play in Italy, based on the rigidity of the catenaccio defence with a low ratio of goals, rarely causes the passion of the support to wane, particularly in the two football capitals of Milan and Turin. The glamour of Italian football has been heightened, particularly in the 1960s, by the expensive importing of some of the world's best players, and in 1980 a ban on foreigners was again lifted.

Italy enjoyed a golden era in the 1930s, when an Olympic gold medal was sandwiched between the World Cup triumphs of 1934 and 1938. The presence of Mussolini fanning the passion in the home crowd made the first success globally unpopular, but no-one could deny Italy's right to the World Cup in France with Inter's Giuseppe Meazza at the helm of a superb side.

After the Second World War Italy found it hard to recapture the same glory. They could not overcome Northern Ireland in the qualifying groups for the 1958 World Cup, but an even greater humiliation lay in store in 1966, when they were eliminated after losing 1-0 to North Korea—a result greeted with such derision in Italy that even the somewhat fortunate success in the European Championship two years later could not obliterate its memory.

In 1970 Italy, with the gifted Sandro Mazzola in midfield, reached the World Cup final in Mexico City, only to lose 4-1 to a combination of Brazil's ability to beat a catenaccio defence, and Italy's own tiredness after a pulsating semi-final win over West Germany. In Argentina eight years later Italy again produced a realistic challenge but once more their obsession with defending rather than looking to add to a one-goal lead was exploited by Holland in a virtual semi-final, and by Brazil in the play-off for third place.

Yet such tactics have served Italian clubs well in the European competitions, with AC Milan and their rivals Internazionale each winning the European Cup twice in the 1960s. Fiorentina, AS Roma and Juventus have also been successful competitors in the European tournaments.

The Italian League system is based on two national divisions, Serie A and Serie B, at the top of a huge pyramid of regional football. With only 18 teams in the top division, Italy's best players face less physical demand in terms of matches played than their British counterparts.

But the pressure to win is arguably greater than anywhere else in the world, and off the

LUXEMBOURG

Year	Champions	Cup winners
1910	Racing Luxembourg	....
1911	Sporting Luxembourg	....
1912	US Hollerich-B'voie	....
1913	*No competition*	....
1914	US Hollerich-B'voie	....
1915	US Hollerich-B'voie	....
1916	US Hollerich-B'voie	....
1917	US Hollerich-B'voie	....
1918	Fola Esch	....
1919	Sporting Luxembourg	....
1920	Fola Esch	....
1921	Jeunesse Esch	....
1922	Fola Esch	Racing Luxembourg
1923	Red Boys Dif'dange	Fola Esch
1924	Fola Esch	Fola Esch
1925	Spora Luxembourg	Red Boys Dif'dange
1926	Red Boys Dif'dange	Red Boys Dif'dange
1927	US Luxembourg	Red Boys Dif'dange
1928	Spora Luxembourg	Spora Luxembourg
1929	Spora Luxembourg	Red Boys Dif'dange
1930	Fola Esch	Red Boys Dif'dange
1931	Red Boys Dif'dange	Red Boys Dif'dange
1932	Red Boys Dif'dange	Spora Luxembourg
1933	Red Boys Dif'dange	Progres Niedercorn
1934	Spora Luxembourg	Red Boys Dif'dange
1935	Spora Luxembourg	Jeunesse Esch
1936	Spora Luxembourg	Red Boys Dif'dange
1937	Jeunesse Esch	Jeunesse Esch
1938	Spora Luxembourg	Stade Dudelange
1939	Stade Dudelange	US Dudelange
1940	Stade Dudelange	Spora Luxembourg
1941-44	*No competition*	*No competition*
1945	Stade Dudelange	Progres Niedercorn
1946	Stade Dudelange	Jeunesse Esch
1947	Stade Dudelange	US Luxembourg

Roberto Bettega's header in Rome helped put England out of the 1978 World Cup.

Year	Champions	Cup winners
1948	Stade Dudelange	US Luembourg
1949	Spora Luxembourg	Stade Dudelange
1950	Stade Dudelange	Spora Luxembourg
1951	Jeunesse Esch	Sport Club Tetange
1952	National Schifflge	Red Boys Dif'dange
1953	Progres Niedercorn	Red Boys Dif'dange
1954	Jeunesse Esch	Jeunesse Esch
1955	Stade Dudelange	Fola Esch
1956	Sport Luxembourg	Stade Dudelange
1957	Stade Dudelange	Spora Luxembourg
1958	Jeunesse Esch	Red Boys Dif'dange
1959	Jeunesse Esch	US Luxembourg
1960	Jeunesse Esch	National Schifflge
1961	Spora Luxembourg	Alliance Dudelange
1962	US Luxembourg	Alliance Dudelange
1963	Jeunesse Esch	US Luxembourg
1964	Aris Bonnevoie	Spora Luxembourg
1965	Stade Dudelange	Spora Luxembourg
1966	Aris Bonnevoie	Spora Luxembourg
1967	Jeunesse Esch	Aris Bonnevoie
1968	Jeunesse Esch	US Remelange
1969	Avenir Beggen	US Luxembourg
1970	Jeunesse Esch	US Luxembourg
1971	US Luxembourg	Jeun'se Hautcharage
1972	Aris Bonnevoie	Red Boys Dif'dange
1973	Jeunesse Esch	Jeunesse Esch
1974	Jeunesse Esch	Jeunesse Esch
1975	Jeunesse Esch	US Rumelange
1976	Jeunesse Esch	Jeunesse Esch
1977	Jeunesse Esch	Progres Niedercorn
1978	Progres Niedercorn	Progres Niedercorn
1979	Red Boys Dif'dange	Red Boys Dif'dange
1980	Jeunesse Esch	Spora Luxembourg
1981	Progres Niedercorn	Jeunesse Esch
1982	Avenir Beggen	Red Boys Dif'dange
1983	Jeunesse Esch	Avenir Beggen

field club discipline places great restriction on life outside football. On the field the knowledge that one goal so often decides a match increases the intensity of competition.

The big city clubs have dominated the Italian championship, but in 1970 Cagliari of Sardinia were champions thanks to the scoring prowess of Luigi Riva; and Paolo Rossi, the golden boy of Italian football in the late 1970s, played first with Lanerossi Vicenza and then with Perugia after being rejected by Juventus.

Liechtenstein

The tiny principality of Liechtenstein supports only seven major clubs, six of which compete in Swiss leagues. Liechtenstein was only registered with FIFA and UEFA in 1974, and has never produced a representative for a major European competition. Its only national side is at Under-21 level. In 1975 a cup tournament was established, and won in the first year by USV Eschen/Mauren. The 1,200 registered players are all amateurs, and the participation in Swiss football is restricted to the regional third and fourth divisions.

Luxembourg

Against great odds tiny Luxembourg continues to compete at international level, despite only the most sporadic success—like the 4-2 win over Portugal in 1961 (in Eusebio's first international) and a victory over Holland in the qualifying groups for the 1964 European Championship.

Football in Luxembourg is entirely amateur throughout the four major divisions, the first division of which is restricted to 12 clubs.

Luxembourg was affiliated to FIFA in 1910 and the following year lost its first international 4-1 at home to France. Jeunesse Esch have been the most successful club since the war but the standard of football has regularly been put into context by heavy defeats in the European competitions. Preparation is also handicapped by the shift-work of so many players in the industrial towns, making it difficult to hold full-scale training sessions. Luxembourg's best known player was Louis Pilot, who became a professional in Belgium and later managed the Luxembourg national side.

Malta

The inherent weakness in Maltese football has at times been compensated by the difficulty encountered by visiting clubs and countries. The island sports only one major stadium, at Gzira, where all the Maltese League matches are played. The sanded pitch which covers a rockbed has proved troublesome to those who are not used to it and has been responsible for a number of surprising results.

In February 1979 West Germany could only draw in Gzira in a European Championship qualifying game. Five years earlier West Germany had only won 1-0, as had England in 1971. Then the difference in standard was totally emphasized in the return match at Wembley when the only times Gordon Banks touched the ball were from four back passes!

In Malta itself there remains continual debate as to whether their teams should compete in Europe; rarely do they progress beyond the opening round, though club sides like Sliema Wanderers, Floriana and Valletta also benefit from their knowledge of the Gzira pitch—and several experienced sides have been happy to come away with a draw, invariably to win the second leg.

Originally a British colony, the growth of the game in Malta has been as a direct result of the British influence. Even now, the Maltese retain a passionate interest in British football and the Malta branches of the Manchester United and Leeds United supporters clubs are extremely active.

Malta play hosts to Wales on their tiny grassless pitch at Gzira in 1979.

MALTA

Year	Champions	Cup winners
1910	Floriana	....
1911	*No competition*	....
1912	Floriana	....
1913	Floriana	....
1914	Hamrun Spartans	....
1915	Valletta United	....
1916	*No competition*	....
1917	St George's	....
1918	Hamrun Spartans	....
1919	KOMR Milizia	....
1920	Sliema Wanderers	....
1921	Floriana	....
1922	Floriana	....
1923	Sliema Wanderers	....
1924	Sliema Wanderers	....
1925	Floriana	....
1926	Sliema Wanderers	....
1927	Floriana	....
1928	Floriana	....
1929	Floriana	....
1930	Sliema Wanderers	....
1931	Floriana	....
1932	Valletta	....
1933	Sliema Wanderers	....
1934	Sliema Wanderers	....
1935	Floriana	Sliema Wanderers
1936	Sliema Wanderers	Sliema Wanderers
1937	Floriana	Sliema Wanderers
1938	Sliema Wanderers	Floriana
1939	Sliema Wanderers	Melita
1940	Sliema Wanderers	Sliema Wanderers
1941-44	*No competition*	*No competition*
1945	Valletta	Floriana
1946	Valletta	Sliema Wanderers
1947	Hamrun Spartans	Floriana
1948	Valletta	Sliema Wanderers
1949	Sliema Wanderers	Floriana
1950	Floriana	Floriana
1951	Floriana	Sliema Wanderers
1952	Floriana	Sliema Wanderers
1953	Floriana	Floriana
1954	Sliema Wanderers	Floriana
1955	Floriana	Floriana
1956	Floriana	Sliema Wanderers
1957	Sliema Wanderers	Floriana
1958	Floriana	Floriana
1959	Valletta	Sliema Wanderers
1960	Valletta	Valletta
1961	Hibernians	Floriana
1962	Floriana	Hibernians
1963	Valletta	Sliema Wanderers
1964	Sliema Wanderers	Valletta
1965	Sliema Wanderers	Sliema Wanderers
1966	Sliema Wanderers	Floriana
1967	Hibernians	Floriana
1968	Floriana	Sliema Wanderers
1969	Hibernians	Floriana
1970	Floriana	Hibernians
1971	Sliema Wanderers	Hibernians
1972	Sliema Wanderers	Floriana
1973	Floriana	Gzira United
1974	Valletta	Sliema Wanderers
1975	Floriana	Valletta
1976	Sliema Wanderers	Floriana
1977	Floriana	Valletta
1978	Valletta	Valletta
1979	Hibernians	Sliema Wanderers
1980	Valletta	Hibernians
1981	Hibernians	Floriana
1982	Hibernians	Hibernians
1983	Hamrun Spartans	Hamrun Spartans

Norway

In 1936 Norway shocked the Berlin crowd, which included Adolf Hitler, by knocking Germany out of the Olympic football tournament. Norway went on to win a bronze medal and two years later the Scandinavian country qualified, for the only time to date, for the World Cup finals. In France they narrowly lost to Italy, the holders, who then successfully defended their title.

Since then Norway have made little impact on the international stage; unlike Sweden they have never managed to overcome the disadvantages of a lack of full-time professionalism and the Scandinavian summer season.

The initial competition in Norway was on a knock-out basis, and a national league did not start until 1938. Fredrikstad and Viking Stavanger have been the most successful clubs in the league, which is limited to 12 sides at the head of a regional structure.

Norwegian clubs naturally compete in the major European competitions, and in 1969 Lyn Oslo reached the quarter-finals of the Cup Winners Cup, when only a narrow 5-4 aggregate defeat by Barcelona ended a gallant run.

Football is the most popular summer sport in Norway, and the followers have a deep knowledge of the game in more fashionable countries. The interest dates back into the 19th century, and Norway became affiliated to FIFA as early as 1908.

NORWAY

Year	Champions	Cup winners
1902	....	Grane Arendal
1903	....	Odds Skien
1904	....	Odds Skien
1905	....	Odds Skien
1906	....	Odds Skien
1907	....	Mercantile Oslo
1908	....	Lyn Oslo
1909	....	Lyn Oslo
1910	....	Lyn Oslo
1911	....	Lyn Oslo
1912	....	Mercantile Oslo
1913	....	Lyn Skien
1914	....	Frigg Oslo
1915	....	Odds Skien
1916	....	Frigg Oslo
1917	....	Sarpsborg
1918	....	Kvik Halden
1919	....	Odds Skien
1920	....	Orn Horten
1921	....	Frigg Oslo
1922	....	Odds Skien
1923	....	Brann Bergen
1924	....	Odds Skien
1925	....	Brann Bergen
1926	....	Odds Skien
1927	....	Orn Horten
1928	....	Orn Horten
1929	....	Sarpsborg
1930	....	Orn Horten
1931	....	Odds Skien
1932	....	Fredrikstad
1933	....	Mjondalen IF
1934	....	Mjondalen IF
1935	....	Fredrikstad
1936	....	Fredrikstad
1937	....	Mjondalen IF
1938	Fredrikstad	Fredrikstad
1939	Fredrikstad	Sarpsborg
1940	*No competition*	Fredrikstad
1941-44	*No competition*	*No competition*
1945	*No competition*	Lyn Oslo
1946	*No competition*	Lyn Oslo
1947	*No competition*	Skeid Oslo
1948	SK Freidig	Sarpsborg
1949	Fredrikstad	Sarpsborg
1950	IF Fram	Fredrikstad
1951	Fredrikstad	Sarpsborg
1952	Fredrikstad	Sparta Sarpsborg
1953	Larvik TIF	Viking Stavangar
1954	Fredrikstad	Skeid Oslo
1955	Larvik TIF	Skeid Oslo
1956	Larvik TIF	Skeid Oslo
1957	Fredrikstad	Fredrikstad
1958	Viking Stavangar	Skeid Oslo
1959	Lillestrom	Viking Stavangar
1960	Fredrikstad	Ros. Trondheim
1961	Fredrikstad	Fredrikstad
1962	Brann Bergen	Gjovik-Lyn
1963	Brann Bergen	Skeid Oslo
1964	Lyn Oslo	Ros. Trondheim
1965	Valerengen Oslo	Skeid Oslo
1966	Skeid Oslo	Fredrikstad
1967	Ros. Trondheim	Lyn Oslo
1968	Lyn Oslo	Lyn Oslo
1969	Ros. Trondheim	Strom. Drammen
1970	Strom. Drammen	Strom. Drammen
1971	Ros. Trondheim	Ros. Trondheim
1972	Viking Stavangar	Brann Bergen
1973	Viking Stavangar	Strom. Drammen
1974	Viking Stavangar	Skeid Oslo
1975	Viking Stavangar	Bodo Glimt
1976	Lillestrom SK	Brann Bergen
1977	Lillestrom SK	Lillestrom SK
1978	Start Kristiansand	Lillestrom SK
1979	Viking Stavangar	Viking Stavangar
1980	Start Kristiansand	Valerengen Oslo
1981	Valerengen Oslo	Lillestrom SK
1982	Viking Stavangar	Brann Bergen
1983	Valerengen Oslo	Moss FC

Poland

After a World Cup history noted only for playing a losing part in the memorable tie with Brazil in the 1938 series—Ernest Willimowski scoring four goals in the 6-5 defeat—Poland's stature rose considerably in the 1970s. The core of the side which had won the gold medal in the 1972 Olympics, with two goals from Kazimierz Deyna, the attacking midfield player from Legia Warsaw, attained more glory by eliminating England in the qualifying group for the 1974 finals.

In Lato and Szarmach, the latter the replacement for the injured Lubanski, Poland produced two strikers whose combined talents took the nation to the very brink of the final. But in swamp-like conditions after a freak storm in Frankfurt, Poland lost by the game's only goal in a virtual semi-final against West Germany. Series top scorer Lato, however, manufactured one more goal to clinch third place over Brazil.

Poland surrendered their Olympic title to East Germany in the 1976 final, and though Deyna, to win his 100th cap in the tournament, Lato, Szarmach and the giant goalkeeper Tomaszewski remained, Poland were on the decline and struggled to beat Tunisia in the 1978 World Cup.

Football became popular in Poland at the turn of the century, fostered by British engineers. But the game only took on a stable organization then the country became independent after the First World War. The first international match was played in Budapest in 1921, a 1-0 defeat by Hungary.

Much of the early domestic football was dominated by Wisla Krakow and Ruch Chorzow, and remarkably Polonia's championship in 1946 was the first won by a Warsaw club, before another nine-year break.

Gornik Zabrze led the way into Europe after 1956 and between 1957 and 1972 they won the Polish championship nine times, and also produced five successive Cup wins between 1968 and 1972.

In 1970 Gornik became the only Polish team to reach the final of a European competition after progress that combined both skill (they beat Rangers 3-1 in both legs in the second round) and good fortune (their place in the final was secured on the toss of a coin after a replay with Roma in Strasburg had ended level). In the Vienna final the free-scoring Lubanski could not penetrate the Manchester City defence and Gornik were beaten 2-1.

The best performance by a Polish club in

POLAND

Year	Champions	Cup winners
1921	Cracovia	....
1922	Pogon Lvov	....
1923	Pogon Lvov	....
1924	*No competition*	....
1925	Pogon Lvov	....
1926	Pogon Lvov	....
1927	Wisla Krakow	....
1928	Wisla Krakow	....
1929	Warta	....
1930	Cracovia	....
1931	Garbarnia Krakow	....
1932	Cracovia	....
1933	Ruch Chorzow	....
1934	Ruch Chorzow	....
1935	Ruch Chorzow	....
1936	Ruch Chorzow	....
1937	Cracovia	....
1938	Ruch Chorzow	....
1939	*Not completed*	....
1940-45	*No competition*	....
1946	Polonia Warsaw	....
1947	Warta	....
1948	Cracovia	....
1949	Wisla Krakow	....
1950	Wisla Krakow	....
1951	Wisla Krakow	Ruch Chorzow
1952	Ruch Chorzow	Polonia Warsaw
1953	Ruch Chorzow	*No competition*
1954	Polonia Bytom	Gwardia Warsaw

Polish joy after victory over Hungary in the Olympic final of 1972 in Munich.

Year	Champions	Cup winners
1955	Legia Warsaw	Legia Warsaw
1956	Legia Warsaw	Legia Warsaw
1957	Gornik Zabrze	LKS Lodz
1958	LKS Lodz	*No competition*
1959	Gornik Zabrze	*No competition*
1960	Ruch Chorzow	*No competition*
1961	Gornik Zabrze	*No competition*
1962	Polonia Bytom	Zaglebie Sosnowiec
1963	Gornik Zabrze	Zaglebie Sosnowiec
1964	Gornik Zabrze	Legia Warsaw
1965	Gornik Zabrze	Gornik Zabrze
1966	Gornik Zabrze	Legia Warsaw
1967	Gornik Zabrze	Wisla Krakow
1968	Ruch Chorzow	Gornik Zabrze
1969	Legia Warsaw	Gornik Zabrze
1970	Legia Warsaw	Gornik Zabrze
1971	Gornik Zabrze	Gornik Zabrze
1972	Gornik Zabrze	Gornik Zabrze
1973	Stal Mielec	Legia Warsaw
1974	Ruch Chorzow	Ruch Chorzow
1975	Ruch Chorzow	Stal Rzeszow
1976	Stal Mielec	Slask Wroclaw
1977	Slask Wroclaw	Zaglebie Sosnowiec
1978	Wisla Krakow	Zaglebie Sosnowiec
1979	Ruch Chorzow	Arka Gdynia
1980	Szombierki Bytom	Legia Warsaw
1981	Widzew Lodz	Legia Warsaw
1982	Widzew Lodz	Lech Poznan
1983	Lech Poznan	Lechia Gdansk

the European Cup came the same season, when Legia Warsaw reached the semi-finals before losing 2-0 on aggregate to Feyenoord, the eventual winners.

The Polish League championship was increased from 14 to 16 clubs in 1973 and the season, in common with the rest of Eastern Europe, takes a midwinter break in December, January and February. Poland rewards its senior players by allowing them to spend the latter days of their careers in western Europe, the most recent examples being Deyna in England, Gadocha in the United States, and Tomaszewski and Lubanski in Belgium.

The First Division is now supported by a 32-club Second Division in two sections, a similar Third Division, and district leagues. But the remarkable domination of both League and Cup by the clubs from the Silesia region—mainly from the coal centres of Katowice, Chorzow, Sosnowiec, Mielec, Bytom and Zabrze—continues despite the larger format.

In 1979 Poland ended the decade in disappointment, failing to qualify for the European Championship finals in a group which was narrowly won by Holland. Poland, in fact, took three points off the Dutchmen, but in turn lost three to East Germany.

Portugal

The reputation of Portuguese football is linked with the success of Benfica, the nation's leading club. Portugal have reached the finals of the World Cup, only once, in 1966, with a side heavily dependent on players who had won the European Cup with Benfica in 1961 and 1962 and been losing finalists in 1963 and 1965.

Eusebio, who was to make a record 77 international appearances, was the central figure for both club and country. Introduced by Benfica for their World Club Championship play-off against Penarol in 1965, the lithe striker from Mozambique outshone the ageing stars from Real Madrid when his two magnificently struck shots in the second half of the 1962 European Cup finally shored up a memorable 5-3 success. Eusebio scored again in the 1963 final, though Benfica lost their chance of a hat-trick of wins by 2-1 to AC Milan at Wembley. Two years later Inter-Milan's cast-iron defence again pushed Benfica into second place.

But in 1966 it was Portugal and Eusebio who ran a romantic thread through the World Cup finals in England. The Portuguese, with Torres, Augusto, Simoes and Coluna ably supporting Eusebio, decisively beat Hungary, who were much-fancied, and Bulgaria in group 2. In their next match Eusebio's superb touch in front of goal sparked a performance that eliminated Brazil, the holders.

But it was the quarter-final that remains one of the most dramatic of World Cup ties North Korea, who had already beaten Italy, raced into a 3-0 lead before Eusebio almost single-handedly turned the tide. His four goals, out of Portugal's five, restored sanity to the match. In the semi-final Portugal were on the wrong end of England's most fluent performance, though Eusebio's penalty made for an enthralling finish. His ninth and final goal of the tournament helped win third place for Portugal over Russia.

A type of football was first played in Portugal in 1866; the Lisbon Football Club was founded nine years later. The national league did not begin until 1935, by which time Portugal had established a reputation as a difficult side to beat at home but vulnerable in away matches. Defeats by Northern Ireland in 1957 and by Luxembourg in 1961 in the World Cup qualifiers endorsed a similar view in later times.

Benfica's defeat of Barcelona at Berne in 1961 put Portugal on the football map.

Benfica continued to dominate the domestic competitions—they were also losing finalists in the European Cup to Manchester United in 1968—but in the 1970s the club exerted less influence on the European competitions. Sporting Lisbon won the Cup Winners Cup in 1964, surviving a 4-1 mauling at Old Trafford in the first leg of the quarter-final to beat Manchester United 5-0 in Portugal.

In 1979 Portugal seemed well placed to reach the finals of the European Championships until a disastrous home defeat by Austria in the group that was finally won by Belgium.

PORTUGAL

Year	Champions	Cup winners
1922	....	FC Porto
1923	....	Sporting Lisbon
1924	....	Olhanense
1925	....	FC Porto
1926	....	Maritimo
1927	....	Belenenses
1928	....	Carcavelinhos
1929	....	Belenenses
1930	....	Benfica
1931	....	Benfica
1932	....	FC Porto
1933	....	Belenenses
1934	....	Sporting Lisbon
1935	FC Porto	Benfica
1936	Benfica	Sporting Lisbon
1937	Benfica	FC Porto
1938	Benfica	Sporting Lisbon
1939	FC Porto	Academica Coimbra
1940	FC Porto	Benfica
1941	Sporting Lisbon	Sporting Lisbon
1942	Benfica	Belenenses
1943	Benfica	Benfica
1944	Sporting Lisbon	Benfica
1945	Benfica	Sporting Lisbon
1946	Belenenses	Sporting Lisbon
1947	Sporting Lisbon	*No competition*
1948	Sporting Lisbon	Sporting Lisbon
1949	Sporting Lisbon	Benfica
1950	Benfica	*No competition*
1951	Sporting Lisbon	Benfica
1952	Sporting Lisbon	Benfica

Year	Champions	Cup winners
1953	Sporting Lisbon	Benfica
1954	Sporting Lisbon	Sporting Lisbon
1955	Benfica	Benfica
1956	FC Porto	FC Porto
1957	Benfica	Benfica
1958	Sporting Lisbon	FC Porto
1959	FC Porto	Benfica
1960	Benfica	Belenenses
1961	Benfica	Leixoes Porto
1962	Sporting Lisbon	Benfica
1963	Benfica	Sporting Lisbon
1964	Benfica	Benfica
1965	Benfica	Vitoria Setubal
1966	Sporting Lisbon	Sporting Braga
1967	Benfica	Vitoria Setubal
1968	Benfica	FC Porto
1969	Benfica	Benfica
1970	Sporting Lisbon	Benfica
1971	Benfica	Sporting Lisbon
1972	Benfica	Benfica
1973	Benfica	Sporting Lisbon
1974	Sporting Lisbon	Sporting Lisbon
1975	Benfica	Boavista
1976	Benfica	Boavista
1977	Benfica	FC Porto
1978	FC Porto	Sporting Lisbon
1979	FC Porto	Boavista
1980	Sporting Lisbon	Benfica
1981	Benfica	Benfica
1982	Sporting Lisbon	Sporting Lisbon
1983	Benfica	Benfica

Rumania

Three Balkan Cup victories between 1931 and 1936 is the total of Rumania's success in international competition. The country and its leading clubs have regularly promised more than was actually achieved.

The Rumanian monarchy encouraged the growth of football, notably Prince (later King) Carol who, in 1930, insisted that Rumania should be represented in distant Uruguay in the initial World Cup. The first tie against Peru, was won 3-1 but Uruguay, who were to become champions, ended Rumania's progress with a decisive 4-0 victory in Montevideo.

In 1934 Rumania lost with credit to the fancied Czechs in the first round, but four years later were surprise victims of Cuba after a replay. Since then Rumania have only reached the final stages once, in 1970.

The national league has a history that extends back to 1910, but it was more formally constituted in 1930 when Rumania also became affiliated to FIFA.

Chinezul Timisoara dominated the League in the twenties but more recently Dynamo Bucharest, the first Rumanian club to enter the European Cup, Rapid and Steaua have formed a formidable trio in the capital city. Universitatea Craiova, a team of 'students', have also been entrants in European competitions—they beat Leeds United in the UEFA Cup in 1978–79—but as with the national team, there has not been sufficient strength in depth in club football to make a genuine challenge to win a major honour.

RUMANIA

Year	Champions	Cup winners
1910	Olimpia Bucharest	....
1911	Olimpia Bucharest	....
1912	United Ploesti	....
1913	Colentina Bucharest	....
1914	Colentina Bucharest	....
1915	Soc.RA Bucharest	....
1916	Prahova Ploesti	....
1917-19	*No competition*	....
1920	Venus Bucharest	....
1921	Venus Bucharest	....
1922	Chinezul Timisoara	....
1923	Chinezul Timisoara	....
1924	Chinezul Timisoara	....
1925	Chinezul Timisoara	....
1926	Chinezul Timisoara	....
1927	Chinezul Timisoara	....
1928	Coltea Brasov	....
1929	Venus Bucharest	....
1930	Juventus Bucharest	....
1931	SUD Resita	....
1932	Venus Bucharest	....
1933	Ripensia Timisoara	....
1934	Venus Bucharest	Ripensia Timisoara
1935	Ripensia Timisoara	CFR Bucharest
1936	Ripensia Timisoara	Ripensia Timisoara
1937	Venus Bucharest	Rapid Bucharest
1938	Ripensia Timisoara	Rapid Bucharest
1939	Venus Bucharest	Rapid Bucharest
1940	Venus Bucharest	Rapid Bucharest
1941	Tricolor	Rapid Bucharest
1942	Rapid Bucharest	Rapid Bucharest
1943	Craiova Bucharest	CFR Turnu Severin
1944-46	*No competition*	*No competition*
1947	UT Arad	*No competition*
1948	UT Arad	UT Arad
1949	ICO Oradea	CCA Bucharest
1950	UT Arad	CCA Bucharest
1951	CCA Bucharest	CCA Bucharest
1952	CCA Bucharest	CCA Bucharest
1953	CCA Bucharest	UT Arad
1954	UT Arad	Metalul Resita
1955	Dynamo Bucharest	CCA Bucharest
1956	CCA Bucharest	ICO Oradea
1957	*No competition*	*No competition*
1958	Petrolul Ploesti	Stinta Timisoara
1959	Petrolul Ploesti	Dynamo Bucharest
1960	CCA Bucharest	Progresul
1961	Steaua Bucharest	Progresul
1962	Dynamo Bucharest	Steaua Bucharest
1963	Dynamo Bucharest	Petrolul Ploesti
1964	Dynamo Bucharest	Dynamo Bucharest
1965	Dynamo Bucharest	Stinta Cluj
1966	Petrolul Ploesti	Steaua Bucharest
1967	Rapid Bucharest	Steaua Bucharest
1968	Steaua Bucharest	Dynamo Bucharest
1969	UT Arad	Steaua Bucharest
1970	UT Arad	Steaua Bucharest
1971	Dynamo Bucharest	Steaua Bucharest
1972	Arges Pitesti	Rapid Bucharest
1973	Dynamo Bucharest	Chimia Vilcea
1974	Univ.Craiova	Jiul Petroseni
1975	Dynamo Bucharest	Rapid Bucharest
1976	Steaua Bucharest	Steaua Bucharest
1977	Dynamo Bucharest	Univ.Craiova
1978	Steaua Bucharest	Univ.Craiova
1979	Arges Pitesti	Steaua Bucharest
1980	Univ.Craiova	Poli Timisoara
1981	Univ.Craiova	Univ.Craiova
1982	Dynamo Bucharest	Dynamo Bucharest
1983	Dynamo Bucharest	Univ.Craiova

Scotland

It has been said, with some reason, that the history of Scottish football is basically one of three great clubs (in modern times just two), of annual skirmishes with the enemy south of the border and very little else.

It was after the humiliating 7-0 defeat by Uruguay in the 1954 World Cup in Switzerland, that a member of the Scottish FA committee is reputed to have said to the team: 'Never mind lads, it doesn't matter so long as we defeat England next season.' That indeed does seem to sum up what was, for so long, the Scots' attitude towards international football.

Scotland have little or nothing of substance to show for their century of international existence, apart from a fair number of successes over England generally regarded as significant only by themselves. By 1979 English fans had effectively abandoned even attending these games because of the appalling but deserved reputation that Scottish fans had gained in odd years with their drunken cavortings in the West End, the ritual demolition of tube trains and British Rail specials south, and the tedious tearing

SCOTLAND

Year	Champions	Cup winners
1874	....	Queen's Park
1875	....	Queen's Park
1876	....	Queen's Park
1877	....	Vale of Leven
1878	....	Vale of Leven
1879	....	Vale of Leven
1880	....	Queen's Park
1881	....	Queen's Park
1882	....	Queen's Park
1883	....	Dumbarton
1884	....	Queen's Park
1885	....	Renton
1886	....	Queen's Park
1887	....	Hibernian
1888	....	Renton
1889	....	Third Lanark
1890	....	Queen's Park
1891	Dumbarton/Rangers	Heart of Midlothian
1892	Dumbarton	Celtic
1893	Celtic	Queen's Park
1894	Celtic	Rangers
1895	Heart of Midlothian	St Bernard's
1896	Celtic	Heart of Midlothian
1897	Heart of Midlothian	Rangers
1898	Celtic	Rangers
1899	Rangers	Celtic
1900	Rangers	Celtic
1901	Rangers	Heart of Midlothian
1902	Rangers	Hibernian
1903	Hibernian	Rangers
1904	Third Lanark	Celtic
1905	Celtic	Third Lanark
1906	Celtic	Heart of Midlothian
1907	Celtic	Celtic
1908	Celtic	Celtic
1909	Celtic	*Cup withheld*
1910	Celtic	Dundee
1911	Rangers	Celtic
1912	Rangers	Celtic
1913	Rangers	Falkirk
1914	Celtic	Celtic
1915	Celtic	*No competition*
1916	Celtic	*No competition*
1917	Celtic	*No competition*
1918	Rangers	*No competition*
1919	Celtic	*No competition*
1920	Rangers	Kilmarnock
1921	Rangers	Partick Thistle
1922	Celtic	Morton
1923	Rangers	Celtic
1924	Rangers	Airdrieonians
1925	Rangers	Celtic

SWITZERLAND

Year	Champions	Cup winners
1898	Grasshoppers	....
1899	Anglo-American FC	....
1900	Grasshoppers	....
1901	Grasshoppers	....
1902	FC Zurich	....
1903	Young Boys Berne	....
1904	St Gallen	....
1905	Grasshoppers	....
1906	Winterthur	....
1907	Servette	....
1908	Winterthur	....
1909	Young Boys Berne	....
1910	Young Boys Berne	....
1911	Young Boys Berne	....
1912	Aarau	....
1913	Lausanne	....
1914	Aarau	....
1915	SC Bruhl St Gallen	....
1916	Cantonal-Neuchatel	....
1917	Winterthur	....
1918	Servette	....
1919	La Chaux de Fonds	....
1920	Young Boys Berne	....
1921	Grasshoppers	....
1922	Servette	....
1923	*No competition*	....
1924	FC Zurich	....
1925	Servette	....
1926	Servette	Grasshoppers
1927	Grasshoppers	Grasshoppers
1928	Grasshoppers	Servette
1929	Young Boys Berne	Urania Geneva
1930	Servette	Young Boys Berne
1931	Grasshoppers	Lugano
1932	Lausanne	Grasshoppers
1933	Servette	Basle
1934	Servette	Grasshoppers
1935	Lausanne	Lausanne
1936	Lausanne	Y'g Fellows Zurich
1937	Grasshoppers	Grasshoppers
1938	Lugano	Grasshoppers
1929	Grasshoppers	Lausanne
1940	Servette	Grasshoppers
1941	Lugano	Grasshoppers
1942	Grasshoppers	Grasshoppers
1943	Grasshoppers	Grasshoppers
1944	Lausanne	Lausanne
1945	Grasshoppers	Young Boys Berne
1946	Servette	Grasshoppers
1947	FC Biel	Basle
1948	Bellinzona	La Chaux de Fonds
1949	Lugano	Servette
1950	Servette	Lausanne
1951	Lausanne	La Chaux de Fonds
1952	Grasshoppers	Grasshoppers
1953	Basle	Young Boys Berne
1954	La Chaux de Fonds	La Chaux de Fonds
1955	La Chaux de Fonds	La Chaux de Fonds
1956	Grasshoppers	Grasshoppers
1957	Young Boys Berne	La Chaux de Fonds
1958	Young Boys Berne	Young Boys Berne
1959	Young Boys Berne	Grenchen
1960	Young Boys Berne	Lucerne
1961	Servette	La Chaux de Fonds
1962	Servette	Lausanne
1963	FC Zurich	Basle
1964	La Chaux de Fonds	Lausanne
1965	Lausanne	Sion
1966	FC Zurich	FC Zurich
1967	Basle	Basle
1968	FC Zurich	Lugano
1969	Basle	St Gallen
1970	Basle	FC Zurich
1971	Grasshoppers	Servette
1972	Basle	FC Zurich
1973	Basle	FC Zurich
1974	FC Zurich	Sion
1975	FC Zurich	Basle
1976	FC Zurich	FC Zurich
1977	Basle	Young Boys Berne
1978	Grasshoppers	Servette
1979	Servette	Servette
1980	Basle	Sion
1981	FC Zurich	Lausanne
1982	Grasshoppers	Sion
1983	Grasshoppers	Grasshoppers

Grasshoppers' Claudio Sulser led the European Cup scorers with 11 goals in 1978-79.

Switzerland

The neutrality of Switzerland has made the country a perfect home for the headquarters of FIFA and UEFA, and Switzerland, a founder member of FIFA, has always acquitted itself well in international football.

Karl Rappan, who guided the Swiss to four successive World Cup final series, was responsible for a tactical innovation, the 'bolt' defence, which often sustained Switzerland against more illustrious opposition. In 1938 Rappan's side eliminated Germany; in 1950 the Swiss 'bolt' shut the door in Brazil's face for a 2-2 draw; in 1954 Italy were beaten twice before Austria were allowed to score five goals in seven minutes and win a 7-5 thriller. In 1960 Rappan was recalled once more as coach and led Switzerland through a heroic run in the qualifying group for the 1962 World Cup, finally gaining a place in Chile after a play-off with Sweden in Berlin.

The Swiss League remains one of the world's most complex. In the top division, which has only 12 clubs, the first part of the season is spent as an orthodox league, with each team playing each other home and away. In the second half of the season the top six then play each other to determine who is the champion, while the bottom six do the same to decide who is relegated. But an added complication is that to each team's total of points in this mini-league is added half of the points gained in the first half of the season. In 1964 FC Zurich emulated Young Boys Berne (1959) in reaching the semi-finals of the European Cup, beating Dundalk, Galatasaray and PSV Eindhoven; but even in decline Real Madrid proved too strong in an 8-1 aggregate victory. In 1978-79 Claudio Sulser, like most top Swiss players a highly-paid part-timer, scored 11 goals in six games in the European Cup for neighbours Grasshoppers, including three against Real.

Grasshoppers' championship in 1978 was a rare break from the domination of Zurich and Basle. Beneath the top level of clubs is a strong regional formation which also incorporates the Liechtenstein sides.

Turkey

In 1954 Turkey qualified for the World Cup finals in Switzerland, eliminating Spain along the way. Under today's rules their superior goal difference—aided by a 7-0 win over South Korea—would have taken them through the first group stage at the expense of West Germany, who went on to win the competition! Instead they faced a play-off which the Germans won 7-2.

Turkey's adoption of professionalism shortly after the Second World War was responsible for this greater competitiveness at international level. It was Turkey, with a 3-1 win in Istanbul, who ended Hungary's run of 18 games without defeat after the 1954 World Cup final.

Galatasaray, along with Fenerbahce, Turkey's most successful club, played a strong part in the game's development when

TURKEY

Year	Champions	Cup winners
1924	Harbuje	....
1925-26	*No competition*	....
1927	Mahafiz Gucu	....
1928-31	*No competition*	....
1932	Instanbulspor	....
1933	Fenerbahce	....
1934	Besiktas	....
1935	Fenerbahce	....
1936-39	*No competition*	....
1940	Demispor	....
1941	Genclerbirligi	....
1942	Harb Okulu Gucu	....
1943	*No competition*	....
1944	Genclerbirligi	....
1945	Harb Okulu Gucu	....
1946	Genclerbirligi	....
1947	Demispor	....
1948	*No competition*	....
1949	Ankara Gucu	....
1950	Goztepe Izmir	....
1951-58	*No competition*	....
1959	Fenerbahce	....
1960	Besiktas	....
1961	Fenerbahce	....
1962	Galatasaray	....
1963	Galatasaray	Galatasaray
1964	Fenerbahce	Galatasaray
1965	Fenerbahce	Galatasaray
1966	Besiktas	Galatasaray
1967	Besiktas	Altay Izmir
1968	Fenerbahce	Fenerbahce
1969	Fenerbahce	Goztepe Izmir
1970	Fenerbahce	Goztepe Izmir
1971	Galatasaray	Eskisehirspor
1972	Galatasaray	Ankara Gucu
1973	Galatasaray	Galatasaray
1974	Fenerbahce	Fenerbahce
1975	Fenerbahce	Besiktas
1976	Trabzonspor	Galatasaray
1977	Trabzonspor	Trabzonspor
1978	Fenerbahce	Trabzonspor
1979	Trabzonspor	Fenerbahce
1980	Trabzonspor	Altay Izmir
1981	Trabzonspor	Ankara Gucu
1982	Besiktas	Galatasaray
1983	Fenerbahce	Fenerbahce

political forces tried to ban it at the turn of the century. But it was not until the fall of the Turkish Empire that football was formalized. The national championship was founded in 1923, the same year that Turkey was affiliated to FIFA.

The passion of the home support makes Turkey a difficult place for visiting teams. Manchester City were eliminated from the 1969 European Cup by Fenerbahce and 10 years later Wales slumped to a controversial defeat in the European Championship in Istanbul, while Turkey had already held West Germany to a goalless draw.

USSR

The Soviet Union has never quite translated its resources as a nation into being a real power in the world of football, their stilted style always being a handicap. Hindered by politics, its contacts with the game in the West only began after the Second World War, notably when the Dynamo Moscow tour of Britain in 1945 totally captured the public imagination.

USSR

Year	Champions	Cup winners
1936	Dynamo Moscow*	....
1936	Spartak Moscow†	Lokomotiv Moscow
1937	Dynamo Moscow	Dynamo Moscow
1938	Spartak Moscow	Spartak Moscow
1939	Spartak Moscow	Spartak Moscow
1940	Dynamo Moscow	*No competition*
1941-43	*No competition*	*No competition*
1944	*No competition*	Zenit Leningrad
1945	Dynamo Moscow	CSKA Moscow
1946	CSKA Moscow	Spartak Moscow
1947	CSKA Moscow	Spartak Moscow
1948	CSKA Moscow	CSKA Moscow
1949	Dynamo Moscow	Torpedo Moscow
1950	CSKA Moscow	Spartak Moscow
1951	CSKA Moscow	CSKA Moscow
1952	Spartak Moscow	Torpedo Moscow
1953	Spartak Moscow	Dynamo Moscow
1954	Dynamo Moscow	Dynamo Moscow
1955	Dynamo Moscow	CSKA Moscow
1956	Spartak Moscow	*No competition*
1957	Dynamo Moscow	Lokomotiv Moscow
1958	Spartak Moscow	Spartak Moscow
1959	Dynamo Moscow	*No competition*
1960	Torpedo Moscow	Torpedo Moscow
1961	Dynamo Kiev	Shaktor Donetz
1962	Spartak Moscow	Shaktor Donetz
1963	Dynamo Moscow	Spartak Moscow
1964	Dynamo Tbilisi	Dynamo Kiev
1965	Torpedo Moscow	Spartak Moscow
1966	Dynamo Kiev	Dynamo Kiev
1967	Dynamo Kiev	Dynamo Moscow
1968	Dynamo Kiev	Torpedo Moscow
1969	Spartak Moscow	Karpaty Lvov
1970	CSKA Moscow	Dynamo Moscow
1971	Dynamo Kiev	Spartak Moscow
1972	S. Voroshilovgrad	Torpedo Moscow
1973	Ararat Erevan	Ararat Erevan
1974	Dynamo Kiev	Dynamo Kiev
1975	Dynamo Kiev	Ararat Erevan
1976	Dynamo Moscow*	Dynamo Tbilisi
1976	Torpedo Moscow†	....
1977	Dynamo Kiev	Dynamo Moscow
1978	Dynamo Tbilisi	Dynamo Kiev
1979	Spartak Moscow	Dynamo Tbilisi
1980	Dynamo Kiev	Shaktor Donetz
1981	Dynamo Kiev	SKA Rostov
1982	Dynamo Minsk	Torpedo Moscow
1983	Dnepropetrovsk	Shaktor Donetz

*Spring †Autumn

Though Russia took part in the 1912 Olympic Games, they did not reappear until 1952. But in 1956 they won the gold medal, beating Yugoslavia in the Melbourne final.

The Russians first entered the World Cup in the 1958 series. With Lev Yashin in goal they came through the group matches at the expense of England after a play-off before losing to Sweden in the quarter-final.

Two years later, however, Russia won the first, somewhat truncated, version of the European Championship, aided by Spain's refusal to meet them in the quarter-final. In the final goals from Metreveli and Ponedelnik beat Yugoslavia. Four years later Russia were losing finalists to Spain, as they would be again to West Germany in 1972. Their impressive record in the tournament was dented, however, when Greece overcame them to reach the 1980 finals. The Soviet side, in fact, came bottom of their group, also losing to Finland and Hungary.

Fourth place in 1966 remains Russia's best World Cup placing, and political considerations in 1974 and defeats by Hungary in 1978 kept them out of the two most recent series in West Germany and Argentina.

The bitterness of the Russian winter creates a staggered season which varies from region to region, but basically runs from February to November. To encourage more enterprising play, a team's first eight draws of the season only are rewarded by the traditional one point—but none are given for subsequent draws.

There was certainly no lack of enterprise in the Dynamo Kiev side which won the Cup Winners Cup in 1975, and in Oleg Blokhin produced a European Footballer of the Year. For a short spell the Kiev players were chosen en bloc to represent Russia. In 1972 Dynamo Moscow finished runners-up to Rangers in the Cup Winners Cup, and in 1979 Dynamo Tbilisi reflected the growth of the game in Georgia by coolly eliminating Liverpool from the European Cup.

Wales

Welsh international football has been a history of defeats by England and Scotland interspersed with the occasional success and hints of glories never quite fulfilled. Perhaps the cruellest moment came in Liverpool on 12 October 1977 when, with 12 minutes left of what was effectively a final qualifying game for the 1978 World Cup finals, Joe Jordan handled the ball in the Welsh penalty area and French referee Robert Wurtz mistakenly gave the Scots a penalty. The Welsh were out of the World Cup yet again, leaving their appearance in 1958 in Sweden as the only time they had qualified for the final stages of a major tournament.

Just 18 months before the Scotland game they had suffered a similar disappointment in the quarter-finals of the European

Dynamo Moscow's brilliant Lev Yashin starred in two European finals and three World Cups.

WELSH CUP

Year	Winners	Year	Winners	Year	Winners	Year	Winners
1878	Wrexham	1903	Wrexham	1931	Wrexham	1961	Swansea Town
1879	Newtown	1904	Druids	1932	Swansea Town	1962	Bangor City
1880	Druids	1905	Wrexham	1933	Chester	1963	Borough U.
1881	Druids	1906	Wellington	1934	Bristol City	1964	Cardiff City
1882	Druids	1907	Oswestry	1935	Tranmere R.	1965	Cardiff City
1883	Wrexham	1908	Chester	1936	Crewe Alex.	1966	Swansea Town
1884	Oswestry	1909	Wrexham	1937	Crewe Alex.	1967	Cardiff City
1885	Druids	1910	Wrexham	1938	Shrewsbury T.	1968	Cardiff City
1886	Druids	1911	Wrexham	1939	South Liverpool	1969	Cardiff City
1887	Chirk	1912	Cardiff City	1940	Wellington	1970	Cardiff City
1888	Chirk	1913	Swansea Town	1941-6	*No competition*	1971	Cardiff City
1889	Bangor	1914	Wrexham	1947	Chester	1972	Wrexham
1890	Chirk	1915	Wrexham	1948	Lovells Athletic	1973	Cardiff City
1891	Shrewsbury T.	1916-9	*No competition*	1949	Merthyr Tydfil	1974	Cardiff City
1892	Chirk	1920	Cardiff City	1950	Swansea Town	1975	Wrexham
1893	Wrexham	1921	Wrexham	1951	Methyr Tydfil	1976	Cardiff City
1894	Chirk	1922	Cardiff City	1952	Rhyl	1977	Shrewsbury T.
1895	Newtown	1923	Cardiff City	1953	Rhyl	1978	Wrexham
1896	Bangor	1924	Wrexham	1954	Flint Town	1979	Shrewsbury T.
1897	Wrexham	1925	Wrexham	1955	Barry Town	1980	Newport C.
1898	Druids	1926	Ebbw Vale	1956	Cardiff City	1981	Swansea City
1899	Druids	1927	Cardiff City	1957	Wrexham	1982	Swansea City
1900	Aberystwyth	1928	Cardiff City	1958	Wrexham	1983	Swansea City
1901	Oswestry	1929	Connah's Quay	1959	Cardiff City		
1902	Wellington	1930	Cardiff City	1960	Wrexham		

Terry Yorath's drive characterized some fine Welsh performances in the 1970s.

Championship when another disputed penalty had given Yugoslavia a 1-1 draw in Cardiff and led to crowd riots that initially had Wales banned from playing internationals at home for a prolonged period. That year, 1976, managed by Englishman Mike Smith, Wales had gone further than any of the other home countries.

Wales' other great spell was in the 1930s, under secretary-manager Ted Robbins. They won the Home Championship in 1933 and 1934 (being undefeated for two consecutive seasons) and again in 1937, though this was the last time they won the title outright. They had won the Championship outright on just four previous occasions (1906-07, 1919-20, 1923-24, 1927-28) and have since had a share in it five times, the last in 1970. It is perhaps odd that they did not do better during that fine spell in the mid to late 1970s. More typical of Welsh performances over the years had, however, been the spell from April 1970 to January 1973 when they even failed to score a single goal against the other home countries.

The Welsh played their first international against Scotland in 1876 and, in fact, did not play against non-British opposition until just months before the outbreak of the Second World War, when France beat them 2-1 in Paris. Their first victory was recorded against England at Blackburn in 1881 but the early period is generally one of massive defeats by England and Scotland with Welsh revenge being exacted on Ireland.

The principality's proudest moment came in the 1958 World Cup. They qualified by eliminating East Germany and Israel and then went on to the quarter-finals with draws against Hungary, Mexico and eventual finalists Sweden. The climax was a group play-off win against Hungary, losing finalists in 1954, for the right to meet Brazil in the quarter-finals. But John Charles was injured, 17-year-old Pelé scored in the dying minutes and Wales were out.

The prominent Welsh clubs—Cardiff City, Swansea City, Wrexham and Newport County—play in the Football League, while neighbouring English clubs participate in the Welsh Cup. The success of Cardiff (who also won the FA Cup in 1927) in that competition has produced 11 ventures in the European Cup Winners Cup, including a magnificent run to a narrow defeat in the semi-finals in 1968.

Yugoslavia

Yugoslavia's commitment to professionalism, rare in Iron Curtain countries, has been an important factor in the competitiveness of both the national side and the leading clubs.

In the initial European Nations Cup, which ran from 1958 to 1960, Yugoslavia were too strong for Bulgaria, Portugal and France and lost only in the final, to Russia. Eight years later in the more established European Championship, Yugoslavia eliminated England, then the World Cup holders, in a bruising semi-final, and in the final Italy needed a replay to make full use of home advantage.

In the Olympic Games, Yugoslavia reached every final from 1948 to 1960, though they were silver medallists in 1948, 1952 and 1956. In 1960 they beat Denmark 3-1 to reach the winners' rostrum at last and take the gold medal.

Yugoslavia's World Cup experiences have been more mixed. Part of the small European entry in 1930, they beat Brazil and Bolivia before a crushing defeat by Uruguay, the eventual winners. In 1954 and 1958 Yugoslavia's progress took them to the quarter-finals, and in 1962 they lost to Czechoslovakia in the semi-finals. It was 12 years before they qualified again, and then a 9-0 win over Zaire and a 1-1 draw with Scotland combined to eliminate the Scots. But in the second groupings Yugoslavia finished bottom after disappointing performances against West Germany, Poland and Sweden.

YUGOSLAVIA

Year	Champions	Cup winners
1923	Gradjanski Zagreb	....
1924	J'slavia Belgrade	....
1925	J'slavia Belgrade	....
1926	Gradjanski Zagreb	....
1927	Hajduk Split	....
1928	Gradjanski Zagreb	....
1929	Hajduk Split	....
1930	Concordia Zagreb	....
1931	BSK Belgrade	....
1932	Concordia Zagreb	....
1933	BSK Belgrade	....
1934	*No competition*	....
1935	BSK Belgrade	....
1936	BSK Belgrade	....
1937	Gradjanski Zagreb	....
1938	HASK Zagreb	....
1939	BSK Belgrade	....
1940	Gradjanski Zagreb	....
1941-46	*No competition*	....
1947	Partizan Belgrade	Partizan Belgrade
1948	Dynamo Zagreb	Red Star Belgrade
1949	Partizan Belgrade	Red Star Belgrade
1950	Hajduk Split	Red Star Belgrade
1951	Red Star Belgrade	Dynamo Zagreb
1952	Hajduk Split	Partizan Belgrade
1953	Red Star Belgrade	BSK Belgrade
1954	Dynamo Zagreb	Partizan Belgrade
1955	Hajduk Split	BSK Belgrade
1956	Red Star Belgrade	*No competition*
1957	Red Star Belgrade	Partizan Belgrade
1958	Dynamo Zagreb	Red Star Belgrade
1959	Red Star Belgrade	Red Star Belgrade
1960	Red Star Belgrade	Dynamo Zagreb
1961	Partizan Belgrade	Vardar Skopje
1962	Partizan Belgrade	OFK Belgrade
1963	Partizan Belgrade	Dynamo Zagreb
1964	Red Star Belgrade	Red Star Belgrade
1965	Partizan Belgrade	Partizan Belgrade
1966	Vojvodina Novi Sad	OFK Belgrade
1967	FC Sarajevo	Hajduk Split
1968	Red Star Belgrade	Red Star Belgrade
1969	Red Star Belgrade	Dynamo Zagreb
1970	Red Star Belgrade	Red Star Belgrade
1971	Hajduk Split	Red Star Belgrade
1972	Zeljeznicar Sarajevo	Hajduk Split
1973	Red Star Belgrade	Hajduk Split
1974	Hajduk Split	Hajduk Split
1975	Hajduk Split	Hajduk Split
1976	Partizan Belgrade	Hajduk Split
1977	Red Star Belgrade	Hajduk Split
1978	Partizan Belgrade	NK Rijeka
1979	Hajduk Split	NK Rijeka
1980	Red Star Belgrade	Dynamo Zagreb
1981	Red Star Belgrade	Velez Mostar
1982	Dynamo Zagreb	Red Star Belgrade
1983	Partizan Belgrade	Dynamo Zagreb

Established Yugoslav internationals like Dzajic, Oblak and Bogicevic became the target of Western European interest, which was encouraged with a policy of allowing players to move at later stages in their career. Golac at Southampton, Jankovic at Middlesbrough and Jovanovic with Manchester United also exhibited the high degree of technical skill instilled at home.

Dynamo Zagreb remain the only club side to have won a major European honour. In 1967 they held on to a two-goal lead achieved at home to beat Leeds United in the final of the Fairs Cup. Dynamo had previously been losing finalists in the same competition to Valencia four years earlier. In 1966 Partizan Belgrade produced a spirited run in the European Cup, including a shock success over Manchester United, but in the final they were beaten by Real Madrid 2-1 at Brussels.

A-Z OF SOUTH AMERICA

Nowhere is the passion for soccer more pronounced than in South America. We analyse the 'top 10' of the continent, from Argentina to Venezuela . . .

Argentina

Argentina can boast the first club, the first league and the first national governing body in South America—while the continents' first international was played in Buenos Aires in 1905. Argentina has the best record in South American international competition and in the Libertadores Cup. But until 1978 she had never won the World Cup.

Argentinian football probably achieved its sublime peak in the 1940s, when most of the rest of the world was at war. By the time World Cup competition was resumed, in 1950, the country had lost many of its leading players to the outlawed Colombian League—and the Asociación del Fútbol Argentino declined to enter anyway.

By the 1940s the difficult transition to legalized professionalism had been accomplished and the country's stars, for a short while at least, were not prey to the usual lucrative blandishments of the Italian League. The upsurge was led by River Plate, the club that had been founded by British players in 1901. They had been the moving force behind the adoption of professionalism, confident in the drawing power of Bernabé Ferreyra, their hard-shooting centre-forward and the idol of Argentinian soccer during the 1930s.

On Ferreyra's retirement the club put together a forward line whose awesome effectiveness caused it to be named 'la maquina' (the machine). Among its components was Angel Labruna, the coach of the present River team, who figured in nine championship winning sides in his 20 years as the club's inside-left. Alongside him, at centre-forward, was Adolfo Pedernera, whose mastery of all phases of the game earned him the title 'el maestro'. Remarkably, his successor was Alfredo di Stefano, who won even greater fame in a similar role.

Argentina's World Cup failures of 1958 and 1962 heralded an era of grim pragmatism. Argentinian clubs dominated the Libertadores Cup, but the ferocity of their challenge for the Intercontinental Cup all but killed the competition.

The violence has now receded, thanks in part to Menotti's World Cup success with a positive and attractive national side that did not contain one single player from the very negative 1978 Libertadores Cup winners, Boca Juniors. And Boca's surprise failure in the 1979 Libertadores final proved devastating—the club announced its intentions to cut its staff by half, refuse all signing-on bonuses and—in the face of a 140% annual inflation rate—freeze all salaries. Other major metropolitan clubs also faced financial difficulties—the exception being River, double winners in 1975 and 1979.

But the emerging powers in Argentinian football are provincial. Since the national championship started as an end-of-season tournament in 1967, clubs from the various regional leagues have won the trophy.

Argentina's sensational Diego Maradona reduces Kenny Dalglish to fruitless pursuit.

Bolivia

Bolivia is traditionally one of the weaker South American footballing countries. The national team failed to score a goal in either

ARGENTINA

Year	Metropolitan
1893	Lomas
1894	Lomas
1895	Lomas
1896	Lomas
1897	Lomas
1898	Lomas
1899	Belgrano
1900	English High School
1901	Alumni
1902	Alumni
1903	Alumni
1904	Belgrano
1905	Alumni
1906	Alumni
1907	Alumni
1908	Belgrano
1909	Alumni
1910	Alumni
1911	Alumni
1912	Quilmes/Porteno
1913	Racing Club/ Estudiantes
1914	Racing Club/Porteno
1915	Racing Club
1916	Racing Club
1917	Racing Club
1918	Racing Club
1919	Boca Juniors
	Racing Club (AAAF)
1920	Boca Juniors
	River Plate (AAAF)
1921	Huracan
	Racing Club (AAAF)
1922	Huracan
	Independiente (AAAF)
1923	Boca Juniors
	San Lorenzo (AAAF)
1924	Boca Juniors
	San Lorenzo (AAAF)
1925	Huracan
	Racing Club (AAAF)
1926	Boca Juniors
	Independiente (AAAF)

Year	Metropolitan
1927	San Lorenzo
1928	Huracan
1929	Gimnasia y Esgrima La Plata
1930	Boca Juniors
1931	Boca Juniors (LAF)
	Estudiantil Porteno (AAF)
1932	River Plate (LAF)
	Sportivo Barracas (AAF)
1933	San Lorenzo (LAF)
	Dock Sud (AAF)
1934	Boca Juniors (AAF)
	Estudiantil Porteno (AAF)
1935	Boca Juniors
1936	River Plate
1937	River Plate
1938	Independiente
1939	Independiente
1940	Boca Juniors
1941	River Plate
1942	River Plate
1943	Boca Juniors
1944	Boca Juniors
1945	River Plate
1946	San Lorenzo
1947	River Plate
1948	Independiente
1949	Racing Club
1950	Racing Club
1951	Racing Club
1952	River Plate
1953	River Plate
1954	Boca Juniors
1955	River Plate
1956	River Plate
1957	River Plate
1958	Racing Plate
1959	San Lorenzo
1960	Independiente
1961	Racing Club
1962	Boca Juniors

Year	Metropolitan
1963	Independiente
1964	Boca Juniors
1965	Boca Juniors
1966	Racing Club
1967	Estudiantes
1968	San Lorenzo
1969	Charcarita Juniors
1970	Independiente
1971	Independiente
1972	San Lorenzo
1973	Huracan
1974	Newell's Old Boys
1975	River Plate
1976	Boca Juniors
1977	River Plate
1978	Quilmes
1979	River Plate
1980	River Plate
1981	Boca Juniors
1982	Estudiantes
1983	Independiente

Year	National
1967	Independiente
1968	Velez Sarsfield
1969	Boca Juniors
1970	Boca Juniors
1971	Rosario Central
1972	San Lorenzo
1973	Rosario Central
1974	San Lorenzo
1975	River Plate
1976	Boca Juniors
1977	Independiente
1978	Independiente
1979	River Plate
1980	Rosario Central
1981	River Plate
1982	FC Oeste
1983	Estudiantes

AAF – Argentinian Football Association AAAF – Argentinian Amateur Football Association LAF – Argentinian Football League

BOLIVIA

Year	Champions
1914	The Strongest
1915	Colegio Militar
1916	The Strongest
1917	The Strongest
1918-19	*No competition*
1920	The Strongest
1921-22	*No competition*
1923	Universitario
1924	The Strongest
1925	*No competition*
1926	Universitario
1927	Nimbles Sport
1928	Deportivo Militar
1929	The Strongest
1930	The Strongest
1931	Nimbles Rail
1932	The Strongest
1933-34	*No competition*
1935	The Strongest
1936	Ayacucho
1937	The Strongest
1938	The Strongest
1939	Bolivar

Year	Champions
1940	Bolivar
1941	Bolivar
1942	Bolivar
1943	The Strongest
1944	Ferroviario
1945	The Strongest
1946	*No competition*
1947	Litoral
1948	Litoral
1949	Litoral
1950	Bolivar
1951	Always Ready
1952	The Strongest
1953	Bolivar
1954	Litoral
1955	San Jose
1956	Bolivar
1957	Always Ready
1958	Jorge Wilsterman
1959	Jorge Wilsterman
1960	Deportivo Municipal
1961	Deportivo Municipal
1962	Deportivo Municipal

Year	Champions
1963	The Strongest
1964	The Strongest
1965	Deportivo Municipal
1966	Jorge Wilsterman
1967	Jorge Wilsterman
1968	Bolivar
1969	Universitario
1970	Chaco Petrolero
1971	Oriente Petrolero
1972	Jorge Wilsterman
1973	Jorge Wilsterman
1974	Oriente Petrolero
1975	The Strongest
1976	Bolivar
1977	The Strongest
1978	Bolivar
1979	Oriente Petrolero
1980	Jorge Wilsterman
1981	The Strongest
1982	Bolivar
1983	Blooming

of its two appearances in World Cup finals and has won the South American Cup just once, in 1963, when it was favoured by the familiar thin air of La Paz, 12,000 feet above sea level.

The La Paz League, founded in 1914, adopted professionalism in 1950 and formed the basis of the Liga Mayor, which the Federación Boliviana de Fútbol intended to be a national league. The league resisted the claims of clubs from the remoter regions and for a short time it seemed as though the FBF would enter non-league clubs in the 1979 Libertadores Cup. Eventually champions Bolivar and runners-up Jorge Wilsterman were allowed to compete and two clubs from provincial associations joined the top four from the Liga Mayor to play off for the 1979 national championship, won by the league club Oriente Petrolero of Santa Cruz.

The enigmatic, chain-smoking Cesar Luis Menotti steered his talented but unpredictable Argentina squad to their World Cup win in Buenos Aires in 1978.

Brazil

Such is the stature of football in Brazil that it is often, without hyperbole, referred to as the 'religião brasileira'—literally the Brazilian religion.

According to legend, it was the São Paulo-born Englishman, Charles Miller, who brought the game to Brazil, when he returned from school in Southampton with two footballs among his luggage.

The game caught on quickly, aided by European coaches and touring teams. Southern League Exeter City were the opponents in the first ever game played by a selection representing Brazil in 1914. Centre-forward Artur Friedenreich lost two teeth in a collision with an Exeter full-back, but Brazil won 2-0.

Born of a German father and a black Brazilian mother, Friedenreich was the first idol of Brazilian football. In a career spanning four clubs and 27 years, he scored an estimated 1,329 goals.

But it was not until their third-place finish in the 1938 World Cup, when the disputes over race and over professionalism had been settled, that Brazil made an impact on the world game. Top scorer in that competition was Leonidas da Silva, Botafogo's 'black diamond', expert practitioner of the bicycle kick and the new Brazilian hero.

Brazil were to go on to win the trophy outright after their third World Cup triumph in 1970. But it took them until 1958 to get everything right.

The lessons of the disappointing 1956 European tour were digested. The Rio-São Paulo rivalry was defused, at least temporarily. Team manager Vicente Feola adopted the still-innovatory 4-2-4 formation that was to prove ideally suited to what was an extravagantly talented team.

After the competition, Pelé was declared 'a national treasure' by the Congress of Brazil, forestalling his transfer abroad. In

BRAZIL

National

Year	Champions
1967	Palmeiras
1968	Santos
1969	Palmeiras
1970	Fluminense
1971	Atletico Mineiro
1972	Palmeiras
1973	Palmeiras
1974	Vasco da Gama
1975	Internacional
1976	Internacional
1977	Sao Paulo FC
1978	Guarani
1979	Internacional
1980	Flamengo
1981	Gremio
1982	Flamengo
1983	Flamengo

Rio de Janeiro

Year	Champions
1906	Fluminense
1907	Fluminense/Botafogo
1908	Fluminense
1909	Fluminense
1910	Botafogo
1911	Fluminense
1912	Paissandu
1913	America
1914	Flamengo
1915	Flamengo
1916	America
1917	Fluminense
1918	Fluminense
1919	Fluminense
1920	Flamengo
1921	Flamengo
1922	America
1923	Vasco da Gama
1924	Vasco da Gama/ Fluminense
1925	Flamengo
1926	Sao Cristovao
1927	Flamengo
1928	America
1929	Vasco da Gama
1930	Botafogo
1931	America
1932	Botafogo
1933	Bangu Botafogo
1934	Vasco da Gama Botafogo
1935	America Botafogo
1936	Fluminense Vasco da Gama
1937	Fluminense
1938	Fluminense
1939	Flamengo
1940	Fluminense
1941	Fluminense
1942	Flamengo
1943	Flamengo
1944	Flamengo
1945	Vasco da Gama
1946	Fluminense
1947	Vasco da Gama
1948	Botafogo
1949	Vasco da Gama
1950	Vasco da Gama
1951	Fluminense
1952	Vasco da Gama
1953	Flamengo
1954	Flamengo
1955	Flamengo
1956	Vasco da Gama
1957	Botafogo
1958	Vasco da Gama
1959	Fluminense
1960	America
1961	Botafogo
1962	Botafogo
1963	Flamengo
1964	Fluminense
1965	Flamengo
1966	Bangu
1967	Botafogo
1968	Botafogo
1969	Fluminense
1970	Vasco da Gama
1971	Fluminense
1972	Flamengo
1973	Fluminense
1974	Flamengo
1975	Fluminense
1976	Fluminense
1977	Vasco da Gama
1978	Flamengo
1979	Flamengo
1980	Flamengo
1981	Flamengo
1982	Vasco da Gama
1983	Fluminense

Sao Paulo

Year	Champions
1902	Sao Paulo AC
1903	Sao Paulo AC
1904	Sao Paulo AC
1905	Paulistano
1906	Internacional (SP)
1907	Germania
1908	Paulistano
1909	AA das Palmeiras
1910	AA das Palmeiras
1911	Sao Paulo AC
1912	Americano
1913	Americano
1914	Corinthians Sao Bento
1915	Germania AA das Palmeiras
1916	Corinthians Paulistano
1917	Paulistano
1918	Paulistano
1919	Paulistano
1920	Palestra Italia
1921	Paulistano
1922	Corinthians
1923	Corinthians
1924	Corinthians
1925	Sao Bento
1926	Palestra Italia Paulistano
1927	Palestria Italia Paulistano
1928	Corinthians Internacional (SP)
1929	Corinthians Paulistano
1930	Corinthians
1931	Sao Paulo FC
1932	Palestra Italia
1933	Palestra Italia
1934	Palestra Italia
1935	Portuguesa Santos
1936	Portuguesa Palestra Italia
1937	Corinthians
1938	Corinthians
1939	Corinthians
1940	Palastria Italia
1941	Corinthians
1942	Palmeiras
1943	Sao Paulo FC
1944	Palmeiras
1945	Sao Paulo FC
1946	Sao Paulo FC
1947	Palmeiras
1948	Sao Paulo FC
1949	Sao Paulo FC
1950	Palmeiras
1951	Corinthians
1952	Corinthians
1953	Sao Paulo FC
1954	Corinthians
1955	Santos
1956	Santos
1957	Sao Paulo FC
1958	Santos
1959	Palmeiras
1960	Santos
1961	Santos
1962	Santos
1963	Palmeiras
1964	Santos
1965	Santos
1966	Palmeiras
1967	Santos
1968	Santos
1969	Santos
1970	Sao Paulo FC
1971	Sao Paulo FC
1972	Palmeiras
1973	Santos/ Portuguesa
1974	Palmeiras
1975	Sao Paulo FC
1976	Palmeiras
1977	Corinthians
1978	Santos
1979	Corinthians
1980	Sao Paulo FC
1981	Sao Paulo FC
1982	Corinthians
1983	Corinthians

four games, the 17-year-old had scored six goals and captured the imagination of the soccer world.

With the most celebrated player of all time in their ranks, Santos, a previously unheralded club from the port city 30 miles from São Paulo, embarked on a period of sustained success. They won the São Paulo championship eight times in 11 seasons, and in 1962 and 1963 they swept all before them, winning the Libertadores and Intercontinental Cups. Their Intercontinental Cup final in 1962 provided the classic highlight of the dark history of the competition. After beating Benfica 3-2 in São Paulo (Pelé 2), they played brilliantly in Lisbon to win 5-2 (Pelé scoring a hat-trick).

Santos also won the Brazilian national championship in 1968. It was only the second season of what came to be known as the Campeonato Nacional—a competition involving all the leading clubs of Brazil's many state championships. Recent editions have included more than 80 clubs drawn from 22 different state leagues.

The national championships reflected the growing power of clubs from outside the Rio de Janeiro-São Paulo axis. Cruzeiro of Belo Horizonte competed in the Libertadores in 1967, with a team that included several of the squad that were to win the World Cup in 1970—most notably Tostão.

Chile

Football has long been a well-established sport in Chile, but the country's international record is distinguished only by its third-place finish in the 1962 World Cup, when it hosted the tournament.

Chile entered the first South American Cup in 1916, but it was 1926—in San-

An emotional Gerson, whose spectacular goal had begun the rout of Italy, is escorted off the pitch after Brazil had won the Jules Rimet Trophy for the third time to take permanent possession in 1970.

tiago—before they won a game. They have never won the competition, though they were beaten finalists in 1979. Colo Colo (the name means 'wild cat') came closer than any Chilean club before or since to winning the Libertadores when they took Independiente to a replay in the 1973 final.

The professional national league was set up in 1933 by eight clubs from the Santiago area, but in recent years only the clubs backed by large immigrant communities (like Santiago's Union Española and Palestino) or by mining industries (like O'Higgins of Rancagua and Cobreloa from the small northern desert town of Chuquicamata) have proved immune from financial or other embarrassments.

The plight of Chilean club football was most starkly realised by Santiago's Colo Colo, Chile's most popular club since their successful and innovatory early years. In 1979 they won the national championship for a record 12th time—and immediately announced that their nearly £2 million debts put their very existence in jeopardy.

CHILE

Year	Champions	Year	Champions	Year	Champions
1933	Magallanes	1951	Union Espanole	1969	Universidad de Chile
1934	Magallanes	1952	Everton	1970	Colo Colo
1935	Magallanes	1953	Colo Colo	1971	Universidad San Felipe
1936	Audax Italiano	1954	Universidad Catolica	1972	Colo Colo
1937	Colo Colo	1955	Palestino	1973	Union Espanole
1938	Magallanes	1956	Colo Colo	1974	Huachipata
1939	Colo Colo	1957	Audax Italiano	1975	Union Espanola
1940	Universidad de Chile	1958	Santiago Wanderers	1976	Everton
1941	Colo Colo	1959	Universidad de Chile	1977	Union Espanola
1942	Santiago Morning	1960	Colo Colo	1978	Palestino
1943	Union Espanole	1961	Universidad Catolica	1979	Colo Colo
1944	Colo Colo	1962	Universidad de Chile	1980	Cobreloa
1945	Green Cross	1963	Colo Colo	1981	Colo Colo
1946	Audax Italiano	1964	Universidad de Chile	1982	Cobreloa
1947	Colo Colo	1965	Universidad de Chile	1983	Colo Colo
1948	Audax Italiano	1966	Universidad Catolica		
1949	Universidad Catolica	1967	Universidad de Chile		
1950	Everton	1968	Santiago Wanderers		

Colombia

After years of fumbling progress, Colombian football suddenly splashed over the front and back pages of British newspapers in April 1950.

Two of England's best-known footballers were leaving Stoke City for Bogota—Independiente Santa Fé had signed right-winger George Mountford and Neil Franklin, England's centre-half in all 27 internationals since the war. Because the renegade Colombian League operated outside the sanction of FIFA, there was no transfer fee involved. Because the Colombians were offering £50 a week plus a substantial signing-on fee to players who had been restricted to £12 a week in England, it seemed likely that many others would follow.

Some did, though for Franklin at least the reality of Colombia did not match the promise. He was back in less than two months. 'If my memory isn't playing tricks on me, it rained almost every day . . . every match was a mud bath,' he was to recall later. After this episode, Alfonso Senior, president of the Millonarios club that had signed Everton's Bill Higgins, pronounced the signing of English players 'simply suicidal'.

Colombia had only adopted professionalism in 1948. In 1949 Bogota's Millonarios signed Alfredo di Stefano from River Plate and won the championship. In 1950 the breakaway league was formed and the gold rush was on. Soon most of the players in the league were foreigners, almost all of them South Americans. But by 1953 di Stefano had left for Spain and the bubble had burst.

Since that heady era, Colombia's influence on world football has been minimal. They qualified for the World Cup finals for the first and only time in 1962 and caused something of an upset by coming back from 4-1 down against the USSR to draw 4-4. Their best performance in the South American Cup was in 1975, when they took Peru to a play-off in the final.

In 1978 coach Carlos Bilardo, a member of the notorious Estudiantes de la Plata side of 1968, took Deportivo Cali to the final of the Libertadores Cup and was subsequently appointed manager of the national team.

COLOMBIA

Year	Champions	Year	Champions	Year	Champions
1948	Independiente Santa Fe	1961	Milionarios de Bogota	1974	Deportivo Cali
1949	Milionarios de Bogota	1962	Milionarios de Bogota	1975	Independiente Santa Fe
1950	Deportes Caldes	1963	Milionarios de Bogota	1976	Atletico Nacional
1951	Milionarios de Bogota	1964	Milionarios de Bogota	1977	Junior Barranquilla
1952	Milionarios de Bogota	1965	Deportivo Cali	1978	Milionarios de Bogota
1953	Milionarios de Bogota	1966	Independiente Santa Fe	1979	America
1954	Atletico Nacional	1967	Deportivo Cali	1980	Junior Barranquilla
1955	Independiente Medellin	1968	Union Magdalena	1981	Atletico Nacional
1956	Atletico Quindio	1969	Deportivo Cali	1982	America
1957	Independiente Medellin	1970	Deportivo Cali	1983	America
1958	Independiente Santa Fe	1971	Independiente Santa Fe		
1959	Milionarios de Bogota	1972	Milionarios de Bogota		
1960	Independiente Santa Fe	1973	Atletico Nacional		

Ecuador

South America's most densely populated country has never made an impact on international football. Since losing on its international debut (9-1 to Peru) in 1938, the country's national side has compiled a record that betters only Venezuela's in South American competition.

The professional national league was set up in 1957 and has never been won from a club outside Quito (the capital) or Guayaquil (the main port and commercial centre), though Deportivo Cuenca have come close.

The Quito-Guayaquil rivalry has sometimes turned bitter, the most recent occasion coming at the conclusion of the 1979 championship. Universidad Catolica of Quito looked to have won the league with a point to spare, until the Guayaquil-based Asociación Ecuatoriana de Fútbol ordered that an earlier defeat for Emelec of Guayaquil should be replayed. This time Emelec won and took the title, sending the Quito clubs into a fury.

Emelec, backed by the state electrical company, are Ecuador's most prosperous club. Their overall record in the Libertadores ranks among the best of Ecuador's clubs, though neighbours Barcelona have the unmatched distinction of twice reaching the semi-final round—only Liga Deportiva Universitaria of Quito have ever gone as far in the competition.

Ecuador's most celebrated player of all time was Alberto Spencer, the brilliant centre-forward of the great Penarol sides of the 1960s. Spencer was top scorer in the first three Libertadores tournaments (1960-62) and scored two goals against Benfica in 1961 and three goals against Real in 1966 on the occasions that Penarol won the World Club Championship.

ECUADOR

Year	Champions	Year	Champions	Year	Champions
1957	Emelec	1969	Liga Deportive Universitaria	1977	Nacional
1958-59	*No competition*	1970	Barcelona	1978	Nacional
1960	Emelec	1971	Barcelona	1979	Universidad Catolica
1961	Everest	1972	Emelec	1980	Barcelona
1962	Everest	1973	Liga Deportive Universitaria	1981	Barcelona
1963	Barcelona	1974	Nacional	1982	Nacional
1964	Deportivo Quito	1975	Liga Deportive Universitaria	1983	Nacional
1965	Emelec	1976	Nacional		
1966	Barcelona				
1967	Nacional				
1968	Deportivo Quito				

Paraguay

Paraguay has occasionally overcome the disadvantages of grinding poverty and a tiny population to astonish the world of football.

There was an amazing South American Cup win in 1953 in Lima, Peru. Paraguay went undefeated in the competition—and twice beat their closest rivals Brazil.

In the 1958 World Cup the national team beat Uruguay in the qualifying round by 7-0 on aggregate.

And—most remarkably of all—in 1979 Paraguayan teams achieved an astonishing international double—champions Olimpia of Asuncion won the Libertadores Cup and the national team carried off the South American Championship.

Just as in 1953 (when Fleitas Solich was the man in charge), it was a coach who took much of the credit. Luis Cubilla, once a pudgy Uruguayan international winger, instituted an unprecedentedly tough training regime at Olimpia and apparently persuaded such players as winger Evaristo Isasi and midfielder Luis Torres to employ their undoubted talent to greater and more consistent effect. After their efficient win over Boca Juniors in the Libertadores final, many of the Olimpia side figured in the national team that first shocked Brazil in the semi-finals and then dealt with Chile in the final of the South American Championship.

Despite the claims of all the Olimpia players, Sportivo Luqueño's young midfielder Julio Cesar Romero finished as the best-placed Paraguayan in the polling for the Latin American Footballer of the Year, finishing second only to Diego Maradona. Romero scored two goals in the final, whereupon he joined Cosmos.

Because no Paraguayan club can match the salaries paid to professionals in other parts of the world, the country's leading players must usually seek their livings elsewhere. In fact, the player generally regarded as the greatest Paraguay has ever produced —Arsenio Erico—never played for a senior club in his own country. He earned his fame with the River Plate side of the 1930s.

PARAGUAY

Year	Champions
1906	Guarani
1907	Guarani
1908	*No competition*
1909	Nacional
1910	Libertad
1911	Nacional
1912	Olimpia
1913	Cerro Porteno
1914	Olimpia
1915	Cerro Porteno
1916	Olimpia
1917	Libertad
1918	Cerro Porteno
1919	Cerro Porteno
1920	Libertad
1921	Guarani
1922	*No competition*
1923	Guarani
1924	Nacional
1925	Olimpia
1926	Nacional
1927	Olimpia
1928	Olimpia
1929	Olimpia
1930	Libertad
1931	Olimpia
1932-34	*No competition*
1935	Cerro Porteno
1936	Olimpia
1937	Olimpia
1938	Olimpia
1939	Cerro Porteno
1940	Cerro Porteno
1941	Cerro Porteno
1942	Nacional
1943	Libertad
1944	Cerro Porteno
1945	Libertad
1946	Nacional
1947	Olimpia
1948	Olimpia
1949	Guarani
1950	Cerro Porteno
1951	Sportivo Luqueno
1952	President Hayes
1953	Sportivo Luqueno
1954	Cerro Porteno
1955	Libertad
1956	Olimpia
1957	Olimpia
1958	Olimpia
1959	Olimpia
1960	Olimpia
1961	Cerro Porteno
1962	Olimpia
1963	Cerro Porteno
1964	Guarani
1965	Olimpia
1966	Cerro Porteno
1967	Guarani
1968	Olimpia
1969	Olimpia
1970	Cerro Porteno
1971	Olimpia
1972	Cerro Porteno
1973	Cerro Porteno
1974	Cerro Porteno
1975	Olimpia
1976	Libertad
1977	Cerro Porteno
1978	Olimpia
1979	Olimpia
1980	Olimpia
1981	Olimpia
1982	Olimpia
1983	Olimpia

PERU

Year	Champions
1926	CS Progreso
1927	Alianza Lima
1928	Alianza Lima
1929	Universitario
1930	Atletico Chalaco
1931	Alianza Lima
1932	Alianza Lima
1933	Alianza Lima
1934	Alianza Lima
1935	Sport Boys
1936	*No competition*
1937	Sport Boys
1938	Deportivo Municipal
1939	Universitario
1940	Deportivo Municipal
1941	Universitario
1942	Sport Boys
1943	Deportivo Municipal
1944	Mariscal Sucre
1945	Universitario
1946	Universitario
1947	Atletico Chalaco
1948	Alianza Lima
1949	Universitario
1950	Deportivo Municipal
1951	Sport Boys
1952	Alianza Lima
1953	Mariscal Sucre
1954	Alianza Lima
1955	Alianza Lima
1956	Sporting Cristal
1957	Alianza Lima
1958	Sport Boys
1959	Universitario
1960	Universitario
1961	Sporting Cristal
1962	Alianza Lima
1963	Alianza Lima
1964	Universitario
1965	Alianza Lima
1966	Universitario
1967	Universitario
1968	Sporting Cristal
1969	Universitario
1970	Sporting Cristal
1971	Universitario
1972	Sporting Cristal
1973	Sporting Cristal
1974	Defensor Lima
1975	Universitario
1976	Union Huaral
1977	Alianza Lima
1978	Alianza Lima
1979	Sporting Cristal
1980	Sporting Cristal
1981	Melgar
1982	Universitario
1983	Sporting Cristal

Peru

The 1970s were a good decade for Peruvian football. Despite losing most of their top players to foreign clubs at various times during the 10 years, they put together enough talent and experience to thrill their fans in two World Cups and one South American Championship.

At the heart of their team for most of the decade has been their brilliant inside-forward Teofilo Cubillas. A magnificent striker of the ball, he was just an unknown 20-year-old from Alianza Lima when Peru's marvellously talented attacking side eliminated Argentina to qualify for the 1970 World Cup finals in Mexico. In the opening game against Bulgaria, Cubillas scored the winning goal—his dashing, elusive dribble culminating in a powerful right-foot shot. He scored twice against Morocco, missed the game against West Germany and added one more in Peru's quarter-final loss to eventual winners Brazil.

Cubillas joined the players' exodus after the World Cup, signing for Basle in 1973, and was missing when Peru won the South American Championship in 1975. It was Hugo Sotil, a winger who had returned to Peru after a spell with Real Madrid, who scored the clinching goal against Colombia in the final.

But Cubillas had returned to Alianza—scoring 22 goals in their 1977 championship win—by the time Peru were qualifying for the 1978 World Cup. He scored two wicked long-range goals against Scotland and added a hat-trick against Iran as Peru finished top of their first round group.

Peruvian clubs have provided fewer highlights. In recent years the national league has been dominated by three Lima clubs—the traditional powers Alianza and Universitario and the less popular Sporting Cristal, whose success in persuading exiled stars to return home owes something to their sponsorship by a brewery. Only Unión Huaral have recently broken the capital's hold.

Three goals from Teofilo Cubillas, including two in this game against Morocco, helped Peru to the quarter-finals of the 1970 World Cup. Cubillas was again prominent when Peru did well in Argentina in 1978.

Uruguay's second World Cup winning side, of 1950. *Back row (players only):* ***Varela, Tejera, Gambetta, Gonzales, Maspoli, Andrade;*** *Front row:* ***Ghiggia, Perez, Miguez, Schiaffino, Moran.***

Uruguay

A tiny country of under three million people, Uruguay has produced a series of brilliant players and an extravagant, disproportionate record of international success.

In 1924, after a series of successes in the fledgling South American Championship, Uruguay sent a team to the Paris Olympics. The 'celestos' crushed Yugoslavia 7-1 in the first game and went on to take the gold medal. Europe was dazzled by its first real look at South American football. The black half-back, José Andrade, was acclaimed as the outstanding player of the tournament.

It was the first leg of an outstanding treble—completed by the gold medal in the 1928 Olympics in Amsterdam and the winning of the first World Cup in 1930. Andrade and inside-right Hector Scarone, nicknamed 'el magico', were the only players to figure in all three triumphs.

The shape of Uruguayan club football was already well set; a small league, made up exclusively of clubs from Montevideo, dominated by the two giants—Peñarol and Nacional.

Andrade and Scarone had both been Nacional players, but Peñarol players predominated in Uruguay's next World Cup team in 1950. The 'oro y negro' (gold and black) won the 1949 League title without losing a game. Goalkeeper Roque Maspoli and the slight but deadly inside-forward Juan Schiaffino were among the stars of the side that shocked Brazil in the World Cup 'final' in Rio.

By 1960 Peñarol had built another great side. They won the first Libertadores Cup without losing a game, then retained the trophy in 1961 and won again in 1966. In 1961 they won the Intercontinental Cup with the help of a dazzling 5-0 win over Benfica.

But Uruguayan football was soon to go into decline. Salaries failed to keep pace with inflation and what top-class players were turned up—most notably the Peñarol forward Fernando Morena—were likely to be tempted abroad.

URUGUAY

Year	Champions	Year	Champions	Year	Champions
1900	Penarol	1928	Penarol	1956	Nacional
1901	Penarol	1929	Penarol	1957	Nacional
1902	Nacional	1930	Penarol	1958	Penarol
1903	Nacional	1931	Wanderers Montevideo	1959	Penarol
1904	*No competition*	1932	Penarol	1960	Penarol
1905	Penarol	1933	Nacional	1961	Penarol
1906	Wanderers Montevideo	1934	Nacional	1962	Penarol
1907	Penarol	1935	Penarol	1963	Nacional
1908	River Plate	1936	Penarol	1964	Penarol
1909	Wanderers Montevideo	1937	Penarol	1965	Penarol
1910	River Plate	1938	Nacional	1966	Nacional
1911	Penarol	1939	Nacional	1967	Penarol
1912	Nacional	1940	Nacional	1968	Penarol
1913	River Plate	1941	Nacional	1969	Nacional
1914	River Plate	1942	Nacional	1970	Nacional
1915	Nacional	1943	Nacional	1971	Nacional
1916	Nacional	1944	Penarol	1972	Nacional
1917	Nacional	1945	Penarol	1973	Penarol
1918	Penarol	1946	Nacional	1974	Penarol
1919	Nacional	1947	Nacional	1975	Penarol
1920	Nacional	1948	*No competition*	1976	Defensor
1921	Penarol	1949	Penarol	1977	Nacional
1922	Nacional	1950	Nacional	1978	Penarol
1923	Nacional	1951	Penarol	1979	Penarol
1924	Nacional	1952	Penarol	1980	Nacional
1925	*No competition*	1953	Penarol	1981	Penarol
1926	Penarol	1954	Penarol	1982	Penarol
1927	Rampla Juniors	1955	Nacional	1983	Nacional

VENEZUELA

Year	Champions	Year	Champions	Year	Champions
1956	Lasalle	1966	Deportivo Italia	1975	Portuguesa Acarigua
1957	Tiquire Aragua	1967	Deportivo Portugues	1976	Portuguesa Acarigua
1958	Deportivo Portugues	1968	Union Deportiva Canarias	1977	Portuguesa Acarigua
1959	Celta Deportivo	1969	Deportivo Galicia	1978	Portuguesa Acarigua
1960	Deportivo Portugues	1970	Deportivo Galicia	1979	Deportivo Tachira
1961	Deportivo Italia	1971	Valencia	1980	Estudiantes Merida
1962	Deportivo Portugues	1972	Deportivo Italia	1981	Deportivo Tachira
1963	Deportivo Italia	1973	Portuguesa Acarigua	1982	San Cristobal
1964	Deportivo Galicia	1974	Portuguesa Acarigua	1983	Universidad de los Andes
1965	Lara Barquisimeto				

Venezuela

Venezuela did not join CONMEBOL until 1952, and a professional league was not set up until 1957. The game remains some way behind baseball in popularity, though the Federación Venezolana de Fútbol and the leading clubs have made determined efforts to improve the game's status. The senior provincial club, Portuguesa of Acarigua, signed the Brazilian World Cup star Jairzinho in 1977 and performed creditably in the Libertadores that year. Portuguesa's run of four successive championships was ended in 1979 when they were debarred from the final play-offs as they owed money to the FVF. Instead, Deportivo Tachira, one of several non-ethnic clubs admitted to the league in recent seasons, took the championship by the narrowest of margins from Venezuela's most popular club, Deportivo Galicia of Caracas.

UPDATE FOR 1984

Rarely has the confusing status of the United Kingdom's international sides been so well illustrated as it was at the end of the 1983-84 season. While none of the four home countries, nor Eire, had qualfied for the European Championships to be held in France in June 1984, no less than six of the twelve European club semi-finalists were from England and Scotland. In the European Cup, dominated by England for much of the past decade, both Liverpool and Dundee United had produced a convincing series of displays. Liverpool won in Bilbao after the Athletic club of that city had drawn on Merseyside, and then went back to the Iberian peninsula to crush Benfica 4-1 in the celebrated Stadium of Light.

Dundee United, competing for the first time, had shown remarkable maturity in easily subduing pre-scandal Standard Liege (4-0 at home after a goalless draw away) and knocking out Rapid Vienna in the quarter-finals. They saved their best for the first leg of the semis, however, when favourites Roma were lucky to escape with only a 2-0 defeat at Tannadice. The second leg, sadly for the Taysiders, was a different story as Roma came back to win 3-0. But had Ralph Milne not missed an excruciatingly easy chance in the early minutes then the result may well have been very different.

Liverpool, however, were much more experienced than Dundee United and this was to show in their semi-final in Bucharest. Leading with only a single Sammy Lee goal at home against the thuggish Dynamo Bucharest, Liverpool won their fourth consecutive away game in the competition, 2-1, in Rumania. Ian Rush had another excellent match, scoring both Liverpool's goals.

In the Cup Winners Cup Manchester United made a little history by pulling back a two goal deficit to beat Barcelona 3-0 at home in the second leg. Bryan Robson scored twice and it was the first time Barcelona had ever conceded a two-goal lead in 25 years of European football—Dukla Prague and Spartak Varna had been United's other conquests, but a team badly depleted by injuries could only draw 1-1 at home against Juventus (Platini scoring a lucky goal with a deflection) and out they went in Turin to a last minute Rossi goal which made it 2-1 on the night and 3-2 on aggregate. In the previous round Juventus had played in one of the Cup Winners Cup's oddest games. Finnish club Valkeakosken Haka had become the first club from their country to reach any European quarter-final, but could not play at home because of icebound pitches. Juventus refused to play the tie indoors so Haka's home leg was actually conducted in Strasbourg, where Michel Platini was the only Frenchman on the pitch.

Aberdeen were Great Britain's other Cup Winners Cup semi-finalist. By this stage of the season they already had the Scottish Championship tied up and were on the way to their first double but they had not looked as good in Europe as they had the previous season, when they won the Cup Winners Cup in Gothenburg. Tiny Akranes of Iceland held them to a 1-1 draw at Pittodrie, then Beveren drew in Belgium but lost 4-1 in Aberdeen. Only a hat-trick by Mark McGhee kept Aberdeen in the quarter-finals after a strangely inept performance against Ujpest Dozsa in Budapest. In the semis they drew Porto, seemingly the easiest of all the British club draws. Losing only 1-0 in Opor-

to, the return seemed to be well within their capabilities. But, in a major surprise, the Dons could not score and Porto made the game safe with a quite magnificent individual goal by Vermelhinho.

Perhaps the most impressive displays had been by two UEFA Cup semi-finalists, Tottenham and Nottingham Forest. Spurs, after an easy game against Drogheda, beat Feijenoord home and away and then, having lost only 1-0 in Munich, beat Bayern 2-0 at White Hart Lane. Nottingham Forest had conducted another thoroughly impressive European campaign, even going so far as to win their first three away matches—1-0 v Vorwaerts in East Germany, 1-0 v PSV in Eindhoven and 2-1 at Celtic Park (after a 0-0 home leg had appeared to put them out of contention). And while Spurs were losing their first leg of their semi-final 2-1 to Hadjuk Split, Forest scored a surprise 2-0 victory over UEFA Cup holders Anderlecht. Both Forest's goals came in the last five minutes, both headers from young Steve Hodge, after Anderlecht had given an almost faultless display of how to defend in a European away leg and drive fans away in their millions.

In the tense second-leg games the roles were to be reversed. Anderlecht played well to knock out Forest 3-0, though they were helped by a palpably absurd penalty, while Spurs beat Hadjuk Split 1-0 with a Mike

Everton and Wales keeper Neville Southall looks surprised after Graeme Souness's shot beat him for the only goal of the 1984 Milk Cup final replay, Liverpool's fourth consecutive win in the competition. Southall was to cheer up after the FA Cup final, which Everton won by beating Watford 2-0 to become the third consecutive Milk Cup runner-up to win the FA Cup in the same year. It also meant that all three English trophies went to Merseyside, only the second time that a single city had swept the board.

Hazard free-kick. Spurs were, therefore, one of only two of the six British semi-finalists to reach a final. Spurs' popular manager, Keith Burkinshaw, had reached four cup finals in four seasons but had already resigned by the time his side reached the UEFA final. When Bill Nicholson resigned from the same job in 1974, he too had reached four cup finals in the previous four years and yet also felt himself to have failed by the club's high standards. Nicholson's last final, of course, had also been in the UEFA Cup.

But while all of this was going on in the club arena, the real interest was centred on the European Championship. The qualifiers were France (as hosts), Denmark, Belgium, Yugoslavia, West Germany, Portugal, Rumania and Spain. With the sole exception of Denmark, none of these sides had looked particularly convincing in qualification. Spain won an astonishing last match 12-1 against Malta to qualify over Holland after having required, strangely, an 11 goal margin of victory. The Dutch, and everyone else, were inclined to reach for the rule-book but television replays suggested that the game was legitimate. At one point it was 1-1 and was only 3-1 at half-time.

The West Germans, World Cup runners-up, had managed to lose both home and away to Northern Ireland and the Irish were desperately unlucky, both to be drawn with the Germans and not to qualify on goal difference. The general rounding down and coming together of international abilities, particularly defensive, were best illustrated by Italy's complete collapse after the glories of the World Cup. It was not until the eighth and last game of their European qualifying group that they managed to win a game—and then against lowly Cyprus. In order, they drew with the Czechs, Rumanians and Cypriots, lost 1-0 in Bucharest, 2-0 in Sweden and then collapsed 3-0 at home to the Swedes and 2-0 to the Czechs. It was difficult to know what to make of it. The credible explanation was probably that the Italians had somehow got lucky in Spain and played, for just four vital games, way beyond their squad's real abilities.

In any event, with West Germany playing so poorly, Portugal surprisingly pipping the USSR 1-0 in their last group game, the Dutch going out so oddly to Spain, England knocked out by Denmark and Yugoslavia struggling against Wales and losing to Norway, there were no favourites except, perhaps, hosts France.

The English performance was lamentable. It began with a lucky 2-2 draw in Copenhagen and reached its highspot with a good 3-0 win in Greece. After that it was downhill all the way. Wins home and away against Luxembourg (9-0 at home) and Hungary, in the throes of a gambling scandal, were to be expected, but it was really a dreadful 0-0 against the Greeks at Wembley which sank England. The Danes later won 1-0 at Wembley with a Simonsen penalty and a solid, if not inspired, display under their excellent West German manager Sepp Piontek, but if England had scored a goal against Greece they would still have gone through on goal difference.

The finest margin was to keep the Welsh out of the European Championships just as it had done out of the 1982 World Cup. With just one minute of the Yugoslavia v Bulgaria game left in Split, the Welsh were home and dry. The Yugoslavs were drawing 2-2 and the Welsh, one goal better off and with the same number of points, were through. But a Radanovic extra-time header made it 3-2 and Wales, who had conceded a late goal and a 1-1 draw to the Yugoslavs a week before in Cardiff, were the last of the home countries to be eliminated. Such statistical leaves, blowing in the wind, had apparently come to dominate international competition.

The Scots had been the first to go, and probably the less said about that the better. They finished bottom of their group below Belgium, Switzerland and East Germany and won but a single match—2-0 against Switzerland with a fine debut goal from Charlie Nicholas. Otherwise it was perhaps Scotland's worst set of results since qualifying groups were introduced for international tournaments thirty years before. Belgium had been the most convincing of the qualifiers, heading Scotland's group with only one defeat and nine points out of 12, but their ambitions were to be dramatically damaged on 29 February 1984 when it emerged that Belgian police were investigating members of the Standard Liege team for bribing Waterschei in the last fixture of the 1981-82 season. Standard won that game and, partially in consequence, the Belgian League. The upshot of an inevitably involved affair was that most of the Standard team was suspended, leaving the national side less most of its defence, captain Eric Gerets, and its high hopes for the European Championship.

The Belgian scandal was certainly the story of the year, but elsewhere things were rather quiet. In South America the game appeared to reflect the rapidly declining economic situation. The great stars continued to leave—Maradona was in Barcelona, Zico in Udine, Falcao in Roma and even Socrates said he might leave for Italy or Spain at year end. Attendances followed—in one Argentinian Second Division match a new record low was established when precisely no-one turned out to see the game.

Things were still a little better in Europe—though sometimes not by much. Attendances of under 10,000 were commonplace in the First Division in England in 1984 and Wolves even dropped below 7,000 on a couple of occasions, their lowest crowds for 50 years. The appeal of European finals, was nonetheless, undeniable.

After their impressive 3-0 defeat of Forest (in their three seasons of European competition since Clough's arrival Forest had never previously abandoned even a one-goal lead) Anderlecht were firm favourites to beat Spurs in the UEFA Cup final. The first leg was in Brussels on 9 May and Keith Burkinshaw chose to complete his Tottenham career with the tactics that had stood him in good stead throughout. Instead of trying to contain the Belgians, Spurs attacked throughout and looked the better side. They went ahead via a Paul Miller header from a Mike Hazard corner in the 59th minute, but Olsen equalised for Anderlecht with just four minutes left to give the Flemings some hope in the second leg.

When, two weeks later, the teams took the field at White Hart Lane for Burkinshaw's last match the portents were good for the home side. This was the 20th time that Spurs had taken the field in a major cup final (7 FA Cup plus 3 replays, 3 League Cup, one Cup Winners Cup and 3 two-legged UEFA Cup Finals). Of the previous 19 they had lost just two—the away leg of the 1974 UEFA final in Rottedam and the 1982 Milk Cup final against Liverpool.

Spurs had never lost a European game at White Hart Lane; of 38 pervious matches 32 had been won and six drawn. A goalless draw on the night would have sufficed for Spurs, but the Belgians went ahead through a Czerniatinski breakaway after 62 minutes and Spurs seemed deflated until six minutes from time. Ardiles, on as a sub, hit the bar after a scramble and, when the ball was pushed back, Roberts, captaining the side in place of the suspended Perryman, delicately touched the ball into the corner of the net.

Despite thirty minutes of extra-time, there were no further goals and the game had to be decided on penalties. It was only the second European cup final to be decided this way— the first had also, strangely, involved a North London club when Valencia defeated Arsenal in the Cup Winners Cup final in 1980.

This time the fates smiled on the English. Hackney born Tony Parks, who had taken over in goal from Ray Clemence earlier in the season, took the Alan Mullery role by saving two of the five Anderlecht penalties, those from Olsen and Gudjohnsen. Roberts, Falco, Stevens and Archibald all scored confidently for Spurs and Danny Thomas's miss (an excellent save by Munaron) with the ninth penalty did not matter in the end. For Keith Burkinshaw, scorer Graham Roberts and keeper Tony Parks it was a fairytale end to their season, though an odd one, with both Spurs' goals in the final being scored by their centre-backs.

Sandwiched between the two legs of the UEFA Cup Final came the finale of the Cup Winners Cup, again played in what seemed to have become its permanent home, that most European of cities, Basel. Unlike most recent Cup Winners finals, this one was played before a full house, most of the crowd coming from nearby Turin. There were few present from distant and much poorer Porto.

The game was, perhaps surprisingly, rather open and enjoyable, though notable for some dreadful goalkeeping. Juventus went ahead in the 12th minute when Vignola scored left-footed from the edge of the area, though the keeper should have saved easily. Another goalkeeping error allowed Sousa to equalise for Porto with a long, speculative shot. Before half-time Juventus went 2-1 ahead when Boniek touched the ball home, though he owed his goal to a stranded keeper. There were no more goals, though one clear penalty for each side was strangely turned down by the East German referee, and the trophy went back with the fans across the Alps.

The highlight of the season was in Rome. Only Real Madrid in 1957 and Inter Milan in 1965 had actually won the premier prize at home, but, in nearly 30 years of European competition, no side had ever lost a single-legged European final on their own ground. There had already been riots at the 1960 Olympic Stadium when tens of thousands queued for scarce tickets in the hope of seeing Roma win their second European trophy (they won the Fairs Cup back in 1961). Liverpool, who had won five trophies so far, and lost only one final (against Borussia Dortmund in the 1966 Cup Winners Cup), had just won a third consecutive League Championship and a record fourth consecutive Milk Cup, but the game in Rome was surely to be their toughest task.

In front of nearly 70,000 spectators, 60,000 of them supporting the home side, Liverpool clinched their fourth European cup victory by beating a Roma team boasting Italian World Cup stars Graziani and Conti, and Brazil's Falcao and Cerezo. The outcome hinged not on an authentic climax but the ordeal of another penalty shootout—the first in this competition's history. Goals by Neal and Pruzzo had left the scores equal at full time, and with extra time settling nothing, the cooler experience of Neal, Souness, Rush and Alan Kennedy saw Liverpool triumph 4-2 from the penalty spot. However, it must be said that except for this dramatic if artificial way of concluding the match, most of the preceding 120 minutes were in the mould of their recent predecessors—emascalated in fear of defeat. At least the penalty shootout spared a repeat.

INDEX

A

B

C

D

E

F

G

H

I

J

K

L

M

N

O

P

Q

R

S

T

U

V

W

Y

Z

SBB

SOM ELS D
ORRIUS
VISCA EL BARÇA